THE WEB COLLECTION PREMIUM EDITION: ADOBE DREAMWEAVER® CS3, FLASH® CS3, AND PHOTOSHOP® CS3

REVEALED

THE WEB COLLECTION PREMIUM EDITION: ADOBE DREAMWEAVER® CS3, FLASH® CS3, AND PHOTOSHOP® CS3

REVEALED

Bishop/Shuman/Reding

COURSE TECHNOLOGY
CENGAGE Learning

The Web Collection Premium Edition—Revealed

Bishop/Shuman/Reding

Vice President, Technology and Trades ABU: David Garza

Director of Learning Solutions: Sandy Clark

Managing Editor: Larry Main

Senior Acquisitions Editor: James Gish

Product Managers: Jane Hosie-Bounar, Nicole Bruno

Editorial Assistant: Sarah Timm

Marketing Director: Deborah Yarnell

Marketing Manager: Kevin Rivenburg

Marketing Specialist: Victoria Ortiz

Content Product Managers: Heather Furrow, Menaka Gupta

Developmental Editors: Barbara Waxer, Pam Conrad, Rachel Bunin

Technical Editors: Ann Fisher, John Shanley, Sasha Vodnik, Elizabeth Gorman

Art Director: Bruce Bond

Cover Design: Lisa Kuhn, Curio Press, LLC

Cover Photo: © Eric & David Hosking/CORBIS

Text Designer: Ann Small

Proofreader: Kim Kosmatka

Indexer: Alexandra Nickerson

For product information and technology assistance, contact us at
Cengage Learning Customer & Sales Support, 1-800-354-9706

For permission to use material from this text or product, submit all requests online at cengage.com/permissions. Further permissions questions can be emailed to
permissionrequest@cengage.com

Some of the product names and company names used in this book have been used for identification purposes only and may be trademarks or registered trademarks of their respective manufacturers and sellers.

Adobe® InDesign®, Adobe® Photoshop®, Adobe® Illustrator®, Adobe® Flash®, Adobe® Dreamweaver®, and Adobe® Creative Suite® are trademarks or registered trademarks of Adobe Systems, Inc. in the United States and/or other countries. Third party products, services, company names, logos, design, titles, words, or phrases within these materials may be trademarks of their respective owners.

The Adobe Approved Certification Courseware logo is a proprietary trademark of Adobe. All rights reserved.

ISBN-13: 978-1-4283-4083-1
ISBN-10: 1-4283-4083-1

Course Technology
25 Thomson Place,
Boston, Massachusetts, 02210.

Cengage Learning is a leading provider of customized learning solutions with office locations around the globe, including Singapore, the United Kingdom, Australia, Mexico, Brazil and Japan. Locate your local office at:
international.cengage.com/region

Cengage Learning products are represented in Canada by Nelson Education, Ltd.

For your lifelong learning solutions, visit course.cengage.com
Visit our corporate website at cengage.com

Course Technology , a part of Cengage Learning, and *Adobe Dreamweaver CS3—Revealed* are independent from ProCert Labs, LLC and Adobe Systems Incorporated, and are not affiliated with ProCert Labs and Adobe in any manner. This publication may assist students to prepare for an Adobe Certified Expert exam, however, neither ProCert Labs nor Adobe warrant that use of this material will ensure success in connection with any exam.

Printed in China by China Translation & Printing Services Limited
4 5 6 7 8 9 11 10 09

Revealed Series Vision

The Revealed Series is your guide to today's hottest multimedia applications. These comprehensive books teach the skills behind the application, showing you how to apply smart design principles to multimedia products such as dynamic graphics, animation, Web sites, software authoring tools, and digital video.

A team of design professionals including multimedia instructors, students, authors, and editors worked together to create this series. We recognized the unique learning environment of the multimedia classroom and created a series that:

- Gives you comprehensive step-by-step instructions
- Offers in-depth explanation of the "Why" behind a skill
- Includes creative projects for additional practice
- Explains concepts clearly using full-color visuals

It was our goal to create a book that speaks directly to the multimedia and design community—one of the most rapidly growing computer fields today. We think we've done just that, with a sophisticated and instructive book design.

—The Revealed Series

Authors' Vision

What a joy it has been to be a part of such a creative and energetic team. The Revealed Series is a great format for teaching and learning Adobe Dreamweaver CS3, Flash CS3, and Photoshop CS3. We would like to thank Jane Hosie-Bounar for her management expertise, and everyone at Course Technology and Delmar Learning for their professional guidance.

A special thanks to Barbara Waxer, Pam Conrad, and Rachel Bunin for their editorial expertise and encouragement.

—The authors

Special thanks go to my husband, Don, who continues to support and encourage me every day, as he has for the last thirty-seven years. Our travels with our children and grandchildren provide happy memories for me and content for the Web sites. This book leans fairly strongly in the direction of my precious grandchildren Jacob, Emma, Thomas, and Caroline. You will see their faces peeking out from some of the pages.

—Sherry Bishop

I would like to thank Jane Hosie-Bounar for her management expertise in guiding us through this project. A very special thanks to Pam Conrad for her editorial expertise and encouragement and to my co-authors Barbara, Sherry and Liz. I also want to give a heartfelt thanks to my wife, Barbara, for her patience and support.

—Jim Shuman

The Revealed Series is different from some other textbooks in that its target audience is a savvy student who wants important information and needs little hand-holding. This student has a sense of adventure, an interest in design, and a healthy dose of creativity. This person is fun to write for because he or she wants to learn.

I would like to thank my husband, Michael, who is used to my disappearing acts when I'm facing deadlines, and Phoebe, Bix, and Jet, who know when it's time to take a break for some good old-fashioned head-scratching.

—Elizabeth Eisner Reding

SERIES & AUTHORS' VISION

v

Introduction to The Web Collection, Premium Edition

Welcome to *The Web Collection Premium Edition: Adobe Dreamweaver CS3, Flash CS3, and Photoshop CS3—Revealed*. This book offers creative projects, concise instructions, and coverage of basic Dreamweaver, Flash, Photoshop, and Creative Suite integration skills, helping you to create polished, professional-looking Web sites and art work. Use this book both in the classroom and as your own reference guide.

This text is organized into 17 chapters. In these chapters, you will learn many skills, including how to move amongst the Creative Suite applications, which, in this release, provide familiar functionality from one application to the next.

What You'll Do

A What You'll Do figure begins every lesson. This figure gives you an at-a-glance look at what you'll do in the chapter, either by showing you a file from the current project or a tool you'll be using.

Comprehensive Conceptual Lessons

Before jumping into instructions, in-depth conceptual information tells you "why" skills are applied. This book provides the "how" and "why" through the use of professional examples. Also included in the text are tips and sidebars to help you work more efficiently and creatively, or to teach you a bit about the history or design philosophy behind the skill you are using.

Step-by-Step Instructions

This book combines in-depth conceptual information with concise steps to help you learn CS3. Each set of steps guides you through a lesson where you will create, modify, or enhance a CS3 file. Step references to large colorful images and quick step summaries round out the lessons. The Data Files for the steps are provided on the CD at the back of this book.

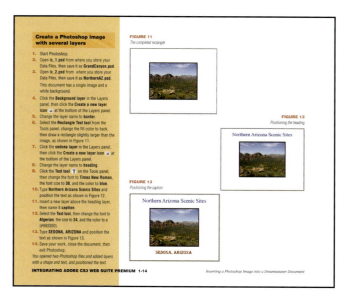

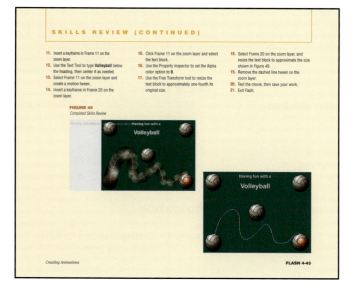

Projects

This book contains a variety of end-of-chapter materials for additional practice and reinforcement. The Skills Review contains hands-on practice exercises that mirror the progressive nature of the lesson material. The chapter concludes with four projects; two Project Builders, one Design Project, and one Group Project or Portfolio Project. The Project Builders and the Design Project require you to apply the skills you've learned in the chapter. Group and Portfolio Projects encourage students to address and solve challenges based on the content explored in the chapter in order to create portfolio-quality work.

CHAPTER 3   WORKING WITH TEXT AND IMAGES

CHAPTER 4 WORKING WITH LINKS

CHAPTER 5 USING HTML TABLES TO LAY OUT A PAGE

Flash CS3

CHAPTER 1	GETTING STARTED WITH ADOBE FLASH CS3

| CHAPTER 3 | **WORKING WITH SYMBOLS AND INTERACTIVITY** |

CHAPTER 4   CREATING ANIMATIONS

CHAPTER 5   CREATING SPECIAL EFFECTS

CONTENTS

Photoshop CS3

| CHAPTER 1 | GETTING STARTED WITH ADOBE PHOTOSHOP |

CHAPTER 2   WORKING WITH LAYERS

CONTENTS

CHAPTER 3   MAKING SELECTIONS

CHAPTER 4   INCORPORATING COLOR TECHNIQUES

CONTENTS

Integrating Adobe CS3 Web Premium

What Instructor Resources Are Available with This Book?

The Instructor Resources CD-ROM is Course Technology's way of putting the resources and information needed to teach and learn effectively into your hands. All the resources are available for both Macintosh and Windows operating systems.

Instructor's Manual

Available as an electronic file, the Instructor's Manual includes chapter overviews and detailed lecture topics for each chapter, with teaching tips. The Instructor's Manual is available on the Instructor Resources CD-ROM.

PowerPoint Presentations

Each chapter has a corresponding PowerPoint presentation that you can use in lectures, distribute to your students, or customize to suit your course.

Data Files for Students

To complete most of the chapters in this book, your students will need Data Files. The Data Files are available on the CD at the back of this text book. Instruct students to use the Data Files List at the end of this book. This list gives instructions on organizing files.

Solutions to Exercises

Solution Files are Data Files completed with comprehensive sample answers. Use these files to evaluate your students' work. Or distribute them electronically so students can verify their work. Sample solutions to all lessons and end-of-chapter material are provided.

Test Bank and Test Engine

ExamView is a powerful testing software package that allows instructors to create and administer printed, computer (LAN-based), and Internet exams. ExamView includes hundreds of questions that correspond to the topics covered in this text, enabling students to generate detailed study guides that include page references for further review. The computer-based and Internet testing components allow students to take exams at their computers, and also save the instructor time by grading each exam automatically.

Intended Audience

This text is designed for the beginner or intermediate user who wants to learn how to use Dreamweaver CS3, Flash CS3, and Photoshop CS3. The book is designed to provide basic and in-depth material that not only educates, but also encourages you to explore the nuances of these exciting programs.

Approach

The text allows you to work at your own pace through step-by-step tutorials. A concept is presented and the process is explained, followed by the actual steps. To learn the most from the use of the text, you should adopt the following habits:

- Proceed slowly: Accuracy and comprehension are more important than speed.
- Understand what is happening with each step before you continue to the next step.
- After finishing a skill, ask yourself if you could do it on your own, without referring to the steps. If the answer is no, review the steps.

Icons, Buttons, and Pointers

Symbols for icons, buttons, and pointers are shown in the step each time they are used. Icons may look different in the files panel depending on the file association settings on your computer.

Skills Reference

As a bonus, a Power User Shortcuts table is included at the end of Dreamweaver and Photoshop chapters. This table contains the quickest method of completing tasks covered in the chapter. It is meant for the more experienced user, or for the user who wants to become more experienced. Tools are shown, not named.

Fonts

The Data Files contain a variety of commonly used fonts, but there is no guarantee that these fonts will be available on your computer. In a few cases, fonts other than those common to a PC or a Macintosh are used. If any of the fonts in use is not available on your computer, you can make a substitution, realizing that the results may vary from those in the book.

Windows and Macintosh

Adobe Creative Suite works virtually the same on Windows and Macintosh operating systems. In those cases where there is a significant difference, the abbreviations (Win) and (Mac) are used.

Data Files

To complete the lessons in this book, you need the Data Files on the CD in the back of this book. Your instructor will tell you where to store the files as you work, such as the hard drive, a network

server, or a USB storage device. The instructions in the lessons will refer to "where you store your Data Files" when referring to the Data Files for the book.

When you copy the Data Files to your computer, you may see lock icons that indicate that the files are read-only when you view them in the Dreamweaver Files panel. To unlock the files, right-click on the locked file name in the Files panel, then click Turn off Read Only.

Images vs Graphics

Many times these terms seem to be used interchangeably. For the purposes of the Dreamweaver chapters, the term images is used when referring to pictures on a Web page. The term graphics is used as a more encompassing term that refers to non-text items on a Web page such as photographs, logos, navigation bars, Flash animations, graphs, background images, and drawings. You may define these terms in a slightly different way, depending on your professional background or business environment.

Preference Settings

The learning process will be much easier if you can see the file extensions for the files you will use in the lessons. To do this in Windows, open Windows Explorer, click Organize, Folder and Search Options, click the View tab, then uncheck the box Hide Extensions for Known File Types. To do this for a

Mac, go to the Finder, click the Finder menu, and then click Preferences. Click the Advanced tab, then select the Show all file extensions check box.

To view the Flash content that you will be creating, you must set a preference in your browser to allow active content to run. Otherwise, you will not be able to view objects such as Flash buttons. To set this preference in Internet Explorer, click Tools, Internet Options, Advanced, then check the box Allow active content to run in files on My Computer. Your browser settings may be slightly different, but look for similar wording. When using Windows Internet Explorer 7, you can also click the information bar when prompted to allow blocked content.

Creating a Portfolio

The Portfolio Project, Group Project, and Project Builders allow students to use their creativity to come up with original Dreamweaver, Flash, and Photoshop designs. You might suggest that students create a portfolio in which they can store their original work.

Dreamweaver CS3
System Requirements
For a Windows operating system:

- Intel® Pentium® 4, Intel Centrino®, Intel Xeon®, or Intel Core™ Duo (or compatible) processor

- Microsoft® Windows® XP with Service Pack 2 or Windows Vista™ Home Premium, Business, Ultimate, or Enterprise (certified for 32-bit editions)

- 512MB of RAM

- 1GB of available hard-disk space (additional free space required during installation)

- 1,024×768 monitor resolution with 16-bit video card

- DVD-ROM drive

- Internet or phone connection required for product activation

- Broadband Internet connection required for Adobe Stock Photos* and other services

For a Macintosh operating system:

- PowerPC® G4 or G5 or multicore Intel® processor

- Mac OS X v.10.4.8

- 512MB of RAM

- 1.4GB of available hard-disk space (additional free space required during installation)

- 1,024×768 monitor resolution with 16-bit video card

- DVD-ROM drive

- Internet or phone connection required for product activation

- Broadband Internet connection required for Adobe Stock Photos* and other services

Dreamweaver CS3 Workspace

If you are starting Dreamweaver for the first time after installing it, you will see the Workspace Setup dialog box, which asks you to choose between two workspace layouts. This text uses the Designer workspace layout throughout.

Building a Web Site

You will create and develop a Web site called The Striped Umbrella in the lesson material in this book. Because each chapter builds off of the previous chapter, it is recommended that you work through the chapters in consecutive order.

Flash CS3
System Requirements
For a Windows operating system:

- Intel® Pentium® 4, Intel Centrino®, Intel Xeon®, or Intel Core™ Duo (or compatible) processor

- Microsoft® Windows® XP with Service Pack 2 or Windows Vista™ Home Premium, Business, Ultimate, or Enterprise (certified for 32-bit editions)

- 512MB of RAM (1GB recommended)

- 2.5GB of available hard-disk space (additional free space required during installation)

- 1,024×768 monitor resolution with 16-bit video card

- DVD-ROM drive
- QuickTime 7.1.2 software required for multimedia features

For a Macintosh operating system:

- 1GHz PowerPC® G4 or G5 or multicore Intel® processor
- Mac OS X v.10.4.8
- 512MB of RAM (1GB recommended)
- 2.5GB of available hard-disk space (additional free space required during installation)
- 1,024×768 monitor resolution with 16-bit video card
- DVD-ROM drive
- QuickTime 7.1.2 software required for multimedia features

Projects

Several projects are presented that allow students to apply the skills they have learned in a chapter. Two projects, Ultimate Tours and the Portfolio, build from chapter to chapter. You will need to contact your instructor if you plan to work on these without having completed the previous chapter's project.

Photoshop CS3
System Requirements

Windows

- Intel® Pentium® 4, Intel Centrino®, Intel Xeon®, or Intel Core™ Duo (or compatible) processor

- Microsoft® Windows® XP with Service Pack 2 or Windows Vista™ Home Premium, Business, Ultimate, or Enterprise (certified for 32-bit editions)
- 512MB of RAM
- 64MB of video RAM
- 1GB of available hard-disk space (additional free space required during installation)
- 1,024×768 monitor resolution with 16-bit video card
- DVD-ROM drive
- QuickTime 7 software required for multimedia features
- Internet or phone connection required for product activation
- Broadband Internet connection required for Adobe Stock Photos* and other services

Macintosh

- PowerPC® G4 or G5 or multicore Intel processor
- Mac OS X v.10.4.8
- 512MB of RAM
- 64MB of video RAM
- 2GB of available hard-disk space (additional free space required during installation)
- 1,024x768 monitor resolution with 16-bit video card
- DVD-ROM drive
- QuickTime 7 software required for multimedia features

- Internet or phone connection required for product activation
- Broadband Internet connection required for Adobe Stock Photos* and other services

File Identification

Instead of printing a file, the owner of a Photoshop image can be identified by reading the File Info dialog box. Use the following instructions to add your name to an image:

1. Click File on the menu bar, then click File Info.
2. Click the Description, if necessary.
3. Click the Author text box.
4. Type your name, course number, or other identifying information.
5. Click OK.

There are no instructions with this text to use the File Info feature other than when it is introduced in Chapter 1. It is up to each user to use this feature so that his or her work can be identified.

Measurements

When measurements are shown, needed, or discussed, they are given in pixels. Use the following instructions to change the units of measurement to pixels:

1. Click Edit on the menu bar, point to Preferences, then click Units & Rulers.

2. Click the Rulers list arrow, then click pixels.

3. Click OK.

You can display rulers by clicking View on the menu bar, then clicking Rulers, or by pressing [Ctrl][R] (Win) or ⌘[R] (Mac). A check mark to the left of the Rulers command indicates that the Rulers are displayed. You can hide visible rulers by clicking View on the menu bar, then clicking Rulers, or by pressing [Ctrl][R] (Win) or ⌘[R] (Mac).

Menu Commands in Tables

In tables, menu commands are abbreviated using the following format: Edit ➤ Preferences ➤ Units & Rulers. This command translates as follows: Click Edit on the menu bar, point to Preferences, then click Units & Rulers.

Grading Tips

Many students have Web-ready accounts where they can post their completed assignments. The instructor can access the student accounts using a browser and view the images online. Using this method, it is not necessary for the student to include his/her name on a type layer, because all of their assignments are in an individual password-protected account.

Creating a Portfolio

One method for students to submit and keep a copy of all of their work is to create a portfolio of their projects that is linked to a simple Web page that can be saved on a CD-ROM. If it is necessary for students to print completed projects, work can be printed and mounted at a local copy shop; a student's name can be printed on the back of the image.

GETTING STARTED WITH
DREAMWEAVER

1. Explore the Dreamweaver workspace

2. View a Web page and use Help

3. Plan and define a Web site

4. Add a folder and pages and set the home page

5. Create and view a site map

GETTING STARTED WITH
DREAMWEAVER

Introduction

Adobe Dreamweaver CS3 is a Web development tool that lets you create dynamic, interactive Web pages containing text, images, hyperlinks, animation, sounds, video, and other elements. You can use Dreamweaver to create individual Web pages or complex Web sites consisting of many Web pages. A **Web site** is a group of related Web pages that are linked together and share a common interface and design. You can use Dreamweaver to create design elements such as text, tables, and interactive buttons, or you can import elements from other software programs. You can save Dreamweaver files in many different file formats, including XHTML, HTML, JavaScript, CSS, or XML, to name a few. **XHTML** is the acronym for eXtensible HyperText Markup Language, the current standard language used to create Web pages. You can still use **HTML** (HyperText Markup Language) in Dreamweaver; however, it is no longer considered the standard language. In Dreamweaver, you can easily convert existing HTML code to XHTML-compliant code. You use a browser to view your Web pages on the Internet. A **browser** is a program, such as Microsoft Internet Explorer

or Mozilla Firefox, that lets you display HTML-developed Web pages.

Using Dreamweaver Tools

Creating an excellent Web site is a complex task. Fortunately, Dreamweaver has an impressive number of tools that can help. Using Dreamweaver's design tools, you can create dynamic and interactive Web pages without writing a word of code. However, if you prefer to write code, Dreamweaver makes it easy to type and edit the code directly and see the visual results of the code instantly. Dreamweaver also contains organizational tools that help you work with a team of people to create a Web site. You can also use Dreamweaver's management tools to help you manage a Web site. For instance, you can use the **Files panel** to create folders to organize and store the various files for your Web site, add pages to your Web site, and set the **home page**, the first page that viewers see when they visit the site. You can also use the **site map**, a graphical representation of how the pages within a Web site relate to each other, to view and edit the navigation structure of your Web site. The **navigation structure** is the way viewers navigate from page to page in your Web site.

Tools You'll Use

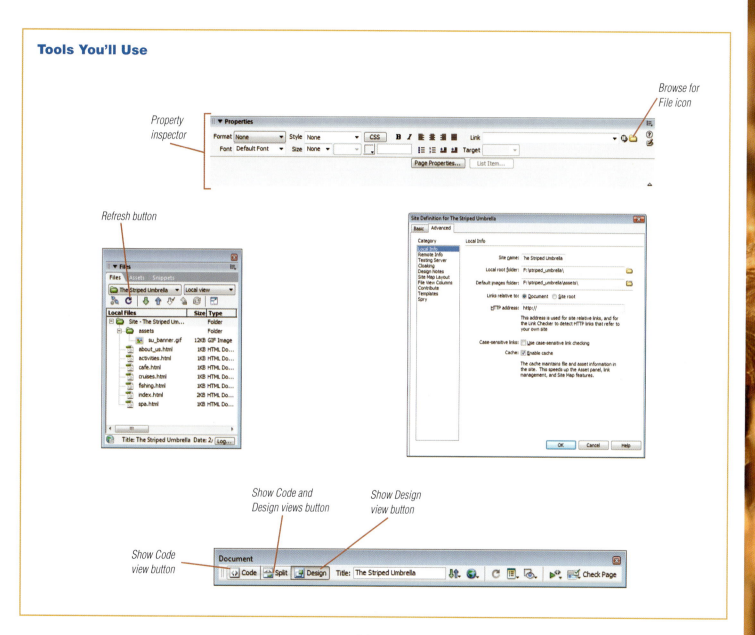

Property inspector

Browse for File icon

Refresh button

Show Code and Design views button

Show Design view button

Show Code view button

EXPLORE THE
DREAMWEAVER WORKSPACE

What You'll Do

In this lesson, you will start Dreamweaver, examine the components that make up the Dreamweaver workspace, and change views.

Examining the Dreamweaver Workspace

The **Dreamweaver workspace** is designed to provide you with easy access to all the tools you need to create Web pages. Refer to Figure 1 as you locate the components described below.

The **Document window** is the large white area in the Dreamweaver program window where you create and edit Web pages. The **menu bar**, located above the Document window, includes menu names, each of which contains Dreamweaver commands. To choose a menu command, click the menu name to open the menu, then click the menu command. Directly below the menu bar is the Insert bar. The **Insert bar** includes seven groups of buttons displayed as tabs: Common, Layout, Forms, Data, Spry, Text, and Favorites. Clicking a tab on the Insert bar displays the buttons and menus associated with that group. For example, if you click the Layout tab, you will find buttons for using div tags, used for creating blocks of content on pages, the Table button, used for inserting a table, and the

Frames button, used for selecting one of thirteen different frame layouts.

QUICKTIP

To display the categories using a drop-down menu as in previous versions of Dreamweaver, click the current Insert bar list arrow, and then click Show as Menu. To change back to the tab display, click the Insert bar list arrow, and then click Show as Tabs.

The **Document toolbar** contains buttons and drop-down menus you can use to change the current work mode, preview Web pages, debug Web pages, choose visual aids, and view file-management options. The **Standard toolbar** contains buttons you can use to execute frequently used commands also available on the File and Edit menus. The **Style Rendering toolbar** contains buttons that can be used to render different media types, but is available only if your document uses media-dependent style sheets. An example of a media-dependent style sheet would be one used to create and format pages for a cell phone. The **Coding toolbar** contains buttons that are used when working directly in the code. These, along with the Standard toolbar, are not part of the default workspace setup and might not be displayed when you open Dreamweaver.

The **Property inspector**, located at the bottom of the Dreamweaver window, lets you view and change the properties of a selected object. The Property inspector is context sensitive, which means it changes according to what is selected in the Document window. The **status bar** is located below the Document window. The left side of the status bar displays the **tag selector**, which shows the HTML tags used at the insertion point location. The right side displays the window size and estimated download time for the current page, as well as the Select tool, used for page editing, the Hand tool, used for panning, and the Zoom tool, used for magnifying.

A **panel** is a window that displays information on a particular topic or contains related commands. **Panel groups** are sets of related panels that are grouped together. To view the contents of a panel in a panel group, click the panel tab. Panel groups can be collapsed and docked on the right side of the screen, or undocked by dragging the gripper on the left side of the panel group title bar. To collapse or expand a panel group, click the expander arrow on the left side of the panel group title bar, as shown in Figure 2, or just click the name of the panel group. When you first start Dreamweaver, the CSS, Application, Tag Inspector, and Files panel groups appear by default. Panels can be opened using the Window menu commands or the corresponding shortcut keys.

Working with Dreamweaver Views

A **view** is a particular way of displaying page content. Dreamweaver has three working views. **Design view** shows the page as it would appear in a browser and is primarily used for designing and creating a Web page. **Code view** shows the underlying HTML code for the page; use this view to read or edit the underlying code. **Code and Design view** is a combination of Code view and Design view. Code and Design view is the best view for **debugging** or correcting errors because you can immediately see how code modifications change the appearance of the page. The view buttons are located on the Document toolbar.

FIGURE 1

Dreamweaver CS3 workspace

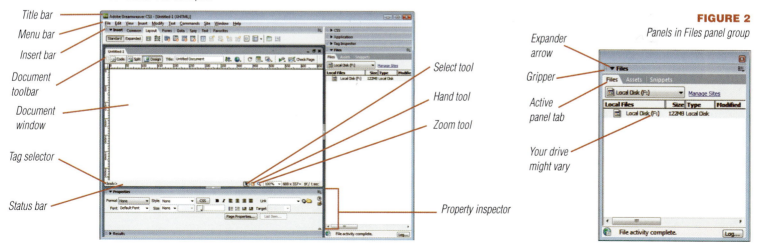

FIGURE 2

Panels in Files panel group

Start Dreamweaver (Windows)

1. Click the **Start button** 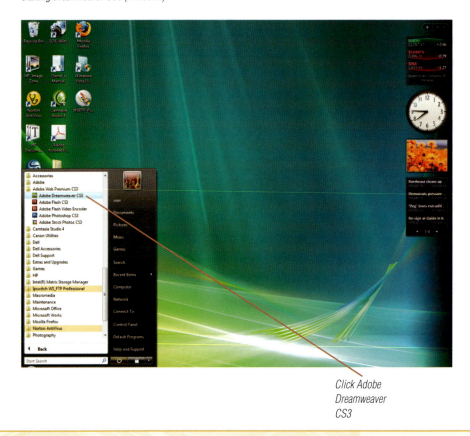 on the taskbar.

2. Point to **All Programs**, click **Adobe Web Premium CS3**, then click **Adobe Dreamweaver CS3**, as shown in Figure 3.

   TIP The name of your Adobe suite may differ from the figure.

3. If the Default Editor dialog box opens, click **OK**.

You started Dreamweaver CS3 for Windows.

FIGURE 3
Starting Dreamweaver CS3 (Windows)

Click Adobe Dreamweaver CS3

Choosing a workspace layout (Windows)

If you are starting Dreamweaver in Windows for the first time after installing it, you might see the Workspace Setup dialog box, which asks you to choose between the Designer, Coder, or Dual Screen layouts. All three layouts are built with an integrated workspace using the Multiple Document Interface (MDI). The **Multiple Document Interface** means that all document windows and panels are positioned within one large application window. In the Designer workspace layout, the panels are docked on the right side of the screen and the Design view is the default view. In the Coder workspace layout, the panels are docked on the left side of the screen and the Code view is the default view. However, the panels may be docked on either side of the screen in both Coder and Designer layouts. To change the workspace layout, click Window on the menu bar, point to Workspace Layout, and then click the desired layout.

FIGURE 4

Starting Dreamweaver CS3 (Macintosh)

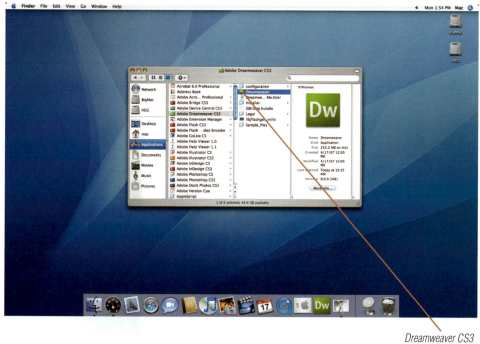

Dreamweaver CS3
application

Start Dreamweaver (Macintosh)

1. Click **Finder** in the Dock, then click **Applications**.

2. Click the **Adobe Dreamweaver CS3 folder**, then double-click the **Dreamweaver CS3 application,** as shown in Figure 4.

   TIP Once Dreamweaver is running, you can add it to the Dock permanently by [control]-clicking the Dreamweaver icon, then clicking Keep In Dock.

You started Dreamweaver CS3 for Macintosh.

Change views and view panels

1. Click **HTML** in the Create New category on the Dreamweaver Welcome Screen.

   The Dreamweaver Welcome Screen provides shortcuts for opening files or for creating new files or Web sites.

   > TIP If you do not want the Dreamweaver Welcome Screen to appear each time you start Dreamweaver, click the Don't show again check box on the Welcome Screen or remove the check mark next to Show Welcome Screen in the General category of the Preferences dialog box.

2. Click the **Show Code view button** 🔲 Code on the Document toolbar.

   The default code for a new document appears in the Document window, as shown in Figure 5.

   > TIP The Coding toolbar is available only in Code view.

3. Click the **Show Code and Design views button** 🔲 Split on the Document toolbar.

4. Click the **Show Design view button** 🔲 Design on the Document toolbar.

   (continued)

FIGURE 5
Code view for new document

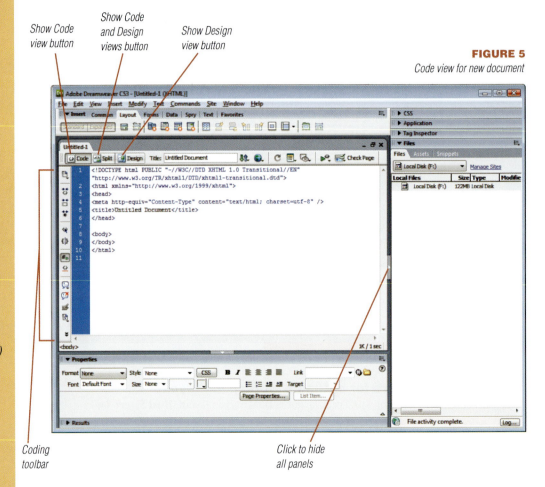

Show Code view button

Show Code and Design views button

Show Design view button

Coding toolbar

Click to hide all panels

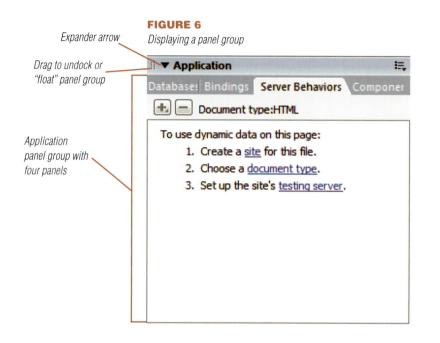

FIGURE 6

Displaying a panel group

Expander arrow

Drag to undock or "float" panel group

Application panel group with four panels

5. Click **Application** on the panel group title bar, then compare your screen to Figure 6.

   TIP If the Application panel group is not displayed, click Window on the menu bar, then click Server Behaviors. The Server Behaviors panel is in the Application panel group.

6. Click each panel name tab to display the contents of each panel.

7. Click **Application** on the panel group title bar to collapse the Application panel group.

8. View the contents of the CSS and Files panel groups, then collapse the CSS panel group.

9. Close the open document.

You viewed a new Web page using three views, opened panel groups, viewed their contents, then closed panel groups.

Hiding and Displaying Toolbars

To hide or display the Insert, Style Rendering, Document, or Standard toolbars, click View on the menu bar, point to Toolbars, then click Insert, Style Rendering, Document, or Standard. The Coding toolbar is available only in Code view and appears vertically in the Document window. By default, the Insert and Document toolbars appear in the workspace.

VIEW A WEB PAGE
AND USE HELP

In this lesson, you will open a Web page, view several page elements, and access the Help system.

Opening a Web Page

After starting Dreamweaver, you can create a new Web site, create a new Web page, or open an existing Web site or Web page. The first Web page that appears when viewers go to a Web site is called the **home page**. The home page sets the look and feel of the Web site and directs viewers to the rest of the pages in the Web site.

Viewing Basic Web Page Elements

There are many elements that make up Web pages. Web pages can be very simple and designed primarily with text, or they can be media-rich with text, images sound, and movies, creating an enhanced interactive Web experience. Figure 7 is an example of a Web page with several different page elements that work together to create a simple and attractive page.

Most information on a Web page is presented in the form of **text**. You can type text directly onto a Web page in Dreamweaver or import text created in other programs. You can then use the Property inspector to format text so that it is attractive and easy to read. Text should be short and to the point to prevent viewers from losing interest and leaving your site.

Hyperlinks, also known as **links**, are image or text elements on a Web page that users click to display another location on the page, another Web page on the same Web site, or a Web page on a different Web site.

Images add visual interest to a Web page. The saying that "less is more" is certainly true with images, though. Too many images cause the page to load slowly and discourage viewers from waiting for the page to download. Many pages have **banners**, which are images displayed across the top of the screen that can incorporate a company's logo, contact information, and links to the other pages in the site.

Navigation bars are bars that contain multiple links that are usually organized in rows or columns. Sometimes navigation bars are used with an image map. An **image map** is an image that has been divided into sections, each of which contains a link.

Flash button objects are Flash objects that can be created in Dreamweaver and can serve as links to other files or Web pages. You can insert them onto a Web page without requiring the Adobe Flash program to be installed. They add visual interest to a Web page.

Getting Help

Dreamweaver has an excellent Help feature that is both comprehensive and easy to use.

When questions or problems arise, you can use the commands on the Help menu to find the answers you need. Clicking the Using Dreamweaver command opens the Adobe Help Viewer that contains two links you can use to search for answers in different ways. The Contents link lists Dreamweaver Help topics by category. The Index link lets you view topics in alphabetical order. The Search text box at the top of the window lets you enter a keyword to search for a specific topic.

You can use the Browse box to view other Adobe products' Help topics. On a Macintosh, you can view topics by Index or Table of Contents, and use Search text box. Context-specific help can be accessed by clicking the Help button on the Property inspector.

Images

Text

Small form for signing in and checking out

Navigation structure includes several sets of text links

Form to sign up for free shipping

Gap Web site used with permission from Gap Inc. – www.gap.com

Open a Web page and view basic page elements

1. Click **File** on the Menu bar, then click **Open**.

2. Click the **Look in list arrow** (Win), or **navigation list arrow** (Mac), locate the drive and folder where you store your Data Files, then double-click the **chapter_1 folder** (Win), or click the **chapter_1 folder** (Mac).

3. Click **dw1_1.html**, then click **Open**.

   TIP If you want your screen to match the figures in this book, make sure the Document window is maximized.

4. Locate each of the Web page elements shown in Figure 8.

   TIP Because you are opening a single page that is not in a Web site with access to the other pages, the links will not work.

5. Click the **Show Code view button** 【🔘 Code】 to view the code for the page.

6. Scroll down to view all the code, then click the **Show Design view button** 【🔘 Design】 to return to Design view.

   TIP To view the code for a particular page element, select the page element in Design view, then click the Show Code view button.

7. Click **File** on the menu bar, then click **Close** to close the page without saving it.

You opened a Web page, located several page elements, viewed the code for the page, then closed the Web page without saving it.

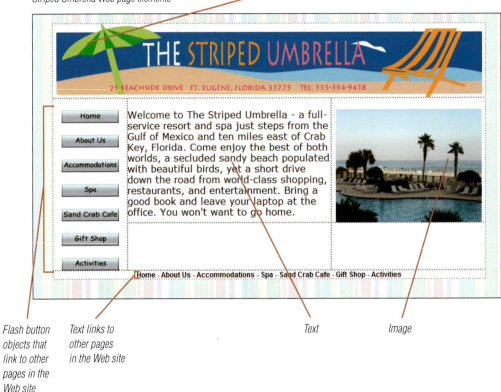

FIGURE 8
Striped Umbrella Web page elements

Banner

Flash button objects that link to other pages in the Web site

Text links to other pages in the Web site

Text

Image

FIGURE 9

Dreamweaver Help window

Use Dreamweaver Help

1. Click **Help** on the menu bar, then click **Dreamweaver Help.**

   The Adobe Help Viewer window opens with Dreamweaver CS3 as the active program to browse for help.

   TIP You can also open the Help feature by pressing [F1] (Win).

2. Click to place the insertion point in the Search text box.

3. Type **saving** in the Search text box (Win).

4. Press **[Enter]** (Win) or **[return]** (Mac), then scroll down to view the topics.

   TIP You may have to select "Dreamweaver CS3" from the list of available programs in the list.

5. If necessary, select **saving** in the Search text box, type **"save files"** (be sure to type the quotation marks), then press **[Enter]** (Win) or **[return]** (Mac).

   Because you placed the keywords in quotation marks, Dreamweaver listed fewer topics found.

6. Click the second topic in the topic list.

   Information on accessing sites, a server, and local drives appears in the right frame, as shown in Figure 9.

7. Scroll down and scan the text.

8. Close the Dreamweaver Help window.

You used Dreamweaver Help to read information about connecting to a server to edit files.

PLAN AND DEFINE A
WEB SITE

What You'll Do

In this lesson, you will review a Web site plan for The Striped Umbrella, a beach resort and spa. You will also create a root folder for The Striped Umbrella Web site, and then define the Web site.

Understanding the Total Process

Creating a Web site is a complex process. It can often involve a large team of people working in various roles to ensure that the Web site contains accurate information, looks good, and works smoothly.

Figure 10 illustrates the phases in a Web site development project.

Planning a Web Site

Planning is probably the most important part of any successful project. Planning is an *essential* part of creating a Web site, and is a

FIGURE 10
Phases of a Web site development project

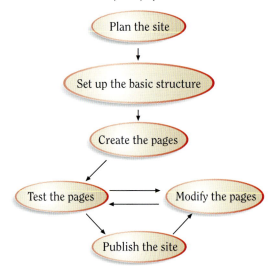

Getting Started with Dreamweaver

continuous process that overlaps the subsequent phases. To start planning your Web site, you need to create a checklist of questions and answers about the site. For example, what are your goals for the Web site? Who is the audience you want to target? Teenagers? Children? Sports Enthusiasts? Senior citizens? How can you design the site to appeal to the target audience? The more questions you can answer about the site, the more prepared you will be when you begin the developmental phase. Because of the public demand for "instant" information, your plan should include not just how to get the site up and running, but how to keep it current. Table 1 lists some of the basic questions you need to answer during the planning phase for almost any type of Web site. From your checklist, you should create a statement of purpose and scope, a timeline for all due dates, a budget, a task list with work assignments, and a list of resources needed. You should also include a list of deliverables, such as a preliminary storyboard, page drafts, and art-work for approval. The due dates for each deliverable should be included in the timeline.

Setting Up the Basic Structure

Once you complete the planning phase, you need to set up the structure of the site by creating a storyboard. A **storyboard** is a small sketch that represents every page in a Web site. Like a flowchart, a storyboard shows the relationship of each page in the Web site to all the other pages. Storyboards are very

TABLE 1: Web Site Planning Checklist

question	examples
1. Who is the target audience?	Seniors, teens, children
2. How can I tailor the Web site to reach that audience?	Specify an appropriate reading level, decide the optimal amount of multimedia content, use formal or casual language
3. What are the goals for the site?	Sell a product, provide information
4. How will I gather the information?	Recruit other employees, write it myself, use content from in-house documents
5. What are my sources for rich media content?	Internal production department, outside production company, my own photographs
6. What is my budget?	Very limited, well financed
7. What is the timeline?	Two weeks, one month, six months
8. Who is on my project team?	Just me, a complete staff of designers
9. How often should the site be updated?	Every 10 minutes, once a month
10. Who will update the site?	Me, other team members

helpful when planning a Web site, because they allow you to visualize how each page in the site is linked to others. You can sketch a storyboard using a pencil and paper or using a graphics program on a computer. The storyboard shown in Figure 11 shows all the pages that will be contained in The Striped Umbrella Web site that you will create in this book. Notice that the home page appears at the top of the storyboard, and that it has four pages linked to it. The home page is called the **parent page**, because it is at a higher level in the Web hierarchy and has pages linked to it. The pages linked below it are called **child pages**. The Activities page, which is a child page to the home page, is also a parent page to the Cruises and Fishing pages. You can refer to this storyboard as you create the actual links in Dreamweaver. More detailed storyboards will also include all document names, images, text files, and link information.

QUICKTIP
You can create a storyboard on a computer using a software program such as Microsoft Word, PowerPoint, or Paint; Corel Paintshop Pro; or Adobe Illustrator. You might find it easier to make changes to a computer-generated storyboard than to one created on paper.

In addition to creating a storyboard for your site, you should also create a folder hierarchy for all of the files that will be used in the Web site. Start by creating a folder for the Web site with a descriptive name, such as the name of the company.

This folder, known as the **root folder** or **local root folder**, will store all the Web pages or HTML files for the site. Then create a subfolder called **assets** in which you store all of the files that are not Web pages, such as images and sound files. You should avoid using spaces, special characters, or uppercase characters in your folder names to ensure that all your files can be read and linked successfully on all Web servers, whether they are Windows- or UNIX-based.

After you create the root folder, you need to define your Web site. When you **define** a Web site, the root folder and any folders and files it contains appear in the **Files**

panel, the panel you use to manage your Web site's files and folders. Using the Files panel to manage your files ensures that the site links work correctly when the Web site is published. You also use the Files panel to add or delete pages.

Creating the Web Pages and Collecting the Page Content
This is the fun part! After you create your storyboard, you need to gather the files that will be used to create the pages, including text, images, buttons, video, and animation. Some of these files will come

FIGURE 11
The Striped Umbrella Web site storyboard

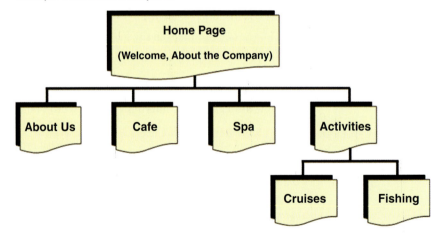

from other software programs, and some will be created in Dreamweaver. For example, you can create text in a word-processing program and insert it into Dreamweaver, or you can create and format text in Dreamweaver. Images, tables, colors, and horizontal rules all contribute to making a page attractive and interesting. In choosing your elements, however, you should always carefully consider the file size of each page. A page with too many graphical elements might take a long time to load, which could cause visitors to leave your Web site. Before you actually add content to each page, however, it is a good idea to use the Files panel to add all the pages to the site according to the structure you specified in your storyboard. Once all the blank pages are in place, you can add the content you collected. This will allow you to create and test the navigation links you will need for the site. The blank pages will act as placeholders. Some designers prefer to add pages as they are created and build the links as they go. It is a personal preference.

Testing the Pages

Once all your pages are completed, you need to test the site to make sure all the links work and that everything looks good. It is important to test your Web pages using different browser software. The two most common browsers are Microsoft Internet Explorer and Mozilla Firefox. You should also test your Web site using different versions of each browser. Older versions of Internet Explorer do not support the latest Web technology. You should also test your Web site using a variety of screen sizes. Some viewers may have small monitors, while others may have large, high-resolution monitors. You should also consider connection download time. Although more people use cable modems or DSL (digital subscriber line) Delete and close-up some still use slower dial-up modems. Testing is a continuous process, for which you should allocate plenty of time.

Modifying the Pages

After you create a Web site, you'll probably find that you need to keep making changes to it, especially when information on the site needs to be updated. Each time you make a change, such as adding a new button or image to a page, you should test the site again. Modifying and testing pages in a Web site is an ongoing process.

Publishing the Site

Publishing a Web site means that you transfer all the files for the site to a **Web server**, a computer that is connected to the Internet with an IP (Internet Protocol) address, so that it is available for viewing on the Internet. A Web site must be published or users of the Internet cannot view it. There are several options for publishing a Web site. For instance, many Internet Service Providers (ISPs) provide space on their servers for customers to publish Web sites, and some commercial Web sites provide limited free space for their viewers. Although publishing happens at the end of the process, it's a good idea to set up Web server access in the planning phase. Use the Files panel to transfer your files using the FTP (File Transfer Protocol) capability. **FTP** is the process of uploading and downloading files to and from a remote site.

Dreamweaver also gives you the ability to transfer files using the FTP process without creating a Web site first. You simply enter login information to an FTP site to establish a connection by clicking New in the Manage Sites dialog box, and then clicking the FTP option.

Create a root folder (Windows)

1. Click the **Start button** 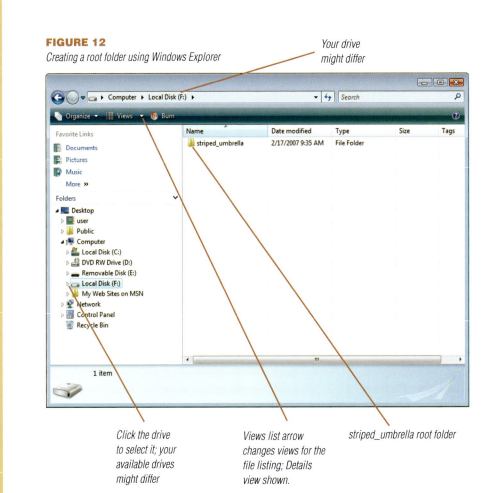 on the taskbar, point to **All Programs**, click **Accessories**, then click **Windows Explorer**.

    TIP You can also right-click the Start button, then click **Explore.**

2. Navigate to the drive and folder where you will create a folder to store your files for The Striped Umbrella Web site.

3. Click **Organize** on the toolbar, then click **New Folder**.

4. Type **striped_umbrella,** to rename the folder, then press **[Enter]**.

    The folder is renamed striped_umbrella, as shown in Figure 12.

    TIP Your desktop will look different from Figure 12 if you are not using Windows Vista.

5. Close Windows Explorer.

    TIP You can also use the Files panel to create a new folder by clicking the Site list arrow, selecting the drive and folder where you want to create the new folder, right-clicking, selecting New Folder, then typing the new folder name.

You created a new folder to serve as the root folder for The Striped Umbrella Web site.

FIGURE 12

Creating a root folder using Windows Explorer

Your drive might differ

Click the drive to select it; your available drives might differ

Views list arrow changes views for the file listing; Details view shown.

striped_umbrella root folder

Getting Started with Dreamweaver

FIGURE 13

Creating a root folder using a Macintosh

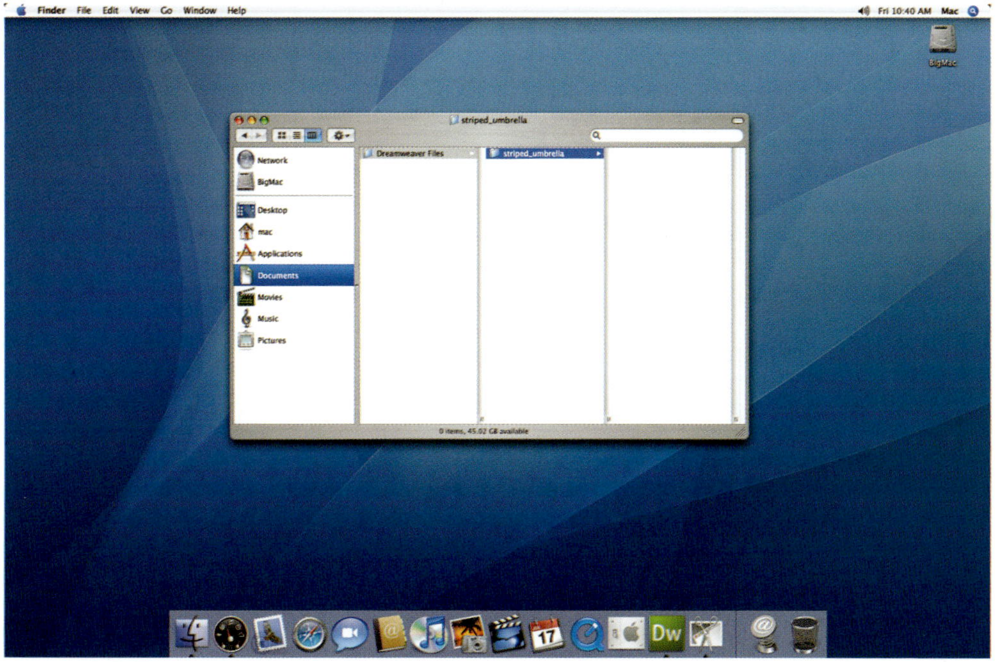

Create a root folder (Macintosh)

1. Double-click the **hard drive icon** on the desktop, then use Finder to navigate to the drive and folder where you will create a folder to store your files for The Striped Umbrella Web site.

2. Click **File** on the menu bar, then click **New Folder**.

3. Type **striped_umbrella** to rename the folder, as shown in Figure 13.

You created a new folder to serve as the root folder for The Striped Umbrella Web site.

Define a Web site

1. Return to Dreamweaver, then click **Dreamweaver Site** in the Create New category on the Welcome Screen.

2. Click the **Advanced tab** (if necessary), then type **The Striped Umbrella** in the Site name text box.

   The Basic tab can be used instead of the Advanced tab if you prefer to use a wizard.

   TIP It is acceptable to use uppercase letters in the site name because it is not the name of a folder or a file.

3. Click the **Browse for File icon** 📁 next to the Local root folder text box, click the **Select list arrow** (Win) or the **navigation list arrow** (Mac) in the **Choose local root folder for site The Striped Umbrella dialog box,** click the **drive and folder** where your Web site files will be stored, then click the **striped_umbrella folder**.

4. Click **Open** (Win) or **Choose** (Mac), then click **Select** (Win).

5. Verify that the Enable cache check box is checked, as shown in Figure 14.

6. Verify that the Links relative to option button is set to Document.

   This setting is very important to make sure your links work correctly.

You created a Web site and defined it with the name The Striped Umbrella. You then verified that the correct options were selected in the Site Definition dialog box.

FIGURE 14
Site Definition for The Striped Umbrella dialog box

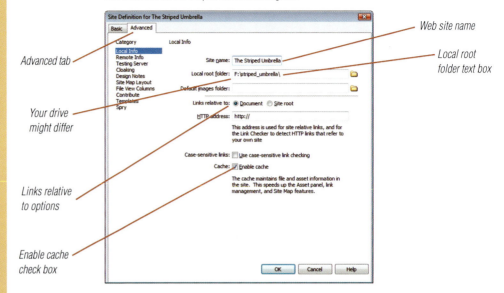

Advanced tab

Your drive might differ

Links relative to options

Enable cache check box

Web site name

Local root folder text box

Understanding IP addresses and domain names

To be accessible over the Internet, a Web site must be published to a Web server with a permanent IP address. An **IP address** is an assigned series of numbers, separated by periods, that designates an address on the Internet. To access a Web page, you can enter either an IP address or a domain name in the address text box of your browser window. A **domain name** is a Web address that is expressed in letters instead of numbers and usually reflects the name of the business represented by the Web site. For example, the domain name of the Adobe Web site is *www.adobe.com,* but the IP address is 192.150.20.61. Because domain names use descriptive text instead of numbers, they are much easier to remember. Compare an IP address to your Social Security number and a domain name to your name. Both your Social Security number and your name are used to refer to you as a person, but your name is much easier for your friends and family to use than your Social Security number. You can type the IP address or the domain name in the address text box of the browser window to access a Web site. The domain name is also referred to as a URL, or Uniform Resource Locator.

1. Click **Remote Info** in the Category list, click the **Access list arrow**, then choose the method you will use to publish your Web site, as shown in Figure 15.

TIP If you do not have the information to publish your Web site, choose None. You can specify this information later.

2. Enter any necessary information in the Site Definition dialog box based on the setting you chose in Step 1, then click **OK**.

TIP Your instructor will give you the necessary information to publish your Web site.

You set up the remote access information to prepare you for publishing your Web site.

FIGURE 15

Setting the Remote Access for The Striped Umbrella Web site

Access list arrow

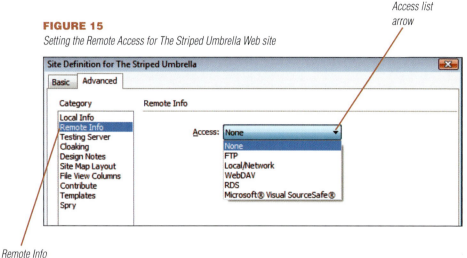

Remote Info category

Understanding the process of publishing a Web site

Before publishing a Web site so that viewers of the Web can access it, you should first create a local root folder, called the **local site**, to house all the files for your Web site. This folder usually resides on your hard drive. Next, you need to gain access to a remote server. A **remote server** is a Web server that hosts Web sites and is not directly connected to the computer housing the local site. Many Internet Service Providers, or ISPs, provide space for publishing Web pages on their servers. Once you have access to a remote server, you can then use the Remote Info category in the Site Definition dialog box to enter information such as the FTP host, host directory, login, and password. After entering this information, you can then use the Put File(s) button in the Files panel to transfer the files to the designated remote server. Once the site is published to a remote server, it is called a **remote site**.

ADD A FOLDER AND PAGES
AND SET THE HOME PAGE

What You'll Do

In this lesson, you will set the home page. You will also create a new folder and new pages for the Web site, using the Files panel.

Adding a Folder to a Web Site

After defining a Web site, you need to create folders to organize the files that will make up the Web site. Creating a folder called **assets** is a good beginning. You can use the assets folder to store all non-HTML files, such as images or sound files. After you create the assets folder, it is a good idea to set it as the default location to store the Web site images. This saves a step when you import new images into the Web site.

DESIGNTIP   **Creating an effective navigation structure**

When you create a Web site, it's important to consider how your viewers will navigate from page to page within the site. A navigation bar is a critical tool for moving around a Web site, so it's important that all text, buttons, and icons used in a navigation bar have a consistent look across all pages. If a complex navigation bar is used, such as one that incorporates JavaScript or Flash, it's a good idea to include plain text links in another location on the page for accessibility. Otherwise, viewers might become confused or lost within the site. A navigation structure can include more links than those included in a navigation bar, however. For instance, it can contain other sets of links that relate to the content of a specific page and which are placed at the bottom or sides of a page in a different format. No matter what navigation structure you use, make sure that every page includes a link back to the home page. Don't make viewers rely on the Back button on the browser toolbar to find their way back to the home page. It's possible that the viewer's current page might have opened as a result of a search and clicking the Back button will take the viewer out of the Web site.

Getting Started with Dreamweaver

Setting the Home Page

The home page of a Web site is the first page that viewers see when they visit your Web site. Most Web sites contain many other pages that all connect back to the home page. Dreamweaver uses the home page that you have designated as a starting point for creating a **site map**, a graphical representation of the Web pages in a Web site. When you **set** the home page, you tell Dreamweaver which page you have designated to be your home page. The home page filename usually has the name index.html (.htm), or default.html (.htm).

Adding Pages to a Web Site

Web sites might be as simple as one page or might contain hundreds of pages. When you create a Web site, you can add all the pages and specify where they should be placed in the Web site folder structure in the root folder. Once you add and name all the pages in the Web site, you can then add the content, such as text and graphics, to each page. It is better to add as many blank pages as you think you will need in the beginning, rather than adding them one at a time with all the content in place. This will enable you to set up the navigation structure of the Web site at the beginning of the development process and view how each page is linked to others. When you are satisfied with the overall structure, you can then add the content to each page. This is strictly a personal preference, however. You can also choose to add and link

pages as they are created, and that will work just fine, too.

You have a choice of several default document types you can generate when you create new HTML pages. The default document type is designated in the Preferences dialog box. XHTML 1.0 Transitional is the default document type when you install Dreamweaver and will be used throughout this book. It's important to understand the terminology—the pages are still called HTML pages and the file extension is still HTML, but the document type will be XHTML 1.0 Transitional.

Using the Files panel for file management

You should definitely use the Files panel to add, delete, move, or rename files and folders in a Web site. It is very important that you perform these file-maintenance tasks in the Files panel rather than in Windows Explorer (Win) or in the Finder (Mac). Working outside of Dreamweaver, such as in Windows Explorer, can cause linking errors. You cannot take advantage of Dreamweaver's simple yet powerful site-management features unless you use the Files panel for all file-management activities. You may choose to use Windows Explorer (Win) or the Finder (Mac) only to create the root folder or to move or copy the root folder of a Web site to another location. If you move or copy the root folder to a new location, you will have to define the Web site again in the Files panel, as you did in Lesson 3 of this chapter. Defining a Web site is not difficult and will become routine for you after you practice a bit. If you are using Dreamweaver on multiple computers, such as in labs or at home, you will have to define your sites the first time you change to a different computer.

Add a folder to a Web site (Windows)

1. Right-click **The Striped Umbrella site** in the Files panel, then click **New Folder**.

2. Type **assets** in the folder text box, then press **[Enter]**.

   TIP To rename a folder, double-click the folder name, then type the new name.

3. Compare your screen to Figure 16.

You used the Files panel to create a new folder in the striped_umbrella folder and named it 'assets'.

Add a folder to a Web site (Macintosh)

1. Press and hold **[control]**, click the **striped_umbrella folder**, then click **New Folder**.

2. Type **assets** in the new folder name text box, then press **[return]**.

   TIP To rename a folder, click the folder name text box, then press **[return]**.

3. Compare your screen to Figure 17.

You used the Files panel to create a new folder under the striped_umbrella folder and named it 'assets'.

FIGURE 16
The Striped Umbrella site in Files panel with assets folder created (Windows)

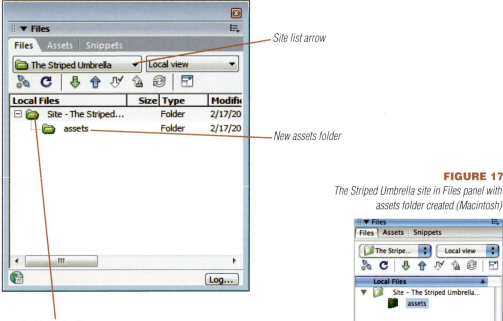

Site list arrow

New assets folder

Root folder for The Striped Umbrella Web site

FIGURE 17
The Striped Umbrella site in Files panel with assets folder created (Macintosh)

FIGURE 18

Site Definition for The Striped Umbrella dialog box with assets folder set as the default images folder

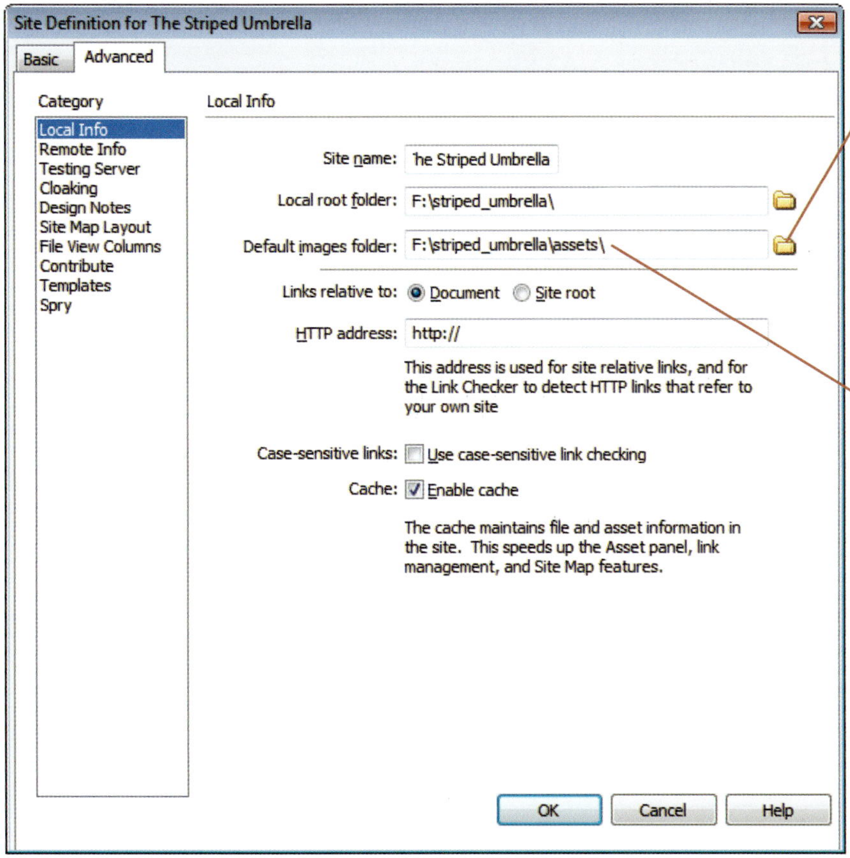

Default images folder text box

Browse for File icon

Site Definition for The Striped Umbrella

| Basic | Advanced |

Category
- Local Info
- Remote Info
- Testing Server
- Cloaking
- Design Notes
- Site Map Layout
- File View Columns
- Contribute
- Templates
- Spry

Local Info

Site name: he Striped Umbrella

Local root folder: F:\striped_umbrella\

Default images folder: F:\striped_umbrella\assets\

Links relative to: ● Document ○ Site root

HTTP address: http://

This address is used for site relative links, and for the Link Checker to detect HTTP links that refer to your own site

Case-sensitive links: ☐ Use case-sensitive link checking

Cache: ☑ Enable cache

The cache maintains file and asset information in the site. This speeds up the Asset panel, link management, and Site Map features.

[OK] [Cancel] [Help]

---

1. Click the **Site list arrow** next to The Striped Umbrella in the Site text box on the Files panel, click **Manage Sites**, then click **Edit**.

2. Click the **Browse for File icon** 📁 next to the Default images folder text box.

3. If necessary, navigate to your striped_umbrella folder, double-click the **assets folder** (Win) or click the **assets folder** (Mac), then click **Select** (Win) or **Choose** (Mac).

   Compare your screen to Figure 18.

4. Click **OK**, then click **Done**.

You set the assets folder as the default images folder so that imported images will be automatically saved in it.

Set the home page

1. Open **dw1_2.html** from where you store your Data Files.

   The file has several elements in it, including a banner image.

2. Click **File** on the menu bar, click **Save As**, click the **Save in list arrow** (Win) or the **Where list arrow** (Mac), navigate to the striped_umbrella folder, select **dw1_2.html** in the File name text box (Win) or select **dw1_2** in the Save As text box (Mac), then type **index**.

3. Click **Save**.

   The file extension .html is automatically added to the filename. As shown in Figure 19, the title bar displays the drive where the root folder is stored, the root folder name, the filename of the page (index.html), and the document type (XHTML) in parentheses. (Win) The information within the brackets is called the **path**, or location of the open file in relation to other folders in the Web site.

4. When asked to update links, click **No.**

   The banner image is no longer visible and the page contains a broken link to the image. This is because although you saved the .html file under a new name in the Web site's root folder, you have not yet copied the image file into the Web site's assets folder. The link to the banner image is still linked to the Data Files folder. You will fix this in the next set of steps.

5. Right-click (Win) or [control]-click (Mac) **index.html** in the Files panel, then click **Set as Home Page**.

You opened a file, saved it with the filename index, then set it as the home page.

FIGURE 19

index.html copied to the striped_umbrella root folder   Path for file

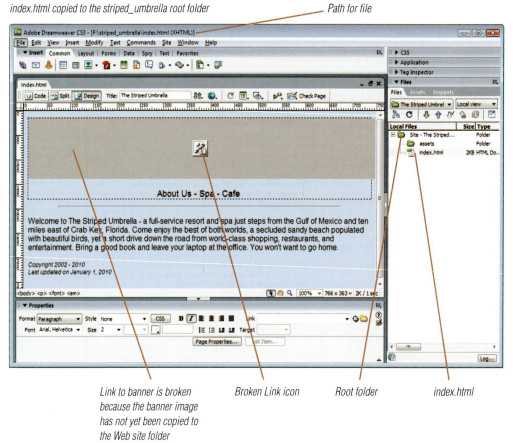

Link to banner is broken because the banner image has not yet been copied to the Web site folder   Broken Link icon   Root folder   index.html

FIGURE 20
Property inspector showing properties of The Striped Umbrella banner

Selection
handles

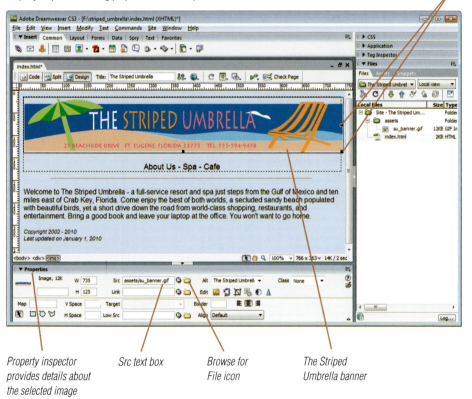

Property inspector
provides details about
the selected image

Src text box

Browse for
File icon

The Striped
Umbrella banner

1. Click **The Striped Umbrella banner broken link placeholder** to select it.

    Selection handles appear around the broken link. To correct the broken link, you must copy the image file from the Data Files folder into the assets folder of your Web site.

2. Click the **Browse for File icon** 📁 next to the Src text box in the Property inspector, click the **Look in list arrow** (Win) or **navigation list arrow** (Mac), navigate to the assets folder in your Data Files folder for this chapter, click **su_banner.gif**, click **OK** (Win) or **Choose** (Mac), then click in a blank part of the page.

    TIP If you do not see the su-banner.gif file listed in the Files panel, click the Refresh button 🔃 on the Files panel toolbar.

    The file for the Striped Umbrella banner, su_banner.gif, is automatically copied to the assets folder of The Striped Umbrella Web site, the folder that you designated as the default images folder. The Src text box shows the path of the banner to the assets folder in the Web site, and the banner image is visible on the page.

3. Compare your screen to Figure 20.

    TIP Until you copy a graphic from an outside folder to your Web site, the graphic is not part of the Web site, and the image will appear as a broken link.

You saved The Striped Umbrella banner in the assets folder.

Add pages to a Web site (Windows)

1. Click the **plus sign** to the left of the assets folder (if necessary) to open the folder and view its contents, su_banner.gif.

   TIP If you do not see a file listed in the assets folder, click the Refresh button 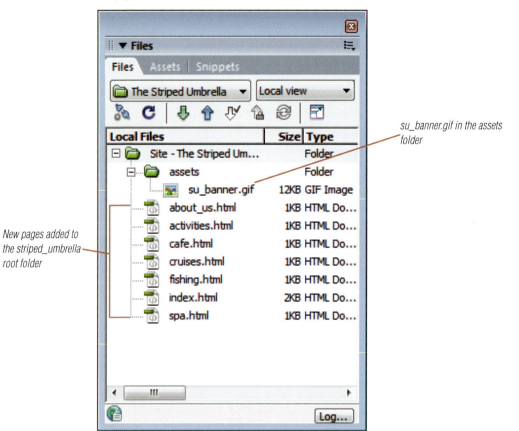 on the Files panel toolbar.

2. Right-click the **striped_umbrella root folder**, click **New File**, type **about_us.html** to replace untitled.html, then press **[Enter]**.

   Each new file is a page in the Web site.

   TIP If you create a new file in the Files panel, you must type the filename extension (.html) manually. If you create a new file using the File menu or the Welcome Screen the filename extension will be added automatically.

3. Repeat Step 2 to add five more blank pages to The Striped Umbrella Web site, then name the new files **spa.html**, **cafe.html**, **activities.html**, **cruises.html**, and **fishing.html**.

   TIP Make sure to add the new files to the root folder, not the assets folder. If you accidentally add them to the assets folder, just drag them to the root folder.

4. Click the **Refresh button** on the Files panel to list the files alphabetically, then compare your screen to Figure 21.

You added the following six pages to The Striped Umbrella Web site: about_us, activities, cafe, cruises, fishing, and spa.

FIGURE 21

New pages added to The Striped Umbrella Web site (Windows)

su_banner.gif in the assets folder

New pages added to the striped_umbrella root folder

Getting Started with Dreamweaver

FIGURE 22

New pages added to The Striped Umbrella Web site (Macintosh)

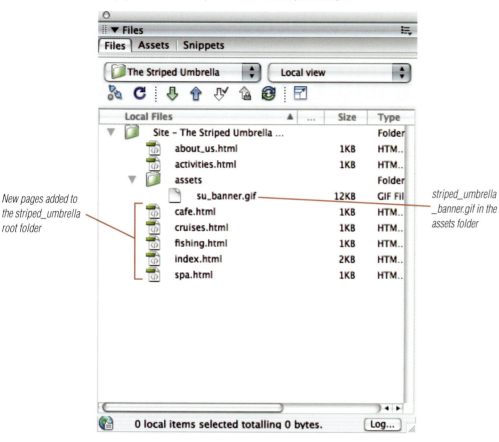

New pages added to the striped_umbrella root folder

striped_umbrella _banner.gif in the assets folder

1. Click the **triangle** to the left of the assets folder to open the folder and view its contents.

   TIP If you do not see a file listed in the assets folder, click the Refresh button ⟳ on the Files panel.

2. [control]-click the **striped_umbrella root folder**, click **New File**, type **about_us.html** to replace untitled.html, then press **[return]**.

   TIP If you create a new file in the Files panel, you must type the filename extension (.html) manually.

3. Repeat Step 3 to add five more blank pages to The Striped Umbrella Web site, then name the new files **spa.html**, **cafe.html**, **activities.html**, **cruises.html**, and **fishing.html**.

4. Click the **Refresh button** ⟳ to list the files alphabetically, then compare your screen to Figure 22.

You added six pages to The Striped Umbrella Web site: about_us, activities, cafe, cruises, fishing, spa.

CREATE AND VIEW
A SITE MAP

What You'll Do

In this lesson, you will create and view a site map for The Striped Umbrella Web site.

Creating a Site Map

As you add new Web pages to a Web site, it is easy to lose track of how they all link together. You can use the site map feature to help you keep track of the relationships between pages in a Web site. A **site map** is a graphical representation of the pages in the Web site and shows the folder structure for the Web site. You can find out details about each page by viewing the visual clues in the site map. For example, the site map uses icons to indicate pages with broken links, e-mail links, and links to external Web sites. It also indicates which pages are currently **checked out**, or being used by other team members.

Viewing a Site Map

You can view a site map using the Map view in the Files panel. You can expand the Files panel to display both the site map and the Web site file list. You can specify that the site map show a filename or a page title for each page. You can also edit page titles in the site map. Figure 23 shows the site map and file list for The Striped Umbrella Web site. Only the home page and pages that are linked to the home page will display in the site map. As more child pages are added, the site map will display them using a **tree structure**, or a diagram that visually represents the way the pages are linked to each other.

> **DESIGN**TIP **Verifying page titles**
>
> When you view a Web page in a browser, its page title is displayed in the browser window title bar. The page title should reflect the page content and set the tone for the page. It is especially important to use words in your page title that are likely to match keywords viewers might enter when using a search engine. Search engines compare the text in page titles to the keywords typed into the search engine. When a title bar displays "Untitled Document," the designer has neglected to give the page a title. This is like giving up free "billboard space" and looks very unprofessional.

Using Site Maps to Help Visitors Find Your Pages

It is very helpful to include an image of the site map, or a site listing, in a Web site to help viewers understand the navigation structure of the site. Using Dreamweaver, you have the options of saving a site map for printing purposes or for displaying a site map on a page in a Web site. Windows users can save site maps as either a BMP (bitmapped) file or as a PNG (Portable Network Graphics) file. Macintosh users can save site maps as PICT or JPEG files. The PNG and JPEG formats are best for inserting the site map on a Web page. Another option to help search engines find your Web pages is to create an **XML site map**, or a listing of the Web site links that can be made available to search engines such as Google, MSN, or Yahoo.

Submitting a site map to search engines is intended to help visitors find your pages, but does not replace the standard methods that search engines use to locate pages based on information entered in search text boxes. For more information on XML site maps, visit *http://www.sitemaps.org/*. This is a Web site sponsored jointly by Google, Yahoo, and Microsoft.

FIGURE 23

The Striped Umbrella site map

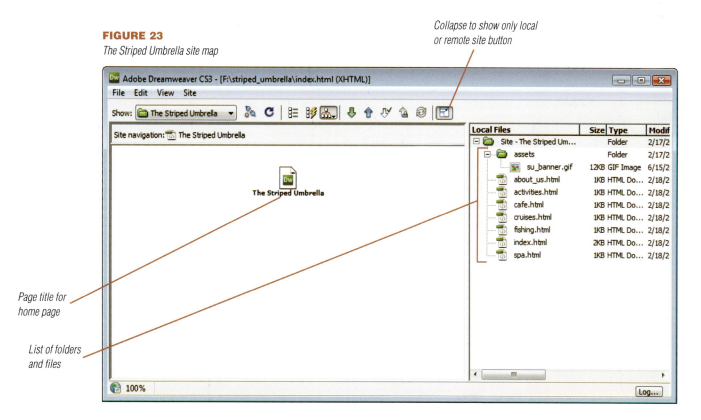

Collapse to show only local or remote site button

Page title for home page

List of folders and files

Select site map options

1. Click the **Site list arrow** next to The Striped Umbrella in the Files panel, click **Manage Sites**, click **The Striped Umbrella** (if necessary), then click **Edit** to open the Site Definition dialog box.

2. Click **Site Map Layout** in the Category list.

3. Verify that index.html is specified as the home page in the Home page text box, as shown in Figure 24.

   TIP If the index.html file is not specified as your home page, click the Browse for File icon next to the Home page text box, then locate and double-click index.html.

4. Click the **Page titles option button**.

5. Click **OK**, then click **Done**.

You designated index.html as the home page for The Striped Umbrella Web site to create the site map. You also specified that page titles are displayed in the site map instead of filenames.

FIGURE 24
Options for the site map layout

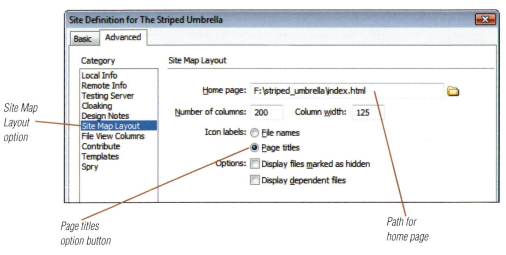

Site Map Layout option

Page titles option button

Path for home page

POWER USER SHORTCUTS

to do this:	use this shortcut:
Open a file	[Ctrl][O] (Win) or ⌘ [O] (Mac)
Close a file	[Ctrl][W] (Win) or ⌘ [W] (Mac)
Create a new file	[Ctrl][N] (Win) or ⌘ [N] (Mac)
Save a file	[Ctrl][S] (Win) or ⌘ [S] (Mac)
Dreamweaver Help	F1
Show panels	F4
Show page titles in Site Map	[Ctrl][Shift][T] (Win) or [Shift]⌘[T] (Mac)

FIGURE 25

Expanding the site map

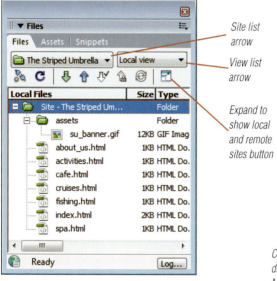

Site list
arrow

View list
arrow

Expand to
show local
and remote
sites button

Click to choose between
displaying Map Only or
Map and Files

FIGURE 26

Viewing the site map options

Drag the border
between the panes
to change the way
the space is
allocated

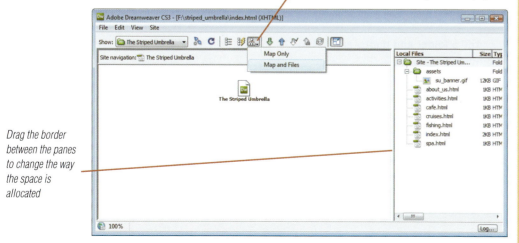

View a site map

1. Click the **Expand to show local and remote sites button** on the Files panel toolbar, as shown in Figure 25, to display the expanded site map.

   The site map shows the home page and pages that are linked to it. Because there are no pages linked to the home page, the site map shows only the home page.

   TIP You can drag the border between the two panes on the screen to resize them.

2. Click the **Site map button**, then click **Map and Files** if you don't see the index page icon on the site map, as shown in Figure 26.

3. Click **View** on the menu bar, point to **Site Map Options**, then click **Show Page Titles** to deselect it (Win) or click **View,** point to **Site Map Options,** then click **Show Page Titles** (Mac).

   The filename, index.html, is now displayed instead of the page title, The Striped Umbrella.

4. Click the **Collapse to show only local or remote site button** on the toolbar to collapse the site map.

   The file list appears again in the Files panel.

5. Click **File** on the menu bar, then click **Exit** (Win) or click **Dreamweaver** on the menu bar, and then click **Quit Dreamweaver** (Mac).

   TIP If you are prompted to save changes, click No.

You expanded the site map and viewed the index page with the page title and then the filename. You then collapsed the site map.

Explore the Dreamweaver workspace.

1. Start Dreamweaver.
2. Create a new document.
3. Change the view to Code view.
4. Change the view to Code and Design views.
5. Change the view to Design view.
6. Expand the Application panel group.
7. View each panel in the Application panel group.
8. Collapse the Application panel group.
9. Close the page without saving it.

View a Web page and use Help.

1. Open the file dw1_3.html from where you store your Data Files.
2. Locate the following page elements: a table, a banner, an image, and some formatted text.
3. Change the view to Code view.
4. Change the view to Design view.
5. Use the Dreamweaver Help command to search for information on panel groups.
6. Display and read one of the topics you find.
7. Close the Dreamweaver Help Viewer window.
8. Close the page without saving it.

Plan and define a Web site.

1. Select the drive and folder where you will store your Web site files using Windows Explorer or the Macintosh Finder.
2. Create a new root folder called **blooms**.
3. Close Windows Explorer or the Finder (Mac), then activate the Dreamweaver application.
4. Create a new site called **blooms & bulbs**.
5. Specify the blooms folder as the Local root folder.
6. Verify that the Enable cache check box is selected.
7. Use the Remote Info category in the Site Definition for the blooms & bulbs dialog box to set up Web server access. (*Hint*: Specify None if you do not have the necessary information to set up Web server access.)
8. Click **OK**, then click Done to close the Site Definition for the blooms & bulbs dialog box.

Add a folder and pages and set the home page.

1. Create a new folder in the blooms root folder called **assets**.
2. Edit the site to set the assets folder as the default location for the Web site images.

3. Open the file dw1_4.html from where you store your Data Files, save this file in the blooms root folder as **index.html**, then click No to updating the links.
4. Set index.html as the home page.
5. Select the broken image link for the blooms & bulbs banner on the page.
6. Use the Property inspector to browse for blooms_banner.jpg, then select it to automatically save it in the assets folder of the blooms & bulbs Web site.
7. Create seven new pages in the Files panel, and name them: **plants.html**, **classes.html**, **newsletter.html**, **annuals.html**, **perennials.html**, **water_plants.html**, and **tips.html**.
8. Refresh the view to list the new files alphabetically.

Create and view a site map.

1. Use the Site Definition dialog box to verify that the index.html file is shown as the home page.
2. View the expanded site map for the Web site.
3. Show the page titles, as shown in Figure 27.
4. Show the file names.
5. Collapse the site map, then close index.html.

FIGURE 27
Completed Skills Review

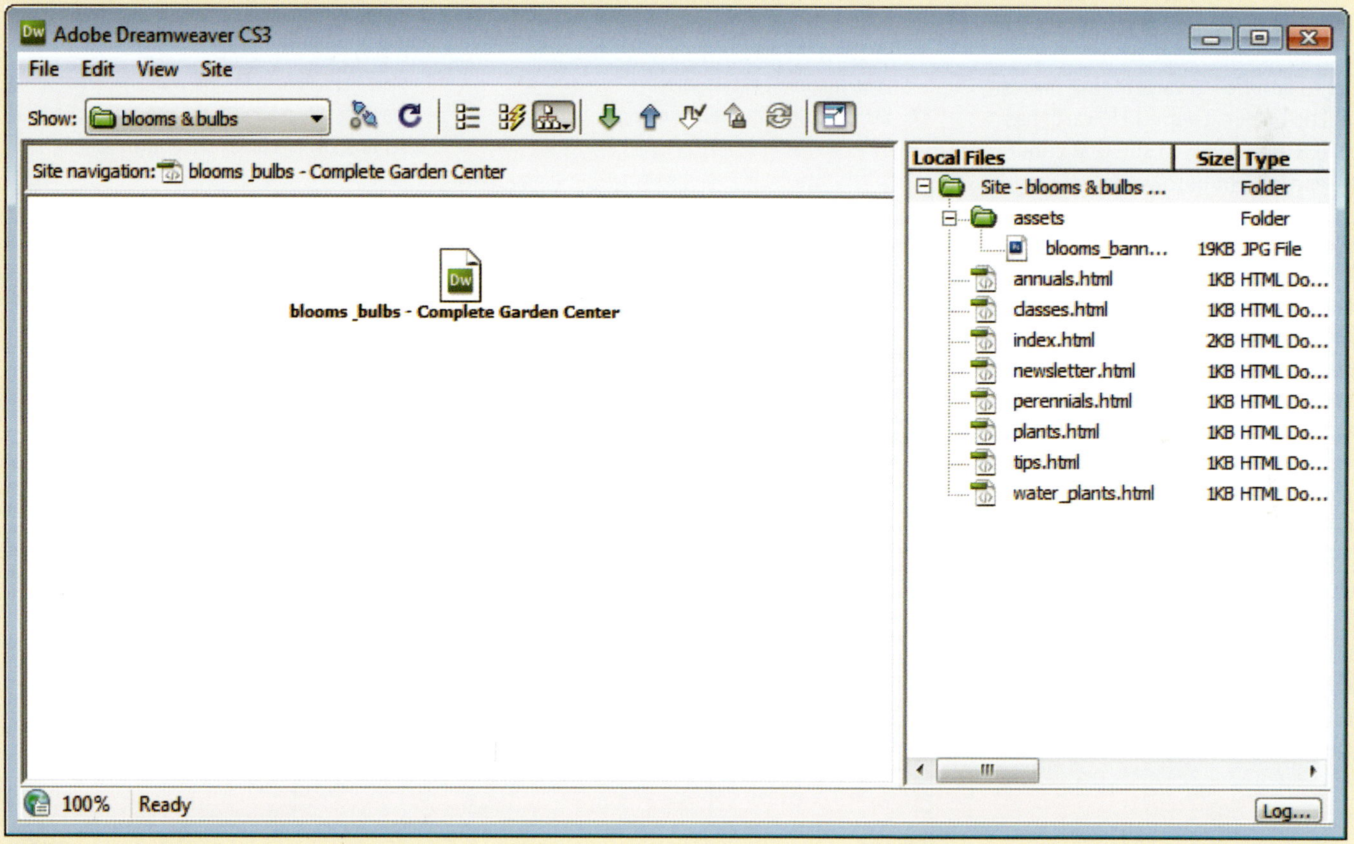

You have been hired to create a Web site for a travel outfitter called TripSmart. TripSmart specializes in travel products and services. In addition to selling travel products, such as luggage and accessories, they sponsor trips and offer travel advice. Their clients range from college students to families to vacationing professionals. The owner, Thomas Howard, has requested a dynamic Web site that conveys the excitement of traveling.

1. Using the information in the preceding paragraph, create a storyboard for this Web site, using either a pencil and paper or a software program such as Microsoft Word. Include the home page with links to four child pages named **catalog.html**, **newsletter.html**, **services.html**, and **destinations.html**. Include two child pages under the destinations page named **amazon.html** and **kenya.html**.
2. Create a new root folder named **tripsmart** in the drive and folder where you store your Web site files.
3. Start Dreamweaver, then create a Web site with the name **TripSmart**. Set the tripsmart folder as the local root folder for the Web site.
4. Create an assets folder and set it as the default location for images.

5. Open the file dw1_5.html from where you store your Data Files, then save it in the tripsmart root folder as **index.html**.
6. Correct the path for the banner by selecting the banner on the page, browsing to the original source in the Data Files folder, then selecting the file to copy it automatically to your TripSmart assets folder.
7. Set index.html as the home page.

FIGURE 28
Completed Project Builder 1

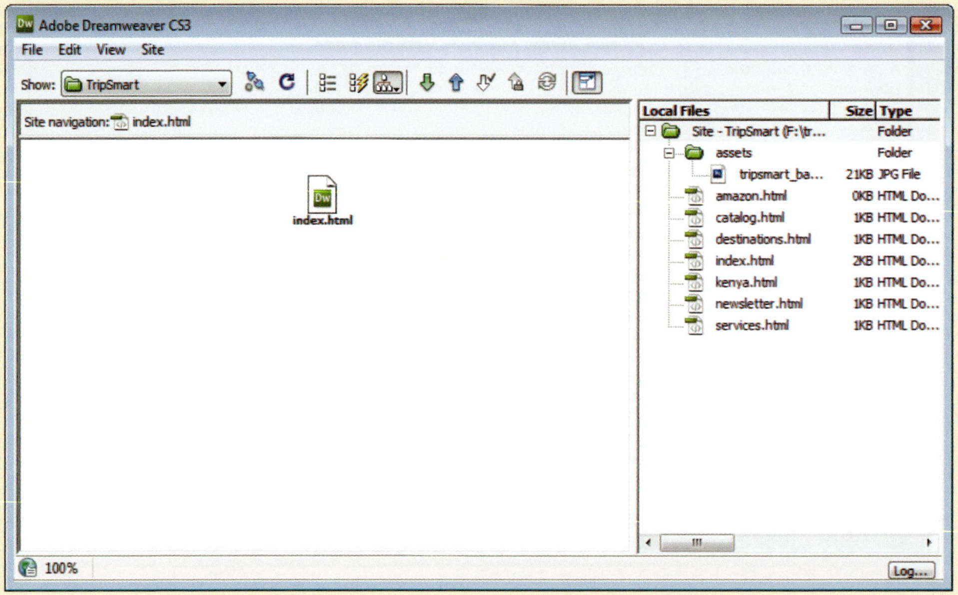

8. Create six additional pages for the site, and name them as follows: **catalog.html**, **newsletter.html**, **services.html**, **destinations.html**, **amazon.html**, and **kenya.html**. Use your storyboard and Figure 28 as a guide.
9. Refresh the Files panel.
10. View the site map for the Web site. (*Hint*: View the site map with the site map option set to show filenames rather than page titles.)
11. Collapse the site map, then close any open pages.

Your company has been selected to design a Web site for a catering business called Carolyne's Creations. In addition to catering, Carolyne's services include cooking classes and daily specials available as take-out meals. She also has a retail shop that stocks gourmet treats and kitchen items.

1. Create a storyboard for this Web site that includes a home page and child pages named **shop.html, classes.html, catering.html**, and **recipes.html**. Create two more child pages under the classes.html page called **children.html** and **adults.html**.

2. Create a new root folder for the Web site in the drive and folder where you save your Web site files, then name it **cc**.

3. Create a Web site with the name Carolyne's Creations, using the cc folder for the root folder.

4. Create an assets folder for the Web site and set the assets folder as the default location for images.

5. Open dw1_6.html from the where you store your Data Files then save it as **index.html** in the cc folder.

6. Save the cc_banner.jpg file in the assets folder.

7. Set index.html as the home page.

8. Using Figure 29 and your storyboard as guides, create the additional pages shown for the Web site.

9. View the site map with page titles displayed, as shown in Figure 29, then show the filenames before you collapse the site map.

10. Close the index file.

FIGURE 29
Completed Project Builder 2

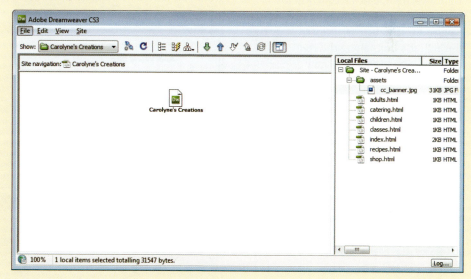

Figure 30 shows the Audi Web site, a past selection for the Adobe Site of the Day. To visit the current Audi Web site, connect to the Internet, then go to *www.audi.com*. The current page might differ from the figure because dynamic Web sites are updated frequently to reflect current information. The main navigation structure is accessed through the links along the right side of the page. The page title is Audi Worldwide > Home.

Go to the Adobe Web site at *www.adobe.com,* click the Showcase link (at the bottom right corner of the page), then click the current Site of the Day. Explore the site and answer the following questions:

1. Do you see page titles for each page you visit?
2. Do the page titles accurately reflect the page content?
3. View the pages using more than one screen resolution, if possible. For which resolution does the site appear to be designed?

4. Is the navigation structure clear?
5. How is the navigation structure organized?

6. Why do you think this site was chosen as a Site of the Day?

FIGURE 30
Design Project

Audi Web site used with permission from Audi AG – www.audi.com

PORTFOLIO PROJECT

The Portfolio Project will be an ongoing project throughout the book, in which you will plan and create an original Web site without any Data Files supplied. The focus of the Web site can be on any topic, organization, sports team, club, or company that you would like. You will build on this Web site from chapter to chapter, so you must do each Portfolio Project assignment in each chapter to complete your Web site. When you finish this book, you should have a completed Web site that would be an excellent addition to a professional portfolio.

1. Decide what type of Web site you would like to create. It can be a personal Web site about you, a business Web site that promotes a fictitious or real company, or an informational Web site that provides information about a topic, cause, or organization.

2. Write a list of questions and answers about the Web site you have decided to create.

3. Create a storyboard for your Web site to include at least four pages. The storyboard should include the home page with at least three child pages under it.

4. Create a root folder and an assets folder to house the Web site assets, then set it as the default location for images.

5. Create a blank page named **index.html** as a placeholder for the home page, then set it as the home page.

6. Begin collecting content, such as pictures or text to use in your Web site. You can use a digital camera to take photos, scan pictures, or create your own graphics using a program such as Adobe Fireworks or Adobe Illustrator. Gather the content in a central location that will be accessible to you as you develop your site.

chapter

2

DEVELOPING A
WEB PAGE

1. Create head content and set page properties

2. Create, import, and format text

3. Add links to Web pages

4. Use the History panel and edit code

5. Modify and test Web pages

2 DEVELOPING A
WEB PAGE

Introduction

The process of developing a Web page requires several steps. If the page is a home page, you need to spend some time crafting the head content. The head content contains information used by search engines to help viewers find your Web site. You also need to choose the colors for the page background and text. You then need to add the page content, format it attractively, and add links to other pages in the Web site or to other Web sites. Finally, to ensure that all links work correctly and are current, you need to test them regularly.

Understanding Page Layout

Before you add content to a page, consider the following guidelines for laying out pages:

Use White Space Effectively. A living room crammed with too much furniture makes it difficult to appreciate the individual pieces. The same is true of a Web page. Too many text blocks, links, animations, and images can be distracting. Consider leaving some white space on each page. White space, which is not necessarily white, is the area on a Web page that contains no text or graphics.

Limit Multimedia Elements. Too many multimedia elements, such as images,

video clips, or sounds, may result in a page that takes too much time to load. Viewers may leave your Web site before the entire page finishes loading. Use multimedia elements only if you have a good reason.

Keep It Simple. Often the simplest Web sites are the most appealing and are also the easiest to create and maintain. A simple, well-designed Web site that works well is far superior to a complex one that contains errors.

Use an Intuitive Navigation Structure. Make sure the navigation structure is easy to use. Viewers should always know where they are in the site and be able to easily find their way back to the home page. If viewers get lost, they may leave the site rather than struggle to find their way around.

Apply a Consistent Theme. To help give pages in your Web site a consistent appearance, consider designing your pages using elements that relate to a common theme. Consistency in the use of color and fonts, the placement of the navigation links, and the overall page design gives a Web site a unified look and promotes greater ease-of-use and accessibility. Template-based pages and style sheets make this task much easier.

Tools You'll Use

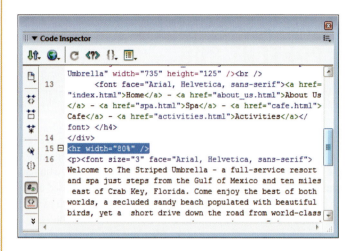

CREATE HEAD CONTENT AND
SET PAGE PROPERTIES

What You'll Do

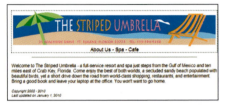

▶ *In this lesson, you will learn how to enter titles, keywords, and descriptions in the head content section of a Web page. You will also change the background color for a Web page.*

Creating the Head Content

A Web page is composed of two distinct sections: the head content and the body. The **head content** includes the page title that is displayed in the title bar of the browser and some important page elements, called meta tags, that are not visible in the browser. Page titles are not to be confused with filenames, the name used to store each file on the server. **Meta tags** are HTML codes that include information about the page, such as keywords and descriptions. Meta tags are read by screen readers (for viewers who have visual impairments) and are also used to provide the server information such as the PICS rating for the page. PICS is the acronym for **Platform for Internet Content Selection**. This is a rating system for Web pages that is similar to rating systems used for movies. **Keywords** are words

DESIGNTIP Using Web-safe colors

Prior to 1994, colors appeared differently on different types of computers. In 1994, Netscape developed the first **Web-safe color palette**, a set of colors that appears consistently in all browsers and on Macintosh, Windows, and UNIX platforms. The evolution of video cards has made this less relevant today, although understanding Web-safe colors may still prove important given the limitations of other online devices, such as cell phones and PDAs. If you want your Web pages to be viewed across a wide variety of computer platforms, choose Web-safe colors for all your page elements. Dreamweaver has two Web-safe color palettes, Color Cubes and Continuous Tone, each of which contains 216 Web-safe colors. Color Cubes is the default color palette. To choose a different color palette, click Modify on the menu bar, click Page Properties, click the Appearance category, click the Background, Text, or Links color box to open the color picker, click the color picker list arrow, and then click the color palette you want.

that relate to the content of the Web site. A **description** is a short paragraph that describes the content and features of the Web site. For instance, the words "beach" and "resort" would be appropriate keywords for The Striped Umbrella Web site. Search engines find Web pages by matching the title, description, and keywords in the head content of Web pages with keywords that viewers enter in search engine text boxes. Therefore, it is important to include concise, useful information in the head content. The **body** is the part of the page that appears in a browser window. It contains all the page content that is visible to viewers, such as text, images, and links.

Setting Web Page Properties

When you create a Web page, one of the first design decisions that you should make is choosing the **background color**, or the color that fills the entire Web page. The background color should complement the colors used for text, links, and images that are placed on the page. Many times, images are used for backgrounds for either the entire page or a part of the page, such as a table background. A strong contrast between the text color and the background color makes it easier for viewers to read the text on your Web page. You can choose a light background color with a dark text color, or a dark background color with a light text color. A white background with dark text, though not terribly exciting, provides good contrast and is the easiest to read for most viewers. Another design decision you need to make is whether to change the **default font** and **default link colors**, which are the colors used by the browser to display text, links, and

visited links. The default color for **unvisited links**, or links that the viewer has not clicked yet, is blue. In Dreamweaver, unvisited links are simply called **links**. The default color for **visited links**, or links that have been previously clicked, is purple. You change the background color, text, and link colors using the color picker in the Page Properties dialog box. You can choose colors from one of the five Dreamweaver color palettes, as shown in Figure 1.

QUICK TIP

Many design decisions are implemented through the use of Cascading Style Sheets, or CSS. We will initially use the Page Properties dialog box to set page properties such as the background color. Later we will learn to do this using Cascading Style Sheets.

FIGURE 1
Color picker showing color palettes

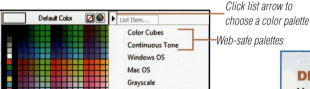

Click list arrow to choose a color palette

Web-safe palettes

DESIGNTIP   **Making pages accessible to viewers of all abilities**
Not all of your viewers will have perfect vision and hearing or full use of both hands. There are several techniques you can use to ensure that your Web site is accessible to individuals with disabilities. These techniques include using alternate text with images, avoiding certain colors on Web pages, and supplying text as an alternate source for information that is presented in an audio file. Adobe provides much information about Web site compliance with Section 508 accessibility guidelines. For more information, visit the Adobe Web site at *www.adobe.com/accessibility/*. Here you will find suggestions for creating accessible Web sites, an explanation of Section 508, and information on how people with disabilities use assistive devices to navigate the Internet.

Edit a page title

1. Start Dreamweaver, click the **Site list arrow** on the Files panel, then click **The Striped Umbrella** (if necessary).

2. Double-click **index.html** in the Files panel to open The Striped Umbrella home page, click **View** on the menu bar, then click **Head Content**.

   The Title icon and Meta icon are now visible in the head content section, as shown in Figure 2.

3. Click the **Title icon** in the head content section.

   The page title The Striped Umbrella appears in the Title text box in the Property inspector.

4. Click the end of The Striped Umbrella text in the Title text box in the Property inspector, press **[Spacebar]**, type **beach resort and spa, Ft. Eugene, Florida**, then press **[Enter]** (Win) or **[return]** (Mac).

   Compare your screen with Figure 3. The new title is better, because it incorporates the words "beach resort" and "spa" and the location of the resort—words that potential customers might use as keywords when using a search engine.

   TIP   You can also change the page title using the Title text box on the Document toolbar.

   You opened The Striped Umbrella Web site, opened the home page in Design view, viewed the head content section, and changed the page title.

FIGURE 2
Viewing the head content

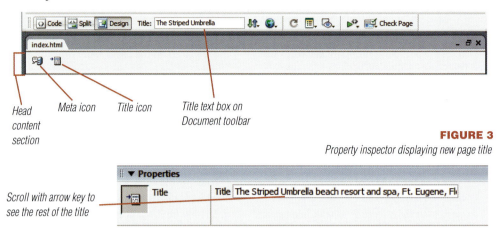

Head content section

Meta icon

Title icon

Title text box on Document toolbar

FIGURE 3
Property inspector displaying new page title

Scroll with arrow key to see the rest of the title

DESIGN TIP   Using appropriate content for your target audience

When you begin developing the content for your Web site, you need to decide what content to include and how to arrange each element on each page. You must design the content with the audience in mind. What is the age group of your audience? What reading level is appropriate? Should you use a formal or informal tone? Should the pages be simple, containing mostly text, or rich with images and multimedia files? Your content should fit your target audience. Look at the font sizes used, the number and size of images and animations used, the reading level, and the amount of technical expertise needed to navigate your site, and then evaluate them to see if they fit your audience. If they do not, you will be defeating your purpose. Usually, the first page that your audience will see when they visit your Web site is the home page. The home page should be designed so that viewers will understand your site's purpose and feel comfortable finding their way around the pages in your site. To ensure that viewers do not get lost in your Web site, make sure you design all the pages with a consistent look and feel. You can use templates and Cascading Style Sheets to maintain a common look for each page.

Templates are Web pages that contain the basic layout for each page in the site, including the location of a company logo or a menu of buttons. **Cascading Style Sheets** are sets of formatting attributes that are used to format Web pages to provide a consistent presentation for content across the site.

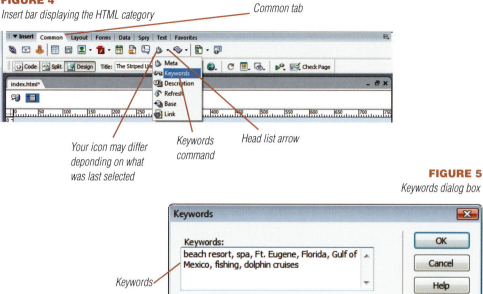

FIGURE 4
Insert bar displaying the HTML category

Common tab

Your icon may differ
depending on what
was last selected

Keywords
command

Head list arrow

FIGURE 5
Keywords dialog box

Keywords

Enter keywords

1. Click the **Common tab** on the Insert bar (if necessary).

2. Click the **Head list arrow**, as shown in Figure 4, then click **Keywords**.

   TIP   Some buttons on the Insert bar include a list arrow indicating that there is a menu of choices beneath the current button. The button that you select last will appear on the Insert bar until you select another.

3. Type **beach resort, spa, Ft. Eugene, Florida, Gulf of Mexico, fishing, dolphin cruises** in the Keywords text box, as shown in Figure 5, then click OK

   The Keywords icon 🔍 appears in the head content section and the keywords appear in the Keywords text box in the Property inspector.

   You added keywords relating to the beach to the head content of The Striped Umbrella home page.

DESIGNTIP   **Entering keywords and descriptions**

Search engines use keywords, descriptions, and titles to find pages after a user enters search terms. Therefore, it is very important to anticipate the search terms your potential customers would use and include these words in the keywords, description, and title. Many search engines display page titles and descriptions in their search results. Some search engines limit the number of keywords that they will index, so make sure you list the most important keywords first. Keep your keywords and descriptions short and concise to ensure that all search engines will include your site. To choose effective keywords, many designers incorporate the use of focus groups to have a more representative sample of words that potential customers or clients might use. A **focus group** is a marketing tool that asks a group of people for feedback about a product, such as its impact in a television ad or the effectiveness of a Web site design.

Enter a description

1. Click the **Head list arrow** on the Insert bar, then click **Description**.

2. In the Description text box, type **The Striped Umbrella is a full-service resort and spa just steps from the Gulf of Mexico in Ft. Eugene, Florida**.

   Your screen should resemble Figure 6.

3. Click **OK**.

   The Description icon appears in the Head Content section and the keywords appear in the Description text box in the Property inspector.

4. Click the **Show Code view button** on the Document toolbar.

   Notice that the title, keywords, and description appear in the HTML code in the document window, as shown in Figure 7.

   TIP You can also enter and edit the meta tags directly in the code in Code view.

5. Click the **Show Design view button** to return to Design view.

6. Click **View** on the menu bar, then click **Head Content** to close the head content section.

You added a description of The Striped Umbrella resort to the head content of the home page. You then viewed the home page in Code view and examined the HTML code for the head content.

FIGURE 6
Description dialog box

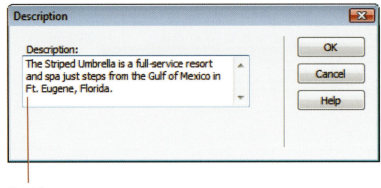

Description

FIGURE 7
Head Content displayed in Code view

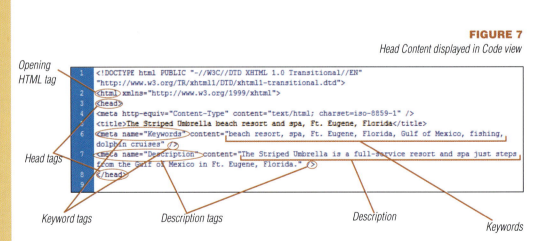

Opening HTML tag

Head tags

Keyword tags

Description tags

Description

Keywords

FIGURE 8

Page Properties dialog box

Default Color button

Background color box

Hexadecimal number for white

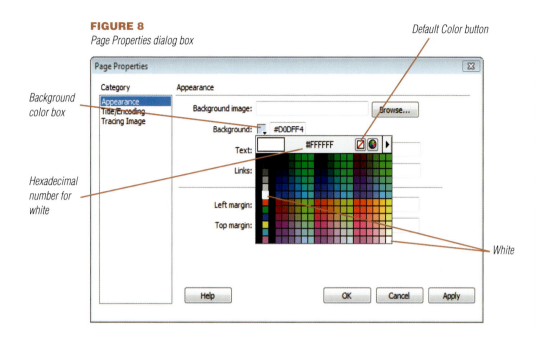

White

1. Click **Modify** on the menu bar, then click **Page Properties** to open the Page Properties dialog box.

2. Click the **Background color box** ⬜ to open the color picker, as shown in Figure 8.

3. Click the last color in the bottom row (white).

4. Click **Apply**, then click **OK**.

   Clicking Apply lets you see the changes you made to the Web page without closing the Page Properties dialog box.

   > TIP If you don't like the color you chose, click the Default Color button ☒ in the color picker to switch back to the default color.

   The background color of the Web page is now white. The black text against the white background provides a nice contrast and makes the text easy to read.

   You used the Page Properties dialog box to change the background color to white.

Understanding hexadecimal values

Each color is assigned a **hexadecimal value**, a value that represents the amount of red, green, and blue present in the color. For example, white, which is made of equal parts of red, green, and blue, has a hexadecimal value of FFFFFF. Each pair of characters in the hexadecimal value represents the red, green, and blue values. The hexadecimal number system is based on 16, rather than 10 in the decimal number system. Because the hexadecimal number system includes only numbers up to 9, values after 9 use the letters of the alphabet. "A" represents the number 10 in the hexadecimal number system. "F" represents the number 15.

CREATE, IMPORT, AND
FORMAT TEXT

What You'll Do

▶ In this lesson, you will apply HTML heading styles and HTML text styles to text on The Striped Umbrella home page. You will also import a file and set text properties for the text on the new page.

Creating and Importing Text

Most information in Web pages is presented in the form of text. You can type text directly in Dreamweaver, import, or copy and paste it from another software program. When using a Windows computer to import text from a Microsoft Word file, you use the Import Word Document command. Not only will the formatting be preserved, but Dreamweaver will generate clean HTML code. When you import text, it is important to keep in mind that visitors to your site must have the same fonts installed on their computers as the fonts applied to the imported text. Otherwise, the text may appear incorrectly. Some software programs may be able to convert text into graphics so that the text retains the same appearance no matter which fonts are installed. However, text converted into graphics is no longer editable. If text does not have a font specified, the default font

Using keyboard shortcuts

When working with text, the standard Windows keyboard shortcuts for Cut, Copy, and Paste are very useful. These are [Ctrl][X] (Win) or ⌘[X] (Mac) for Cut, [Ctrl][C] (Win) or ⌘[C] (Mac) for Copy, and [Ctrl][V] (Win) or ⌘[V] (Mac) for Paste. You can view all Dreamweaver keyboard shortcuts using the Keyboard Shortcuts dialog box, which lets you view existing shortcuts for menu commands, tools, or miscellaneous functions, such as copying HTML or inserting an image. You can also create your own shortcuts or assign shortcuts that you are familiar with from using them in other software programs. To view or modify keyboard shortcuts, click the Keyboard Shortcuts command on the Edit menu (Win) or Dreamweaver menu (Mac), then select the shortcut key set you want. The Keyboard Shortcuts feature is also available in Adobe Fireworks and Flash. Each chapter includes a list of keyboard shortcuts relevant to that chapter.

will apply. This means that the default font on the user's computer will be used to display the text. Keep in mind that some fonts may not display the same on both a Windows and a Macintosh computer. It is wise to stick to the standard fonts that work well with both systems.

Formatting Text Using the Property Inspector

Because text is more difficult and tiring to read on a computer screen than on a printed page, you should make the text in your Web site attractive and easy to read. You can format text in Dreamweaver by changing its font, size, and color, just as you would in other software programs. To apply formatting to text, you first select the text you want to enhance, and then use the Property inspector to apply formatting attributes, such as font type, size, color, alignment, and indents.

Changing Fonts

You can format your text with different fonts by choosing a font combination from the Font list in the Property inspector. A **font combination** is a set of three fonts that specify which fonts a browser should use to display the text of your Web page. Font combinations are used so that if one font is not available, the browser will use the next one specified in the font combination. For

example, if text is formatted with the font combination Arial, Helvetica, sans serif, the browser will first look on the viewer's system for Arial. If Arial is not available, then it will look for Helvetica. If Helvetica is not available, then it will look for a sans-serif font to apply to the text. Using fonts within the default settings is wise, because fonts set outside the default settings may not be available on all viewers' computers.

Changing Font Sizes

There are two ways to change the size of text using the Property inspector. You can select a font size between 1 and 7 (where 1 is the smallest and 7 is the largest), or you can change the font size relative to the default base font. The **default base font** is size 3. For example, choosing +1 in the Size list increases the font size from 3 to 4. Font sizes on Windows and Macintosh computers may differ slightly, so it's important to view your page on both platforms, if possible.

Formatting Paragraphs

You can format blocks of text as paragraphs or as different sizes of headings. To format a paragraph as a heading, click anywhere in the paragraph, and then select the heading size you want from the Format list in the Property inspector. The Format list contains six different heading formats. Heading 1 is the largest size, and

Heading 6 is the smallest size. Browsers display text formatted as headings in bold, setting them off from paragraphs of text. You can also align paragraphs with the alignment buttons on the Property inspector and indent paragraphs using the Text Indent and Text Outdent buttons on the Property inspector.

QUICKTIP

Mixing too many different fonts and formatting attributes on a Web page can result in pages that are visually confusing or difficult to read.

Using HTML Tags Compared to Using CSS

The standard practice today is to use Cascading Style Sheets (CSS) to handle most of the formatting and placement of Web page elements. In fact, the default preference in Dreamweaver is to use CSS rather than HTML tags. However, this is a lot to learn when you are just beginning, so we are going to disable this preference temporarily until we study CSS in depth in the next chapter. At that point, we will again set the default preference to using CSS instead of HTML tags by clicking Edit (Win) or Dreamweaver (Mac) on the menu bar, clicking Preferences, and then checking the Use CSS instead of HTML tags check box.

Enter text

1. Position the insertion point directly after "want to go home." at the end of the paragraph, press **[Enter]** (Win) or **[return]** (Mac), then type **The Striped Umbrella**.

   Pressing [Enter] (Win) or [return] (Mac) creates a new paragraph. The HTML code for a paragraph break is <p>. The tag is closed with </p>.

   > TIP If the new text does not assume the formatting attributes as the paragraph above it, click the Show Code and Design views button 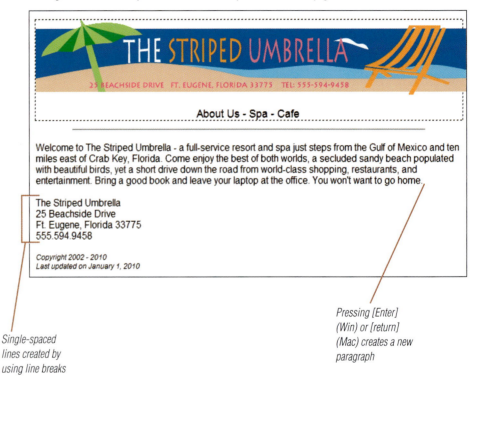 position the cursor between the period after "home" and the font tag, then go back to the page in Design view and insert a new paragraph.

2. Press and hold **[Shift]**, press **[Enter]** (Win) or **[return]** (Mac), then type **25 Beachside Drive**.

   Pressing and holding [Shift] while you press [Enter] (Win) or [return] (Mac) creates a line break. A line break places a new line of text on the next line down without creating a new paragraph. Line breaks are useful when you want to add a new line of text directly below the current line of text and keep the same formatting. The HTML code for a line break is <br />.

3. Add the following text below the 25 Beachside Drive text, using line breaks after each line:

   Ft. Eugene, Florida 33775

   555.594.9458

4. Compare your screen with Figure 9.

   You entered text for the address and telephone number on the home page.

FIGURE 9

Entering the address and telephone number on The Striped Umbrella home page

Welcome to The Striped Umbrella - a full-service resort and spa just steps from the Gulf of Mexico and ten miles east of Crab Key, Florida. Come enjoy the best of both worlds, a secluded sandy beach populated with beautiful birds, yet a short drive down the road from world-class shopping, restaurants, and entertainment. Bring a good book and leave your laptop at the office. You won't want to go home.

The Striped Umbrella
25 Beachside Drive
Ft. Eugene, Florida 33775
555.594.9458

Copyright 2002 - 2010
Last updated on January 1, 2010

Single-spaced lines created by using line breaks

Pressing [Enter] (Win) or [return] (Mac) creates a new paragraph

FIGURE 10

Formatting the address on The Striped Umbrella home page

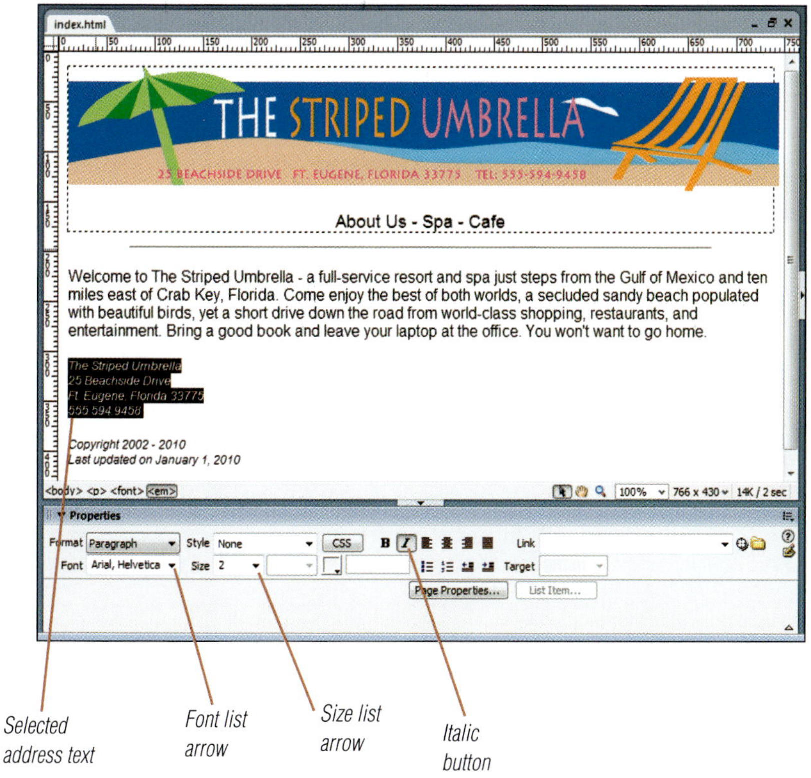

Selected address text

Font list arrow

Size list arrow

Italic button

Format text

1. Select the entire address and telephone number, as shown in Figure 10, then click the **Italic button** $\boxed{I}$ in the Property inspector to italicize the text.

   When you have applied the italic style to selected text, the HTML code is <em>.

   TIP   To create bold text, the HTML tag is <strong></strong>; to underline text, the HTML code is <u></u>.

2. With the text still selected, click the **Size list arrow**, click **2**, then compare your screen to Figure 10.

3. Save your work, then close the document.

You formatted the address and phone number for The Striped Umbrella by changing the font style to Italic and changing the size to 2.

Preventing data loss

When you are ready to stop working with a file in Dreamweaver, it is a good idea to save your changes, close the page or pages on which you are working, and exit Dreamweaver. Doing this will prevent the loss of data if power is interrupted. In some cases, loss of power can corrupt an open file and render it unusable.

Save an image file in the assets folder

1. Open dw2_1.html from where you store your Data Files, save it as **spa.html** in the striped_umbrella folder, overwriting the existing file, then click **No** in the Update Links dialog box.

2. Select **The Striped Umbrella** banner.

   Updating links ties the image or hyperlink to the Data Files folder. Because you already copied su_banner.gif to the Web site, the banner image is visible. Notice that the Src text box shows the link is to the Web site assets folder, not to the Data Files folder.

3. Click the **Spa image broken link placeholder** to select it, click the **Browse for File icon** 📁 in the Property inspector, navigate to the chapter_2 assets folder, click **the_spa.jpg**, click beside the icon to deselect it, then click **OK** (Win) or **Choose** (Mac).

   Because this image was not in the Web site, it appears as a broken link. Using the Browse for File icon 📁 selects the source of the original image file. Dreamweaver automatically copies the file to the assets folder of the Web site and it is visible on the page. You may have to deselect the new image to see it replace the broken link.

4. Click the **Refresh button** 🔄 on the Files panel toolbar, then click the **plus sign** (Win) or **expander arrow** (Mac) next to the assets folder in the Files panel, (if necessary).

   A copy of the_spa.jpg file appears in the assets folder, as shown in Figure 11.

   You opened a new file, saved it as the new spa page, and fixed a broken link by copying the image to the assets folder.

FIGURE 11
Image file added to The Striped Umbrella assets folder

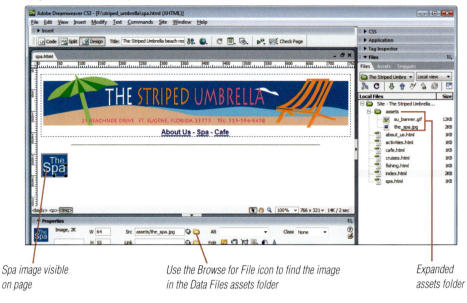

Spa image visible on page

Use the Browse for File icon to find the image in the Data Files assets folder

Expanded assets folder

Choosing filenames for Web pages

When you choose a name for a Web page, you should use a descriptive name that reflects the contents of the page. For example, if the page is about your company's products, you could name it products.html. You should also follow some general rules for naming Web pages, such as naming the home page **index.html**. Most file servers look for the file named index.html to use as the initial page for a Web site. Do not use spaces, special characters, or punctuation in Web page filenames or in the names of any images that will be inserted in your Web site. Spaces in filenames can cause errors when a browser attempts to read a file, and may cause your images to load incorrectly. You should also never use a number for the first character of a filename. To ensure that everything will load properly on all platforms, including UNIX, assume that filenames are case-sensitive and use lowercase characters. Files are saved with the .htm or .html file extension. Although either file extension is appropriate, the default file extension is .html. Use underscores in place of spaces. Forbidden characters include * & ^ % $ # @ ! / and \.

FIGURE 12

Clean Up Word HTML dialog box

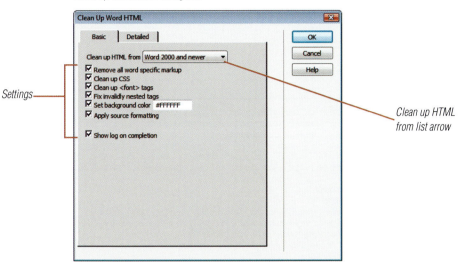

Settings —

Clean up HTML
from list arrow

Importing and Linking Microsoft Office documents (Windows)

Adobe makes it easy to transfer data between Microsoft Office documents and Dreamweaver Web pages. When importing a Word or Excel document, click File on the menu bar, point to Import, then click either Word Document or Excel Document. Select the file want to import, then click the Formatting list arrow to choose between importing Text only (unformatted text); Text with structure (paragraphs, lists, and tables); Text, structure, basic formatting (bold, italic and Text), structure, full formatting (bold, italic, styles) before you click Open. The option you choose depends on the importance of the original structure and formatting. Always use the Clean Up Word HTML command after importing a Word file. You can also create a link to a Word or Excel document on your Web page. To do so, drag the Word or Excel document from its current location to the location on the Web page where you would like the link to appear. (If the document is located outside the Web site, you can browse for it using the Site list arrow on the Files panel.) Next, select the Create a link option button in the Insert Document dialog box, then save the file in your root folder so it will be uploaded when you publish your site. If it is not uploaded, the link will be broken.

Import text

1. Click **Edit** (Win) or **Dreamweaver** (Mac) on the menu bar, click **Preferences**, then click **General** on the left (if necessary).

2. Verify that the Use CSS instead of HTML tags check box is not checked, then click **OK**.

   TIP   It is very important to remove the check mark in the Use CSS instead of HTML tags check box at this time. After we explore CSS, we will restore this default preference. This is not a recommended practice. It is being suggested only to facilitate the learning process for a beginning Web designer.

3. Click to the right of the spa graphic on the spa.html page, then press **[Enter]** (Win) or **[return]** (Mac).

4. Click **File** on the menu bar, point to **Import**, click **Word Document**, double-click the **chapter_2 folder** from where you store your Data Files, then double-click **spa.doc** (Win), or double-click **spa.doc** from where you store your Data Files, select all, copy, close spa.doc, then paste the copied text on the spa page in Dreamweaver (Mac).

5. Click **Commands** on the menu bar, then click **Clean Up Word HTML**.

   TIP   If a dialog box appears stating that Dreamweaver was unable to determine the version of Word used to generate this document, click OK, click the Clean up HTML from list arrow, then choose a version of Word.

6. Make sure each check box in the Clean Up Word HTML dialog box is checked, as shown in Figure 12, click **OK**, then click **OK** again to close the Clean Up Word HTML Results window.

You imported a Word document, then used the Clean Up Word HTML command.

Set text properties

1. Expand the Insert bar (if necessary), click the Common tab, then place the insertion point anywhere within the words "Spa Services."

2. Click the **Format list arrow** in the Property inspector, click **Heading 4**, click the **Show Code and Design views button** [Split] on the Document toolbar, then compare your screen to Figure 13.

   The Heading 4 format is applied to the paragraph. Even a single word is considered a paragraph if there is a hard return or paragraph break after it. The HTML code for a Heading 4 tag is <h4>. The tag is then closed with </h4>. The level of the heading tag follows the h, so the code for a Heading 1 tag is <h1>.

3. Click the **Align Center button** [≡] in the Property inspector to center the heading.

   When the paragraph is centered, the HTML code 'align="center"' is added to the <h4> tag.

4. Select the words **Spa Services**, click the **Font list arrow**, then click **Arial, Helvetica, sans-serif**.

   Because setting a font is a character command, you must select all the characters you want to format before applying a font.

   TIP You can modify the font combinations in the Font list by clicking Text on the menu bar, pointing to Font, then clicking Edit Font List.

   (continued)

FIGURE 13
Code for Headings 4 tags

Code for <h4> tags

```
1   <!DOCTYPE html PUBLIC "-//W3C//DTD XHTML 1.0 Transitional//EN"
    "http://www.w3.org/TR/xhtml1/DTD/xhtml1-transitional.dtd">
2   <html xmlns="http://www.w3.org/1999/xhtml">
3   <head>
4   <meta http-equiv="Content-Type" content="text/html; charset=iso-8859-1" />
5   <title>The Striped Umbrella beach resort and spa, Ft. Eugene, Florida</title>
6   </head>
7   <body bgcolor="#FFFFFF">
8   <div align="center">
9     <h4><img src="assets/su_banner.gif" width="736" height="125" /><br />
10      <font face="Arial, Helvetica, sans-serif"><a href="about_us.html">About Us</a> - <a href
    ="spa.html">Spa</a> - <a href="cafe.html">Cafe</a></font></h4>
11  </div>
12  <hr width="600" />
13  <p><img src="assets/the_spa.jpg" width="64" height="55" /></p>
14  <h4>Spa Services</h4>
15  <p>Our spa services include numerous skin care treatments, body  treatments, and massages.
    We also have some spa packages that combine several  spa services into economical packages.
    </p>
```

Insertion point within the Spa Services text

FIGURE 14
Formatted Spa Services text

DESIGNTIP **Choosing fonts**

There are two classifications of fonts: sans-serif and serif. **Sans-serif fonts** are block-style characters that are often used for headings and subheadings. The headings in this book use a sans-serif font. Examples of sans-serif fonts include Arial, Verdana, and Helvetica. **Serif fonts** are more ornate and contain small extra strokes at the beginning and end of the characters. Some people consider serif fonts easier to read in printed material, because the extra strokes lead your eye from one character to the next. This paragraph you are reading uses a serif font. Examples of serif fonts include Times New Roman, Times, and Georgia. Many designers feel that a sans-serif font is preferable when the content of a Web site is primarily intended to be read on the screen, but that a serif font is preferable if the content will be printed. When you choose fonts, you need to keep in mind the amount of text each page will contain and whether most viewers will read the text on-screen or print it. A good rule of thumb is to limit each Web site to no more than three font variations. Using more than three may make your Web site look unprofessional and suggest the "ransom note effect." The phrase **ransom note effect** implies that fonts have been randomly used in a document without regard to style, similar to a ransom note made up of words cut from various sources and pasted onto a page.

5. With the heading still selected, click the **Text Color button** ☐ in the Property inspector to open the color picker, then click the first **dark blue color** in the third row (#000066).

   The HTML code added when the font color is designated is `<font color="#000066">`. The font color tag is closed with `</font>`.

   TIP You can also type #000066 in the color text box in the Property inspector to select the color in Step 5.

6. Click to the left of the "O" in Our spa services, press and hold **[Shift]**, scroll to the end of the text, click to place the insertion point after the end of the last sentence on the page, then release **[Shift]**.

7. Click the **Font list arrow** in the Property inspector, click **Arial, Helvetica, sans-serif**, click the **Size list arrow** in the Property inspector, then click **3**.

   TIP To change the size of selected text, use either the Format list arrow or the Size list arrow, but not both.

8. Click anywhere on the page to deselect the text, save your work, then compare your screen to Figure 14.

9. Close the spa page.

You formatted the Spa Services text using the Heading 4 style and the Arial, Helvetica, sans-serif font combination. Next, you centered the heading on the page and changed the text color to a dark blue. You then selected the rest of the text on the page and changed it to the Arial, Helvetica, sans-serif font combination with a text size of 3.

ADD LINKS TO
WEB PAGES

What You'll Do

In this lesson, you will open the home page and add links to the navigation bar that link to the About Us, Spa, Cafe, and Activities pages. You will then insert an e-mail link at the bottom of the page and create page titles for the untitled pages in the site map.

Adding Links to Web Pages

Links provide the real power for Web pages. Links make it possible for viewers to navigate all the pages in a Web site and to connect to other pages anywhere on the Web. Viewers are more likely to return to Web sites that have a user-friendly navigation structure. Viewers also enjoy Web sites that have interesting links to other Web pages or other Web sites.

To add links to a Web page, first select the text or image that you want to serve as a link, and then specify a path to the page to which you want to link in the Link text box in the Property inspector. After you add all your links, you can open the site map to see a diagram of how the linked pages relate to each other.

When you create links on a Web page, it is important to avoid **broken links**, or links that cannot find their intended destinations. You can accidentally cause a broken link by typing the incorrect address for the link in the Link text box. Broken links are often caused by companies merging, going out of business, or simply moving their Web site addresses.

In addition to adding links to your pages, you should provide a **point of contact**, or a place on a Web page that provides viewers with a means of contacting the company. A common point of contact is a **mailto: link**, which is an e-mail address that viewers with questions or problems can use to contact someone at the company's headquarters.

Using Navigation Bars

A **navigation bar** is an area on a Web page that contains links to the main pages of a Web site. Navigation bars are usually located at the top or side of the main pages of a Web site and can be created with text, images, or a combination of the two. To make navigating a Web site as easy as possible, you should place navigation bars in the same position on each Web page. Navigation bars are the backbone of a Web site's navigation structure, which includes all navigation aids for moving around a Web site. You can, however, include additional links to the main pages of the Web site elsewhere on the page. The Web page in Figure 15 shows an example of a navigation bar that contains both text and image links that use JavaScript. Notice that when the mouse is placed on an item in the navigation bar, the image expands to include more information.

Navigation bars can also be simple and contain only text-based links to the pages in the site. You can create a simple navigation bar by typing the names of your Web site's pages at the top of your Web page, formatting the text, and then adding links to each page name. It is always a good idea to provide plain text links for accessibility, regardless of the type of navigation structure you choose to use.

FIGURE 15

The Coca-Cola Web site

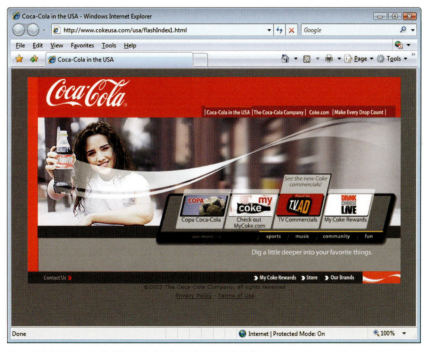

Coca-Cola Web site used with permission from The Coca-Cola Company - www.coca-cola.com

Create a navigation bar

1. Open **index.html** (the home page).

2. Position the insertion point to the left of "A" in About Us, then drag to select **About Us - Spa - Cafe**.

3. Type **Home - About Us - Spa - Cafe - Activities,** as shown in Figure 16.

   These five text labels will serve as a navigation bar. You will add the links later.

You created a new navigation bar using text, replacing the original navigation bar.

Format a navigation bar

1. Select **Home - About Us - Spa - Cafe - Activities** (if necessary), click the **Size list arrow** in the Property inspector, then click **None**.

   None is equal to size 3, the default text size. The None setting eliminates any prior size formatting that was applied to the text.

   TIP If your Property inspector is not visible, click Window on the menu bar, then click Properties to open it.

2. Click the **Format list arrow** in the Property inspector, then click **Heading 4**.

3. Click the **Font list arrow** in the Property inspector, click **Arial, Helvetica, sans-serif** (if necessary), compare your screen to Figure 17, then deselect the text.

   TIP An asterisk after the filename in the title bar indicates that you have altered the page since you last saved it. After you save your work, the asterisk does not appear.

You formatted the new navigation bar, using a heading and a font combination.

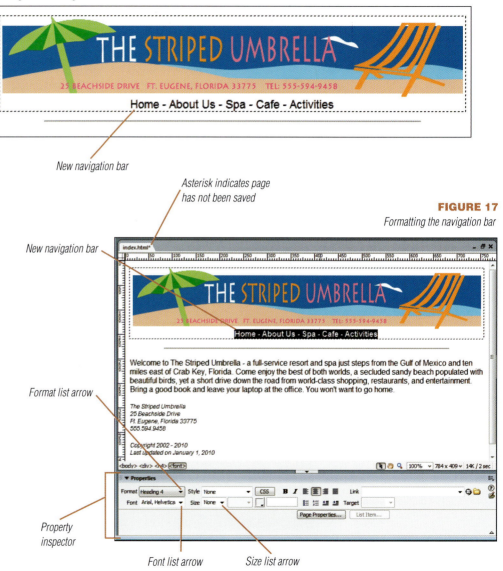

FIGURE 16
Viewing the new navigation bar

New navigation bar

Asterisk indicates page has not been saved

FIGURE 17
Formatting the navigation bar

New navigation bar

Format list arrow

Property inspector

Font list arrow

Size list arrow

FIGURE 18
Selecting the Home link

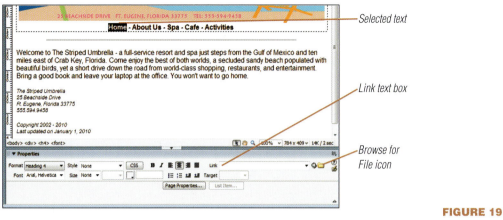

Selected text

Link text box

Browse for
File icon

FIGURE 19
Select File dialog box

Striped Umbrella
local root folder

index.html
page

Relative to
list arrow

Click OK to
set link

FIGURE 20
Links added to navigation bar

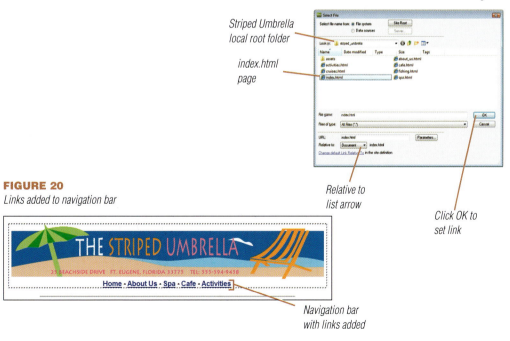

Navigation bar
with links added

1. Double-click **Home** to select it, as shown in Figure 18.

2. Click the **Browse for File icon** 📁 next to the Link text box in the Property inspector, then navigate to the striped_umbrella root folder (if necessary).

3. Verify that the link is set Relative to Document in the Relative to: list.

4. Click **index.html** as shown in Figure 19, click **OK** (Win) or **Choose** (Mac), then click anywhere on the page to deselect Home.

   Home now appears in blue with an underline, indicating it is a link. However, clicking Home will not open a new page because the link is to the home page. It might seem odd to create a link to the same page on which the link appears, but this will be helpful when you copy the navigation bar to other pages in the site. Always provide viewers a link to the home page.

5. Repeat Steps 1–4 to create links for About Us, Spa, Cafe, and Activities to their corresponding pages in the striped_umbrella root folder.

6. When you finish adding the links to the other four pages, deselect all, then compare your screen to Figure 20.

You created a link for each of the five navigation bar elements to their respective Web pages in The Striped Umbrella Web site.

Create an e-mail link

1. Place the insertion point after the last digit in the telephone number, then insert a line break.

2. Click the **Common tab** on the Insert bar (if necessary), then click the **Email Link button** to insert an e-mail link.

3. Type **Club Manager** in the Text text box, type **manager@stripedumbrella.com** in the E-Mail text box, as shown in Figure 21, then click **OK** to close the Email Link dialog box.

   If you do not retain the formatting from the previous line (Size 2, Italic), use the History panel to undo Steps 1–3. Switch to Code view and place the insertion point immediately to the right of the telephone number, then repeat the steps again in Design view.

4. Save your work.

   Notice that the text "mailto:manager@striped_umbrella.com," appears in the Link text box in the Property inspector. When a viewer clicks this link, a blank e-mail message window opens in the viewer's default e-mail software, where the viewer can type a message. See Figure 22.

   TIP You must enter the correct e-mail address in the E-Mail text box for the link to work. However, you can enter any descriptive name, such as customer service or Bob Smith in the Text text box. You can also enter the e-mail address as the text if you want to show the actual e-mail address on the Web page.

You inserted an e-mail link to serve as a point of contact for The Striped Umbrella.

FIGURE 21
Email Link dialog box

Text for e-mail link on the page (this could also be a person's name or position or the actual e-mail link)

Link information

FIGURE 22
mailto: link on the Property inspector

mailto: link

FIGURE 23

The Striped Umbrella site map

Site Map button

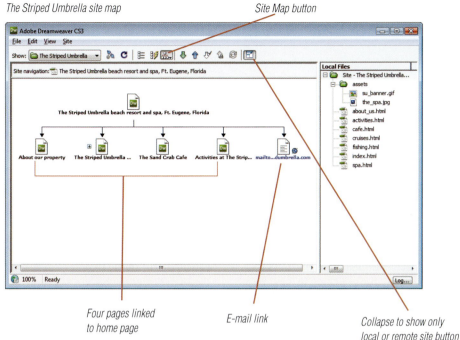

Four pages linked
to home page

E-mail link

Collapse to show only
local or remote site button

1. Click the **Expand to show local and remote sites button** on the Files panel to expand the site map.

   The site map shows the home page, the four pages that are linked to it, and the e-mail link on the home page.

   > **TIP** If you don't see the site map on the left window, click the Site Map button list arrow, then click Map and Files.

2. Click **View** on the Files panel menu bar, point to **Site Map Options**, then click **Show Page Titles** (Win), or click the **Options menu,** point to **View**, point to **Site Map Options**, then click **Show Page Titles** (Mac) (if necessary).

3. Select the first Untitled Document page in the site map, select the words **Untitled Document**, type **About our property**, then press **[Enter]** (Win) or **[return]** (Mac).

   When you select a page title in the site map, the corresponding file is selected in the Local Files panel. Be careful before entering a new page title in the Site map. If the option is set to filenames rather than page titles, you will accidentally change the filename.

4. Repeat Step 3 for the other two Untitled Document pages, naming them **The Sand Crab Cafe** and **Activities at The Striped** Umbrella, respectively, as shown in Figure 23.

5. Click the **Collapse to show only local or remote site button** on the toolbar to collapse the site map.

You viewed the site map and added page titles to the untitled pages.

USE THE HISTORY
PANEL AND EDIT CODE

What You'll Do

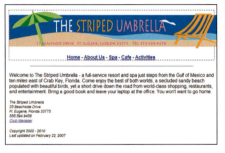

 In this lesson, you will use the History panel to undo formatting changes you make to a horizontal rule. You will then use the Code Inspector to view the HTML code for the horizontal rule. You will also insert a date object and then view its code in the Code Inspector.

Using the History Panel

Throughout the process of creating a Web page, it's likely that you will make mistakes along the way. Fortunately, you have a tool named the History panel to undo your mistakes. The **History panel** records each editing and formatting task performed and displays them in a list in the order in which they were completed. Each task listed in the History panel is called a **step**. You can drag the **slider** on the left side of the History panel to undo or redo steps, as shown in Figure 24. You can also click in the bar to the left of a step to undo all steps below it. You click the step to select it. By default, the History panel records 50 steps. You can change the number of steps the History panel records in the General category of the Preferences dialog box. However, keep in mind that setting this number too high might require additional memory and could affect Dreamweaver's performance.

Understanding other History panel features

Dragging the slider up and down in the History panel is a quick way to undo or redo steps. However, the History panel offers much more. It has the capability to "memorize" certain tasks and consolidate them into one command. This is a useful feature for steps that are executed repetitively on Web pages. Some Dreamweaver features, such as drag and drop, cannot be recorded in the History panel and are noted by a red "x" placed next to them. The History panel does not show steps performed in the Files panel.

Viewing HTML Code in the Code Inspector

If you enjoy writing code, you occasionally might want to make changes to Web pages by entering the code rather than using the panels and tools in Design view. You can view the code in Dreamweaver using Code view, Code and Design views, or the Code Inspector. The **Code Inspector**, shown in Figure 25, is a separate window that displays the current page in Code view. The advantage of using the Code Inspector is that you can see a full-screen view of your page in Design view while viewing the underlying code in a floating window that you can resize and position wherever you want.

You can add advanced features, such as JavaScript functions, to Web pages by copying and pasting code from one page to another in the Code Inspector. A **JavaScript** function is a block of code that adds dynamic content such as rollovers or interactive forms to a Web page. A **rollover** is a special effect that changes the appearance of an object when the mouse moves over it.

QUICKTIP

If you are new to HTML, you can use the Reference panel to find answers to your HTML questions. The Reference panel is part of the Code panel group and contains many resources besides HTML help, such as JavaScript help.

FIGURE 24
The History panel

FIGURE 25
Code Inspector

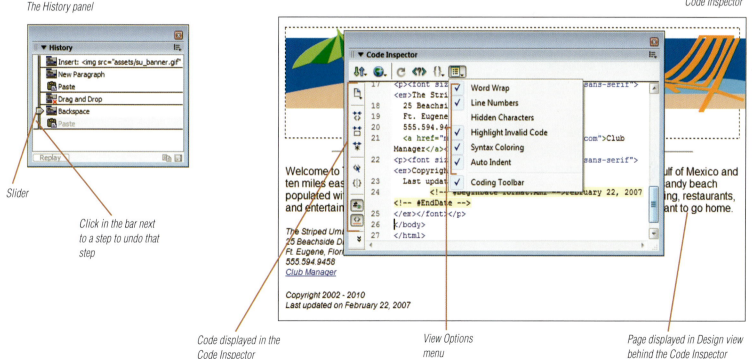

Slider

Click in the bar next to a step to undo that step

Code displayed in the Code Inspector

View Options menu

Page displayed in Design view behind the Code Inspector

Use the History panel

1. Click **Window** on the menu bar, then click **History**, **if necessary**.

   The History panel opens and displays steps you have recently performed.

2. Click the **History panel options menu**, click **Clear History**, as shown in Figure 26, then click **Yes** to close the warning box (if necessary).

3. Select the **horizontal rule** on the home page.

   A **horizontal rule** is a line used to separate page elements or to organize information on a page.

4. Select the number in the W text box in the Property inspector, type **90**, click the **list arrow** next to the W text box, click **%**, then compare your Property inspector to Figure 27.

5. Using the Property inspector, change the width of the horizontal rule to 80%, click the **Align list arrow**, then click **Left**.

6. Drag the **slider** on the History panel up to Set Width: 90%, as shown in Figure 28.

   The bottom two steps in the History panel appear gray, indicating that these steps have been undone.

7. Click the **History panel options menu,** then click **Close panel group** to close the History panel.

You formatted the horizontal rule, made changes to it, then used the History panel to undo some of the changes.

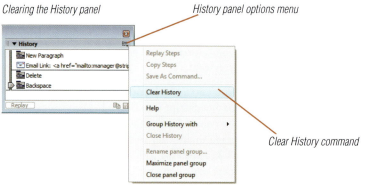

History panel options menu

Clear History command

FIGURE 27
Property inspector settings for horizontal rule

Width set to 90% of width of window

FIGURE 28
Undoing steps using the History panel

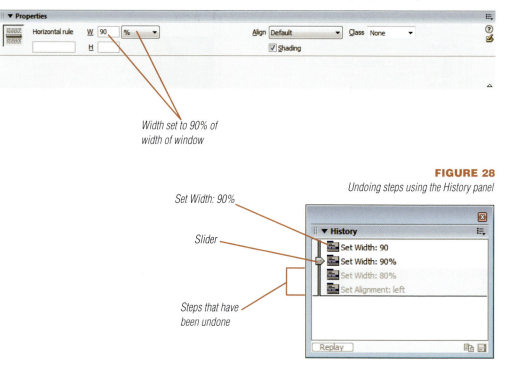

Set Width: 90%

Slider

Steps that have been undone

Developing a Web Page

FIGURE 29
Viewing the View Options menu in the Code Inspector

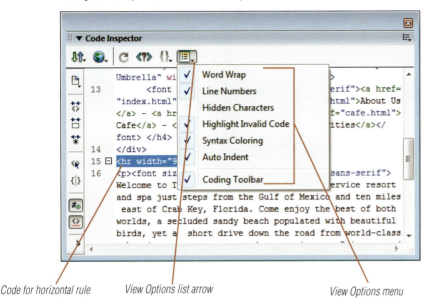

Code for horizontal rule   View Options list arrow   View Options menu

POWER USER SHORTCUTS

to do this:	use this shortcut:
Select All	[Ctrl][A] (Win) or ⌘ [A] (Mac)
Copy	[Ctrl][C] (Win) or ⌘ [C] (Mac)
Cut	[Ctrl][X] (Win) or ⌘ [X] (Mac)
Paste	[Ctrl][V] (Win) or ⌘ [V] (Mac)
Line Break	[Shift][Enter] (Win) or [Shift][return] (Mac)
Show or hide the Code Inspector	[F10] (Win) or [option][F10] (Mac)
Preview in browser	[F12] (Win) or [option][F12] (Mac)

Use the Code Inspector

1. Click the **horizontal rule** to select it (if necessary), click **Window** on the menu bar, then click **Code Inspector**.

   The Code Inspector highlights the code for the horizontal rule.

   > TIP You can also press [F10](Win) or [option][F10] (Mac) to display the Code Inspector.

2. Click the **View Options list arrow** on the Code Inspector toolbar to display the View Options menu, then click **Word Wrap** (if necessary), to activate Word Wrap.

   The Word Wrap feature forces text to stay within the confines of the Code Inspector window, allowing you to read without scrolling sideways.

3. Click the **View Options list arrow**, then verify that the Word Wrap, Line Numbers, Highlight Invalid Code, Syntax Coloring, Auto Indent, and the Coding Toolbar menu items are checked, as shown in Figure 29.

4. Select **90%** in the horizontal rule width code, then type **80%**.

5. Click **Refresh** in the Property inspector.

   After typing in the Code Inspector, you must refresh your changes to see them.

You changed the width of the horizontal rule by changing the code in the Code Inspector.

Use the Reference panel

1. Click the **Reference button** 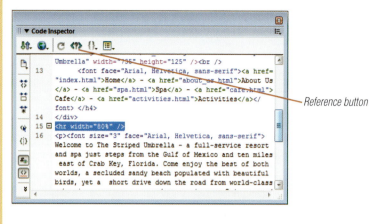 on the Code Inspector toolbar, as shown in Figure 30, to open the Results panel group with the Reference panel visible.

   TIP   Verify that the horizontal rule is still selected, or you will not see the horizontal rule description in the Reference panel.

2. Read the information about horizontal rules in the Reference panel, as shown in Figure 31, right-click the **Results panel group title bar,** then click **Close panel group** (Win) or click the **Results panel option list** in the Results panel title bar, then click **Close panel group** (Mac) to close the Results panel group.

3. Close the Code Inspector.

You read information about horizontal rule settings in the Reference panel.

FIGURE 30
Reference button on the Code Inspector toolbar

Reference button

FIGURE 31
Viewing the Reference panel

Information on HR (horizontal rule) tag

Inserting comments

A handy Dreamweaver feature is the ability to insert comments into HTML code. Comments can provide helpful information describing portions of the code, such as a JavaScript function. You can create comments in any Dreamweaver view, but you must turn on Invisible Elements to see them in Design view. Use the Edit, Preferences, Invisible Elements, Comments option to enable viewing of comments; then use the View, Visual Aids, Invisible Elements menu option to display them on the page. To create a comment, click the Common tab on the Insert bar, click the Comment button, type a comment in the Comment dialog box, and then click OK. Comments are not visible in browser windows.

Developing a Web Page

FIGURE 32

Insert Date dialog box

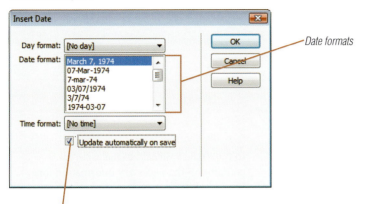

Date formats

Update automatically
on save check box

FIGURE 33

Viewing the date object in Code view

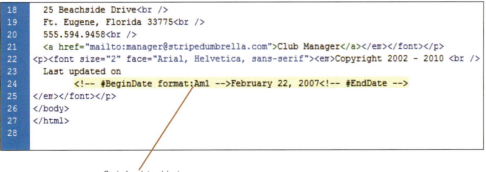

Code for date object

Insert a date object

1. Scroll down the page (if necessary), to select **January 1, 2010**, then press **[Delete]** (Win) or **[delete]** (Mac).

2. Click the **Date button** on the Insert bar, then click **March 7, 1974** in the Date format text box.

3. Click the **Update automatically on save checkbox**, as shown in Figure 32, click **OK**, then deselect the text.

4. Click the **Show Code and Design views button** .

   Notice that the code has changed to reflect the date object, which is set to today's date, as shown in Figure 33. (Your date will be different.) The new code is highlighted with a light yellow background, indicating that it is a date object, automatically coded by Dreamweaver, rather than a date that has been manually typed on the page by the designer.

5. Return to Design view.

You inserted a date object that will be updated automatically when you open and save the home page.

MODIFY AND TEST
WEB PAGES

What You'll Do

In this lesson, you will preview the home page in the browser to check for typographical errors, grammatical errors, broken links, and overall appearance. After previewing, you will make slight formatting adjustments to the page to improve its appearance.

Testing and Modifying Web Pages

Testing Web pages is a continuous process. You never really finish a Web site, because there are always additions and corrections to make. As you add and modify pages, you must test each page as part of the development process. The best way to test a Web page is to preview it in a browser window to make sure that all text and image elements appear the way you expect them to. You should also test your links to make sure they work properly. You also need to proofread your text to make sure it contains all the necessary information for the page with no typographical or grammatical errors. Designers typically view a page in a browser, return to Design view to make necessary changes, and then view the page in a browser again. This process may be repeated many times before the page is ready for publishing. In fact, it is sometimes difficult to stop making improvements to a page and move on to another project. You need to strike a balance among quality, creativity, and productivity.

DESIGNTIP   **Using "Under Construction" pages**

Many people are tempted to insert an unfinished page as a placeholder for a page that will be finished later. Rather than have real content, these pages usually contain text or an image that indicates the page is not finished, or "under construction." You should not publish a Web page that has a link to an unfinished page. It is frustrating to click a link for a page you want to open only to find an "under construction" note or image displayed. You want to make the best possible impression on your viewing audience. If you cannot complete a page before publishing it, at least provide enough information on it to make it "worth the trip."

Testing a Web Page Using Different Browsers and Screen Sizes

Because users access the Internet using a wide variety of computer systems, it is important to design your pages so that all browsers and screen sizes can display them well. You should test your pages using different browsers and a wide variety of screen sizes to ensure the best view of your page by the most people possible. Although the most common screen size that designers use today is 1024×768, many viewers restore down individual program windows to a size comparable to 800×600 to be able to have more windows open simultaneously on their screen. In other words, people use their "screen real estate" according to their personal work style. To view your page using different screen sizes, click the Window Size pop-up menu in the status bar (Win) or at the bottom of the document window (Mac), then choose the setting you want to use. Table 1 lists the Dreamweaver default window screen sizes. Remember also to check your pages using Windows and Macintosh platforms. Some page elements such as fonts, colors, table borders, layers, and horizontal rules may not appear consistently in both.

Testing a Web Page As Rendered in a Mobile Device

There is another preview feature with Dreamweaver that allows you to see what a page would look like if it were viewed on a mobile hand-held device, such as a Blackberry. To use this feature, click the Preview/Debug in Browser button on the Document toolbar, then click Preview in Device Central.

TABLE 1: Dreamweaver Default Window Screen Sizes

window size (inside dimensions of the browser window without borders)	monitor size
592W	
536×196	640×480, default
600×300	640×480, maximized
760×420	800×600, maximized
795×470	832×624, maximized
955×600	1024×768, maximized
544×378	Web TV

Modify a Web page

1. Click the **Restore Down button** on the index.html title bar to decrease the size of the home page window (Win) or skip to Step 2 (Mac).

   TIP   You cannot use the Window Size options if your Document window is maximized (Win).

2. Click the **Window Size list arrow** on the status bar, as shown in Figure 34, then click **600 × 300 (640 × 480, Maximized)**, (if necessary).

   A viewer using this setting will be forced to use the horizontal scroll bar to view the entire page.

3. Click the **Window Size list arrow**, then click **760 × 420 (800 × 600, Maximized)**.

4. Replace the period after the last sentence, "You won't want to go home." with an exclamation point.

5. Shorten the horizontal rule to 75%.

6. Click the **Maximize button** on the index.html title bar to maximize the home page window.

7. Save your work.

You viewed the home page using two different window sizes and you made simple formatting changes to the page.

FIGURE 34
Window screen sizes

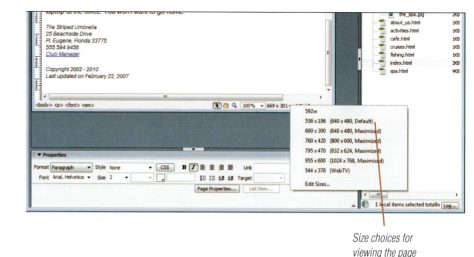

Size choices for viewing the page

Using smart design principles in Web page layout

As you view your pages in the browser, take a critical look at the symmetry of the page. Is it balanced? Are there too many images compared to text, or vice versa? Does everything "heavy" seem to be on the top or bottom of the page, or do the page elements seem to balance with the weight evenly distributed between the top, bottom, and sides? Use design principles to create a site-wide consistency for your pages. Horizontal symmetry means that the elements are balanced across the page. Vertical symmetry means that they are balanced down the page. Diagonal symmetry balances page elements along the invisible diagonal line of the page. Radial symmetry runs from the center of the page outward, like the petals of a flower. These principles all deal with balance; however, too much balance is not good, either. Sometimes it adds interest to place page elements a little off center or to have an asymmetric layout. Color, white space, text, and images should all complement each other and provide a natural flow across and down the page. The rule of thirds—dividing a page into nine squares like a tic-tac-toe grid—states that interest is increased when your focus is on one of the intersections in the grid. The most important information should be at the top of the page where it is visible without scrolling, or "above the fold," as they say in the newspaper business.

FIGURE 35
Viewing The Striped Umbrella home page in the Firefox browser

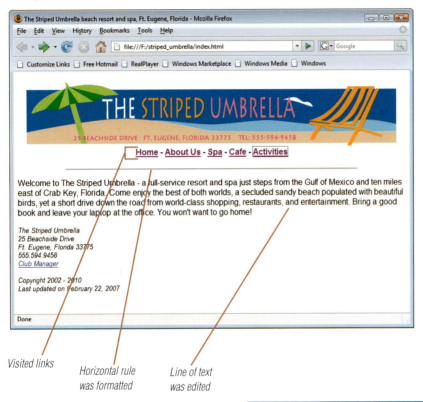

Visited links

Horizontal rule
was formatted

Line of text
was edited

Test Web pages by viewing them in a browser

1. Click the **Preview/Debug in browser button** on the Document toolbar, then choose your browser from the menu that opens.

   The Striped Umbrella home page opens in your default browser.

   TIP If previewing the page in Internet Explorer 7, click the Information bar when prompted to allow blocked content.

2. Click each link on the navigation bar, then after each click, use the Back button on the browser toolbar to return to the home page.

   Pages with no content at this point will appear as blank pages. Compare your screen to Figure 35.

3. Close your browser window, then close all open pages.

You viewed The Striped Umbrella home page in your browser and tested each link on the navigation bar.

DESIGNTIP **Choosing a window size**

Today, the majority of viewers are using a screen resolution of 1024×768 or higher. Because of this, more content can be displayed at one time on a computer monitor. Some people may use their whole screen to view pages on the Internet. Others may choose to allocate a smaller area of their screen to the browser window. In other words, people tend to use their "screen real estate" in different ways. The ideal Web page will not be so small that it tries to spread out over a larger screen size or so large that the viewer has to use horizontal scroll bars to read the page content. Achieving the best balance is one of the design decisions that must be made during the planning process.

Create head content and set Web page properties.

1. Open the blooms & bulbs Web site.
2. Open the index page and view the head content.
3. Change the page title to **blooms & bulbs - Your Complete Garden Center**.
4. Insert the following keywords: **garden**, **plants**, **nursery**, **flowers**, **landscape**, **blooms & bulbs**.
5. Insert the following description: **blooms & bulbs is a premier supplier of garden plants for both professional and home gardeners.**
6. Switch to Code view to view the HTML code for the head content, then switch back to Design view.
7. Open the Page Properties dialog box to view the current page properties.
8. Change the background color to a color of your choice.
9. Change the background color to white again, then save your work.

Create, import, and format text.

1. Select the current navigation bar and replace it with **Home**, **Featured Plants**, **Garden Tips**, and **Classes**. Use the [Spacebar] and a hyphen to separate the items.
2. Using the Property inspector, apply the Heading 4 format to the navigation bar.

3. Create a new paragraph after the paragraph of text and type the following text, inserting a line break after each line.
   blooms & bulbs
   Highway 43 South
   Alvin, Texas 77511
   555.248.0806
4. Italicize the address and phone number lines and change the font to Arial, Helvetica, sans-serif and the size to 2.
5. Change the copyright and last updated statements to size 2.
6. Save your work, then close the home page.
7. Open dw2_2.html and save it as **tips.html** in the blooms & bulbs Web site, overwriting the existing file, but not updating links.
8. Click the broken image link below the blooms & bulbs banner, browse to the chapter_2 Data Files folder, select the garden_tips.jpg in the assets folder, then click OK to save a copy of it in the blooms & bulbs Web site.
9. Place the insertion point under the Garden Tips graphic.
10. Import gardening_tips.doc from where you store your Data Files, using the Import Word Document command, then use the Clean Up Word HTML command. (*Hint*: The Use CSS instead of HTML tags option should be turned off before executing the following steps.)
11. Format all of the text on the page using the following attributes: Font: Arial, Helvetica, sans-serif, Alignment: Align Left, and Style: None.

12. Select the Seasonal Gardening Checklist heading, then use the Property inspector to center the text.
13. Use the Property inspector to format the selected text with a Heading 3 format.
14. Apply the color #003366 (the dark blue color in the third row) to the text.
15. Select the rest of the text on the page except for the Seasonal Gardening Checklist heading, then set the size to 3.
16. Select the Basic Gardening Tips heading, then format this text in bold, with the color #003366.
17. Save your work and close the tips page.

Add links to Web pages.

1. Open the index page, then use the Property inspector to link Home on the navigation bar to the index.html page in the blooms & bulbs Web site.
2. Link Featured Plants on the navigation bar to the plants.html page.
3. Link Garden Tips on the navigation bar to the tips.html page.
4. Link Classes on the navigation bar to the classes.html page.
5. Using the Insert bar, create an e-mail link under the telephone number.
6. Type **Customer Service** in the Text text box and **mailbox@blooms.com** in the E-Mail text box.
7. Open the plants.html page, add a page title called **Our Featured Plants**, then save the page.
8. Open the classes.html page and add the page title **Classes Offered**, then save your work.

Use the History panel and edit code.

1. Open the History panel, then clear its contents.
2. Delete the current date in the Last updated on statement on the home page and replace it with a date that will update automatically when the file is saved.
3. Change the font for the last updated on statement using the font of your choice.
4. Use the History panel to go back to the original font and style settings for the last updated on statement.
5. Close the History panel.

6. Examine the code for the last updated on statement.
7. Save your work.

Modify and test Web pages.

1. Using the Window Size pop-up menu, view the home page at 600 × 300 (640 × 480, Maximized) and 760 × 420 (800 × 600, Maximized), then maximize the Document window.
2. View the page in your browser. (*Hint:* If previewing the page in Internet Explorer 7, click the Information bar when prompted to allow blocked content.)

3. Verify that all links work correctly, then close the browser.
4. On the home page, change the text "Stop by and see us soon!" to **We ship overnight**.
5. Save your work, then view the pages in your browser, comparing your screens to Figure 36 and Figure 37.
6. Close your browser.
7. Adjust the spacing (if necessary), save your work, then preview the home page in the browser again.
8. Close the browser, then save and close all open pages.

FIGURE 36
Completed Skills Review, home page

FIGURE 37
Completed Skills Review, tips page

You have been hired to create a Web site for a TripSmart, a travel outfitter. You have created the basic framework for the Web site and are now ready to format and edit the home page to improve the content and appearance.

1. Open the TripSmart Web site, then open the home page.
2. Enter the following keywords: **travel**, **traveling**, **trips**, and **vacations**.
3. Enter the following description: **TripSmart is a comprehensive travel store. We can help you plan trips, make travel arrangements, and supply you with travel gear.**
4. Change the page title to **TripSmart - Serving All Your Travel Needs**.

5. Select the existing navigation bar and replace it with the following text links: **Home**, **Catalog**, **Services**, **Destinations**, and **Newsletter**. Type hyphens between each text link.
6. Replace the date in the last updated statement with a date that will update automatically on save.
7. Type the following address two lines below the paragraph about the company, using line breaks after each line:
   TripSmart
   1106 Beechwood
   Fayetteville, AR 72704
   555.848.0807

8. Insert an e-mail link in the line below the telephone number, using **Customer Service** for the Text text box and **mailbox@tripsmart.com** for the E-mail text box in the Email Link dialog box.
9. Italicize TripSmart, the address, phone number, and e-mail link and format it to size 2, Arial, Helvetica, sans-serif.
10. Link the navigation bar entries to index.html, catalog.html, services.html, destinations.html, and newsletter.html.
11. View the HTML code for the page.
12. View the page using two different window sizes, then test the links in your browser window.
13. View the site map.

14. Create the following page titles:

catalog.html = **TripSmart Catalog**

services.html = **TripSmart Services**

destinations.html = **TripSmart Featured Destinations**

newsletter.html = **TripSmart Newsletter**

15. Verify that all the page titles are entered correctly, then collapse the site map.

16. Preview the home page in your browser, then test all the links. (*Hint:* If previewing the page in Internet Explorer 7, click the Information bar when prompted to allow blocked content.).

17. Compare your page to Figure 38, close the browser, then save and close all open pages.

FIGURE 38

Completed Project Builder 1

Home - Catalog - Services - Destinations - Newsletter

Welcome to TripSmart - the smart choice for the savvy traveler. We're here to help you with all your travel needs. Choose customized trips to any location or our Five-Star Tours, recently rated number one in the country by Traveler magazine. With over 30 years of experience, we can bring you the best the world has to offer.

TripSmart
1106 Beechwood
Fayetteville, AR 72704
555.848.0807
Customer Service

Copyright 2002 - 2010
Last updated on March 10, 2007

PROJECT BUILDER 2

Your company has been selected to design a Web site for a catering business named Carolyne's Creations. You are now ready to add content to the home page and apply formatting options to improve the page appearance, using Figure 39 as a guide.

1. Open the Carolyne's Creations Web site, then open the home page.
2. Place the insertion point in front of the sentence beginning "Give us a call" and type **Feel like a guest at your own party**.

3. Center the navigation bar.
4. Change the navigation bar to the Heading 4 format.
5. Add the following address below the paragraph using line breaks after each line:
   Carolyne's Creations
   496 Maple Street
   Seven Falls, Virginia 52404
   555.963.8271
6. Enter another line break after the telephone number and type **E-mail**, then add an e-mail link using Carolyne Kate for the text and carolyne@carolynescreations.com for the e-mail address.

7. Apply the Verdana, Arial, Helvetica, sans-serif font to the contact information, then apply any other formatting of your choice.
8. Create links from each navigation bar element to its corresponding Web page.
9. Replace the date that follows the text "Last updated on" with a date object, then save your work.

10. View the completed page in your default browser, then test each link. (*Hint*: If previewing the page in Internet Explorer 7, click the Information bar when prompted to allow blocked content.)

11. Close your browser.

12. View the site map, then title any untitled pages with appropriate titles.

13. Save your work, then close all pages.

FIGURE 39
Completed Project Builder 2

Home | Shop | Classes | Catering | Recipes

Let Carolyne's Creations be your personal chef, your one stop shop for the latest in kitchen items and fresh ingredients, and your source for new and innovative recipes. We enjoy planning and executing special events for all occasions - from children's birthday parties to corporate retreats. Feel like a guest at your own party. Give us a call or stop by our shop to browse through our selections.

Carolyne's Creations
496 Maple Avenue
Seven Falls, Virginia 52404
555.963.8271
E-mail Carolyne Kate

Copyright 2001 - 2010
Last updated on March 10, 2007

Angela Lou is a freelance photographer. She is searching the Internet looking for a particular type of paper to use in printing her digital images. She knows that Web sites use keywords and descriptions in order to receive "hits" with search engines. She is curious about how they work. Follow the steps below and write your answers to the questions.

1. Connect to the Internet, then go to *www.snapfish.com* to see the Snapfish Web site's home page, as shown in Figure 40.
2. View the page source by clicking View on the menu bar, then clicking Source (Internet Explorer) or Page Source (Netscape Navigator or Mozilla Firefox).
3. Can you locate a description and keywords? If so, what are they?
4. How many keywords do you find?
5. Is the description appropriate for the Web site? Why or why not?
6. Look at the numbers of keywords and words in the description. Is there an appropriate number? Or are there too many or not enough?

7. Use a search engine such as Google at *www.google.com*, then type the words **photo quality paper** in the Search text box.

8. Click the first link in the list of results and view the source code for that page. Do you see keywords and a description? Do any of them match the words you used in the search?

FIGURE 40
Design Project

Snapfish Web site used with permission from Snapfish - www.snapfish.com

Developing a Web Page

In this assignment, you will continue to work on the Web site you defined in Chapter 1. In Chapter 1, you created a storyboard for your Web site with at least four pages. You also created a local root folder for your Web site and an assets folder to store the Web site asset files. You set the assets folder as the default storage location for your images. You began to collect information and resources for your Web site and started working on the home page.

1. Think about the head content for the home page. Add the title, keywords, and a description.

2. Create the main page content for the home page and format it attractively.

3. Add the address and other contact information to the home page, including an e-mail address.

4. Consult your storyboard and design the navigation bar.

5. Link the navigation bar items to the appropriate pages.

6. Add a last updated on statement to the home page with a date that will automatically update when the page is saved.

7. Edit and format the page content until you are satisfied with the results.

8. Verify that each page has a page title by viewing the site map.

9. Verify that all links, including the e-mail link, work correctly.

10. When you are satisfied with the home page, review the checklist questions shown in Figure 41, then make any necessary changes.

11. Save your work.

FIGURE 41
Portfolio Project checklist

Web Site Checklist

1. Do all pages have a page title?
2. Does the home page have a description and keywords?
3. Does the home page contain contact information, including an e-mail address?
4. Do all completed pages in the Web site have consistent navigation links?
5. Does the home page have a "last updated on" statement that will automatically update when the page is saved?
6. Do all pages have attractively formatted text?
7. Do all paths for links and images work correctly?
8. Does the home page view well using at least two different screen resolutions?

chapter

3

WORKING WITH TEXT
AND IMAGES

1. Create unordered and ordered lists

2. Create, apply, and edit Cascading Style Sheets

3. Add styles and attach Cascading Style Sheets

4. Insert and align images

5. Enhance an image and use alternate text

6. Insert a background image and perform site maintenance

3
WORKING WITH TEXT
AND IMAGES

Introduction

Most Web pages contain a combination of text and images. Dreamweaver provides many tools for working with text and images that you can use to make your Web pages attractive and easy to read. Dreamweaver also has tools that help you format text quickly and ensure a consistent appearance of text elements across all your Web pages.

Formatting Text as Lists

If a Web page contains a large amount of text, it can be difficult for viewers to digest it all. You can break up the monotony of large blocks of text by breaking them up into smaller paragraphs or organizing them as lists. You can create three types of lists in Dreamweaver: unordered lists, ordered lists, and definition lists.

Using Cascading Style Sheets

You can save time and ensure that all your page elements have a consistent appearance by using **Cascading Style Sheets (CSS)**. CSS are sets of formatting instructions, usually stored in a separate file, that control the appearance of content on a Web page or throughout a Web site. You can use CSS to

define consistent formatting attributes for page elements such as text and tables throughout your Web site. You can then apply the formatting attributes you define to any element in a single document or to all of the pages in a Web site.

Using Images to Enhance Web Pages

Images make Web pages visually stimulating and more exciting than pages that contain only text. However, you should use images sparingly. If you think of text as the meat and potatoes of a Web site, the images would be the seasoning. You should add images to a page just as you would add seasoning to food. A little seasoning enhances the flavor and brings out the quality of the dish. Too much seasoning overwhelms the dish and masks the flavor of the main ingredients. Too little seasoning results in a bland dish. There are many ways to work with images so that they complement the content of pages in a Web site. There are specific file formats used to save images for Web sites to ensure maximum quality with minimum file size. You should store images in a separate folder in an organized fashion.

Tools You'll Use

H Space text box

Border text box

Align list arrow

Alt text box

CREATE UNORDERED AND ORDERED LISTS

What You'll Do

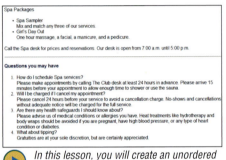

In this lesson, you will create an unordered list of spa services on the spa page. You will also import text with questions and format them as an ordered list.

Creating Unordered Lists

Unordered lists are lists of items that do not need to be placed in a specific order. A grocery list that lists items in a random order is a good example of an unordered list. Items in unordered lists are usually preceded by a **bullet**, or a small raised dot or similar icon. Unordered lists that contain bullets are sometimes called **bulleted lists**. Although you can use paragraph indentations to create an unordered list, bullets can often make lists easier to read. To create an unordered list, first select the text you want to format as an unordered list, then use the Unordered List button in the Property inspector to insert bullets at the beginning of each paragraph of the selected text.

Formatting Unordered Lists

In Dreamweaver, the default bullet style is a round dot. To change the bullet style to a square, expand the Property inspector to its full size, as shown in Figure 1, click List Item in the Property inspector to open the List Properties dialog box, and then set the style for bulleted lists to Square. Be aware, however, that not all browsers display square bullets correctly, in which case the bullets will appear differently.

Creating Ordered Lists

Ordered lists, which are sometimes called **numbered lists**, are lists of items that are presented in a specific order and that are preceded by numbers or letters in sequence. An ordered list is appropriate for a list in which each item must be executed according to its specified order. A list that provides numbered directions for driving from Point A to Point B or a list that provides instructions for assembling a bicycle are both examples of ordered lists.

Formatting Ordered Lists

You can format an ordered list to show different styles of numbers or letters by using the List Properties dialog box, as shown in Figure 2. You can apply numbers, Roman numerals, lowercase letters, or uppercase letters to an ordered list.

Creating Definition Lists

Definition lists are similar to unordered lists but do not have bullets. They are often used with terms and definitions, such as in a dictionary or glossary. To create a definition list, select the text to use for the list, click Text on the menu bar, point to List, and then click Definition List.

FIGURE 1
Expanded Property inspector

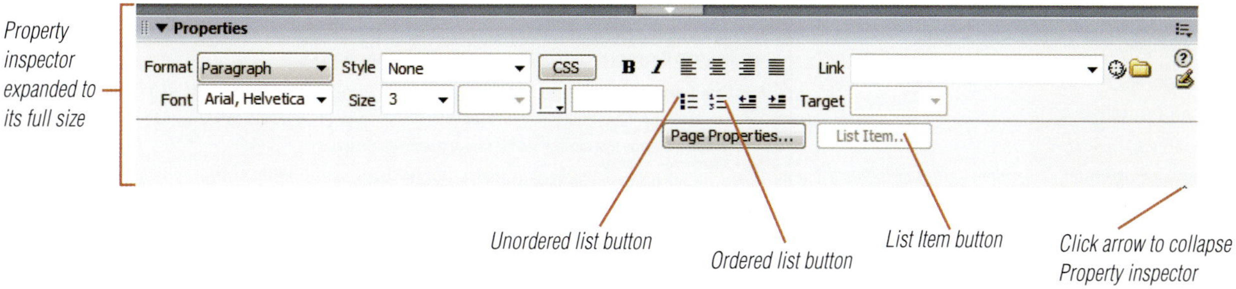

Property inspector expanded to its full size

Unordered list button
Ordered list button
List Item button
Click arrow to collapse Property inspector

List type list arrow

FIGURE 2
Choosing a numbered list style in the List Properties dialog box

Numbered list styles

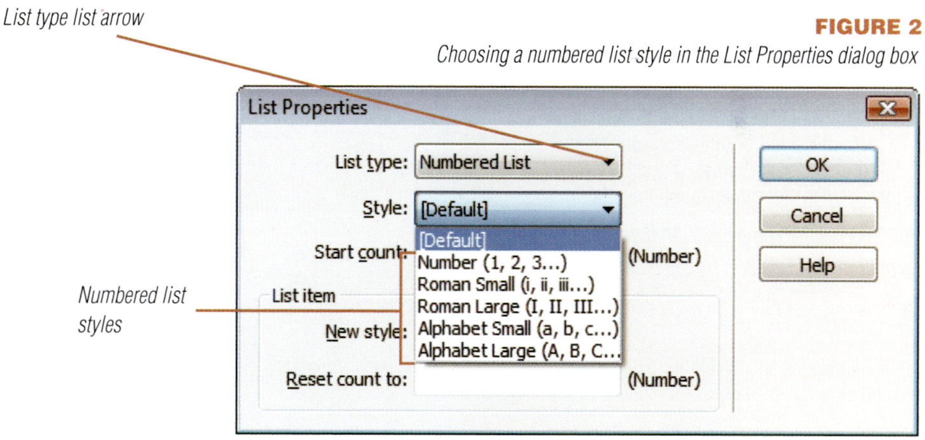

Create an unordered list

1. Open the spa page in The Striped Umbrella Web site.

2. Select the three items under the Skin Care Treatments heading.

3. Click the **Unordered List button** 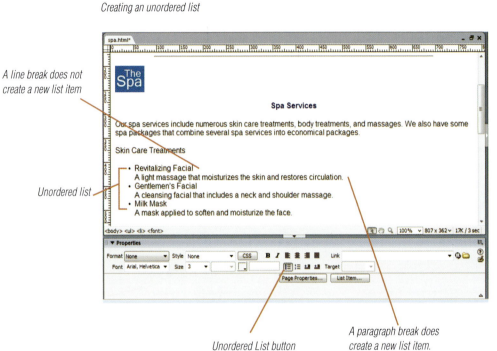 in the Property inspector to format the selected text as an unordered list, click anywhere to deselect the text, then compare your screen to Figure 3.

   Each spa service item and its description is separated by a line break. That is why each description is indented under its corresponding item, rather than formatted as a new list item. You must enter a paragraph break to create a new list item.

4. Repeat Step 3 to create unordered lists of the items under the Body Treatments, Massages, and Spa Packages headings, being careful not to include the contact information in the last sentence on the page as part of your last list.

   TIP Pressing [Enter] (Win) or [return] (Mac) once at the end of an unordered list creates another bulleted item. To end an unordered list, press [Enter] (Win) or [return] (Mac) twice.

You opened the spa page in Design view and formatted four spa services lists as unordered lists.

FIGURE 3
Creating an unordered list

A line break does not create a new list item

Unordered list

Unordered List button

A paragraph break does create a new list item.

FIGURE 4
List Properties dialog box

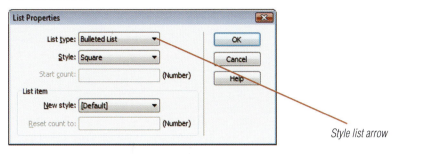

Style list arrow

FIGURE 5
HTML tags in Code view for unordered list

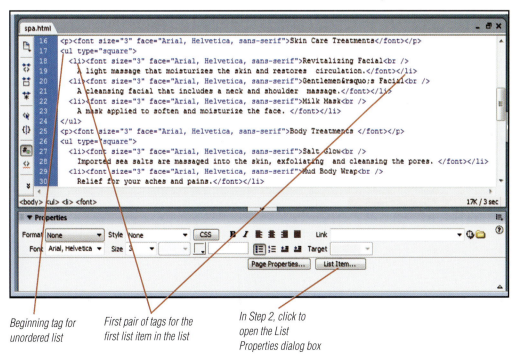

Beginning tag for unordered list

First pair of tags for the first list item in the list

In Step 2, click to open the List Properties dialog box

Format an unordered list

1. Click any of the items in the first unordered list to place the insertion point in the list.

2. Expand the Property inspector (if necessary), click **List Item** in the Property inspector to open the List Properties dialog box, click the **Style list arrow**, click **Square**, as shown in Figure 4, then click **OK**.

   The bullets in the unordered list now have a square shape.

3. Repeat Step 2 to format the next three unordered lists.

4. Position the insertion point to the left of the first item in the first unordered list, then click the **Show Code view button** <> Code toolbar to view the code for the unordered list, as shown in Figure 5.

   Notice that there is a pair of HTML codes, or tags, surrounding each type of element on the page. The first tag in each pair begins the code for a particular element, and the last tag ends the code for the element. For instance, the tags <ul></ul> surround the unordered list. The tags <li> and </li> surround each item in the list.

5. Click the **Show Design view button** Design on the toolbar.

You used the List Properties dialog box to apply the Square bullet style to the unordered lists. You then viewed the HTML code for the unordered lists in Code view.

Create an ordered list

1. Place the insertion point at the end of the page, after the word "5:00 p.m."

2. Use the Import Word Document command to import questions.doc from where you store your Data Files (Win) or open questions.doc from where you store your Data Files, select all, copy, then paste the copied text on the page (Mac).

   The inserted text appears on the same line as the existing text.

   TIP Remember to remove the check mark in the Use CSS instead of HTML tags check box in the General section of the Preferences dialog box before importing Word text.

3. Place the insertion point to the left of the text "Questions you may have," click **Insert** on the menu bar, point to **HTML**, then click **Horizontal Rule**.

   A horizontal rule appears and helps to separate the unordered list from the text you just imported.

4. Select the text beginning with "How do I schedule" and ending with the last sentence on the page.

5. Click the **Ordered List button** ⊟ in the Property inspector to format the selected text as an ordered list.

6. Deselect the text, then compare your screen to Figure 6.

You imported text on the spa page. You also added a horizontal rule to help organize the page. Finally, you formatted selected text as an ordered list.

FIGURE 6
Creating an ordered list

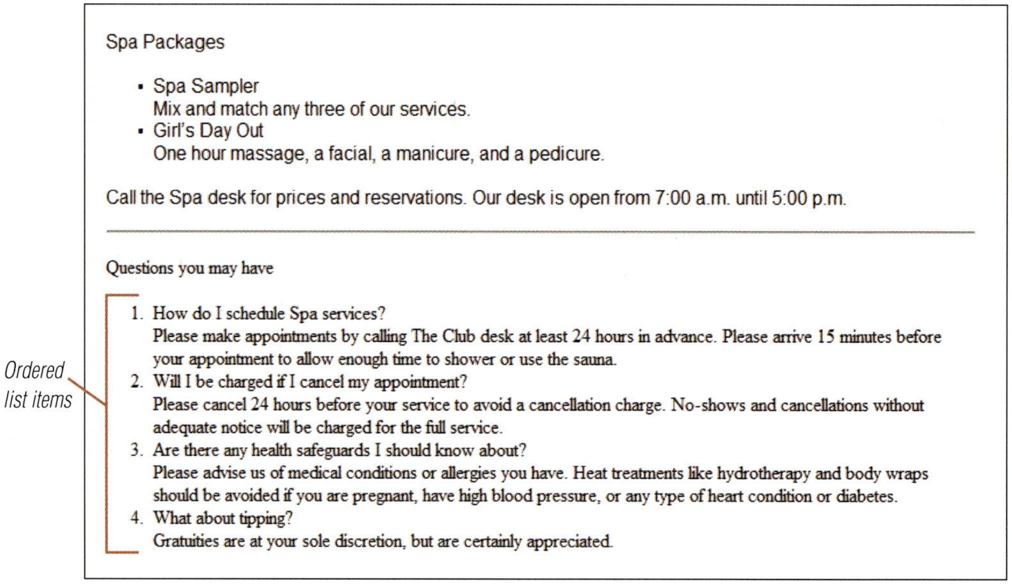

Spa Packages

- Spa Sampler
  Mix and match any three of our services.
- Girl's Day Out
  One hour massage, a facial, a manicure, and a pedicure.

Call the Spa desk for prices and reservations. Our desk is open from 7:00 a.m. until 5:00 p.m.

Questions you may have

Ordered list items

1. How do I schedule Spa services?
   Please make appointments by calling The Club desk at least 24 hours in advance. Please arrive 15 minutes before your appointment to allow enough time to shower or use the sauna.
2. Will I be charged if I cancel my appointment?
   Please cancel 24 hours before your service to avoid a cancellation charge. No-shows and cancellations without adequate notice will be charged for the full service.
3. Are there any health safeguards I should know about?
   Please advise us of medical conditions or allergies you have. Heat treatments like hydrotherapy and body wraps should be avoided if you are pregnant, have high blood pressure, or any type of heart condition or diabetes.
4. What about tipping?
   Gratuities are at your sole discretion, but are certainly appreciated.

FIGURE 7

Spa page with ordered list

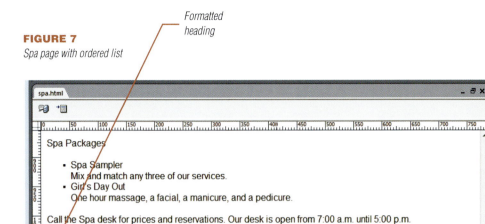

Formatted
heading

Spa Packages

- Spa Sampler
  Mix and match any three of our services.
- Girl's Day Out
  One hour massage, a facial, a manicure, and a pedicure.

Call the Spa desk for prices and reservations. Our desk is open from 7:00 a.m. until 5:00 p.m.

Questions you may have

1. How do I schedule Spa services?
   Please make appointments by calling The Club desk at least 24 hours in advance. Please arrive 15 minutes before your appointment to allow enough time to shower or use the sauna.
2. Will I be charged if I cancel my appointment?
   Please cancel 24 hours before your service to avoid a cancellation charge. No-shows and cancellations without adequate notice will be charged for the full service.
3. Are there any health safeguards I should know about?
   Please advise us of medical conditions or allergies you have. Heat treatments like hydrotherapy and body wraps should be avoided if you are pregnant, have high blood pressure, or any type of heart condition or diabetes.
4. What about tipping?
   Gratuities are at your sole discretion, but are certainly appreciated.

Formatted
body text

Text Color button

Bold button

Click arrow to collapse
Property inspector

Format an ordered list

1. Select all the text below the horizontal rule, then change the font to Arial, Helvetica, sans-serif, size 3.
2. Select the heading "Questions you may have," then click the **Bold button** **B** in the Property inspector.
3. Click the **Text Color button** in the Property inspector to open the color picker, click the first **dark blue color** in the third row, color #000066, deselect the text, then compare your screen to Figure 7.

   TIP If you want to see more of your Web page in the Document window, you can collapse the Property inspector.

5. Save your work.

You applied a new font and font size to the ordered list. You also formatted the "Questions you may have" heading.

CREATE, APPLY, AND EDIT
CASCADING STYLE SHEETS

What You'll Do

In this lesson, you will create a Cascading Style Sheet file for The Striped Umbrella Web site. You will also create styles named bullets and heading and apply them to the spa page.

Understanding Cascading Style Sheets

CSS are made up of sets of formatting attributes called rules, which define the formatting attributes for individual styles, and are classified by where the code is stored. Sometimes the terms "style" and "rule" seem to be used interchangeably to refer to a rule in a style sheet. The code can be saved in a separate file (**external style sheets**), as part of the head content of an individual Web page (**internal or embedded styles**) or as part of the body of the HTML code (**inline styles**). External CSS style sheets are saved as files with the .css extension and are stored in the directory structure of a Web site, as shown in Figure 8. They are the preferred method for creating and using styles.

CSS are also classified by their function. A **Class style** can be used to format any page element. An **HTML style** is used to redefine an HTML tag. An **Advanced style** is used to format combinations of page elements. In this chapter, we will use class styles stored in external style sheet files.

Using the CSS Styles Panel

You use the buttons on the CSS Styles panel to create, edit, and apply styles. To add a style, use the New CSS Rule dialog box to name the style and specify whether to add it to a new or existing style sheet. You then use the CSS Rule definition dialog box to set the formatting attributes for the style. Once you add a new style to a style sheet, it appears in a list in the CSS Styles panel. To apply a style, you select the text to which you want to apply the style, and then choose a style from the Style list in the Property inspector. You can apply CSS styles to elements on a single Web page or to all of the pages in a Web site. When you make a change to a style, all page elements formatted with that style are automatically updated. Once you create a CSS style sheet, you can attach it to the remaining pages in your Web site.

The CSS Styles panel is used for managing your styles. The Properties pane displays properties for a selected style at the bottom of the panel. You can easily change a property's value by clicking an option from a drop-down list.

Comparing the Advantages of Using Style Sheets

You can use CSS styles to save an enormous amount of time. Being able to define a rule and then apply it to page elements on all the pages of your Web site means that you can make hundreds of formatting changes in a few minutes. In addition, style sheets create a more uniform look from page to page and they generate cleaner code. Using style sheets separates the development of content from the way the content is presented. Pages formatted with CSS styles are much more compliant with current accessibility standards than those with manual formatting.

QUICKTIP

For more information about Cascading Style Sheets, visit *www.w3.org* or view a tutorial at *www.adobe.com/go/vid0152*.

Understanding CSS Style Sheet Code

You can see the code for a CSS style by opening a style sheet file. A CSS style consists of two parts: the selector and the declaration. The **selector** is the name of the tag to which the style declarations have been assigned. The **declaration** consists of the property and the value. For example, Figure 9 shows the code for the su_styles.css style sheet. In this example,

the first property listed for the .bullets style is font-family. The value for this property is Arial, Helvetica, sans-serif. When you create a new CSS, you will see it as an open document in the Document window. Save this file as you make changes to it.

FIGURE 8

Cascading Style Sheet file created in striped_umbrella root folder

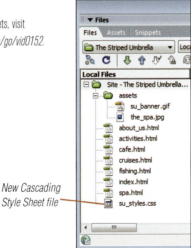

New Cascading Style Sheet file

FIGURE 9

su_styles.css style sheet file

```
1  .bullets {
2      font-family: Arial, Helvetica, sans-serif;
3      font-size: 14px;
4      font-style: normal;
5      font-weight: bold;
6      color: #000066;
7  }
8
```

Create a Cascading Style Sheet and a style

1. Click **Edit** (Win) or **Dreamweaver** (Mac) on the menu bar, click **Preferences**, click the **General category**, if necessary, click the **Use CSS instead of HTML tags check box**, then click **OK** to turn this default option back on.

   From this point forward, we will use CSS rather than HTML tags to format text. The Property inspector font sizes will be shown in pixels rather than HTML text sizes, as shown in Figure 10. You can also set font sizes using values such as "small" or "medium."

2. Expand the CSS panel group, then click the **CSS Styles panel tab** (if necessary).

3. Click the **Switch to All (Document) Mode button** **All** , click the **New CSS Rule button** in the CSS Styles panel to open the New CSS Rule dialog box, verify that the Class option button is selected, then type **bullets** in the Name text box.

   TIP Class names are preceded by a period. If you don't enter a period when you type the name, Dreamweaver will add the period for you.

4. Click the **Define in list arrow**, click **(New Style Sheet File)** (if necessary), compare your screen with Figure 11, then click **OK**.

5. Type **su_styles** in the File name text box (Win) or the Save As text box (Mac), then click **Save** to open the CSS Rule Definition for .bullets in su_styles.css dialog box.

   The .bullets rule will be stored within the su_styles.css file.

(continued)

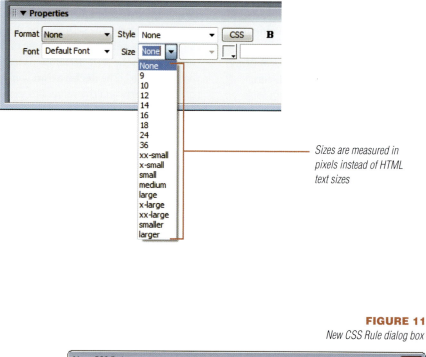

Sizes are measured in pixels instead of HTML text sizes

FIGURE 11
New CSS Rule dialog box

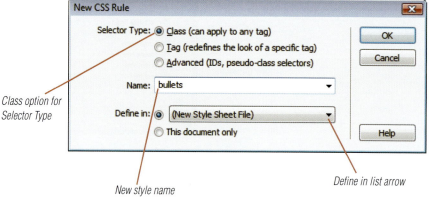

Class option for Selector Type

New style name

Define in list arrow

FIGURE 12

CSS Rule Definition for .bullets in su_styles.css dialog box

Type category selected

CSS Rule Definition for .bullets in su_styles.css

Category	Type
Type	
Background	
Block	
Box	
Border	
List	
Positioning	
Extensions	

Font: Arial, Helvetica, sans-serif

Size: 12 pixels   Weight: bold

Style: normal   Variant:

Line height: pixels   Case:

Decoration: ☐ underline   Color: ■ #000066
☐ overline
☐ line-through
☐ blink
☐ none

Help   OK   Cancel   Apply

FIGURE 13

CSS Styles panel with bullets style added

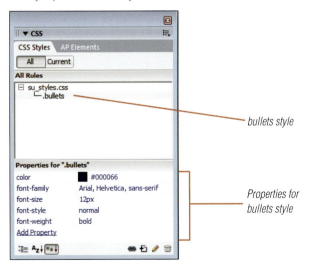

bullets style

Properties for bullets style

6. Verify that Type is selected in the Category list, set the Font to **Arial, Helvetica, sans-serif,** set the Size to **12 pixels**, set the Weight to **bold**, set the Style to **normal**, set the Color to **#000066**, compare your screen to Figure 12, then click **OK**.

7. Click the **plus sign** (Win) or the **expander arrow** (Mac) next to su_styles.css in the CSS Styles panel and expand the panel (if necessary) to list the .bullets style, then select the **bullets style**.

   The CSS style named .bullets and the style properties appear in the CSS Styles panel, as shown in Figure 13.

You created a Cascading Style Sheet file named su_styles.css and a style called .bullets.

Apply a Cascading Style Sheet

1. Click **View** on the menu bar, point to **Toolbars**, then click **Style Rendering**.

2. Verify that the **Toggle Displaying of CSS Styles button** on the Style Rendering toolbar is active, as shown in Figure 14.

   TIP You can determine if the Toggle Displaying of CSS Styles button is active if it has an outline around the button. As long as this button is active, you do not have to display the toolbar on the screen.

   You can use the Toggle Displaying of CSS Styles button to see how styles affect your page.

3. Select the text "Revitalizing Facial," as shown in Figure 15, then use the Property inspector to set the Font to **Default Font**, the Size to **None**, and the Style to **bullets**.

   TIP Before you apply a style to selected text, you need to remove all formatting attributes such as font and color from that text, or the style will not be applied correctly.

4. Repeat Step 1 to apply the bullets style to each of the spa services bulleted items in the unordered lists, then compare your screen to Figure 16.

   The font size is too small, which you will fix in the next lesson.

You applied the bullets style to each item in the Spa Services category lists.

FIGURE 14
Style Rendering toolbar

Toggle Displaying of CSS Styles button

FIGURE 15
Applying a CSS style to selected text

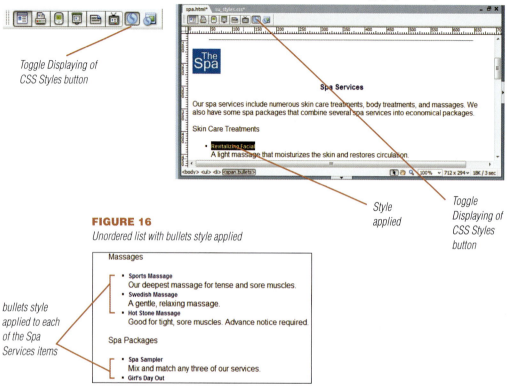

Style applied

Toggle Displaying of CSS Styles button

FIGURE 16
Unordered list with bullets style applied

bullets style applied to each of the Spa Services items

Using the Style Rendering toolbar

The Style Rendering toolbar allows you to render your page as different media types, such as print, TV, or handheld. To display it when a page is open, click View on the menu bar, point to Toolbars, and then click Style Rendering. The buttons on the Style Rendering toolbar allow you to see how your page will look as you select different media types. The next to the last button on the toolbar is the Toggle Displaying of CSS Styles button, which you can use to view how a page looks with styles applied. It works independently of the other buttons. The last button is the Design-time Style Sheets button, which you can use to show or hide particular combinations of styles while you are working in the Document window.

FIGURE 17

Editing a style

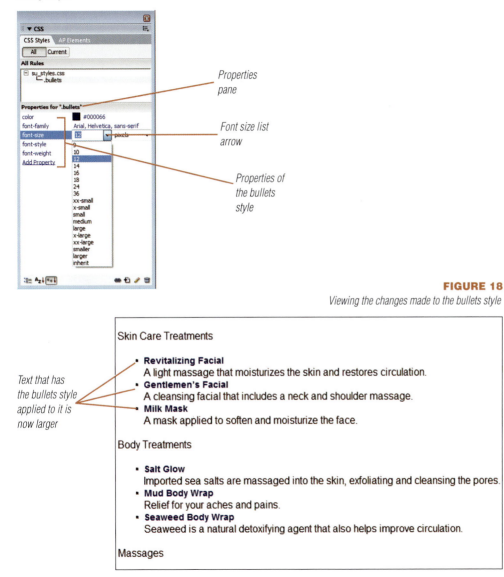

Properties pane

Font size list arrow

Properties of the bullets style

FIGURE 18

Viewing the changes made to the bullets style

Text that has the bullets style applied to it is now larger

Skin Care Treatments

- **Revitalizing Facial**
  A light massage that moisturizes the skin and restores circulation.
- **Gentlemen's Facial**
  A cleansing facial that includes a neck and shoulder massage.
- **Milk Mask**
  A mask applied to soften and moisturize the face.

Body Treatments

- **Salt Glow**
  Imported sea salts are massaged into the skin, exfoliating and cleansing the pores.
- **Mud Body Wrap**
  Relief for your aches and pains.
- **Seaweed Body Wrap**
  Seaweed is a natural detoxifying agent that also helps improve circulation.

Massages

Edit a Cascading Style Sheet

1. Click **.bullets** in the CSS Styles panel.

   The style's properties and values are displayed in the Properties pane, the bottom part of the CSS Styles panel, as shown in Figure 17. You can also click the **Edit Style button** 🖉 in the CSS Styles panel to open the CSS Rule Definition for .bullets dialog box.

   > TIP Click the plus sign (Win) or expander arrow (Mac) to the left of su_styles.css in the CSS Styles panel if you do not see .bullets. Click the plus sign (Win) or expander arrow (Mac) to the left of <style> if you do not see su_styles.css.

2. Click **12px** in the CSS Styles panel, click the **font-size list arrow**, click **14**, then compare your screen to Figure 18.

   The text is larger, reflecting the changes you made to the bullets style.

   > TIP If you position the insertion point in text that has a CSS style applied to it, that style is displayed in the Style text box on the Property inspector.

You edited the bullets style to change the font size to 14 pixels. You then viewed the results of the edited style in the unordered list.

ADD STYLES AND ATTACH
CASCADING STYLE SHEETS

What You'll Do

In this lesson, you will add a style to a Cascading Style Sheet. You will then attach the style sheet file to the index page and apply one of the styles to text on the page.

Understanding External and Embedded Style Sheets

When you are first learning about CSS, the terminology can be very confusing. In the last lesson, you learned that external style sheets are a separate file in a Web site saved with the .css file extension. You also learned that CSS can be part of an html file, rather than a separate file. These are called internal, or embedded, style sheets. External CSS files are created by the Web designer. Embedded style sheets are created automatically by Dreamweaver when the Preference is set to Use CSS instead of HTML tags. When this preference is set, any formatting choices you make using the Property inspector will automatically create a style. The code for these styles will reside in the head content for that page. These styles will be automatically named style1, style2, and so on. You can rename the styles as they are created to make them more recognizable for you to use, for example, body_text, subheading, or address. Embedded style sheets apply only to a single page, although you can copy them into the code in other pages. Remember that style sheets can be used to format much more than text objects. They can be used to set the page background, link properties, tables, or determine the appearance of almost any object on the page. Figure 19 shows the code for some embedded styles. The code resides in the head content of the Web page.

When you have several pages in a Web site, you will probably want to use the same CSS style sheet for each page to ensure that all your elements have a consistent appearance. To attach a style sheet to another document, click the Attach Style Sheet button on the CSS Styles panel to open the Attach External Style Sheet dialog box, make sure the Add as Link option is selected, browse to locate the file you want to attach, and then click OK. The styles contained in the attached style sheet will appear in the CSS Styles panel, and you can use them to apply styles to text on the page. External style sheets can be attached, or linked, to any page. This is an extremely powerful tool. If you decide to make a change in a style, it will automatically be made to every object that it formats.

FIGURE 19

Code for embedded styles shown in Code view

```
1   <!DOCTYPE html PUBLIC "-//W3C//DTD XHTML 1.0 Transitional//EN"
    "http://www.w3.org/TR/xhtml1/DTD/xhtml1-transitional.dtd">
2   <html xmlns="http://www.w3.org/1999/xhtml">
3   <head>
4   <meta http-equiv="Content-Type" content="text/html; charset=utf-8" />
5   <title>Welcome to the Striped Umbrella</title>
6   <style type="text/css">
7   <!--
8   .style1 {
9       font-family: Arial, Helvetica, sans-serif;
10      font-size: 10px;
11  }
12  .style2 {font-family: Arial, Helvetica, sans-serif;
13      font-size: 18px; }
14  body {
15      background-color: #99CCCC;
16  }
17  a:link {
18      color: #990000;
19  }
20  -->
21  </style>
22  </head>
23
```

Add a style to a Cascading Style Sheet

1. Click the **New CSS Rule button** in the CSS Styles panel.

2. Type **heading** in the Name text box, as shown in Figure 20, then click **OK**.

3. Set the Font to **Arial**, **Helvetica**, **sans-serif**, set the Size to **16**, set the Style to **normal**, set the Weight to **bold**, set the Color to **#000066**, compare your screen to Figure 21, then click **OK**.

4. Click the **Edit Style button**.

5. Click the **Block category** in the CSS Rule Definition for .heading in su_styles.css dialog box, click the **Text align list arrow**, click **center**, as shown in Figure 22, then click **OK**.

6. Select the heading text "Spa Services," then use the Property inspector to set the Format to **None** and the Font to **Default Font**.

7. With the heading still selected, click the **Text Color button** to open the color picker, then click the **Default Color button**.

8. Click the **Style list arrow** in the Property inspector, then click **heading** to apply it to the Spa Services heading.

9. Repeat Steps 1 through 3 to add another style called **body_text** with the **Arial**, **Helvetica**, **sans-serif** font, size **14**, and **normal** style.

10. Repeat Steps 6 through 8 to apply the body_text style to the all the text on the page except for the blue text that already has the bullets style applied to it and the heading text "Questions you may have."

FIGURE 20

Adding a style to a CSS Style sheet

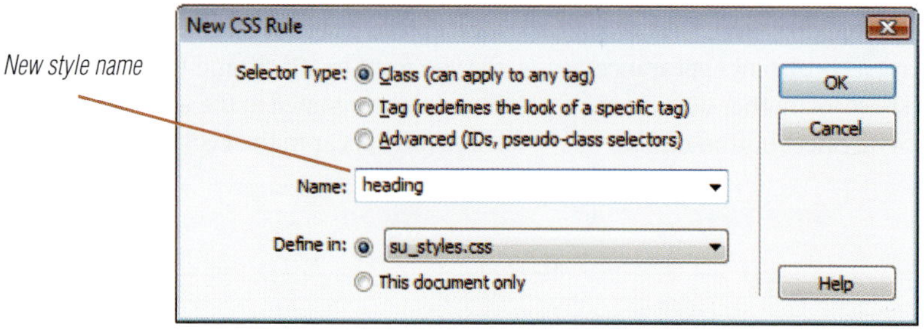

New style name

FIGURE 21

Formatting options for heading style

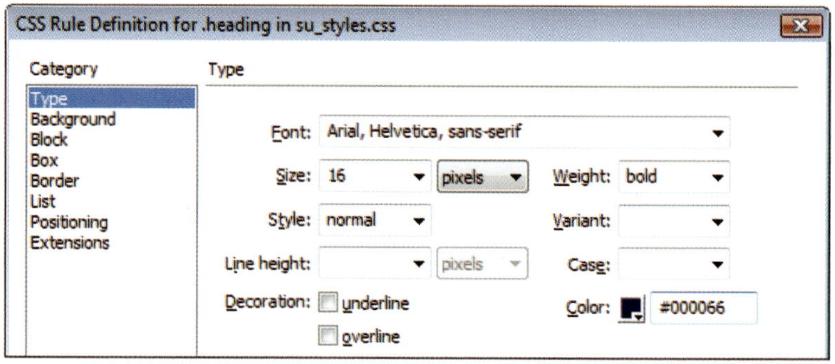

FIGURE 22

Setting text alignment for heading style

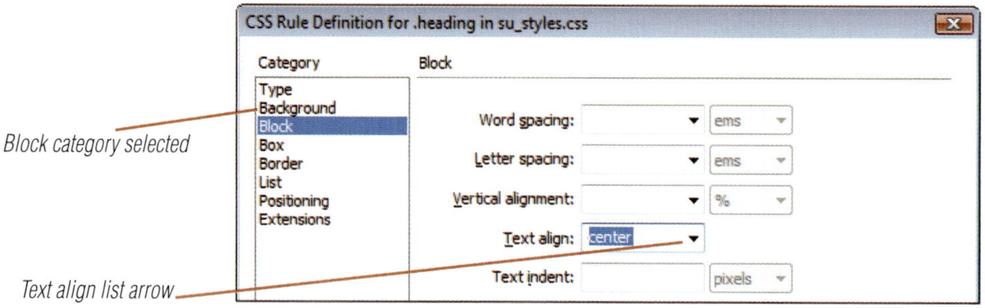

Block category selected

Text align list arrow

FIGURE 23

Spa page with styles applied

heading
style applied

body_text
style applied

Spa Services

Our spa services include numerous skin care treatments, body treatments, and massages. We also have some spa packages that combine several spa services into economical packages.

Skin Care Treatments

- **Revitalizing Facial**
  A light massage that moisturizes the skin and restores circulation.
- **Gentlemen's Facial**
  A cleansing facial that includes a neck and shoulder massage.
- **Milk Mask**
  A mask applied to soften and moisturize the face.

FIGURE 24

Attaching a style sheet to a page

su_styles.css

Link option
button

FIGURE 25

Viewing the code to link the CSS style sheet file

Code linking external style
sheet file to the index page

Code that applies the body_text
style to the paragraph

11. Click **File** on the menu bar, then click **Save All**, to save both the spa page and the su_styles.css file.

The styles are saved and applied to the text, as shown in Figure 23.

> TIP   You must save the open su_styles.css file after editing it, or you will lose your changes.

You added two new styles called heading and body_text to the su_styles.css file. You then applied the two styles to selected text.

Attach a style sheet

1. Close the spa page and open the index page.

2. Click the **Attach Style Sheet button** 🖳 on the CSS Styles panel.

3. Browse to select the file su_styles.css (if necessary), click **Choose** (Mac) verify that the **Link option button** is selected, as shown in Figure 24, then click **OK**.

4. Select the opening paragraph text, then set the Font to **Default Font** and the Size to **None** to clear prior formatting.

5. Click the **Style list arrow**, then click **body_text**.

6. Click the **Show Code view button** ‹› Code and view the code that links the su_styles.css file to the index page, as shown in Figure 25.

7. Click the **Show Design view button** 🖳 Design , save your work, then close the index page.

You attached the su_styles.css file to the index.html page.

INSERT AND ALIGN
GRAPHICS

What You'll Do

 In this lesson, you will insert five graphics on the about us page in The Striped Umbrella Web site. You will then stagger the alignment of the images on the page to make the page more visually appealing.

Understanding Graphic File Formats

When you add graphics to a Web page, it's important to choose the appropriate graphic file format. The three primary graphic file formats used in Web pages are **GIF** (Graphics Interchange Format), **JPEG** (Joint Photographic Experts Group), and **PNG** (Portable Network Graphics). GIF files download very quickly, making them ideal to use on Web pages. Though limited in the number of colors they can represent, GIF files have the ability to show transparent areas. JPEG files can display many colors. Because they often contain many shades of the same color, photographs are often saved in JPEG format. Files saved with the PNG format can display many colors and use various degrees of transparency, called **opacity**. While the GIF format is subject to licensing restrictions, the PNG format is free to use. However, not all browsers support the PNG format.

QUICKTIP

The status bar displays the download time for the page. Each time you add a new graphic to the page, you can see how much additional time is added to the total download time.

Understanding the Assets Panel

When you add a graphic to a Web site, it is automatically added to the Assets panel. The **Assets panel**, located in the Files panel group, displays all the assets in a Web site. The Assets panel contains nine category buttons that you use to view your assets by category. These include Images, Colors, URLs, Flash, Shockwave, Movies, Scripts, Templates, and Library. To view a particular type of asset, click the appropriate category button. The Assets panel is split into two panes. When you click the Images button, as shown in Figure 26, the lower pane displays a list of all the images in your site and contains four columns. The top pane displays a thumbnail of the selected image in the list. You can view assets in each category in two ways. You can use the Site option button to view all the assets in a Web site, or you can use the Favorites option button to view those assets that you have designated as **favorites**, or assets that you expect to use repeatedly while you work on the site. You can use the Assets panel to add an

Working with Text and Images

asset to a Web page by dragging the asset from the Assets panel to the page or by using the Insert button on the Assets panel.

Inserting Files with Adobe Bridge

You can manage project files, including video and Camera Raw files, with a file-management tool called Adobe Bridge. Bridge is an easy way to view files outside the Web site before bringing them into the Web site. It is an integrated application, working with other Adobe programs such as Photoshop and Illustrator. You can also use Bridge to add meta tags and search text to your files. To open Bridge, click the Browse in Bridge command on the File menu or click the Browse In Bridge button on the Standard toolbar.

Aligning Images

When you insert an image on a Web page, you need to position it in relation to other elements on the page. Positioning an image is referred to as **aligning** an image. By default, when you insert an image in a paragraph, its bottom edge aligns with the baseline of the first line of text or any other element in the same paragraph. When you select an image, the Align text box in the Property inspector displays the alignment setting for the image. You can change the alignment setting using the options in the Align menu in the Property inspector.

FIGURE 26
The Assets panel

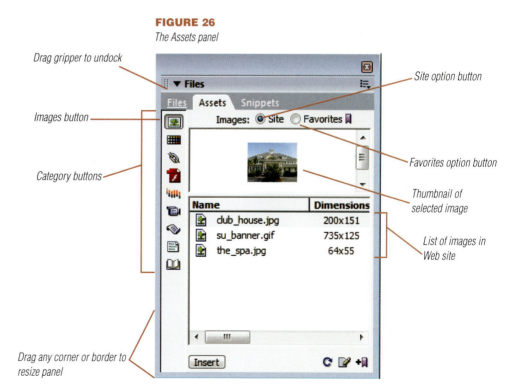

Drag gripper to undock

Images button

Category buttons

Site option button

Favorites option button

Thumbnail of selected image

List of images in Web site

Drag any corner or border to resize panel

Insert a graphic

1. Open dw3_1.html from where you store your Data Files, then save it as **about_us.html** in the striped_umbrella root folder.

2. Click **Yes** (Win) or **Replace** (Mac) to overwrite the existing file, then click **No** to Update Links.

3. Click the **Attach Style Sheet button** 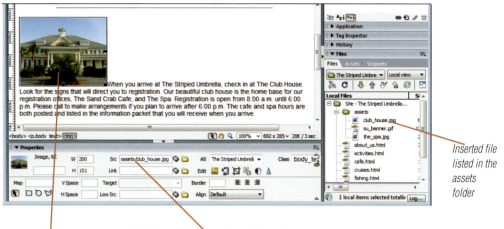 in the CSS Styles panel, attach the su_styles.css style sheet, then apply the body_text style to all of the paragraph text on the page.

4. Place the insertion point before "When" in the first paragraph, click the **Common tab** on the Insert bar (if necessary), click the **Images list arrow**, then click **Image** to open the Select Image Source dialog box.

5. Navigate to the assets folder where you store your Data Files, double-click **club_house.jpg,** type the alternate text **Club House** if prompted, click **OK,** then verify that the file was copied to your assets folder in the striped_umbrella root folder.

   Compare your screen to Figure 27.

6. Click the **Assets panel tab** in the Files panel group, click the **Images button** 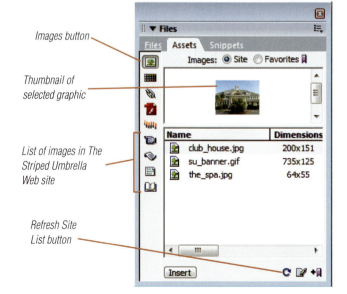 on the Assets panel (if necessary), then click the **Refresh Site List button** on the Assets panel to update the list of images in The Striped Umbrella Web site.

   The Assets panel displays a list of all the images in The Striped Umbrella Web site, as shown in Figure 28.

You inserted one image on the about_us page and copied it to the assets folder of the Web site.

FIGURE 27
The Striped Umbrella about us page with inserted image

club_house.jpg file inserted   *Path should begin with the word "assets"*   *Inserted file listed in the assets folder*

FIGURE 28
Image files for The Striped Umbrella Web site listed in Assets panel

Images button

Thumbnail of selected graphic

List of images in The Striped Umbrella Web site

Refresh Site List button

FIGURE 29

Using Adobe Bridge

*boardwalk.jpg
image is selected*

FIGURE 30

Assets panel with seven images

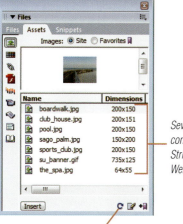

*Seven image files
contained in The
Striped Umbrella
Web site*

Click Refresh Site List button to refresh file list

Use Adobe Bridge

1. Click to place the insertion point before the word "After" at the beginning of the second paragraph.

2. Click **File** on the menu bar, click **Browse in Bridge,** navigate to where you store your Data Files, then click the thumbnail image **boardwalk.jpg** in the assets folder, as shown in Figure 29.

   Bridge is divided into several panels; files and folders are listed in the Folders Panel. The files in the selected folder appear in the Content Panel. A picture of the file appears in the Preview Panel. The Metadata and Keywords Panels list any tags that have been added to the file.

3. Click **File** on the menu bar, point to **Place,** then click **In Dreamweaver**.

4. Type the alternate text **Boardwalk to the beach,** if prompted.

   The image appears on the page.

   > TIP: You can also click the Browse in Bridge button  on the Standard toolbar to open Bridge.

5. Repeat Steps 1–4 to place the **pool.jpg, sago_palm.jpg**, and **sports_club.jpg** files at the beginning of each of the succeeding paragraphs, adding appropriate alternate text if prompted for the pool, sago palm, and sports club images.

   After refreshing, your Assets panel should resemble Figure 30.

You inserted four images using Adobe Bridge on the about_us page and copied each image to the assets folder of The Striped Umbrella Web site.

Align an image

1. Scroll to the top of the page, click the **club house image**, then expand the Property inspector (if necessary).

   Because an image is selected, the Property inspector displays tools for setting the properties of an image.

2. Click the **Align list arrow** in the Property inspector, then click **Left**.

   The club house photo is now left-aligned with the text and the paragraph text flows around its right edge, as shown in Figure 31.

   (continued)

FIGURE 31
Left-aligned club house image

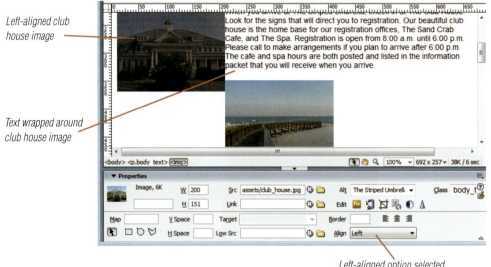

Left-aligned club house image

Text wrapped around club house image

Left-aligned option selected

Using Favorites in the Assets panel

The assets in the Assets panel can be listed two ways: Site and Favorites. The Site option lists all of the assets in the Web site in the selected category in alphabetical order. As your list of assets grows, you can designate some of the assets that are used more frequently as Favorites for quicker access. To add an asset to the Favorites list, right-click (Win) or [control]-click (Mac) the asset name in the Site list, and then click Add to Favorites. When an asset is placed in the Favorites list, it is still included in the Site list. To delete an asset from the Favorites list, select the asset you want to delete, and then press [Delete] or the Remove from Favorites button on the Assets panel. You can further organize your Favorites list by creating folders for similar assets and grouping them inside the folders.

FIGURE 32
Aligned images on the about us page

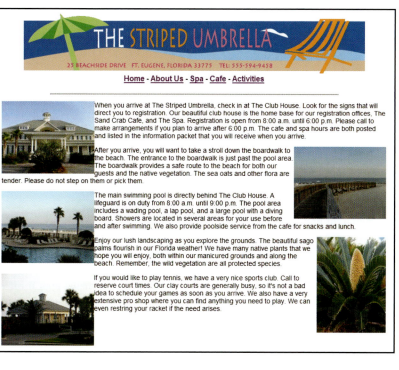

3. Select the boardwalk image, click the **Align list arrow** in the Property inspector, then click **Right**.

4. Align the pool image, using the **Left Align** option.

5. Align the sago palm image, using the **Right Align** option.

6. Align the sports club image, using the **Left Align** option.

7. Save your work.

8. Preview the Web page in your browser, compare your screen to Figure 32, then close your browser.

9. Close Adobe Bridge.

You used the Property inspector to set the alignment for the five images. You then previewed the page in your browser.

Graphics versus images

Two terms that sometimes seem to be used interchangeably are graphics and images. For the purposes of discussion in this text, we will use the term **graphics** to refer to the appearance of most non-text items on a Web page such as photographs, logos, navigation bars, Flash animations, graphs, background images, and drawings. A file that produces any of these page elements is called a graphic file. Files that produce images on a page are referred to by their file type, or graphic file format, such as JPEG (Joint Photographic Experts Group), GIF (Graphics Interchange Format), or PNG (Portable Network Graphics). We will refer to the actual pictures that you see on the pages as images. Don't worry about which term to use. Many people use one term or the other according to habit or region, or use them interchangeably.

ENHANCE AN IMAGE AND
USE ALTERNATE TEXT

What You'll Do

 In this lesson, you will add borders to images, add horizontal and vertical space to set them apart from the text, and then add alternate text to each image on the page.

Enhancing an Image

After you place an image on a Web page, you have several options for **enhancing** it, or improving its appearance. To make changes to the image itself, such as removing scratches from it, or erasing parts of it, you need to use an image editor such as Adobe Fireworks or Adobe Photoshop. To edit an image directly in Fireworks from Dreamweaver, first select the image, and then click Edit on the Property inspector. This will open the Fireworks program.

Complete your editing, and then click Done to return to Dreamweaver.

QUICKTIP

You can copy a Photoshop PSD file directly into Dreamweaver. After inserting the image, Dreamweaver will prompt you to optimize the image for the Web.

You can use Dreamweaver to enhance certain aspects of how images appear on a page. For example, you can add borders around an image or add horizontal and

---

DESIGNTIP   **Resizing graphics using an external editor**

Each image on a Web page takes a specific number of seconds to download, depending on the size of the file. Larger files (in kilobytes, not width and height) take longer to download than smaller files. It's important to determine the smallest acceptable size for an image on your Web page. Then, if you need to resize an image to reduce the file size, use an external image editor to do so, *instead* of resizing it in Dreamweaver. Although you can adjust the width and height settings of an image in the Property inspector to change the size of the image as it appears on your screen, these settings do not affect the file size. Decreasing the size of an image using the H (height) and W (width) settings in the Property inspector does *not* reduce the time it will take the file to download. Ideally you should use images that have the smallest file size and the highest quality possible, so that each page downloads as quickly as possible.

vertical space. **Borders** are frames that surround an image. Horizontal and vertical space is blank space above, below, and on the sides of an image that separates the image from text or other elements on the page. Adding horizontal or vertical space is the same as adding white space, and helps images stand out on a page. In the Web page shown in Figure 33, the horizontal and vertical space around the images in the center column helps make these images more prominent. Adding horizontal or vertical space does not affect the width or height of the image. Spacing around Web page objects can also be created by using "spacer" images, or clear images that act as placeholders.

Using Alternate Text

One of the easiest ways to make your Web page viewer-friendly and accessible to people of all abilities is to use alternate text. **Alternate text** is descriptive text that appears in place of an image while the image is downloading or when the mouse pointer is placed over it. You can program some browsers to display only alternate text and to download images manually. Alternate text can be "read" by a **screen reader**, a device used by persons with visual impairments to convert written text on a computer monitor to spoken words. Screen readers and alternate text make it possible for viewers who have visual impairments to have an image described to them in detail. One of the

default preferences in Dreamweaver is to prompt you to enter alternate text whenever you insert an image on a page.

The use of alternate text is the first checkpoint listed in the World Wide Web Consortium (W3C) list of Priority 1 checkpoints. The Priority 1 checkpoints

dictate the most basic level of accessibility standards to be used by Web developers today. The complete list of these and the other priority-level checkpoints are listed on the W3C Web site, *www.w3.org*. You should always strive to meet these criteria for all Web pages.

FIGURE 33
Lands' End Web site

Lands' End Web site used with permission from Lands' End, Inc. - www.landsend.com

Add a border

1. Select the club house image, then expand the Property inspector (if necessary).

2. Type **1** in the Border text box, then press **[Tab]** to apply the border to the club house image, as shown in Figure 34.

   The border setting is not visible until you preview the page in a browser.

3. Repeat Step 2 to add borders to the other four images.

You added a 1-pixel border to each image on the about_us page.

Add horizontal space

1. Select the club house image, type **7** in the V Space text box in the Property inspector, press **[Tab]**, type **7** in the H Space text box, then compare your screen to Figure 35.

   The text is more evenly wrapped around the image and is easier to read, because it is not so close to the edge of the image.

2. Repeat Step 1 to set the V Space and H Space to 7 for the other four images.

   The spacing under each picture differs because of the difference in the lengths of the paragraphs.

You added horizontal spacing and vertical spacing around each image on the about_us page.

FIGURE 34

Using the Property inspector to add a border

Selected image with 1-pixel border

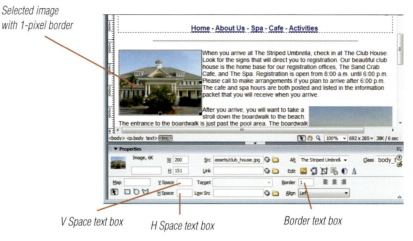

V Space text box   H Space text box   Border text box

FIGURE 35

Comparing images with and without horizontal and vertical space

Image with horizontal and vertical space

Image without horizontal and vertical space

FIGURE 36

Brightness and contrast settings for the boardwalk image

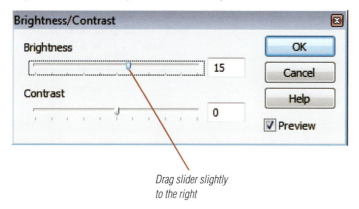

*Drag slider slightly
to the right*

Apply the Brightness/Contrast feature to graphics

1. Select the **boardwalk image**.

2. Click the **Brightness and Contrast button** ◐ in the Property inspector, then click **OK** to close the warning dialog box to open the Brightness/Contrast dialog box.

3. Drag the **Brightness slider** to the right until **15** appears in the text box, as shown in Figure 36, then click **OK**.

   The image is now lighter.

4. Repeat Step 3 to adjust any of the other images if desired.

   TIP   In addition to using brightness and contrast features, you can also scale an image. First, select the image, then drag one of the borders toward the center of the image to reduce it, or drag away from the center of the image to enlarge it.

You used the Brightness/Contrast dialog box to lighten an image.

Integrating Photoshop CS3 with Dreamweaver

Dreamweaver has many functions integrated with Photoshop CS3. This new partnership includes the ability to copy and paste a Photoshop PSD file directly from Photoshop into Dreamweaver. After using the Paste command, Dreamweaver will prompt you to optimize the image by choosing a file format and settings for the Web. After optimization, Dreamweaver will then paste the image on the page. If you want to edit the image later, simply double-click the image in Dreamweaver and it will open in Photoshop.

Photoshop users can set Photoshop as the default image editor in Dreamweaver. Click Edit on the menu bar, click Preferences, click Dreamweaver (Mac), click File Types/Editors, click the Editors plus sign button to add Photoshop, (if you don't see it listed already) and then click Make Primary. You can view a tutorial for Photoshop and Dreamweaver integration on the Adobe Web site at *www.adobe.com/go/vid0200*.

Edit alternate text

1. Select the club house image, select any existing text in the Alt text box in the Property inspector (if necessary), type **The Striped Umbrella Club House** as shown in Figure 37, then press **[Enter]** (Win) or **[return]** (Mac).

2. Save your work, preview the page in your browser, then point to the **club house image** until the alternate text appears, as shown in Figure 38.

3. Close your browser.

4. Select the boardwalk image, type **The boardwalk to the beach** in the Alt text box, replacing any existing text, then press **[Enter]** (Win) or **[return]** (Mac).

5. Repeat Step 4 to add the alternate text **The pool area** to the pool image.

6. Repeat Step 4 to add the alternate text **Sago palm** to the sago palm image.

7. Repeat Step 4 to add the alternate text **The Sports Club** to the sports club image.

8. Save your work.

9. Preview the page in your browser, view the alternate text for each image, then close your browser.

You edited the alternate text for five images on the page, then you viewed the alternate text in your browser.

FIGURE 37
Alternate text setting in the Property inspector

Alt text box

FIGURE 38
Alternate text displayed in browser

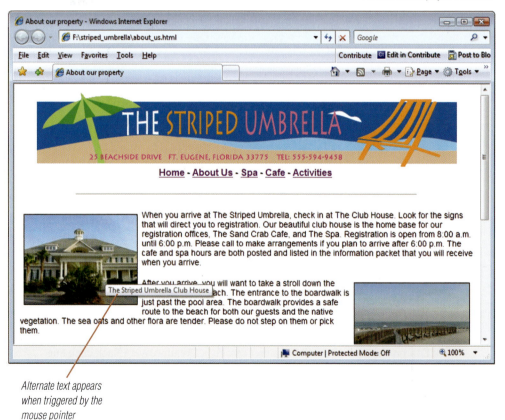

Alternate text appears when triggered by the mouse pointer

Working with Text and Images

FIGURE 39
Preferences dialog box with Accessibility category selected

Accessibility category

Check boxes for Form objects, Frames, Media, and Images

This option is not available in Mac OS X

POWER USER SHORTCUTS

To do this:	Use this shortcut:
Switch views	[Ctrl][`] (Win) or [control][`] (Mac)
Insert image	[Ctrl][Alt][I] (Win) or [⌘][option][I] (Mac)
Indent text	[Ctrl][Alt][]] (Win) or [⌘][option][]] (Mac)
Outdent text	[Ctrl][Alt][[] (Win) or [⌘][option][[] (Mac)
Align Left	[Ctrl][Alt][Shift][L] (Win) or [⌘][option][shift][L] (Mac)
Align Center	[Ctrl][Alt][Shift][C] (Win) or [⌘][option][shift][C] (Mac)
Align Right	[Ctrl][Alt][Shift][R] (Win) or [⌘][option][shift][R] (Mac)
Align Justify	[Ctrl][Alt][Shift][J] (Win) or [⌘][option][shift][J] (Mac)
Bold	[Ctrl][B] (Win) or [⌘][B] (Mac)
Italic	[Ctrl][I] (Win) or [⌘][I] (Mac)
Refresh	[F5]
Browse in Bridge	[Ctrl][At][O] (Win) or [⌘][option][O] (Mac)

Lesson 5 Enhance an Image and Use Alternate Text

Set the alternate text accessibility option

1. Click **Edit** (Win) or **Dreamweaver** (Mac) on the menu bar, click **Preferences** to open the Preferences dialog box, then click the **Accessibility category**.

2. Verify that the four check boxes are checked, as shown in Figure 39, check them if they are not checked, then click **OK**.

   TIP Once you set the Accessibility preferences, they will be in effect for all Web sites that you develop, not just the one that's open when you set them.

You set the Accessibility preferences to prompt you to enter alternate text each time you insert a form object, frame, media, image, or object on a Web page.

INSERT A BACKGROUND IMAGE
AND PERFORM SITE
MAINTENANCE

What You'll Do

▶ In this lesson, you will insert two types of background images. You will then use the Assets panel to delete them both from the Web site. You will also check for Non-Websafe colors in the Assets panel.

Inserting a Background Image

You can insert a background image on a Web page to provide depth and visual interest to the page, or to communicate a message or mood. **Background images** are image files used in place of background colors. Although you can use background images to create a dramatic effect, you should avoid inserting them on Web pages where they would not provide the contrast necessary for reading a well-designed page. Even though they might seem too plain, standard white backgrounds are usually the best choice for Web pages. If you choose to use a background image on a Web page, it should be small in file size. You can insert either a small image file that is tiled, or repeated, across the page or a larger image that is not repeated across the page. A tiled image will download much faster than a large image. A **tiled image** is a small image that repeats across and down a Web page, appearing as individual squares or rectangles. When you create a Web page, you can use either a background color or a background image, but

not both, unless you have a need for the background color to be displayed while the background image finishes downloading. The background in the Web page shown in Figure 40 is a gray-green color, along with an image faded to become the background for a large portion of the page.

Managing Images

As you work on a Web site, you might find that you accumulate files in your assets folder that the Web site does not use. To avoid accumulating unnecessary files, it's a good idea to look at an image first, before you place it on the page and copy it to the assets folder. If you inadvertently copy an unwanted file to the assets folder, you should delete it or move it to another location. This is a good Web-site management practice that will prevent the assets folder from filling up with unwanted image files.

Removing an image from a Web page does not remove it from the assets folder in the local root folder of the Web site. To remove an asset from a Web site, you first locate the file you want to remove in the Assets panel. You then use the Locate in Site command to open the Files panel with the unwanted file selected. You can then use the Delete command to remove the file from the site.

Removing Colors from a Web Site

You can use the Assets panel to locate Non-Websafe colors in a Web site. **Non-Websafe** colors are colors that may not be displayed uniformly across computer platforms. After you replace a Non-Websafe color with another color, you should use the Refresh Site List button on the Assets panel to verify that the color has been removed. Sometimes it's necessary to press [Ctrl] (Win) or ⌘ (Mac) while you click the Refresh Site List button. If refreshing the Assets panel does not work, try re-creating the site cache, and then refreshing the Assets panel again.

FIGURE 40
The Mansion on Turtle Creek

The Mansion on Turtle Creek Web site used with permission from The Mansion on Turtle Creek, A Rosewood Hotel - www.mansiononturtlecreek.com

Insert a background image

1. Click **Modify** on the menu bar, then click **Page Properties** to open the Page Properties dialog box.

2. Click the **Appearance category**, if necessary.

3. Click **Browse** next to the Background image text box, navigate to the assets folder where you store your Data Files, then double-click **umbrella_back.gif**.

   The umbrella_back.gif file is automatically copied to The Striped Umbrella assets folder.

4. Click **OK** to close the Page Properties dialog box, then click the **Refresh Site List button**  to refresh the file list in the Assets panel.

   A file with a single umbrella forms a background made up of individual squares, replacing the white background, as shown in Figure 41. It is much too busy and makes it difficult to read the page.

5. Repeat Steps 1–4 to replace the umbrella_back.gif background image with stripes_back.gif, located in the chapter_3 assets folder.

   As shown in Figure 42, the striped background is also tiled, but with vertical stripes, so you aren't aware of the small squares making up the pattern. It is still too busy, though.

You applied a tiled background to the about us page. Then you replaced the tiled background with another tiled background that was not as busy.

FIGURE 41
The about_us page with a busy tiled background

Each umbrella is a small square that forms a tiled background

FIGURE 42
The about_us page with a more subtle tiled background

It is harder to tell where each square ends

Working with Text and Images

FIGURE 43

Removing a background image

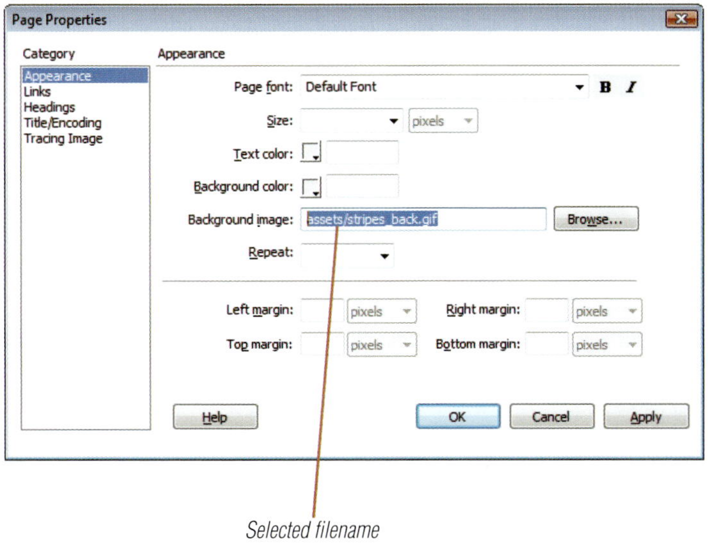

Selected filename

1. Click **Modify** on the menu bar, click **Page Properties**, then click **Appearance**.

2. Select the text in the Background image text box, as shown in Figure 43, press **[Delete]**, then click **OK**.

   The background of the about us page is white again.

You deleted the link to the background image file to change the about us page background back to white.

Understanding HTML body tags

When you are setting page preferences, it is helpful to understand the HTML tags that are being generated. Sometimes it's much easier to make changes to the code, rather than use menus and dialog boxes. The <body> </body> tags define the beginning and end of the body section of a Web page. The page content falls between these two tags. If you want to change the page properties, additional codes must be added to the <body> tag. The tag to add a color to the page background is bgcolor, so the tag will read <body bgcolor="#000000">, where the numbers following the pound sign indicate a color. If you insert an image for a background, the code will read <body background="assets/stripes.gif">. The filename between the quotation marks is the name of the image file used for the background.

Delete files from a Web site

1. Click the **Assets panel tab**, then click the **Images button** 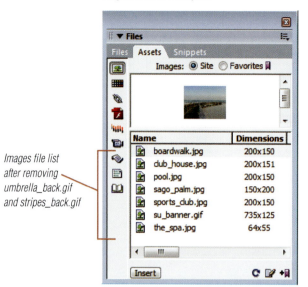 (if necessary).

2. Right-click (Win) or [control]-click (Mac) **stripes_back.gif** in the Assets panel, click **Locate in Site** to open the Files panel, select **stripes_back.gif** in the Files panel (if necessary), press **[Delete]**, then click **Yes** in the dialog box that appears.

   TIP Refresh the Assets panel if you still see the file listed.

3. Repeat Step 2 to remove umbrella_back.gif from the Web site, open the Assets panel, then refresh the Assets panel.

   TIP If you delete a file in the Files panel that has an active link to it, you will receive a warning message. If you rename a file in the Files panel that has a link to it, the Files panel will update the links to correctly link to the renamed file. To rename a file, right-click (Win) or [control]-click (Mac) the file you want to rename, point to Edit, click Rename, then type the new name.

   Your Assets panel should resemble Figure 44.

   You removed two image files from The Striped Umbrella Web site, then refreshed the Assets panel.

FIGURE 44
Images listed in Assets panel

Images file list after removing umbrella_back.gif and stripes_back.gif

Name	Dimensions
boardwalk.jpg	200x150
club_house.jpg	200x151
pool.jpg	200x150
sago_palm.jpg	150x200
sports_club.jpg	200x150
su_banner.gif	735x125
the_spa.jpg	64x55

Managing image files

It is a good idea to store original unedited copies of your Web site image files in a separate folder, outside the assets folder of your Web site. If you edit the original files, save them again using different names. Doing this ensures that you will be able to find a file in its original, unaltered state. You may have files on your computer that you are currently not using at all, however, you may need to use them in the future. Storing currently unused files also helps keep your assets folder free of clutter. Storing copies of original Web site image files in a separate location also ensures that you have backup copies in the event that you accidentally delete a file from the Web site.

FIGURE 45
Colors listed in Assets panel

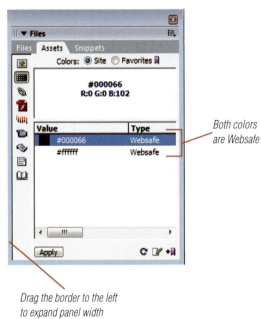

Both colors are Websafe

Drag the border to the left to expand panel width

Check for Non-Websafe colors

1. Click the **Colors button** in the Assets panel to display the colors used in the Web site, then drag the left border of the Assets panel (if necessary) to display the second column, as shown in Figure 45.

   The Assets panel does not list any Non-Websafe colors.

2. Save your work, preview the page in your browser, close your browser, then close all open files.

   TIP If previewing the page in Internet Explorer 7, click the Information bar when prompted to allow blocked content.

You checked for Non-Websafe colors in the Assets panel list of colors.

Using color in compliance with accessibility guidelines

The second guideline listed in the World Wide Web Consortium (W3C) list of Priority 1 Checkpoints is to not rely on the use of color alone. This means that if your Web site content is dependent on your viewer correctly seeing a color, then you are not providing for those people who cannot distinguish between certain colors or do not have monitors that display color.

Be especially careful when choosing color used with text to provide a good contrast between the text and the background. It is better to reference colors as numbers, rather than names. For example, use "#FFFFFF" instead of "white." Using style sheets for specifying color formats is the preferred method for coding. For more information, see the complete list of priority level checkpoints listed on the W3C Web site, *www.w3.org*.

Create unordered and ordered lists.

1. Open the blooms & bulbs Web site.
2. Open the tips page.
3. Select the four lines of text below the Seasonal Gardening Checklist heading and format them as an unordered list. (*Hint:* If each line does not become a separate list item, enter a paragraph break between each line, then remove any extra spaces.)
4. Select the lines of text below the Basic Gardening Tips heading and format them as an ordered list.
5. Save your work.

Create, apply, and edit Cascading Style Sheets.

1. Create a new CSS rule named **seasons**, making sure that the Class option button is selected in the Selector Type section and that the (New Style Sheet File) option button is selected in the Define in section of the New CSS Rule dialog box.
2. Click OK, name the style sheet file **blooms_styles** in the Save Style Sheet File As dialog box, then click Save.
3. Choose the following settings for the seasons style: Font = Arial, Helvetica, sans-serif, Size = medium, Style = normal, Weight = bold, and Color = #003366.
4. Change the Font setting to Default Font and the Size setting to None for the following words in the Seasonal Gardening Checklist: "Fall," "Winter," "Spring," and "Summer."

Apply the seasons style to Fall, Winter, Spring, and Summer.

5. Edit the seasons style by changing the font size to 16 pixels.

Add styles and attach cascading style sheets.

1. Add an additional style called **headings** in the blooms_styles.css file and define this style choosing the following type settings: Font = Arial, Helvetica, sans-serif, Size = large Style = normal, Weight = bold, and Color = #003366.
2. Apply the headings style to the two sub-headings on the page: Seasonal Gardening Checklist and Basic Gardening Tips. (*Hint:* Make sure you remove any manual formatting before applying the style.)
3. Click File on the menu bar, click Save All, then view the page in the browser. (*Hint:* If previewing the page in Internet Explorer 7, click the Information bar when prompted to allow blocked content.)
4. Close the browser and all open pages.

Insert and align graphics.

1. Open dw3_2.html from where you store your Data Files, then save it as **plants.html** in the blooms & bulbs Web site, overwriting the existing plants.html. Do not update links.
2. Verify that the path of the blooms & bulbs banner is set correctly to the assets folder in the blooms root folder.
3. Set the Accessibility preferences to prompt you

to add alternate text to images (if necessary).

4. Use Adobe Bridge to insert the petunias.jpg file from the assets folder where you store your Data Files to the left of the words "Pretty petunias" and add **Petunias** as alternate text.
5. Insert the verbena.jpg file from assets folder where you store your Data Files in front of the words "Verbena is one" and add **Verbena** as alternate text.
6. Insert the lantana.jpg file from the assets folder where you store your Data Files in front of the words "Dramatic masses" and add **Lantana** as alternate text.
7. Refresh the Files panel to verify that all three images were copied to the assets folder.
8. Left-align the petunias image.
9. Right-align the verbena image.
10. Left-align the lantana image.
11. Save your work.

Enhance an image and edit alternate text.

1. Apply a 1-pixel border and horizontal spacing of 20 pixels around the verbana image.
2. Apply a 1-pixel border and horizontal spacing of 20 pixels around the verbana image.
3. Apply a 1-pixel border and horizontal spacing of 20 pixels around the lantana image.
4. Save your work, preview it in the browser, then compare your screen to Figure 46.
5. Close the browser and open the tips page and add H Space of 10 and V Space of 10 to the garden_tips.jpg image.

6. Left-align the garden tips image, then compare your screen to Figure 47.

7. Save your work.

Insert a background image and manage graphics.

1. Switch to the plants page, then insert the **daisies.jpg** file as a background image from the assets folder where you store your Data Files.

2. Save your work.

3. Preview the Web page in your browser, then close your browser.

4. Remove the daisies.jpg file from the background.

5. Open the Assets panel, then refresh the Files list.

6. Use the Files panel to delete the daisies.jpg file from the list of images.

7. Refresh the Assets panel, then verify that the daisies.jpg file has been removed from the Web site.

8. View the colors used in the site in the Assets panel, then verify that all are Websafe.

9. Save your work, then close all open pages.

FIGURE 46
Completed Skills Review

Drop by to see our Featured Spring Plants

Pretty petunias blanket your beds with lush green leaves and bright blooms in assorted colors. Shown is the Moonlight White Petunia (Mini-Spreading). This variety is fast-growing and produces spectacular blooms. Cut them back in July for blooms that will last into the fall. Full sun to partial shade. Great for border plants or hanging baskets.

Verbena is one of our all-time favorites. The variety shown is Blue Silver. Verbena grows rapidly and is a good choice for butterfly gardens. The plants can spread up to two feet wide, so it makes excellent ground cover. Plant in full sun. Heat resistant. Beautiful also in rock gardens. We have several other varieties equally as beautiful.

Dramatic masses of Lantana display summer color for your beds or containers. The variety shown is Golden Dream. Blooms late spring through early fall. This variety produces outstanding color. Plant in full sun with well-drained soil. We carry tall, dwarf, and trailing varieties. You can also overwinter with cuttings.

Stop by to see us soon. We will be happy to help you with your selections.

FIGURE 47
Completed Skills Review

We have some planting tips we would like to share with you as you prepare your gardens this season. Remember, there is always something to be done for your gardens, no matter what the season. Our experienced staff is here to help you plan your gardens, select your plants, prepare your soil, assist you in the planting, and maintain your beds. Check out our calendar for a list of our scheduled classes. All classes are free of charge and on a first-come, first-served basis!

Seasonal Gardening Checklist:

- **Fall** – The time to plant trees and spring blooming bulbs.
- **Winter** – The time to prune fruit trees and finish planting your bulbs.
- **Spring** – The time to prepare your beds, plant annuals, and apply fertilizer to established plants.
- **Summer** – The time to supplement rainfall so that plants get one inch of water per week.

Basic Gardening Tips

1. Select plants according to your climate.
2. In planning your garden, consider the composition, texture, structure, depth, and drainage of your soil.
3. Use compost to improve the structure of your soil.
4. Choose plant foods based on your garden objectives.
5. Generally, plants should receive one inch of water per week.
6. Use mulch to conserve moisture, keep plants cool, and cut down on weeding.

Use Figures 48 and 49 as guides to continue your work on the TripSmart Web site that you began in Project Builder 1 in Chapter 1, and continued to work on in Chapter 2. You are now ready to format text on the newsletter page and begin work on the destinations page that showcases one of the featured tours to Kenya. You want to include some colorful pictures and attractively formatted text on the page.

1. Open the TripSmart Web site.
2. Open dw3_3.html from where you store your Data Files and save it in the tripsmart root folder as **newsletter.html**, overwriting the existing newsletter.html file and not updating the links.
3. Verify that the path for the banner is correctly set to the assets folder of the TripSmart Web site. Create an unordered list from the text beginning "Expandable clothesline" to the end of the page.
4. Create a new CSS rule called **body_text** making sure that the Class option button is selected in the Selector Type section and that the (New Style Sheet File) option button is selected in the Define in section of the New CSS Rule dialog box.
5. Save the style sheet file as **tripsmart_styles.css** in the TripSmart Web site root folder.
6. Choose a font, size, style, color, and weight of your choice for the body_text style.
7. Apply the **body_text** style to all of the text on the page except the "Ten Packing Essentials" heading on the newsletter page.
8. Create another style called **heading** with a font, size, style, color, and weight of your choice and apply it to the "Ten Packing Essentials" heading.
9. Type **Travel Tidbits** in the Title text box on the Document toolbar, then save and close the newsletter page.
10. Open dw3_4.html from where you store your Data Files and save it in the tripsmart root folder as **destinations.html**, overwriting the existing destinations.html file. Do not update links.
11. Insert **zebra_mothers.jpg** from the assets folder where you store your Data Files to the left of the sentence beginning "Our next," then add appropriate alternate text.
12. Insert **lion.jpg** from the assets folder where you store your Data Files to the left of the sentence beginning "This lion," then add appropriate alternate text.
13. Align both images using the Align list arrow in the Property inspector with alignments of your choice, then add horizontal spacing, vertical spacing, or borders if desired.
14. Apply the **heading** style to the "Destination: Kenya" heading and the **body_text** style to the rest of the text on the page.
15. Apply any additional formatting to enhance the page appearance, then add the page title **Destination: Kenya**.
16. Verify that the Accessibility Preference option is turned on.
17. Save your work, then preview the destinations page in your browser. (*Hint:* If previewing the page in Internet Explorer 7, click Information bar when prompted to allow blocked content.)
18. Close your browser, then close all open files.

FIGURE 48

Sample Project Builder 1

Ten Packing Essentials

The next time you are packing for a trip, whether it is for an adventure-backpacking trip to the jungles of Panama or for a weekend in New York , consider our list of "can't do without these" items:

- Expandable clothesline and clothespins – These are handy after you have hand-washed your clothes in the river or hotel sink.
- Paperback book – A book will help pass the time on a long plane trip or a wait in a customs line.
- Small hotel-size shampoo bottle – Shampoo is actually a mild detergent, handy for washing your hair, of course, but also for washing your clothes.
- Travel alarm clock – Don't depend on wake-up calls or a hotel clock to keep you from an important meeting time.
- Small flashlight – You never know when a flashlight will come in handy. Even five-star hotels have been known to lose power at times. Invaluable for snake spotting at night in the woods!
- Zippered plastic bags – These are so handy for storing a number of things: snacks, dirty clothes, wet clothes, small items that would get "lost" in your bag, like pens, tape, and your expandable clothesline and clothespins!
- Guidebook – There are many great guidebooks that range from guides for students on a shoestring budget to guides on shopping for fine antiques in Italy . Take advantage of available research to obtain general background knowledge of your destination.
- Backpack – Backpacks are versatile, easy to carry, and have enough style variations to appeal to all ages and sexes. They hold a lot of your essential items!
- Packing cubes – Packing cubes are zippered nylon bags that are great for organizing your packed items. You can squeeze the air out of the packed cubes, conserving space in your bag.

FIGURE 49

Sample Project Builder 2

Destination: Kenya

Our next Photo Safari to Kenya has now been scheduled with a departure date of May 5 and a return date of May 23. Come join us and take some beautiful pictures like these two Grevy's zebras nursing their young at Samburu National Reserve. Our flight will leave New York for London, where you will have dayrooms reserved before flying all night to Nairobi, Kenya. To provide the finest in personal attention, this tour will be limited to no more than sixteen persons. Game drives will take place early each morning and late afternoon to provide maximum opportunity for game viewing, as the animals are most active at these times. We will visit five game reserves to allow for a variety of animal populations and scenery.

This lion is relaxing in the late afternoon sun. Notice the scar under his right ear. He might have received that when he was booted out of his pride as a young lion. We will be spending most nights in tented camps listening to the night sounds of hunters such as this magnificent animal. Enjoy visiting native villages and trading with the local businessmen. Birding enthusiasts will enjoy adding to their bird lists with Kenya's over 300 species of birds. View the beginning of the annual migration of millions of wildebeest, a spectacular sight. The wildebeest are traveling from the Serengeti Plain to the Mara in search of water and grass. Optional excursions include  ballooning over the Masai Mara, fishing on Lake Victoria, camel rides at Amboseli Serena Lodge, and golfing at the Aberdare Country Club. Lake Victoria is the largest freshwater lake

In this exercise, you continue your work on the Carolyne's Creations Web site that you started in Project Builder 2 in Chapter 1, and continued to build in Chapter 2. You are now ready to add two new pages to the Web site. One page will display featured items in the kitchen store and one will be used to showcase a recipe. Figures 50 and 51 show possible solutions for this exercise. Your finished pages will look different if you choose different formatting options.

1. Open the Carolyne's Creations Web site.
2. Open dw3_5.html from where you store your Data Files, save it to the Web site root folder as **recipes.html**, overwriting the existing file and not updating the links.
3. Format the list of ingredients as an unordered list.
4. Create a CSS rule named **body_text** and save the style sheet file as **cc_styles.css** in the Web site root folder. Use any formatting options that you like, and then apply the body_text style to all text except the text "Cranberry Ice" and "Directions."
5. Create another style called **headings** using appropriate formatting options and apply it to the text "Cranberry Ice" and "Directions."
6. Insert the file **cranberry_ice.jpg** from where you store your Data Files, then place it on the page, using alignment, horizontal space, and vertical space settings. (*Hint*: In Figure 50 the align setting is set to left, H space is set to 30, and V space is set to 10.
7. Add appropriate alternate text to the banner, then save and close the file.
8. Open dw3_6.html from where you store your Data Files and save it as **shop.html**, overwriting the existing file and not updating the links.
9. Attach the **cc_styles.css** style sheet and create a new style named **sub_head** to use in formatting the text "January Specials - Multifunctional Pot and Cutlery Set." Use any formatting options that you like. Apply the **body_text** style to the rest of the text on the page.
10. Insert the **pot_knives.jpg** image from the assets folder where you store your Data Files next to the paragraph beginning "We try," choosing your own alignment and spacing settings and adding appropriate alternate text.
11. Save all pages, then preview both new pages in the browser, (*Hint:* If previewing the page in Internet Explorer 7, click the Information bar when prompted to allow blocked content.)
12. Close your browser, then close all open pages.

FIGURE 50

Completed Project Builder 2

Home | Shop | Classes | Catering | Recipes

This is one of our most requested desserts. It is simple, elegant, and refreshing. You will need a small electric ice cream maker to produce the best results.

Cranberry Ice

- 3 pts. fresh cranberries
- 1 1/2 pts. sugar
- juice of 1 1/2 lemons
- 1 cup whipping cream
- dash salt

Directions:

Boil cranberries in 3 pints of water. When soft, strain. Add the sugar to the juice and bring to a brisk boil. Cool. Add the lemon juice and freeze to a soft mush. Stir in whipping cream and freeze in an ice cream maker. Serves 14.

This recipe was given to us by Cosie Simmons, who served it as one of her traditions at Thanksgiving and Christmas family gatherings.

FIGURE 51

Completed Project Builder 2

Home | Shop | Classes | Catering | Recipes

Our small storefront is filled with wonderful kitchen accessories and supplies. We also have a large assortment of gourmet items from soup mixes to exotic teas and coffee — perfect for gift baskets for any occasion. We deliver to homes and offices, as well as dorms and hospitals.

January Specials: Multifunctional Pot and Cutlery Set

We try to feature special items each month and love to promote local foods. This month's features: A large multifunctional pot for tempting soups and stews and a professional grade cutlery set.

The pot is made of polished stainless steel with a tempered glass lid so you can peak without lifting the lid to monitor progress. A pasta insert lifts out for draining. Each piece is dishwasher safe. The handles remain cool to the touch while the pot is heating on the stovetop.

The knife blades are solid stainless steel, precision forged as one single piece. The heavy bolsters provide balance and control. The cutting edge holds its sharpness well. The five knives come with a handsome butcher block knife stand. They are dishwasher safe, but hand washing is recommended.

Working with Text and Images

Don Chappell is a new sixth-grade history teacher. He is reviewing educational Web sites for information he can use in his classroom.

1. Connect to the Internet, then navigate to the Library of Congress Web site at *www.loc.gov*. The Library of Congress Web site is shown in Figure 52.
2. Which fonts are used for the main content on the home—serif or sans-serif? Are the same fonts used consistently on the other pages in the Web site?
3. Do you see ordered or unordered lists on any pages in the Web site? If so, how are they used?
4. Use the Source command on the View menu to view the source code to see if a style sheet was used.
5. Do you see the use of Cascading Style Sheets noted in the source code?
6. Select another site from the list and compare the use of text on the two sites.

FIGURE 52
Design Project

Library of Congress Web site - www.loc.gov

PORTFOLIO PROJECT

In this assignment, you will continue to work on the Web site that you started in Chapter 1, and continued to build in Chapter 2. No Data Files are supplied. You are building this Web site from chapter to chapter, so you must do each Portfolio Project assignment in each chapter to complete your Web site.

You continue building your Web site by designing and completing a page that contains a list, headings, body text, images, and a background. During this process, you will develop a style sheet and add several styles to it. You will insert appropriate images on your page and enhance them for maximum effect. You will also check for Non-Websafe colors and remove any that you find.

1. Consult your storyboard and decide which page to create and develop for this chapter.

2. Plan the page content for the page and make a sketch of the layout. Your sketch should include at least one ordered or unordered list, appropriate headings, body text, several images, and a background color or image. Your sketch should also show where the body text and headings should be placed on the page and what styles should be used for each type of text. You should plan on creating at least two styles.

3. Create the page using your sketch for guidance.

4. Create a Cascading Style Sheet for the Web site and add to it the styles you decided to use. Apply the styles to the appropriate content.

5. Access the images you gathered in Chapter 2, and place them on the page so that the page matches the sketch you created in Step 2. Add a background image if you want, and appropriate alternate text for each image.

6. Remove any Non-Websafe colors.

7. Identify any files in the Assets panel that are currently not used in the Web site. Decide which of these assets should be removed, then delete these files.

8. Preview the new page in a browser, then check for page layout problems and broken links. Make any necessary corrections in Dreamweaver, then preview the page again in the browser. Repeat this process until you are satisfied with the way the page looks in the browser. (*Hint:* If previewing the page in Internet Explorer 7, click the Information bar when prompted to allow blocked content.)

9. Use the checklist in Figure 53 to check all the pages in your site.

10. Close the browser, then close the open pages.

FIGURE 53
Portfolio Project check list

Web Site Checklist

1. Does each page have a page title?
2. Does the home page have a description and keywords?
3. Does the home page contain contact information?
4. Does every page in the Web site have consistent navigation links?
5. Does the home page have a last updated statement that will automatically update when the page is saved?
6. Do all paths for links and images work correctly?
7. Do all images have alternate text?
8. Are all colors Websafe?
9. Are there any unnecessary files you can delete from the assets folder?
10. Is there a style sheet with at least two styles?
11. Did you apply the styles to all text blocks?
12. Do all pages view well using at least two different browsers?

4

WORKING WITH
LINKS

1. Create external and internal links

2. Create internal links to named anchors

3. Insert rollovers with Flash text

4. Create, modify, and copy a navigation bar

5. Create an image map

6. Manage Web site links

4 WORKING WITH
LINKS

Introduction

What makes Web sites so powerful are the links that connect one page to another within a Web site or to any page on the Web. Although you can add graphics, animations, movies, and other enhancements to a Web site to make it visually attractive, the links you include are often a site's most essential components. Links that connect the pages within a Web site are always very important because they help viewers navigate between the pages of the site. However, if one of your goals is to keep viewers from leaving your Web site, you might want to avoid including links to other Web sites. For example, most e-commerce sites include only links to other pages in the site to discourage shoppers from leaving the site. In this chapter, you will create links to other pages in The Striped Umbrella Web site and to other sites on the Web. You will also insert a navigation bar that contains images instead of text, and check the links in The Striped Umbrella

Web site to make sure they all work correctly.

Understanding Internal and External Links

Web pages contain two types of links: internal links and external links. **Internal links** are links to Web pages in the same Web site, and **external links** are links to Web pages in other Web sites or to e-mail addresses. Both internal and external links have two important parts that work together. The first part of a link is the element that viewers see and click on a Web page, for example, text, an image, or a button. The second part of a link is the **path**, or the name and location of the Web page or file that will open when the element is clicked. Setting and maintaining the correct paths for all your links is essential to avoid having broken links in your site, which can easily cause a visitor to click away immediately.

Tools You'll Use

Insert | Common | Layout | Forms | Data | Spry | Text | Favorites

Named anchor button

Insert Navigation Bar

Add button

Nav bar elements: home

Element name: home
Up image: [   ] Browse...
Over image: [   ] Browse...
Down image: [   ] Browse...
Over while down image: [   ] Browse...
Alternate text: [   ]
When clicked, Go to URL: [   ] Browse... in Main window
Options: ☑ Preload images
☐ Show "Down image" initially
Insert: Horizontally ☐ Use tables

OK
Cancel
Help

Named anchor

Named Anchor

Anchor name: top

OK
Cancel
Help

Properties

Image, 52K   W 756   Src _banner_with_text.jpg   Alt Carolyne's banner   Class None
            H 151   Link [   ]   Edit

Image map buttons

Map recipes   V Space [   ]   Target [   ]   Border 0
              H Space [   ]   Low Src [   ]   Align Default

CREATE EXTERNAL AND
INTERNAL LINKS

What You'll Do

 In this lesson, you will create external links on The Striped Umbrella activities page that link to Web sites related to area attractions. You will also create internal links to other pages within The Striped Umbrella Web site.

Creating External Links

A good Web site usually includes a variety of external links to other related Web sites so that viewers can get more information on a particular topic. To create an external link, you first select the text or object that you want to serve as a link, then you type the absolute path to the destination Web page in the Link text box in the Property inspector. An **absolute path** is a path used for external links that includes the complete address for the destination page, including the protocol (such as http://)

and the complete **URL** (Uniform Resource Locator), or address, of the destination page. When necessary, the Web page file-name and folder hierarchy are also part of an absolute path. Figure 1 shows an example of an absolute path showing the protocol, URL, and filename. After you enter external links on a Web page, you can view them in the site map. An example for the code for an external link would be <a href="http://www.adobe.com" Adobe Web site </a>.

FIGURE 1

An example of an absolute path

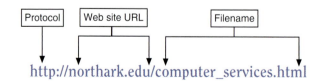

Creating Internal Links

Each page in a Web site usually focuses on an individual category or topic. You should make sure that the home page provides links to each major page in the site, and that all pages in the site contain numerous internal links so that viewers can move easily from page to page. To create an internal link, you first select the text element or image that you want to use to make a link, and then use the Browse for File icon next to the Link text box in the Property inspector to specify the relative path to the destination page. A **relative path** is a type of path used to reference Web pages and image files within the same Web site. Relative paths include the filename and folder location of a file. Figure 2 shows an example of a relative path. Table 1 describes absolute paths and relative paths. Relative paths can either be site-root relative or document-relative. You can also use the Point to File icon in the Property inspector to point to the file you want to use for the link, or drag the file you want to use for the link from the Files panel into the Link text box on the Property inspector.

You should take great care in managing your internal links to make sure they work correctly and are timely and relevant to the page content. You should design the navigation structure of your Web site so that viewers are never more than three or four clicks away from the page they are seeking. An example for the code for an internal link would be <a href="activities.html" Activities page </a>.

FIGURE 2
An example of a relative path

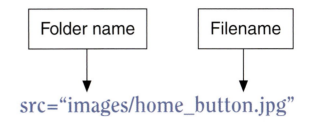

TABLE 1: Description of absolute and relative paths

type of path	description	examples
Absolute path	Used for external links and specifies protocol, URL, and filename of destination page	*http://www.yahoo.com/recreation*
Relative path	Used for internal links and specifies location of file relative to the current page	spa.html or assets/heron.gif
Root-relative path	Used for internal links when publishing to a server that contains many Web sites or where the Web site is so large it requires more than one server	/striped_umbrella/activities.html
Document-relative path	Used in most cases for internal links and specifies the location of file relative to current page	cafe.html or assets/heron.gif

Create an external link

1. Open The Striped Umbrella Web site, open dw4_1.html from where you store your Data Files, then save it as **activities** in the striped_umbrella root folder, overwriting the existing activities page, but not updating links.

2. Attach the su_style.css file, then apply the **body_text style** to the paragraphs of text on the page (not to the navigation bar).

3. Select the first broken image, click the **Browse for File icon** 📁 next to the Src text box, then select the **heron_waiting_small.jpg** in the Data Files folder to save the image in your assets folder.

4. Repeat Step 3 for the second image, **two_dolphins_small.jpg.**

5. Scroll down, then select the text "Blue Angels."

6. Click in the Link text box in the Property inspector, type **http://www.blueangels. navy.mil**, press [**Enter**] (Win) or [**return**] (Mac), then compare your screen to Figure 3.

7. Repeat Steps 5 and 6 to create a link for the USS Alabama site in the next paragraph: **http://www.ussalabama.com.**

8. Save your work, preview the page in your browser, test all the links to make sure they work, then close your browser.

> TIP You must have an active Internet connection to test the links. If clicking a link does not open a page, make sure you typed the URL correctly in the Link text box.

You opened The Striped Umbrella Web site, replaced the existing activities page, attached the su_styles.css.file, applied the body_text style to the text, then added two external links to other sites on the page. You also tested each link in your browser.

FIGURE 3

Creating an external link to the Blue Angels Web site

Selected text   URL for link

Typing URLs

Typing URLs in the Link text box in the Property inspector can be very tedious. When you need to type a long and complex URL, it is easy to make mistakes and create a broken link. You can avoid such mistakes by copying and pasting the URL from the Address text box (Internet Explorer) or Location bar (Mozilla Firefox) to the Link text box in the Property inspector. Copying and pasting a URL ensures that the URL is entered correctly.

FIGURE 4

Site map displaying external links on the activities page

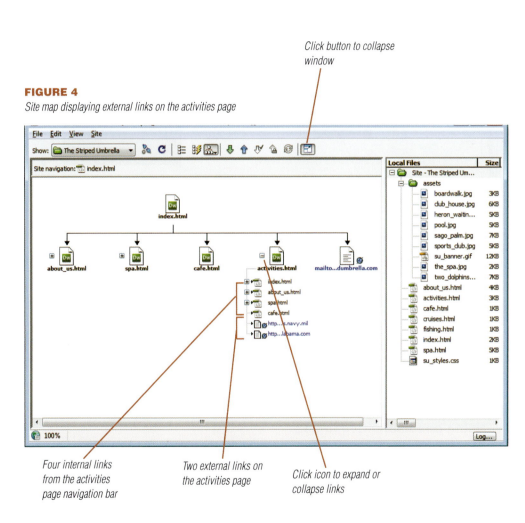

Click button to collapse window

Four internal links from the activities page navigation bar

Two external links on the activities page

Click icon to expand or collapse links

1. Click the **Expand to show local and remote sites button** 🖳 on the Files panel to expand the Files panel.

2. Click the **Site Map list arrow** on the toolbar, then click **Map and Files**.

   Four links from the navigation bar appear as internal links.

   > TIP If you want to view or hide page titles in the site map, click View on the menu bar, point to Site Map Options, then click Show Page Titles (Win) or click the Options button in the Files panel group title bar, point to View, then click Show Page Titles (Mac).

3. Click the **plus sign** to the left of the activities page icon in the site map (if necessary) to view a list of the two external links you created, as shown in Figure 4.

4. Click the **minus sign** to the left of the activities page icon in the site map to collapse the list of links.

5. Click the **Collapse to show only local or remote site button** 🖳 on the toolbar.

You viewed The Striped Umbrella site map and expanded the view of the activities page to display the two external links you added.

Create an internal link

1. Select the text "fishing excursions" in the third paragraph.

2. Click the **Browse for File icon** next to the Link text box in the Property inspector, then double-click **fishing.html** in the Select File dialog box to set the relative path to the fishing page.

   Notice that fishing.html appears in the Link text box in the Property inspector, as shown in Figure 5.

   TIP To collapse all open panels below the Document window, such as the Link Checker or the Property inspector, click the expander arrow in the center of the bottom border of the Document window. Pressing [F4] will hide all panels, including the ones on the right side of the screen.

3. Select the text "dolphin cruises" in the same sentence.

4. Click the **Browse for File icon** next to the Link text box in the Property inspector, then double-click **cruises.html** in the Select File dialog box to specify the relative path to the cruises page.

   The words "dolphin cruises" are now a link to the cruises page.

5. Save your work, preview the page in your browser to verify that the internal links work correctly, then close your browser.

   The fishing and cruises pages do not have page content yet, but serve as placeholders until they do.

You created two internal links on the activities page, and then tested the links in your browser.

FIGURE 5
Creating an internal link on the activities page

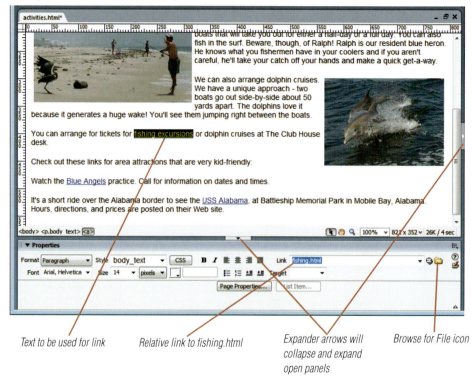

Text to be used for link

Relative link to fishing.html

Expander arrows will collapse and expand open panels

Browse for File icon

Using case-sensitive links

When text is said to be "case sensitive," it means that the text will be treated differently when it is typed using uppercase letters rather than lowercase letters, or vice-versa. With some operating systems, such as Windows, it doesn't matter which case you use when you enter URLs. However, with other systems, such as UNIX, it does matter. To be sure that your links will work with all systems, use lowercase letters for all links. This is another good reason to select and copy a URL from the browser address bar, and then paste it in the link text box or code in Dreamweaver when creating an external link. You won't have to worry about missing a case change.

FIGURE 6

Site map displaying external and internal links on the activities page

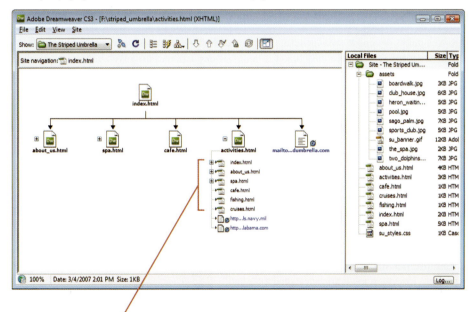

Six internal links, four from the navigation
bar and two from text links

View internal links in the site map

1. Click the **Expand to show local and remote sites button** on the Files panel.

2. Click the **Site Map list arrow**, then click **Map and Files** (if necessary).

   TIP Under Site Map Options on the View menu, verify that Show Page Titles is not selected.

3. Click the **plus sign** to the left of the activities page icon.

   A list of eight links appears below the activities page icon, as shown in Figure 6. Two are external links, and six are internal links.

   TIP If your links do not display correctly, re-create the site cache. To re-create the site cache, click Site on the menu bar, click Advanced, then click Re-create Site Cache.

4. Click the **Collapse to show only local or remote site button**.

5. Close the activities page.

You viewed the links on the activities page in the site map.

CREATE INTERNAL LINKS
TO NAMED ANCHORS

What You'll Do

In this lesson, you will insert five named anchors on the spa page: one for the top of the page and four for each of the spa services lists. You will then create internal links to each named anchor.

Inserting Named Anchors

Some Web pages have so much content that viewers must scroll repeatedly to get to the bottom of the page and then back up to the top of the page. To make it easier for viewers to navigate to specific areas of a page without scrolling, you can use a combination of internal links and named anchors. A **named anchor** is a specific location on a Web page that has a descriptive name. Named anchors act as targets for internal links and make it easy for viewers to jump to a particular place on the same page quickly. A **target** is the location on a Web page that a browser displays when an internal link is clicked. For example, you can insert a named anchor called "top" at the top of a Web page, and then create a link to it from the bottom of the page. You can also insert named anchors in strategic places on a Web page, such as at the beginning of paragraph headings.

You insert a named anchor using the Named Anchor button in the Common category of the Insert bar, as shown in Figure 7. You then enter the name of the anchor in the Named Anchor dialog box. You should choose short names that describe the named anchor location on the page. Named anchors are represented by yellow anchor icons on a Web page. Selected anchors are represented by blue icons. You can show or hide named anchor icons by clicking View on the menu bar, pointing to Visual Aids, and then clicking Invisible Elements.

Creating Internal Links to Named Anchors

Once you create a named anchor, you can create an internal link to it using one of two methods. You can select the text or image on the page that you want to use to make a link, and then drag the Point to File icon from the Property inspector to the named anchor icon on the page. Or, you can select the text or image to which you want to use to make a link, then type # followed by the named anchor name (such as "#top") in the Link text box in the Property inspector.

QUICKTIP

To avoid possible errors, you should create a named anchor before you create a link to it.

FIGURE 7
Named Anchor button on the Insert bar

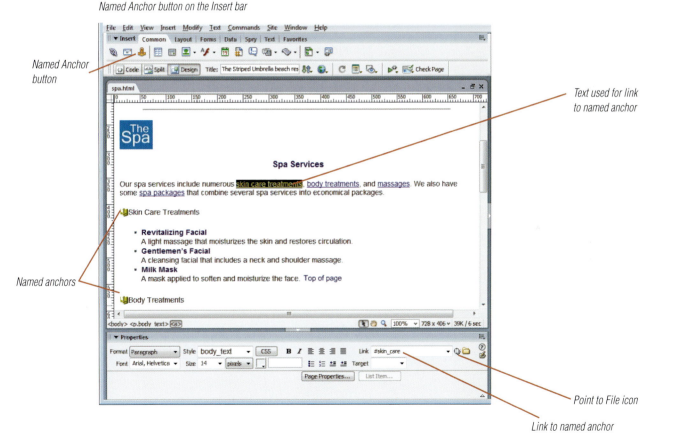

Named Anchor button

Text used for link to named anchor

Named anchors

Point to File icon

Link to named anchor

Insert a named anchor

1. Open the spa page, click the **banner image** to select it, then press [←] to place the insertion point to the left of the banner.

2. Click **View** on the menu bar, point to **Visual Aids**, then verify that Invisible Elements is checked.

   TIP If there is no check mark next to Invisible Elements, this feature is turned off. Click Invisible Elements to turn this feature on.

3. Click the **Common tab** on the Insert bar (if necessary).

4. Click the **Named Anchor button** on the Insert bar to open the Named Anchor dialog box, type **top** in the Anchor name text box, compare your screen with Figure 8, then click **OK**.

   An anchor icon now appears before The Striped Umbrella banner.

   TIP Use lowercase letters, no spaces, and no special characters in named anchor names. You should also avoid using a number as the first character in a named anchor name.

   (continued)

FIGURE 8
Named Anchor dialog box

Name of new anchor

Working with Links

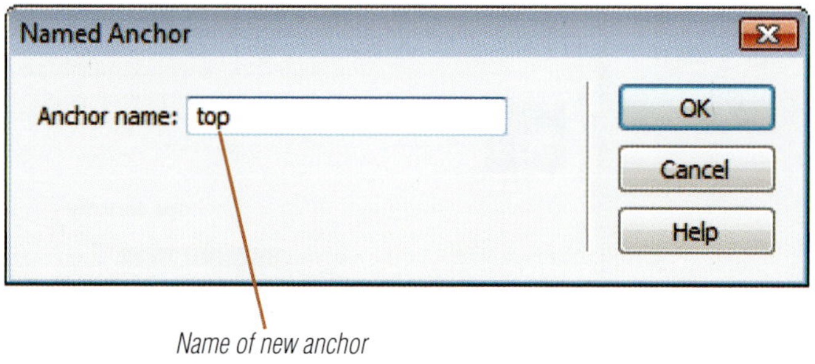

FIGURE 9

Named anchors on the activities page

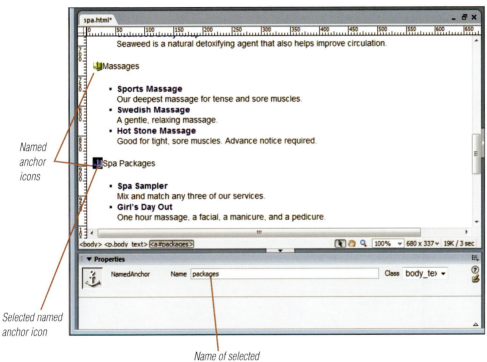

Named anchor icons

Selected named anchor icon

Name of selected named anchor

5. Click to the left of the Skin Care Treatments heading, then insert a named anchor named **skin_care**.

6. Insert named anchors to the left of the Body Treatments, Massages, and Packages headings using the following names: **body_treatments**, **massages**, and **packages**.

   Your screen should resemble Figure 9.

You created five named anchors on the activities page; one at top of the page, and four that will help viewers quickly access the Spa Services headings on the page.

Create an internal link to a named anchor

1. Select the words "skin care treatments" in the first paragraph, then drag the **Point to File icon** ☺ from the Property inspector to the anchor named skin_care, as shown in Figure 10.

   The words "skin care treatments" are now linked to the skin_care named anchor. When viewers click the words "skin care treatments" the browser will display the Skin Care Treatments heading at the top of the browser window.

   TIP The name of a named anchor is always preceded by a pound (#) sign in the Link text box in the Property inspector.

2. Create internal links for body treatments, massages, and spa packages in the first paragraph by first selecting each of these words or phrases, then dragging the **Point to File icon** ☺ to the appropriate named anchor icon.

   The words "body treatments," "massages," and "spa packages" are now links that connect to the Body Treatments, Massages, and Spa Packages headings.

   TIP Once you select the text on the page you want to link, you might need to scroll down to view the named anchor on the screen. Once you see the named anchor on your screen, you can drag the Point to File icon on top of it.

   (continued)

FIGURE 10

Dragging the Point to File icon to a named anchor

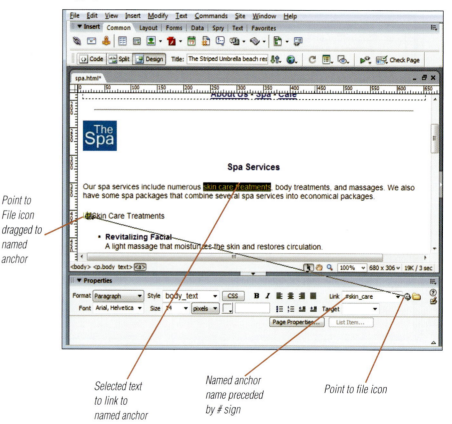

Point to File icon dragged to named anchor

Selected text to link to named anchor

Named anchor name preceded by # sign

Point to file icon

FIGURE 11

Spa page in Mozilla Firefox with internal links to named anchors

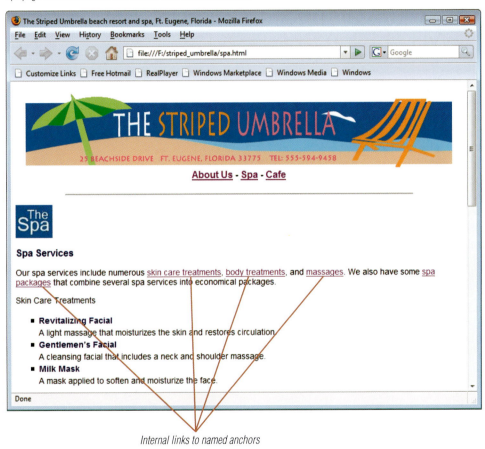

Internal links to named anchors

3. Save your work, preview the page in your browser, as shown in Figure 11, then test the links to each named anchor.

Notice that when you click the spa packages link in the browser, the associated named anchor appears in the middle of the page instead of at the top. This happens because the spa page is not long enough to position this named anchor at the top of the page.

4. Close your browser.

You created internal links to the named anchors next to the Spa Services headings on the spa page. You then previewed the page in your browser and tested each link.

INSERT ROLLOVERS
WITH FLASH TEXT

What You'll Do

▶ In this lesson, you will use the Insert Flash Text dialog box to create a button that links to the top named anchor on the spa page. You will copy this button to several locations on the spa page, and then change the alignment of each button.

Understanding Flash Text

Flash is an Adobe software application that you can use to create vector-based graphics and animations. **Vector-based graphics** are graphics that are based on mathematical formulas, as opposed to other types of graphic files such as JPG and GIF which are based on pixels. Vector-based graphics have a smoother look and are smaller in file size than pixel-based graphics. Because they download quickly, vector-based graphics are ideal for Web sites. **Flash text** is a vector-based graphic file that contains text. You can insert Flash text to add visual interest to an otherwise dull Web page or to help deliver or reinforce a message. You can use Flash text to create internal or external links. Flash text files are saved with the .swf filename extension.

When Flash text is inserted on a Web page, JavaScript code is added to the page to control the rollover. Dreamweaver automatically creates a folder named Scripts in the root folder, which stores the new JavaScript code

file, AC-RunActiveContent.js. When a viewer views a Web page with Flash text, the JavaScript that runs is stored on the user's, or client's, computer.

QUICKTIP

To view Flash animations, you must have the Flash player installed on your computer. The Flash player is free software that lets you play streaming video and audio.

Inserting Flash Text on a Web Page

You can create Flash text in Dreamweaver without opening the Flash program. To insert Flash text on a Web page, you choose the Common tab on the Insert bar, click the Media list arrow, and then click Flash Text, as shown in Figure 12. Clicking this button opens the Insert Flash Text dialog box, which you use to specify the settings for the Flash text. You first need to specify the text you want to create as Flash text by typing it in the Text text box. You can then specify the font, size, and color of the Flash text, apply bold or italic styles to it, and align it using left, center, or right alignment options. You can also specify a **rollover color**, or the color in which the text will appear when the mouse pointer is placed on it. You also need to enter the path for the destination link in the Link text box. The destination link can be an internal link to another page in the site, to a named anchor on the same page, or to an external link to a page on another Web site. You then use the Target list to specify how to open the destination page. The four options are described in Table 2.

QUICKTIP

Notice that the _parent option in the table displays the page in the parent frameset. A **frameset** is a group of Web pages displayed using more than one **frame** or window.

Before you close the Insert Flash Text dialog box, you need to type a descriptive name for your Flash text file in the Save as text box. Because Flash text files must be saved in the same folder as the page that contains the Flash text, you should save your Flash text files in the root folder of the Web site.

Using Flash Player

To play Flash movies in Dreamweaver and in your browser, you must have the Flash Player installed on your computer. If the Flash Player is not installed, you can download it from the Adobe Web site at *www.adobe.com*. In addition, you need to choose a specific setting in your browser. If you are using Internet Explorer, click Tools on the menu bar, click Internet Options, click the Advanced tab, click the Allow active content to run in files on my computer check box, and then click OK. If you are using another browser, look for a similar setting in your Options or Preferences dialog boxes.

FIGURE 12
Media menu on the Common group

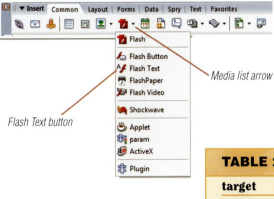

Flash Text button

Media list arrow

TABLE 2: Options in the Target list	
target	**result**
_blank	Displays the destination page in a separate browser window
_parent	Displays the destination page in the parent frameset (replaces the frameset)
_self	Displays the destination page in the same frame or window
_top	Displays the destination page in the whole browser window

Create Flash text

1. Click after the last sentence on the spa page, then press **[Enter]** (Win) or **[return]** (Mac) twice to end the ordered list.

2. Click the **Common tab** on the Insert bar (if necessary), click the **Media list arrow**, then click **Flash Text** to open the Insert Flash Text dialog box.

3. Set the Font to **Arial,** set the Size to **14,** set the Color to **#000066,** set the Rollover color to **#66CCFF,** type **Top of page** in the Text text box, type **spa.html#top** in the Link text box, use the Target list arrow to set the Target to **_top,** type **top.swf** in the Save as text box, as shown in Figure 13, then click **OK**.

4. Type **Link to top of page** in the Flash Accessibility Attributes dialog box, then click **OK**.

   The Top of page Flash text appears as a button at the bottom of the page. When clicked, the browser will display the top of the page.

5. Click **Assets** in the Files panel group, click the **Flash button** on the Assets panel, as shown in Figure 14, click the **Refresh button** (if necessary), click the **top.swf** file, then click the **Play button** to see the Flash text preview.

6. Drag **top.swf** from the Assets panel to the end of the last bulleted entry in each of the spa services groups to insert four top links adding **Link to top of page** in the Object Tag Accessibility Attributes dialog box.

7. Click the **Files panel tab**, then refresh the Files panel (if necessary).

8. Switch to Show Code and Design views to view the JavaScript code shown in Figure 15, then switch back to Design view.

(continued)

FIGURE 13
Insert Flash Text dialog box

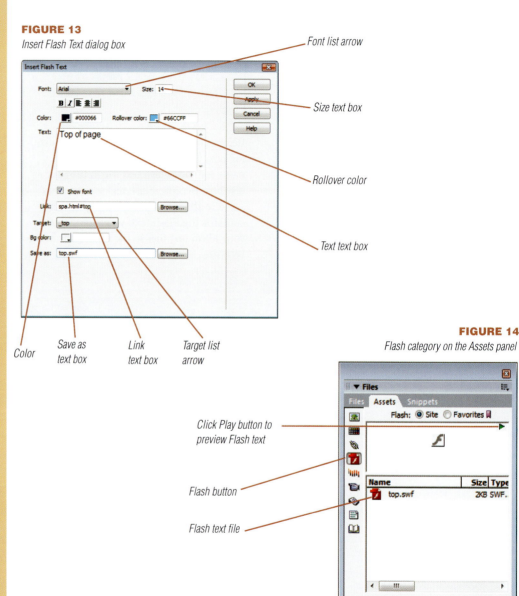

Font list arrow

Size text box

Rollover color

Text text box

Color

Save as text box

Link text box

Target list arrow

FIGURE 14
Flash category on the Assets panel

Click Play button to preview Flash text

Flash button

Flash text file

FIGURE 15

Script added to code and script file added to root folder

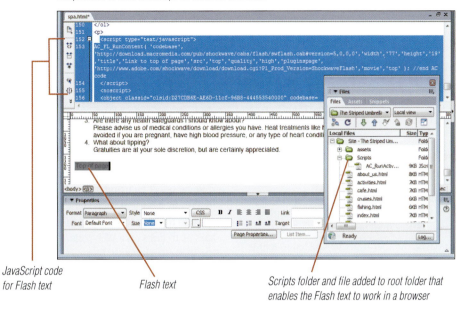

JavaScript code
for Flash text

Flash text

Scripts folder and file added to root folder that
enables the Flash text to work in a browser

FIGURE 16

Flash text aligned to top

Flash text aligned with top of
paragraph text line

9. Save your work, click **OK** in the Copy Dependent Files dialog box to copy the script to the root folder, preview the spa page in your browser, test each Top of page link, then close your browser.

Dreamweaver added the file AC_RunActiveContent.js in a new Scripts folder to the root folder. This file enables the Flash file to be viewed in a browser. See Figure 15.

TIP If the top of the page is already displayed, the window will not move when you click the Flash text.

You used the Insert Flash Text dialog box to create a Top of page Flash text button that links to the top named anchor on the spa page. You also inserted the Top of page button at the end of each spa service.

Align Flash text

1. Click the **Top of page button** at the end of the Skin Care Treatments section, expand the Property inspector, click the **Align list arrow** in the Property inspector, then click **Top**.

The Top of page button is now aligned with the top of the line of text. See Figure 16.

2. Apply the Top alignment setting to the Top of page button located at the end of the Body Treatments, Massages, and Spa Packages sections.

3. Collapse the Property inspector, turn off Invisible Elements, then save your work.

4. Preview the spa page in a browser, test each Top of page button, then close the browser.

You aligned the Flash text.

CREATE, MODIFY, AND COPY
A NAVIGATION BAR

What You'll Do

▶ *In this lesson, you will create a navigation bar on the spa page that can be used to link to each major page in the Web site. The navigation bar will have five elements: home, about us, cafe, spa, and activities. You will also copy the new navigation bar to other pages in the Web site. On each page you will modify the appropriate element state to reflect the current page.*

Creating a Navigation Bar Using Images

To make your Web site more visually appealing, you can create a navigation bar with images rather than text. Any images you use in a navigation bar must be created in a graphics software program, such as Adobe Fireworks or Adobe Illustrator. For a browser to display a navigation bar correctly, all image links in the navigation bar must be exactly the same size. You insert a navigation bar by clicking Insert on the menu bar, pointing to Image Objects, then clicking Navigation Bar. The Insert Navigation Bar dialog box appears. You use this dialog box to specify the appearance of each link, called an **element**, in each of four possible states. A **state** is the condition of the element relative to the mouse pointer. The four states are as follows: **Up image** (the state when the mouse pointer is not on top of the element), **Over image** (the state when the mouse pointer is positioned on top of the element), **Down image** (the state when you click the element), and **Over while down image** (the state when the mouse pointer is positioned over an element that has been clicked). You can create a rollover effect by using different colors or images to represent each element state. You can add many special effects to navigation bars or to links on a Web page. For instance, the Web site shown in Figure 17 contains a navigation bar that uses rollovers and also contains images that link to featured items in the Web site.

When a navigation bar is inserted on a Web page using the Insert Navigation Bar command, JavaScript code is added to the page to make the interaction work with the navigation bar elements. Dreamweaver also creates a Scripts folder and adds it to the root folder to store the newly created AC-RunActiveContent.js file.

QUICKTIP

You can insert only one navigation bar using the Insert Navigation Bar dialog box or by clicking the Common tab and then selecting Navigation Bar from the Images menu.

Working with Links

Copying and Modifying a Navigation Bar

After you create a navigation bar, you can reuse it and save time by copying and pasting it to the other main pages in your site. Make sure you place the navigation bar in the same position on each page. This practice ensures that the navigation bar will look the same on each page, making it much easier for viewers to navigate to all the pages in a Web site. If you are even one line or one pixel off, the navigation bar will "jump" as it changes position from page to page.

You can then use the Modify Navigation Bar dialog box to customize the appearance of the copied navigation bar on each page. For example, you can change the appearance of the spa navigation bar element on the spa page so that it appears in a different color. Highlighting the navigation element for the current page provides a visual reminder so that viewers can quickly tell which page they are viewing. This process ensures that the navigation bar will not only look consistent across all pages, but will be customized for each page.

FIGURE 17
Ohio Historical Society Web site

Navigation bar with rollovers

Images serving as links

Ohio Historical Society Web site used with permission from Ohio Historical Society - www.ohiohistory.org

Create a navigation bar using images

1. Select the navigation bar (About Us - Spa - Cafe) on the spa page, then delete it.

   The insertion point is now positioned between the banner and the horizontal rule.

2. Click the **Common** tab on the Insert bar (if necessary), click the **Images list arrow**, then click **Navigation Bar**.

3. Type **home** in the Element name text box, click the **Insert list arrow** in the dialog box, click **Horizontally** (if necessary), to specify that the navigation bar be placed horizontally on the page, then remove the check mark in the Use tables check box.

   Be sure to choose Horizontally for the navigation bar orientation and uncheck the Use tables check box. These two options (below the horizontal rule) will not be available in the Modify Navigation Bar dialog box. If you miss these settings now, you will either have to make your corrections directly in the code or start over.

4. Click **Browse** next to the Up image text box, navigate to the assets folder where you store your Data Files, then double-click **home_up.gif**.

   The path to the file home_up.gif appears in the Up image text box, as shown in Figure 18.

5. Click **Browse** next to the Over image text box to specify a path to the file home_down.gif located in the chapter_4 assets folder.

6. Click **Browse** next to the Down image text box to specify a path to the file home_down.gif

(continued)

FIGURE 18

Insert Navigation bar dialog box

Element name text box

Image file specified for Up image state

Insert list arrow

Remove check mark

Click to select an image for each element state

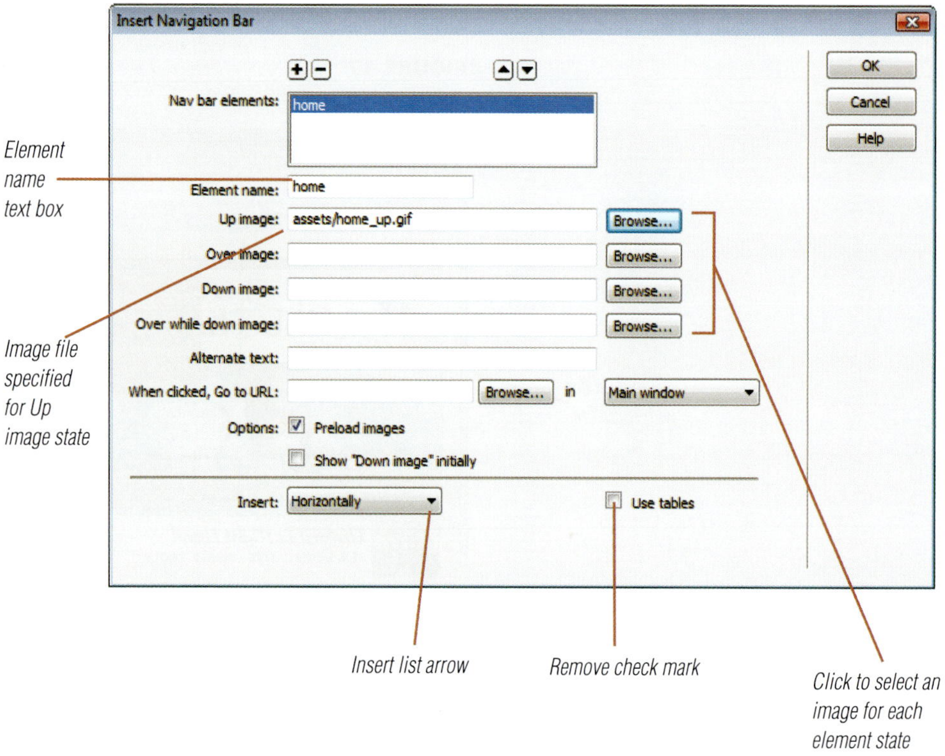

FIGURE 19

Insert Navigation bar dialog box

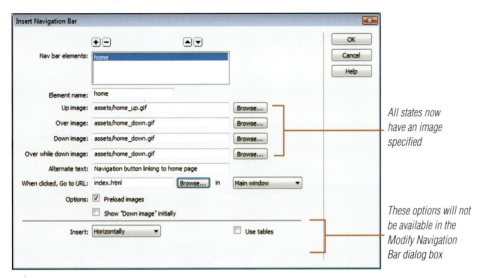

All states now
have an image
specified

These options will not
be available in the
Modify Navigation
Bar dialog box

FIGURE 20

Home element of the navigation bar

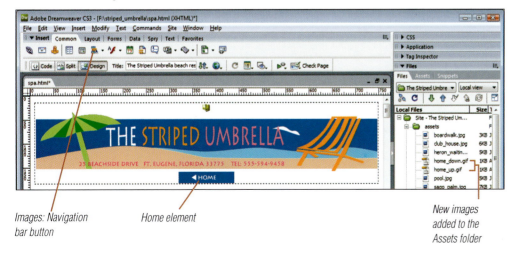

Images: Navigation
bar button

Home element

New images
added to the
Assets folder

located in the chapter_4 assets folder, over-writing the existing file.

Because this is a simple navigation bar, you use the home_down.gif image for the Over, Down, and Over while down image states.

> TIP   Instead of clicking Browse in Steps 6 and 7, you could copy the path of the home_down.gif file in the Over image text box and paste it to the Down image and Over while down image text boxes. You could also reference the home_down.gif file in The Striped Umbrella assets folder once it is copied there in Step 5.

7. Click **Browse** next to the Over while down image text box to specify a path to the file home_down.gif located in the chapter_4 assets folder, overwriting the existing file.

   By specifying one graphic for the Up image state, and another graphic for the Over image, Down image, and Over while down image states, you will create a rollover effect.

8. Type **Navigation button linking to home page** in the Alternate text text box, click **Browse** next to the When clicked, Go to URL text box, double-click **index.html** in the striped_umbrella root folder, then compare your screen to Figure 19.

9. Click **OK**, refresh the Files panel to view the new images you added to The Striped Umbrella assets folder, deselect the button, place the insertion point in front of the button, press **[Backspace]** (Win) or **[delete]** (Mac), press **[Shift][Enter]** (Win) or **[Shift][return]** (Mac), compare your screen to Figure 20, then save your work.

You used the Insert Navigation Bar dialog box to create a navigation bar for the spa page and added the home element to it. You used one image for the Up state and one for the other three states.

Add elements to a navigation bar

1. Click **Modify** on the menu bar, then click **Navigation Bar**.

2. Click the **Add button** ⊞ in the Modify Navigation Bar dialog box, then type **about_us** in the Element name text box.

   TIP You use the Add button ⊞ to add a new navigation element to the navigation bar, and the Delete button ⊟ to delete a navigation element from the navigation bar.

3. Click **Browse** next to the Up image text box, navigate to the chapter_4 assets folder, click **about_us_up.gif**, then click **OK** (Win) or **Choose** (Mac).

   TIP If a dialog box appears asking if you would like to copy the file to the root folder, click Yes, then click Save (Mac).

4. Click **Browse** next to the Over image text box to specify a path to the file **about_us_down.gif** located in the chapter_4 assets folder.

5. Click **Browse** next to the Down image text box to specify a path to the file **about_us_down.gif** located in the chapter_4 assets folder, overwriting the existing file.

6. Repeat Step 5 for the **Over while down** image.

7. Type **Navigation button linking to about_us page** in the Alternate text text box, click **Browse** next to the When clicked, Go to URL text box, double-click **about_us.html**, then compare your screen to Figure 21.

   (continued)

FIGURE 21
Add elements to a navigation bar

Settings for about_us button

Add button

Delete button

New about_us element

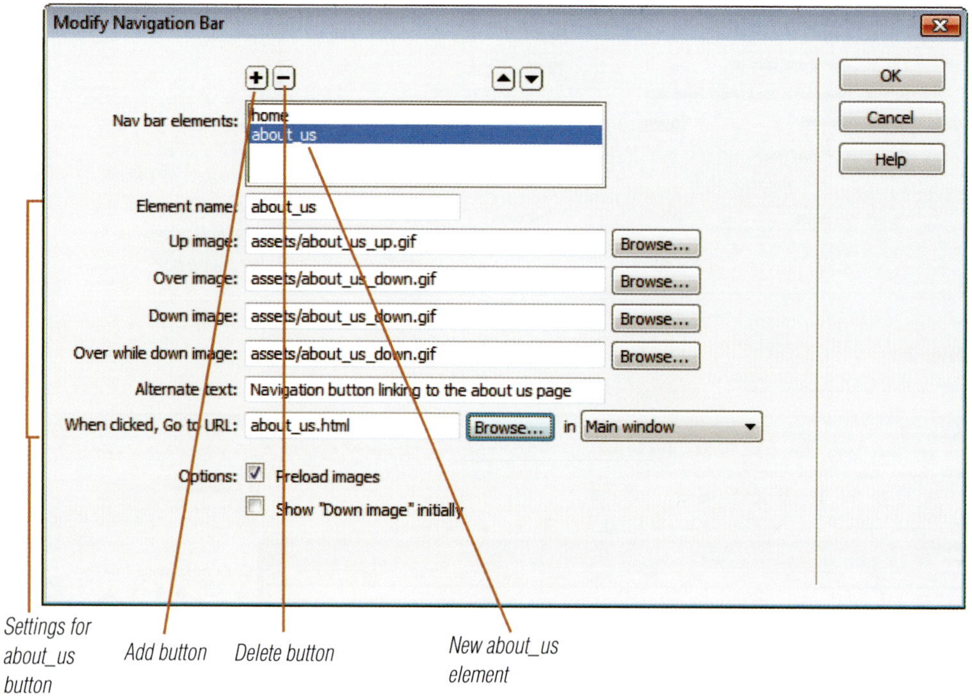

FIGURE 22
Navigation bar with all elements added

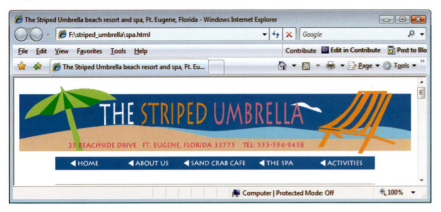

TABLE 3: Settings to use in the Modify Navigation Bar dialog box for each new element

dialog box item	cafe element	spa element	activities element
Up image file	cafe_up.gif	spa_up.gif	activities_up.gif
Over image file	cafe_down.gif	spa_down.gif	activities_down.gif
Down image file	cafe_down.gif	spa_down.gif	activities_down.gif
Over while down image file	cafe_down.gif	spa_down.gif	activities_down.gif
Alternate text	Navigation button linking to cafe page	Navigation button linking to the spa page	Navigation button linking to activities page
When clicked, Go to URL	cafe.html	spa.html	activities.html

8. Using the information provided in Table 3, add three more navigation bar elements in the Modify Navigation Bar dialog box called **cafe**, **spa**, and **activities.**

   TIP All files listed in the table are located in the assets folder of the chapter_4 folder where you store your Data Files.

9. Click **OK** to close the Modify Navigation Bar dialog box.

10. Save your work, preview the page in your browser, compare your screen to Figure 22, check each link to verify that each element works correctly, then close your browser.

    TIP If you see spaces between each button in your browser, select the first button, press [→], then press delete. Continue for each button to remove each space after the button.

You completed The Striped Umbrella navigation bar by adding four more elements to it, each of which contain links to four pages in the site. All images added to the navigation bar are now stored in the assets folder of The Striped Umbrella Web site.

Copy and paste a navigation bar

1. Place the insertion point to the left of the navigation bar, press and hold **[Shift]**, then click to the right of the navigation bar.
2. Click **Edit** on the menu bar, then click **Copy**.
3. Double-click **activities.html** in the Files panel to open the activities page.
4. Select the original navigation bar on the page, click **Edit** on the menu bar, click **Paste**, then compare your screen to Figure 23.
5. Click in front of the navigation bar, press **[Backspace]** (Win) or **[delete]** (Mac), then press **[Shift][Enter]** (Win) or **[shift][return]** (Mac).

You copied the navigation bar from the spa page and pasted it on the activities page.

Customize a navigation bar

1. Click **Modify** on the menu bar, then click **Navigation Bar** to open the Modify Navigation Bar dialog box.
2. Click **activities** in the Nav bar elements text box, then click the **Show "Down image" initially check box**, as shown in Figure 24.

   An asterisk appears next to activities in the Nav bar elements text box, indicating that this element will be displayed in the Down image state initially. The sand-colored activities navigation element normally used for the Down image state of the activities navigation bar element will remind viewers that they are on the activities page.

(continued)

FIGURE 23
Navigation bar copied to the activities page

FIGURE 24
Changing settings for the activities element

Asterisk is placed next to the element name

Show "Down image" initially is selected

FIGURE 25

about_us page with the modified navigation bar

When you arrive at The Striped Umbrella, check in at The Club House. Look for the signs that will direct you to registration. Our beautiful club house is the home base for our registration offices, The Sand Crab Cafe, and The Spa. Registration is open from 8:00 a.m. until 6:00 p.m. Please call to make arrangements if you plan to arrive after 6:00 p.m. The cafe and spa hours are both posted and listed in the

3. Click **OK** to save the new settings and close the Modify Navigation Bar dialog box, then save and close the activities page.

4. Repeat Steps 1 through 3 to modify the navigation bar on the spa page to show the Down image initially for the spa element, then save and close the spa page.

    TIP The Show "Down image" initially check box should be checked only for the element that links to the current page.

5. Open the home page, paste the navigation bar on top of the original navigation bar, remove any spaces before the navigation bar, add a line break, then modify the navigation bar to show the Down image initially for the home element.

6. Save and close the home page.

7. Open the about us page, paste the navigation bar on top of the original navigation bar, then use the Modify Navigation Bar dialog box to specify that the Down image be displayed initially for the about_us element, then compare your screen to Figure 25.

8. Save your work, preview the current page in your browser, test the navigation bar on the home, about us, spa, and activities pages, then close your browser.

    The cafe page is blank at this point, so use the Back button when you test the spa link to return to the page you were viewing previously.

You modified the navigation bar on the activities page to show the activities element in the Down state initially. You then copied the navigation bar to two additional pages in The Striped Umbrella Web site, modifying the navigation bar elements each time to show the Down image state initially.

CREATE AN
IMAGE MAP

 In this lesson, you will create an image map by placing a hotspot on The Striped Umbrella banner that will link to the home page.

Another way to create links for Web pages is to combine them with images by creating an image map. An **image map** is an image that has one or more hotspots placed on top of it. A **hotspot** is a clickable area on an image that, when clicked, links to a different location on the page or to another Web page. For example, a map of the United States could have a hotspot placed on each individual state so that viewers could click a state to link to information about that state. The National Park Service Web site is shown in Figure 26. As you place your mouse over a state, the state name, a photo, and introductory sentences from that state's page are displayed. When you click a state, you will be linked to information about national parks in

that state. You can create hotspots by first selecting the image on which you want to place a hotspot, and then using one of the hotspot tools in the Property inspector to define its shape.

There are several ways to create image maps to make them more user-friendly and accessible. One way is to be sure to include alternate text for each hotspot. Another is to draw the hotspot boundaries a little larger than they need to be to cover the area you want to set as a link. This allows viewers a little leeway when they place their mouse over the hotspot by creating a larger target area for them.

The hotspot tools in Dreamweaver make creating image maps a snap. In addition to the Rectangular Hotspot tool, there is an Oval Hotspot tool and a Polygon Hotspot tool for creating different shapes. These tools can be used to create any shape hotspot that you need. For instance, on a map of the United States, you can draw an outline around each state with the Polygon Hotspot tool. You can then make each state "clickable." Hotspots can be easily changed and rearranged on the image. Use the Pointer Hotspot tool to select the hotspot you would like to edit. You can drag one of the hotspot selector handles to change the size or shape of a hotspot. You can also move the hotspot by dragging it to a new position on the image. It is a good idea to limit the number of complex hotspots in an image because the code can become too lengthy for the page to download in a reasonable length of time.

FIGURE 26

Viewing an image map on the National Park Service Web site

The pointer is over Arkansas, which results in a window with a photo and introductory text about Arkansas to display

Clicking an individual state will link to information about parks in that state

National Park Service Web site: www.nps.gov

Create an image map

1. Open or switch to the activities page, if necessary, select the banner, then click the **Rectangular Hotspot tool** in the Property inspector.

2. Drag the **pointer** to create a rectangle over the umbrella in the banner, as shown in Figure 27, then click **OK** to close the dialog box that reminds you to supply alternate text for the hotspot.

   TIP To adjust the shape of a hotspot, click the Pointer Hotspot tool in the Property inspector, then drag a sizing handle on the hotspot.

3. Use the **Point to File icon** in the Property inspector to link the index page to the hotspot.

4. Type **home** in the Map text box in the Property inspector to give the image map a unique name.

5. Click the **Target list arrow** in the Property inspector, then click **_top**.

   When the hotspot is clicked, the home page will open in the same window.

   (continued)

FIGURE 27
Properties of the rectangular hotspot on the banner

Hotspot

Rectangular
Hotspot tool

FIGURE 28

Properties of the hotspot

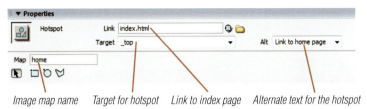

Image map name   Target for hotspot   Link to index page   Alternate text for the hotspot

FIGURE 29

Preview of the image map on the activities page in the browser

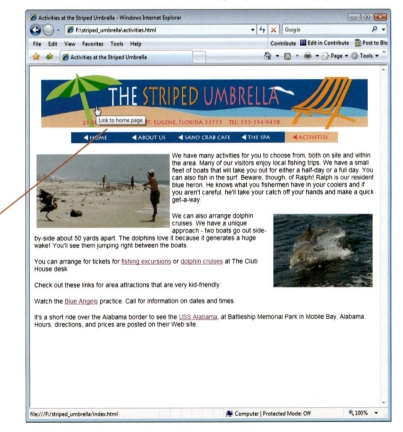

Alternate text
for hotspot

6. Type **Link to home page** in the Alt text box in the Property inspector, as shown in Figure 28. then press **[Enter]** (Win) or **[return]** (Mac).

7. Save your work, then preview the page in your browser to test the link on the image map.

As you place the pointer over the hotspot, you see the alternate text displayed and the pointer indicates the link (Win), as shown in Figure 29.

8. Close the browser, then close all open pages.

You created an image map on the banner of the activities page using the Rectangular Hotspot tool. You then linked the hotspot to the home page.

MANAGE WEB SITE
LINKS

In this lesson, you will use some of Dreamweaver's reporting features to check The Striped Umbrella Web site for broken links and orphaned files.

Managing Web Site Links

Because the World Wide Web changes constantly, Web sites may be up one day and down the next. If a Web site changes server locations or goes down due to technical difficulties or a power failure, the links to it become broken. Broken links, like misspelled words on a Web page, indicate that a Web site is not being maintained diligently.

Checking links to make sure they work is an ongoing and crucial task you need to perform on a regular basis. You must check external links manually by reviewing your Web site in a browser and clicking each link to make sure it works correctly. The Check Links Sitewide feature is a helpful tool for managing internal links. You can use it to check your entire Web site for the total number of links and the number of links that are okay, external, or broken, and then view the results in the Link Checker panel. The Link Checker panel also provides a list of all of the files used in a Web site, including those that are **orphaned files**, or files that are not linked to any pages in the Web site.

> **DESIGN**TIP **Considering navigation design issues**
>
> As you work on the navigation structure for a Web site, you should try to limit the number of links on each page to no more than is necessary. Too many links may confuse visitors to your Web site. You should also design links so that viewers can reach the information they want within a few clicks. If finding information takes more than three or four clicks, the viewer may become discouraged or lost in the site. It's a good idea to provide visual clues on each page to let viewers know where they are, much like a "You are here" marker on a store directory at the mall, or a bread crumbs trail. A **bread crumbs trail** is a list of links that provides a path from the initial page you opened in a Web site to the page that you are currently viewing.

FIGURE 30

Link Checker panel displaying external links

List of external links

Show list arrow

FIGURE 31

Link Checker panel displaying no orphaned files

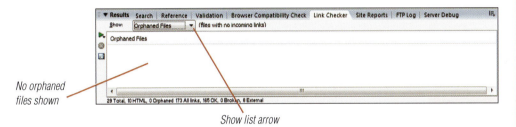

No orphaned
files shown

Show list arrow

FIGURE 32

Assets panel displaying links

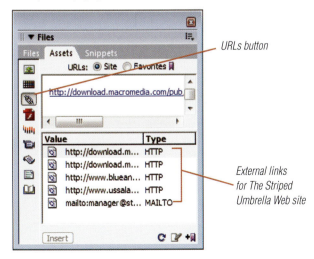

URLs button

External links
for The Striped
Umbrella Web site

1. Click **Site** on the menu bar, point to **Advanced**, then click **Re-create Site Cache**.

2. Click **Site** on the menu bar, then click **Check Links Sitewide**.

   The Results panel group opens with the Link Checker panel displayed. By default, the Link Checker panel initially displays any broken internal links found in the Web site. The Striped Umbrella Web site has no broken links.

3. Click the **Show list arrow** in the Link Checker panel, click **External Links**, then compare your screen to Figure 30.

   Some external links are listed more than once because the Link Checker displays each instance of an external link.

4. Click the **Show list arrow**, then click **Orphaned Files** to view the orphaned files in the Link Checker panel, as shown in Figure 31.

   The Striped Umbrella Web site has no orphaned files.

5. Click the **Options button** in the Results panel group title bar, then click **Close panel group**.

6. Display the Assets panel (if necessary), then click the **URLs button** in the Assets panel to display the list of links in the Web site.

   The Assets panel displays the external links used in the Web site, as shown in Figure 32.

You used the Link Checker panel to check for broken links, external links, and orphaned files in The Striped Umbrella Web site.

Update a page

1. Open dw4_2.html from where you store your Data Files, then save it as **fishing.html** in the striped_umbrella root folder, overwriting the existing fishing page, but not updating the links.

2. Click the broken link image placeholder, click the **Browse for File icon** next to the Src text box on the Property inspector, then browse to the chapter_4 assets folder and select the file **heron_small.jpg** to copy the file to the striped_umbrella assets folder.

3. Deselect the image placeholder and the image will appear as shown in Figure 33.

   Notice that the text is automatically updated with the body_text style. The code was already in place on the page linking the su_styles.css to the file.

4. Save and close the page.

FIGURE 33

Fishing page updated

POWER USER SHORTCUTS

to do this:	use this shortcut:
Close a file	[Ctrl][W] (Win) or ⌘[W] (Mac)
Close all files	[Ctrl][Shift][W] (Win) or ⌘[Shift][W] (Mac)
Print Code	[Ctrl][P] (Win) or ⌘[P] (Mac)
Check page links	[Shift][F8]
Undo	[Ctrl][Z], [Alt][BkSp] (Win) or ⌘[Z], [option][delete] (Mac)
Redo	[Ctrl][Y], [Ctrl][Shift][Z] (Win) or ⌘[Y], ⌘[Shift][Z] (Mac)
Refresh Design View	[F5]
Hide all Visual Aids	[Ctrl][Shift][I] (Win) or ⌘[Shift][I] (Mac)
Insert a Flash file	[Ctrl][Alt][F] (Win) or ⌘[option][F] (Mac)
Insert a Named Anchor	[Ctrl][Alt][A] (Win) or ⌘[option][A] (Mac)
Make a Link	[Ctrl][L] (Win) or ⌘[L] (Mac)
Remove a Link	[Ctrl][Shift][L] (Win) or ⌘[Shift][L] (Mac)
Check Links Sitewide	[Ctrl][F8] (Win) or ⌘[F8] (Mac)
Show Assets panel	[F11]
Show Files panel	[F8]

FIGURE 34

Cruises page updated

THE STRIPED UMBRELLA

25 BEACHSIDE DRIVE   FT. EUGENE, FLORIDA 33775   TEL: 555-594-9458

◄ HOME   ◄ ABOUT US   ◄ SAND CRAB CAFE   ◄ THE SPA   ◄ ACTIVITIES

This is the Dolphin Racer at dock. We leave daily at 4:00 p.m. and 6:30 p.m. for 1 1/2 hour cruises. There are snacks and restrooms available on board. We welcome children of all ages. Our ship is a U.S. Coast Guard approved vessel and our captain is a former member of the Coast Guard. Call The Club desk for reservations.

5. Open dw4_3.html from where you store your Data Files, then save it as **cruises.html** in the striped_umbrella root folder, overwriting the existing cruises page, but not updating the links.

6. Click the broken link graphic placeholder, click the **Browse for File icon** 🗀 next to the Src text box on the Property inspector, then browse to the chapter_4 assets folder and select the file **boats.jpg** to copy the file to the striped_umbrella assets folder.

7. Deselect the image placeholder and the image will appear as shown in Figure 34.

   Notice that the text is automatically updated with the body_text style. The code was already in place on the page linking the su_styles.css to the file.

8. Save and close the page.

Create external and internal links.

1. Open the blooms & bulbs Web site.
2. Open dw4_4.html from where you store your Data Files, then save it as **newsletter.html** in the blooms & bulbs Web site, overwriting the existing file without updating the links.
3. Verify that the banner path is set correctly to the assets folder in the Web site and correct it, if it is not.
4. Scroll to the bottom of the page, then link the National Gardening Association text to *http://www.garden.org*.
5. Link the Better Homes and Gardens Gardening Home Page text to *http://bhg.com/gardening*.
6. Link the Southern Living text to *http://www.southernliving.com/southern*.
7. Save the file, then preview the page in your browser, verifying that each link works correctly.
8. Close your browser, then return to the newsletter page in Dreamweaver.
9. Scroll to the paragraph about gardening issues, select the gardening tips text in the last sentence, then link the selected text to the tips.html file in the blooms root folder.
10. Add a new rule to the blooms_styles.css file called **bodytext** using the following formatting choices: Font: **Arial**, Helvetica, **sans-serif**; Style: **normal**; Weight: **normal**; and Size: **medium**.
11. Apply the headings style to the text "Gardening Matters," the seasons style to the subheadings on the page, and the bodytext style to the descriptions under each subheading and the three external links.
12. Center the "Gardening Matters" text.
13. Change the page title to **Gardening Matters**, then save your work.
14. Open the plants page and add the following sentence to the end of the last paragraph: **We have many annuals, perennials, and water plants that have just arrived**.
15. Link the "annuals" text to the annuals.html file, link the "perennials" text to the perennials.html file, and the "water plants" text to the water_plants.html file.
16. Save your work, test the links in your browser, then close your browser.

Create internal links to named anchors.

1. Show Invisible Elements (if necessary).
2. Click the Common tab on the Insert bar.
3. Switch to the newsletter page, then insert a named anchor in front of the Grass heading named **grass**.
4. Insert a named anchor in front of the Plants heading named **plants**.
5. Insert a named anchor in front of the Trees heading named **trees**.
6. Insert a named anchor at the top of the page named **top**.
7. Use the Point to File icon in the Property inspector to create a link from the word "grass" in the Gardening Issues paragraph to the anchor named "grass."
8. Create a link from the word "trees" in the Gardening Issues paragraph to the anchor named "trees."
9. Create a link from the word "plants" in the Gardening Issues paragraph to the anchor named "plants."
10. Save your work, view the page in your browser, test all the links to make sure they work, then close your browser.

Insert Flash text.

1. Insert Flash text at the bottom of the page that will take you to the top of the page. Use the following settings: Font: **Arial**, Size: **16**, Color: **#000066**, Rollover color: **#3366FF**, Text: **Top of page**, Link: **newsletter.html#top**, Target: _top.
2. Save the Flash text file as **top.swf** and enter the title **Link to top of page** in the Flash Accessibility Attributes dialog box.
3. Save all open files, view the page in your browser, test the Flash text link, then close your browser.

Create, modify, and copy a navigation bar.

1. Place your insertion point right under the banner, click the Images list arrow on the Insert bar, then click Navigation Bar to insert a horizontal navigation bar at the top of the newsletter page below the banner. Uncheck the option to use tables.

2. Type **home** as the first element name, then use the b_home_up.jpg file for the Up image state. This file is in the assets folder where you store your Data Files.

3. Specify the file **b_home_down.jpg** for the three remaining states. This file (and all files for the remainder of this exercise) are in the assets folder where you store your Data Files.

4. Enter **Link to home page** as the alternate text, then set the **index.html** file as the link for the home element.

5. Create a new element named **plants** and use the **b_plants_up.jpg** file for the Up image state and the **b_plants_down.jpg** file for the remaining three states.

6. Enter **Link to plants page** as the alternate text, then set the **plants.html** file as the link for the plants element.

7. Create a new element named **tips** and use the **b_tips_up.jpg** file for the Up image state and the **b_tips_down.jpg** file for the remaining three states.

8. Enter **Link to tips page** as the alternate text, then set the **tips.html** file as the link for the tips element.

9. Create a new element named **classes** and use the **b_classes_up.jpg** file for the Up image state and the **b_classes_down.jpg** file for the remaining three states.

10. Enter **Link to classes page** as the alternate text, then set the **classes.html** file as the link for the classes element.

11. Create a new element named **newsletter**, then use the **b_newsletter_up.jpg** file for the Up image state and the **b_newsletter_down.jpg** file for the remaining three states.

12. Enter the alternate text **Link to newsletter page**, then set the **newsletter.html** file as the link for the newsletter element.

13. Center the navigation bar (if necessary), save the page and test the links in your browser, then close the browser.

14. Select and copy the navigation bar, then open the home page.

15. Delete the current navigation bar on the home page, then paste the new navigation bar under the banner. (*Hint*: Insert a line break after the banner before you paste so that the navigation bar is directly below the banner.)

16. Modify the home element on the navigation bar to show the Down image state initially.

17. Save the page, test the links in your browser, then close the browser and the page.

18. Modify the navigation bar on the newsletter page so the Down image is shown initially for the newsletter element, then save and close the newsletter page.

19. Paste the navigation bar on the plants page and the tips page, making the necessary modifications so that the Down image is shown initially for each element.

20. Save your work, preview all the pages in your browser, compare your newsletter page to Figure 35, test all the links, then close your browser.

Create an image map

1. Use the Rectangular Hotspot tool to draw an image map across the left side of the banner on the newsletter page that will link to the home page.
2. Name the image map **home** and set the target to **_top**.
3. Add the alternate text **Link to home page**, save the page, then preview it in the browser to test the link.
4. Close the page.

Manage Web site links.

1. Use the Link Checker panel to view and fix broken links, external links, and orphaned files in the blooms & bulbs Web site.
2. Open **dw4_5.html** from where you store your Data Files, then save it as **annuals.html**, replacing the original file. Do not update links, but save the file **fuschia.jpg** in the assets folder of the Web site.
3. Repeat Step 2 using **dw4_6.html** to replace **perennials.html,** saving the **iris.jpg** file in the assets folder and using **dw4_7.html** to replace **water_plants.html,** saving the **water_hyacinth.jpg** file in the assets folder.
4. Save your work, then close all open pages.

FIGURE 35
Completed Skills Review

Use Figure 36 as a guide to continue your work on the TripSmart Web site that you began in Project Builder 1 in Chapter 1 and developed in the previous chapters. You have been asked to create a new page for the Web site that lists helpful links for customers. You will also add content to the destinations, kenya, and amazon pages.

1. Open the TripSmart Web site.
2. Open **dw4_8.html** from where you store your Data Files, then save it as **services.html** in the TripSmart Web site root folder, not updating links.
3. Verify that the TripSmart banner is in the assets folder of the root folder.
4. Apply the **body_text** style to the paragraphs of text and the heading style to the paragraph headings.
5. Create named anchors named **reservations, outfitters, tours**, and **links** in front of the respective headings on the page, then link each named anchor to "Reservations,"

"Travel Outfitters," "Escorted Tours," and "Helpful Links in Travel Planning" in the first paragraph.
6. Link the text "on-line catalog" in the Travel Outfitters paragraph to the catalog.html page.
7. Link the text "CNN Travel Channel" under the heading Travel Information Sites to *http://www.cnn.com/TRAVEL*.
8. Repeat Step 7 to create links for the rest of the Web sites listed:
US Department of State: *http://travel.state.gov*
Yahoo! : *http://yahoo.com/Recreation/Travel*
MapQuest: *http://www.mapquest.com*
Rand McNally: *http://www.randmcnally.com*
AccuWeather: *http://www.accuweather.com*
The Weather Channel: *http://www.weather.com*
9. Save the services page, then open the index page.

10. Attach the style sheet to the index page and assign a style to all text. Create new styles if you need them.
11. Reformat the navigation bar on the home page with a style of your choice, then place it on each completed page of the Web site. If you decide to use graphics for the navigation bar, you will have to create your own graphic files using a graphics program. There are no data files for you to use. (*Hint*: If you create your own graphic files, be sure to create two graphic files for each element: one for the Up image state and one for the Down image state.) To design a navigation bar using text, you simply type the text for each navigation bar element, format the text appropriately, and insert links to each text element as you did in Chapter 2. The navigation bar should contain the following elements: Home, Catalog, Services, Destinations, and Newsletter.

12. Save each page, then check for broken links and orphaned files. (*Hint*: The two orphaned files will be removed after completing the next steps.)

13. Open the destinations.html file in your root folder and save it as **kenya.html**, overwriting the existing file, then close the file.

14. Open dw4_9.html from where you store your Data Files, then save it as **amazon.html**, overwriting the existing file. Do not update links, but save the **water_lily.jpg** and **sloth.jpg** files in the assets folder of the Web site, then save and close the file.

15. Open dw4_10.html from where you store your Data Files, then save the file as **destinations.html**, overwriting the existing file. Do not update links, but save the **parrot.jpg** and **giraffe.jpg** files in the assets folder of the Web site.

16. Link the text "Amazon" in the second sentence of the first paragraph to the **amazon.html** file.

17. Link the text "Kenya" in the first sentence in the second paragraph to the **kenya.html** file.

18. Copy your customized navigation bar to the two new pages so they will match the other pages.

19. Check all text on all pages to make sure each text block uses a style for formatting. Correct those that don't.

20. Save all files.

21. Test all links in your browser, close your browser, then close all open pages.

FIGURE 36
Sample Project Builder 1

You are continuing your work on the Carolyne's Creations Web site that you started in Project Builder 2 in Chapter 1 and developed in the previous chapters. Chef Carolyne has asked you to create a page describing her cooking classes offered every month. You will create the content for that page and individual pages describing the children's classes and the adult classes. Refer to Figures 37–40 for possible solutions.

1. Open the Carolyne's Creations Web site.
2. Open **dw4_11.html** from where you store your Data Files, save it as **classes.html** in the root folder of the Carolyne's Creations Web site, overwriting the existing file and not updating the links.
3. Check the path of the banner to make sure it is linking to the banner in the assets folder of the Web site. Notice that styles have already been applied to the text, because the CSS code was already in the Data File.
4. Select the text "adults' class" in the last paragraph, then link it to the adults.html page. (*Hint*: This page has not been developed yet.)
5. Select the text "children's class" in the last paragraph and link it to the children.html page. (*Hint*: This page has not been developed yet.)

6. Create an e-mail link from the text "Sign me up!" that links to **carolyne@carolynes-creations.com**
7. Insert the file **fish.jpg** from the assets folder where you store your Data Files at the beginning of the second paragraph, add

appropriate alternate text, then choose your own alignment and formatting settings.
8. Add the file **children_cooking.jpg** from the assets folder where you store your Data Files at the beginning of the third paragraph.

FIGURE 37
Completed Project Builder 2

Cooking Classes are fun!

Chef Carolyne loves to offer a fun and relaxing cooking school each month in her newly refurbished kitchen. She teaches an **adult class** on the fourth Saturday of each month from 6:00 to 8:00 pm. Each class will learn to cook a complete dinner and then enjoy the meal at the end of the class with a wonderful wine pairing. This is a great chance to get together with friends for a fun evening. .

Chef Caroline also teaches a **children's class** on the second Tuesday of each month from 4:00 to 5:30 pm. Our young chefs will learn to cook two dishes that will accompany a full meal served at 5:30 pm. Kids aged 5–8 years accompanied by an adult are welcome. We also host small birthday parties where we put the guests to work baking and decorating the cake! Call for times and prices.

We offer several special adult classes throughout the year. The **Valentine Chocolate Extravaganza** is a particular favorite. You will learn to dip strawberries, make truffles, and bake a sinful Triple Chocolate Dare You Torte. We also host the **Not So Traditional Thanksgiving** class and the **Super Bowl Snacks** class each year with rave reviews. Watch the Web site for details!

Prices are $40.00 for each adult class and $15.00 for each children's class. Sign up for classes by calling 555-963-8271 or by emailing us: Sign me up!

See what's cooking this month for the adults' class and children's class.

9. Compare your work to Figure 37 for a possible solution, then save and close the file.

10. Open dw4_12.html from where you store your Data Files, then save it as **children.html**, overwriting the existing file and not updating links. Save the image **cookies_oven.jpg** from the assets folder where you store your Data Files to the Web site assets folder.

11. Add your own alignment and formatting settings, compare your work to Figure 38 for a possible solution, then save and close the file.

12. Repeat Steps 10 and 11 to open the dw4_13.html file and save it as **adults.html**, overwriting the existing file and saving the files **dumplings1.jpg**, **dumplings2.jpg**, and **dumplings3.jpg** in the assets folder, then use alignment settings of your choice. Compare your work to Figure 39 for a possible solution, then save and close the file.

13. Open the **index** page and delete the banner and navigation bar.

14. Insert the file **cc_banner_with_text.jpg** from where you store your Data Files in its place, adding appropriate alternate text.

15. Create an image map for each word at the bottom of the navigation bar to be used as a link to that page, as shown in Figure 40. Use **_top** as the target, the names of the "buttons" as the image map names, and appropriate alternate text. Link each image map to its corresponding page.

16. Copy the new navigation bar to each completed page, deleting existing navigation bars and banners.

17. Save all the pages, then check for broken links and orphaned files.

18. Preview all the pages in your browser, check to make sure the links work correctly, close your browser, then close all open pages.

FIGURE 38

Completed Project Builder 2

Children's Cooking Class for March: Oven Chicken Fingers, Chocolate Chip Cookies

This month we will be baking oven chicken fingers that are dipped in a milk and egg mixture, then coated with breadcrumbs. The chocolate chip cookies are based on a famous recipe that includes chocolate chips, M&Ms, oatmeal, and pecans. Yummy! We will be learning some of the basics like how to cream butter and crack eggs without dropping shells into the batter.

We will provide French fries, green beans, fruit salad, and a beverage to accompany the chicken fingers.

FIGURE 39

Completed Project Builder 2

Adult Cooking Class for March: Chinese Cuisine

The class in March will be cooking several traditional Chinese dishes: Peking dumplings, wonton soup, fried rice, Chinese vegetables, and shrimp with lobster sauce. For dessert: banana spring rolls.

This looks easier than it is! Chef Carolyne is demonstrating the first steps in making Chinese dumplings, known as *jiaozi* (pronounced geeow dz). Notice that she is using a traditional wooden rolling pin to roll out the dough. These dumplings were stuffed with pork and then steamed, although other popular fillings are made with chicken and leeks or vegetables with spiced tofu and cellophane noodles. Dumplings can be steamed, boiled, or fried, and have unique names depending on the preparation method.

FIGURE 40

Completed Project Builder 2

Let Carolyne's Creations be your personal chef, your one stop shop for the latest in kitchen items and fresh ingredients, and your source for new and innovative recipes. We enjoy planning and executing special events for all occasions - from children's birthday parties to corporate retreats. Feel like a guest at your own party. Give us a call or stop by our shop to browse through our selections.

Carolyne's Creations
496 Maple Avenue
Seven Falls, Virginia 52404
555.963.8271
E-mail Carolyne Kate

Copyright 2001 - 2010
Last updated on March 14, 2007

Grace Keiko is a talented young water-color artist who specializes in botanical works. She wants to develop a Web site to advertise her work, but isn't sure what she would like to include in a Web site or how to tie the pages together. She decides to spend several hours looking at other artists' Web sites to help her get started.

1. Connect to the Internet, then navigate to the Kate Nessler Web site pictured in Figure 41, *www.katenessler.com*.

2. Spend some time looking at several of the pages in the site to get some ideas.

3. What categories of page content would you include on your Web site if you were Grace?

4. What external links would you consider including?

5. Describe how you would place external links on the pages and list examples of ones you would use.

6. Would you use text or images for your navigation bar?

7. Would you include rollover effects on the navigation bar elements? If so, describe how they might look.

8. How could you incorporate named anchors on any of the pages?

9. Would you include an image map on a page?

10. Sketch a Web site plan for Grace, including the pages that you would use as links from the home page.

11. Refer to your Web site sketch, then create a home page for Grace that includes a navigation bar, a short introductory paragraph about her art, and a few external links.

FIGURE 41
Design Project

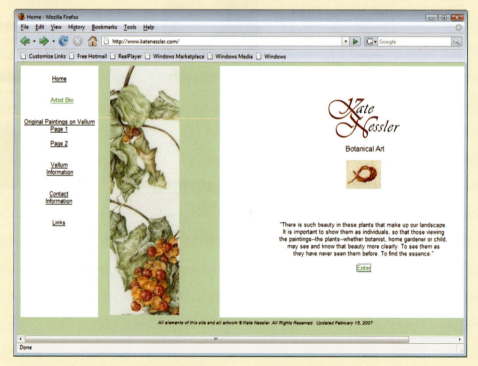

Kate Nessler Web site used with permission from Kate Nessler - www.katenessler.com

PORTFOLIO PROJECT

In this assignment, you will continue to work on the Web site that you started in Chapter 1 and developed in the previous chapters.

You will continue building your Web site by designing and completing a page with a navigation bar. After creating the navigation bar, you will copy it to each completed page in the Web site. In addition to the navigation bar, you will add several external links and several internal links to other pages as well as to named anchors. You will also link Flash text to a named anchor. After you complete this work, you will check for broken links and orphaned files.

1. Consult your storyboard to decide which page or pages you would like to develop in this chapter. Decide how to design and where to place the navigation bar, named anchors, Flash text, and any additional page elements you decide to use. Decide which reports should be run on the Web site to check for accuracy.

2. Research Web sites that could be included on one or more of your pages as external links of interest to your viewers. Create a list of the external links you want to use. Using your storyboard as a guide, decide where each external link should be placed in the site.

3. Add the external links to existing pages or create any additional pages that contain external links.

4. Create named anchors for key locations on the page, such as the top of the page, then link appropriate text on the page to them.

5. Insert at least one Flash text object that links to either a named anchor or an internal link.

6. Decide on a design for a navigation bar that will be used on all pages of the Web site.

7. Create the navigation bar and copy it to all finished pages on the Web site. If you decided to use graphics for the navigation bar, create the graphics that will be used.

8. Think of a good place to incorporate an image map, then add it to a page.

9. Use the Link Checker panel to check for broken links and orphaned files.

10. Use the checklist in Figure 42 to make sure your Web site is complete, save your work, then close all open pages.

FIGURE 42
Portfolio Project checklist

Web Site Checklist

1. Do all pages have a page title?
2. Does the home page have a description and keywords?
3. Does the home page contain contact information?
4. Does every page in the Web site have consistent navigation links?
5. Does the home page have a last updated statement that will automatically update when the page is saved?
6. Do all paths for links and images work correctly?
7. Do all images have alternate text?
8. Are all colors Websafe?
9. Are there any unnecessary files that you can delete from the assets folder?
10. Is there a style sheet with at least two styles?
11. Did you apply the style sheet to page content?
12. Does at least one page contain links to one or more named anchors?
13. Does at least one page contain Flash text that links to either a named anchor or an internal link?
14. Do all pages view well using at least two different browsers?

5

USING HTML TABLES
TO LAY OUT
A PAGE

1. Create a table

2. Resize, split, and merge cells

3. Insert and align images in table cells

4. Insert text and format cell content

chapter 5

USING HTML TABLES
TO LAY OUT A PAGE

Introduction

You have learned how to place and align elements on a page and enhance them using various formatting options. However, page layout options are fairly limited without the use of tables, AP Elements, or Cascading Style Sheets. Tables offer one solution for organizing text and graphics on a page. **Tables** are placeholders made up of small boxes called **cells**, into which you can insert text and graphics. Cells in a table are arranged horizontally in **rows** and vertically in **columns**. Using tables on a Web page gives you total control over the placement of each object on the page. In this chapter, you will learn how to create and format tables, work with table rows and columns, and format the contents of table cells. You will also learn how to select and format table cells using table tags on the tag selector. Clicking a table tag on the tag selector selects the table element associated with that tag. In later chapters, we will use AP Elements and Cascading Style Sheets for page layout.

Inserting Graphics and Text in Tables

Once you insert a table on a Web page, it becomes very easy to place text and graphics exactly where you want them on the page. You can use a table to control both the placement of elements in relation to each other and the amount of space between them. Before you insert a table, however, you should always plan how you would like your table to look with all the text and graphics in it. Even a rough sketch before you begin will save you time as you add content to the page.

Tools You'll Use

Table properties

Cell properties

Row properties

CREATE A
TABLE

What You'll Do

In this lesson, you will create a table for the cafe page in The Striped Umbrella Web site to provide the framework for the page layout.

Understanding Table Modes

There are two ways to create a table in Dreamweaver. Each method requires working in Design view. The first method is to click the Table button on the Insert bar. The Table button is available in the Common category of the Insert bar and in the Layout category of the Insert bar, whenever the Standard mode button is enabled. The second method is to click View, Table Mode, Layout Mode; then click the Draw Layout Table button or the Draw Layout Cell button. When the Layout category of the Insert bar is displayed, you can choose Standard mode or Expanded Table mode by clicking the appropriate button on the Insert bar.

Creating a Table in Standard Mode

Creating a table in Standard mode is useful when you want to create a table with a specific number of columns and rows. To create a table in Standard mode, click the Table button on the Insert bar to open the Table dialog box. Enter values for the number of rows and columns, the border thickness, table width, cell padding, and cell spacing. The **border** is the outline or frame around the table and the individual cells and is measured in pixels. The table width can be specified in pixels or as a percentage. When the table width is specified as a percentage, the table width will adjust to the width of the browser window. Figure 1 could either be a page based on a table set to 100% width (of the browser window), or it could be a page that is not based on a table at all. The content spreads across the entire browser window, without a container to set boundaries. When the table width is specified in pixels, the table width stays the same, regardless of the size of the browser window. The page in Figure 2 is an example of a page based on a table with a fixed width of 750 pixels. The content will not spread outside the table borders unless it contains images that are wider than the table. **Cell padding** is the distance between the cell content and the **cell walls**, the lines inside the cell borders. **Cell spacing** is the distance between cells.

Planning a Table

Before you create a table, you should sketch a plan for it that shows its location on the Web page and the placement of text and graphics in its cells. You should also decide whether to include borders around the tables and cells. Setting the border value to 0 causes the table to appear invisible, so that viewers will not realize that you used a table for the page layout unless they look at the code. Figure 3 shows a sketch of the table you will create on The Striped Umbrella cafe page to organize graphics and text.

Setting Table Accessibility Preferences for Tables

You can make a table more accessible to visually handicapped viewers by adding a table caption and a table summary that screen readers can read. The table caption appears on the screen. The table summary does not. These features are especially useful for tables that are used for tabular data.

Table headers are another way to provide accessibility. Table headers can be placed at the top or sides of a table with data. They are automatically centered and bold and are used by screen readers to help viewers identify the table content. Table captions, summaries, and headers are all created in the Table dialog box.

Drawing a Table in Layout Mode

You use Layout mode when you want to draw your own table. Drawing a table is ideal when you want to place page elements on a Web page and have no need for a specific number of rows and columns. You can use the Draw Layout Cell button or the Draw Layout Table button in the Layout category of the Insert bar to draw a cell or a table. After you draw the first cell, Dreamweaver plots a table for you automatically.

FIGURE 1

Page shown without using tables or using a table based on a 100% width

FIGURE 2

Same page shown using a fixed-width table for layout

FIGURE 3

Sketch of table on cafe page

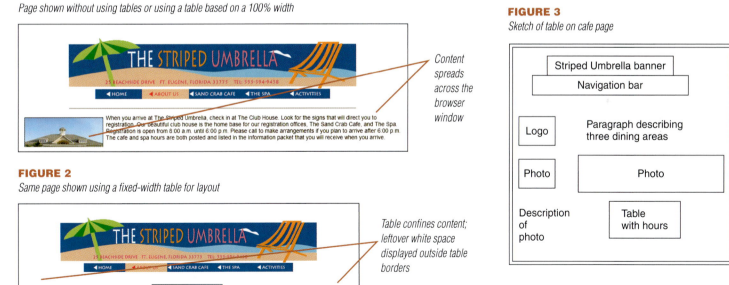

Content spreads across the browser window

Table confines content; leftover white space displayed outside table borders

Create a table

1. Open The Striped Umbrella Web site that you completed in Chapter 4.

2. Double-click **cafe.html** in the Files panel to open the cafe page in Design view.

   The cafe page is blank.

3. Click the **Layout tab** on the Insert bar, click the **Standard mode button** Standard , then click the **Table button** .

   The Table dialog box opens.

4. Type **7** in the Rows text box, type **3** in the Columns text box, type **750** in the Table width text box, click the **Table width list arrow**, click **pixels**, then type **0** in the Border thickness text box, as shown in Figure 4.

   TIP It is better to add more rows than you think you will need when you create your table. After they are filled with content, it is far easier to delete rows than to add rows if you decide later to split or merge cells in the table.

   (continued)

FIGURE 4
Table dialog box

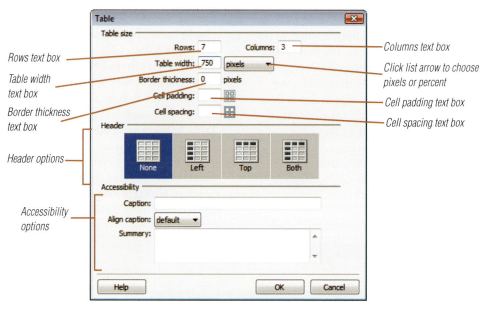

Rows text box →

Table width text box →

Border thickness text box →

Header options →

Accessibility options →

← Columns text box

← Click list arrow to choose pixels or percent

← Cell padding text box

← Cell spacing text box

Expanded Tables mode

Expanded Tables mode is a feature that allows you to change to a table view with expanded table borders and temporary cell padding and cell spacing. This mode makes it much easier to actually see how many rows and columns you have in your table. Many times, especially after splitting empty cells, it is difficult to place the insertion point precisely in a table cell. The Expanded Tables mode allows you to see each cell clearly. However, most of the time you will want to work in Standard mode to maintain the WYSIWYG environment. **WYSIWYG** is the acronym for What You See Is What You Get. This means that your Web page should look the same in the browser as it does in the Web editor. You can toggle between Expanded Tables mode and Standard mode by pressing [F6]. You can access Layout mode by holding the [Ctrl] (Win) or [option] (Mac) key and then pressing [F6].

Working with Tables

FIGURE 5
Table dialog box

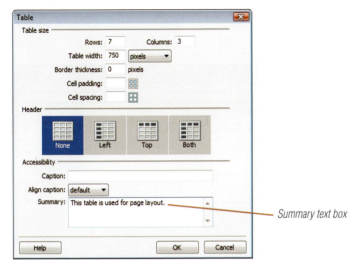

Summary text box

FIGURE 6
Expanded Tables mode

Click to exit
Expanded
Tables mode

Expanded Tables
mode displays more
space between cells
for easier editing

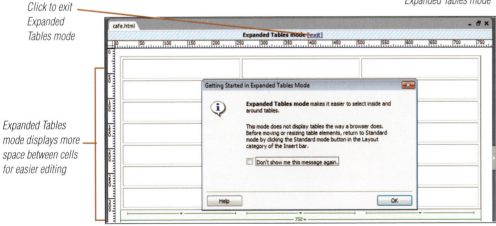

5. Type **This table is used for page layout.** in the Summary text box, then compare your screen to Figure 5.

6. Click **OK**.

   The table appears on the page, but the table summary is not visible. The summary will not appear in the browser but will be read by screen readers.

   > TIP   To edit accessibility preferences for a table, switch to Code view to edit the code directly.

7. Click the **Expanded Tables mode button** Expanded on the Layout tab, then click **OK** in the Getting Started in Expanded Tables Mode dialog box, as shown in Figure 6.

   The Expanded Tables mode makes it easier to select and edit tables.

8. Click the **Standard mode button** Standard to return to Standard mode.

   > TIP   You can also return to Standard mode by clicking [exit] at the top of the table.

You opened the cafe page in The Striped Umbrella Web site. You then created a table containing seven rows and three columns and set the width to 750 pixels so it will appear in the same size regardless of the browser window size. Finally, you entered a table summary that will be read by screen readers.

Set table properties

1. Move the pointer slowly to the top or bottom edge of the table until you see the pointer change to a Table pointer 🔀 , then click the **table border** to select the table.

   TIP You can also select a table by: (1) clicking the insertion point in the table, then clicking Modify, Table, Select Table; (2) selecting a cell in the table, then clicking Edit, Select All twice; or (3) clicking the table tag <table> on the tag selector.

2. Expand the Property inspector (if necessary) to display the current properties of the new table.

   TIP The Property inspector will display information about the table only when the table is selected.

3. Click the **Align list arrow** on the Property inspector, then click **Center** to center the table on the page, as shown in Figure 7.

   The center alignment formatting ensures that the table will be centered in all browser windows, regardless of the screen size.

   TIP The position of the left edge of the table on the ruler will depend on the size of the Document window.

You selected and center-aligned the table.

FIGURE 7

Property inspector showing properties of selected table

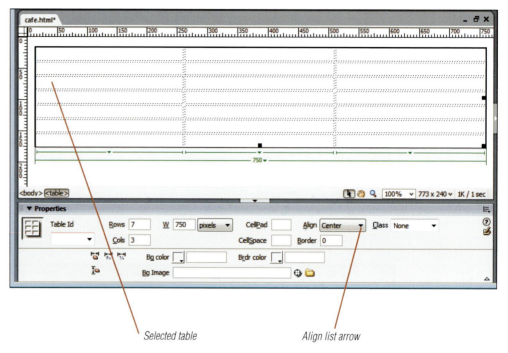

Selected table   Align list arrow

FIGURE 8

Table in Layout mode

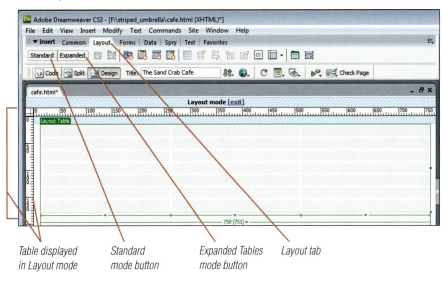

Table displayed   Standard   Expanded Tables   Layout tab
in Layout mode   mode button   mode button

DESIGNTIP   **Setting table and cell widths**

If you use a table to place all the text and graphics contained on a Web page, it is wise to set the width of the table in pixels. This ensures that the table will not resize itself proportionally if the browser window size is changed. If you set the width of a table using pixels, the table will remain one size, regardless of the browser window size. For instance, if the width of a table is set to slightly less than 800, the table will stretch across the whole width of a browser window set at a resolution of 800×600. The same table would be the same size on a screen set at 1024×768 and therefore would not stretch across the entire screen. Most designers use a resolution of 800×600 or higher. Be aware, however, that if you set the width of your table at 800 pixels, your table will be too wide to print the entire width of the page, and part of the right side of the page will be cut off. If you are designing a table layout for a page that is likely to be printed by the viewer, you should make your table narrower to fit on a printed page. If you set a table width as a percentage, however, the table would resize itself proportionally in any browser window, regardless of the resolution. You can also set each cell width as either a percentage of the table or as fixed pixels.

View the table in Layout mode

1. Click **View** on the menu bar, point to **Table Mode,** then click **Layout Mode.**

   The table appears in Layout mode, as shown in Figure 8.

   TIP   The Getting Started in Layout Mode dialog box might open, providing instructions on creating and editing a table in Layout mode.

2. Click **OK** (if necessary) to close the Getting Started in Layout Mode dialog box.

3. Click the **Standard mode button** `Standard` to return to Standard mode.

4. Click the **Common tab** on the Insert bar.

You viewed the table in Layout mode, then returned to Standard mode.

RESIZE, SPLIT, AND
MERGE CELLS

What You'll Do

> In this lesson, you will set the width of the table cells to be split across the table in predetermined widths. You will then split one cell. You will also merge some cells to provide space for the banner.

Resizing Table Elements

You can resize the rows or columns of a table manually. To resize a table, row, or column, you must first select the table, then drag one of the table's three selection handles. To change all the columns in a table so that they are the same size, drag the middle-right selection handle. To resize the height of all rows simultaneously, drag the middle-bottom selection handle. To resize the entire table, drag the right-corner selection handle. To resize a row or column individually, drag the interior cell borders up, down, to the left, or to the right. You can also resize selected columns, rows, or individual cells by entering specific measurements in the W and H text boxes in the Property inspector specified either in pixels or as a percentage. Cells whose width or height is specified as a percentage will maintain that percentage in relation to the width or height of the entire table if the table is resized.

Adding or deleting a row

As you add new content to your table, you might find that you have too many or too few rows or columns. You can add or delete one row or column at a time or several at once. You use commands on the Modify menu to add and delete table rows and columns. When you add a new column or row, you must first select the existing column or row to which the new column or row will be adjacent. The Insert Rows or Columns dialog box lets you choose how many rows or columns you want to insert or delete, and where you want them placed in relationship to the selected row or column. The new column or row will have the same formatting and number of cells as the selected column or row.

Splitting and Merging Cells

Using the Table button creates a new table with evenly spaced columns and rows. Sometimes you might want to adjust the cells in a table by splitting or merging them. To split a cell means to divide it into multiple rows or columns. To merge cells means to combine multiple cells into one cell. Using split and merged cells gives you more flexibility and control in placing page elements on a page and can help you create a more visually exciting layout. When you merge cells, the HTML tag used to describe the merged cell changes from a width size tag to a column span or row span tag. For example, <td colspan="2"> is the code for two cells that have been merged into one cell that spans two columns.

QUICKTIP
You can split merged cells and merge split cells.

DESIGNTIP   **Using nested tables**

A nested table is a table inside a table. To create a nested table, you place the insertion point in the cell where you want to insert the nested table, then click the Table button on the Insert bar. The nested table is a separate table that can be formatted differently from the table in which it is placed. Nested tables are useful when you want part of your table data to have visible borders and part to have invisible borders. For example, you can nest a table with red borders inside a table with invisible borders. You need to plan carefully when you insert nested tables. It is easy to get carried away and insert too many nested tables, which makes it more difficult to apply formatting and rearrange table elements. Before you insert a nested table, consider whether you could achieve the same result by adding rows and columns or by splitting cells.

Resize columns

1. Click inside the **first cell** in the bottom row, then click **<td>** on the tag selector, as shown in Figure 9.

   Clicking the cell tag <td> (the HTML tag for that cell) selects the corresponding cell in the table.

   > TIP You can also click inside a cell to select it. To select the entire table, click the <table> tag on the tag selector.

2. Type **30%** in the W text box in the Property inspector, then press **[Enter]** (Win) or **[return]** (Mac) to change the width of the cell to 30 percent of the table width.

   Notice that the column width is shown as a percentage at the bottom of the first column in the table, along with the table width of 750 pixels.

   > TIP You need to type the % sign next to the number you type in the W text box. Otherwise, the width will be expressed in pixels.

3. Repeat Steps 1 and 2 for the next two cells in the last row, using **30%** for the middle cell and **40%** for the last cell.

   The combined widths of the three cells add up to 100 percent. As you add content to the table, the columns will remain in this proportion unless you insert a graphic that is larger than the table cell. If a larger graphic is inserted, the cell width will expand to display it.

   > TIP Changing the width of a single cell changes the width of the entire column.

You set the width of each of the three cells in the bottom row to set the column sizes for the table. This will keep the table from resizing when you add content.

FIGURE 9
Selecting a cell 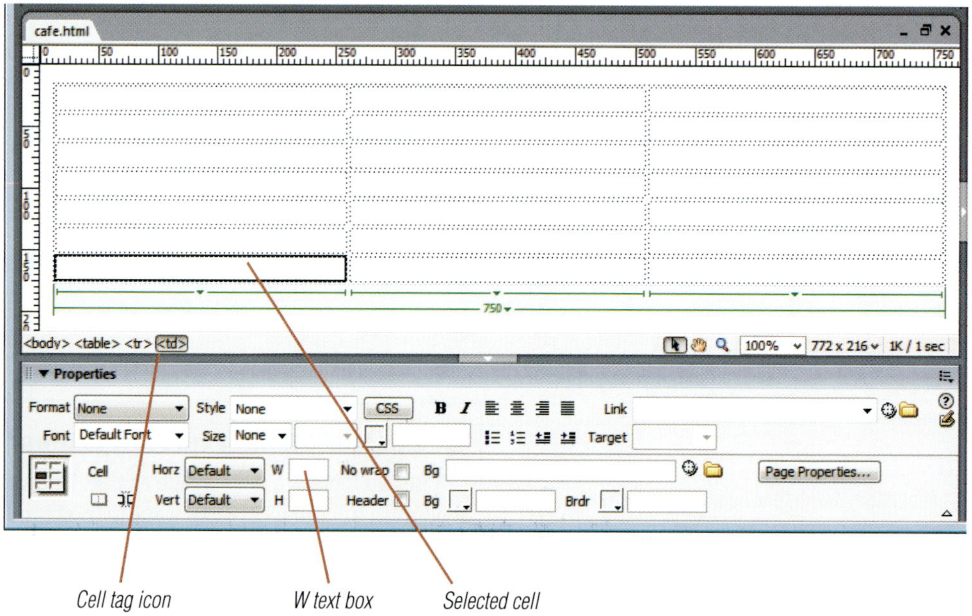

Cell tag icon   W text box   Selected cell

Resetting table widths and heights

After resizing columns and rows in a table, you might want to change the sizes of the columns and rows back to their previous sizes. To reset columns and rows to their previous widths and heights, click Modify on the menu bar, point to Table, then click Clear Cell Heights or Clear Cell Widths. Using the Clear Cell Heights command also forces the cell border to snap to the bottom of any inserted graphics, so you can also use this command to tighten up extra white space in a cell.

FIGURE 10

Resizing the height of a row

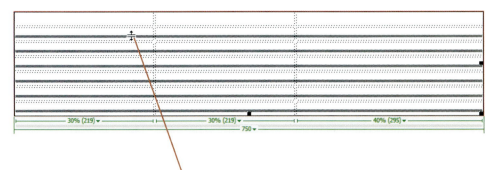

Resizing pointer

1. Place the pointer over the bottom border of the first row until it changes to a resizing pointer ⬍, as shown in Figure 10, then click and drag down about ¼ of an inch (approximately 24 pixels on the vertical ruler) to increase the height of the row.

   The border turns darker when you select and drag it.

2. Click **Window** on the menu bar, click **History**, then drag the **slider** in the History panel up one line to the **Set Height: 40%** mark to return the row to its original height. (Explanatory text for under step 2)

   The percentage shown in the Set Height state in the History panel will depend on how much you resized the row.

3. Close the History panel group.

You changed the height of the top row, then used the History panel to change it back it to its original height.

HTML table tags

When formatting a table, it is important to understand the basic HTML table tags. The tags used for creating a table are <table> </table>. The tags used to create table rows are <tr></tr>. The tags used to create table cells are <td></td>. Dreamweaver places the   code into each empty table cell at the time it is created. The   code represents a nonbreaking space, or a space that a browser will display on the page. Some browsers will collapse an empty cell, which can ruin the look of a table. The nonbreaking space will hold the cell until content is placed in it, at which time it will be automatically removed.

Split cells

1. Click inside the first cell in the fifth row, then click the **<td>** in the tag selector.

2. Click the **Splits cell into rows or columns button** ⊐⊏ in the Property inspector.

3. Click the **Split cell into Rows option button** (if necessary), type **2** in the Number of rows text box (if necessary), as shown in Figure 11, click **OK,** then click in the cell to deselect it.

   The cell is split, as shown in Figure 12.

   > TIP   To create a new row identical to the one above it, place the insertion point in the last cell of a table, then press [Tab].

You split a cell into two rows.

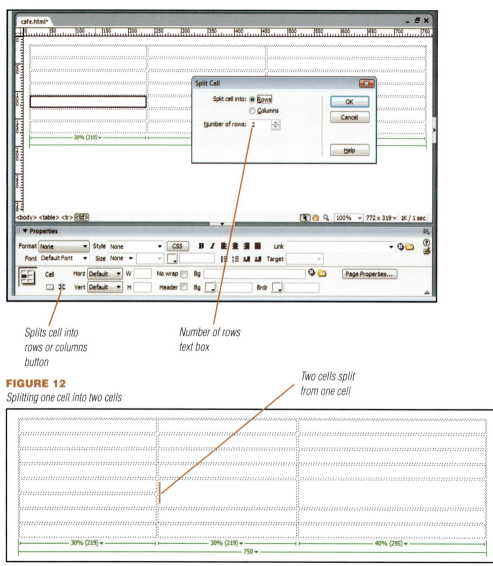

FIGURE 11
Splitting a cell into two rows

Splits cell into
rows or columns
button

Number of rows
text box

FIGURE 12
Splitting one cell into two cells

Two cells split
from one cell

FIGURE 13
Merging selected cells into one cell

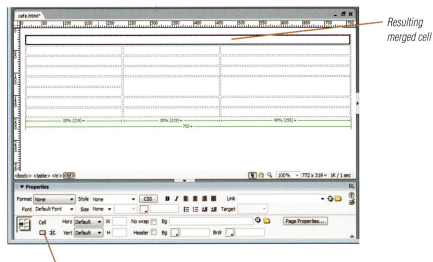

Resulting merged cell

Merges selected cells using spans button

1. Click the insertion point in the first cell in the top row, then drag to the right to select the second and third cells in the top row.

2. Click the **Merges selected cells using spans button** ▣ in the Property inspector.

   The three cells are merged into one cell, as shown in Figure 13. Merged cells are good placeholders for banners or page headings.

   TIP You can only merge cells that are adjacent to each other.

3. Click the **Show Code view button** ‹› Code, then view the code for the merged cells, as shown in Figure 14.

   Notice the table tags denoting the column span (td colspan="3") and the nonbreaking spaces ( ) inserted in the empty cells.

   TIP The nonbreaking space is a special character that is inserted automatically in an empty cell to serve as a placeholder until content is added. A nonbreaking space will override automatic word wrap, or prevent a line break from being inserted in HTML code.

4. Click the **Show Design view button** 🔲 Design, then save your work.

You merged three cells in the first row to make room for The Striped Umbrella banner.

FIGURE 14
Code view for merged cells

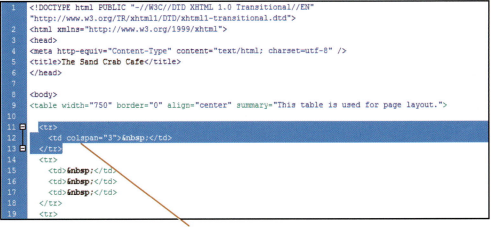

```
1  <!DOCTYPE html PUBLIC "-//W3C//DTD XHTML 1.0 Transitional//EN"
   "http://www.w3.org/TR/xhtml1/DTD/xhtml1-transitional.dtd">
2  <html xmlns="http://www.w3.org/1999/xhtml">
3  <head>
4  <meta http-equiv="Content-Type" content="text/html; charset=utf-8" />
5  <title>The Sand Crab Cafe</title>
6  </head>
7
8  <body>
9  <table width="750" border="0" align="center" summary="This table is used for page layout.">
10
11 <tr>
12   <td colspan="3"> </td>
13 </tr>
14 <tr>
15   <td> </td>
16   <td> </td>
17   <td> </td>
18 </tr>
19 <tr>
```

colspan tag

Lesson 2   Resize, Split, and Merge Cells

INSERT AND ALIGN
IMAGES IN TABLE CELLS

What You'll Do

In this lesson, you will insert The Striped Umbrella banner in the top row of the table. You will then insert three images in three different cells. After placing the three images, you will align them within their cells.

Inserting Images in Table Cells

You can insert images in the cells of a table using the Image command in the Images menu on the Insert bar. If you already have images saved in your Web site that you would like to insert in a table, you can drag them from the Assets panel into the table cells. When you add a large image to a cell, the cell expands to accommodate the inserted image. If you select the Show attributes when inserting Images check box in the Accessibility category of the Preferences dialog box, the Image Tag Accessibility Attributes dialog box will open after you insert an image, prompting you to enter alternate text. Figure 15 shows the John Deere Web site, which uses several tables for page layout and contains several images in its table cells. Notice that some images appear in cells by themselves, and some appear in cells containing text or other graphics. Some cells have a white background, and some have a green background.

Working with Tables

Aligning Images in Table Cells

You can align images both horizontally and vertically within a cell. You can align an image horizontally using the Horz (horizontal) alignment options in the Property inspector. This option is used to align the entire contents of the cell, whether there is one object or several. You can also align an image vertically by the top, middle, bottom, or baseline of a cell. To align an image vertically within a cell, use the Vert (vertical) Align list arrow in the Property inspector, then choose an alignment option, as shown in Figure 16. To control spacing between cells, you can use cell padding and cell spacing. Cell padding is the space between a cell's border and its contents. Cell spacing is the distance between adjacent cells.

FIGURE 15
John Deere Web site

John Deere Web site used with permission from Deere & Company – www.johndeere.com

FIGURE 16
Vertically aligning cell contents

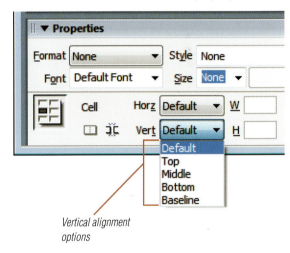

Vertical alignment options

Insert images in table cells

1. Open the index page, click the **banner image** to select it, press and hold **[Shift],** then click to the right of the navigation bar to select both the banner and the navigation bar.

2. Click **Edit** on the menu bar, click **Copy**, then close the index page.

3. Click in the top cell on the cafe page, click **Edit** on the menu bar, then click **Paste.**

4. Compare your screen to Figure 17.

   The banner and navigation bar are copied to the page. We will adjust the alignment in the next lesson.

   (continued)

FIGURE 17
Banner and navigation bar copied from the home page into table

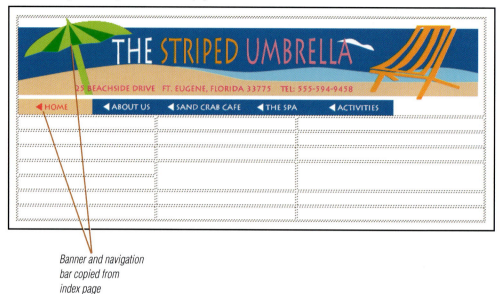

Banner and navigation
bar copied from
index page

Using visual aids
Dreamweaver has an option for turning on and off various features, such as table borders, that are displayed in Design view but are not displayed in the browser. This tool is called Visual Aids and can be accessed through the View menu or through the Visual Aids button on the Document toolbar. Most of the time, these features are very helpful while you are editing and formatting a page. However, turning them off is a quick way to see how the page will be viewed in the browser without having to open it in the browser window.

FIGURE 18
Images inserted into table cells

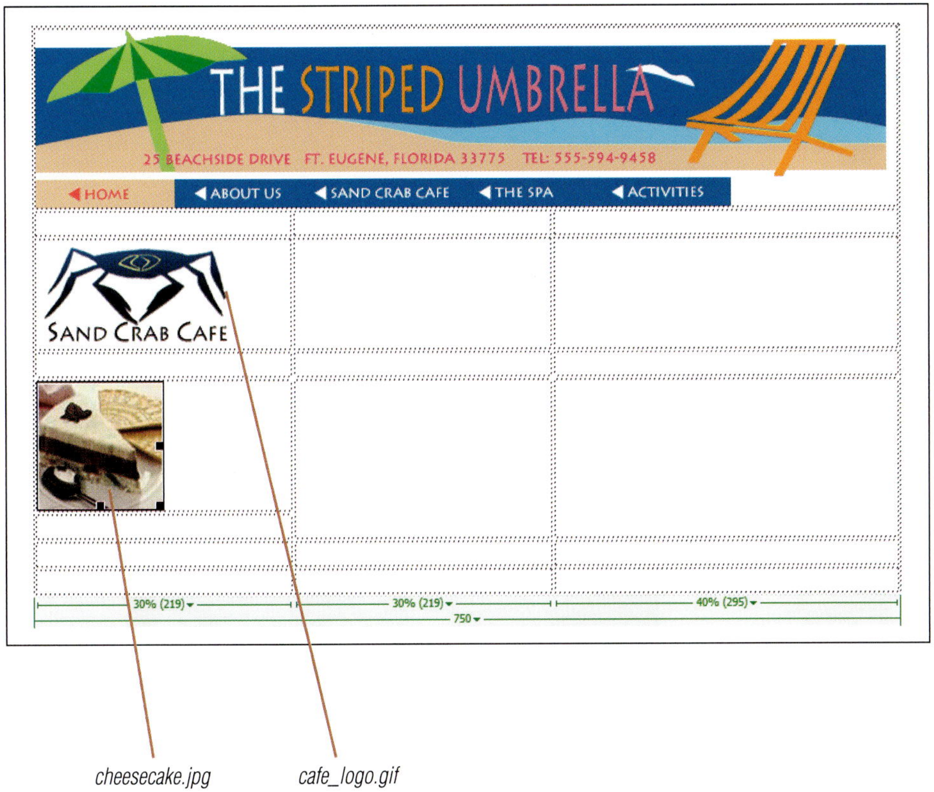

cheesecake.jpg   cafe_logo.gif

5. Click inside the first cell in the third row and insert **cafe_logo.gif** from the assets folder where you store your Data Files, then type **Sand Crab Cafe logo** as the alternate text.

   TIP   Remember to count the banner and nav bar as the first row.

6. Repeat Step 5 to insert **cheesecake.jpg** in the first cell in the fifth row (the top row in the set of split cells), using **Banana Chocolate Cheesecake** for the alternate text.

7. Compare your screen to Figure 18.

(continued)

8. Merge the two cells to the right of the cheesecake graphic, repeat Step 5 to insert the **cafe_photo.jpg** in the newly merged cells, using **The Sand Crab Cafe** as the alternate text, then compare your screen to Figure 19.

   TIP Press [Tab] to move the insertion point to the next cell in a row. Press [Shift][Tab] to move the insertion point to the previous **cell**.

9. Refresh the Assets panel to verify that the three new images were copied to The Striped Umbrella Web site assets folder.

10. Save your work, then preview the page in your browser.

   Notice that the page would look better if the new images had better placement on the **page**.

11. Close your browser.

You inserted images into four cells of the table on the cafe page.

FIGURE 19
Cafe photo inserted into table cell

cafe_photo.jpg

FIGURE 20
Aligning images in cells

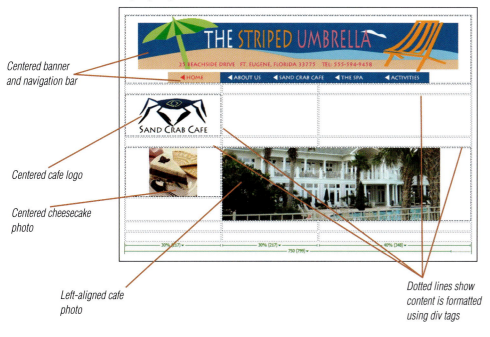

Centered banner
and navigation bar

Centered cafe logo

Centered cheesecake
photo

Left-aligned cafe
photo

Dotted lines show
content is formatted
using div tags

Align graphics in table cells

1. Click the **banner**, then click the **Align Center button** ≣ in the Property inspector.

   The banner and navigation bar move together to become centered in the cell. You may have copied the center alignment tag when you copied the banner and navigation bar from the index page. In that case, the banner and navigation bar will already be centered on the cafe page.

2. Center-align the logo and cheesecake images, then left-align the cafe photo, as shown in Figure 20.

   Notice the extra dotted lines surrounding the four images. Each one represents a div tag that was generated when the alignment button was applied to the image.

3. Save your work.

4. Preview the page in your browser, view the aligned images, then close your browser.

You center-aligned The Striped Umbrella banner and two other images within their respective cells. You left-aligned the fourth image.

Working with div tags

Div tags are used for formatting blocks of content, similar to the way P tags are used to format paragraphs of text. Div tags, however, are more flexible in that they can be used as a container for any type of block content. They are used in various ways, such as centering content on a page or applying color to an area of a Web page. One of the benefits of using div tags is that they are combined easily with Cascading Style Sheets for formatting and positioning. When alignment is assigned to a block of content, Dreamweaver will automatically add a div tag. They are frequently used in style sheets to specify formatting attributes.

INSERT TEXT AND FORMAT
CELL CONTENT

What You'll Do

 In this lesson, you will insert text that describes the restaurant in a cell, type text in two cells, and then type the cafe hours in a nested table. You will also format the text to enhance its appearance on the page. Last, you will add formatting to some of the cells and cell content.

Inserting Text in a Table

You can enter text in a table either by typing it in a cell, copying it from another source and pasting it into a cell, or importing it from another program. Once you place text in a table cell, you can format it to make it more readable and more visually appealing on the page.

Formatting Cell Content

Making modifications and formatting changes to a table and its contents is easier to do in Standard mode than in Layout mode. To format the contents of a cell in Standard mode, select the contents in the cell, then apply formatting to it. For example, you can select an image in a cell and center it, add a border, or add V space.

Or, you can select text in a cell and apply a style or use the Text Indent or Text Outdent buttons in the Property inspector to move the text farther away from or closer to the cell walls.

If a cell contains multiple objects of the same type, such as text, you can either format each item individually or select the entire cell and apply formatting that will be applied identically to all items. You can tell whether you have selected the cell contents or the cell by looking to see what options are showing in the Property inspector. Figure 21 shows a selected image in a cell. Notice that the Property inspector displays options for formatting the object, rather than options for formatting the cell.

Formatting Cells

Formatting a cell is different from formatting a cell's contents. Formatting a cell can include setting properties that visually enhance the cell's appearance, such as setting a cell width and assigning a background color. You can also set global alignment properties for the cell content, using the Horz or Vert list arrows on the Property inspector. These options set the alignment for cell content horizontally or vertically. To format a cell, you need to either select the cell or place the insertion point inside the cell you want to format, then choose the cell formatting options you want in the Property inspector. For example, to choose a fill color for a selected cell, click the Background Color button in the Property inspector, then choose a color from the color picker. To set a background image for a cell, use the Browse for file button or the Point to file button in the Property inspector next to the Background URL of cell button to link to an image. To format a cell, you must expand the Property inspector to display the cell formatting options. In Figure 22, notice that the insertion point is positioned in the cafe logo cell, but the logo is not selected. The Property inspector displays the formatting options for cells.

FIGURE 21

Property inspector showing options for formatting cell contents

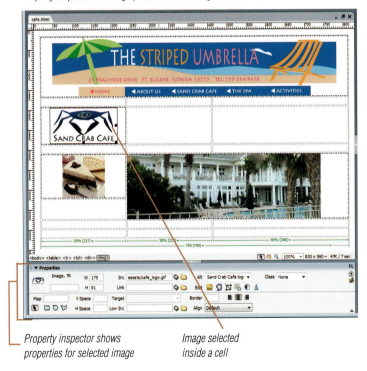

Property inspector shows
properties for selected image

Image selected
inside a cell

FIGURE 22

Property inspector showing options for formatting a cell

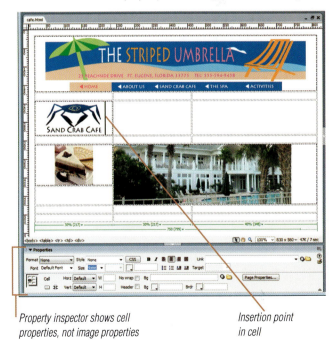

Property inspector shows cell
properties, not image properties

Insertion point
in cell

Insert text

1. Merge the two cells to the right of the cafe logo, click in the newly merged cell, then import the Word document, cafe.doc, from where you store your Data Files (Win) or copy and paste (Mac).

2. Click in the cell below the cheesecake photo, type **Banana Chocolate**, press **[Shift][Enter]** (Win) or **[shift][return]** (Mac), type **Cheesecake**, press **[Shift][Enter]** (Win) or **[shift][return]** (Mac), then type **Our signature dessert**.

3. Click in the next cell down and type **Reservations are recommended for The Dining Room during the peak summer season.**, as shown in Figure 23.

4. Use the Clean Up Word HTML command to correct the code from the cafe.doc file.

You imported a Word document describing the restaurant into one cell and typed two descriptive paragraphs into two cells.

FIGURE 23
Importing and typing text into cells

Imported text describing the cafe

Text typed into cells

Importing and exporting data from tables

You can import and export tabular data into and out of Dreamweaver. Tabular data is data that is arranged in columns and rows and separated by a **delimiter**: a comma, tab, colon, semicolon, or similar character. **Importing** means to bring data created in another software program into Dreamweaver, and **exporting** means to save data created in Dreamweaver in a special file format that can be inserted into other programs. Files that are imported into Dreamweaver must be saved as delimited files. **Delimited files** are database or spreadsheet files that have been saved as text files with delimiters such as tabs or commas separating the data. Programs such as Microsoft Access and Microsoft Excel offer many file formats for saving files. To import a delimited file, click File on the menu bar, point to Import, then click Tabular Data. The Import Tabular Data dialog box opens, offering you formatting options for the imported table. To export a table that you created in Dreamweaver, click File on the menu bar, point to Export, then click Table. The Export Table dialog box opens, letting you choose the type of delimiter you want for the delimited file.

FIGURE 24

Table dialog box settings for nested table

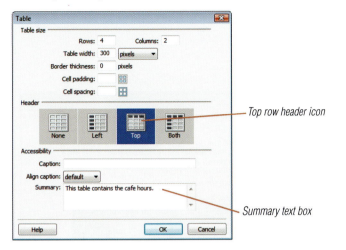

Top row header icon

Summary text box

FIGURE 25

Adding a nested table

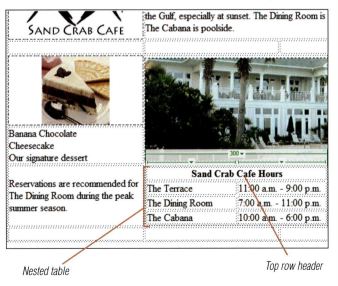

Nested table

Top row header

Insert text using a nested table

1. Merge the two empty cells below the cafe photo.

2. Place the insertion point inside the newly merged cells, then click the **Table button** on the Common tab to open the Table dialog box.

3. Type **4** in the Rows text box, type **2** in the Columns text box, type **300** in the Table width text box, click the **Table width list arrow**, click **pixels**, type **0** in the Border thickness text box, click the **Top row header icon** in the Header section, type **This table contains the cafe hours.** in the Summary text box, compare your Table dialog box to Figure 24, then click **OK**.

   The Top row header option will automatically center and bold the text that is typed into the top cells of the table. The header will be read by screen readers, providing more accessibility for the table.

4. Merge the two cells in the top row of the nested table, click in the cell, then type **Sand Crab Cafe Hours**.

5. Enter the cafe dining area names and hours, as shown in Figure 25.

You inserted a nested table and entered a schedule for the cafe hours.

Format cell content

1. Expand the CSS panel group (if necessary).
2. Click the **Attach Style Sheet button** 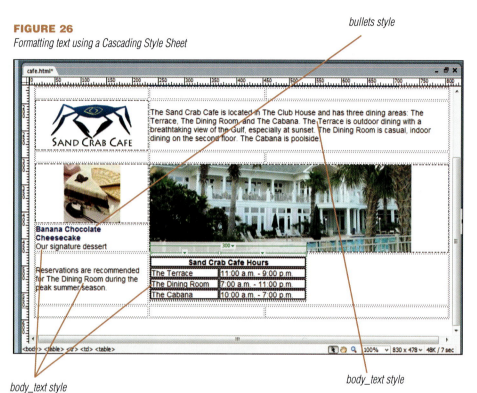 to attach the **su_styles.css** file to the cafe page.
3. Select the paragraph next to the cafe logo, then use the Property inspector to apply the **body_text style**.
4. Select the text "Banana Chocolate Cheesecake," then apply the bullets style.
5. Select the text "Our Signature dessert" and apply the **body_text style**, then select all of the text about reservations in the cell below and apply the **body_text style**.
6. Repeat Step 5 to apply the **body_text** style to the nested table text.

   Your screen should resemble Figure 26.

You formatted text in table cells using a Cascading Style Sheet.

FIGURE 26

Formatting text using a Cascading Style Sheet

bullets style

body_text style

body_text style

FIGURE 27

Formatting cells using horizontal alignment

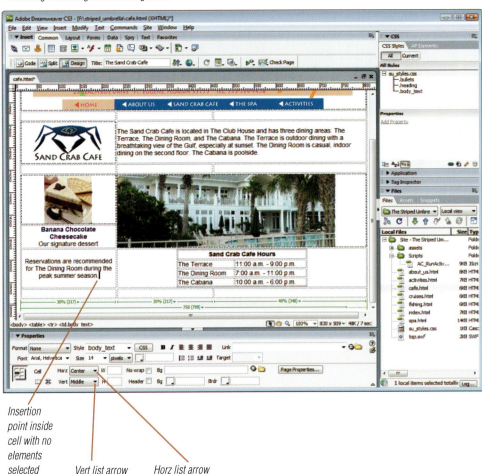

Insertion point inside cell with no elements selected

Vert list arrow

Horz list arrow

Format cells

1. Click to place the insertion point in the cell with the cheesecake name.

2. Click the **Horz list arrow** in the Property inspector, then click **Center** to center the cell contents.

   You do not need to select the text because you are setting the alignment for all contents in the cell.

3. Repeat Steps 1 and 2 for the cell with the reservations text and the cell with the nested table.

   TIP   Click to the right of the nested table to easily select the cell.

4. Click in the cell with the reservations text, click the **Vert list arrow**, then click **Middle**, as shown in Figure 27.

   TIP   Setting alignment can be helpful if you need to troubleshoot a page later.

5. Save your work.

You formatted table cells by adding horizontal and vertical alignment.

Modify cell content

1. Click **Modify** on the menu bar, then click **Navigation Bar** to open the Modify Navigation Bar dialog box.

2. Click the **Show "Down image" initially check box** to remove the check mark for the home button.

3. Click **cafe** in the Nav bar elements box, click the **Show "Down image" initially check box** to add a check mark, then click **OK**.

   The button now shows viewers that they are on the cafe page by displaying the down state when the page is open, as shown in Figure 28.

4. Save your work.

You edited the navigation bar to show the correct initial down state.

FIGURE 28
Edited navigation bar on the cafe page

Correct button is shown in the down state

Power User Shortcuts

To do this:	Use this shortcut:
Toggle between table modes	F6
Access layout mode	[Ctrl][F6] (Win) or [option][F6] (Mac)
Insert table	[Ctrl][Alt][T] (Win) or ⌘[option][T] (Mac)
Select table	[Ctrl][A] (Win) or ⌘[A] (Mac)
Merge cells	[Ctrl][Alt][M] (Win) or ⌘[option][M] (Mac)
Split cell	[Ctrl][Alt][S] (Win) or ⌘[option][S] (Mac)
Insert row	[Ctrl][M] (Win) or ⌘[M] (Mac)
Insert column	[Ctrl][Shift][A] (Win) or ⌘[Shift][A] (Mac)
Delete row	[Ctrl][Shift][M] (Win) or ⌘[Shift][M] (Mac)
Delete column	[Ctrl][Shift][-] (Win) or ⌘[Shift][-] (Mac)
Increase column span	[Ctrl][Shift][]] (Win) or ⌘[Shift][]] (Mac)
Decrease column span	[Ctrl][Shift][[] (Win) or ⌘[Shift][[] (Mac)

FIGURE 29
Hiding visual aids

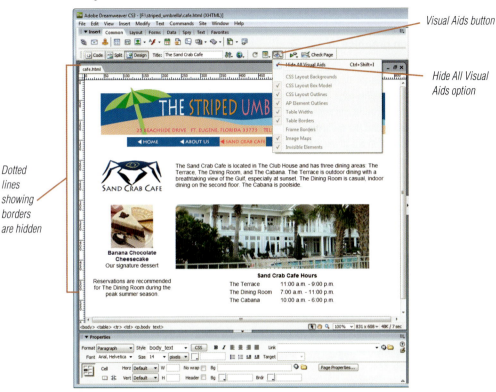

Visual Aids button

Hide All Visual
Aids option

Dotted
lines
showing
borders
are hidden

Use visual aids to check layout

1. Click the **Visual Aids button** on the Document toolbar, then click **Hide All Visual Aids**, as shown in Figure 29.

   The borders around the table, table cells, and div tags (where you used alignment options) are all hidden, allowing you to see more clearly how the page will look in the browser.

2. Repeat Step 1 to show the visual aids again.

3. Save your work, preview the cafe page in the browser, then close the browser.

You used the Hide All Visual Aids command to hide the table borders and layout block outlines, then showed them again.

Using grids and guides for positioning page content

There are some other options available to help you position your page content that are available through the View menu. **Grids** provide a graph paper-like view of a page. Horizontal and vertical lines fill the page when this option is turned on. You can edit the colors of the lines, the distance they are apart, whether they are displayed using lines or dots, and whether or not objects "snap" to them. **Guides** are horizontal or vertical lines that you drag onto the page from the rulers. You can edit both the colors of the guides and the color of the distance, a feature that shows you the distance between two guides. You can lock the guides so you don't accidentally move them and you can set them either to snap to page elements or have page elements snap to them. To display either feature, click View on the menu bar, then click Grids or Guides.

Create a table.

1. Open the blooms & bulbs Web site.
2. Open classes.html from the Web site.
3. Insert a table on the page with the following settings: Rows: **5**, Columns: **3**, Table width: **750 pixels**, Border thickness: **0**, Cell padding: **5**, and Cell spacing: **5**.
4. Enter the text **This table is used for page layout.** in the Summary text box.
5. Center-align the table on the page, then use Figure 30 as a guide for completing this exercise.
6. Replace the existing page title with the title **Master Gardener classes begin soon!**, then save your work.

Resize, split, and merge cells.

1. Select the first cell in the first row, then set the cell width to **25%**.
2. Select the second cell in the first row, then set the cell width to **40%**.
3. Select the third cell in the first row, then set the cell width to **35%**.
4. Merge the three cells in the first row.
5. Merge the first two cells in the second row.
6. Merge the third cell in the third row with the third cell in the fourth row.
7. Split the first cell in the fourth row into two columns.
8. Merge the three cells in the last row.
9. Save your work.

Insert and align graphics in table cells.

1. Copy the banner and the navigation bar together from the home page and paste them into the first row of the table.
2. Center the banner and the navigation bar.
3. Modify the navigation bar to show the classes element in the Down image state and the home element in the Up image state.
4. Use the Insert bar to insert **flower_bed.jpg** in the last row. You can find the flower_bed.jpg file in the assets folder where you store your Data Files. Add the alternate text **Flower bed in downtown Alvin** to the flower_bed.jpg image when prompted, then center the image in the cell.
5. Use the tag selector to select the cell containing the flower_bed.jpg image, then set the vertical alignment to **Top**.
6. Save your work.

Insert text and format cell content.

1. Type **Master Gardener Classes Beginning Soon!** in the first cell in the second row.
2. Type **Who are Master Gardeners?** in the second cell in the second row.
3. Type **Schedule** in the first cell in the third **row**.
4. Type **Registration** in the second cell in the third row.

5. Type the dates and times for the classes from Figure 30 in the first and second cells in the fourth row. (*Hint*: You can drag the border between columns to adjust the cells to display the hours correctly.)
6. Use the Import Word Document command on the File menu to import the file **registration.doc** into the third cell in the fourth row, (or use copy and paste) then use the Clean up Word HTML command on the Commands menu to remove any unnecessary code.
7. Repeat Step 6 to place the text from the **gardeners.doc** file into the next empty cell.
8. Attach the **blooms_styles.css** file, then apply the **bodytext** style to the dates, times, and two paragraphs of text describing the program.
9. Create a new style in the blooms_styles.css style sheet named **subheadings** with the following settings: Font: **Arial, Helvetica, sans-serif**; Size: **14**; Style: **normal**; Weight: **bold**; Color: **#003366**.
10. Create another new style in the blooms_styles.css style sheet named **reverse_text** with the following settings: Font: **Arial, Helvetica, sans-serif**; Size: **14**; Style: **normal**; Weight: **bold**; Color: **#FFFFFF**.
11. Select each cell that contains text and set the vertical alignment to **Top**.
12. Center-align the four headings (Master Gardener Classes Beginning Soon!, Who are Master Gardeners?, Schedule, and Registration).

13. Set the horizontal alignment for the cell with the dates to **Center**.

14. Set the horizontal alignment for the cell with the times and the cells describing registration and Master Gardeners to **Left**.

15. Select the cell with the word "Registration" in it, then change the cell background color to **#000099**.

16. Apply the **subheadings style** to the text "Schedule" and "Who are Master Gardeners?"

17. Apply the **reverse_text** style to the heading "Registration," then apply the seasons style to the text "Master Gardener Classes Beginning Soon!"

18. Save your work, preview the page in your browser, then close your browser.

19. Close all open pages.

FIGURE 30
Completed Skills Review

Master Gardener Classes Beginning soon!

Who are Master Gardeners?

Schedule		Registration
8/4	5:00 - 9:00	
8/6	5:00 - 9:00	
8/8	9:00 - 5:00	
8/11	5:00 - 9:00	
8/13	5:00 - 9:00	
8/15	9:00 - 5:00	
8/18	5:00 - 9:00	
8/20	5:00 - 9:00	

The registration fee is $50.00. Make checks payable to the county extension office. You also must fill out a registration form and turn it in with your check. The registration deadline is August 1. The registration fee is $50.00. Make checks payable to the county extension office. You also must fill out a registration form and turn it in with your check. The registration deadline is August 1. You may pick up and turn in the registration forms at either the county extension office or here at blooms & bulbs.

Master Gardeners were conceived by the extension agent in Snohomish County, Washington, in 1972 to assist him with the growing requests from urban farmers in that area. Today Master Gardener programs exist in every state and in six Canadian provinces. It is a program designed to "grow" volunteers that contribute thousands of volunteer hours in their communities by planting and maintaining public gardens, conducting research, and speaking on gardening issues.

In this exercise, you will continue your work on the TripSmart Web site that you began in Project Builder 1 in Chapter 1 and developed in the previous chapters. You are ready to begin work on a page that will feature catalog items. You plan to use a table for page layout.

1. Open the TripSmart Web site.
2. Open catalog.html from the Web site.
3. Insert a table with the following settings: Rows: **6**, Columns: **3**, Table width: **750 pixels**, Border thickness: **0**. Enter an appropriate table summary, then center-align the table.
4. Set the cell widths in the bottom row to **33%**, **33%**, and **34%**.
5. Merge the cells in the top row, copy the TripSmart banner and navigation bar from the home page, then paste them into the resulting merged cell. Add the following alternate text to the image: **TripSmart banner**, then center the banner.
6. Center the navigation bar, if necessary.
7. Merge the three cells in the second row, type **Our products are backed with a 100% guarantee.**, then center the text.
8. Type **Protection from harmful UV rays, Cool, light-weight, versatile**, and **Pockets for everything** in the three cells in the third row.
9. Place the files hat.jpg, pants.jpg, and vest.jpg from the assets folder where you store your Data Files in the three cells in the fourth row, add the following alternate text to the images: **Safari hat, Kenya convertible pants**, and **Photographer's vest,** then center the three images.
10. Type **Safari Hat, Kenya Convertible Pants**, and **Photographer's Vest** in the three cells in the fifth row, then center each label.
11. Type **Item number 50501** and **$29.00** with a line break between them in the first cell in the sixth row.
12. Repeat Step 11 to type **Item number 62495** and **$39.50** in the second cell in the sixth row.
13. Repeat Step 11 to type **Item number 52301** and **$54.95** in the third cell in the sixth row.
14. Attach the **tripsmart_styles.css** file to the page, apply the **body_text style** to the three descriptions in the third row, then center each description.
15. Create a new style in the tripsmart_styles.css style sheet named **reverse_text** with the following settings: Font, **Verdana, Arial, Helvetica, sans-serif**; Size, **14 px**; Style, **normal**; Weight, **bold**; Color, **#FFFFFF**.
16. Apply the **reverse_text style** to the text "Our products are backed by a 100% guarantee.", then change the cell background color to **#666666**.

17. Apply the **reverse_text style** to the three item names under the images, then change the cell background color to **#999999**.

18. Create a new style called **item_numbers** with the following settings: Font:

Verdana, Arial, Helvetica, sans-serif; Size: **10 px**; Style: **normal**; Weight: **bold**.

19. Apply the **item_numbers style** to the three items' numbers and prices.

20. Save your work, view the page in your browser, compare your screen with Figure 31, then close the browser.

21. Save your work, then close all open pages.

FIGURE 31

Sample Project Builder 1

Use Figure 32 as a guide to continue your work on the Carolyne's Creations Web site that you started in Chapter 1 and developed in the previous chapters. You are now ready to begin work on a page that will showcase the catering services. You decide to use a table to lay out the page.

1. Open the Carolyne's Creations Web site, then open catering.html.
2. Type **Carolyne's Catering** for the page title, replacing the original title.
3. Create a table on the page with the following settings: Rows: **11**, Columns: **3**, Table width: **770 pixels**, Cell Pad: **3**, Cell Space: **0**, Border thickness: **0**, adding an appropriate table summary.
4. Center-align the table and set the width of the three cells to **33%** each.
5. Merge the cells in the first row, then insert the banner with links from another page in the site. Enter appropriate alternate text for the banner, then center-align the banner (if necessary).
6. Type **Catering for All Occasions** in the second cell in the third row and **Dinner to Go** in the second cell in the seventh row.
7. Attach the **cc_styles.css** file to the page, then apply the **sub_head** style to the text you typed in Step 6 and center the text.
8. Merge the cells in the 6th and 10th rows, then Insert rules that are 100% wide. (*Hints*: Change the view to Expanded Tables mode to be able to see the cells easier and use the Insert, HTML, Horizontal Rule command to insert a horizontal rule.)
9. Type **Lunch Boxes**, **Brunch Boxes**, and **Gift Baskets** in the three cells in the fourth row.
10. Type **Soups**, **Entrees**, and **Desserts** in the three cells in the eighth row.
11. Apply the **sub_head** style to the text you typed in Steps 9 and 10, then center each heading.
12. Use the file cell_back.jpg from your Data Files folder to serve as the background for each cell in the fourth and eighth rows. (*Hint*: Use the Browse for File icon next to the Bg text box.)

13. Type the text **Call/fax by 9:00 a.m. for lunch orders, Call/fax by 1:00 p.m. for dinner orders, Fax number: 555-963-5938** in the first cell in the last row using a line break to separate the first two lines and a paragraph break to separate the last line.

14. Apply the **body_text style** to the text you typed in Step 13.

15. Open the file menu items.doc from your Data Files folder. Copy and paste each text block into the cells in the fifth and ninth rows, then apply the **body_text style** to each text block, using Figure 32 as a guide.

16. Merge the last two cells in the last row, then insert the image muffins.jpg with any additional formatting of your choice.

17. Save your work, preview the page in your browser, then close all open files.

FIGURE 32
Completed Project Builder 2

Catering For All Occasions

Lunch Boxes	Brunch Boxes	Gift Baskets
Sandwich, Chips, Cookie	Muffin, Fresh Fruit, Yogurt	Holiday Rolls & Honey Butter
Tortilla Rollups, Chips & Fresh Salsa	Lox, Cream Cheese & Bagel	Muffins, Breads, & Assorted Jams
Chicken Salad, Fruit, Cookie	Quiche, Fresh Fruit, Muffin	Assorted Cookies of the Day
Fruit Smoothie or Tea included	Coffee/Tea of the Day included	Gourmet Chocolates included
$6.95 + tax	$4.95 + tax	From $12.00

Dinner To Go

Soups	Entrees	Desserts
Chicken Taco	Chicken Enchiladas	Peanut Butter Chocolate Pie
Broccoli Cheese	Oven Swiss Steak	Red Velvet Cake
Cream of Mushroom	Shrimp & Grits	White Peach Cobbler with Hard Sauce
Baked Potato	Stuffed Pork Chops	Chocolate Mousse
Chicken Artichoke	Buttermilk Pecan Chicken	Seasonal Fruit Sorbets
$4.50 individual serving	From $10.00	$3.50 individual/$16.00 whole

Call/fax by 9:00 am for lunch orders
Call/fax by 1:00 pm for dinner orders

Fax number: 555-963-5938

Working with Tables

DESIGN PROJECT

Vesta Everitt has opened a new shop called CollegeFandz, an online source for college clothing and collectibles. She is considering creating a Web site to promote her services and products and would like to gather some ideas before she hires a Web designer. She decides to visit retail Web sites to look for design ideas. Figures 33 and 34 show the Teva and L.L. Bean Web sites.

1. Connect to the Internet, then go to *www.teva.com*.

2. Click View on your browser's menu bar, then click the Source or View Source command to view the source code for the Web site you selected.

3. Search the code for table tags. Note the number that you find.

4. Browse to *www.llbean.com* next and repeat Steps 2 and 3.

5. Using a word processor or paper, list five design ideas that you like from either of these pages. Be sure to specify which page was the source of each idea.

FIGURE 33
Design Project

FIGURE 34
Design Project

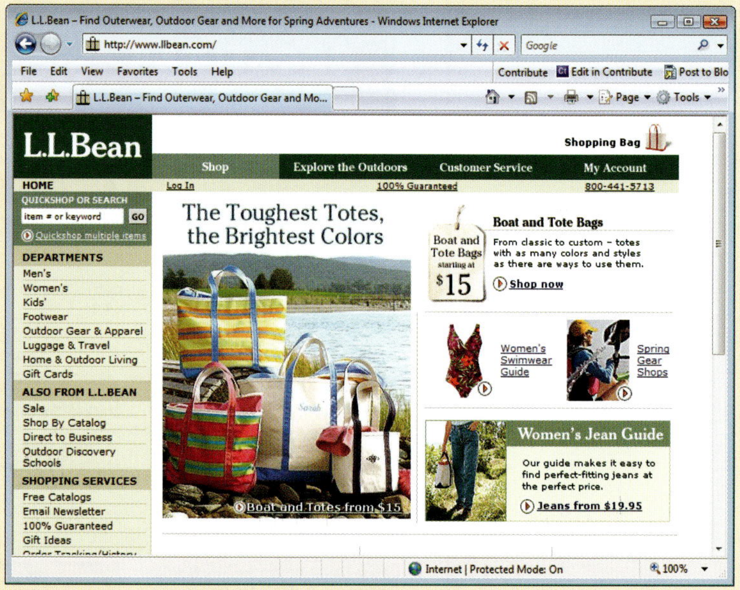

Teva Web site used with permission from Deckers Outdoor Corporation – www.teva.com

LL. Bean Web site used with permission from L.L. Bean – www. llbean.com

PORTFOLIO PROJECT

In this assignment, you will continue to work on the Web site that you started in Chapter 1 and developed in Chapters 2 through 4. There will be no data files supplied. You are building this Web site from chapter to chapter, so you must do each Portfolio Project assignment in each chapter to complete your Web site.

You will continue building your Web site by designing and completing a page that contains a table used for page layout. After completing your page, you will run several reports to test the Web site.

1. Take a few minutes to evaluate your storyboard. Choose a page or pages to develop in which you will use a table for page layout.

2. Plan the content for the new page (or pages) by making a sketch of the table that shows where the content will be placed in the table cells. Split and merge cells and align each element as necessary to create a visually attractive layout.

3. Create the table and place the content in the cells using the sketch for guidance.

4. After you complete the pages, run a report that checks for broken links in the Web site. Correct any broken links that appear in the report.

5. Run a report on the Web site for orphaned files and correct any if found.

6. Check for any Non-Websafe colors in the Web site. If any are found, replace them with Websafe colors.

7. Preview all the pages in your browser and test all links. Evaluate the pages for both content and layout, then use the checklist in Figure 35 to make sure your Web site is completed.

8. Make any modifications necessary to improve the pages.

FIGURE 35
Portfolio Project checklist

Web Site Checklist
1. Title any pages that have no page titles.
2. Check to see that all pages have consistent navigation links.
3. Check to see that all links work correctly.
4. Check to see that all images have alternate text.
5. Remove any Non-Websafe colors.
6. Delete any unnecessary files.
7. Remove any orphaned files.
8. Use tables for layout when possible.
9. View all pages using at least two different browsers.
10. Verify that the home page has keywords, a description, and a point of contact.

chapter

6

MANAGING A WEB
SERVER AND FILES

1. Perform Web site maintenance

2. Publish a Web site and transfer files

3. Check files out and in

4. Cloak files

5. Import and export a site definition

6. Evaluate Web content for legal use

6 MANAGING A WEB
SERVER AND FILES

Introduction

Once you have created all the pages of your Web site, finalized all the content, and performed site maintenance, you are ready to publish your site to a remote server so the rest of the world can access it. In this chapter, you will start by running some reports to make sure the links in your site work properly, that the colors are Websafe, and that orphaned files are removed. Next, you will set up a connection to the remote site for The Striped Umbrella Web site. You will then transfer files to the remote site and learn how to keep them up to date. You will also check out a file so that it is not available to other team members while you are editing it and you will learn how to cloak files. When a file is **cloaked**, it is excluded from certain processes, such as being transferred to the remote site. Next, you will export the site definition file from The Striped Umbrella Web site so that other designers can import the site. Finally, you will research important copyright issues that affect all Web sites.

Preparing to Publish a Site

Before you publish a site to a remote server so that it is available to others, it is extremely important that you test it regularly to make sure the content is accurate and up to date and that everything is functioning properly. When viewing pages over the Internet, it is very frustrating to click a link that doesn't work or have to wait for pages that load slowly because of large graphics and animations. Remember that a typical Web viewer has a short attention span and limited patience. Before you publish your site, make sure to use the Link Checker panel to check for broken links and orphaned files. Make sure that all image paths are correct and that all images load quickly and have alternate text. Verify that all pages have titles, and remove all Non-Websafe colors. View the pages in at least two different browsers and different versions of the same browser to ensure that everything works correctly. The more frequently you test, the better the chance that your viewers will have a positive experience at your site and want to return. All content must be original to the Web site, have been obtained legally, or used properly without violating the copyright of someone else's work.

Tools You'll Use

PERFORM WEB SITE
MAINTENANCE

What You'll Do

In this lesson, you will use some of Dreamweaver's site management tools to check for broken links, orphaned files, and missing alternate text. You will also verify that all colors are Websafe. You will then correct any problems that you find.

Maintaining a Web Site

As you add pages, links, and content to a Web site, it can quickly become difficult to manage. It's important to perform maintenance tasks frequently to make sure your Web site operates smoothly and remains "clean." You have already learned about some of the tools described in the following paragraphs. Although it is important to use them as you create and modify your pages, it is also important to run them at periodic intervals after publishing your Web site to make sure your Web site is always error-free.

Using the Assets Panel

You should use the Assets panel to check the list of images and colors used in your Web site. If you see images listed that are not being used, you should move them to a storage folder outside the Web site until you need them. If you are concerned about using only Websafe colors, you should also check the Colors list to make sure that all colors in the site are Websafe. If there are non-Websafe colors in the list, locate the elements to which

these colors are applied and apply Websafe colors to them.

Checking Links Sitewide

Before and after you publish your Web site, you should use the Link Checker panel to make sure all internal links are working. If the Link Checker panel displays any broken links, you should repair them. If the Link Checker panel displays any orphaned files, you should evaluate whether to delete them or link them with existing pages.

Using Site Reports

You can use the Reports command in the Site menu to generate six different HTML reports that can help you maintain your Web site. You choose the type of report you want to run in the Reports dialog box, shown in Figure 1. You can specify whether to generate the report for the current document, the entire current local site, selected files in the site, or a selected folder. You can also generate Workflow reports to see files that have been checked out by others or recently modified or you can view the Design Notes attached to files.

Design Notes are separate files in a Web site that contain additional information about a page file or a graphic file. In a collaborative situation, designers can record notes to exchange information with other designers. Design Notes can also be used to record sensitive information that would not be included in files that could be viewed on the Web site. Information about the source files for graphic files, such as Flash files or Fireworks files, are also stored in Design Notes.

Using the Site Map

You can use the site map to check your navigation structure. Does the site map show that you have followed the file hierarchy in the storyboard and flow chart? Does the navigation structure shown in the site map reflect a logically organized flowchart? Is each page three or four clicks from the home page? If the answer is no to any of these questions, make adjustments to improve the navigation structure.

Validating Markup

One of the report features in Dreamweaver is the ability to validate markup. This means that Dreamweaver will go through the code to look for errors that could occur with different language versions, such as XHTML or XML. To validate code for a page, click File on the menu bar, point to Validate, and then click Markup. The Results panel opens and lists any pages with errors, the line numbers where the errors occur, and an explanation of the errors. The Validate button on the

Results panel offers the choice of validating a single document, an entire local Web site, or selected files in a local Web site.

Testing Pages

Finally, you should test your Web site using many different types and versions of browsers, platforms, and screen resolutions. You can use the Check Page button on the Document toolbar to check browser compatibility. This feature lists issues with the pages in your site that may cause problems when the pages are viewed using certain

browsers, such as the rendering of square bullets in Mozilla Firefox. If you find such issues, you then have the choice to make changes to your page to eliminate the problems. The Reports panel includes a URL that you can visit to find the solutions to problems. You should test every link to make sure it connects to valid, active Web sites. Pages that download slowly should be reduced in size to improve performance. You should analyze all feedback on the Web site objectively, saving both positive and negative comments for future reference to help you make improvements to the site.

FIGURE 1
Reports dialog box

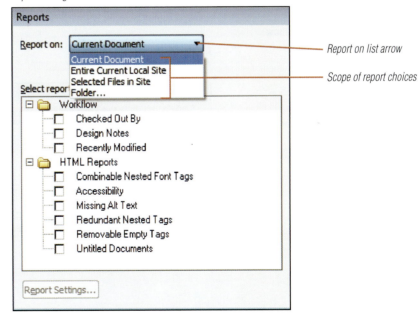

Report on list arrow

Scope of report choices

Check for broken links

1. Open The Striped Umbrella Web site.

2. Show the Files panel (if necessary).

3. Click **Site** on the menu bar, point to **Advanced**, then click **Recreate Site Cache**.

4. Click **Site** on the menu bar, then click **Check Links Sitewide**.

   No broken links are listed in the Link Checker panel of the Results panel group, as shown in Figure 2.

You verified that there are no broken links in the Web site.

Check for orphaned files

1. In the Link Checker panel, click the **Show list arrow**, then click **Orphaned Files**.

   As Figure 3 shows, there are no orphaned files.

2. Close the Results panel group.

You verified that there are no orphaned files in the Web site.

FIGURE 2

Link Checker panel displaying no broken links

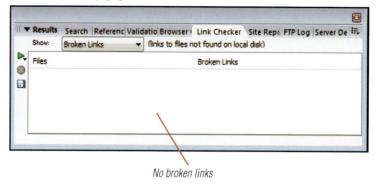

No broken links

FIGURE 3

Link Checker panel displaying no orphaned files

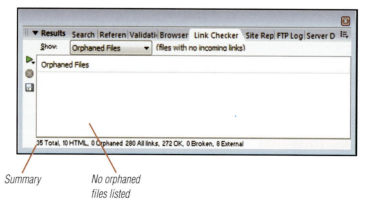

Summary   *No orphaned files listed*

FIGURE 4

Assets panel displaying Websafe colors

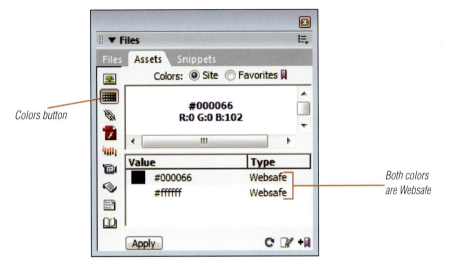

Colors button

Both colors
are Websafe

1. Click the **Assets tab**, then click the **Colors button** to view the Web site colors, as shown in Figure 4.

   The Assets panel shows that all colors used in the Web site are Websafe.

   You verified that the Web site contains all Websafe colors.

Using Find and Replace to Locate Non-Websafe Colors

As with many software applications, Dreamweaver has a Find and Replace feature that can be used both in Design view and in Code view under the Edit menu. If you are looking for a non-Websafe color, you will probably save time by using the Find and Replace feature to locate the hexadecimal color code in Code view. If a site has very many pages, this will be the fastest way to locate it. The Find and Replace feature can also be used to locate other character combinations, such as a phrase that begins or ends with a particular word or tag. These patterns of character combinations are referred to as **regular expressions**. To find out more, search for "regular expressions" in Dreamweaver Help.

Check for untitled documents

1. Click **Site** on the menu bar, then click **Reports** to open the Reports dialog box.

2. Click the **Untitled Documents check box**, click the **Report on list arrow**, click **Entire Current Local Site**, as shown in Figure 5, then click **Run**.

   The Site Reports panel opens in the Results panel group, and shows no files, indicating that all documents in the Web site contain titles.

You verified that the Web site contains no untitled documents.

FIGURE 5

Reports dialog box with Untitled Documents option selected

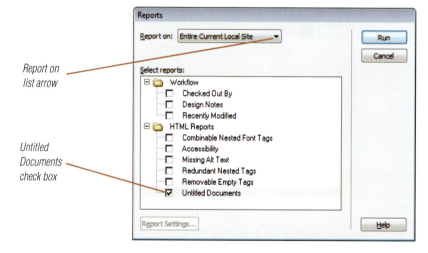

Report on list arrow

Untitled Documents check box

FIGURE 6

Reports dialog box with Missing Alt Text option selected

Missing Alt Text
check box
checked

FIGURE 7

Site Reports panel displaying missing "alt" tags

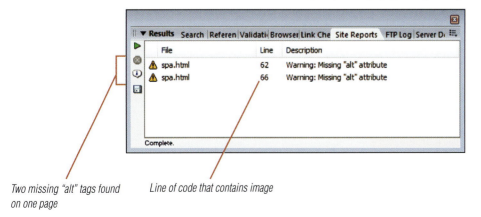

Two missing "alt" tags found
on one page

Line of code that contains image

Check for missing alternate text

1. Using Figure 6 as a guide, run another report that checks the entire current local site for missing alternate text.

The results show that the spa page contains images that are missing alternate text, as shown in Figure 7.

2. Open the spa page, then find the images that are missing alternate text.

> TIP   The Site Reports panel documents the code line numbers where the missing alt tags occur. Sometimes it is faster to locate the errors in Code view, rather than in Design view.

3. Add appropriate alternate text to the images.

4. Save your work, then run the report again to check the entire site for missing alternate text.

No files should appear in the Site Reports panel.

5. Close the Results panel group, then close all open pages.

You ran a report to check for missing alternate text in the entire site. You then added alternate text to two images and ran the report again.

Enable Design Notes

1. Click **Site** on the menu bar, point to **Manage Sites**, click **Edit**, click the **Advanced tab** (if necessary), then click the **Design Notes category**.

2. Click the **Maintain Design Notes check box**, to select it (if necessary), as shown in Figure 8.

3. Click the **File View Columns category**, then click **Notes** in the File View Columns list.

4. Click the **Options**: **Show check box**, to select it (if necessary), click **OK**, then click **Done** in the Manage Sites dialog box.

   The Notes column now displays the word "Show" in the Show column, as shown in Figure 9, indicating that the Notes column will be visible in the Files panel.

You set the preference to use Design Notes in the Web site. You also set the option to display the Notes column in the Files panel.

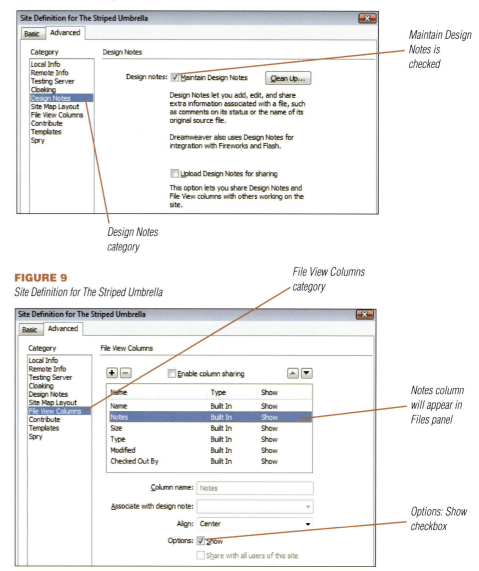

FIGURE 8
Site Definition for The Striped Umbrella

Maintain Design Notes is checked

Design Notes category

FIGURE 9
Site Definition for The Striped Umbrella

File View Columns category

Notes column will appear in Files panel

Options: Show checkbox

FIGURE 10
Design Notes dialog box

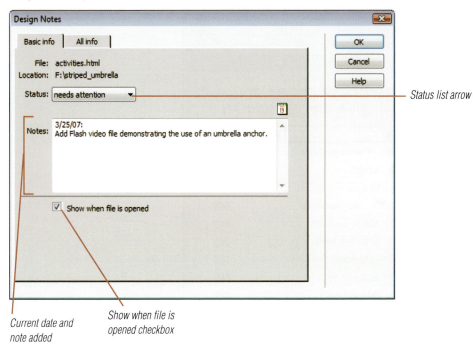

Status list arrow

Current date and note added

Show when file is opened checkbox

Associate a Design Note with a file

1. Open the activities page, click **File** on the menu bar, click **Design Notes**, then click the **Basic Info tab** (if necessary).

   The Design Notes dialog box opens with a text box to record a note related to the open file, the option to display the note each time the file is opened, an option to include the current date, and a status indicator.

2. Click the **Date icon** 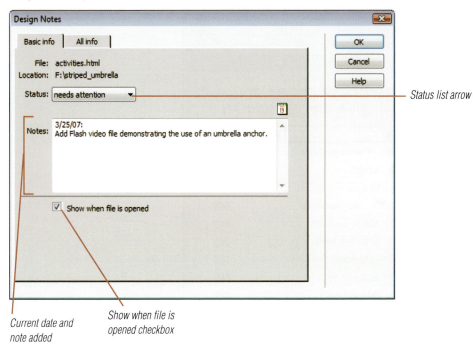 above the Notes text box on the right.

   The current date is added to the Notes text box.

3. Type **Add Flash video file demonstrating the use of an umbrella anchor**. in the Notes text box beneath the date.

4. Click the **Status list arrow**, then click **needs attention**.

5. Click the **Show when file is opened** check box to select it, as shown in Figure 10, then click **OK**.

You added a design note to the activities page with the current date and a status indicator. The note will open each time the file is opened.

Using Version Cue to Manage Assets

Another way to collaborate with team members is through Adobe Version Cue, a workgroup collaboration system that is included in Adobe Creative Suite 3. You can perform such functions such as managing security, backing up data, and using metadata to search files. **Metadata** includes information about a file such as keywords, descriptions, and copyright information. Adobe Bridge also organizes files with metadata.

Edit a Design Note

1. Click **File** on the menu bar, then click **Design Notes** to open the Design Note associated with the activities page.

   You can also right-click (Windows) or control-click (Mac) the filename in the Files panel, then click Design Notes, or double-click the yellow Design Notes icon in the Files panel next to the filename to open a Design Note, as shown in Figure 11.

2. Edit the note by adding the sentence **Ask Jane Pinson to send the files.** beneath the existing text in the Notes section, then click **OK** to close it.

   A file named activities.html.mno has been created in a new folder called_notes. This folder and file will not display in the Files panel unless you have the option to show hidden files and folders selected. However, you can switch to Windows Explorer to see them without selecting this option.

FIGURE 11

Files panel with Notes icon displayed

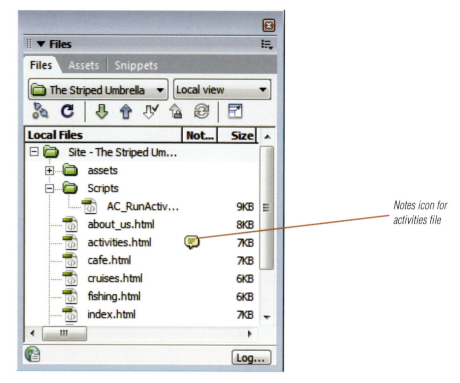

Notes icon for activities file

Deleting a Design Note

There are two steps to deleting a design note that you don't need anymore. The first step is to delete the file. To delete a Design Note, right-click the filename in the Files panel that is associated with the Design Note you want to delete, and then click Explore (Win) or Reveal in Finder (Mac) to open your file management system. Delete the .mno file in the files list, and then close Explorer (Win) or Finder (Mac). The second step is done in Dreamweaver. Click Site on the menu bar, click Manage Sites, click Edit, and then select the Design Notes category. Click the Clean Up button. (*Note*: Don't do this if you deselect Maintain Design Notes first or it will delete all of your design notes!) The Design Notes icon will be removed from the Notes column in the Files panel.

FIGURE 12

Windows Explorer displaying the notes file and folder

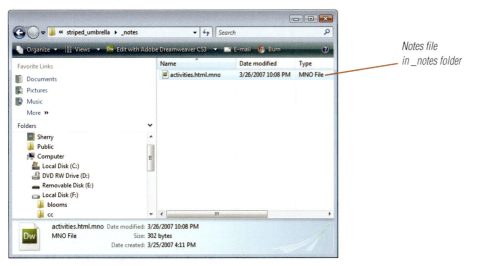

Notes file
in _notes folder

3. Right-click (Win) or control-click (Mac) **activities.html** in the Files panel, then click **Explore** (Win) or **Reveal in Finder** (Mac).

4. Double-click the folder **_notes** to open it, then double-click the file **activities.html.mno**, shown in Figure 12, to open the file in Dreamweaver.

   The notes file opens in Code view in Dreamweaver, as shown in Figure 13.

5. Read the file, close it, then close Explorer (Win) or Finder (Mac).

You opened the Design Notes dialog box and edited the note in the Notes text box. Next, you viewed the .mno file that Dreamweaver created when you added the Design Note.

FIGURE 13

Code for the activities.html.mno file

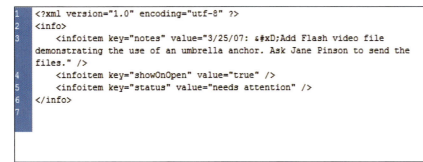

```
1  <?xml version="1.0" encoding="utf-8" ?>
2  <info>
3    <infoitem key="notes" value="3/25/07: &#xD;Add Flash video file
   demonstrating the use of an umbrella anchor. Ask Jane Pinson to send the
   files." />
4    <infoitem key="showOnOpen" value="true" />
5    <infoitem key="status" value="needs attention" />
6  </info>
7
```

Lesson 1   Perform Web Site Maintenance

PUBLISH A WEB SITE
AND TRANSFER FILES

What You'll Do

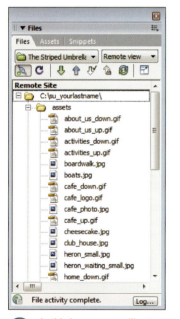

▶ *In this lesson, you will set up remote access to either an FTP folder or a local/network folder for The Striped Umbrella Web site. You will also view a Web site on a remote server, upload files to it, and synchronize the files.*

Defining a Remote Site

As you learned in Chapter 1, publishing a site means transferring all the site's files to a Web server. A **Web server** is a computer that is connected to the Internet with an IP (Internet Protocol) address so that it is available on the Internet. Before you can publish a site to a Web server, you must first define the remote site by specifying the Remote Info settings in the Advanced section of the Site Definition dialog box. You can specify remote settings when you first create a new site and define the root folder (as you did in Chapter 1 when you defined the remote access settings for The Striped Umbrella Web site), or you can do it after you have completed all of your pages and are confident that your site is ready for public viewing. To specify the remote settings for a site, you must first choose an Access setting, which specifies the type of server you will use. The most common Access setting is FTP (File Transfer Protocol). If you specify FTP, you will need to specify an address for the server and the name of the folder on the FTP site in which your root folder will be stored. You will also need to enter login and password information. Figure 14 shows an example of FTP settings in the Remote Info category of the Site Definition dialog box.

QUICKTIP

If you do not have access to an FTP site, you can publish a site to a local/network folder. This is referred to as a **LAN**, or a Local Area Network. Use the alternate steps provided in this lesson to publish your site to a local/network folder.

Viewing a Remote Site

Once you have defined a site to a remote location, you can then view the remote folder in the Files panel by choosing Remote view from the View list. If your remote site is located on an FTP server, Dreamweaver will connect to it. You will see the File Activity dialog box showing the progress of the connection. You can also use the Connects to remote host button on the Files panel toolbar to connect to the remote site. If you defined your site on a local/network folder, then you don't need to use the Connects to remote host button; the root folder and any files and folders it contains will appear in the Files panel when you switch to Remote view.

Transferring Files to and from a Remote Site

After you define a remote site, you will need to transfer or **upload** your files from the local version of your site to the remote host. To do this, view the site in Local view, select the files you want to upload, and then click the Put File(s) button on the Files panel toolbar. Once you click this button, the files will be transferred to the remote site. To view the uploaded files, switch to Remote view, as shown in Figure 15. Or, you can expand the Files panel to view both the Remote Site and the Local Files panes.

If a file you select for uploading requires additional files, such as graphics, a dialog box will open after you click the Put File(s) button and ask if you want those files (known as **dependent files**) to be uploaded. By clicking Yes, all dependent files in the selected page will be uploaded to the appropriate folder in the remote site. If a file that you want to upload is located in a folder in the local site, the entire folder will be automatically transferred to the remote site.

QUICKTIP

To upload an entire site to a remote host, select the root folder, then click the Put File(s) button. Sometimes you will need to move the files you want to upload to an intermediary folder before transferring them to the remote site.

If you are developing or maintaining a Web site in a group environment, there might be times when you want to transfer or **download** files that other team members have created from the remote site to your local site. To do this, switch to Remote view,

FIGURE 14

FTP settings in the Site Definition for The Striped Umbrella dialog box

FIGURE 15

Files panel with Remote view selected

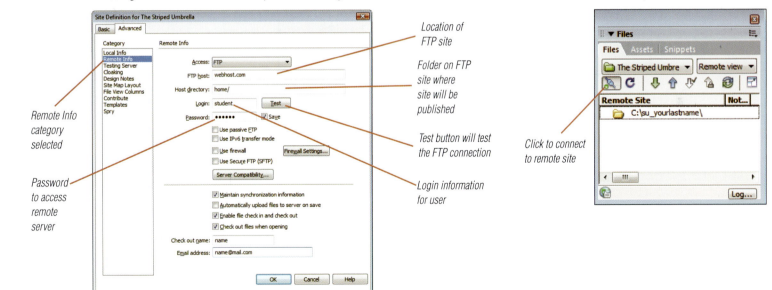

Remote Info category selected

Password to access remote server

Location of FTP site

Folder on FTP site where site will be published

Test button will test the FTP connection

Login information for user

Click to connect to remote site

select the files you want to download, then click the Get File(s) button on the Files panel toolbar.

Synchronizing Files

To keep a Web site up to date—especially one that contains several pages and involves several team members—you will need to update and replace files. Team members might make changes to pages on the local version of the site or make additions to the remote site. If many people are involved in maintaining a site, or if you are constantly making changes to the pages, ensuring that both the local and remote sites have the most up-to-date files could get confusing. Thankfully, you can use the Synchronize command to keep things straight. The Synchronize command instructs Dreamweaver to compare the dates of the saved files in both versions of the site, then transfers only the files that have changed. To synchronize files, use the Synchronize Files dialog box, as shown in Figure 16. You can synchronize an entire site or just selected files. You can also specify whether to upload newer files to the remote site, download newer files from the remote site, or both.

FIGURE 16

Synchronize Files dialog box

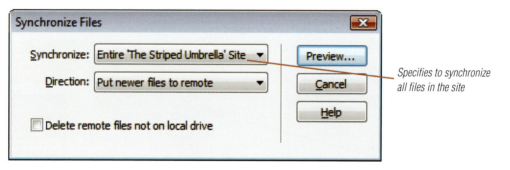

Specifies to synchronize all files in the site

Understanding Dreamweaver connection options for transferring files

The connection types with which you are probably the most familiar are FTP and Local/Network. Other connection types that you can use with Dreamweaver are VSS, WebDav, and RDS. **VSS** refers to Microsoft Visual SafeSource, and is used only with the Windows operating system with Microsoft Visual SafeSource Client version 6. **WebDav** stands for Web-based Distributed Authoring and Versioning. This type of connection is used with the WebDav protocol. An example would be a Web site residing on an Apache Web server. **RDS** stands for Remote Development Services, and is used with Web servers using Cold Fusion.

FIGURE 17

*FTP settings specified in the Site Definition
for The Striped Umbrella dialog box*

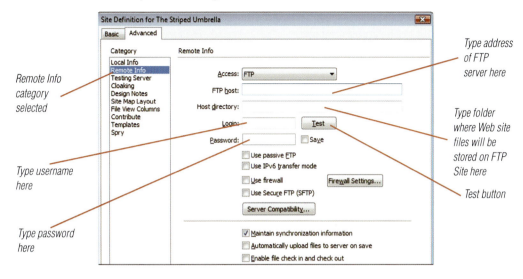

Remote Info
category
selected

Type username
here

Type password
here

Type address
of FTP
server here

Type folder
where Web site
files will be
stored on FTP
Site here

Test button

Set up Web server access on an FTP site

NOTE: Complete these steps only if you know you can store The Striped Umbrella files on an FTP site and you know the login and password information. If you do not have access to an FTP site, complete the exercise called Set up Web server access on a local or network folder on Page 6-18.

1. Click **Site** on the menu bar, then click **Manage Sites**.

2. Click **The Striped Umbrella** in the Manage Sites dialog box (if necessary), then click **Edit**.

3. Click the **Advanced tab**, click **Remote Info** in the Category list, click the **Access list arrow**, click **FTP**, then compare your screen to Figure 17.

4. Enter the FTP host, Host directory, Login, and Password information in the dialog box.

> TIP   You must have file and folder permissions to use FTP.

5. Click the **Test button** to test the connection to the remote site.

6. If the connection is successful, click **Done** to close the dialog box; if it is not successful, repeat Step 4.

7. Click **OK**, then click **Done** to close the Manage Sites dialog box.

You set up remote access information for The Striped Umbrella Web site using an FTP site folder.

Comparing two files for differences in content

There are situations where it would be helpful to be able to compare the contents of two files, such as a local file and the remote version of the same file; or an original file and the same file that has been saved with a different name. Once the two files are compared and differences are detected, you can merge the information in the files. A good time to compare files is before you upload them to a remote server to prevent accidentally writing over a file with more recent information. To compare files, you must first locate and install a third-party file comparison utility, or "dif" tool, such as FileMerge or BBEdit. (Dreamweaver does not have a file comparison tool included as part of the software. You will have to download one. If you are not familiar with these tools, find one using your favorite search engine.)

After installing the files comparison utility, use the Preferences command on the Edit menu, and then select the File Compare category. Next, browse to select the application to compare files. After you have set your Preferences, click the Compare with Remote command on the File menu to compare an open file with the remote version.

Set up Web server access on a local or network folder

NOTE: Complete these steps if you do not have the ability to post files to an FTP site and could not complete the previous objective.

1. Using Windows Explorer (Win) or Finder (Mac), create a new folder on your hard drive or on a shared drive named **su_yourlastname** (e.g., if your last name is Jones, name the folder **su_jones**.)

2. Switch back to Dreamweaver, open The Striped Umbrella Web site, click **Site** on the menu bar, then click **Manage Sites** to open the Manage Sites dialog box.

3. Click **The Striped Umbrella**, click **Edit** to open the Site Definition for The Striped Umbrella dialog box, click the **Advanced tab**, then click **Remote Info** in the Category list.

4. Click the **Access list arrow**, then click **Local/Network**.

5. Click the **Browse for File icon** 🗀 next to the Remote folder text box to open the Choose remote root folder for site The Striped Umbrella dialog box, navigate to the folder you created in Step 1, select the folder, click **Open**, then click **Select** (Win) or **Choose** (Mac).

6. Compare your screen to Figure 18, click **OK**, click **OK** in the message window about the site cache, then click **Done**.

You created a new folder and specified it as the remote location for The Striped Umbrella Web site, then set up remote access to a local or network folder.

FIGURE 18
Local/Network settings specified in the Site Definition for The Striped Umbrella dialog box

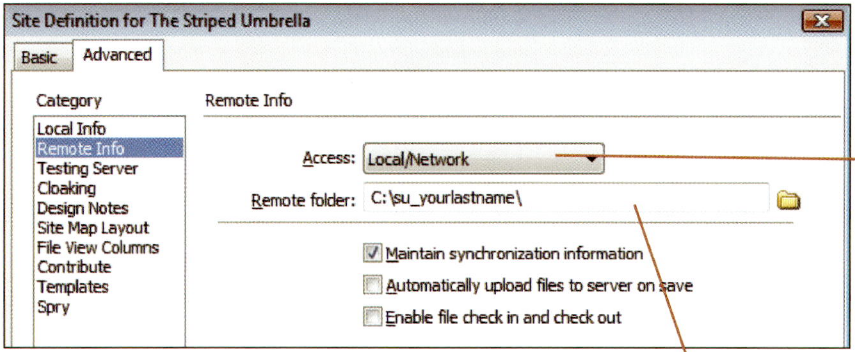

Local/Network setting selected

Local or network drive and folder where remote site will be published (your drive may differ and the folder name should end with your last name)

FIGURE 19
Connecting to the remote site

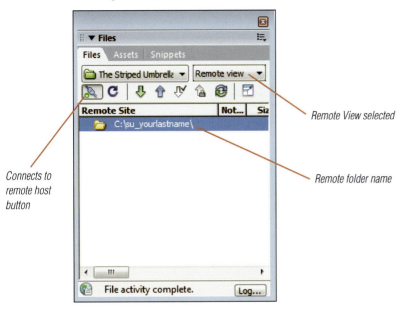

Remote View selected

Remote folder name

Connects to remote host button

View a Web site on a remote server

1. Click the **View list arrow** in the Files panel, then click **Remote view**, as shown in Figure 19.

   If you specified your remote access to a local or network folder, then the su_yourlastname folder will now appear in the Files panel. If your remote access is set to an FTP site, Dreamweaver will connect to the host server to see the remote access folder.

2. Click the **Expand to show local and remote sites button** to view both the Remote Site and Local Files panes. The su_yourlastname folder appears in the Remote Site portion of the Files panel.

   TIP   If you don't see your remote site files, click the Connects to remote host button or the Refresh button.

3. Click the **Collapse to show only local or remote site button** to return to Design view.

You used the Files panel to set the view for The Striped Umbrella site to Remote view. You then connected to the remote server to view the contents of the remote folder you specified.

Using a site usability test to test your site

Once you have at least a prototype of the Web site ready to evaluate, it is a good idea to conduct a site usability test. This is a process that involves asking unbiased people, who are not connected to the design process, to use and evaluate the site. A comprehensive usability test will include pre-test questions, participant tasks, a post-test interview, and a post-test survey. This will provide much-needed information as to how usable the site is to those unfamiliar with it. Typical questions include: "What are your overall impressions?"; "What do you like the best and the least about the site?"; and "How easy is it to navigate inside the site?" For more information, go to *www.w3.org* and search for "site usability test."

Upload files to a remote server

1. Click the **about_us.html file**, then click the **Put File(s) button** 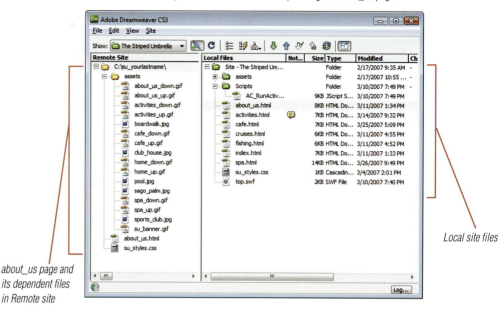 on the Files panel toolbar.

   The Dependent Files dialog box opens, asking if you want to include dependent files.

2. Click **Yes**.

   The about_us file and the other image files used in the about_us page are copied to the remote server. The Status dialog box appears and flashes the names of each file as they are uploaded.

3. Expand the assets folder (if necessary), then compare your screen to Figure 20.

   The remote site now contains the about_us page as well as several images, and the striped_umbrella external style sheet file, all of which are needed by the about_us page.

   TIP   You might need to expand the su_yourlastname folder in order to view the assets folder.

You used the Put File(s) button to upload the about_us file and all files that are dependent files of the about_us page.

FIGURE 20
Remote view of The Striped Umbrella Web site after uploading the about_us page

about_us page and its dependent files in Remote site

Local site files

Continuing to work while transferring files to a remote server

During the process of uploading files to a remote server, there are many Dreamweaver functions that you can continue to use while you wait. For example, you can create a new site, create a new page, edit a page, add files and folders, and run reports. However, there are some functions that you cannot use while transferring files, many of which involve accessing files on the remote server or using Check In/Check Out.

FIGURE 21
Synchronize Files dialog box

FIGURE 22
Files that need to be uploaded to the remote site

1. Click **Site** on the menu bar, click **Synchronize Sitewide** to open the Synchronize Files dialog box (Win) or click the **Options list arrow**, point to **Site**, then click **Synchronize** to open the Synchronize Files dialog box (Mac).

2. Click the **Synchronize list arrow**, then click **Entire 'The Striped Umbrella' Site**.

3. Click the **Direction list arrow**, click **Put newer files to remote** (if necessary), then compare your screen to Figure 21.

4. Click **Preview**.

   The Status dialog box might appear and flash the names of all the files from the local version of the site that need to be uploaded to the remote site. The dialog box shown in Figure 22 then opens and lists all the files that need to be uploaded to the remote site.

5. Click **OK**.

   All the files from the local The Striped Umbrella Web site are now contained in the remote version of the site. The dialog box changes to show the files that were uploaded.

   TIP   If you want to keep a record of your synchronizations, click Save Log, specify a location and name for the synchronization log, then click Save.

6. Refresh the Files panel to place the files and folders in alphabetical order.

You synchronized The Striped Umbrella Web site files to copy all remaining files from the local root folder to the remote root folder.

CHECK FILES
OUT AND IN

What You'll Do

In this lesson, you will use the Site Definition dialog box to enable the Check In/Check Out feature. You will then check out the cafe page, make a change to it, and then check it back in.

Managing a Web Site with a Team

When you work on a large Web site, chances are that many people will be involved in keeping the site up to date. Different individuals will need to make changes or additions to different pages of the site by adding or deleting content, changing graphics, updating information, and so on. If everyone had access to the pages at the same time, problems could arise. For instance, what if you and another team member both made edits to the same page at the same time? If you post your edited version of the file to the site after the other team member posts his edited version of the same file, the file that you upload will overwrite his version and none of his changes will be incorporated.

Not good! Fortunately, you can avoid this scenario by using Dreamweaver's collaboration tools.

Checking Out and Checking In Files

Checking in and out files is similar to checking in and out library books or video/DVD rentals. No one else can read the same copy that you have checked out. Using Dreamweaver's Check In/Check Out feature ensures that team members can not overwrite each other's pages. When this feature is enabled, only one person can work on a file at a time. To check out a file, click the file you want to work on in the Files panel, and then click the Check Out File(s) button on the Files panel toolbar. Files that you have checked out are marked with green check marks in the Files panel. Files that have been checked in are marked with padlock icons.

After you finish editing a checked-out file, you need to save and close the file, and then click the Check In button to check the file back in and make it available to other users.

When a file is checked in, you cannot make edits to it unless you check it out again. Figure 23 shows the Check Out File(s) and Check In buttons on the Files panel toolbar.

Enabling the Check In/Check Out Feature

To use the Check In /Check Out feature with a team of people, you must first enable it. To turn on this feature, check the Enable file check in and check out check box in the Remote Info settings of the Site Definition dialog box.

FIGURE 23

Check Out File(s) and Check in buttons on the Files Panel toolbar

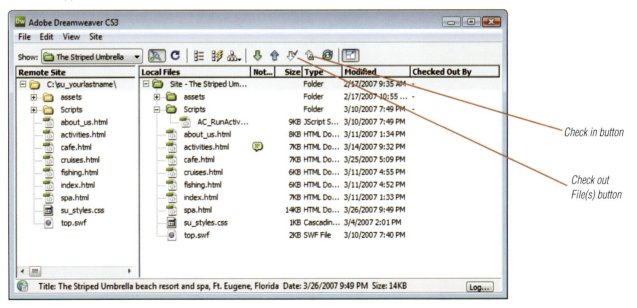

Check in button

Check out File(s) button

Enable the Check In/Check Out feature

1. Verify that the Site panel is in expanded view, click **Site** on the menu bar, click **Manage Sites** to open the Manage Sites dialog box, click **The Striped Umbrella** in the list, then click **Edit** to open the Site Definition for The Striped Umbrella dialog box.

2. Click **Remote Info** in the Category list, then click the **Enable file check in and check out check box** to select it.

3. Check the **Check out files when opening check box** to select it (if necessary).

4. Type **your name** using lowercase letters and no spaces in the Check out name text box.

5. Type your **e-mail address** in the Email address text box.

6. Compare your screen to Figure 24, click **OK** to close the Site Definition for The Striped Umbrella dialog box, then click **Done** to close the Manage Sites dialog box.

You used the Site Definition for The Striped Umbrella dialog box to enable the Check In/Check Out feature to let site collaborators know when you are working with a file in the site.

Check out a file

1. Click the **cafe page** in the Local Files list in the Files panel to select it.

(continued)

FIGURE 24
Enabling the Check In/Check Out feature

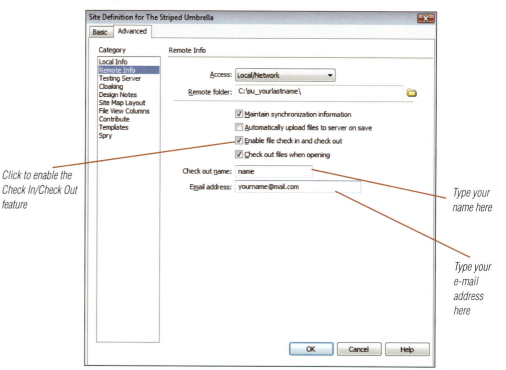

Click to enable the Check In/Check Out feature

Type your name here

Type your e-mail address here

FIGURE 25
Files panel in Local view after checking out cafe page

Check mark indicates file is checked out

Dependent file

Date: 2/17/2007 9:35 AM   Log...

Padlock icon indicates file is read-only and cannot be edited unless it is checked out

Dependent file is also locked

FIGURE 26
Files panel after checking in cafe page

2. Click the **Check Out File(s) button** on the Files panel toolbar.

   The Dependent Files dialog box appears, asking if you want to include all files that are needed for the cafe page.

3. Click **Yes**, click another file in the Files panel to deselect the cafe page, collapse the Files panel, switch to Local view, then compare your screen to Figure 25.

   The cafe file has a check mark next to it indicating you have checked it out. The dependent file has a padlock icon.

   TIP   If a dialog box appears asking "Do you wish to overwrite your local copy of cafe.html?", click Yes.

You checked out the cafe page so that no one else can use it.

Check in a file

1. Open the cafe page, change the closing hour for the The Cabana in the nested table to **7:00 p.m.**, then save your changes.

2. Close the cafe page, then click the **cafe page** in the Files panel to select it.

3. Click the **Check In button** on the Files panel toolbar.

   The Dependent Files dialog box opens, asking if you want to include dependent files.

4. Click **Yes**, click another file in the Files panel to deselect the cafe page, then compare your screen to Figure 26.

   A padlock icon appears instead of a green check mark next to the cafe page on the Files panel.

You made a content change on the cafe page, then checked in the cafe page, making it available for others to check it out.

CLOAK
FILES

What You'll Do

 In this lesson, you will cloak the assets folder so that it is excluded from various operations, such as the Put, Get, Check In, and Check Out commands. You will also use the Site Definition dialog box to cloak all .gif files in the site.

Understanding Cloaking Files

There may be times when you want to exclude a particular file or files from being uploaded to a server. For instance, suppose you have a page that is not quite finished and needs more work before it is ready to be viewed by others. You can exclude such files by **cloaking** them, which marks them for exclusion from several commands, including Put, Get, Synchronize, Check In, and Check Out. Cloaked files are also excluded from site-wide operations, such as checking for links or updating a template or library item. You can cloak a folder or specify a type of file to cloak throughout the site.

QUICKTIP

By default, the cloaking feature is enabled. However, if for some reason it is not turned on, open the Site Definition dialog box, click the Advanced tab, click the Cloaking category, then click the Enable cloaking check box.

Cloaking a Folder

There may be times when you want to cloak an entire folder. For instance, if you are not concerned with replacing outdated image files, you might want to cloak the assets folder of a Web site to save time when synchronizing files. To cloak a folder, select the folder, click the Options list arrow in the Files panel, point to site, point to Cloaking, and then click Cloak. The folder you cloaked and all the files it contains appear with red slashes across them, as shown in Figure 27. To uncloak a folder, click the Options list arrow in the Files panel, point to Site, point to Cloaking, and then click Uncloak.

QUICKTIP

To uncloak all files in a site, click the Files panel Options list arrow, point to Site, point to Cloaking, then click Uncloak All.

Cloaking Selected File Types

There may be times when you want to cloak a particular type of file, such as a

.swf file. To cloak a particular file type, open the Site Definition dialog box, click the Cloaking category, click the Cloak files ending with check box, and then type a file extension in the text box below the check box. All files throughout the site that have the specified file extension will be cloaked.

FIGURE 27

Cloaked assets folder in the Files panel

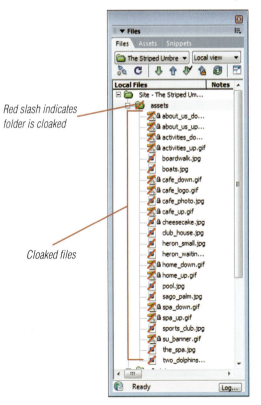

Red slash indicates folder is cloaked

Cloaked files

Cloak and uncloak a folder

1. Verify that Local view is displayed in the Files panel, click **Site** on the menu bar, then click **Manage Sites**.

2. Click **The Striped Umbrella** (if necessary), click **Edit** to open the Site Definition for The Striped Umbrella dialog box, click **Cloaking** in the Category list, verify that the Enable cloaking check box is checked, click **OK**, then click **Done**.

3. Click the **assets folder** in the Files panel, click the **Options list arrow** 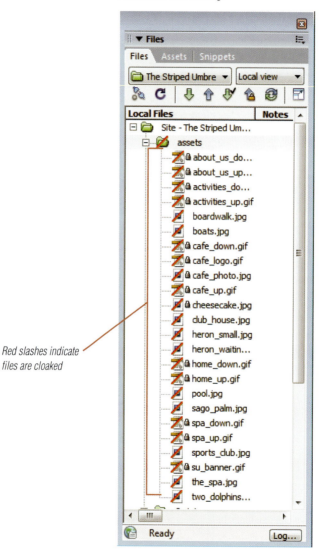, point to **Site**, point to **Cloaking**, click **Cloak**, expand the assets folder (if necessary), then compare your screen to Figure 28.

   A red slash now appears on top of the assets folder in the Files panel, indicating that all files in the assets folder are cloaked and will be excluded from putting, getting, checking in, checking out, and many other operations.

   > TIP   You can also cloak a folder by right-clicking (Win) or [control]-clicking (Mac) the folder, pointing to Cloaking, then clicking Cloak.

4. Right-click (Win) or [control]-click (Mac) the **assets folder**, point to **Cloaking**, then click **Uncloak**.

   The assets folder and all the files it contains no longer appear with red slashes across them, indicating they are no longer cloaked.

You cloaked the assets folder so that this folder and all the files it contains would be excluded from many operations, including uploading and downloading files. You then uncloaked the assets folder.

FIGURE 28
Assets folder after cloaking

Red slashes indicate files are cloaked

Managing a Web Server and Files

FIGURE 29
Specifying a file type to cloak

Site Definition for The Striped Umbrella

Basic | Advanced

Category | Cloaking

Local Info
Remote Info
Testing Server
Cloaking
Design Notes
Site Map Layout
File View Columns
Contribute
Templates
Spry

Options: ☑ Enable cloaking

Cloaking lets you exclude specified folders and files from all site operations.

☑ Cloak files ending with:

.gif

FIGURE 30
Assets folder in Files panel after cloaking .gif files

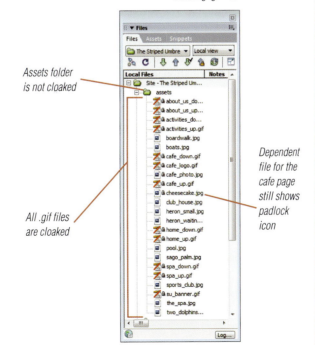

Assets folder
is not cloaked

All .gif files
are cloaked

Dependent
file for the
cafe page
still shows
padlock
icon

1. Right-click (Win) or [control]-click (Mac) the **assets folder** in the Files panel, point to **Cloaking**, then click **Settings** to open the Site Definition for The Striped Umbrella dialog box with the Cloaking category selected.

2. Click the **Cloak files ending with check box**, select the text in the text box that appears, type **.gif** in the text box, then compare your screen to Figure 29.

3. Click **OK**.

   A dialog box opens, indicating that the site cache will be re-created.

4. Click **OK**, open the assets folder (if necessary), then compare your screen to Figure 30.

   All of the .gif files in the assets folder appear with red slashes across them, indicating that they are cloaked. Notice that the assets folder is not cloaked.

You cloaked all the .gif files in The Striped Umbrella Web site.

IMPORT AND EXPORT
A SITE DEFINITION

What You'll Do

In this lesson, you will export the site definition file for The Striped Umbrella Web site. You will then import The Striped Umbrella Web site.

Exporting a Site Definition

When you work on a Web site for a long time, it's likely that at some point you will want to move it to another machine or share it with other collaborators who will help you maintain it. The site definition for a Web site contains important information about the site, including its URL, preferences that you've specified, and other secure information, such as login and password information. You can use the Export command to export the site definition file to another location. To do this, click Site on the menu bar, click Manage Sites, click the site you want to export, and then click Export. Because the site definition file contains password information that you will want to keep secret from other site users, you should never save the site definition file in the Web site. Instead, save it in an external file.

Importing a Site Definition

If you want to set up another user with a copy of your Web site, you can import the site definition file. To do this, click Import in the Manage Sites dialog box to open the Import Site dialog box, navigate to the .ste file you want to import, then click Open.

FIGURE 31

Saving The Striped Umbrella.ste file in the su_site_definition folder

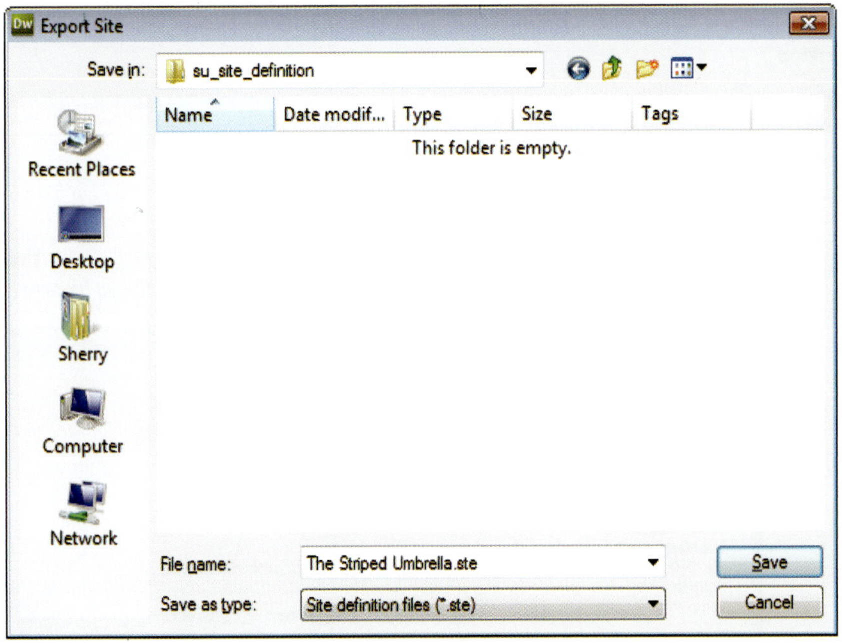

Export a site definition

1. Use Windows Explorer (Win) or Finder (Mac) to create a new folder on your hard drive or external drive named **su_site_definition**.

2. Switch back to Dreamweaver, click **Site** on the menu bar, click **Manage Sites**, click **The Striped Umbrella**, then click **Export** to open the Export Site dialog box.

3. Navigate to and select the **su_site_definition folder** that you created in Step 1, as shown in Figure 31, click **Save**, then click **Done**.

You used the Export command to create the site definition file and saved it in the su_site_definition folder.

Import a site definition

1. Click **Site** on the menu bar, click **Manage Sites**, click **The Striped Umbrella**, then click **Import** to open the Import Site dialog box.

2. Navigate to the su_site_definition folder, compare your screen to Figure 32, select **The Striped Umbrella.ste**, then click **Open**.

   A dialog box opens and says that a site named The Striped Umbrella already exists. It will name the imported site The Striped Umbrella 2 so that it has a different name.

3. Click **OK**.

4. Click **The Striped Umbrella 2** (if necessary), click **Edit**, then compare your screen to Figure 33.

   The settings show that the The Striped Umbrella 2 site has the same root folder and default images folder as the The Striped Umbrella site. Both of these settings are specified in the The Striped Umbrella.ste file that you imported. Importing a site in this way makes it possible for multiple users with different computers to work on the same site.

   TIP Make sure you know who is responsible for which files to keep from overwriting the wrong files when they are published. The Synchronize Files and Check In/Check Out features are good procedures to use with multiple designers.

5. Click **OK**, click **OK** to close the warning message, then click **Done**.

   TIP If a dialog box opens warning that the root folder chosen is the same as the folder for the site "The Striped Umbrella," click OK.

You imported The Striped Umbrella.ste file and created a new site, The Striped Umbrella 2.

FIGURE 32
Import Site dialog box

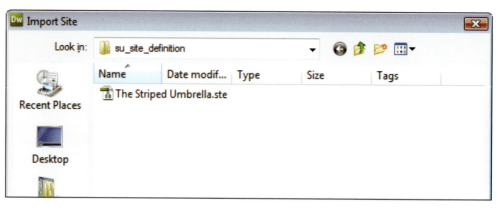

FIGURE 33
Site Definition for the The Striped Umbrella 2 dialog box

Name of
imported site

FIGURE 34
Viewing The Striped Umbrella 2 Web site files

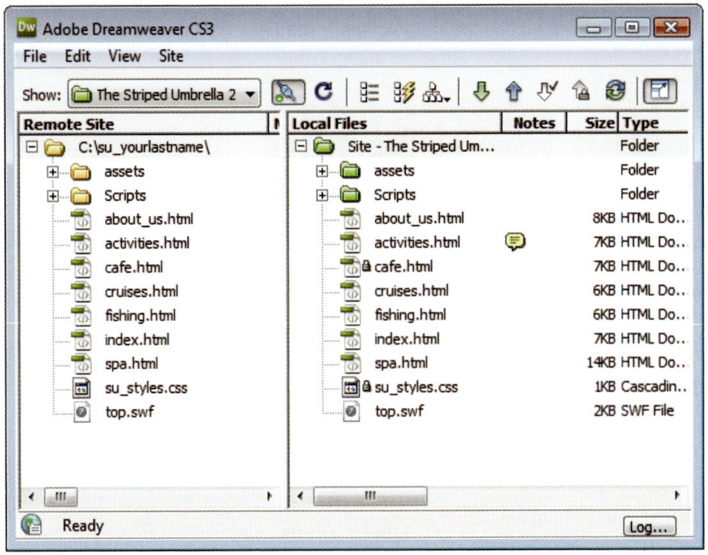

Power User Shortcuts

To do this:	Use this shortcut:
Validate Markup	[Shift][F6]
Get	[Ctrl][Shift][D] (Win) or ⌘[Shift][D] (Mac)
Check Out	[Ctrl][Alt][Shift][D] (Win) or ⌘[option][Shift][D] (Mac)
Put	[Ctrl][Shift][U] (Win) or ⌘[Shift][U] (Mac)
Check In	[Ctrl][Alt][Shift][U] (Win) or ⌘[option][U] (Mac)
Check Links	[Shift][F8]
Check Links Sitewide	[Ctrl][F8] (Win) or ⌘[F8] (Mac)

View the imported site

1. Click the **Expand to show local and remote sites button** on the Files panel toolbar to expand the Files panel.

2. Expand the Site root folder to view the contents (if necessary).

3. Click the **Refresh button** to view the files in the Remote Site pane.

   As shown in Figure 34, the site looks identical to the original The Striped Umbrella site, except the name has been changed to The Striped Umbrella 2.

   TIP   If you don't see your remote site files, click the Connects to remote host button.

4. Click the **Collapse to show only local or remote site button** to collapse the Files panel.

5. Click **Site** on the menu bar, click **Manage Sites**, click **Remove**, click **Yes** to clear the warning dialog box, then click **Done** to delete The Striped Umbrella 2 Web site.

You viewed the expanded Files panel for The Striped Umbrella 2 Web site and then deleted The Striped Umbrella 2 Web site.

EVALUATE WEB CONTENT FOR
LEGAL USE

What You'll Do

In this lesson, you will examine copyright issues in the context of using content gathered from sources such as the Internet.

Can You Use Downloaded Media?

The Internet has made it possible to locate compelling and media-rich content to use in Web sites. A person who has learned to craft searches can locate a multitude of interesting material, such as graphics, animations, sounds, and text. Just because you can find it easily does not mean that you can use it however you want or under any circumstance. Learning about copyright law can help you decide whether or how to use content created and published by someone other than yourself.

Understanding Intellectual Property

Intellectual property is a product resulting from human creativity. It can include inventions, movies, songs, designs, clothing, and so on.

Understanding Copyright Law

The purpose of copyright law is to promote progress in society, not expressly to protect the rights of copyright owners. However, the vast majority of work you might want to download is protected by either copyright or trademark law.

Copyright protects the particular and tangible *expression* of an idea, not the idea itself. If you wrote a story using the idea about aliens crashing in Roswell, New Mexico, no one could copy or use your story without permission. However, anyone could write a story using a similar plot or characters—the idea of aliens crashing in Roswell is not copyright-protected. Copyright attaches to a work as soon as you create it; you do not have to register it with the U.S. Copyright Office.

Trademark protects an image, word, slogan, symbol, or design used to identify goods or services. For example, the Nike swoosh, Disney characters, or the shape of a classic Coca-Cola bottle are works protected by trademark.

What Exactly Does the Copyright Owner Own?

The Copyright Act of 1976 provided the copyright owner with a "bundle" of six rights, consisting of:

1) reproduction (including downloading)
2) creation of **derivative works** (for example, a movie version of a book)
3) distribution to the public
4) public performance
5) public display
6) public performance by digital audio transmission of sound recordings.

By default, only a copyright holder can create a derivative work of his or her original by transforming or adapting it. For example, the film *Hairspray* has gone from movie to musical play back to movie musical, all under the creative guidance of its writer, John Waters.

Understanding Fair Use

The law builds in limitations to copyright protection. One limitation to copyright is **fair use**. Fair use allows limited use of copyright-protected work. For example, you could excerpt short passages of a film or song for a class project or parody a television show. Determining if fair use applies to a work depends on the *purpose* of its use, the *nature* of the copyrighted work, *how much* you want to copy, and the *effect* on the market or value of the work. However, there is no clear formula on what constitutes fair use. It is always decided on a case by case basis.

How Do I Use Work Properly?

Being a student doesn't mean you can use any amount of any work for class. On the other hand, the very nature of education means you need to be able to use or reference different work in your studies. There are many situations that allow you to use protected work.

In addition to applying a fair use argument, you can obtain permission, pay a fee, use work that does not have copyright protection, or use work that has a flexible copyright license, where the owner has given the public permission to use the work in certain ways. For more information about open-access licensing, visit *www.creativecommons.org*. Work that is no longer protected by copyright is in the **public domain**; anyone can use it however they wish for any purpose. In general, the photos and other media on federal government Web sites are in the public domain.

For example, say you need to create a presentation about volcanoes for a class. Because your topic is about volcanoes, it makes sense that you would insert photos or video about volcanoes, quote from articles or books, and of course give proper credit for all your sources.

However, if you were designing a Web page for a client and wanted to insert a volcano photo that fit the site's design, you couldn't just insert your favorite volcano photo. In this case, you would need to obtain permission or pay a fee to use it, find a photo that is in the public domain, or find a photo with a Creative Commons license that permits commercial use.

Understanding Licensing Agreements

Before you decide whether to use a work you find on a Web site, such as an image or a sound file, you must decide whether you can comply with its licensing agreement. A **licensing agreement** is the permission given by a copyright holder that conveys the right to use the copyright holder's work under certain conditions.

Web sites have rules that govern how a user may use its text and media, known as **terms of use**. Figures 35 and 36 are great examples of clear terms of use for the Library of Congress Web site.

A site's terms of use do not override your right to apply fair use. Also, someone cannot compile public domain images in a Web site and then claim they own them or dictate how the images can be used. Conversely, someone can erroneously state in their terms of use that you can use work on the site freely, but they may not know the work's copyright status. The burden is on you to research the veracity of anyone claiming you can use work.

Obtaining Permission or a License

The **permissions process** is specific to what you want to use (text, photographs, music, trademarks, merchandise, and so on) and how you want to use it (school term paper, personal Web site, fabric pattern). And, getting permission from an amateur photographer whose work you found on a photo-sharing Web site may prove to be quite different from getting permission from a large corporation. How you want to use the work will determine the level and scope of permissions you need to secure. The fundamentals, however, are the same. Your request should contain the following:

- Your full name, address, and complete contact information.
- A specific description of your intended use. Sometimes including a sketch, storyboard, or link to a Web site is helpful.
- A signature line for the copyright holder.
- A target date when you would like the copyright holder to respond. This can be important if you're working under deadline.

Posting a Copyright Notice

The familiar © symbol or "Copyright" is no longer required to indicate copyright, nor does it automatically register your work, but it does serve a useful purpose. When you post or publish it, you are stating clearly to those who may not know anything about copyright law that this work is claimed by you and is not in the public domain. Your case is made even stronger if someone violates your copyright and your notice is clearly visible. A violator can never

FIGURE 35

The Library of Congress home page

Link to legal information regarding the use of content on the Web site

Library of Congress Web site: www.loc.gov

claim ignorance of the law as an excuse for infringing. Common notification styles include:

Copyright 2010
Thomson Course Technology
or © **2010 Thomson Course Technology**
Giving proper attribution for text excerpts is a must; giving attribution for media is excellent practice, but is never a substitute for applying a fair use argument, buying a license, or simply getting permission.

References

Waxer, Barbara M., and Baum, Marsha L. 2006. **Internet Surf and Turf - The Essential Guide to Copyright**, **Fair Use**, **and Finding Media**. Boston: Thomson Course Technology.

You must provide proper citation for the Web materials you incorporate into your own material. This expectation applies even to unsigned material and material that does not display the copyright symbol (©). Moreover, the expectation applies just as certainly to ideas you summarize or paraphrase as to words you quote verbatim.

Here's a list of the elements that make up an APA-style citation of Web-based resources:

- Author's name (if known)
- Date of publication or last revision (if known), in parentheses
- Title of document
- Title of complete work or Web site (if applicable), underlined
- URL, in angled brackets
- Date of access, in parentheses

Here are a few examples as they might appear on a references page in your paper:

References

Citation Guides. (1996). UMUC Information and Library Services. **www.umuc.edu/library/citation guides.html** (19 Feb. 2004).

Harnack, A. and Kleppinger, E. (1996). Beyond the MLA handbook. **http://english.ttu.edu/kairos/1.2/inbox/mla_archive.html** (19 Feb. 2004).

Walker, J. R. and Taylor, T. (1998). *The Columbia Guide to Online Style*. **www.columbia.edu/cu/cup/cgos/idx_basic.html** (19 Feb. 2004).

FIGURE 36
Library of Congress Web site Legal page

Library of Congress Web site: www.loc.gov

About Copyright and the Collections

Whenever possible, the Library of Congress provides factual information about copyright owners and related matters in the catalog records, finding aids and other texts that accompany collections. As a publicly supported institution, the Library generally does not own rights in its collections. Therefore, it does not charge permission fees for use of such material and generally does not grant or deny permission to publish or otherwise distribute material in its collections. Permission and possible fees may be required from the copyright owner independently of the Library. It is the researcher's obligation to determine and satisfy copyright or other use restrictions when publishing or otherwise distributing materials found in the Library's collections. Transmission or reproduction of protected items beyond that allowed by fair use requires the written permission of the copyright owners. Researchers must make their own assessments of rights in light of their intended use.

The Library of Congress wants to hear from any copyright owners who are not properly identified on this Web site so that we may make the necessary corrections.

Perform Web site maintenance.

1. Open the blooms & bulbs Web site, then re-create the site cache.
2. Use the Link Checker panel to check for broken links, then fix any broken links that appear.
3. Use the Link Checker to check for orphaned files. If any orphaned files appear in the report, take steps to link them to appropriate pages or remove them.
4. Use the Assets panel to check for Non-Websafe colors.
5. Run an Untitled Documents report for the entire local site. If the report lists any pages that have no titles, add page titles to the untitled pages. Run the report again to verify that all pages have page titles.
6. Run a report to look for missing alternate text. Add alternate text to any graphics that need it, then run the report again to verify that all images contain alternate text.

7. Enable the Design Notes preference and add a design note to the classes page as follows: **Shoot a video of the hanging baskets class to add to the page**. Add the status **needs attention** and check the **Show when file is opened** option.

Publish a Web site and transfer files.

1. Set up Web server access for the blooms & bulbs Web site on an FTP server or a local/network server (whichever is available to you) using appropriate settings.
2. View the blooms & bulbs remote site in the Files panel.
3. Upload the iris.jpg file to the remote site, then view the remote site.
4. Synchronize all files in the blooms & bulbs Web site, so that all files from the local site are uploaded to the remote site.

Check files out and in.

1. Enable the Check In/Check Out feature.
2. Check out the plants page and all dependent pages.
3. Open the plants page, change the heading style of "Drop by to see our Featured Spring Plants" to **seasons**, center the heading, then save your changes. (*Hint*: You will have to attach the style sheet to the page.)
4. Check in the plants page and all dependent files.

Cloak files.

1. Verify that cloaking is enabled in the blooms & bulbs Web site.
2. Cloak the assets folder, then uncloak it.
3. Cloak all the .jpg files in the blooms & bulbs Web site.

Import and export a site definition.

1. Create a new folder named **blooms_site_ definition** on your hard drive or external drive.
2. Export the blooms & bulbs site definition to the blooms_site_definition folder.

3. Import the blooms & bulbs site definition to create a new site called **blooms & bulbs 2**.
4. Make sure that all files from the blooms & bulbs Web site appear in the Files panel for the imported site, then compare your screen to Figure 37.
5. Remove the blooms & bulbs 2 site.

FIGURE 37
Completed Skills Review

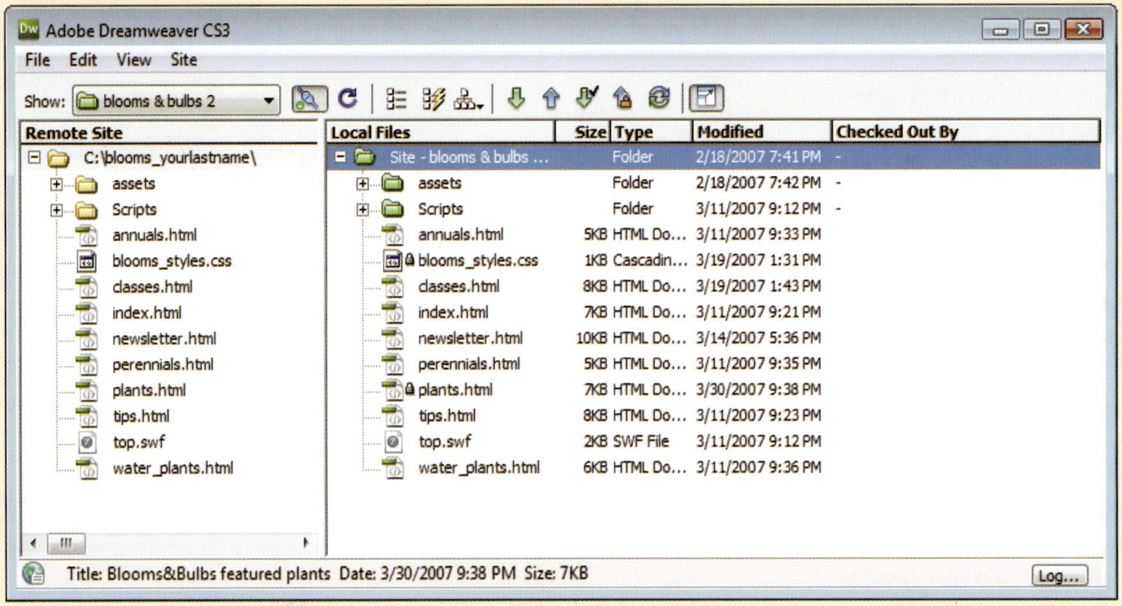

In this Project Builder, you will publish the TripSmart Web site that you have developed throughout this book to a remote server or local/network folder. Mike Andrew has provided the password and login information to publish the site on a remote server. You will first run several reports on the site, specify the remote settings for the site, upload files to the remote site, check files out and in, and cloak files. Finally, you will export and import the site definition.

1. Use the TripSmart Web site that you began in Project Builder 1 in Chapter 1 and developed in previous chapters.

2. Use the Link Checker panel to check for broken links, then fix any broken links that appear.

3. Use the Link Checker to check for orphaned files. If any orphaned files appear in the report, take steps to link them to appropriate pages or remove them.

4. Use the Assets panel to check for non-Websafe colors.

5. Run an Untitled Documents report for the entire local site. If the report lists any pages that lack titles, add page titles to the untitled pages. Run the report again to verify that all pages have page titles.

6. Run a report to look for missing alternate text. Add alternate text to any graphics that

need it, then run the report again to verify that all images contain alternate text.

7. Enable the Design Notes preference, if necessary, and add a design note to the newsletter page as follows: **Add a short video demonstrating how to pack clothing wrinkle-free in a suitcase**. Add the status **needs attention** and check the **Show when file is opened** option.

8. If you did not do so in Project Builder 1 in Chapter 1, use the Site Definition dialog box to set up Web server access for a remote site using either an FTP site or a local or network folder.

9. Upload the index page and all dependent files to the remote site.

10. View the remote site to make sure that all files uploaded correctly.

11. Synchronize the files so that all other files on the local TripSmart site are uploaded to the remote site.

12. Enable the Check In/Check Out feature.

13. Check out the index page and all dependent files.

14. Open the index page, close the index page, then check in the index page and all dependent pages.

15. Cloak all .jpg files in the Web site.

16. Export the site definition to a new folder named **tripsmart_site_definition**.

17. Import the **TripSmart.ste** file to create a new site named TripSmart 2.

18. Expand the assets folder in the Files panel (if necessary), then compare your screen to Figure 38.

19. Remove the TripSmart 2 site.

FIGURE 38

Sample Project Builder 1

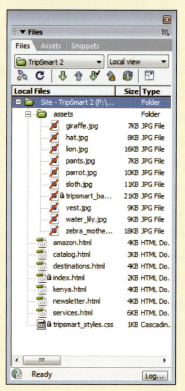

In this Project Builder, you will finish your work on the Carolyne's Creations Web site. You are ready to publish the Web site to a remote server and transfer all the files from the local site to the remote site. First, you will run several reports to make sure the Web site is in good shape. Next, you will enable the Check In/Check Out feature so that other staff members may collaborate on the site. Finally, you will export and import the site definition file.

1. Use the Carolyne's Creations Web site that you began in Project Builder 1 in Chapter 1 and developed in previous chapters.
2. If you did not do so in Project Builder 2 in Chapter 1, use the Site Definition dialog box to set up Web server access for a remote site using either an FTP site or a local or network folder.
3. Run reports for broken links and orphaned files, correcting any errors that you find. The cc_banner.jpg is no longer needed, so delete the file.
4. Run reports for untitled documents and missing alt text, correcting any errors that you find.
5. Check for non-Websafe colors.
6. Upload the classes.html page and all dependent files to the remote site.

7. View the remote site to make sure that all files uploaded correctly.
8. Synchronize the files so that all other files on the local Carolyne's Creations site are uploaded to the remote site.
9. Enable the Check In/Check Out feature.
10. Check out the classes page and all its dependent files.
11. Open the classes page, then change the price of the adult class to **$45.00**.
12. Save your changes, close the page, then check in the classes page and all dependent pages.
13. Export the site definition to a new folder named **cc_site_definition**.

14. Import the Carolyne's Creations.ste file to create a new site named Carolyne's Creations 2.
15. Expand the root folder in the Files panel (if necessary), compare your screen to Figure 39, then remove the Carolyne's Creations2 site.

FIGURE 39
Completed Project Builder 2

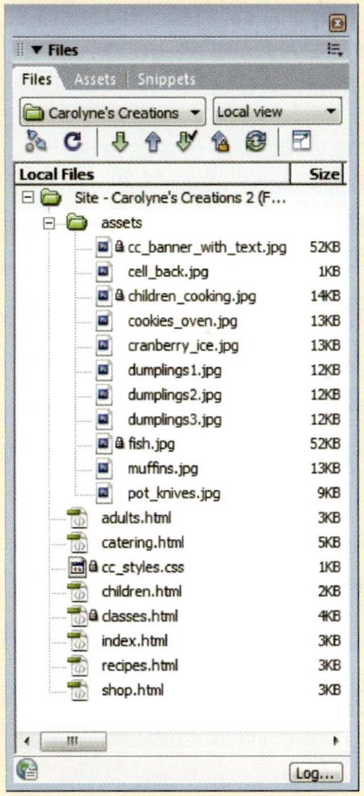

Throughout this book you have used Dreamweaver to create and develop several Web sites that contain different elements, many of which are found in popular commercial Web sites. For instance, Figure 40 shows the National Park Service Web site, which contains photos and information on all the national parks in the United States. This Web site contains many types of interactive elements, such as image maps, Flash content, and tables—all of which you learned to create in this book.

1. Connect to the Internet, then go to the National Park Service Web site at *www.nps.gov*.
2. Spend some time exploring the pages of this site to familiarize yourself with its elements.
3. Type a list of all the elements in this Web site that you have learned how to create in this book. After each item, write a short description of where and how the element is used in the site.
4. Print the home page and one or two other pages that contain some of the elements you described and attach it to your list.

FIGURE 40
Design Project

National Park Service Web site: www.nps.gov

In this project, you will finish your work on the Web site that you created and developed throughout this book.

You will publish your site to a remote server or local or network folder.

1. Before you begin the process of publishing your Web site to a remote server, make sure that it is ready for public viewing. Use Figure 41 to assist you in making sure your Web site is complete. If you find problems, make the necessary changes to finalize the site.

2. Decide where to publish your site. The folder where you will publish your site can be either an FTP site or a local/network folder. If you are publishing to an FTP site, be sure to write down all the information you will need to publish to the site, including the URL of the FTP host, the directory on the FTP server where you will publish your site's root folder, and the login and password information.

3. Use the Site Definition dialog box to specify the remote settings for the site using the information that was decided upon in Step 2.

4. Transfer one of the pages and its dependent files to the remote site, then view the remote site to make sure the appropriate files were transferred.

5. Synchronize the files so that all the remaining local pages and dependent files are uploaded to the remote site.

6. Enable the Check In/Check Out feature.

7. Check out one of the pages. Open the checked-out page, make a change to it, save the change, close the page, then check the page back in.

8. Cloak a particular file type.

9. Export the site definition for the site to a new folder on your hard drive or on an external drive.

10. Import the site to create a new version of the site.

11. Close the imported site, save and close all open pages (if necessary), then exit Dreamweaver.

FIGURE 41
Portfolio Project check list

Web Site Checklist
1. Are you satisfied with the content and appearance of every page?
2. Are all paths for all links and images correct?
3. Does each page have a title?
4. Do all images appear?
5. Are all colors Websafe?
6. Do all images have appropriate alternate text?
7. Have you eliminated any orphaned files?
8. Have you deleted any unnecessary files?
9. Have you viewed all pages using at least two different browsers?
10. Does the home page have keywords and a description?

GETTING STARTED WITH
ADOBE FLASH CS3

1. Understand the Adobe Flash CS3 workspace

2. Open a document and play a movie

3. Create and save a movie

4. Work with the Timeline

5. Distribute an Adobe Flash movie

6. Plan an application or a Web site

GETTING STARTED WITH
ADOBE FLASH CS3

Introduction

Adobe Flash CS3 Professional is a development tool that allows you to create compelling interactive experiences, often by using animation. You can use Flash to create entire Web sites, including e-commerce, entertainment, education, and personal use sites. In addition, Flash can be used to create applications, such as games and simulations, that can be delivered over the Web and on DVDs. They can even be scaled to be displayed on mobile devices, such as cell phones. While it is known as a tool for creating complex animations for the Web, Flash also has excellent drawing tools and tools for creating interactive controls, such as navigation buttons and menus. Furthermore, Flash provides the ability to incorporate sounds and video easily into an application.

Flash has become the standard for both professional and casual applications and Web developers. Flash is popular because the program is optimized for the Web. Web developers need to provide high-impact experiences for the user, to make sites come alive and turn them from static text and pictures to dynamic, interactive experiences. The problem has been that incorporating high-quality graphics and motion into a Web site can dramatically increase the download time and frustrate viewers as they wait for an image to appear or for an animation to play. Flash directly addresses this problem by allowing developers to use vector images, which reduce the size of graphic files. Vector images appeal to designers because they are scalable, which means they can be resized and reshaped without distortion. For example, you could easily have an object, such as an airplane, become smaller as it moves across the screen without having to create the plane in different sizes.

In addition, Flash provides for streaming content over the Internet. Instead of waiting for the entire contents of a Web page to load, the viewer sees a continuous display of images. Streaming allows the movie to start playing when the Web site is opened, and it continues as frames of the movie are delivered to the viewer's computer. Another reason Flash has become a standard is that it is made by Adobe. Adobe makes other programs, such as Dreamweaver, Fireworks, Photoshop, and Illustrator. Together these products can be used to create compelling interactive Web sites and applications. The programs are bundled in various ways in Creative Suite (CS3) products that provide common user interfaces and integration features.

Tools You'll Use

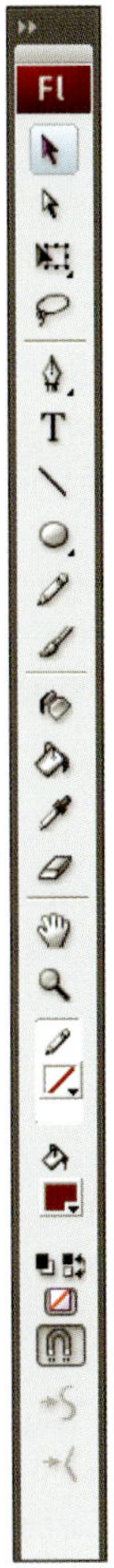

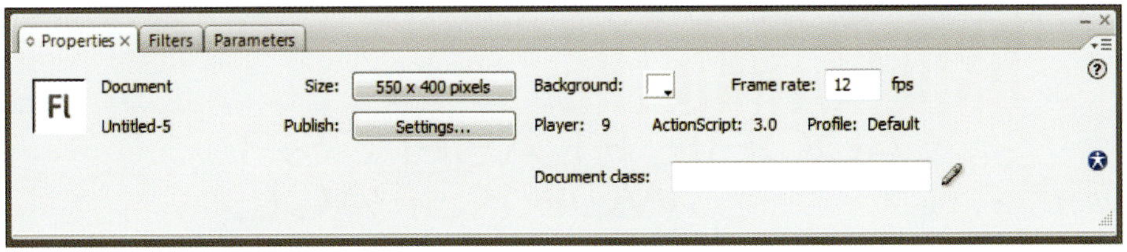

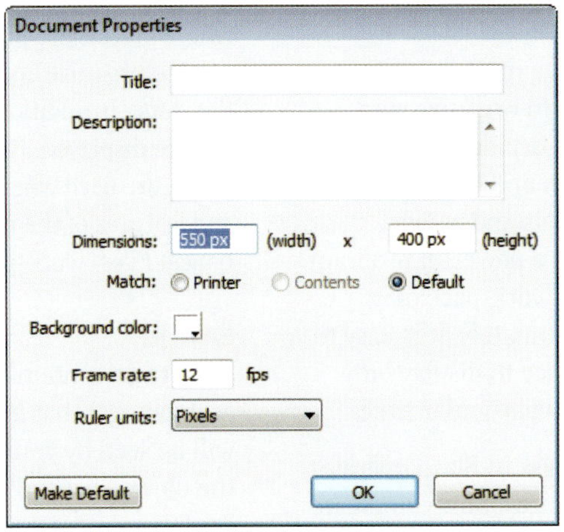

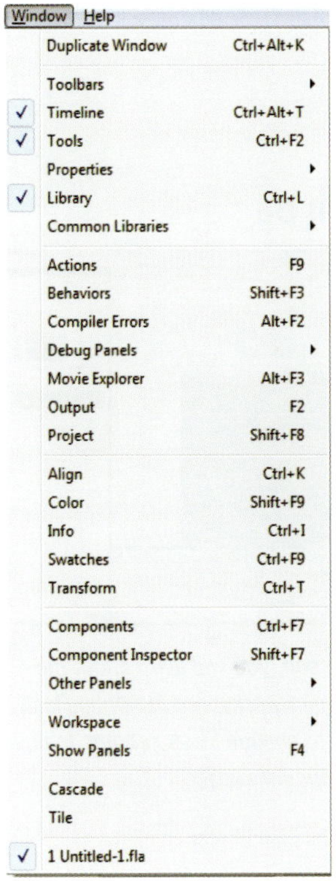

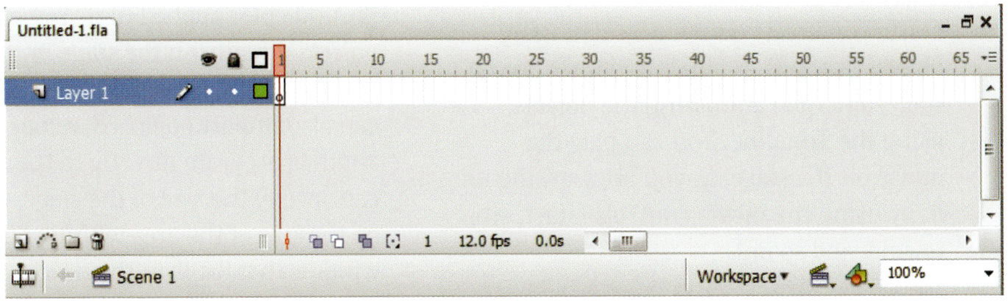

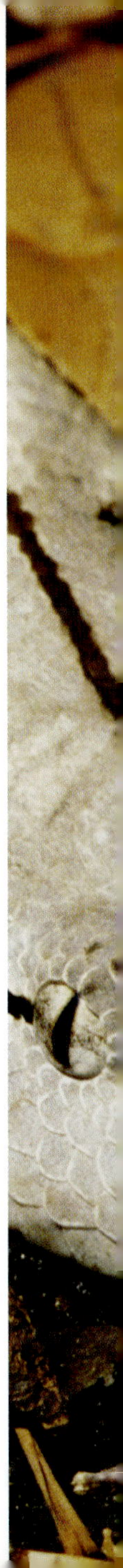

UNDERSTAND THE
ADOBE FLASH CS3
WORKSPACE

What You'll Do

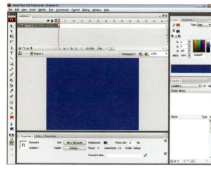

In this lesson, you will learn about the development workspace in Adobe Flash and how to change Flash settings to customize your workspace.

Organizing the Flash Workspace

As a designer, one of the most important things for you to do is to organize your workspace—that is, to decide what to have displayed on the screen and how to arrange the various tools and panels. Because **Flash** is such a powerful program with many tools, your workspace may become cluttered. Fortunately, it is easy to customize the workspace to display only the tools needed at any particular time.

The development process in Flash operates according to a movie metaphor: you create scenes on a stage; these scenes run in frames on a Timeline. As you work in Flash, you create a movie by arranging objects (such as graphics and text) on the stage, and then animating the objects using the Timeline. You can play the movie on the stage, as you are working on it, by using the movie controls (start, stop, rewind, and so on).

When you start Flash, three basic parts of the workspace are displayed: a menu bar that organizes commands within menus, a stage where objects are placed, and a Timeline used to organize and control the objects on the stage. In addition, one or more panels may be displayed. Panels, such as the Tools panel, are used when working with objects and features of the movie. Figure 1 shows a typical Flash workspace.

Stage

The **stage** contains all of the objects (such as drawings) that are part of the movie that will be seen by your viewers. It shows how the objects behave within the movie and how they interact with each other. You can resize the stage and change the background color applied to it. You can draw objects directly on the stage or drag them from the Library panel to the stage. You can also import objects developed in another program directly to the stage. You can specify the size of the stage, which will be the size of the area within your browser window that displays the movie. The gray area surrounding the stage is the Pasteboard. You can place objects on the

Pasteboard as you are creating a movie. However, neither the Pasteboard nor the objects on it will appear when the movie is played in a browser or the Flash Player.

Timeline

The **Timeline** is used to organize and control the movie's contents by specifying when each object appears on the stage. The Timeline is critical to the creation of movies, because a movie is merely a series of still images that appear over time. The images are contained within **frames**, which are segments of the Timeline. Frames in a Flash movie are similar to frames in a motion picture. When a Flash movie is played, a playhead moves from frame to frame in the Timeline, causing the contents of each frame to appear on the stage in a linear sequence.

The Timeline indicates where you are at any time within the movie and allows you to insert, delete, select, and move frames. It shows the animation in your movie and the layers that contain objects. Layers help to organize the objects on the stage. You can draw and edit objects on one layer without affecting objects on other layers. Layers are a way to stack objects so they can overlap and give a 3-D appearance on the stage.

Panels

Panels are used to view, organize, and modify objects and features in a movie. The most commonly used panels are the Tools panel, the Properties panel (also called the Property inspector), and the Library panel. For example, the Property inspector is used

FIGURE 1

A typical Flash workspace

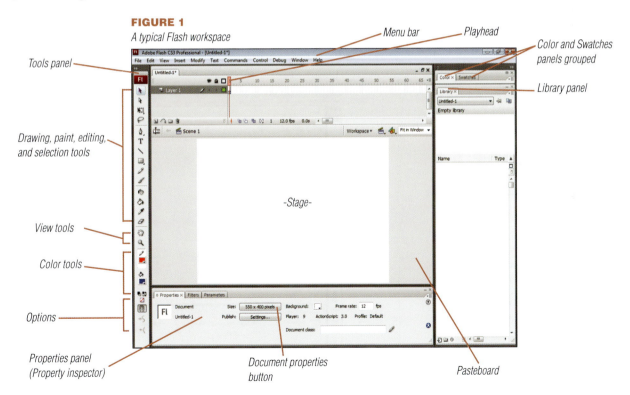

Menu bar

Playhead

Color and Swatches panels grouped

Tools panel

Library panel

Drawing, paint, editing, and selection tools

-Stage-

View tools

Color tools

Options

Properties panel (Property inspector)

Document properties button

Pasteboard

to change the properties of an object, such as the fill color of a circle. The Property inspector is context sensitive, so that if you are working with text it displays the appropriate options, such as font and font size.

You can control which panels are displayed individually or you can choose to display panel sets. Panel sets are groups of the most commonly used panels. In addition, you can control how a panel is displayed. That is, you can expand a panel to show all of its features or collapse it to show only the title bar.

Tools panel

The **Tools panel** contains a set of tools used to draw and edit graphics and text. It is divided into four sections.

Tools—Includes draw, paint, text, and selection tools, which are used to create lines, shapes, illustrations, and text. The selection tools are used to select objects so that they can be modified in several ways.

View—Includes the Zoom tool and the Hand tool, which are used to zoom in on and out of parts of the stage and to pan the stage window, respectively.

Colors—Includes tools and icons used to change the stroke (border of an object) and fill (area inside an object) colors.

Options—Includes options for selected tools, such as allowing you to choose the size of the brush when using the Brush tool.

Although several panels open automatically when you start Flash, you may choose to display them only when they are needed. This keeps your workspace from becoming too cluttered. Panels are floating windows, meaning that you can move them around the workspace. This allows you to group (dock) panels together as a way to organize them in the workspace. You can also make room in the workspace by collapsing panels so only their title bars are displayed. You use the Window menu on the menu bar to display and hide panels.

Arranging panels can be a bit tricky. It's easy to start moving panels around and find that the workspace is cluttered with panels arranged in unintended ways.

While you cannot use the Flash Undo feature in the Edit menu to undo a panel move, you can always close a panel or choose the Default option from the Workspace command in the Windows menu. This command displays the default panel arrangement, which is a good starting position when working with Flash.

If you choose to rearrange panels, first decide if you want a panel to be grouped (docked) with another panel, stacked above or below another panel, a floating panel, or simply a stand-alone panel. An example of each of these is shown in Figure 2.

FIGURE 2
Arranging panels

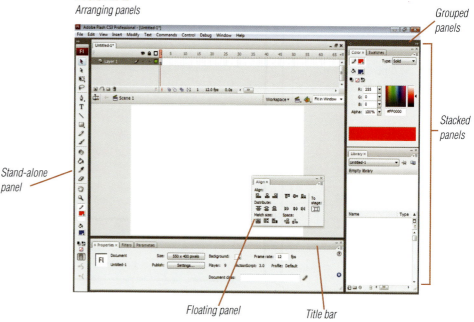

Grouped panels

Stacked panels

Stand-alone panel

Floating panel

Title bar

The key to any rearrangement of panels is the blue drop zone that appears when a panel is being moved. The drop zone is the area to which the panel can move and is indicated by either a blue line or a rectangle with a blue border. A single blue line indicates the position for stacking a panel above or below another panel. A rectangle with a blue border indicates the position for grouping panels. If you move a panel without using a drop zone, the panel becomes a floating panel and is neither grouped nor stacked with other panels. To move a panel, you drag the panel by its tab until the desired blue drop zone appears, then you release the mouse button. (*Note*: Dragging a panel by its tab moves only that panel. To move a grouped panel, you must drag the group by its title bar.)

Figure 3 shows the Library panel being grouped with the Color and Swatches panels. Notice the rectangle with the blue border that surrounds the Color panel. This indicates the drop zone for the Library panel and the other panels included in the group. Figure 4 shows the Library panel being ungrouped and stacked below the Color and Swatches panels. The blue line indicates the drop zone for the Library panel and shows where it will be stacked.

FIGURE 3

Grouping the Library panel

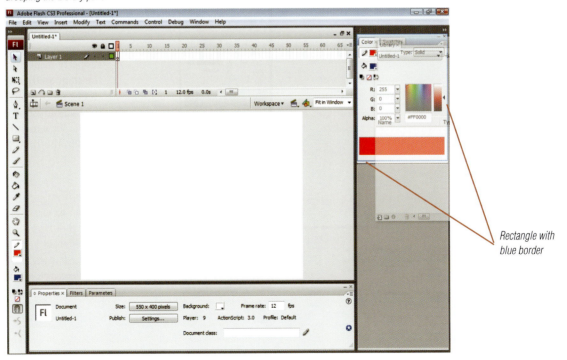

Rectangle with
blue border

In addition to moving panels, you can collapse them so that only the title bar appears, and then you can expand them to display the entire panel. The Collapse button is located in the upper-right corner of each panel, as shown in Figure 4. The Collapse button is a toggle button, which means it changes or toggles between two states. When clicked, the Collapse button changes to theExpand button. One other way to collapse some panels is with the Collapse to Icons button, also shown in Figure 4. Finally, if you want to close a panel, you can use the Close button, as shown in Figure 4.

Regardless of how you decide to customize your development workspace, the stage and the menu bar are always displayed. Usually, you display the Timeline, Tools panel, Library panel, Property inspector, and one or more other panels.

When you start a new Flash document (movie), you can set the document properties, such as the size of the window (stage) the movie will play in, the background color, and the speed of the movie in frames per second. You can change these settings using the Document Properties dialog box, which can be displayed using the Document command on the Modify menu. You can also change the settings using the Property inspector. To increase the size of the stage so that the objects on the stage can be more easily edited, you can change the magnification setting using commands on the View menu or by using the View tools in the Tools panel.

FIGURE 4

Ungrouping the Library panel

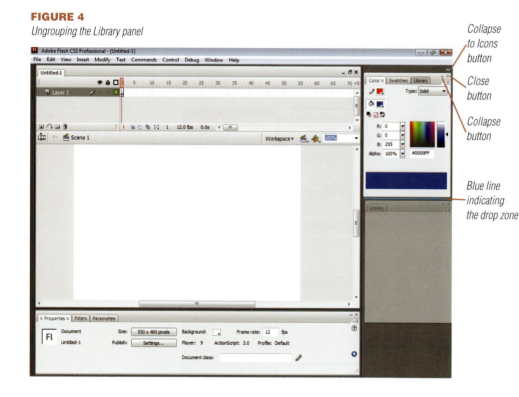

Collapse to Icons button

Close button

Collapse button

Blue line indicating the drop zone

FIGURE 5

The Open/Create screen

1. Start the Adobe Flash CS3 program .

   The Adobe Flash CS3 Open/Create screen appears, as shown in Figure 5. This screen allows you to open a recent document or create a new Flash file.

2. Click **Flash File (ActionScript 3.0)** under Create New.

3. Click **Window** on the menu bar, point to **Workspace**, then click **Default**.

4. Click **Window** on the menu bar, then note the panels with check marks indicating they are displayed. Use the check marks to identify the panels.

   > TIP The Swatches panel may be grouped with the Color panel.

5. With the Windows menu still displayed, click **Hide Panels**.

6. Click **Window** on the menu bar, then click **Color**.

7. Click **Window** on the menu bar, then click **Library**.

8. Click **Window** on the menu bar, point to **Properties**, then click **Properties**.

9. Point to the far left of the workspace until the Tools panel is displayed.

   When the Tools panel is hidden, it can be displayed by pointing to the far left of the workspace. When you move the mouse away from the Tools panel, it hides again.

10. Click the **Library tab**, then drag the **panel** to the stage as a floating panel.

(continued)

11. Click the **Library tab**, drag the panel to on top of the Color tab, then when a rectangle with a blue border appears, release the mouse button.

The Library panel is grouped with the Color and Swatches panels, as shown in Figure 6.

12. Click the **Collapse to Icons button** in the upper-right corner of the grouped panels, as shown in Figure 6.

13. Click the **Color panel icon** to display the grouped panels with the Color panel active, then click the **Color panel icon** again to collapse the panel.

14. Click the **Expand Dock button** in the upper-right corner of the grouped panels to expand the panel group.

15. Click the **Library tab**, drag the **Library panel** below the Color and Swatches panels until the blue line appears, then release the mouse button.

Note: Mac users will not see a blue line. Rather, the tabs switch position as they are dragged.

16. Click the **Properties panel Collapse button** in the title bar, as shown in Figure 6, to collapse the panel.

17. Click the **Properties panel Expand button** in the title bar to expand the panel.

18. Click the **Properties panel Close button** to close the panel.

19. Click **Window** on the menu bar, point to **Properties**, then click **Properties**.

20. Click **Window** on the menu bar, point to **Workspace**, then click **Default**.

The default workspace is displayed.

You started Flash and configured the workspace by hiding, moving, and displaying selected panels.

FIGURE 6
Library panel grouped with the Color and Swatches panels

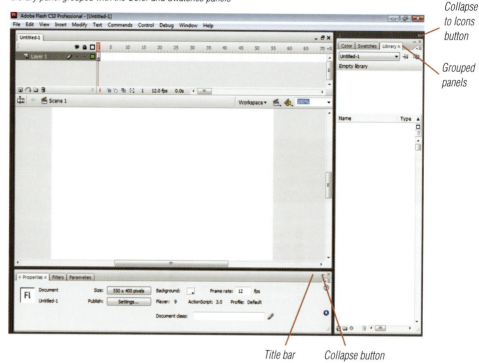

Collapse to Icons button

Grouped panels

Title bar   Collapse button

Understanding your workspace

Organizing the Flash workspace is like organizing your desktop. You may work more efficiently if you have many of the most commonly used items in view and ready to use. Alternately, you may work better if your workspace is relatively uncluttered, giving you more free "desk space." Fortunately, Flash makes it easy for you to decide which items to display and how they are arranged while you work. For example, to toggle the Main toolbar, click Window on the menu bar, point to Toolbars, then click Main. You should become familiar with quickly opening, collapsing, expanding, and closing the various windows, toolbars, and panels in Flash, and experimenting with different layouts and screen resolutions to find the workspace that works best for you.

FIGURE 7
Document Properties dialog box

Document Properties

Title:	My workspace
Description:	This is a typical workspace setup.
Dimensions:	400px (width) x 300px (height)
Match:	○ Printer ○ Contents ● Default
Background color:	■
Frame rate:	12 fps
Ruler units:	Pixels ▼

Make Default   OK   Cancel

FIGURE 8
Completed changes to Document properties

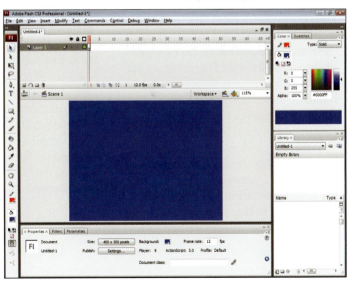

Change the Document Properties

1. Click the **Document properties button** `550 x 400 pixels` in the Property inspector to display the Document Properties dialog box.

2. Click inside the **Title text box**, then type **My workspace**.

3. Click inside the **Description text box**, then type **This is a typical workspace setup**.

   TIP   Text entered into the Title and Description text boxes, which are actually fields, can be used by Web-based search engines to display files developed using Flash.

4. Double-click the number in the **width text box**, type **400**, double-click the number in the **height text box**, then type **300**.

5. Click the **Background color swatch**, then click the **blue color swatch** in the far-left column of the color palette.

6. Review the remaining default values shown in Figure 7, then click **OK**.

7. Drag the scroll bars at the bottom and the right of the stage to center the stage.

8. Click **View** on the menu bar, point to **Magnification**, then click **Fit in Window**. Your screen should resemble Figure 8.

9. Click **File** on the menu bar, then click **Save**.

10. Navigate to the drive and folder where your data files are stored, type **workspace** for the file-name, then click **Save**.

    TIP   Click Browse Folders to open the Navigation pane if it is not open.

11. Click **File** on the menu bar, then click **Close**.

You set the document properties including the size of the stage and background color, then set the magnification and saved the document.

OPEN A DOCUMENT
AND PLAY A MOVIE

What You'll Do

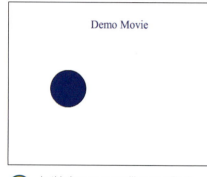

Demo Movie

In this lesson, you will open a Flash document (movie) and then preview, test, and save the movie.

Opening a Movie in Flash

Flash files are called documents and have an .fla file extension. If you have created a movie in Flash and saved it with the name mymovie, the filename will be mymovie.fla. Files with the .fla file extension can only be opened using Flash. After they are opened, you can edit and resave them.

Another file format for Flash movies is the Flash Player (.swf) format. These files are created from Flash movies using the Publish command. Flash .swf movies can be played in a browser without the Flash program, but the Flash Player must be installed on the computer. Flash Players are pre-installed on almost all computers. For those that do not have the player, it can be downloaded free from the Adobe Web site, *www.adobe.com* Because .swf files cannot be edited in the Flash program, you should preview them on the stage and test them before you publish them. Be sure to keep the original .fla file so that you can make changes at a later date.

Previewing a Movie

After opening a Flash movie, you can preview it within the workspace in several ways. When you preview a movie, you play the frames by directing the playhead to move through the Timeline, and you watch the movement on the stage.

Control menu commands (and keyboard shortcuts)

Figure 9 shows the Control menu commands, which resemble common DVD-type options:

- Play ([Enter] (Win) or [return] (Mac)) begins playing the movie frame by frame, from the location of the playhead to the end of the movie. For example, if the playhead is on Frame 5 and the last frame is Frame 40, choosing the Play command will play Frames 5–40 of the movie.

When a movie starts, the Play command changes to a Stop command. You can also stop the movie by pressing [Enter] (Win) or [return] (Mac).

- Rewind ([Ctrl] [Alt] [R] (Win)) or [option] ⌘ [R] (Mac) moves the play-head to Frame 1.
- Step Forward (.) moves the playhead forward one frame at a time.
- Step Backward (,) moves the playhead backward one frame at a time.

You can turn on the Loop Playback setting to allow the movie to continue playing repeatedly. A check mark next to the Loop Playback command on the Control menu indicates that the feature is turned on. To turn off this feature, click the Loop Playback command.

Controller

You can also preview a movie using the Controller. To display the Controller, click the Controller option on the Toolbars command of the Window menu.

QUICKTIP

The decision of which controls to use (the Control menu, keyboard shortcuts, or the Controller) is a matter of personal preference.

Testing a Movie

When you play a movie within the Flash workspace, some interactive functions (such as buttons that are used to jump from one part of the movie to another) do not work. To preview the full functionality of a movie you need to play it using a Flash Player. You can use the Test Movie command on the Control menu to test the movie using a Flash Player.

QUICKTIP

You can drag the Playhead in the Timeline to play frames and display their contents on the stage. This process, called "scrubbing," provides a quick way to view parts of the movie.

FIGURE 9
Control menu commands

DVD-type commands

Documents, Movies, and Applications

As you work in Flash, you are creating a document. When you save your work as an .fla file, you are saving the document. This is consistent with other Adobe products such as Photoshop that use the word *document* to refer to work created in that progam. In addition, because Flash uses a movie metaphor with a stage, Timeline, frames, animations, and so on, the work done in Flash is often referred to as a movie. So, the phrase *Flash document* and the phrase *Flash movie* are synonymous. Applications are products, such as games, that have been developed using Flash. Applications usually contain multiple Flash documents or movies that are linked.

Open and play a movie using the Control menu and the Controller

1. Open fl1_1.fla from the drive and folder where your Data Files are stored, then save it as **demomovie.fla**.

2. Click **View** on the menu bar, point to **Magnification**, then click **Fit in Window**.

3. Click **Control** on the menu bar, then click **Play**. Notice how the playhead moves across the Timeline as the blue circle moves from the left to right, as shown in Figure 10.

4. Click **Control** on the menu bar, then click **Rewind**.

5. Press **[Enter]** (Win) or **[return]** (Mac) to play the movie, then press **[Enter]** (Win) or **[return]** (Mac) again to stop the movie before it ends.

6. Click **Window** on the menu bar, point to **Toolbars**, then click **Controller**.

7. Use all the buttons on the Controller to preview the movie, then close the Controller.

8. Point to the **Playhead** in the Timeline, then click and drag the **Playhead** back and forth to view the contents of the frames and view the movie.

You opened a Flash movie and previewed it, using various controls.

FIGURE 10
Playhead moving across Timeline

Playhead

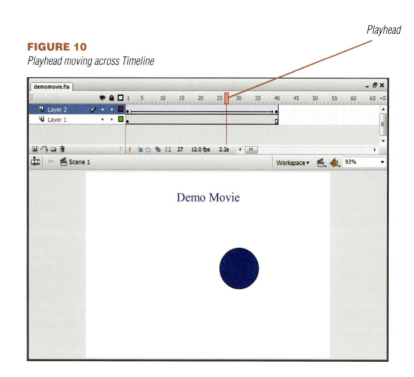

Demo Movie

FIGURE 11
Flash Player window

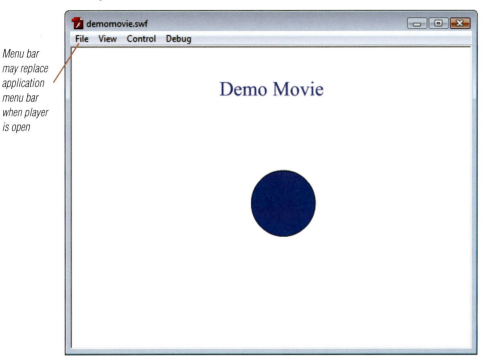

Menu bar may replace application menu bar when player is open

Test a movie

1. Click **Control** on the menu bar, then click **Test Movie** to view the movie in the Flash Player window, as shown in Figure 11.

2. Click **Control** on the menu bar of the Flash Player window (Win) or application menu bar (Mac), then review the available commands.

3. Click **File** on the menu bar of the Flash Player window (Win) or application menu bar (Mac), then click **Close** to close the Flash Player window.

4. Navigate to the drive and folder where you saved the movie and notice the demomovie.swf file that has been created, then close the dialog box.

   TIP When you test a movie, Flash automatically creates a file that has an .swf extension in the folder where your movie is stored and then plays the movie in the Flash Player.

5. Click **File** on the menu bar, then click **Close**, to close the demomovie.fla document, saving changes if prompted.

You tested a movie in the Flash Player window and closed the Flash document.

Using the Flash Player

To view a Flash movie on the Web, your computer needs to have the Flash Player installed. An important feature of multimedia players, such as Flash Player, is the ability to decompress a file that has been compressed to give it a small file size that can be delivered more quickly over the Internet. In addition to Adobe, companies such as Apple, Microsoft, and RealNetworks create players that allow applications, developed with their and other company's products, to be viewed on the Web. The multimedia players are distributed free and can be downloaded from the company's Web site. The Flash Player is created by Adobe and is available at *www.adobe.com*.

CREATE AND SAVE
A MOVIE

What You'll Do

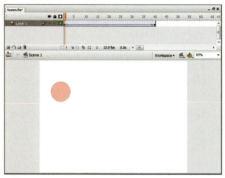

▶ *In this lesson, you will create a Flash movie that will include a simple animation, and then you will save the movie.*

Creating a Flash Movie

Flash movies are created by placing objects (graphics, text, sounds, photos, and so on) on the stage, editing these objects (for example, changing their brightness), animating the objects, and adding interactivity with buttons and menus. You can create graphic objects in Flash using the drawing tools, or you can create them in another program, such as Adobe Fireworks, Illustrator, or Photoshop, and then import them into a Flash movie. In addition, you can acquire clip art and stock photographs and import them into a movie. When objects are placed on the stage, they are automatically placed in a layer and in the currently selected frame of the Timeline.

Figure 12 shows a movie that has an oval object created in Flash. Notice that the playhead is on Frame 1 of the movie. The object placed on the stage appears in Frame 1 and appears on the stage when the playback head is on Frame 1. The dot in Frame 1 on the Timeline indicates that this frame is a keyframe. The concept of

keyframes is critical to understanding how Flash works. A keyframe indicates that there is a change in the movie, such as the start or end of an animation, or the playing of a sound. A keyframe is automatically designated in frame 1 of every layer. In addition, you can designate any frame to be a keyframe.

The oval object in Figure 12 was created using the Oval tool. To create an oval or a rectangle, you select the desired tool and then drag the pointer over an area on the stage. *Note:* Flash groups the Oval and Rectangle tools using one button. To display a menu of the tools available, click and hold the rectangle (or oval) button in the Tools panel until the menu opens, and then click the tool you want to use. If you want to draw a perfect circle or square, press and hold [Shift] after the tool is selected, and then drag the pointer. If you make a mistake, you can click Edit on the menu bar, and then click Undo. To edit an object, you must first select it. You can use the Selection tool to select an entire object or group of objects. You drag the Selection tool pointer around the entire object to make a marquee selection. An object that has been selected displays a dot pattern or a blue border.

Creating an Animation

Figure 13 shows another movie that has 40 frames, as specified in the Timeline. The arrow in the Timeline indicates a motion animation that starts in Frame 1 and ends in Frame 40. In this case, the object will move from left to right across the stage. The movement of the object is caused by having the object in different places on the stage in different frames of the movie. In this case, Frame 20 will display the object midway through the animation. A basic motion animation requires two keyframes. The first keyframe sets the starting position of the object, and the second keyframe sets the ending position of the object. The number of frames between the two keyframes determines the length of the animation. For example, if the starting keyframe is Frame 1 and the ending keyframe is Frame 40, the object will be animated for 40 frames. Once the two keyframes are set, Flash automatically fills in the frames between them, with a process called **motion tweening**.

Adding an Effect to an Object

In addition to animating the location of an object (or objects), you can also animate an object's appearance; for example, its shape, color, brightness, or transparency. The color of the circle on the left of the stage in Figure 13 has been lightened using the Brightness effect on the Property inspector. When the movie is played, the color of the circle will start out light and then become darker as it moves to the right.

FIGURE 12
Oval object in Frame 1

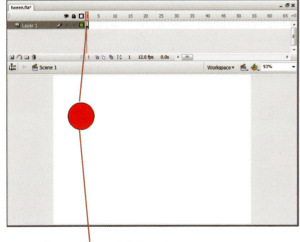

Object on the stage is in Frame 1
on the Timeline

FIGURE 13
Motion animation

Arrow indicates motion animation

The brightness of the object has been changed

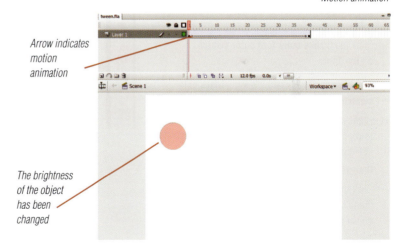

Create objects using drawing tools

1. Click **File** on the menu bar, then click **New**.

2. Click **OK** in the New Document window to choose Flash File (ActiveScript 3.0) as the new document to create, then save the movie as **tween**.

3. Click **View** on the menu bar, point to **Magnification**, then click **Fit in Window**.

4. Click and hold the **Rectangle tool** 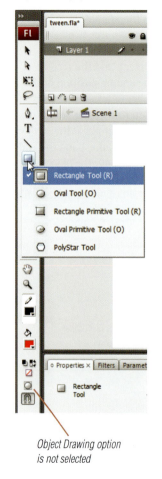 (or the Oval tool if it is displayed) on the Tools panel to display the list of tools, as shown in Figure 14, then click the **Oval tool** .

5. Verify that the Object Drawing option in the Options panel is deselected, as shown in Figure 14.

6. Click the **Fill color tool color swatch** on the Tools panel, then, if necessary, click the **red color swatch** in the left column of the color palette.

7. Click the **Stroke color tool color swatch** on the Tools

   panel, then, if necessary, click the **black color swatch** in the left column of the color palette.

8. Press and hold **[Shift]**, then drag the **Oval tool** on the stage to draw the circle, as shown in Figure 15.

   Pressing and holding [Shift] creates a circle.

9. Click the **Selection tool** on the Tools panel, then drag a **marquee** selection around the object to select it, as shown in Figure 16.

   The object appears covered with a dot pattern.

You created an object using the Oval tool and then selected the object using the Selection tool.

FIGURE 14
Object Drawing option

Object Drawing option
is not selected

FIGURE 15
Drawing a circle

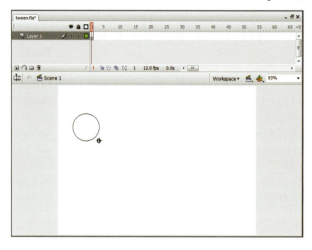

FIGURE 16
Creating a marquee selection

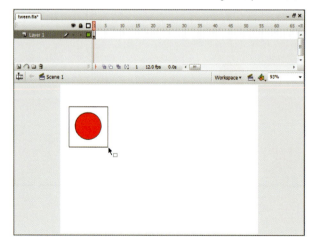

FIGURE 17

The circle on the right side of the stage

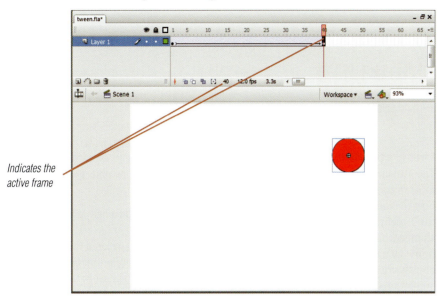

Indicates the
active frame

Using options and shortcuts

There is often more than one way to complete a particular function when using Flash. For example, if you want to change the font for text you have typed, you can use Text menu options or the Property inspector. In addition, Flash provides context menus that are relevant to the current selection. For example, if you point to a graphic and right-click (Win) or [control] click (Mac), a menu appears with graphic-related commands, such as distort and smooth. Shortcut keys are also available for many of the most common commands, such as [Ctrl] [Z] (Win) or ⌘ [Z] (Mac) for Undo.

Create basic animation

1. Click **Insert** on the menu bar, point to **Timeline**, then click **Create Motion Tween**.

   A blue border surrounds the object.

2. Click **Frame 40** on Layer 1 on the Timeline.

3. Click **Insert** on the menu bar, point to **Timeline**, then click **Keyframe**.

   A second keyframe is defined in Frame 40, and Frames 1–40 appear shaded.

4. Click and then drag the **circle** to the right side of the stage, as shown in Figure 17.

5. Press **[Enter]** to play the movie.

   The playhead moves through the Timeline in Frames 1–40, and the circle moves across the stage.

You created a basic motion tween animation by inserting a keyframe and changing the location of an object.

Change the brightness

1. Click **Window** on the menu bar, point to **Properties,** then verify that Properties is checked.

2. Click **Frame 1** on Layer 1, then click the **circle**.

3. Click the **Color Styles list arrow** in the Property inspector, then click **Brightness**.

4. Click the **% list arrow**, then drag the slider up to 70%.

5. Click anywhere on a blank area of the Property inspector to close the slider if necessary.

6. Play the movie, then save your work.

   The circle becomes brighter as it moves across the stage.

You used the Property inspector to change the brightness of the object in one of the keyframes.

WORK WITH THE TIMELINE

What You'll Do

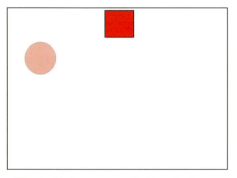

In this lesson, you will add another layer, allowing you to create an additional animation, and you will use the Timeline to help organize your movie.

Understanding the Timeline

The Timeline organizes and controls a movie's contents over time. By learning how to read the information provided in the Timeline, you can determine and change what will be happening in a movie, frame by frame. You can determine which objects are animated, what types of animations are being used, when the various objects will appear in a movie, which objects will appear on top of others, and how fast the movie will play. Features of the Timeline are shown in Figure 18 and explained in this lesson.

Using Layers

Each new Flash movie contains one layer, named Layer 1. **Layers** are like transparent sheets of acetate that are stacked on top of each other. This is shown in Figure 19, which also shows how the stacked objects appear on the stage. Each layer can contain one or more objects. You can add layers using the Layer command on the Insert menu or by clicking the Insert Layer icon on the Timeline. Placing objects on differ-

ent layers helps avoid accidentally making changes in one object while editing another.

When you add a new layer, Flash stacks it on top of the other layer(s) in the Timeline. The stacking order of the layers in the Timeline is important because objects on the stage appear in the same stacking order. For example, if you have two overlapping objects, and the top layer has a drawing of a tree and the bottom layer has a drawing of a house, the tree appears as though it is in front of the house. You can change the stacking order of layers simply by dragging them up or down in the list of layers. You can name layers, hide them so their contents do not appear on the stage, and lock them so that they cannot be edited.

Using Frames

The Timeline is made up of individual segments called **frames**. The content of each layer is displayed in frames as the playhead moves over them while the movie plays. Frames are numbered in increments of five for easy reference, while colors and symbols are used to indicate the type of frame (for example, keyframe or motion animation). The upper-right corner of the Timeline contains a Frame View icon. Clicking this icon displays a menu that provides different views of the Timeline, showing more frames or showing thumbnails of the objects on a layer, for example. The status bar at the bottom of the Timeline indicates the current frame (the frame that the playhead is currently on), the frame rate (frames per second), and the elapsed time from Frame 1 to the current frame.

Using the Playhead

The **playhead** indicates which frame is playing. You can manually move the playhead by dragging it left or right. This makes it easier to locate a frame that you may want to edit. Dragging the playhead also allows you to do a quick check of the movie without having to play it.

Understanding Scenes

When you create a movie, Scene 1 appears in the Timeline. You can add scenes to a movie at any time. Scenes are a way to organize long movies. For example, a movie created for a Web site could be divided into several scenes: an introduction, a home page, and content pages. Each scene has its own Timeline. You can insert new scenes by using the Insert menu. Scenes can be given descriptive names, which will help you find them easily if you need to edit a particular scene. The number of scenes is limited only by the computer's memory. There are some drawbacks to using scenes, including potentially larger file sizes and longer download times for the viewer.

FIGURE 18
Elements of the timeline

FIGURE 19
The concept of layers

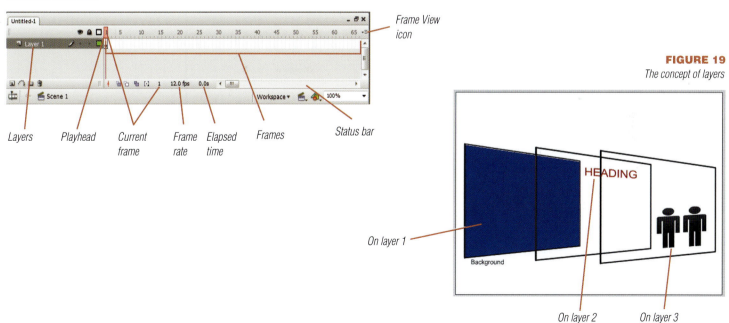

Working with the Timeline

Figure 20 shows the Timeline of a movie created in Lesson 3 with a second object, a square at the top of the stage. By studying the Timeline, you can learn several things about this movie. First, the second object is placed on its own layer, Layer 2. Second, the layer has a motion animation (indicated by the arrow and blue background in the frames). Third, the animation runs from Frame 1 to Frame 40. Fourth, if the objects intersect during the animation, the square will be on top of the circle, because the layer it is placed on (Layer 2) is above the layer that the circle is placed on (Layer 1). Fifth, the frame rate is set to 12, which means that the movie will play 12 frames per second. Sixth, the playhead is at Frame 1, which causes the contents for both layers of Frame 1 to be displayed on the stage.

FIGURE 20
The Timeline of a movie with a second object

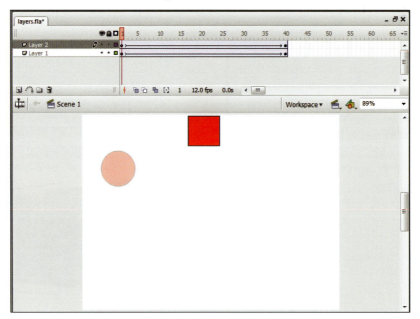

FIGURE 21
Drawing a square

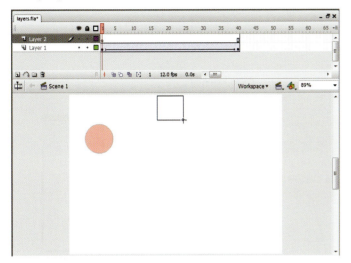

FIGURE 22
Positioning the square at the bottom of the stage

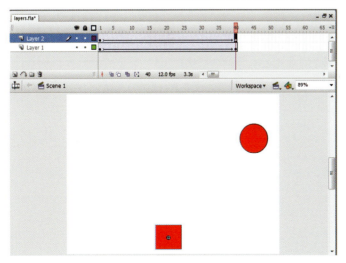

Add a layer

1. Save tween.fla as **layers.fla**.
2. Click **Frame 1** on Layer 1.
3. Click **Insert** on the menu bar, point to **Timeline**, then click **Layer**.

   A new layer—Layer 2—appears at the top of the Timeline.

You added a layer to the Timeline.

Create a second animation

1. Click **Frame 1** on Layer 2.
2. Select the **Rectangle tool** ▣ on the Tools panel, press and hold [**Shift**], then draw a square resembling the dimensions and position of the square, shown in Figure 21.
3. Click the **Selection tool** ▶ on the Tools panel, then drag a **marquee** around the square to select the object.
4. Click **Insert** on the menu bar, point to **Timeline**, then click **Create Motion Tween**.
5. Click **Frame 40** on Layer 2, click **Insert** on the menu bar, point to **Timeline**, then click **Keyframe**.
6. Drag the **square** to the bottom of the stage, as shown in Figure 22, then play the movie.

   The square appears on top if the two objects intersect.

You drew an object and used it to create a second animation.

Lesson 4   Work with the Timeline

Work with layers and view features in the Timeline

1. Click **Layer 2** on the Timeline, then drag it below Layer 1.

   Layer 2 is now the bottom layer.

2. Play the movie and notice how the square appears beneath the circle if the objects intersect.

3. Click **Layer 2** on the Timeline, then drag it above Layer 1.

4. Play the movie and notice how the square appears above the circle if they intersect.

5. Click the **Frame View icon** ≡ on the end of the Timeline to display the menu.

6. Click **Tiny** to display more frames and notice how the frames in the Timeline change.

7. Click the **Frame View icon** ≡, then click **Short,** as shown in Figure 23.

8. Click the **Frame View icon** ≡, click **Preview**, then note the object thumbnails that appear on the Timeline.

9. Click the **Frame View icon** ≡, then click **Normal**.

You changed the order of the layers, the display of frames, and the size of the Timeline.

FIGURE 23
Changing the view of the Timeline

Frame View icon

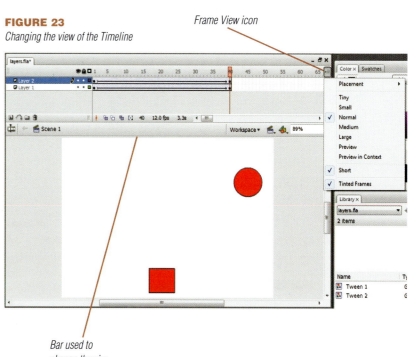

Bar used to change the size of the Timeline

FIGURE 24
Changing the frame rate

New frame rate

Document Properties		
Title:		
Description:		
Dimensions:	550 px (width) x	400 px (height)
Match:	○ Printer ○ Contents ● Default	
Background color:		
Frame rate:	3 fps	
Ruler units:	Pixels	

Make Default   OK   Cancel

Getting Help

Flash provides a comprehensive Help feature that can be very useful when first learning the program. You can access Help by clicking commands on the Help menu. The Help feature includes the Flash manual, which is organized by topic and can be accessed through the index or by using a keyword search. In addition, the Help menu contains samples and tutorials that cover basic Flash features.

Modify the frame rate

1. Double-click the **Frame Rate icon** on the bottom of the Timeline to open the Document Properties dialog box.

2. Double-click **12**, type **3** in the Frame rate text box, then compare your Document Properties dialog box to Figure 24.

3. Click on a blank area of the stage, then click **OK**.

4. Play the **movie** and notice that the speed of the movie changes.

   TIP The letters fps stand for frames per second. Frames per second is the unit of measurement for movies.

5. Verify the Properties panel is displayed. If not, click **Window, Properties, Properties**.

   Notice the Properties panel provides information about the stage, including size and background color.

6. Click the **Size button** 550 x 400 pixels in the Properties panel to display the Document Properties dialog box.

   This is a way to open the dialog box without using the Modify menu.

7. Change the frame rate to **18**, then repeat Steps 3 and 4.

8. Change the frame rate to **12** in the Properties panel.

9. Click **Frame 20** on the Timeline and notice the position of the objects on the stage.

10 Drag the **playhead** left and right to display specific frames.

11. Save your work.

You changed the frame rate of the movie and used the playhead to display the contents of frames.

DISTRIBUTE AN ADOBE
FLASH MOVIE

What You'll Do

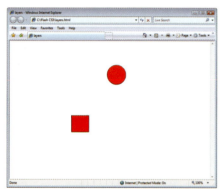

In this lesson, you will prepare a movie for distribution in various formats.

Distributing Movies

When you develop Flash movies, the program saves them in a file format (.fla) that only users who have the Flash program installed on their computers can view. Usually, Flash movies are viewed on the Web as part of a Web site or directly from a viewer's computer using the Flash Player. Flash files (.fla) cannot be viewed on the Web using a Web browser. They must be converted into a Flash Player file (.swf) so that the Web browser knows the type of file to play (.swf) and the program needed to play the file (Flash Player). In addition, the HTML code needs to be created that instructs the Web browser to play the swf file. Fortunately, Flash generates both the swf and HTML files when you use the publish feature of Flash.

The process for publishing a Flash movie is to create and save a movie and then click the Publish command on the File menu. You can also specify various set-tings, such as dimensions for the window in which the movie plays in the browser, before publishing the movie. Publishing a movie creates three files: an HTML file, a Flash Player (.swf) file, and a JavaScript file. The JavaScript file is needed to detect the Flash Player when viewers use certain browsers. Both the HTML and swf files retain the same name as the Flash movie file, but with different file extensions:

- .html—the HTML document
- .swf—the Flash Player file

For example, publishing a movie named layers.fla generates layers.html and layers.swf. The HTML document contains the code that the browser interprets to display the movie on the Web. The code also specifies which Flash Player movie the browser should play. Sample HTML code referencing a Flash Player movie is shown in Figure 25. If you are familiar with HTML code, you will recognize this as a complete HTML document. Even if you are not familiar with HTML code, you might recognize the code, as seen in Figure 25, that the browser uses to display the Flash movie. For example, the movie value is set to layers.swf; the background color is set to white (#ffffff is the code for white), and the display dimensions (determined by the size of the stage) are set to 550x400.

Flash provides several other ways to distribute your movies that may or may not involve delivery on the Web. You can create a stand-alone movie called a **projector**. Projector files, such as Windows .exe files, maintain the movie's interactivity. Alternately, you can create self-running movies, such as QuickTime .mov files, that are not interactive.

You can play projector and non-interactive files directly from a computer, or you can incorporate them into an application, such as a game, that is downloaded or delivered on a CD or DVD. In addition, Flash provides features for creating movies specifically for mobile devices, such as cell phones.

FIGURE 25
Sample HTML code

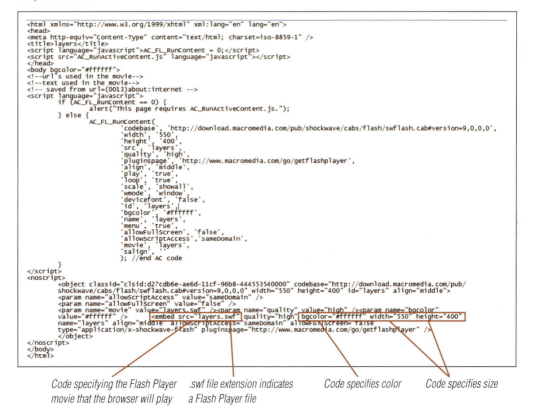

Code specifying the Flash Player movie that the browser will play   .swf file extension indicates a Flash Player file   Code specifies color   Code specifies size

Publish a movie for distribution on the Web

1. Verify layers.fla is open.

2. Click **File** on the menu bar, then click **Publish**.

   The files are automatically generated and saved in the same folder as the Flash document.

3. Use your file management program to navigate to the drive and folder where you save your work, then be sure All Files is selected as the File type to display.

4. Notice the three files that begin with "layers," as shown in Figure 26.

   Layers.fla, the Flash movie; layers.swf, the Flash Player file; and layers.html, the HTML document; and the JScript file appear in the window.

5. Double-click **layers.html** to play the movie in the browser.

   TIP Click the browser button on the taskbar if the movie does not open automatically in your browser.

   Notice the animation takes up only a portion of the browser window, as shown in Figure 27. This is because the stage size is set to 550x440, which is smaller than the browser window.

6. Close the browser.

You used the Publish command to create an HTML document and a Flash Player file, then you displayed the HTML document in a Web browser.

FIGURE 26
The three layers files after publishing the movie

Name	Type	Size
layers.html	HTML Document	2 KB
layers.swf	Flash Movie	1 KB
layers.fla	Flash Document	32 KB
AC_RunActiveContent.js	JScript Script File	9 KB

Your files may be listed in a different order

FIGURE 27
The animation played in a browser window

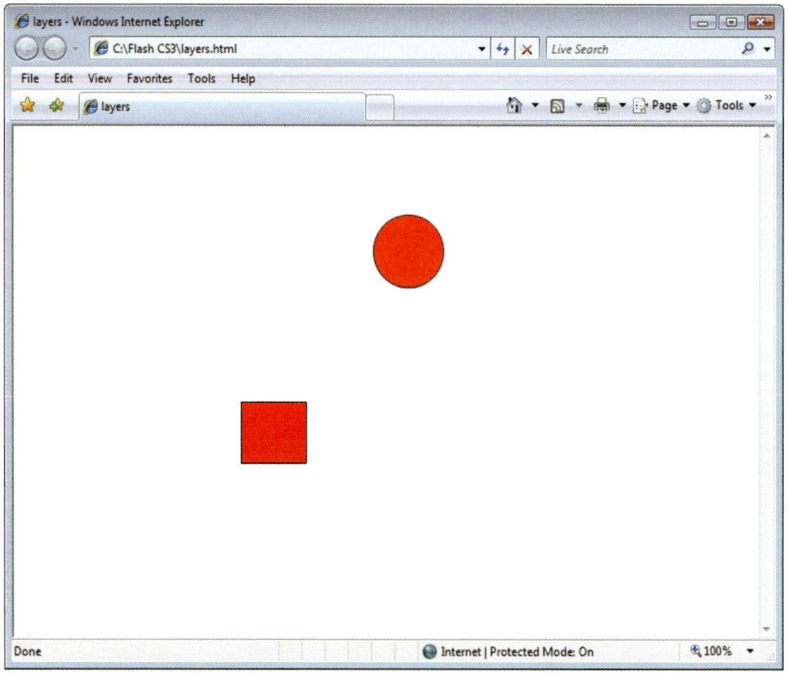

Getting Started with Adobe Flash CS3

FIGURE 28

The Flash Player window playing the Flash Player movie

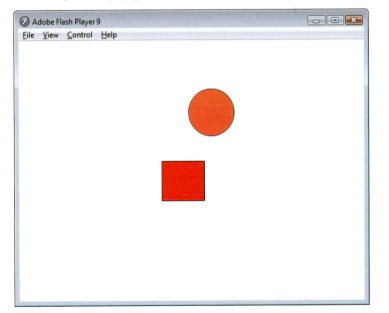

1. Return to Flash, click **File** on the menu bar, then click **Publish Settings** to open the Publish Settings dialog box.

2. Verify the Formats tab is selected.

   Notice the various file formats that can be generated automatically when you publish a Flash document.

3. Click the **Windows Projector (.exe)** (Win) or **Macintosh Projector** (Mac) **check box**.

4. Click **Publish**, then click **OK**.

5. Navigate to the drive and folder where you save your work, then be sure **All Files** is selected as the File type to display.

6. Double-click **layers.exe** (Win), or **layers** (Mac), then notice that the application plays in the Flash Player window, as shown in Figure 28.

   In this case, the Flash Player window is sized to the dimensions of the stage.

   (<u>Note</u>: You must have the Flash Player installed to view the movie.)

7. Close the Flash Player window.

8. Close layers.fla in Flash, saving your changes if prompted.

You created and displayed a stand-alone projector file.

PLAN AN APPLICATION OR A
WEB SITE

What You'll Do

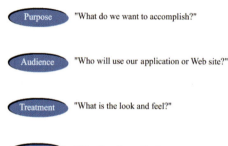

Purpose   "What do we want to accomplish?"

Audience   "Who will use our application or Web site?"

Treatment   "What is the look and feel?"

Specifications   "What does the application include and how does it work?"

In this lesson, you will learn how to plan a Flash application. You will also learn about the guidelines for screen design and the interactive design of Web pages.

Planning an Application or a Web site

Flash can be used to develop animations (movies) that are part of a product, such as a game or educational tutorial, and delivered on CD, DVD, or a mobile device. You can use Flash to create enhancements to Web pages, such as animated logos and interactive navigation buttons. You can also use Flash to create entire Web sites. No matter what the application, the first step is planning. Often, the temptation is to jump right into the program and start developing movies. The problem is that this invariably results in a more time-consuming process at best; and wasted effort, resources, and money at worst. The larger in scope and the more complex the project

is, the more critical the planning process becomes. Planning an application or an entire Web site should involve the following steps:

Step 1: Stating the Purpose (Goals). "What, specifically, do we want to accomplish?"

Determining the goals is a critical step in planning because goals guide the development process, keep the team members on track, and provide a way to evaluate the application or Web site, both during and after its development.

Step 2: Identifying the Target Audience. "Who will use the application or Web site?"

Understanding the potential viewers helps in developing an application or a Web site that can address their needs. For example, children respond to exploration and surprise, so having a dog wag its tail when the mouse pointer rolls over it might appeal to this audience.

Step 3: Determining the Treatment. "What is the look and feel?"

The treatment is how the application or Web site will be presented to the user, including the tone, approach, and emphasis.

Tone. Will the application or Web site be humorous, serious, light, heavy, formal, or informal? The tone of a site can often be used to make a statement, projecting a progressive, high-tech, well-funded corporate image, for instance.

Approach. How much direction will be provided to the user? An interactive game might focus on exploration, while an informational Web site might provide lots of direction, such as menus.

Emphasis. How much emphasis will be placed on the various multimedia elements? For example, a company may want to develop an informational application or Web site that shows the features of its new product line, including animated demonstrations of how each product works. The budget might not allow for the expense of creating the animations, so the emphasis would shift to still pictures with text descriptions.

Step 4: Developing the Specifications and Storyboard. "What precisely does the application or Web site include and how does it work?"

The specifications state what will be included in each screen, including the arrangement of each element and the functionality of each object (for example, what happens when you click the button labeled Skip Intro). Specifications should include the following:

Playback System. The choice of what configuration to target for playback is critical, especially Internet connection speed, browser versions, screen resolution, and plug-ins.

Elements to Include. The specifications should include details about the various elements that are to be included in the site. What are the dimensions for the animations, and what is the frame rate? What are the sizes of the various objects such as photos, buttons, and so on? What fonts, font sizes, and font formatting will be used? Should video or sound be included?

Functionality. The specifications should include the way the program reacts to an action by the user, such as a mouse click. For example, clicking a door (object) might cause a doorbell to ring (sound), the door

Rich Media Content and Accessibility

Flash provides the tools that allow you to create compelling applications and Web sites by incorporating rich media content, such as animations, sound, and video. Generally, incorporating rich media enhances the user's experience. However, accessibility becomes an issue for those persons who have visual, hearing, or mobility impairments, or have a cognitive disability. Designers need to utilize techniques that help ensure accessibility, such as providing consistency throughout the applications and Web site in navigation and layout, labeling graphics, captioning audio content, and providing keyboard access.

to open (an animation), an "exit the program" message to appear (text), or an entirely new screen to be displayed.

User Interface. The user interface involves designing the appearance of objects (how each object is arranged on the screen) and the interactivity (how the user navigates through the site).

A flowchart is a visual representation of how the contents in an application or a Web site are organized and how various screens are linked. It provides a guide for the developer and helps to identify problems with the navigation scheme before work begins. Figure 29 shows a simple flowchart illustrating the site organization and links.

A storyboard shows the layout of the various screens. It describes the contents and illustrates how text, graphics, animation, and other screen elements will be positioned. It also indicates the navigation process, such as menus and buttons. Figure 30 shows a storyboard. The exact content (such as a specific photo) does not have to be decided, but it is important to show where text, graphics, photos, buttons, and other elements, will be placed. Thus, the storyboard includes placeholders for the various elements.

Using Screen Design Guidelines

The following screen design guidelines are used by application and Web developers.

The implementation of these guidelines is affected by the goals of the site, the intended audience, and the content.

Balance—Balance in screen design refers to the distribution of optical weight in the layout. Optical weight is the ability of an object to attract the viewer's eye, as determined by the object's size, shape, color, and so on. Figure 30 shows a fairly well-balanced layout, especially if the logo has as much optical weight as the text description. In general, a balanced design is more appealing to a viewer. However, for a game application or entertainment site, a balanced layout may not be desired.

FIGURE 29
Sample Flowchart

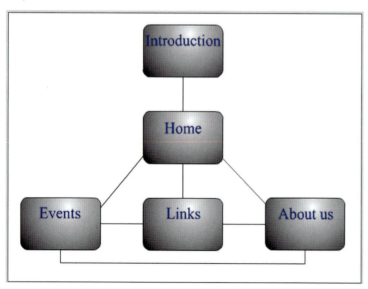

FIGURE 30
Sample Storyboard

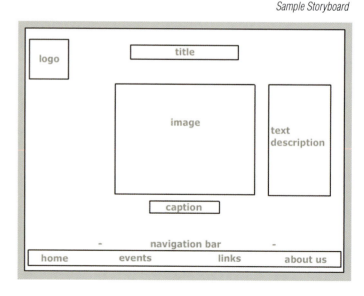

Unity—Intra-screen unity has to do with how the various screen objects relate and how they all fit in. For example, a children's game might only use cartoon characterizations of animals for all the objects—including navigation buttons and sound control buttons, as well as the on-screen characters. Unity helps the screen objects reinforce each other. Inter-screen unity refers to the design that viewers encounter as they navigate from one screen to another, and it provides consistency throughout the site. For example, all navigation buttons are located in the same place on each screen.

Movement—Movement refers to the way the viewer's eyes move through the objects on the screen. Different types of objects and various animation techniques can be used to draw the viewer to a location on the screen.

For example, a photo of a waterfall may cause the viewer's eyes to follow the flow of the water down, especially if the waterfall is animated. The designer could then place an object, such as a logo or link, below the waterfall.

Using Interactive Design Guidelines

In addition to screen design guidelines, interactive guidelines determine the interactivity of the site. The following guidelines are not absolute rules but are affected by the goals of the site, the intended audience, and the content:

- Make it simple, easy to understand, and easy to use so that viewers do not have to spend time learning what the site is about and what they need to do.

- Build in consistency in the navigation scheme. Help the users know where they are in the site and help them avoid getting lost.
- Provide feedback. Users need to know when an action, such as clicking a button, has been completed. Changing its color or shape, or adding a sound can indicate this.
- Give the user control. Allow the user to skip long introductions; provide controls for starting, stopping, and rewinding animations, video, and audio; and provide controls for adjusting audio.

Project Management

Developing Web sites or any extensive application, such as a game, involves project management. A project plan needs to be developed that provides the project scope and identifies the milestones, including analyzing, designing, building, testing, and launching. Personnel and resource needs are identified, budgets built, tasks assigned, and schedules developed. Successful projects are a team effort relying on the close collaboration of designers, developers, project managers, graphic artists, programmers, testers, and others. Adobe provides various product suites, such as their Creative Suite 3 (CS3) Web Collection series, that include programs such as Flash, Dreamweaver, Fireworks, Photoshop, and Illustrator. These are the primary tools needed to develop interactive applications and Web sites. These programs are designed for easy integration. So, a graphic artist can use Photoshop to develop an image that can easily be imported into Flash and used by an animator. In addition, other tools in the suites, such as Adobe Bridge and Adobe Version Cue, help ensure efficient workflow when working in a team environment.

The Flash Workflow Process

After the planning process, you are ready to start work on the Flash documents. Following are steps that can be used as guidelines in a general workflow process suggested by Adobe.

Step 1: Create and/or acquire the elements to be used in the application. The elements include text, photos, drawings, video, and audio. The elements become the raw material for the graphics, animations, menus, buttons, and content that populate the application and provide the interactivity. You can use the various Flash drawing and text tools to create your own images and text content; or, you can use another program, such as Adobe Photoshop, to develop the elements, and then import them into Flash. Alternately, you can acquire stock clip art and photographs. You can produce video and audio content in-house and import it into Flash or you can acquire these elements from a third party.

Step 2: Arrange the elements and create the animations. Arrange the elements (objects) on the Stage and in the Timeline to define when and how they appear in your application. Once the elements are available, you can create the various animations called for in the specifications.

Step 3: Apply special effects. Flash provides innumerable special effects that can be applied to the various media elements and animations. These include graphic and text filters, such as drop shadows, blurs, glows, and bevels. In addition, there are effects for sounds and animations such as fade-ins and fade-outs, acceleration and deceleration, and morphing.

Step 4: Create the interactivity. Flash provides a scripting feature, ActionScript, which allows you to develop programming code to control how the media elements behave, including how various objects respond to user interactions, such as clicking buttons and rolling over images.

Step 5: Test and publish the application. Testing should be done throughout the development process, including using the Test Movie feature in the Control menu to test the movie using the Flash Player and to publish the movie in order to test it in a browser.

Using the Flash Help Feature

Flash provides a comprehensive Help feature that can be very useful when first learning the program. You can access the Help panel from the Help menu. The Help feature is organized by categories, including Using Flash, which have several topics such as Getting Started and Workspace overview. In addition, you can use the Help search feature to search for topics related to keywords, such as Timeline. Other resources not affiliated with Adobe are available through the Web. You may find some by searching the Web for Flash resources.

FIGURE 31

The Flash Help categories

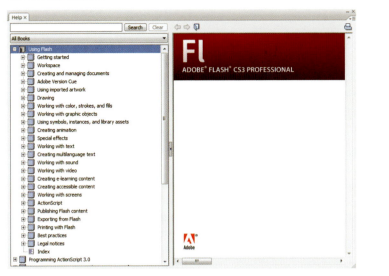

FIGURE 32

The Flash Help Search feature

Use Flash Help

1. Start a new Flash document.

2. Click **Help** on the menu bar, then click **Flash Help**.

3. Click **Using Flash** to expand the category, as shown in Figure 31, then click **Workspace**.

4. Click **The Timeline**, then click **About the Timeline**.

5. Read through the text in About the Timeline.

6. Click **Using Flash** to collapse the list.

7. Click in the **Search text box**, then type **panel,** as shown in Figure 32.

8. Click **Search**, then click **Customize the workspace**.

9. Read the article Customize the workspace.

10. Close the Help panel and exit the Flash program.

You used the Flash Help feature to access information on the Timeline and the workspace.

Start Flash, open a movie, and set the movie properties and magnification.

1. Start Flash, open fl1_2.fla, then save it as **skillsdemo1**.
2. Display the Document Properties dialog box, add a title, **Animated Objects**, then add a description, **A review of skills learned in Chapter 1**.
3. Change the movie window dimensions to width: 550 px and height: 450 px.
4. Change the background color to blue. (*Hint*: Select the blue color swatch in the left column of the color palette.)
5. Close the Document Properties dialog box.
6. Change the magnification to 50% using the View menu (*Hint:* Click View, point to Magnification, then click 50%.).
7. Change the magnification to Fit in Window.

Close, display, and collapse panels.

1. Hide all panels.
2. Display the Property inspector, the Align panel, and the Library panel.
3. Group the Library and Align panels.
4. Ungroup the Library panel from the Align panel and position it below the Align panel.
5. Collapse the Property inspector and Library panels.

6. Close the Library panel to remove it from the screen.
7. Expand the Property inspector.
8. Display the Default workspace.

Play and test a movie.

1. Drag the playhead to view the contents of each frame. Use the commands in the Control menu to play and rewind the movie.
2. Press [Enter] (Win) or [return] (Mac) to play and stop the movie.
3. Use the Controller to rewind, play, stop, and start the movie.
4. Test the movie in the Flash Player window, then close the test movie window.

Create an object, create a basic animation, and apply an effect.

1. Insert a new layer above the heading layer, then select Frame 1 of the new layer.
2. Draw a red circle in the lower-left corner of the stage, approximately the same size as the green ball.
3. Select the circle, then create a Motion Tween to animate the circle so that it moves across the screen from left to right, beginning in Frame 1 and ending in Frame 60. (*Hint*: Add a keyframe in the ending frame.)

4. Use the Selection Tool to select the circle (if necessary), then change the brightness from 0% to 60%, in the last frame of the animation.
5. Play the movie, then rewind it.

Add a layer, change the frame rate, and change the view of the Timeline.

1. Add a new layer above layer 3, select Frame 1, then create a second circle in the lower-right corner of the stage that's approximately the same size as the circle you created in the lower-left corner of the stage.
2. Create a Motion Tween to animate the circle so that it moves across the screen from right to left beginning in Frame 1 and ending in Frame 60.
3. Use the Selection Tool to select the circle, then change the brightness from 0% to –60% in the last frame of the animation.
4. Play the movie.
5. Change the frame rate to 8 frames per second, play the movie, then change the frame rate to 12.

6. Change the view of the Timeline to display more frames.
7. Change the view of the Timeline to display a preview of the object thumbnails.
8. Change the view of the Timeline to display the Normal view.
9. Use the playhead to display each frame, then compare your screens to Figure 33.
10. Save the movie.

Publish a movie.

1. Click File on the menu bar, then click Publish.
2. Open your browser, then open skillsdemo1.html.

   | TIP   Be sure All Files is selected as the File type to display.

3. View the movie, then close your browser.

Create a projector file.

1. Display the Publish Settings dialog box.
2. Select the appropriate projector setting for your operating system and remove all of the other settings.
3. Publish the movie.
4. Navigate to the drive and folder where you save your work, then open the skillsdemo1 projector file.
5. View the movie, then close the Flash Player window.
6. Save and close the Flash document.
7. Exit Flash.

FIGURE 33
Completed Skills Review

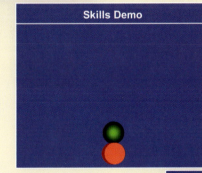

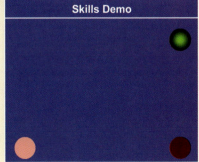

A friend cannot decide whether to sign up for a class in Flash or Dreamweaver. You help her decide by showing her what you already know about Flash. Since you think she'd enjoy a class in Flash, you decide to show her how easy it is to create a simple animation. You decide to animate three objects. The first object enters the stage from the left side and moves to the middle of the stage. The second object starts at the middle of the stage covering the first object and moves to the right and off the stage. The third object moves from above the stage to below it. All three objects intersect at the middle of the stage.

1. Open a Flash document, then save it as **demonstration**.
2. Change the view to 50%.
3. Use the tools on the Tools panel to create a simple shape or design, and place it off the left side of the stage, halfway down the stage.
4. Select the object and insert a motion tween.
5. Insert a keyframe in Frame 20, then move the object to the middle of the stage.
6. Insert a new layer, then select Frame 20 of the layer and insert a keyframe.
7. Create another object that is a different shape and that is slightly larger than the first object and that covers the first object, then select the object and insert a motion tween for the object.
8. Insert a keyframe in Frame 40, then move the object to the right side off the stage.

9. Insert a new layer, then select Frame 1 of the layer.
10. Draw an object off the top of the stage, about midway across the stage.
11. Animate the object to move straight down and off the bottom of the stage for 40 frames.

12. Change the brightness of the object to 70% in Frame 40.
13. Add a background color.
14. Preview the movie and test it.
15. Save the movie, then compare it to the example shown in Figure 34.

FIGURE 34
Sample completed Project Builder 1

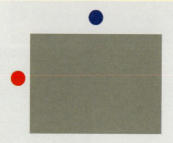
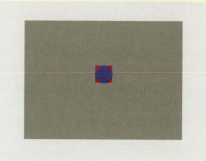

You've been asked to develop a simple movie about recycling for a day care center. For this project, you will add two animations to an existing movie. You will show three objects that appear on the screen at different times, and then move each object to a recycle bin at different times. You can create the objects using any of the Tools on the Tools panel.

1. Open fl1_3.fla, then save it as **recycle**.
2. Play the movie and study the Timeline to familiarize yourself with the movie's current settings. Currently, there are no animations.
3. Insert a new layer above Layer 2, insert a keyframe in Frame 10 of the new layer, then draw a small object in the upper-left corner of the stage.
4. Create a motion animation that moves the object to the recycle bin. (*Note*: The object may appear outside the recycle bin.)
5. Insert a new layer above the top layer, insert a keyframe in Frame 20, draw a small object in the upper-center of the stage, then create a motion animation that moves the object to the recycle bin.
6. Insert a new layer above the top layer, insert a keyframe in Frame 30, draw a small object in the upper-right corner of the stage, then create a motion animation that moves the object to the recycle bin.
7. Move Layer 1 to the top of all the layers.
8. Play the movie and compare it to Figure 35.
9. Save the movie.

FIGURE 35
Sample completed Project Builder 2

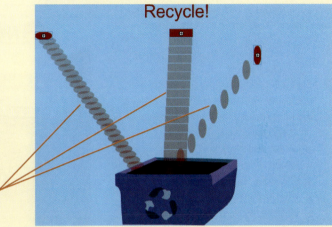

This figure shows the animated objects with outlines of their positions during the animations. Your completed project will not show these outlines

Recycle!

DESIGN PROJECT

Figure 36 shows the home page of a Web site. Study the figure and answer the following questions. For each question, indicate how you determined your answer.

1. Connect to the Internet, then go to *www.argosycruises.com*.
2. Open a document in a word processor or open a new Flash document, save the file as **dpc1**, then answer the following questions. (*Hint*: Use the Flash Text tool.)
   - Whose Web site is this?
   - What is the goal(s) of the site?
   - Who is the target audience?
   - What treatment (look and feel) is used?
   - What are the design layout guidelines being used (balance, movement, etc.)?
   - How can animation enhance this page?
   - Do you think this is an effective design for the company, its products, and its target audience? Why, or why not?
   - What suggestions would you make to improve on the design, and why?

FIGURE 36
Design Project

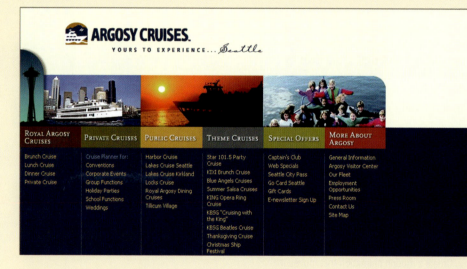

PORTFOLIO PROJECT

There are numerous companies in the business of developing Web sites for others. Many of these companies use Flash as one of their primary development tools. These companies promote themselves through their own Web sites and usually provide online portfolios with samples of their work. Log onto the Internet, then use your favorite search engine (use keywords such as Flash developers and Flash animators) to locate three of these companies, and generate the following information for each one. A sample is shown in Figure 37.

1. Company name:
2. Contact information (address, phone, and so on):
3. Web site URL:
4. Company mission:
5. Services provided:
6. Sample list of clients:
7. Describe three ways they seem to have used Flash in their own sites. Were these effective? Why, or why not?
8. Describe three applications of Flash that they include in their portfolios (or showcases or samples). Were these effective? Why, or why not?
9. Would you want to work for this company? Why, or why not?
10. Would you recommend this company to another company that was looking to enhance its Web site? Why, or why not?

FIGURE 37
Portfolio Project

chapter

2

DRAWING OBJECTS IN
ADOBE FLASH

1. Use the Flash drawing tools

2. Select Objects and Apply Colors

3. Work with drawn objects

4. Work with text and text objects

5. Work with layers and objects

DRAWING OBJECTS IN ADOBE FLASH

Introduction

Computers can display graphics in either a bitmap or a vector format. The difference between these formats is in how they describe an image. Bitmap graphics represent the image as an array of dots, called **pixels**, which are arranged within a grid. Each pixel in an image has an exact position on the screen and a precise color. To make a change in a bitmap graphic, you modify the pixels. When you enlarge a bitmap graphic, the number of pixels remains the same, resulting in jagged edges that decrease the quality of the image. Vector graphics represent the image using lines and curves, which you can resize without losing image quality. Also, the file size of a vector image is generally smaller than the file size of a bitmap image, which makes vector images particularly useful for a Web site. However, vector graphics are not as effective as bitmap graphics for representing photo-realistic images.

One of the most compelling features of Flash is the ability to create and manipulate vector graphics. Images (objects) created using Flash drawing tools have a stroke (border lines), a fill, or both. In addition, the stroke of an object can be segmented into smaller lines. You can modify the size, shape, rotation, and color of each stroke, fill, and segment.

Flash provides two drawing modes, called models. In the Merge Drawing Model, when you draw two shapes and one overlaps the other, a change in the top object may affect the object beneath it. For example, if you draw a circle on top of a rectangle and then move the circle off the rectangle, the portion of the rectangle overlapped by the circle is removed. The Object Drawing Model allows you to overlap shapes which are then kept separate, so that changes in one object do not affect another object. Another way to avoid having changes in one object affect another is to place them on separate layers in the Timeline as you did in Chapter 1.

Tools You'll Use

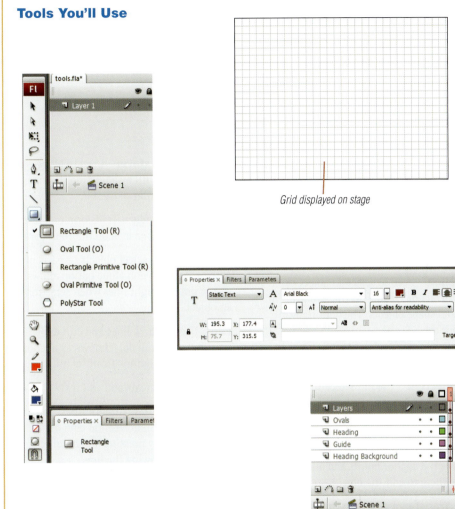

Grid displayed on stage

USE THE FLASH DRAWING TOOLS

What You'll Do

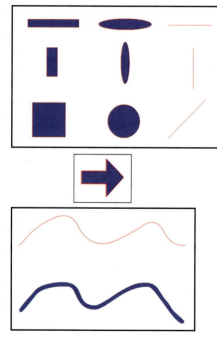

In this lesson, you will use several drawing tools to create various vector graphics.

Using Flash Drawing and Editing Tools

When you point to a tool on the Tools panel, its name appears next to the tool. Figure 1 identifies the tools described in the following paragraphs. Several of the tools have options that modify their use.

Selection—Used to select an object or parts of an object, such as the stroke or fill; and to reshape objects. The options available for the Selection tool are Snap to Objects (aligns objects), Smooth (smoothes lines), and Straighten (straightens lines).

Subselection—Used to select, drag, and reshape an object. Vector graphics are composed of lines and curves (each of which is a segment) connected by **anchor points**. Selecting an object with this tool displays the anchor points and allows you to use them to edit the object.

Free Transform—Used to transform objects by rotating, scaling, skewing, and distorting them.

Gradient Transform—Used to transform a gradient fill by adjusting the size, direction, or center of the fill.

The Free and Gradient Transform tools are grouped within one icon on the Tools panel.

Lasso—Used to select objects or parts of objects. The Polygon Mode option allows you to draw straight lines when selecting an object.

Pen—Used to draw lines and curves by creating a series of dots, known as anchor points, that are automatically connected.

Text—Used to create and edit text.

Line—Used to draw straight lines. You can draw vertical, horizontal, and 45° diagonal lines by pressing and holding [Shift] while drawing the line.

Rectangle—Used to draw rectangular shapes. Press and hold [Shift] to draw a perfect square. The Round Rectangle Radius option in the Property inspector allows you to round the corners of a rectangle.

Oval—Used to draw oval shapes. Press and hold [Shift] to draw a perfect circle.

Primitive Rectangle and Oval—Used to draw objects with properties, such as corner radius or inner radius, that can be changed using the Property inspector.

PolyStar—Used to draw polygons and stars.

The Rectangle, Oval, Primitive and PolyStar tools are grouped within one tool on the Tools panel. To display a list of grouped tools, you click the tool and hold the mouse button until the menu opens. For example, if you want to select the Oval tool and the Rectangle tool is displayed, you click and hold the Rectangle tool. Then, when the menu opens, you click the Oval tool.

Pencil—Used to draw freehand lines and shapes. The options available for the Pencil tool are Straighten (draws straight lines), Smooth (draws smooth curved lines), and Ink (draws freehand with no modification).

Brush—Used to draw (paint) with brush-like strokes. Options allow you to set the size and shape of the brush, and to determine the area to be painted, such as inside or behind an object.

Ink Bottle—Used to apply line colors and thickness to the stroke of an object.

Paint Bucket—Used to fill enclosed areas of a drawing with color. Options allow you to fill areas that have gaps and to make adjustments in a gradient fill.

Eyedropper—Used to select stroke, fill, and text attributes so they can be copied from one object to another.

Eraser—Used to erase lines and fills. Options allow you to choose what part of the object to erase, as well as the size and shape of the eraser.

The Oval, Rectangle, Pencil, Brush, Line, and Pen tools are used to create vector objects.

Displaying Gridlines, Guides, and Rulers and Using Guide Layers

Gridlines, guides, and rulers can be used to position objects on the stage. The Grid, Guides, and Rulers commands, which are found on the View menu, are used to turn on and off these features. You can modify the grid size and color, and you can specify the unit of measure for the rulers. In addition, you can create a new layer as a Guide layer that you use to position objects on the stage.

FIGURE 1
Flash tools

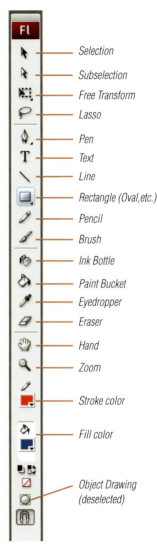

- Selection
- Subselection
- Free Transform
- Lasso
- Pen
- Text
- Line
- Rectangle (Oval, etc.)
- Pencil
- Brush
- Ink Bottle
- Paint Bucket
- Eyedropper
- Eraser
- Hand
- Zoom
- Stroke color
- Fill color
- Object Drawing (deselected)

Show gridlines and check settings

1. Start Flash, create a new Flash Document, then save it as **tools**.

2. Click **Window** on the menu bar, click **Workspace**, then click **Default**.

3. Close all of the panels except for the Tools panel and the Properties panel.

4. Click **View** on the menu bar, point to **Magnification**, then click **Fit in Window**.

5. Click the **Stroke color tool color swatch** on the Tools panel, then click the **red color swatch** in the left column of the Color palette (if necessary).

6. Click the **Fill color tool color swatch** on the Tools panel, then click the **blue color swatch** in the left column of the Color palette (if necessary).

7. Click **View** on the menu bar, point to **Grid**, then click **Show Grid** to display the gridlines.

   A gray grid appears on the stage.

8. Point to each tool on the Tools panel, as shown in Figure 2, then read its name.

You started a new document, saved it, set up the workspace, changed the stroke and fill colors, then displayed the grid and viewed tool names on the Tools panel.

FIGURE 2
Tool name on the Tools panel

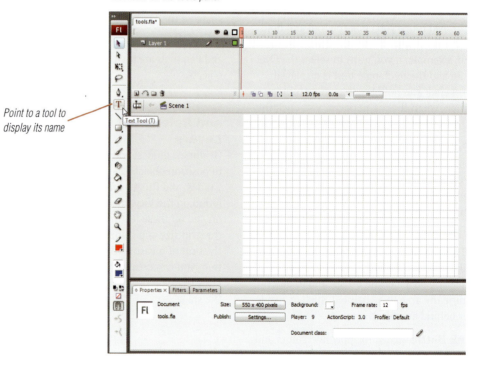

Point to a tool to display its name

FIGURE 3

Objects created with drawing tools

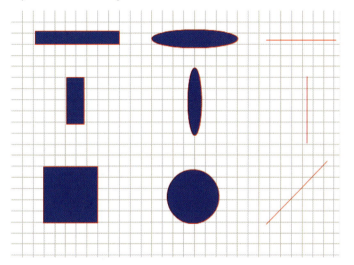

1. Click the **Rectangle tool** on the Tools panel.

   Note: If the Rectangle tool is not displayed, click and hold the Oval tool to display the group of tools.

2. Verify that the **Object Drawing option** in the Options section of the Tools panel is deselected.

   TIP When the Object Drawing option is deselected, the object is drawn so that its stroke and fill can be selected separately.

3. Using Figure 3 as a guide, draw the three rectangle shapes.

   Notice the blue color for the fill and the red color for the strokes (border lines).

   TIP Use the grid to approximate shape sizes and hold down [Shift] to draw a square. To undo an action, click the Undo command on the Edit menu.

4. Click and hold down the **Rectangle tool** on the Tools panel, then click the **Oval tool**.

5. Using Figure 3 as a guide, draw the three oval shapes.

   TIP Hold down [Shift] to draw a perfect circle.

6. Click the **Line tool**, then, using Figure 3 as a guide, draw the three lines.

   TIP Hold down [Shift] to draw a straight line.

You used the Rectangle, Oval, and Line tools to draw objects on the stage.

Use the Pen, Pencil, and Brush tools

1. Click **Insert** on the menu bar, point to **Timeline**, then click **Layer**.

    A new layer—Layer 2—appears above Layer 1.

2. Click **Frame 5** on Layer 2.

3. Click **Insert** on the menu bar, point to **Timeline**, then click **Keyframe**.

    Since the objects were drawn in Frame 1 on Layer 1, they are no longer visible when you insert a keyframe in Frame 5 on Layer 2.

4. Click the **Zoom tool** 🔍 on the Tools panel, point near the upper-left quadrant of the stage, click to zoom in, then scroll as needed to see more of the grid.

5. Click the **Pen tool** ✒️ on the Tools panel, position it in the upper-left quadrant of the stage, as shown in Figure 4, then click to set an anchor point.

6. Using Figure 5 as a guide, click the remaining anchor points to complete drawing an arrow.

    | TIP   To close an object, be sure to re-click the first anchor point as your last action.

7. Click the **Paint Bucket tool** 🪣 , then click inside the arrow.

8. Click **View** on the menu bar, point to **Magnification**, then click **Fit in Window**.

9. Insert a **new layer**, Layer 3, then insert a **keyframe** in Frame 10.

10. Click the **Pencil tool** ✏️ on the Tools panel.

11. Select the **Smooth option** S. in the Options section of the Tools panel, as shown in Figure 6.

    (continued)

FIGURE 4
Positioning the Pen Tool on the stage

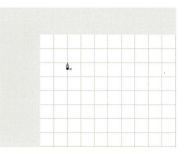

FIGURE 5
Setting anchor points to draw an arrow

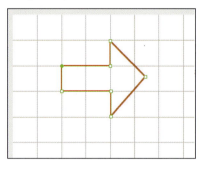

Click on the Smooth icon to display the 3 options. (Note: the Straighten icon might be displayed instead of the Smooth icon)

FIGURE 6
Pencil Tool options

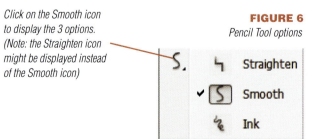

Drawing Objects in Flash

FIGURE 7

Images drawn using drawing tools

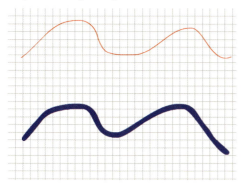

FIGURE 8

The dot pattern indicating the object is selected

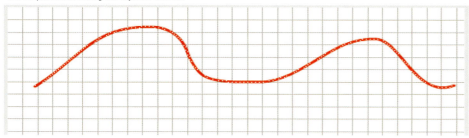

12. Draw the top image, as shown in Figure 7.

13. Click the **Brush tool** on the Tools panel.

14. Click the **Brush Size Icon** in the Options section of the Tools panel, then click the fifth option from the top.

15. Draw the bottom image, as shown in Figure 7.

Notice the Pencil tool displays the stroke color and the Brush tool displays the fill color.

You added a layer, inserted a keyframe, then used the Pen tool to draw an arrow; you selected the Smooth option for the Pencil tool and drew an object; you selected a brush size for the Brush tool and drew an object.

Modify an object using tool options

1. Click the **Selection tool** on the Tools panel, then drag a **marquee** around the top object to select it. The line displays a dot pattern, as shown in Figure 8, indicating that it is selected.

2. Click the **Smooth option icon** S in the Options section of the Tools panel three times. The line becomes smoother.

> TIP Use ScreenTips to help identify icons. (Mac)

3. Use the **Selection tool** to select the bottom object.

4. Click the **Smooth option** S in the Options section of the Tools panel.

5. Use the **Selection tool** to click a blank area of the stage, to deselect the object.

6. Save your work.

You smoothed objects using the tool options.

SELECT OBJECTS
AND APPLY COLORS

What You'll Do

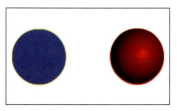

In this lesson, you will use several techniques to select objects, change the color of strokes and fills, and create a gradient fill.

Selecting Objects

Before you can edit a drawing, you must first select the object, or part of the object, on which you want to work. Objects are made up of a stroke(s) and a fill. Strokes can have several segments. For example, a rectangle will have four stroke segments, one for each side of the object. These can be selected separately or as a whole. Flash highlights objects that have been selected, as shown in Figure 9. When the stroke of an object is selected, a colored line appears. When the fill of an object is selected, a dot pattern appears; and when objects are grouped, a bounding box appears.

Using the Selection Tool

You can use the Selection tool to select part or all of an object, and to select multiple objects. To select only the fill, click just the fill; to select only the stroke, click just the stroke. To select both the fill and the stroke, double-click the object or draw a marquee around it. To select part of an object, drag a marquee that defines the area you wish to select, as shown in Figure 9. To select

multiple objects or combinations of strokes and fills, press and hold [Shift], then click each item. To deselect an item(s), click a blank area of the stage.

Using the Lasso Tool

The Lasso tool provides more flexibility than the Selection tool when selecting an area on the stage. You can use the tool in a freehand manner to select any size and shape of an area. Alternately, you can use the Polygon Mode option to draw straight lines and connect them.

Drawing Model Modes

Flash provides two drawing modes, called models. In the Merge Drawing Model mode, the stroke and fill of an object are separate. Thus, as you draw an object such as a circle, the stroke and fill can be selected individually as described earlier. When using the Object Drawing Model mode, the stroke and fill are combined and cannot be selected individually. However, you can use the Break Apart option from the Modify menu to separate the stroke and fill so that they can be selected individually. In addition, you can turn off either the stroke or fill when drawing an object in either mode. You can toggle between the two modes by clicking the Object Drawing option in the options section of the Tools panel.

Working with Colors

Flash allows you to change the color of the stroke and fill of an object. Figure 10 shows the Colors section of the Tools panel. To change a color, you click the color swatch of the Stroke color tool or the color swatch of the Fill color tool, and then select a Color swatch on the Color palette. The Color palette, as shown in Figure 11, allows you to type in a six-character code that represents the values of three colors (red, green, blue),

referred to as RGB. When these characters are combined in various ways, they can represent virtually any color. The values are in a hexadecimal format (base 16), so they include letters and digits (A–F + 0–9 = 16 options), and they are preceded by a pound sign (#). The first two characters represent the value for red, the next two for green, and the last two for blue. For example, #000000 represents black (lack of color); #FFFFFF represents white; and #FFCC66 represents a shade of gold. You do not have to memorize the codes. There are reference manuals with the codes, and many programs allow you to set the values visually by selecting a color from a palette.

You can set the desired colors before drawing an object, or you can change a color of a

previously drawn object. You can use the Ink Bottle tool to change the stroke color, and you can use the Paint Bucket tool to change the fill color. You can also use the Property inspector to change the stroke and fill colors.

Working with Gradients

A gradient is a color fill that makes a gradual transition from one color to another. Gradients can be very useful for creating a 3-D effect, drawing attention to an object, and generally enhancing the appearance of an object. You can apply a gradient fill by using the Paint Bucket tool. The position of the Paint Bucket tool over the object is important because it determines the direction of the gradient fill. The Color palette can be used to create and alter custom gradients.

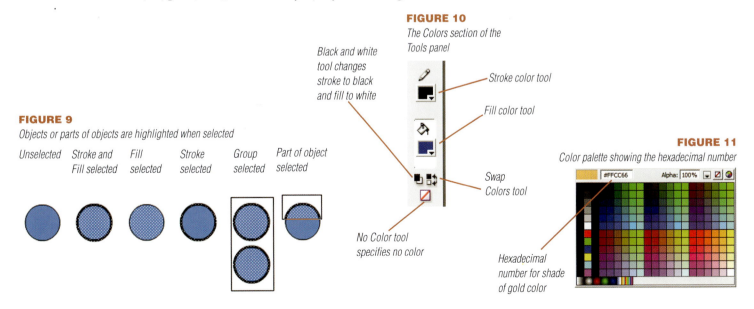

FIGURE 9
Objects or parts of objects are highlighted when selected

Unselected   Stroke and   Fill   Stroke   Group   Part of object
             Fill selected   selected   selected   selected   selected

FIGURE 10
The Colors section of the Tools panel

Black and white tool changes stroke to black and fill to white

Stroke color tool

Fill color tool

Swap Colors tool

No Color tool specifies no color

FIGURE 11
Color palette showing the hexadecimal number

#FFCC66   Alpha: 100%

Hexadecimal number for shade of gold color

Select a drawing using the Selection tool

1. Click **Frame 1** on the Timeline.

   > TIP The actions you perform on the stage will produce very different results, depending on whether you click a frame number on the Timeline or click a frame within a layer.

2. Click the **Selection tool** ⏵ on the Tools panel (if necessary), then drag the **marquee** around the circle to select the entire object (both the stroke and the fill).

3. Click anywhere on the stage to deselect the object. As you continue to select objects, notice how the availability of the Stroke color and Fill color tools in the Properties panel changes depending on what is selected.

4. Click inside the circle to select the fill only, then click outside the circle to deselect it.

5. Click the stroke of the circle to select it, as shown in Figure 12, then deselect it.

6. Double-click the **circle** to select it, press and hold **[Shift]**, double-click the **square** to select both objects, then deselect both objects.

7. Click the right border of the square to select it, as shown in Figure 13, then deselect it.

   Objects, such as rectangles, have border segments that can be selected individually.

8. Drag a **marquee** around the square, circle, and diagonal line to select all three objects.

9. Click a blank area of the stage to deselect the objects.

You used the Selection tool to select the stroke and fill of an object, and to select multiple objects.

FIGURE 12

Using the Selection tool to select the stroke of the circle

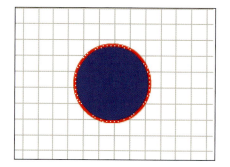

FIGURE 13

Using the Selection tool to select a segment of the stroke of the square

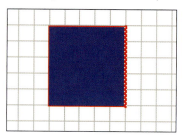

FIGURE 14
Circles drawn with the Oval tool

Change fill and stroke colors

1. Click **Layer 3**, click **Insert** on the menu bar, point to **Timeline**, then click **Layer**.

2. Click **Frame 15** of the new layer, click **Insert** on the menu bar, point to **Timeline**, then click **Keyframe**.

3. Click **View** on the menu bar, point to **Grid**, then click **Show Grid** to remove the gridlines.

4. Select the **Oval tool** ◯ on the Tools panel, then draw two circles similar to those shown in Figure 14.

5. Click the **Fill color tool color swatch** on the Tools panel, then click the **yellow color swatch** in the left column of the Color palette.

6. Click the **Paint Bucket tool** ◇ on the Tools panel, then click the fill of the right circle.

7. Click the **Stroke color tool color swatch** on the Tools panel, then click the **yellow Color swatch** in the left column of the color palette.

8. Click the **Ink Bottle tool** ◇ on the Tools panel, point to the red stroke line of the left circle, as shown in Figure 15, then click to change the stroke color to yellow.

You used the Paint Bucket and Ink Bottle tools to change the fill and stroke colors of an object.

FIGURE 15
Changing the stroke color

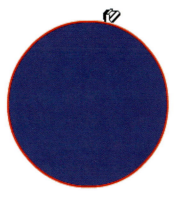

Create a gradient and make changes to the gradient

1. Click the **Fill color tool color swatch** 🪣 on the Tools panel, then click the **red gradient color swatch** in the bottom row of the Color palette, as shown in Figure 16.

2. Click the **Paint Bucket tool** 🪣 on the Tools panel, then click the yellow circle.

3. Click different parts of the right circle to view how the gradient changes.

4. Click the right side of the circle, as shown in Figure 17.

5. Click and hold the **Free Transform tool** on the Tools panel, then click the **Gradient Transform tool** 🔲 .

6. Click the **gradient-filled circle**.

7. Drag each of the four handles, as shown in Figure 18, to determine their effects on the gradient, then click the **stage** to deselect the circle.

8. Click the **Fill color tool color swatch** 🪣, click the **Hex Edit text box**, type **#0000FF** (four zeros), then press **[Enter]** (Win) or **[return]** (Mac).

   The Fill color swatch changes to blue.

9. Save your work.

You applied a gradient fill and you used the Gradient Transform tool to alter the gradient.

FIGURE 16
Selecting the red gradient

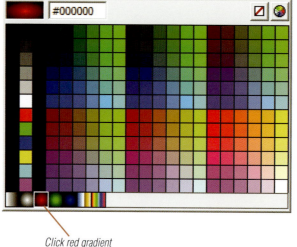

#000000

Click red gradient color swatch to select it

FIGURE 17
Clicking the right side of the circle

FIGURE 18
Gradient Transform handles

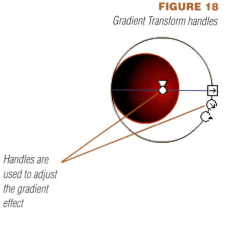

Handles are used to adjust the gradient effect

FIGURE 19

Circle drawn using the Object Drawing Model mode

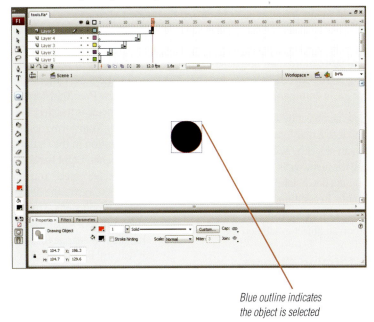

Blue outline indicates
the object is selected

1. Insert a **new layer**, then insert a **keyframe** on Frame 20.

2. Select the **Oval tool** .

3. Click the **Stroke color tool color swatch** , then click the **red swatch**.

4. Click the **Fill color tool color swatch** , then click the **black swatch**.

5. Click the **Object Drawing option** in the Options section of the Tools panel to change the mode to the Object Drawing Model.

6. Draw a **circle** on the stage, as shown in Figure 19.

   Notice that when you use the Object Drawing Model mode, objects are automatically selected, and the stroke and fill areas are combined.

7. Click the **Selection tool** on the Tools panel, then click a blank area of the stage to deselect the object.

8. Click once on the **circle**.

   The entire object is selected, including the stroke and fill areas.

9. Click **Modify** on the menu bar, then click **Break Apart**.

   Breaking apart an object drawn in Object Drawing Model mode allows you to select the strokes and fills individually.

10. Click a blank area on the stage, then save your work.

You used the Object Drawing Model mode to draw an object, deselect it, and then break it apart to display the stroke and fill.

WORK WITH DRAWN OBJECTS

What You'll Do

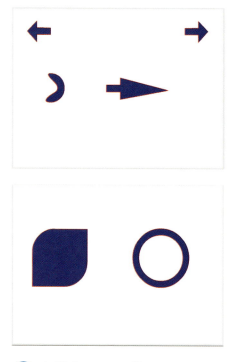

▶ In this lesson, you will copy, move, and transform (resize, rotate, and reshape) objects.

Copying and Moving Objects

To copy an object, select it, and then click the Copy command on the Edit menu. To paste the object, click the Paste command on the Edit menu. You can copy an object to another layer by selecting the frame and layer prior to pasting the object. You can copy and paste more than one object by selecting all the objects before using the Copy or Paste commands.

You move an object by selecting it and dragging it to a new location. You precisely position an object by selecting it and then pressing the arrow keys, which move the selection up, down, left, and right in small increments. In addition, the X and Y coordinates in the Property inspector can be used to position an object exactly on the stage.

Transforming Objects

You use the Free Transform tool and the Transform panel to resize, rotate, skew, and reshape objects. After selecting an object, you click the Free Transform tool to display eight square-shaped handles used to trans-

form the object, and a circle-shaped transformation point located at the center of the object. The transformation point is the point around which the object can be rotated. You can also change its location.

Resizing an Object

You enlarge or reduce the size of an object using the Scale option, which is available when the Free Transform tool is selected. The process is to select the object and click the Free Transform tool, and then click the Scale option in the Options section of the Tools panel. Eight handles appear around the selected object. You drag the corner handles to resize the object without changing its proportions. That is, if the object starts out as a square, dragging a corner handle will change the size of the object, but it will still be a square. On the other hand, if you drag one of the middle handles, the object will be reshaped as taller, shorter, wider, or narrower. In addition, the Width and Height settings in the Property inspector can be used to resize an object in increments of one-tenth of one pixel.

Rotating and Skewing an Object

You use the Rotate and Skew option of the Free Transform tool to rotate an object and to skew it. Select the object, click the Free Transform tool, and then click the Rotate and Skew option in the Options section of the Tools panel. Eight square-shaped handles appear around the object. You drag the corner handles to rotate the object, or you drag the middle handles to skew the object, as shown in Figure 20. The Transform panel can be used to rotate and skew an object in a more precise way; select the object, display the Transform panel, enter the desired rotation or skew in degrees, and then press [Enter] (Win) or [return] (Mac).

Distorting an Object

You can use the Distort and Envelope options to reshape an object by dragging its handles. The Distort option allows you to reshape an object by dragging one corner without affecting the other corners of the object. The Envelope option provides more than eight handles to allow for more precise distortions. These options are accessed through the Transform command on the Modify menu.

Reshaping a Segment of an Object

You use the Subselection tool to reshape a segment of an object. You click an edge of the object to display handles that can be dragged to reshape the object.

You use the Selection tool to reshape objects. When you point to the edge of an object, the pointer displays an arc symbol. Using the Arc pointer, you drag the edge of the object you want to reshape, as shown in Figure 21. If the Selection tool points to a corner of an object, the pointer changes to an L-shape. You drag the pointer to reshape the corner of the object.

Flipping an Object

You use a Flip option on the Transform menu to flip an object either horizontally or vertically. You select the object, click the Transform command on the Modify menu, and then choose Flip Vertical or Flip Horizontal. Other Transform options allow you to rotate and scale the selected object. The Remove Transform command allows you to restore an object to its original state.

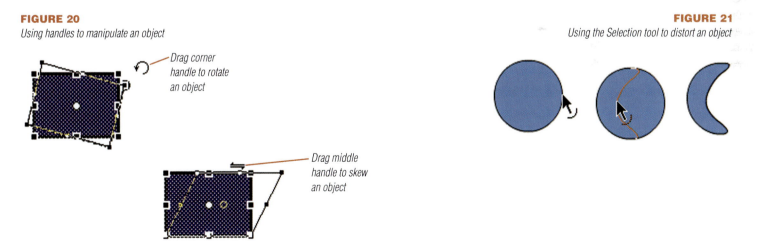

FIGURE 20
Using handles to manipulate an object

Drag corner handle to rotate an object

Drag middle handle to skew an object

FIGURE 21
Using the Selection tool to distort an object

Copy and move an object

1. Click **Frame 5** on the Timeline.

2. Click the **Selection tool** ![arrow] on the Tools panel, then draw a **marquee** around the arrow object to select it.

3. Click **Edit** on the menu bar, click **Copy**, click **Edit** on the menu bar, then click **Paste in Center**.

   A copy of the arrow is pasted on the center of the stage.

4. Drag the newly copied **arrow** to the upper-right corner of the stage, as shown in Figure 22.

5. Verify the right arrow object is selected on the stage, press the **[down arrow key]** ↓ on the keyboard to move the object in approximately one-pixel increments, and notice how the Y coordinate in the Property inspector changes.

6. Press the **[right arrow key]** → on the keyboard to move the object in one-pixel increments, and notice how the X coordinate in the Property inspector changes.

7. Select the **number** in the X coordinate box in the Property inspector, type **450**, as shown in Figure 23, then press **[Enter]** (Win) or **[return]** (Mac).

8. Repeat Step 7 to change the Y coordinate setting to **30**.

9. Select the **left arrow object**, then set the X and Y coordinates to **36** and **30**, respectively.

10. Click a blank area of the stage to deselect the object.

You used the Selection tool to select an object, then you copied and moved the object.

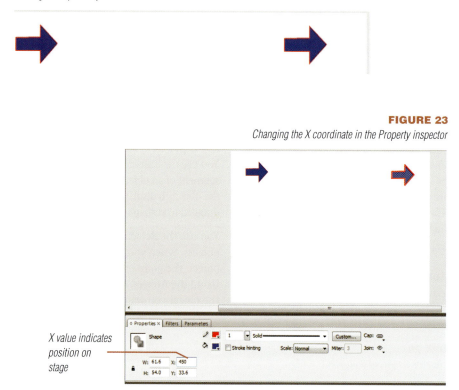

FIGURE 22
Moving the copied object

FIGURE 23
Changing the X coordinate in the Property inspector

X value indicates position on stage

X and Y Coordinates

The stage dimensions are made up of pixels (dots) matching the stage size. So, a stage size of 550×400 would be 550 pixels wide and 400 pixels high. Each pixel has a location on the stage designated as the X (across) and Y (down) coordinates. The location of any object is determined by its position from the upper-left corner of the stage, which is 0,0. So, an object having coordinates of 450,30 would be positioned at 450 pixels across and 30 pixels down the stage. The registration point of an object is used to align it with the coordinates. The registration point is initially set at the upper-left corner of an object.

FIGURE 24

Resizing an object using the corner handles

FIGURE 25

Reshaping an object using the middle handles

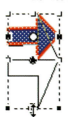

Transform Options

Different transform options, such as rotate, skew, and scale, can be accessed through the Free Transform tool on the Tools panel, the Transform command on the Modify menu, and the Transform panel.

Resize and reshape an object

1. Draw a **marquee** around the arrow object on the right side of the stage to select the object.

2. Select the **Free Transform tool** on the Tools panel

   Note: You may need to click and hold the Gradient tool to display the Free Transform tool.

3. Select the **Scale option** in the Options section of the Tools panel.

4. Drag each **corner handle** toward and then away from the center of the object, as shown in Figure 24.

   As you drag a corner handle, the object's size is changed, but its proportions remain the same.

5. Click **Edit** on the menu bar, then click **Undo Scale.**

6. Repeat Step 5 until the arrow returns to its original size.

   TIP The object is its original size when the option Undo Scale is no longer available on the Edit menu.

7. Verify the arrow is still selected and the handles are displayed, then select the **Scale option** (if necessary).

8. Drag each **middle handle** toward and then away from the center of the object, as shown in Figure 25.

   As you drag the middle handles, the object's size and proportions change.

9. Click **Edit** on the menu bar, then click **Undo Scale**, as needed, to return the arrow to its original size.

You used the Free Transform tool and the Scale option to display an object's handles, and you used the handles to resize and reshape the object.

Rotate, skew, and flip an object

1. Verify that the right arrow is selected (handles displayed), then click the **Rotate and Skew option** 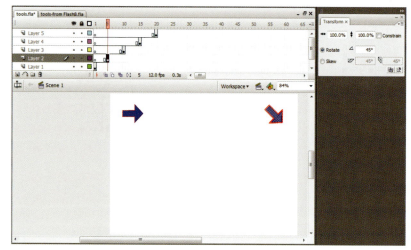 in the Options section of the Tools panel.

2. Click the **upper-right corner handle,** then rotate the object clockwise.

3. Click the **upper-middle handle,** then drag it to the right.

    The arrow slants to the right.

4. Click **Edit** on the menu bar, click the **Undo Rotate** command, then repeat until the arrow is in its original shape and orientation.

5. Click the **Selection tool** ⬉ on the Tools panel, verify that the right arrow is selected, click **Window** on the menu bar, then click **Transform**.

6. Double-click the **Rotate text box**, type **45**, then press **[Enter]** (Win) or **[return]** (Mac).

    The arrow rotates 45°, as shown in Figure 2-26.

7. Click **Edit** on the menu bar, then click **Undo Transform**.

8. Close the Transform panel.

9. Click the **Selection tool** ⬉ on the Tools panel, then draw a **marquee** around the arrow in the upper-left corner of the stage to select the object.

10. Click **Modify** on the menu bar, point to **Transform**, then click **Flip Horizontal**.

11. Save your work.

You used options on the Tools panel, the Transform panel, and Modify menu commands to rotate, skew, and flip an object.

FIGURE 26

Using the Transform panel to rotate an object

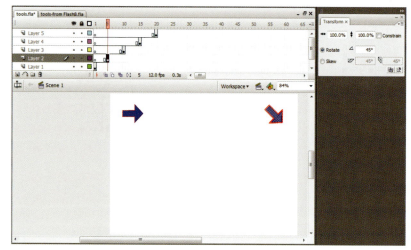

FIGURE 27

Using the Subselection tool to select an object

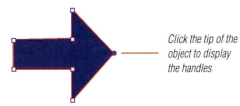

Click the tip of the
object to display
the handles

FIGURE 28

Using the Subselection tool to drag a handle to reshape the object

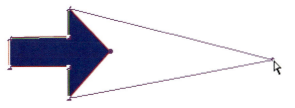

FIGURE 29

Using the Selection tool to drag an edge to reshape the object

Click here, then drag

Lesson 3   Work with Objects

Use the Zoom, Subselection, and Selection tools

1. Select the **arrow** in the upper-right corner of the stage, click **Edit** on the menu bar, click **Copy**, click **Edit** on the menu bar, then click **Paste in Center**.

2. Click the **Zoom tool** 🔍 on the Tools panel, then click the middle of the copied object to enlarge the view.

3. Click the **Subselection tool** on the Tools panel, then click the **tip of the arrow** to display the handles, as shown in Figure 27.

    | TIP   The handles allow you to change any segment of the object.

4. Click the **handle** at the tip of the arrow, then drag it, as shown in Figure 28.

5. Select the **Oval tool** on the Tools panel, then deselect the **Object Drawing option** in the Options section of the Tools panel (if necessary).

6. Verify the Fill color is set to blue, then draw a **circle** to the left of the arrow you just modified.

7. Click the **Selection tool** on the Tools panel, then point to the left edge of the circle until the Arc pointer is displayed.

8. Drag the **pointer** to the position shown in Figure 29.

9. Click **View** on the menu bar, point to **Magnification**, then click **Fit in Window**.

10. Save your work.

You used the Zoom tool to change the view, and you used the Subselection and Selection tools to reshape objects.

Use the Primitive Rectangle and Oval tools

1. Insert a **new layer** above Layer 5, click **Frame 25** on Layer 6, then insert a **Keyframe**.

2. Click and hold down the **Oval tool**  (or the Rectangle tool if it is displayed) to display the menu.

3. Click the **Rectangle Primitive tool** , then click the **Reset button** in the Property inspector to clear all of the settings.

4. Hold down **[Shift]** and draw the **square** shown in Figure 30.

   Notice the four corner handles. These can be dragged to change the radius of the corners. In addition, the Property inspector can be used to make changes in the object.

5. Click the **Selection tool** in the Tools panel, then drag **the upper-right corner handle** toward the center of the object.
   As you drag the corner, the radius of all four corners are changed.

6. Click the **Reset button** in the Property inspector to clear the setting.

7. Click the **Rectangle corner radius list arrow** , as shown in Figure 31.

8. Slowly drag the **slider** up until the radius changes to 40, then slowly drag the **slider** down until the radius changes to −100.
   The slider can be used to quickly change the radius of the corners.

9. Click the **Reset button** in the Property inspector to clear the setting.

FIGURE 30
Drawing an object with the Rectangle Primitive tool

FIGURE 31
Selecting the rectangle corner radius

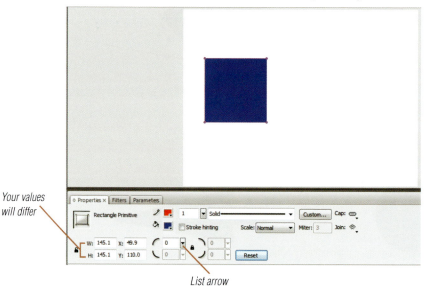

Your values will differ

List arrow

Drawing Objects in Flash

FIGURE 32
Drawing an object with the Oval Primitive tool

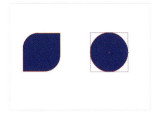

FIGURE 33
Setting the start angle for a circle

10. Click the **lock icon** next to the Rectangle corner radius box to unlock the other settings.

11. Use the corner radius settings to set the upper-left corner radius to **60** and the lower-right corner to **60**.

12. Click a blank area of the stage to deselect the object.

13. Select the **Oval Primitive tool** in the Tools panel, then hold down **[Shift]** and draw the **circle** shown in Figure 32.

> TIP Remember some tools are grouped. Click and hold a grouped tool, such as the Oval tool, to see the menu of tools in the group.

14. Click the **Reset button** to clear any settings.

15. Click the **Start angle list arrow**.

16. Rotate the **circle slider** completely around, then set the angle to **55**, as shown in Figure 33.

17. Click the **Reset button** to clear the setting.

18. Click the **Inner radius list arrow**, then use the **slider** to set the inner radius to **90**.

19. Save your work.

You used the Primitive tools to create objects and the Property inspector to alter them.

Properties × | Filters | Parameters

Oval Primitive

Solid

Custom... | Cap:

Scale: Normal | Miter: 3 | Join:

W: 148.6 X: 313.9 Start angle: 55 Inner radius: 0 Reset

H: 148.7 Y: 108.6 End angle: 0 ✓ Close path

WORK WITH TEXT
AND TEXT OBJECTS

What You'll Do

In this lesson, you will enter text using text blocks. You will also resize text blocks, change text attributes, and transform text.

Learning About Text

Flash provides a great deal of flexibility when using text. Among other settings, you can specify the typeface (font), size, style (bold, italic), and color (including gradients) for text. You can transform the text by rotating, scaling, skewing, and flipping it. You can even break apart a letter and reshape its segments.

Entering Text and Changing the Text Block

It is important to understand that text is entered into a text block, as shown in Figure 34. You use the Text tool to place a text block on the stage and to enter and edit text. A text block expands as more text is entered and may even extend beyond the edge of the stage. You can adjust the size of the text block so that it is a fixed width by dragging the handle in the upper-right corner of the block. Figure 35 shows the process of using the Text tool to enter text and resize the text block. Once you select the tool, you click the pointer on the stage where you want the text to appear. An

insertion point indicates where in the text block the next character will appear when typed. You can reshape the text block by pressing [Enter] (Win) or [return] (Mac) or by dragging the circle handle. After reshaping the text block, the circle handle changes to a square, indicating that the text block now has a fixed width. Then, when you enter more text, it automatically wraps within the text block. You can resize the text block at any time by selecting it with the Selection tool and dragging a handle.

Changing Text Attributes

You can use the Properties panel to change the font, size, and style of a single character or an entire text block. Figure 36 shows the Properties panel when a text object is selected. You select text, display the Properties panel, and make the changes. You use the Selection tool to select the entire text block by drawing a marquee around it. You use the Text tool to select a single character or string of characters by dragging the

I-beam pointer over the text you want to select, as shown in Figure 37.

Working with Paragraphs

When working with large bodies of text, such as paragraphs, Flash provides many of the features found in a word processor. You can align paragraphs (left, right, center, justified) within a text block, set margins (space between the border of a text block and the paragraph text), set indents for the first line of a paragraph, and set line spacing (distance between paragraphs) using the Properties panel.

Transforming Text

It is important to understand that a text block is an object. Therefore, you can transform (reshape, rotate, skew, and so on) a text block in the same way you transform other objects. If you want to transform individual characters within a text block, you must first break apart the text block. Then you use the Selection tool to select the text block, and click the Break Apart command on the Modify menu. Each character (or a group of characters) in the text block can now be selected and transformed.

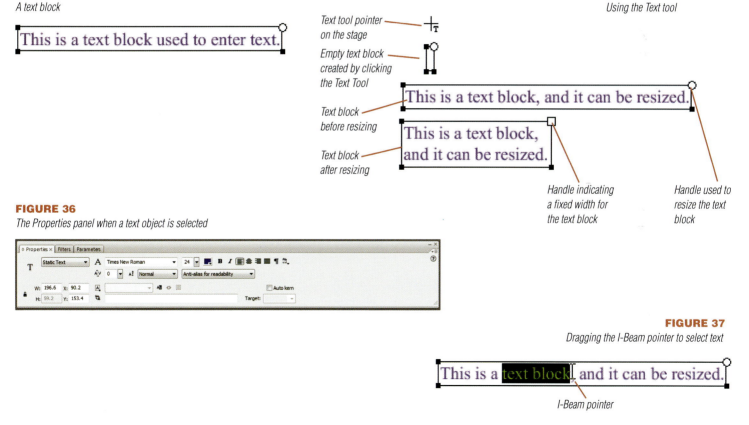

FIGURE 34
A text block

This is a text block used to enter text.

Text tool pointer on the stage

Empty text block created by clicking the Text Tool

FIGURE 35
Using the Text tool

This is a text block, and it can be resized.

Text block before resizing

This is a text block, and it can be resized.

Text block after resizing

Handle indicating a fixed width for the text block

Handle used to resize the text block

FIGURE 36
The Properties panel when a text object is selected

FIGURE 37
Dragging the I-Beam pointer to select text

This is a text block, and it can be resized.

I-Beam pointer

Enter text and change text attributes

1. Click **Layer 6**, insert a **new layer**, then insert a **keyframe** in Frame 30 of the new layer.

2. Click the **Text tool** **T** on the Tools panel, click the center of the stage, then type **We have great events each year including a Rally**!

3. Click the **I-Beam pointer** I before the word "Rally," as shown in Figure 38, then type **Car** followed by a space.

4. Verify that the Property inspector panel is displayed, then drag the I-Beam pointer I across the text to select all the text.

5. Click the **Font list arrow**, click **Arial Black**, click the **Font Size list arrow**, then drag the **slider** to **16**.

6. Click the **Text (fill) color swatch** , click the **Hex Edit text box**, type **#990000**, then press **[Enter]** (Win) or **[return]** (Mac).

7. If necessary, click the text block to select it, position the **text pointer** over the circle handle until the pointer changes to a double arrow ↔, then drag the **handle** to the left, as shown in Figure 39.

8. Select the text using the I-Beam pointer I, then click the **Align Center button** in the Property inspector.

9. Click the **Selection tool** on the Tools panel, click the **text object**, then drag the **object** to the lower-middle of the stage.

   TIP The Selection tool is used to select the text block, and the Text tool is used to select and edit the text within the text block.

You entered text and changed the font, type size, and text color; you also resized the text block and changed the text alignment.

FIGURE 38
Using the Text tool to enter text

We have great events each year including a |Rally!

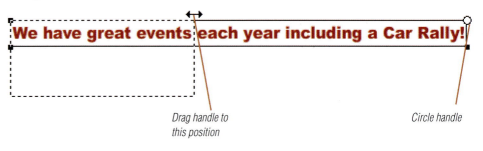

FIGURE 39
Resizing the text block

We have great events each year including a Car Rally!

Drag handle to
this position

Circle handle

FIGURE 40
The Filters options in the Property inspector panel

Using Filters

You can apply special effects, such as drop shadows, to text using options on the Filters panel in the Property inspector. The process is to select the desired text, click the Filters tab in the Property inspector panel, choose the desired effect, and make any adjustments, such as changing the color of a gradient glow. You can copy and paste a filter from one object to another using the Filter panel.

Add a Filter effect to text

1. Click the **Text tool** T on the Tools panel, click the center of the stage twice, then type **Join Us Now**.

2. Drag the **I-Beam pointer** I across the text to select it, then use the Property inspector to change the Font size to **30** and the Fill color to **#003399**.

3. Click the **Selection tool** on the tools panel, verify the text block is selected, then click the **Filters** tab on the title bar of the Property panel.

4. Click the **Add filter icon**, then click **Drop Shadow**.

    TIP If you don't see the Drop Shadow option, hold the mouse pointer over the arrow at the bottom of the menu until Drop Shadow scrolls into view, then click it.

5. Click the **Angle list arrow** in the Filters section of the Property inspector, as shown in Figure 40.

6. Click and rotate the small circle within the larger circle and notice the changes in the drop shadow.

7. Set the Angle to **50**.

8. Click the **Distance list arrow**, then drag the **slider** and notice the changes in the drop shadow.

9. Set the Distance to **5**.

10. Save your work.

You used the Filter panel to create a drop shadow and then made changes to it.

Skew text and align objects

1. Click the **Properties tab**, verify that the **Text tool** T is selected, click the pointer near the top middle of the stage twice, then type **Classic Car Club**.

   The attributes of the new text reflect the most recent settings entered in the Properties panel.

2. Drag the **I-Beam pointer** I to select the text, then change the font size to **40** and the fill color to **#990000**.

3. Click the **Selection tool** on the Tools panel to select the text box, then select the **Free Transform tool** on the Tools panel.

4. Click the **Rotate and Skew option** in the Options section of the Tools panel.

5. Drag the top middle handle to the right, as shown in Figure 41, to skew the text.

6. Click the **Selection tool** on the Tools panel.

7. Drag a **marquee** around all of the objects on the stage to select them.

8. Click **Modify** on the menu bar, point to **Align**, then click **Horizontal Center**.

9. Click a blank area of the stage to deselect the objects.

You entered a heading, changed the type size, and skewed text using the Free Transform tool, then you aligned the objects on the stage.

FIGURE 41
Skewing the text

Drawing Objects in Flash

FIGURE 42
Reshaping a letter

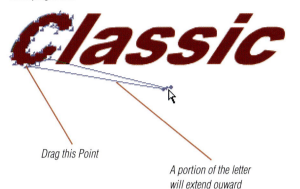

Drag this Point

A portion of the letter
will extend ouward

FIGURE 43
Applying a gradient fill to each letter

Reshape and apply a gradient to text

1. Click the **Selection tool** ![arrow], click the **Classic Car Club text block** to select it, click **Modify** on the menu bar, then click **Break Apart**.

   The letters are now individual text blocks.

2. Click **Modify** on the menu bar, then click **Break Apart**.

   The letters are filled with a dot pattern, indicating that they can now be edited.

3. Click the **Zoom tool** ![zoom] on the Tools panel, then click the **"C"** in Classic.

4. Click the **Subselection tool** ![arrow] on the Tools panel, then click the edge of the letter **"C"** to display the object's segment handles.

5. Drag a lower handle on the "C" in Classic, as shown in Figure 42.

6. Click the **Selection tool** ![arrow], then click a blank area of the stage to deselect the objects.

7. Click the **Fill color tool color swatch** ![swatch] on the Tools panel, then click the **red gradient color swatch** in the bottom row of the Color palette.

8. Click the **Paint Bucket tool** ![bucket] on the Tools panel, then click the top of each letter to change the fill to a red gradient, as shown in Figure 43.

9. Click the **Selection tool** ![arrow], then change the view to **Fit in Window**.

10. Click **Control** on the menu bar, click **Test Movie**, watch the movie, then close the Flash Player window.

11. Save your work, then close the movie.

You broke apart a text block, reshaped text, and added a gradient to the text.

WORK WITH LAYERS
AND OBJECTS

What You'll Do

In this lesson, you will create, rename, reorder, delete, hide, and lock layers. You will also display outline layers, use a Guide layer, distribute text to layers, and create a folder layer.

Learning About Layers

Flash uses two types of spatial organization. First, there is the position of objects on the stage, and then there is the stacking order of objects that overlap. An example of overlapping objects is text placed on a banner. Layers are used on the Timeline as a way to organize objects. Placing objects on their own layer makes them easier to work with, especially when reshaping them, repositioning them on the stage, or rearranging their order in relation to other objects. In addition, layers are useful for organizing other elements such as sounds, animations, and ActionScript.

There are six types of layers, as shown in the Layer Properties dialog box displayed in Figure 44 and discussed next.

Normal—The default layer type. All objects on these layers appear in the movie.

Guide (Standard and Motion)—A Standard Guide layer serves as a reference point for positioning objects on the stage. A Motion Guide layer is used to create a path for animated objects to follow.

Guided—A layer that contains an animated object, linked to a Motion Guide layer.

Mask—A layer that hides and reveals portions of another layer.

Masked—A layer that contains the objects that are hidden and revealed by a Mask layer.

Folder—A layer that can contain other layers.

Motion Guide, Mask, and Masked layer types will be covered in a later chapter.

Working with Layers

The Layer Properties dialog box, accessed through the Timeline command on the Modify menu, allows you to specify the type of layer. It also allows you to name, show (and hide), and lock them. Naming a layer provides a clue to the objects on the layer. For example, naming a layer Logo might indicate that the object on the layer is the company's logo. Hiding a layer(s) may reduce the clutter on the stage and make it easier to work with selected objects from the layer(s) that are not hidden. Locking a layer(s) prevents the objects from being accidentally edited. Other options in the Layer Properties dialog box allow you to view layers as outlines and change the outline color.

Outlines can be used to help you determine which objects are on a layer. When you turn on this feature, each layer has a colored box that corresponds with the color of the objects on its layer. Icons on the Layers section of the Timeline, as shown in Figure 45, correspond to features in the Layer Properties dialog box.

FIGURE 44
The Layer Properties dialog box

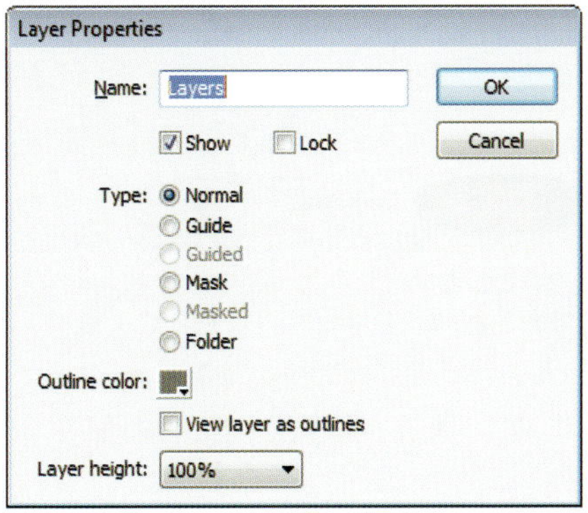

FIGURE 45
The Layers section of the Timeline

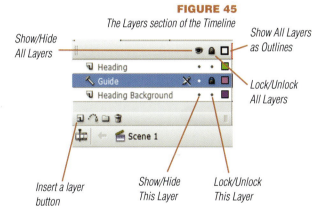

Using a Guide Layer

Guide layers are useful in aligning objects on the stage. Figure 46 shows a Guide layer that has been used to align three buttons along a diagonal path. The buttons are on one layer and the diagonal line is on another layer, the Guide layer. The process is to insert a new layer above the layer containing the objects to be aligned, click the Layer command on the Modify menu to display the Layer Properties dialog box, select Guide as the layer type, and then draw a path that will be used as the guide to align objects. You then display the Guides options from the View menu, turn on Snap to Guides, and drag the desired objects to the Guide line. Objects have a transformation point that is used when snapping to a guide. By default, this point is at the center of the object. Figure 47 shows the process.

FIGURE 46
A Guide layer used to align objects on the stage

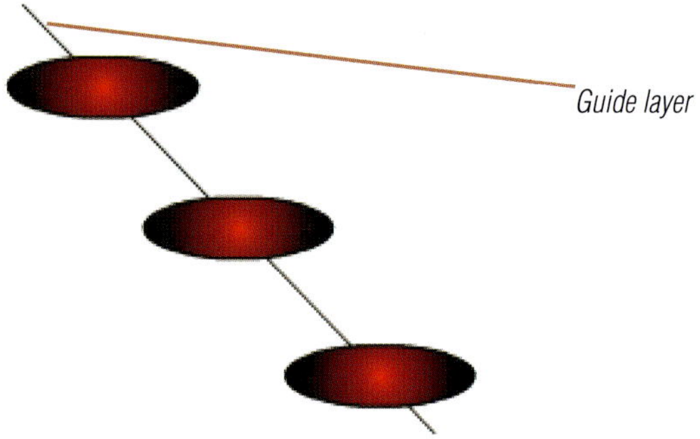

Guide layer

FIGURE 47
The transformation point of an object

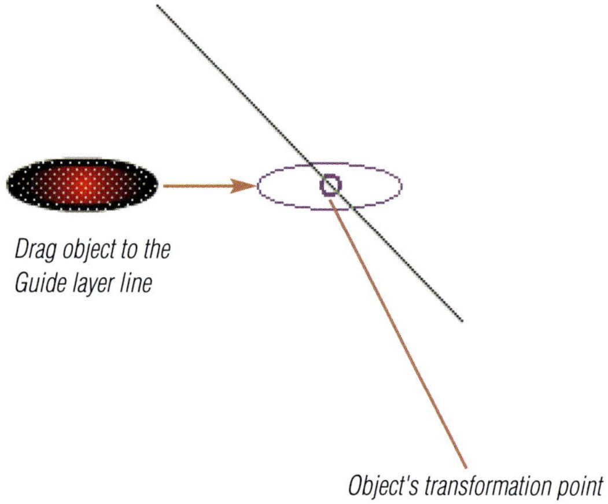

Drag object to the Guide layer line

Object's transformation point

Distributing Text to Layers

Text blocks are made up of one or more characters. When you break apart a text block, each character becomes an object that can be edited independently of the other characters. You can use the Distribute to Layers command to cause each character to automatically be placed on its own layer. Figure 48 shows the seven layers created after the text block containing 55 Chevy has been broken apart and distributed to layers.

Using Folder Layers

As movies become larger and more complex, the number of layers increases.

Flash allows you to organize layers by creating folders and grouping other layers in them. Figure 49 shows a layers folder—Layer 1—with seven layers in it. You click the Folder layer triangle next to Layer 1 to open and close the folder.

FIGURE 48
Distributing text to layers

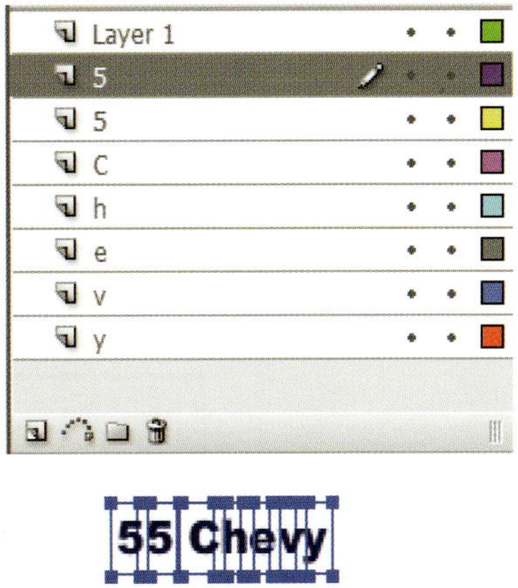

FIGURE 49
A folder layer

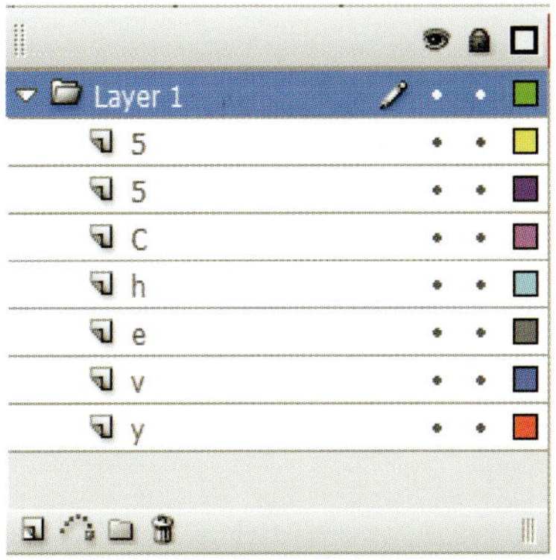

Create and reorder layers

1. Open fl2_1.fla from the drive and folder where your Data Files are stored, then save it as **layers2.fla**.

2. Click **View** on the menu bar, point to **Magnification**, then click **Fit in Window**.

3. Click the **Insert Layer icon** on the bottom of the Timeline (below the layer names) to insert a new layer, Layer 2.

4. Select the **Rectangle tool** on the Tools panel, then set the corner radius to **10** in the Property inspector.

5. Click the **Fill color tool color swatch** on the Tools panel, click the **Hex Edit text box**, type **#999999**, then press **[Enter]** (Win) or **[return]** (Mac).

6. Click the **Stroke color tool color swatch** on the Tools panel, click the **Hex Edit text box**, type **#000000**, then press **[Enter]** (Win) or **[return]** (Mac).

7. Draw the **rectangle** shown in Figure 50 so it masks the text heading.

8. Drag **Layer 1** above Layer 2 on the Timeline, as shown in Figure 51.

You added a layer, drew an object on the layer, and reordered layers.

FIGURE 50
Drawing a rectangle with a rounded corner

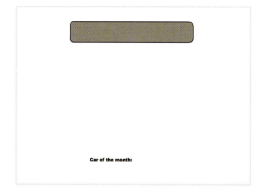

Car of the month:

FIGURE 51
Dragging Layer 1 above Layer 2

Drag Layer 1 above Layer 2

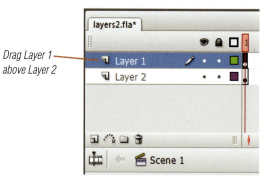

layers2.fla*

Layer 1

Layer 2

Scene 1

Drawing Objects in Flash

FIGURE 52
Renaming layers

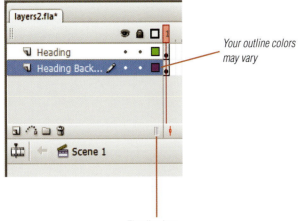

*Your outline colors
may vary*

Timeline icon

FIGURE 53
Expanding the Layer name section of the Timeline

Rename and delete layers and expand the Timeline

1. Double-click **Layer 1** on the Timeline, type **Heading** in the Layer Name text box, then press **[Enter]** (Win) or **[return]** (Mac).

2. Rename Layer 2 as **Heading Background**.

3. Point to the **Timeline icon** below the layer names, as shown in Figure 52.

4. When the pointer changes to a double arrow , drag the **icon** to the right to display all the layer names, as shown in Figure 53.

5. Click the **Heading layer**, then click the **Delete Layer icon** on the bottom of the Timeline.

6. Click **Edit** on the menu bar, then click **Undo Delete Layer**.

You renamed layers to associate them with objects on the layers, then deleted and restored a layer.

Hide, lock, and display layer outlines

1. Click the **Show/Hide All Layers icon** to hide all layers, then compare your image to Figure 54.

2. Click the **Show/Hide All Layers icon** to show all the layers.

3. Click the **Heading layer**, then click the **Show/Hide icon** twice to hide and then show the layer.

4. Click the **Lock/Unlock All Layers icon** to lock all layers.

5. With the layers locked, try to select and edit an object.

6. Click the **Lock/Unlock All Layers icon** again to unlock the layers.

7. Click the **Show All Layers as Outlines icon** twice to display and then turn off the outlines of all objects.

You hid and locked layers and displayed the outlines of objects in a layer.

FIGURE 54

Hiding all the layers

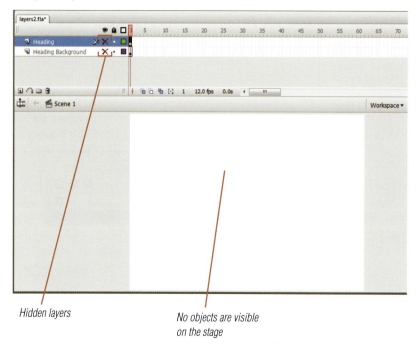

Hidden layers

No objects are visible on the stage

FIGURE 55
Expanding the Timeline

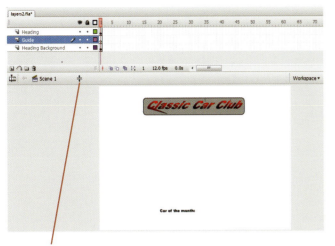

Resize pointer

FIGURE 56
A diagonal line

Create a guide for a Guide layer

1. Click the **Heading Background layer**, then click the **Insert Layer icon** on the Timeline to add a new layer, Layer 3.

2. Rename the layer **Guide**.

3. Point to the bar below the Timeline, when the pointer changes to a double arrow, as shown in Figure 55, drag the **bar** down approximately one-half inch to view all of the layers (if necessary).

4. Verify that the Guide layer is selected.

5. Click **Modify** on the menu bar, point to **Timeline**, then click **Layer Properties** to display the Layer Properties dialog box.

6. Click the **Guide option button**, then click **OK**.

   A symbol appears next to the word Guide indicating that this is a Guide layer.

7. Click **Frame 1** of the Guide layer.

8. Click the **Line tool** on the Tools panel, press and hold **[Shift]**, then draw the diagonal line, as shown in Figure 56.

9. Click the **Lock/Unlock This Layer icon** in the Guide layer to lock it.

You increased the size of the Timeline, created a guide for a Guide layer, and drew a guide line.

Add objects to a Guide layer

1. Add a new layer on the Timeline. Name it **Ovals**, then click **Frame 1** of the Ovals layer.

2. Click the **Fill color tool color swatch** on the Tools panel, then click the **red gradient color swatch** in the bottom row of the Color palette, if necessary.

3. Select the **Oval tool** on the Tools panel, then verify that the **Object Drawing option** in the Options section of the Tools panel is deselected.

4. Draw the **oval,** as shown in Figure 57.

5. Click the **Selection tool** on the Tools panel, then draw a **marquee** around the oval object to select it.

   TIP Make sure the entire object (stroke and fill) is selected.

6. Point to the center of the **oval**, click, then slowly drag it to the Guide layer line, as shown in Figure 58.

7. With the oval object selected, click **Edit** on the menu bar, then click **Copy**.

8. Click **Edit** on the menu bar, click **Paste in Center**, then (if necessary) align the copied object to the Guide layer line beneath the first oval.

9. Click **Edit** on the menu bar, click **Paste in Center**, then align the copied object to the bottom of the Guide layer line.

   TIP When objects are pasted in the center of the stage, one object may cover up another object. Move them as needed.

You created a Guide Layer and used it to align objects on the stage.

FIGURE 57
An oval object

FIGURE 58
Dragging an object to the Guide layer line

FIGURE 59

Adding text to the oval objects

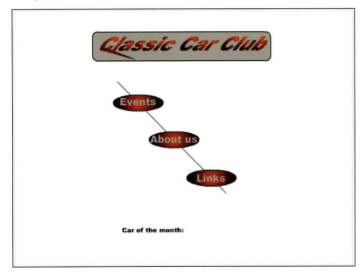

1. Insert a **new layer** on the Timeline, then name it **Labels**.

2. Click **Frame 1** of the Labels layer.

3. Click the **Text tool** T on the Tools panel, click the **top oval**, then type **Events**.

4. Drag the **I-Beam pointer** across Events to select the text, then, using the Property inspector, set the font to **Arial Black**, the font size to **16**, and the fill color to **#999999** (if necessary).

5. Click the **Selection tool** on the Tools panel, click the **text box** to select it, then drag the **text box** to center it on the oval, as shown in Figure 59.

   TIP Use the arrow keys on the keyboard to nudge the text in place (if necessary).

6. Repeat Steps 3 through 5, typing **About us** and **Links** text blocks.

7. Test the movie, then save and close the document.

8. Exit Flash.

You used the Text tool to create text blocks that were placed above objects.

Use the Flash drawing tools.

1. Start Flash, create a new Flash document, then save it as **skillsdemo2**. Refer to Figure 60 as you complete these steps.
2. Display the Grid.
3. Set the stroke color to black (Hex: #000000) and the fill color to blue (Hex: #0000FF).
4. Use the Oval tool to draw an oval on the left side of the stage, then draw a circle beneath the oval.
5. Use the Rectangle tool to draw a rectangle in the middle of the stage, then draw a square beneath the rectangle.
6. Use the Line tool to draw a horizontal line on the right side of the stage, then draw a vertical line beneath the horizontal line and a diagonal line beneath the vertical line.
7. Use the Pen tool to draw an arrow-shaped object above the rectangle.
8. Use the Paint Bucket tool to fill the arrow with the blue color.
9. Use the Pencil tool to draw a freehand line above the oval, then use the Smooth option to smooth out the line.
10. Use the Rectangle Primitive tool to draw a rectangle below the square and then drag a corner to round all the corners.
11. Save your work.

Select objects and apply colors.

1. Use the Selection tool to select the stroke of the circle, then deselect the stroke.
2. Use the Selection tool to select the fill of the circle, then deselect the fill.
3. Use the Ink Bottle tool to change the stroke color of the circle to red (Hex #FF0000).
4. Use the Paint Bucket tool to change the fill color of the square to a red gradient.
5. Change the fill color of the oval to a blue gradient.
6. Save your work.

Work with drawn objects.

1. Copy and paste the arrow object.
2. Move the copied arrow to another location on the stage.
3. Rescale both arrows to approximately half their original size.

4. Flip the copied arrow horizontally.
5. Rotate the rectangle to a 45° angle.
6. Skew the square to the right.
7. Copy one of the arrows and use the Subselection tool to reshape it, then delete it.
8. Use the Selection tool to reshape the circle to a crescent shape, then click Undo on the Edit menu.
9. Save your work.

Work with text and text objects.

1. Enter the following text in a text block at the top of the stage: **Gateway to the Pacific**.
2. Change the text to font: Tahoma, size: 24, color: red.
3. Use the gridlines to help align the text block to the top-center of the stage.
4. Skew the text block to the right.
5. Save your work.

Work with layers.

1. Insert a layer into the document.
2. Change the name on the new layer to **Heading Bkgnd**.
3. Draw a rounded corner rectangle with a blue color that covers the words Gateway to the Pacific.
4. Switch the order of the layers.
5. Lock all layers.
6. Unlock all layers.
7. Hide the Heading Bkgnd layer.
8. Show the Heading Bkgnd layer.
9. Show all layers as outlines.
10. Turn off the view of the outlines.
11. Create a Guide layer and move the arrows to it.
12. Add a layer and use the Text tool to type **Seattle** below the heading.
13. Save your work.

Use the Merge Drawing Model mode.

1. Insert a new layer and name it **MergeDraw**.
2. Click the Rectangle tool and verify that the Object Drawing option is deselected.
3. Draw a square, then use the Oval tool to draw a circle with a different color that covers approximately half of the square.
4. Use the Selection tool to drag the circle off the square.

Use the Object Drawing Model mode.

1. Insert a new layer and name it **ObjectDraw**.
2. Click the Rectangle tool and click the Object Drawing option to select it.
3. Draw a square, then use the Oval tool to draw a circle with a different color that covers approximately half of the square.
4. Use the Selection tool to drag the circle off the square.

FIGURE 60
Completed Skills Review

5. Save your work, then compare your image to the example shown in Figure 60.
6. Test the movie, then save and close the document.
7. Exit Flash.

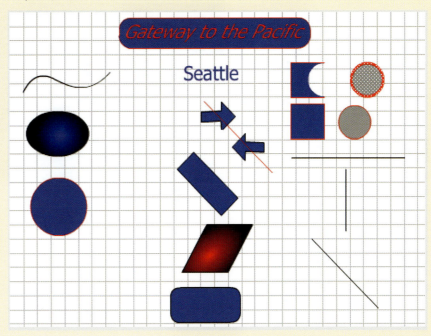

A local travel company, Ultimate Tours, has asked you to design several sample home pages for its new Web site. The goal of the Web site is to inform potential customers of its services. The company specializes in exotic treks, tours, and cruises. Thus, while its target audience spans a wide age range, they are all looking for something out of the ordinary.

1. Open a new Flash document and save it as **ultimatetours2**.
2. Set the document properties, including the size and background color.
3. Create the following on separate layers and name the layers:
   - A text heading; select a font size and font color. Skew the heading, break it apart, then reshape one or more of the characters.
   - A subheading with a different font size and color.
   - A guide path.
   - At least three objects.
4. Snap the objects to the guide path.
5. On another layer, add text to the objects and place them on the guide path.
6. Lock all layers.
7. Compare your image to the example shown in Figure 61.
8. Save your work.
9. Test the movie, then close the movie.

FIGURE 61
Sample completed Project Builder 1

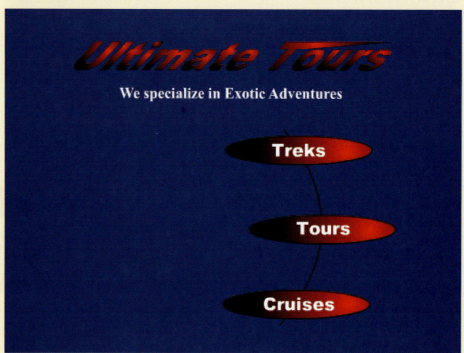

You have been asked to create several sample designs for the home page of a new organization called The Jazz Club. The club is being organized to bring together music enthusiasts for social events and charitable fundraising activities. The club members plan to sponsor weekly jam sessions and a show once a month. Because the club is just getting started, the organizers are looking to you for help in developing a Web site.

1. Plan the site by specifying the goal, target audience, treatment ("look and feel"), and elements you want to include (text, graphics, sound, and so on).
2. Sketch out a storyboard that shows the layout of the objects on the various screens and how they are linked together. Be creative in your design.
3. Open a new Flash document and save it as **thejazzclub2**.
4. Set the document properties, including the size and background color, if desired.
5. Display the gridlines and rulers and use them to help align objects on the stage.
6. Create a heading with a background, text objects, and drawings to be used as links to the categories of information provided on the Web site.
7. Hide the gridlines and rulers.
8. Save your work, then compare your image to the example shown in Figure 62.

FIGURE 62
Sample completed Project Builder 2

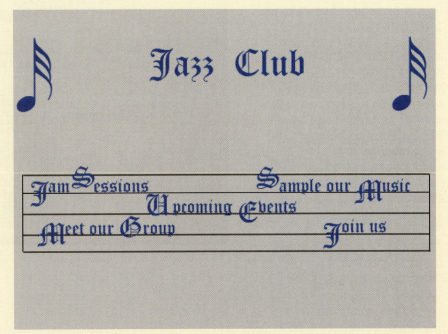

Drawing in Flash

Figure 63 shows the home page of a Web site. Study the figure and complete the following. For each question indicate how you determined your answer.

1. Connect to the Internet, then go to *www.k2skis.com/skis/*.
2. Open a document in a word processor or open a new Flash document, save the file as **dpc2**, then answer the following questions. (*Hint*: Use the Text tool in Flash.)

   ■ Whose Web site is this?

   ■ What is the goal(s) of the site?

   ■ Who is the target audience?

   ■ What is the treatment ("look and feel") that is used?

   ■ What are the design layout guidelines being used (balance, movement, and so on)?

   ■ What may be animated on this home page?

   ■ Do you think this is an effective design for the company, its products, and its target audience? Why or why not?

   ■ What suggestions would you make to improve the design and why?

FIGURE 63
Design Project

You have decided to create a personal portfolio of your work that you can use when you begin your job search. The portfolio will be a Web site done completely in Flash.

1. Research what should be included in a portfolio.
2. Plan the site by specifying the goal, target audience, treatment ("look and feel"), and elements you want to include (text, graphics, sound, and so on).
3. Sketch out a storyboard that shows the layout of the objects on the various screens and how they are linked together. Be creative in your design.
4. Design the home page to include personal data, contact information, previous employment, education, and samples of your work.
5. Open a new Flash document and save it as **portfolio2**.
6. Set the document properties, including the size and background color, if desired.
7. Display the gridlines and rulers and use them to help align objects on the stage.
8. Add a border the size of the stage. (*Hint*: Use the Rectangle tool and set the fill color to none.)

9. Create a heading with its own background, then create other text objects and drawings to be used as links to the categories of information provided on the Web site. (*Hint*: In the example shown here, the Tahoma font is used. You can replace this font with Impact or any other appropriate font on your computer.)
10. Hide the gridlines and rulers.
11. Save your work, then compare your image to the example shown in Figure 64.

FIGURE 64
Sample completed Portfolio Project

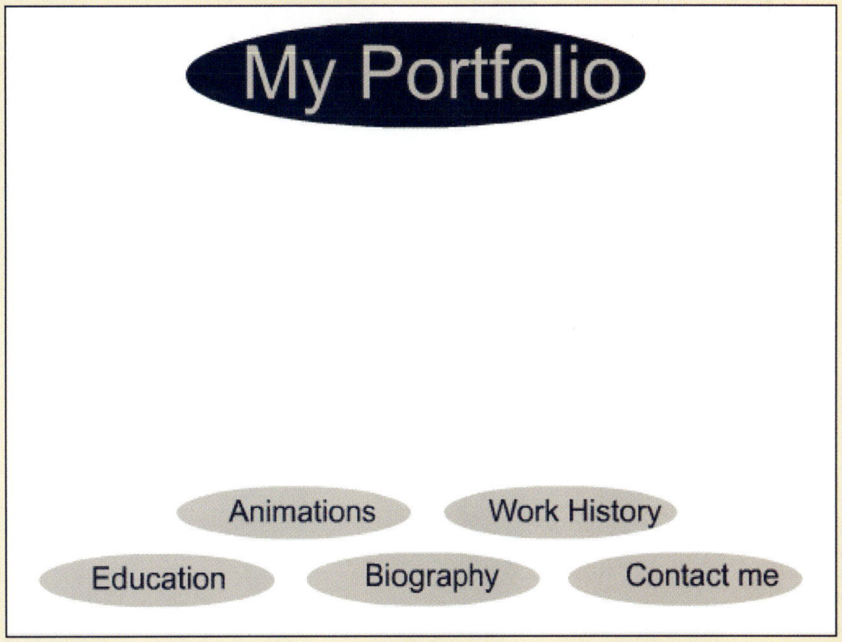

WORKING WITH SYMBOLS
AND INTERACTIVITY

1. Create symbols and instances

2. Work with Libraries

3. Create buttons

4. Assign actions to frames and buttons

3 WORKING WITH SYMBOLS
AND INTERACTIVITY

Introduction

An important benefit of Flash is its ability to create movies with small file sizes. This allows the movies to be delivered from the Web more quickly. One way to keep the file sizes small is to create reusable graphics, buttons, and movie clips. Flash allows you to create a graphic (drawing) and then make unlimited copies, which you can use throughout the current movie and in other movies. Flash calls the original drawing a **symbol** and the copied drawings **instances**. Using instances reduces the movie file size because Flash needs to store only the symbol's information (size, shape, color). When you want to use a symbol in a movie, Flash creates an instance (copy), but does not save the instance in the Flash movie; this keeps down the movie's file size. What is especially valuable about this process is that you can change the attributes (such as color and shape) for each instance. For

example, if your Web site is to contain drawings of cars that are similar, you can create just one drawing, convert it to a symbol, insert as many instances of the car as needed, and then change the individual instances as desired. Flash stores symbols in the Library panel—each time you need a copy of the symbol, you can open the Library panel and drag the symbol to the stage, which creates an instance of the symbol.

There are three categories of symbols: graphic, button, and movie clip. A graphic symbol is useful because you can reuse a single image and make changes in each instance of the image. A button symbol is useful because you can create buttons for interactivity, such as starting or stopping a movie. A movie clip symbol is useful for creating complex animations because you can create a movie within a movie.

Tools You'll Use

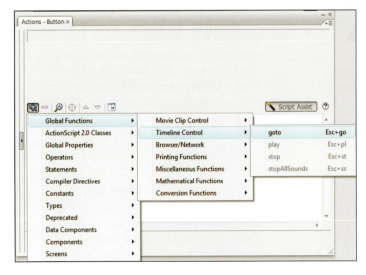

CREATE SYMBOLS
AND INSTANCES

▶ *In this lesson, you will create graphic symbols, turn them into instances, and then edit the instances.*

Creating a Graphic Symbol

You can use the New Symbol command on the Insert menu to create and then draw a symbol. You can also draw an object and then use the Convert to Symbol command on the Modify menu to convert the object to a symbol. The Convert to Symbol dialog box, shown in Figure 1, allows you to name the symbol and specify the type of symbol you want to create (Movie Clip, Button, or Graphic). When naming a symbol, it's a good idea to use a naming convention that allows you to quickly identify the type of symbol and to group like symbols together. For example, you could identify all graphic symbols by naming them g_*name* and all buttons as b_*name*. In Figure 1, the drawing on the stage is being converted into a graphic symbol named g_ball.

After you complete the Convert to Symbol dialog box, Flash places the symbol in the Library panel, as shown in Figure 2. In Figure 2, an icon identifying the symbol as a graphic symbol, the symbol name, and the symbol type are listed in the library panel, along with a preview of the selected symbol.

To create an instance of the symbol, you simply drag a symbol from the Library panel to the stage. To edit a symbol, you select it from the Library panel or you use the Edit Symbols command on the Edit menu. This displays the symbol in an edit window, where changes can be made to it. When you edit a symbol, the changes are reflected in all instances of that symbol in your movie. For example, you can draw a car, convert the car to a symbol, and then create several instances of the car. You can uniformly change the size of all the cars by double-clicking the car symbol in the Library panel to open the symbol edit window, and then rescaling it to the desired size.

Working with Instances

You can have as many instances as needed in your movie, and you can edit each one to make it somewhat different from the others. You can rotate, skew (slant), and resize graphic and button instances. In addition, you can change the color, brightness, and transparency. However, there are some limitations. An instance is a single object with no segments or parts, such as a stroke and a fill. You cannot select a part of an instance. Therefore, any changes to the color of the instance are made to the entire object. Of course, you can use layers to stack other objects on top of an instance to change its appearance. In addition, you can use the Break Apart command on the Modify menu to break the link between an instance and a symbol. Once the link is broken, you can make any changes to the object, such as changing its stroke and fill color. However, because the link is broken,

the object is no longer an instance; if you make any changes to the original symbol, then the object is not affected.

The process for creating an instance is to open the Library panel and drag the desired symbol to the stage. Once the symbol is on the stage, you select the instance by using the Selection tool to draw a marquee around it. A blue border indicates that the object is selected. Then, you can use the Free Transform tool options (such as Rotate and Skew, or Scale) to modify the

entire image, or you can use the Break Apart command to break apart the instance and edit individual strokes and fills.

QUICKTIP

You need to be careful when editing an instance. Use the Selection tool to draw a marquee around the instance, or click the object once to select it. Do not double-click the instance when it is on the stage; otherwise, you will open an edit window that is used to edit the symbol, not the instance.

FIGURE 1
Using the Convert to Symbol dialog box to convert an object to a symbol

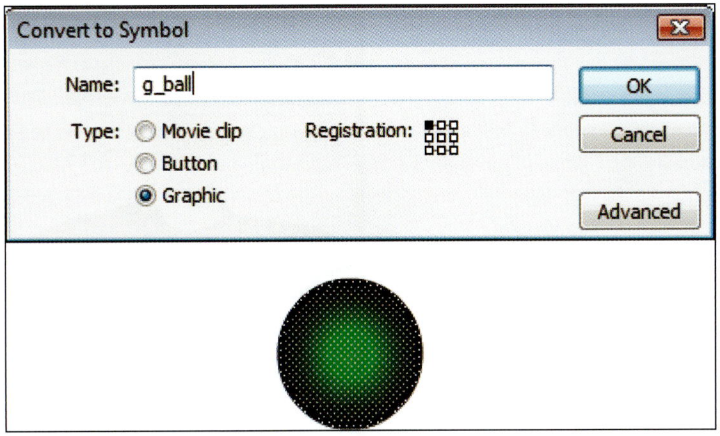

FIGURE 2
A graphic symbol in the Library panel

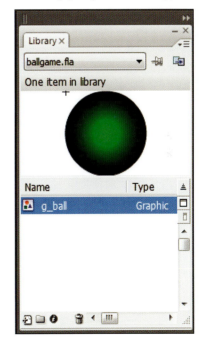

Create a symbol

1. Open fl3_1.fla from the drive and folder where your Data Files are stored, then save it as **coolcar**.

2. Verify the Property inspector, the Library panel, and the Tools panel are displayed.

3. Set the magnification to **Fit in Window**.

   The car was created using the Flash drawing tools.

4. Click the **Selection tool** ▶ on the Tools panel, then drag a **marquee** around the car to select it.

5. Click **Modify** on the menu bar, then click **Convert to Symbol**.

6. Type **g_car** in the Name text box.

7. Click the **Graphic option button** as shown in Figure 3, then click **OK**.

8. Study the Library panel, as shown in Figure 4, and notice it displays the symbol (red car) in the Item Preview window, an icon 🖼 indicating that this is a graphic symbol, the name of the symbol (g_car), and the type (Graphic) of symbol.

   The symbol is contained in the library, and the car on the stage is now an instance of the symbol.

You opened a file with an object, converted the object to a symbol, and displayed the symbol in the Library panel.

FIGURE 3
Options in the Convert to Symbol dialog box

FIGURE 4
Newly created symbol in the Library panel

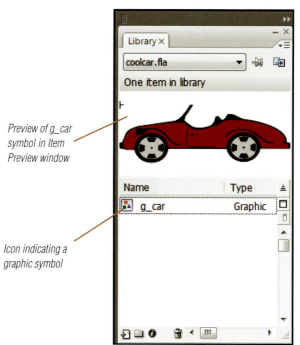

Preview of g_car symbol in Item Preview window

Icon indicating a graphic symbol

Working with Symbols and Interactivity

FIGURE 5

Creating an instance

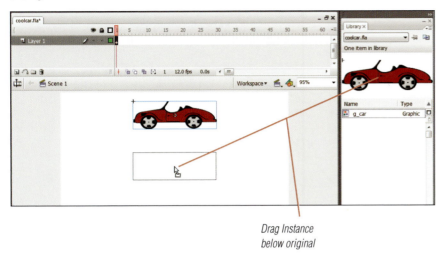

Drag Instance
below original

FIGURE 6

The alpha set to 50%

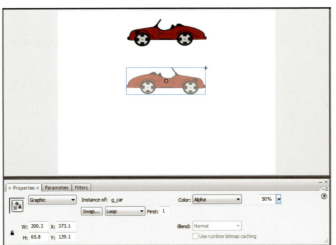

Create and edit an instance

1. Point to the **car image** in the Item Preview window of the Library panel, then drag the **image** to the stage beneath the first car, as shown in Figure 5.

   TIP   You can also drag the name of the symbol from the Library panel to the stage. Both cars on the stage are instances of the graphic symbol in the Library panel.

2. Click the **Selection tool** on the Tools panel (if necessary), verify that the bottom car is selected, click **Modify** on the menu bar, point to **Transform**, then click **Flip Horizontal**.

3. Expand the Property inspector (if necessary).

4. Click the **Color list arrow** on the Property inspector, then click **Alpha**.

5. Click the **% list arrow** ▼ , then drag the slider to **50%**.

   Notice how the transparency changes. Figure 6 shows the transparency set to 50%.

6. Click a blank area of the stage to deselect the object.

   Changing the alpha setting gives the car a more transparent look.

You created an instance of a symbol and edited the instance on the stage.

Edit a symbol in the edit window

1. Double-click the **g_car symbol icon** 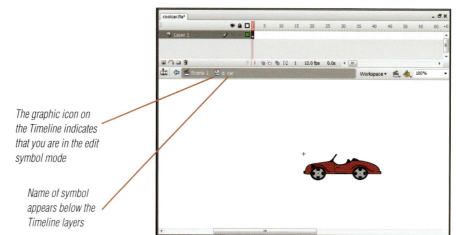 in the Library panel to display the edit window, then compare your screen to Figure 7.

   The g_car symbol appears on the stage below the Timeline layers, indicating that you are editing the g_car symbol.

   > TIP   You can also edit a symbol by clicking Edit on the menu bar, then clicking Edit Symbols.

2. Click a blank area of the stage to deselect the car.

3. Verify that the **Selection tool** ⬉ is selected, then click the **light gray hubcap** inside the front wheel to select it.

4. Press and hold **[Shift]**, then click the **hubcap** inside the back wheel so both hubcap fills are selected.

5. Set the **Fill color** to the **blue gradient color swatch** in the bottom row of the color palette, deselect the image, then compare your image to Figure 8.

   Changes you make to the symbol affect every instance of the symbol on the stage. The hubcap fill becomes a blue gradient in the Library panel and on the stage.

6. Click **Scene 1** below the Timeline layer to exit the symbol edit window and return to the main Timeline and main stage.

   The hubcap color of the instances on the stage reflects the color changes you made to the symbol.

You edited a symbol in the edit window that affected all instances of the symbol.

FIGURE 7
Symbol-editing window

The graphic icon on the Timeline indicates that you are in the edit symbol mode

Name of symbol appears below the Timeline layers

FIGURE 8
Edited symbol

Hubcap fills are blue gradient

Symbol reflects changes

Working with Symbols and Interactivity

FIGURE 9

The car with the maroon body selected

Break apart an instance

1. Click the **Selection tool** on the Tools panel, then drag the **marquee** around the bottom car to select it (if necessary).

2. Click **Modify** on the menu bar, then click **Break Apart**.

   The object is no longer linked to the symbol, and its parts (strokes and fills) can now be edited.

3. Click a blank area of the stage to deselect the object.

4. Click the **blue front hubcap**, press and hold **[Shift]**, then click the **blue back hubcap** so both hubcaps are selected.

5. Set the **Fill color** to the **dark gray color swatch (#333333)** in the left column of the color palette.

6. Double-click the **g_car symbol icon** in the Library window to display the edit window.

7. Click the **maroon front body** of the car to select it, press and hold **[Shift]**, then click the **maroon back body** of the car, as shown in Figure 9.

8. Set the **Fill color** to the **red gradient color swatch** in the bottom row of the color palette.

9. Click **Scene 1** below the Timeline layers, then compare your image to Figure 10.

   The body color of the car in the original instance is a different color, but the one to which you applied the Break Apart command remains unchanged.

10. Save your work.

You used the Break Apart command to break the link of the instance to its symbol, you edited the object, and then you edited the symbol.

FIGURE 10

Changing the symbol affects only the one instance of the symbol

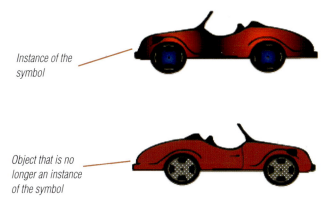

Instance of the symbol

Object that is no longer an instance of the symbol

WORK WITH
LIBRARIES

What You'll Do

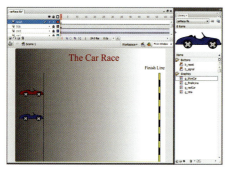

 In this lesson, you will use the Library panel to organize the symbols in a movie.

Understanding the Library

The Library in a Flash movie contains the movie symbols and other assets such as imported graphics, movie clips, and sounds. The Library panel provides a way to view and organize the symbols, and allows you to change the symbol name, display symbol properties, and add and delete symbols. Figure 11 shows the Library panel for a movie. Refer to this figure as you read the following descriptions of the parts of the Library.

Title tab—Identifies this as the Library panel. The list box below the title tab can be used to select an open document and display the Library panel associated with that open document. This allows you to use the objects from one movie in another movie. For example, you may have developed a drawing in one Flash movie and need to use it in the movie you are working on. With both documents open, you simply use the list box to display the Library with the desired drawing, and then drag it to the stage. This will automatically place the drawing in the Library for the current movie. In addition to the movie libraries, you can create permanent libraries that are available whenever you start Flash. Flash also has sample libraries that contain buttons and other objects. The permanent and sample libraries are accessed through the Common Libraries command on the Window menu. All assets in all of these libraries are available for use in any movie.

Options menu—Shown in Figure 12; provides access to several features used to edit symbols (such as renaming symbols) and organize symbols (such as creating a new folder).

Item Preview window—Displays the selected item. If the item is animated or a sound file, a control button appears, allowing you to preview the animation or play the sound.

Toggle Sorting Order icon—Allows you to reorder the list of folders and symbols within folders.

Wide Library View and Narrow Library View icons—Allows you to expand and collapse the Library panel to display more or less of the symbol properties.

Name text box—Lists the folder and symbol names. Each symbol type has a different icon associated with it. Clicking a symbol name or icon displays the symbol in the Item Preview window.

New Symbol icon—Displays the Create New Symbol dialog box, allowing you to create a new symbol.

New Folder icon—Allows you to create a new folder.

Properties icon—Displays the Symbol Properties dialog box for the selected symbol.

Delete Item icon—Deletes the selected symbol or folder. To make changes in a symbol, you can double-click the symbol icon in the Library panel to display the Symbol-editing window.

FIGURE 11

The Library panel

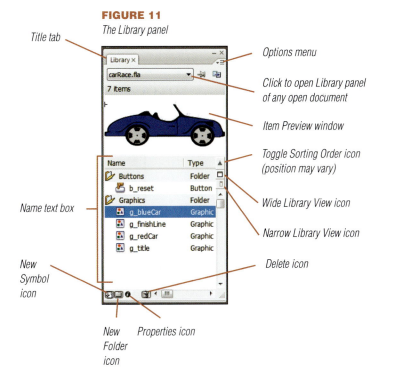

Title tab

Options menu

Click to open Library panel of any open document

Item Preview window

Toggle Sorting Order icon (position may vary)

Wide Library View icon

Narrow Library View icon

Name text box

Delete icon

New Symbol icon

New Folder icon

Properties icon

FIGURE 12

The Options menu

Create folders in the Library panel

1. Open fl3_2.fla, then save it as **carRace**.

2. Verify the Property inspector, the Library panel, and the Tools panel are displayed.

3. Set the magnification to **Fit in Window**.

4. Click each of the items in the Library panel to display them in the Item Preview window.

5. Click the **New Folder icon** 🗋 in the Library panel, as shown in Figure 13.

6. Type **Graphics** in the Name text box, then press [**Enter**] (Win) or [**return**] (Mac).

7. Click the **New Folder icon** 🗋 in the Library panel.

8. Type **Buttons** in the Name text box, then press [**Enter**] (Win) or [**return**] (Mac).

   Your Library panel should resemble Figure 14.

You opened a Flash movie and created folders in the Library panel.

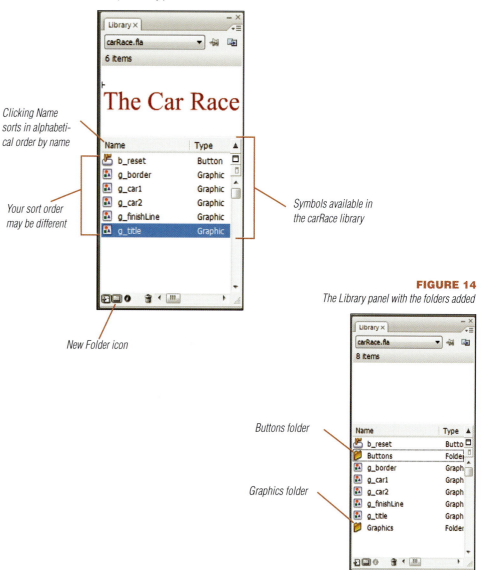

FIGURE 13
The open Library panel

Clicking Name sorts in alphabetical order by name

Your sort order may be different

Symbols available in the carRace library

New Folder icon

FIGURE 14
The Library panel with the folders added

Buttons folder

Graphics folder

Working with Symbols and Interactivity

FIGURE 15

The Library panel after moving the symbols to the folders

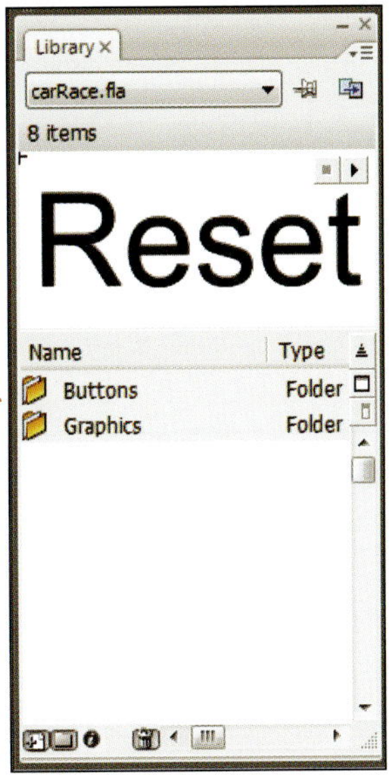

Your folders might be expanded

Organize symbols within Library panel folders

1. Click the **Toggle Sorting Order icon** and notice how the items are sorted.
2. Click the **Toggle Sorting Order icon** again and notice how the items are sorted.
3. Drag the **g_title symbol** in the Library panel to the Graphics folder.
4. Drag the other graphic symbols to the Graphics folder.
5. Drag the **b_reset symbol** to the Buttons folder, then compare your Library panel to Figure 15.
6. Double-click the **Graphics folder** to open it and display the symbols.
7. Double-click the **Buttons folder** to open it and display the symbol (if necessary).
8. Double-click the **Graphics folder** to close the folder.
9. Double-click the **Buttons folder** to close the folder.

You organized the symbols within the folders and opened and closed the folders.

Display the properties of symbols, rename symbols, and delete a symbol

1. Double-click the **Graphics folder icon** to display the symbols.

2. Click the **g_car1 symbol**, then click the **Properties icon** 🛈 to display the Symbol Properties dialog box.

3. Type **g_redCar** in the Name text box, as shown in Figure 16, then click **OK**.

4. Repeat Steps 2 and 3 renaming the g_car2 symbol to **g_blueCar**.

   TIP   Double-click the name to rename it without opening the Symbol Properties dialog box.

5. Click **g_border** in the Library panel to select it.

6. Click the **Delete icon** 🗑 at the bottom of the Library panel.

7. If necessary, click **Yes** to complete the delete process.

   TIP   You can also select an item and press [Delete], or use the Options menu in the Library panel to remove an item from the library. The Undo command in the Edit menu can be used to undelete an item.

You used the Library panel to display the properties of symbols, rename symbols, and delete a symbol.

FIGURE 16
Renaming a symbol

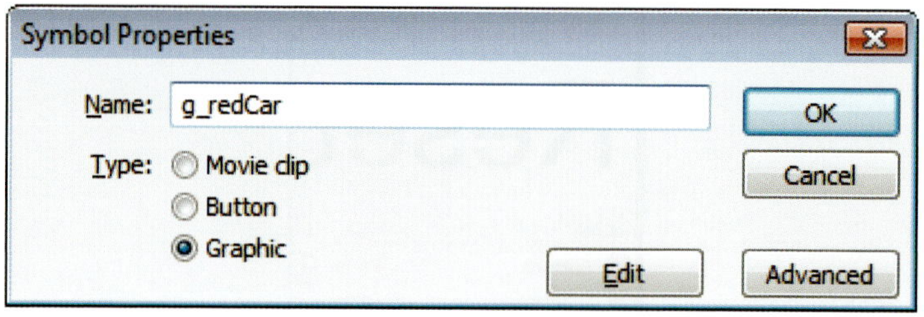

FIGURE 17
The carRace.fla document and the coolCar.fla Library panel

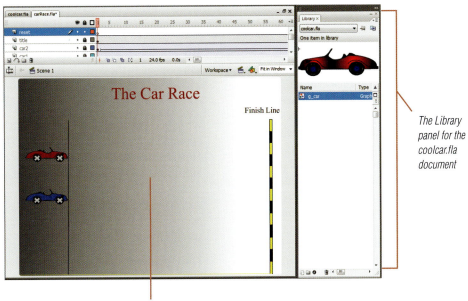

The Library panel for the coolcar.fla document

The carRace.fla document

1. Click the **Library panel list arrow** near the top of the Library panel to display a list of open documents.

2. Click **coolcar.fla**, then click **g_car**.

   The Library panel for the coolcar document is displayed. However, the carRace document remains open, as shown in Figure 17.

3. Click **Frame 1** on the Reset layer, then drag the **car** from the Library panel to the center of the stage.

   The Reset layer is the only unlocked layer. Objects cannot be placed on locked layers.

4. Click the **Library panel list arrow** to display the open documents.

5. Click **carRace.fla** to view the carRace document's Library panel.

   Notice the g_car symbol is automatically added to the Library panel of the carRace document.

6. Click the **g_car symbol** in the Library panel.

7. Click the **Delete icon** 🗑 at the bottom of the Library panel, then (if necessary) click **Yes** to delete the symbol.

   You deleted the g_car symbol from the carRace Library but it still exists in the coolcar library. The car was also deleted from the stage.

8. Save your work.

9. Click the **coolcar.fla tab** above the Timeline to display the document.

10. Close the coolcar document.

You used the Library panel to display the contents of another Library and added an object from that Library to the current document.

CREATE
BUTTONS

What You'll Do

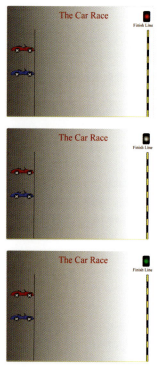

In this lesson, you will create buttons, edit the four button states, and test a button.

Understanding Buttons

Button symbols are used to provide inter-activity. When you click a button, an action occurs, such as starting an animation or jumping to another frame on the Timeline. Any object, including Flash drawings, text blocks, and imported graphic images, can be made into buttons. Unlike graphic symbols, buttons have four states: Up, Over, Down, and Hit. These states correspond to the use of the mouse and recognize that the user requires feedback when the mouse is pointing to a button and when the button has been clicked. This is often shown by a change in the button (such as a different color or different shape). These four states are explained in the following paragraphs and shown in Figure 18.

Up—Represents how the button appears when the mouse pointer is not over it.

Over—Represents how the button appears when the mouse pointer is over it.

Down—Represents how the button appears after the user clicks the mouse.

Hit—Defines the area of the screen that will respond to the click. In most cases, you will want the Hit state to be the same or similar to the Up state in location and size.

When you create a button symbol, Flash automatically creates a new Timeline. The Timeline has only four frames, one for each button state. The Timeline does not play; it merely reacts to the mouse pointer by displaying the appropriate button state and performing an action, such as jumping to a specific frame on the main Timeline.

The process for creating and previewing buttons is as follows:

Create a button symbol—Draw an object or select an object that has already been created and placed on the stage. Use the Convert to Symbol command on the Modify menu to convert the object to a button symbol and to enter a name for the button.

Edit the button symbol—Select the button and choose the Edit Symbols command on the Edit menu or double-click the button symbol in the Library panel. This displays the button Timeline, shown in Figure 19, which allows you to work with the four button states. The Up state is the original button symbol. Flash automatically places it in Frame 1. You need to determine how the original object will change for the other states. To change the button for the Over state, click Frame 2 and insert a keyframe.

This automatically places a copy of the button in Frame 1 into Frame 2. Then, alter the button's appearance for the Over state. Use the same process for the Down state. For the Hit state, you insert a keyframe on Frame 4 and then specify the area on the screen that will respond to the pointer. If you do not specify a hit area, the image for the Up state is used for the hit area.

Return to the main Timeline—Once you've finished editing a button, you choose the Edit Document command on the Edit menu, or click Scene 1 below the Timeline layers, to return to the main Timeline.

Preview the button—By default, Flash disables buttons so that you can manipulate them on the stage. You can preview a button by choosing the Enable Simple Buttons command on the Control menu. You can also choose the Test Movie command on the Control menu to play the movie and test the buttons.

FIGURE 18
The four button states

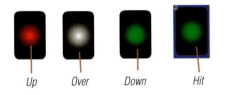

Up   Over   Down   Hit

FIGURE 19
The button Timeline

Create a button

1. Insert a layer above the top layer in the Timeline, then name the layer **signal**.

2. Select the **Rectangle Primitive tool** , click the **Stroke color tool** on the Tools panel, then click the **No Stroke icon** in the upper-right corner of the color palette.

3. Set the **Fill color** to the **red gradient color swatch** in the bottom row of the color palette.

4. Click the **Reset button** in the Property inspector, then set the corner radius to **5**.

5. Draw the **rectangle** shown in Figure 20.

6. Click the **Zoom tool** on the Tools panel, then click the **rectangle** to enlarge it.

7. Select the **Gradient Transform tool** on the Tools panel, then click the **rectangle**.

   You may need to click and hold the Free Transform tool first.

8. Drag the **diagonal arrow** toward the center of the rectangle as shown in Figure 21 to make the red area more round.

9. Click the **Selection tool** on the Tools panel (if necessary), then drag a **marquee** around the rectangle to select it.

10. Click **Modify** on the menu bar, then click **Convert to Symbol**.

11. Type **b_signal** in the Name text box, click the **Button option button**, then click **OK**.

12. Drag the **b_signal symbol** to the Buttons folder in the Library panel.

You created a button symbol on the stage and dragged it to the Buttons folder in the Library panel.

FIGURE 20
The rectangle object

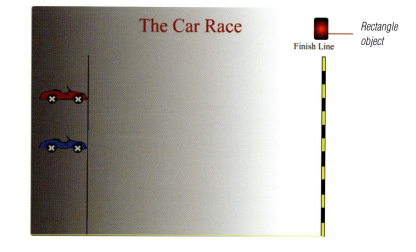

Rectangle object

FIGURE 21
Adjusting the gradient

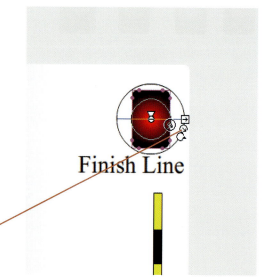

Drag the diagonal arrow from the outside ring toward the center of the rectangle

Working with Symbols and Interactivity

FIGURE 22

Specifying the hit area

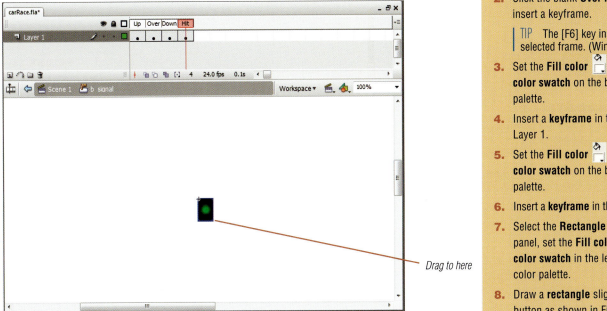

Drag to here

1. Open the Buttons folder (if necessary), right-click (Win) or control-click (Mac) **b_signal** in the Library panel, then click **Edit**.

    Flash displays the symbol-edit window showing the Timeline with four button states.

2. Click the blank **Over frame** on Layer 1, then insert a keyframe.

    > TIP The [F6] key inserts a keyframe in the selected frame. (Win)

3. Set the **Fill color** to the **gray gradient color swatch** on the bottom of the color palette.

4. Insert a **keyframe** in the Down frame on Layer 1.

5. Set the **Fill color** to the **green gradient color swatch** on the bottom of the color palette.

6. Insert a **keyframe** in the Hit frame on Layer 1.

7. Select the **Rectangle tool** on the Tools panel, set the **Fill color** to the **blue color swatch** in the left column of the color palette.

8. Draw a **rectangle** slightly larger than the button as shown in Figure 22.

    > TIP The Hit area is not visible on the stage.

9. Click **Scene 1** below the Timeline layers to return to the main Timeline.

You edited a button by changing the color of its Over and Down states, and you specified the Hit area.

Test a button

1. Click the **Selection tool** ![selection tool], then click a blank area of the stage.

2. Click **Control** on the menu bar, then click **Enable Simple Buttons**.

   This command allows you to test buttons on the stage without viewing the movie in the Test window.

3. Point to the **signal button** on the stage, then compare your image to Figure 23.

   The pointer changes to a hand ![hand], indicating that the object is clickable, and the button changes to a gray gradient, the color you selected for the Over state.

4. Press and hold the **mouse button**, then notice that the button changes to a green gradient, the color you selected for the Down state, as shown in Figure 24.

   (continued)

FIGURE 23
The button's Over state

FIGURE 24
The button's Down state

The Button Hit area

All buttons have an area that responds to the mouse pointer, including rolling over the button and clicking it. This hit area is usually the same size and shape as the button itself. However, you can specify any area of the button to be the hit area. For example, you could have a button symbol that looks like a target with just the bulls-eye center being the hit area.

FIGURE 25
The button's Up state

FIGURE 26

View options from the Timeline

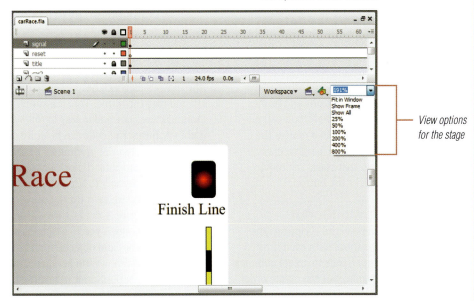

View options
for the stage

5. Release the mouse and notice that the button changes to a gray gradient, the color you selected for the Over state.

6. Move the mouse away from the signal button, and notice that the button returns to a red gradient, the Up state color, as shown in Figure 25.

7. Click **Control** on the menu bar, then click **Enable Simple Buttons** to turn off the command.

8. Click **Window** on the menu bar, then click **Library** to close the Library panel.

9. Click the **View box list arrow** below the Timeline, as shown in Figure 26, then click **Fit in Window**.

    This shortcut allows you to change the magnification view without using the Magnification command on the View menu or the Zoom tool in the Tools panel.

10. Save your work.

You used the mouse to test a button and view the button states.

ASSIGN ACTIONS
TO FRAMES AND BUTTONS

What You'll Do

▶ In this lesson, you will use ActionScripts to assign actions to frames and buttons.

Understanding Actions

In a basic movie, Flash plays the frames sequentially, repeating the movie without stopping for user input. However, you may often want to provide users with the ability to interact with the movie by allowing them to perform actions, such as starting and stopping the movie or jumping to a specific frame in the movie. One way to provide user interaction is to assign an action to the Down state of a button. Then, whenever the user clicks the button, the action occurs. Flash provides a scripting language, called ActionScript, that allows you to add actions to buttons and frames within a movie. For example, you can place a stop action in a frame that pauses the movie, and then you can assign a play action to a button that starts the movie when the user clicks the button.

Analyzing ActionScript

ActionScript is a powerful scripting language that allows those with even limited programming experience to create complex actions. For example, you can create order

forms that capture user input or volume controls that display when sounds are played. A basic ActionScript involves an event (such as a mouse click) that causes some action to occur by triggering the script. The following is an example of a basic ActionScript:

```
on (release) {
        gotoAndPlay(10);
}
```

In this example, the event is a mouse click (indicated by the word release) that causes the movie's playback head to go to Frame 10 and play the frame. This is a simple ActionScript code and is easy to follow. Other ActionScript code can be quite complex and may require programming expertise to understand. Fortunately, Flash provides an easy way to use ActionScripts without having to learn the scripting language. The Script Assist feature within the Actions panel allows you to assign basic actions to frames and objects, such as buttons. Figure 27 shows the Actions panel displaying an ActionScript indicating that when the user clicks the selected object (a button, in this example, b_signal), the movie goes to Frame 2.

The process for assigning actions to buttons, shown in Figure 28, is as follows:

- Select the button on the stage that you want to assign an action to.
- Display the Actions panel, using the Window menu.
- Select the Script Assist button to display the Script Assist panel within the ActionScript panel.
- Click the Add a new item to the script icon to display a list of Action categories.
- Select the appropriate category from a drop-down list. Flash provides several Action categories. The Timeline Control category within the Global Functions menu allows you to create scripts for controlling movies and navigating within movies. You can use these actions to start and stop movies, jump to specific frames, and respond to user mouse movements and keystrokes.
- Select the desired action, such as gotoAndPlay.
- Specify the event that triggers the action, such as on (release).

Button actions respond to one or more mouse events, including:

Release—With the pointer inside the button Hit area, the user presses and releases (clicks) the mouse button. This is the default event.

Key Press—With the button displayed, the user presses a predetermined key on the keyboard.

Roll Over—The user moves the pointer into the button Hit area.

Drag Over—The user holds down the mouse button, moves the pointer out of the button Hit area, and then back into the Hit area.

Using Frame Actions—In addition to assigning actions to buttons, you can assign actions to frames. Actions assigned to frames are executed when the playhead reaches the frame. A common frame action is stop, which is often assigned to the first and last frame in the Timeline.

ActionScript 2.0 and 3.0—The latest version of ActionScript is 3.0. This version can be quite complex and requires some programming knowledge. A main advantage of AS3 is that movies can download quickly. However, AS2 is very similar and, when using Script Assist, does not require programming expertise.

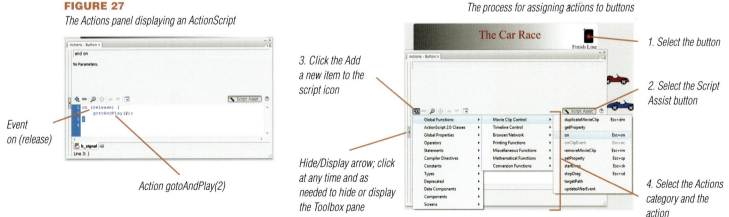

FIGURE 27
The Actions panel displaying an ActionScript

Event
on (release)

Action gotoAndPlay(2)

FIGURE 28
The process for assigning actions to buttons

3. Click the Add a new item to the script icon

Hide/Display arrow; click at any time and as needed to hide or display the Toolbox pane

1. Select the button

2. Select the Script Assist button

4. Select the Actions category and the action

Assign a stop action to frames

1. Click **Control** on the menu bar, then click **Test Movie**.

   The movie plays and continues to loop.

2. Close the test movie window.

3. Insert a **new layer**, name it **stopmovie**, then click **Frame 1** of the layer to select the frame.

4. Click **Window** on the menu bar, then click **Actions** to display the Actions panel.

5. Verify the Script Assist button ![Script Assist] is off, click the **List arrow** for the ActionScript options, point to **ActionScript 1.0 & 2.0**, shown in Figure 29, then click.

   TIP The ActionScript version can also be set using the Flash option in the Publish Settings command of the File menu.

6. Verify stopmovie:1 (indicating the layer and frame to which the action will be applied) is displayed in the lower-left corner of the Actions panel.

7. Click the Hide/Display arrow to hide the Toolbox pane, click the **Add a new item to the script button** ![icon] to display the Script categories, point to **Global Functions**, point to **Timeline Control**, then click **stop**, as shown in Figure 30.

8. Insert a **keyframe** in Frame 66 on the stopmovie layer, then repeat Step 7. Compare your screen to Figure 31. Test the movie.

   The movie does not play because there is a stop action assigned to Frame 1.

9. Close the test movie window.

You inserted a layer and assigned a stop action to the first and last frames on the layer.

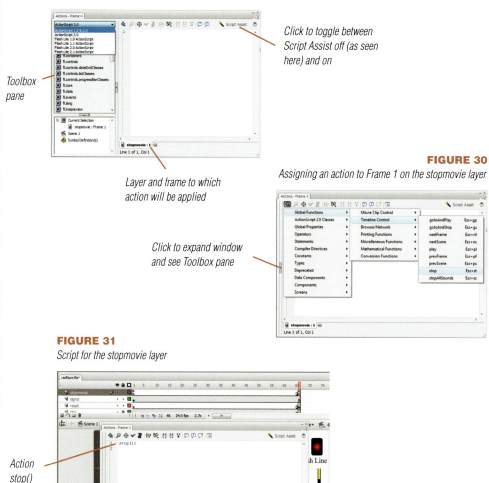

FIGURE 29
Selecting ActionScript 1.0 & 2.0 from the Actions panel

Click to toggle between Script Assist off (as seen here) and on

Toolbox pane

Layer and frame to which action will be applied

FIGURE 30
Assigning an action to Frame 1 on the stopmovie layer

Click to expand window and see Toolbox pane

FIGURE 31
Script for the stopmovie layer

Action stop()

FIGURE 32
Assigning an event to a button

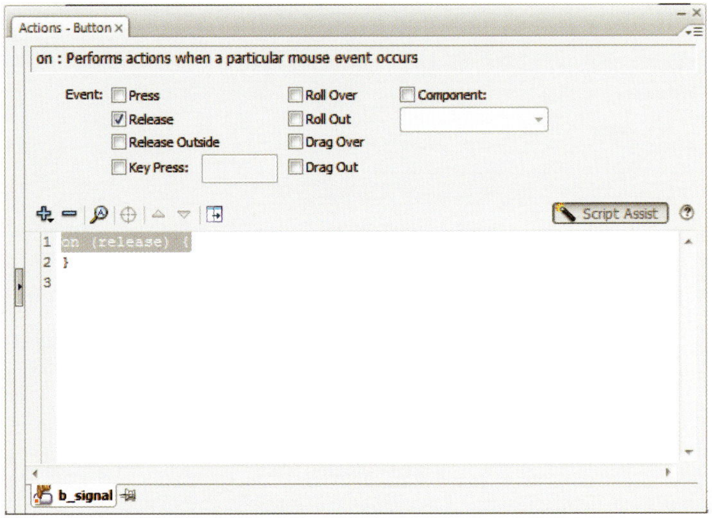

FIGURE 33
Specifying the frame to go to

Change frame
number here

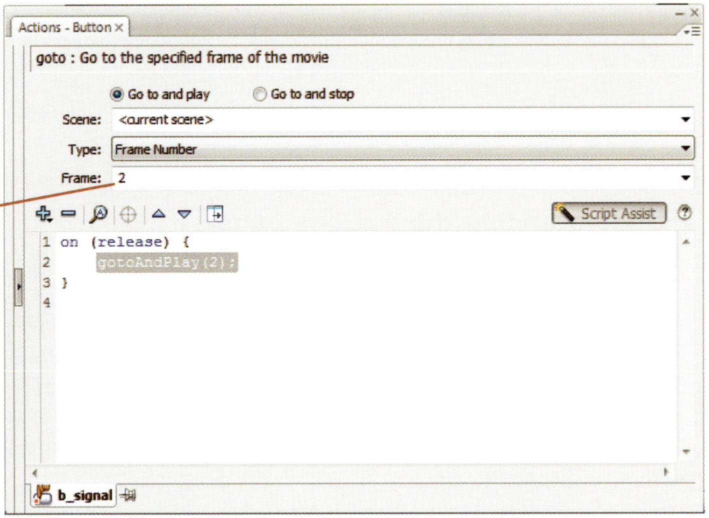

Assign a goto action to a button

1. Click **Frame 1** of the Signal layer.

2. Move the **Actions panel** to view the signal button on the stage (if necessary).

3. Click the **Selection tool** ♦ on the Tools panel, then click the **button** on the stage.

4. Verify that b_signal is displayed in the lower left of the Actions panel.

   This ensures that the actions specified in the Actions panel will apply to the b_signal button.

5. Click the **Script Assist button** ⟍ Script Assist to turn on this feature.

6. Click ⊹ to display the Script categories, point to **Global Functions**, point to **Movie Clip Control**, then click **on**.

   Release is the default event, as shown in Figure 32.

7. Click ⊹, point to **Global Functions**, point to **Timeline Control**, then click **goto**.

   Frame 1 is the default frame to go to.

8. Change the Frame number to **2**, as shown in Figure 33.

9. Click **Control** on the menu bar, then click **Test Movie**.

10. Click the **signal button** to play the animation.

11. Close the test movie window.

You used the Actions panel to assign a play action to a button.

Assign a goto frame action to a button

1. Click **Control** on the menu bar, then click **Test Movie**.

2. Click the **signal button**.

   The movie plays and stops, and the word Reset, which is actually a button, appears.

3. Click the **Reset button** and notice nothing happens because it does not have an action assigned to it.

4. Close the test movie window.

5. Click **Frame 66** of the reset layer to display the Reset button on the stage.

   Note: You many need to move the Actions panel to view the Reset button on the stage.

6. Click the **Reset button** on the stage to select it (if necessary).

7. Verify that **b_reset** is displayed in the lower left of the Actions panel.

8. Verify Script Assist is active, click ![icon], point to **Global Functions**, point to **Timeline Control**, click **goto**, then verify Frame 1 is specified, as shown in Figure 34.

9. Click **Control** on the menu bar, then click **Test Movie**.

10. Click the **signal button** to start the movie, then when the movie stops, click the **Reset button**.

11. Close the test movie window.

You used the Actions panel to assign an action to a button.

FIGURE 34
Assigning a goto action to a button

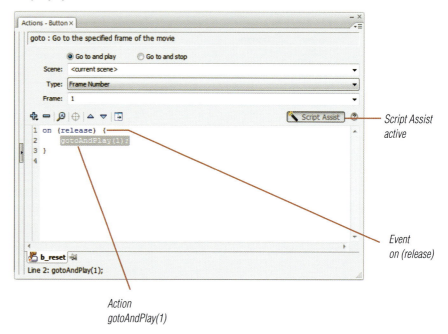

Script Assist active

Event on (release)

Action gotoAndPlay(1)

Understanding the Actions panel

The Actions panel has two panes. The left pane uses folders to display the Action categories. The right pane uses lists to display the categories. The right pane, called the Script pane, is used with the Script Assist feature and it displays the ActionScript code as the code is being generated. When using the Script Assist feature, it is best to close the left window. This is done by clicking the hide/display arrow. The lower-left corner of the Actions panel displays the symbol name or the Frame to which the action(s) will apply. Always verify that the desired symbol or frame is displayed.

FIGURE 35

Assigning a keypress action to a button

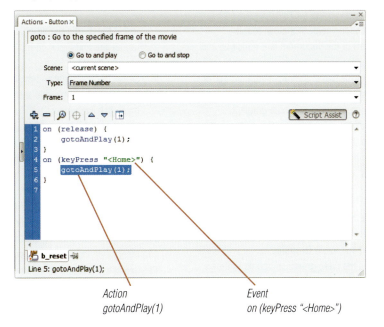

Action
gotoAndPlay(1)

Event
on (keyPress "<Home>")

Script Assist and ActionScript

The Script Assist feature performs differently when using different versions of ActionScript. Starting a new Flash document using ActionScript 2.0 or using the Publish Setting to set the version of ActionScript to 2.0 provides a straightforward way to use Script Assist. However, some actions (such as play and stop) may not be available when using Script Assist. These actions can be used by either turning off the Script Assist feature or typing the code directly into the Script pane.

Assign a second event to a button

1. Click the **right curly bracket** (}) in the Actions panel to highlight the bracket in Step 3 of the ActionScript.

2. Click [icon] in the Script Assist window, point to **Global Functions**, point to **Movie Clip Control**, then click **on**.

   The Script Assist window displays several event options. Release is selected.

3. Click the **Release check box** to deselect the option.

4. Click the **Key Press check box** to select it, then press the [**Home**] key on the keyboard.

   TIP   If your keyboard does not have a [Home] key, use one of the function keys to complete the steps.

5. Click [icon] in the Script Assist window, point to **Global Functions**, point to **Timeline Control**, then click **goto**.

   The ActionScript now indicates that pressing the [Home] key will cause the playhead to go to Frame 1, as shown in Figure 35.

   The Reset button can now be activated by clicking it or by pressing the [Home] key.

6. Click **File** on the menu bar, point to **Publish Preview**, then click **Default – (HTML)**.

   The movie opens in your default browser.

7. Click the **signal button** to start the movie, then when the movie stops, press the [**Home**] key.

8. Close the browser window.

9. Close the Actions panel, save and close the movie, then exit Flash.

You added an event that triggers a goto frame action.

Create a symbol.

1. Start Flash, open fl3_3.fla, then save it as **skillsdemo3**.
2. Change the background color of the document to **#CCCCCC**.
3. Change the heading, Color Spin, to font size **30**.
4. Insert a new layer above the ballspin layer and name it **titlebkgnd**.
5. Draw a primitive rectangle with a black fill and black stroke behind the Color Spin title text with a corner radius of **10**.
6. Verify the rectangle is selected, convert it to a graphic symbol, then name it **g_bkgnd** *Note*: If you use the Selection tool to draw a marquee around the rectangle, you will select the rectangle and the text. To select only the rectangle, point to an edge and single click.
7. Save your work.

Create and edit an instance.

1. Insert a new layer above the title layer and name it **vballs-sm**.
2. Display the Library panel, if necessary.
3. Drag the g_vball-sm symbol to the upper-left corner of the stage.
4. Drag the g_vball-sm symbol three more times to each of the remaining corners of the stage.
5. Double-click the g_vball-sm symbol icon in the Library panel to switch to symbol-editing mode.

6. Change the color of the ball to red.
7. Return to the document and notice how all instances have been changed to red.
8. Select the ball in the upper-right corner of the stage and break apart the object.
9. Change the color to a blue gradient.
10. Select, break apart, and change the bottom-left ball to a green gradient and the bottom-right ball to white.
11. Save your work.

Create a folder in the Library panel.

1. Click the New Folder button at the bottom of the Library panel to create a new folder.
2. Name the folder **Graphics**.
3. Move the three graphic symbols to the Graphics folder.
4. Expand the Graphics folder, if necessary.
5. Save your work.

Work with the Library window.

1. Rename the g_bkgnd symbol to **g_title-bkgnd** in the Library panel.
2. Collapse and expand the folder.
3. Save your work.

Create a button.

1. Insert a new layer above the vballs-sm layer and name it **start**.
2. Drag the g_title-bkgnd symbol from the Library panel to the bottom center of the stage.
3. Create a text block formatted with white, bold, 30-pt Arial, position the text block on

top of the g_title-bkgnd object, type **Start**. Center the text block on top of the g_title-bkgnd object.
4. Select the rectangle and the text. (*Hint*: Click the Selection tool, press and hold [Shift], then click each object.)
5. Convert the selected objects to a button symbol and name it **b_start**.
6. Create a new folder named **Buttons** in the Library panel and move the b_start button symbol to the folder.
7. Display the b_start button Timeline.
8. Insert a keyframe in the Over frame.
9. Select the text and change the color to gray.
10. Insert a keyframe in the Down frame.
11. Select the text and change the color to blue.
12. Insert a keyframe in the Hit frame.
13. Draw a rectangular object that covers the button area for the Hit state.
14. Return to movie-editing mode.
15. Save your work.

Test a button.

1. Turn on Enable Simple Buttons.
2. Point to the button and notice the color change.
3. Click the button and notice the other color change.

Stop a movie.

1. Insert a new layer and name it **stopmovie**.
2. Insert a keyframe in Frame 40 on the new layer.
3. With Frame 40 selected, display the Actions panel.
4. Assign a stop action to the frame.
5. Click Frame 1 on the new layer.
6. Assign a stop action to Frame 1.
7. Save your work.

Assign a goto action to a button.

1. Click Control on the menu bar, then click Enable Simple Buttons to turn off this feature.
2. Use the Selection tool to select the Start button on the stage.
3. Use Script Assist in the Actions panel to assign an event and a goto action to the button. (*Hint*: Refer to the section on assigning a goto action as needed.)
4. Test the movie.
5. Save your work, then compare your image to Figure 36.
6. Exit Flash.

FIGURE 36
Completed Skills Review

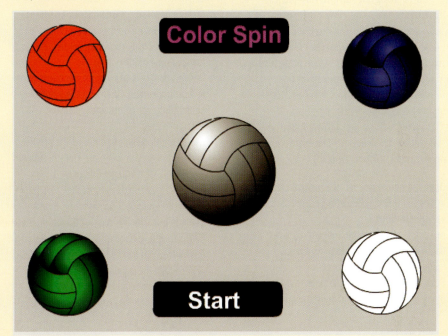

The Ultimate Tours travel company has asked you to design a sample navigation scheme for its Web site. The company wants to see how its home page will link with one of its main categories (Treks). Figure 37 shows a sample home page and Treks screen. Using the figures or the home page you created in Chapter 2 as a guide, you will add a Treks screen and link it to the home page. (*Hint*: Assume that all of the drawings on the home page are on Frame 1, unless noted.)

1. Open ultimatetours2.fla (the file you created in Chapter 2 Project Builder 1), then save it as **ultimatetours3**.
2. Insert a layer above the Subheading layer, name it **logo**, then type **logo** as a place-holder in the upper-left corner of the stage.
3. Select the layer that the Ultimate Tours text block is on, then insert a keyframe on a frame at least five frames farther along the Timeline.
4. Insert a new layer, name it **treks headings**, insert a keyframe on the last frame of the movie, then create the Treks screen, except for the home graphic.
5. Convert the Treks graphic on the home page to a button symbol, then edit the symbol so that different colors appear for the different states.
6. Assign a goto action that jumps the playhead to the Treks screen when the Treks button is clicked. (*Hint*: You need to use ActionScript 2.0. You can set the ActionsScript version by selecting Publish Settings from the File menu, clicking on the Flash tab and specifying ActionScript 2.0. Alternately, you can specify ActionScript 1.0 & 2.0 within the Actions panel.)
7. Insert a new layer and name it **stopmovie**. Add stop actions that cause the movie to stop after displaying the home page and after displaying the Treks page. Make sure there is a keyframe in the last frame of the stopmovie layer.
8. Insert a new layer and name it **homeButton**, insert a keyframe on the last frame of the movie, then draw the home button image with the Home text.
9. Convert the image to a button symbol, then edit the symbol so that different colors appear for the different states. Assign a goto action for the button that jumps the movie to Frame 1.
10. Test the movie.
11. Save your work, then compare your Web page to the sample shown in Figure 37.

FIGURE 37
Sample completed Project Builder 1

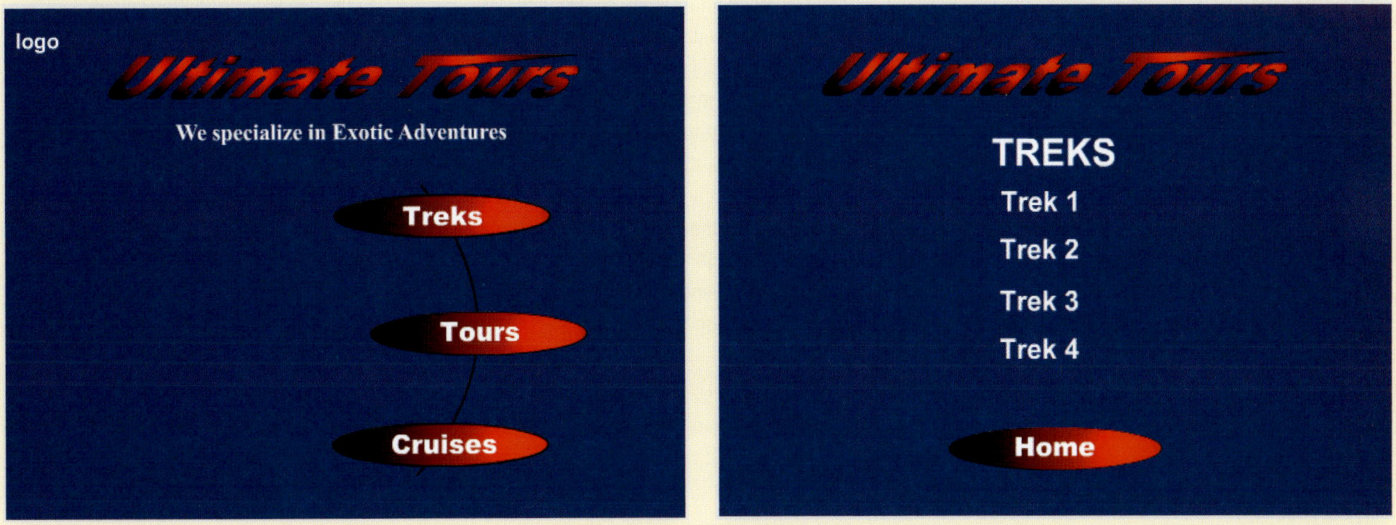

You have been asked to assist the International Student Association (ISA). The association sponsors a series of monthly events, each focusing on a different culture from around the world. The events are led by a guest speaker who makes a presentation, followed by a discussion. The events are free and they are open to everyone. ISA would like you to design a Flash movie that will be used with its Web site. The movie starts by providing information about the series, and then provides a link to the upcoming event.

1. Open a new Flash ActionScript 2.0 document and save it as **isa3**.
2. Create an initial Information screen with general information about the association's series.
3. Assign an action that stops the movie.
4. Add a button on the general information screen that jumps the movie to a screen that presents information about the next event.
5. Add a button on the information screen that jumps the movie to a screen that lists the series (all nine events for the school year—September through May).
6. On the next event and series screens, add a Return button that jumps the movie back to the general information screen.
7. Specify different colors for each state of each button.
8. Test the movie.
9. Save your work, then compare your movie to the sample shown in Figure 38.

FIGURE 38
Sample completed Project Builder 2

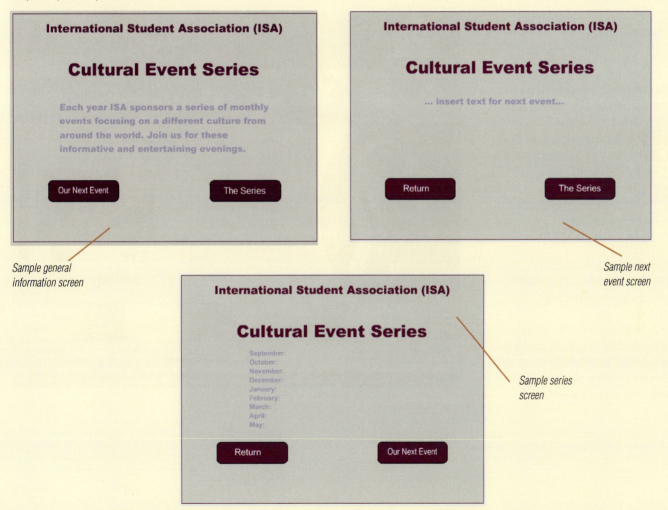

Sample general
information screen

Sample next
event screen

Sample series
screen

DESIGN PROJECT

Figure 39 shows the home page of a Web site. Study the figure and complete the following questions. For each question, indicate how you determined your answer.

1. Connect to the Internet and go to *www.zoo.org*. Notice that this Web site has images that change, and each time you visit the Web site some images change.
2. Open a document in a word processor or open a new Flash document, save the file as **dpc3**, then answer the following questions. (*Hint*: Use the Text tool in Flash.)
   - Whose Web site is this?
   - What is the goal(s) of the site?
   - Who is the target audience?
   - What is the treatment ("look and feel") that is used?
   - What are the design layout guidelines being used (balance, movement, and so on)?
   - What may be animated in this home page?
   - Do you think this is an effective design for the company, its products, and its target audience? Why or why not?
   - What suggestions would you make to improve the design, and why?

FIGURE 39
Design Project

This is a continuation of the Chapter 2 Portfolio Project, which is the development of a personal portfolio. The **home page** has several categories, including the following:

- Personal data
- Contact information
- Previous employment
- Education
- Samples of your work

In this project, you will create a button that will be used to link the **home page** of your portfolio to the animations page. Next, you will create another button to start the animation.

1. Open portfolio2.fla (the file you created in Portfolio Project, Chapter 2), then save it as **portfolio3**. (*Hint*: When you open the file, you may receive a warning message that the font is missing. You can replace this font with the default, or with any other appropriate font on your computer.)

2. Unlock the layers as needed.

3. Change the My Portfolio text to **#003366** and the oval background to **#CCCCCC**.

4. Insert a new layer, insert a keyframe on Frame 3 (or one frame past the last frame of the movie), then create an animation using objects that you create.

5. Insert a new layer, insert a keyframe on Frame 2 (or one frame before the animation frame), then create a Sample Animation screen with a text block that says

Sample Animation at the top of the stage and another text block that says **Home** at the bottom of the stage.

6. Convert each text block into a button symbol, then edit each symbol so that different colors appear for the different states. For the Sample Animation button, assign an action that jumps to the frame that plays an animation. For the Home button, assign an action that jumps to the frame that displays My Portfolio. (*Hint*: You need to use ActionScript 2.0. You can set the ActionsScript version by selecting Publish

Settings from the File menu, clicking on the Flash tab and specifying ActionScript 2.0. Alternately, you can specify ActionScript 1.0 & 2.0 within the Actions panel.)

7. Change the Animations graphic on the homepage to a button, then edit the symbol so that different colors appear for the different states. Assign an action that jumps to the Sample Animation screen.

8. Insert a new layer, then name it **stopmovie**. Insert keyframes and assign stop actions to the appropriate frames.

9. Test the movie.

10. Save your work, then compare your movie to the sample shown in Figure 40.

FIGURE 40
Sample completed Portfolio Project

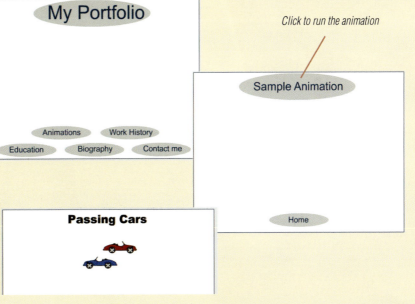

chapter

4

CREATING
ANIMATIONS

1. Create frame-by-frame animations

2. Create motion-tweened animations

3. Work with motion guides

4. Create animation effects

5. Animate text

4 CREATING ANIMATIONS

Introduction

Animation can be an important part of your application or Web site, whether the focus is on e-commerce (attracts attention and provides product demonstrations), education (simulates complex processes such as DNA replication), or entertainment (provides interactive games).

How Does Animation Work?

The perception of motion in an animation is actually an illusion. Animation is like a motion picture in that it is made up of a series of still images. Research has found that our eye captures and holds an image for one-tenth of a second before processing another image. By retaining each impression for one-tenth of a second, we perceive a series of rapidly displayed still images as a single, moving image. This phenomenon is known as persistence of vision and provides the basis for the frame rate in animations. Frame rates of 10–12 frames-per-second (fps) generally provide an acceptably smooth computer-based animation. Lower frame rates result in a jerky image, while higher frame rates may result in a blurred image. Flash uses a default frame rate of 12 fps.

Flash Animation

Creating animation is one of the most powerful features of Flash, yet developing basic animations is a simple process. Flash allows you to create animations that can move and rotate an object around the stage, and change its size, shape, or color. You can also use the animation features in Flash to create special effects, such as an object zooming or fading in and out. You can combine animation effects so that an object changes shape and color as it moves across the stage. Animations are created by changing the content of successive frames. Flash provides two animation methods: frame-by-frame animation and tweened animation. Tweened animations can be either motion tweens or shape tweens.

Tools You'll Use

Insert		
New Symbol...	Ctrl+F8	
Timeline	▶	
Timeline Effects	▶	
Scene		

Assistants	▶
Effects	▶
Transform/Transition	▶

Transform
Transition

Properties ×

Frame   Tween: Motion   ☑ Scale   Sound: None

<Frame Label>   Ease: 100   out   Edit...   Effect: None   Edit...

Label type: Rotate: Auto   0   times   Sync: Event   Repeat   0

Name   ☑ Orient to path   ☑ Sync   ☑ Snap   No sound selected

⦿ 🔒 ☐

🐾 Guide: carRoute   • • ☐

🔲 carRoute   ✎ • • ☐

Advanced Effect ☒

Red = (100% ▼ x R) + 86

Green = (100% ▼ x G) + 0

Blue = (100% ▼ x B) + 0

Alpha = (100% ▼ x A) + 0 ▼

OK   Cancel

CREATE FRAME-BY-FRAME ANIMATIONS

What You'll Do

In this lesson, you will create frame-by-frame animations.

Understanding Frame-by-Frame Animations

A frame-by-frame animation (also called a frame animation) is created by specifying the object that is to appear in each frame of a sequence of frames. Figure 1 shows three images that are variations of a cartoon character. In this example, the head and body remain the same, but the arms and legs change to represent a walking motion. If these individual images are placed into succeeding frames (with keyframes), an animation is created.

Frame-by-frame animations are useful when you want to change individual parts of an image. The images in Figure 1 are simple—only three images are needed for the animation. However, depending on the complexity of the image and the desired movements, the time needed to display each change can be substantial. When creating a frame-by-frame animation, you need to consider the following points:

- The number of different images. The more images there are, the more effort is needed to create them. However, the greater the number of images, the less change you need to make in each image and the more realistic the movement in the animation may seem.
- The number of frames in which each image will appear. If each image appears in only one frame, the animation may appear rather jerky, since the frames change very rapidly. In some cases, you may want to give the impression of a rapid change in an object, such as rapidly blinking colors. If so, you could make changes in the color of an object from one frame to another. Changing the number of frames in which the object appears may change the effect of the animation.
- The movie frame rate. Frame rates below 10 may appear jerky, while those above 30 may appear blurred. The frame rate is easy to change, and you should experiment with different rates until you get the desired effect.

Keyframes are critical to the development of frame animations because they signify a change in the object. Because frame animations are created by changing the object, each frame in a frame animation may need to be a keyframe. The exception is when you want an object displayed in several frames before it changes.

Creating a Frame-by-Frame Animation

To create a frame animation, select the frame on the layer where you want the animation to begin, insert a keyframe, and then place the object on the stage. Next, select the frame where you want the change to occur, insert a keyframe, and then change the object. You can also add a new object in place of the original one. Figure 2 shows the first six frames of an animation in which the front end of a car raises up and down in place. The movement of the animation is shown in the figure as shadows. These shadows are visible because the Onion Skin feature is turned on; this feature will be discussed later in this chapter. In this animation, the car stays in place during the animation, with only the front end of the car moving up and down. However, a frame animation can also involve movement of the object around the stage.

FIGURE 1

Three images used in an animation

FIGURE 2

The first six frames of an animation

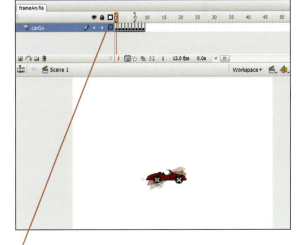

In each frame, the front end of the car is in a different position

Create an in-place frame-by-frame animation

1. Open fl4_1.fla from the drive and folder where your Data Files are stored, then save it as **frameAn**.

2. Verify the Tools panel, Property inspector, and Library panel are the only open panels.

3. Click **View** on the menu bar, point to **Magnification**, then click **Fit in Window**.

4. Click **Frame 2** on the carGo layer, then insert a **keyframe**.

5. Verify that the car is selected, select the **Free Transform tool**  on the Tools panel, then click the **Rotate and Skew option** in the Options section of the Tools panel.

6. Drag the **top-right handle** up one position, as shown in Figure 3.

7. Insert a **keyframe** in Frame 3 on the carGo layer.

8. Drag the **top-right handle** up one more position.

9. Insert a **keyframe** in Frame 4 on the carGo layer, then drag the **top-right handle** down one position.

10. Insert a **keyframe** in Frame 5 on the carGo layer, then drag the **top-right handle** down to position the car to its original horizontal position.

11. Insert a **keyframe** in Frame 6 on the carGo layer, then compare your Timeline to Figure 4.

You created an in-place frame animation by inserting several keyframes and adjusting an object in each of the frames.

FLASH 4-6

FIGURE 3
Rotating the car

Click handle and drag up

FIGURE 4
The Timeline with keyframes

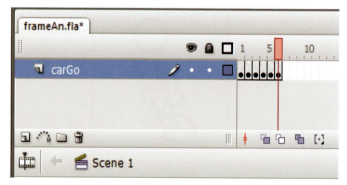

FIGURE 5

Adding lines to the object

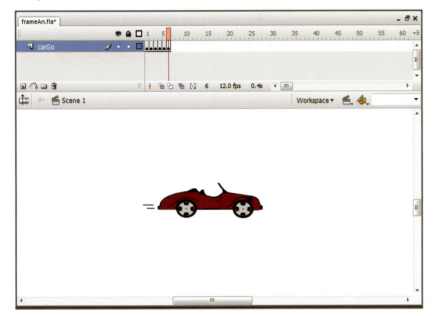

1. Click the **Zoom tool** on the Tools panel, then click the **car** to zoom in on it.

2. Click the **Line tool** on the Tools panel.

3. Set the **Stroke color** to the **black color swatch** in the left column of the color palette (if necessary).

4. Verify Frame 6 is selected, then draw the two lines shown in Figure 5.

5. Click **Frame 1** on the Timeline, then press the **period [.]** on the keyboard five times to move the playhead one frame at a time.

   Notice how the car moves in each frame.

6. Press **[Enter]** (Win) or **[return]** (Mac) to play the movie on the stage.

7. Click **View** on the menu bar, point to **Magnification**, then click F**it in Window**.

You added lines that indicate motion to the animation.

Create a moving frame animation

1. Insert a **keyframe** in Frame 7 on the carGo layer.

2. Click the **Selection tool** on the Tools panel, drag a **marquee** around the car and the lines to select them.

3. Drag the **car** and the **two lines** to the right approximately half the distance to the right edge of the stage, as shown in Figure 6.

4. Insert a **keyframe** in Frame 8 on the carGo layer.

5. Click the **Line tool** on the Tools panel, then draw a third line, as shown in Figure 7.

6. Click the **Selection tool** , drag a **marquee** around the car and lines, then drag the **car** and the **three lines** to the right edge of the stage.

7. Insert a **keyframe** in Frame 9 on the carGo layer, then drag the **car** and the **three lines** completely off the right side of the stage, as shown in Figure 8.

8. Play the movie on the stage.

You created a moving frame animation by dragging the object across the stage.

FIGURE 6
Positioning the car

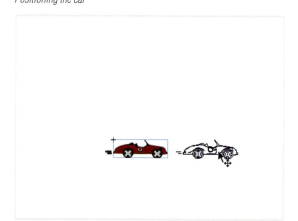

FIGURE 7
The car with a third line

FIGURE 8
Positioning the car off the stage

FIGURE 9
Changing the frame rate

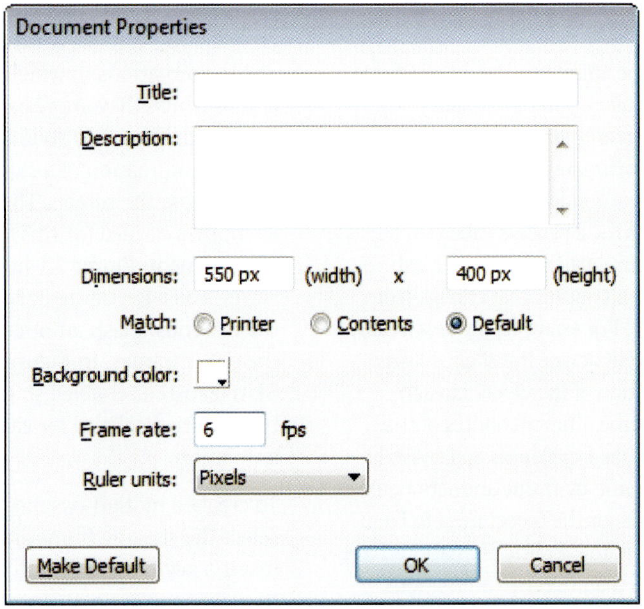

Change the frame rate

1. Click **Control** on the menu bar, then click **Test Movie** to view the movie in the Flash Player window.

   Notice the speed of the car with the frame rate set at 12 fps, the Flash default setting.

2. Close the Flash Player window.
3. Click the **Selection tool** on the Tools panel, then click a **blank area** of the stage.
4. Click the **Size** button in the Property inspector.
5. Type **6** in the Frame rate text box, as shown in Figure 9, then click **OK**.
6. Click **Control** on the menu bar, then click **Test Movie** to view the movie in the Flash Player window.

   Notice the speed of the car with the frame rate set at 6 fps.

7. Close the Flash Player window.
8. Change the frame rate to **18**, then test the movie.
9. Close the Flash player window.
10. Change the frame rate to **12**.
11. Save your work, then close the movie.

You changed the frame rate for the movie to see its effect on the movement of the object.

CREATE MOTION-TWEENED ANIMATIONS

What You'll Do

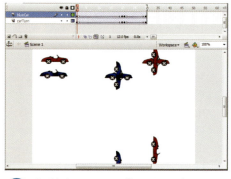

In this lesson, you will create motion-tweened animations.

Understanding Motion Tweening

Frame-by-frame animation can be a tedious process, especially if you have to alter an object's position an infinitesimal amount in every frame. Fortunately, once you create start and end frames, Flash can fill in the in-between frames, a process called **tweening**. In tweened animation, Flash stores only the attributes that change from frame to frame. For example, if you have an object that moves across the stage, Flash stores the location of the object in each frame, but not the other attributes of the object, such as its dimensions and color. In contrast, for frame-by-frame animation, all of the attributes for the object need to be stored in each frame. Frame animations have larger file sizes than tweened animations.

There are two types of tweened animations: shape and motion. Shape-tweened animations are similar to the process of image morphing in which one object slowly turns into another—often unrelated—object, such as a robot that turns into a man. Shape-tweened animations will be covered in the next chapter. You can use **motion tweening** to create animations in which objects move and in which they are resized, rotated, and recolored. Figure 10 shows a motion-tweened animation of a car moving diagonally across the screen. There are only two keyframes needed for this animation: a keyframe in Frame 1 where the car starts, and a keyframe in Frame 30 where the car ends. Flash automatically fills in the other frames. In Figure 10, the Onion Skin feature is enabled so that outlines of the car are displayed for each frame of the animation.

To create a motion-tweened animation, select the starting frame and, if necessary, insert a keyframe. Position the object on the stage and verify that it is selected. Next, choose the Create Motion Tween command from the Timeline option on the Insert menu, and then insert a keyframe in the ending frame of the animation. Figure 10 shows the Timeline after creating a Motion Tween and specifying an ending keyframe. On the Timeline, motion tweening is represented by black dots displayed in the keyframes and a black arrow linking the keyframes against a light blue background. The final step is to move the object and/or make changes to the object, such as changing its size or rotating it.

Keep in mind the following points as you create motion-tweened animations.

- If you change the position of the object, it will move in a direct line from the starting position to the ending position. To move the object on a predetermined path, you can create several motion-tweened animations in succeeding frames, or you can use a motion guide as explained in the next lesson.

- If you reshape an object in the ending keyframe, the object will slowly change from the starting keyframe to the ending keyframe. If this is not the effect you want, you can add a keyframe immediately after the tweened animation and reshape the object at that point.
- When you select an object that is not already a symbol in the Library and create a motion tween, Flash automatically creates a symbol, names it Tween 1, and places it in the Library panel.
- You can remove a motion tween animation by selecting a frame within the tween and using the Remove

Tween command from the Timeline option in the Insert menu.

A motion tween can be copied from one object to another. This saves time when you want two or more objects to have the same animation. The objects must be graphic symbols to copy a motion tween from one object to the other.

FIGURE 10
Sample motion-tweened animation

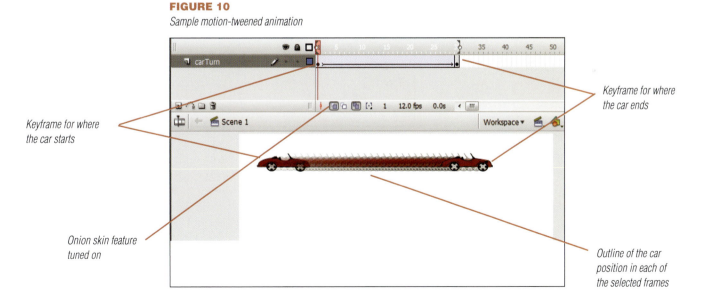

Keyframe for where the car starts

Keyframe for where the car ends

Onion skin feature tuned on

Outline of the car position in each of the selected frames

Create a motion-tweened animation

1. Open fl4_2.fla, then save it as **carAn**.

2. Click **View** on the menu bar, point to **Magnification**, then click **Fit in Window** (if necessary).

   Notice there is one object on the stage, and it is placed in Frame 1 of a layer named carTurn.

3. Click **Frame 1** on the carTurn layer, click **Insert** on the menu bar, point to **Timeline**, then click **Create Motion Tween**.

4. Insert a **keyframe** in Frame 20 on the carTurn layer.

   Notice the arrow indicating a motion tween animation.

5. Click the **Selection tool ▶** on the Tools panel (if necessary), select the **car**, then drag the **car** to the position on the stage shown in Figure 11.

6. Press **[Enter]** (Win) or **[return]** (Mac) to play the movie on the stage.

7. Click **Frame 1** on the Timeline, then press the **period [.]** on the keyboard six times to move the playhead one frame at a time.

   Notice how Flash has filled in the frames between the two keyframes. This process is known as tweening.

You created a motion-tweened animation, causing an object to move across the stage.

FIGURE 11
Final position of the first motion tween

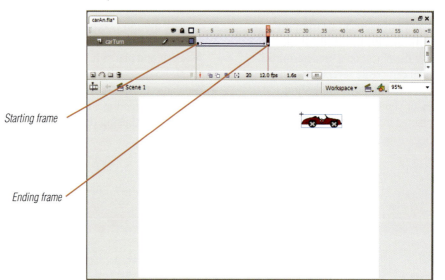

Starting frame

Ending frame

Creating Animations

FIGURE 12

Final position of the combined motion tweens

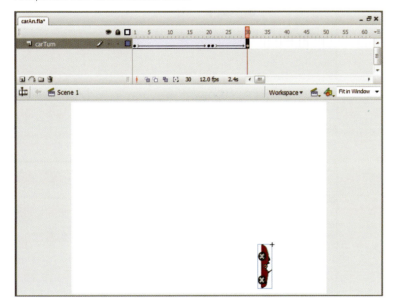

1. Insert a **keyframe** in Frame 21 on the carTurn layer.

2. Verify that the car is selected, click **Modify** on the menu bar, point to **Transform**, then click **Rotate 90° CW**.

   | TIP   CW means clockwise.

3. Insert a **keyframe** in Frame 30 on the carTurn layer.

   A motion tween is automatically inserted in the Timeline because of the previous motion-tween that was created for the object.

   | TIP   If you did not want another motion tween to be automatically inserted, you could add a Blank Keyframe to the frame following the animation. You use the Timeline option from the Insert menu to select and insert a Blank Keyframe.

4. Click the **Selection tool** ⬉ on the Tools panel (if necessary), then drag the **car** to the location shown in Figure 12.

5. Play the movie.

6. Save your work.

You combined two motion-tweened animations with a rotation between the animations.

Copy a motion-tweened animation

1. Insert a **new layer** and name it **blueCar**.

2. Click **Frame 1** of the blueCar layer.

3. Display the Library panel, then drag the **g_blueCar graphic** from the Library panel to just off the stage, as shown in Figure 13.

4. Click a **blank area** of the stage, to deselect the car.

5. Click **Frame 1** of the carTurn layer to select it.

6. Press and hold **[Shift]**, then click **Frame 30** to select the range of frames, as shown in Figure 14.

7. Click **Edit** on the menu bar, point to **Timeline**, then click **Copy Motion**.

8. Click the **blueCar** to select it.

9. Click **Edit** on the menu bar, point to **Timeline**, then click **Paste Motion Special**.

10. Deselect the **Horizontal scale option** and the **Vertical scale option**.

    This prevents the blue car from being resized when the motion is copied.

11. Click **OK** to close the Paste Motion Special dialog box.

    Notice the arrows in the blueCar layer on the Timeline indicating that there are two motion tweens on the layer.

FIGURE 13

Positioning the blue car

Blue car placed off the stage

FIGURE 14

Selecting the animation frames

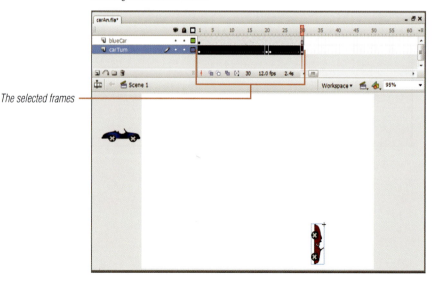

The selected frames

FIGURE 15

FIGURE 15

Repositioning the blue car

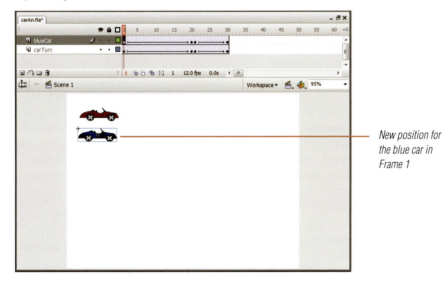

New position for
the blue car in
Frame 1

12. Press **[Enter]** (Win) or **[return]** (Mac) to play the movie on the stage.

    Notice the blue car animation is the same as the red car.

13. Click **Control** on the menu bar, then click **Test Movie** to view the movie in the Flash player window.

14. Close the Flash player window.

15. Click **File** on the menu bar, point to **Publish Preview**, then click **Default** to view the movie in a browser.

16. Close the browser window.

    You can change the location of the objects in any keyframe to change the starting or ending positions of the objects.

17. Click **Frame 1** of the blueCar layer to select the car.

18. Drag the **blue car** to the right and up as needed until it is below the red car, as shown in Figure 15.

19. Press **[Enter]** (Win) or **[return]** (Mac) to play the movie on the stage.

20. Save your work, then close the movie.

You copied a motion tween to another object and changed the starting position of the object.

WORK WITH MOTION GUIDES

What You'll Do

In this lesson, you will create a motion guide and attach an animation to it.

Understanding Motion Guides

In the previous lesson, you combined two motion tween animations to cause an object to change directions. Flash provides a way for you to create a path that will guide moving objects around the stage in any direction, as shown in Figure 16. (Note: The onion skin feature is turned on to show how the car follows the path.) **Motion guide layers** allow you to draw a motion guide path and attach motion-tweened animations to the path. The animations are placed on their own layer beneath the motion guide layer. There are two ways to work with motion guides. One way is to insert a guide layer, draw a path, and then create an animation and attach the animated object to the path. The second way is to create an animation, insert a motion guide layer and draw a path, and then attach the animated object to the path. The process for using the second method is as follows:

- Create a motion-tweened animation.
- Select the layer the animation is on and insert a motion guide layer. The selected layer is indented below the motion

guide layer, as shown in Figure 17. This indicates that the selected layer is associated with the motion guide layer.

- Draw a path using the Pen, Pencil, Line, Circle, Rectangle, or Brush tools.
- Attach the object to the path by clicking the first keyframe of the layer that contains the animation, and then dragging the object by its transformation point to the beginning of the path. Select the end keyframe and then repeat the steps to attach the object to the end of the path.

Depending on the type of object you are animating and the path, you may need to orient the object to the path. This means that the object will rotate in response to the direction of the path. The Property inspector is used to specify that the object will be oriented to the path. The advantages of using a motion guide are that you can have an object move along any path, including a path that intersects itself, and you can easily change the shape of the path, allowing you to experiment with different motions. A consideration when using a motion guide is that, in some instances, orienting the object along the path may result in an unnatural-looking animation. You can fix this by stepping through the animation one frame at a time until you reach the frame where the object is positioned poorly. You can then insert a keyframe and adjust the object as desired.

Working with the Property Inspector When Creating Motion-Tweened Animations

The Property inspector provides the following options when creating motion-tweened animations:

- Tween—specifies Motion, Shape, or None.
- Scale—tweens the size of an object. Select this option when you want an object to grow smaller or larger.
- Ease—specifies the rate of change

between tweened frames. For example, you may want to have an object—such as a car—start out slowly and accelerate gradually. Ease values are between –100 (slow) to 100 (fast).

- Rotate—specifies the number of times an object rotates clockwise (CW) or counterclockwise (CCW).
- Orient to path—orients the baseline of the object to the path.
- Sync—ensures that the object loops properly.
- Snap—attaches the object to the path by its transformation point.

Transformation Point and Registration Point

Each symbol has a transformation point in the form of a circle (O) that is used to

orient the object when it is being animated. For example, when you rotate a symbol, the transformation point is the pivot point around which the object rotates. The transformation point is also the point that snaps to a motion guide, as shown in Figure 16. When attaching an object to a path, you can drag the transformation point to the path. The default position for a transformation point is the center of the object. You can reposition the transformation point while in the symbol edit mode by dragging the transformation point to a different location in the object. Objects also have a registration point (+) that is used to position the object on the stage using ActionScript code. The transformation and registration points can overlap—this is displayed as a plus sign within a circle. ⊕

FIGURE 16
A motion guide with an object (car) attached

Transformation Point

FIGURE 17
A motion guide layer

Motion guide layer

Indented layer containing the animation that will follow the path created on the guide layer

⚬ Guide: carRoute
carRoute

Create an animation without a motion guide

1. Open fl4_3.fla, then save it as **carPath**.

2. Verify the Tools panel and Property inspector are displayed.

3. Set the View to **Fit in Window**.

4. Click **Frame 1** of the carRoute layer.

5. Make sure that the car is selected, click **Insert** on the menu bar, point to **Timeline**, then click **Create Motion Tween**.

6. Insert a **keyframe** in Frame 40 on the carRoute layer.

7. Drag the **car** to the lower-right corner of the stage, as shown in Figure 15.

8. Press **[Enter]** (Win) or **[return]** (Mac) to play the movie.

   The car moves diagonally down to the corner of the stage.

You created a motion animation that moves an object in a diagonal line across the stage.

FIGURE 18
Positioning the car

carRoute layer

FIGURE 19

The completed motion path

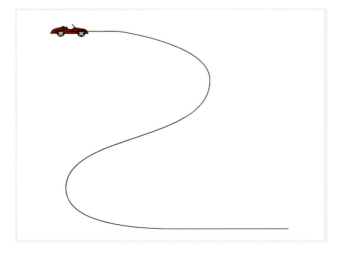

FIGURE 20

Snapping an object to the path

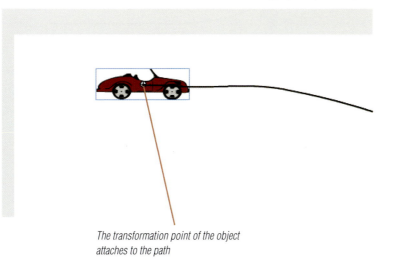

The transformation point of the object attaches to the path

Add a motion guide to an animation

1. Click **Frame 1** on the carRoute layer.

2. Click **Insert** on the menu bar, point to **Timeline**, then click **Motion Guide**.

   The carRoute layer is indented beneath the guide layer on the Timeline.

3. Click **Frame 1** of the Guide layer, click the **Pencil tool** on the Tools panel, click the **Smooth option** $\int$ in the Options section of the Tools panel, then draw a path starting at the middle of the car similar to the one shown in Figure 19.

   TIP   Draw straight lines for the beginning and ending of the path. This will help orient the car to the path.

4. Click the **Selection tool** and click the **lock icon** for the Guide layer to lock the layer.

5. Click **Frame 1** of the carRoute layer. If the transformation point is not on the path, click the **transformation point** ⊕ of the car, then drag it to the beginning of the path, as shown in Figure 20.

   TIP   An object is snapped to the beginning or end of a motion path when the path intersects the object's transformation point.

6. Click **Frame 40** on the carRoute layer.

7. If the car does not snap to the end of the path, click the **Selection tool**, click the **transformation point** ⊕ of the car, then drag it to the end of the path.

8. Play the movie.

You created a motion guide on a path and attached an animation to it.

Orient an object to the path

1. Play the movie again and notice how the car does not turn front-first in response to the turns in the path.

2. Make sure the Property inspector is displayed, then click **Frame 1** on the carRoute layer.

3. Make sure the **car** is selected, then click the **Orient to path check box** in the Property inspector.

4. Play the movie.

   Notice the car is oriented front-first to the turns in the path.

You used the Property inspector to specify that the object is oriented to the path.

Alter the path

1. Click **Frame 1** on the carRoute layer.

2. Click the **Selection tool** ▶, (if necessary).

3. Click the **Lock icon** 🔒 on the Guide layer to unlock the the layer, then point to the middle of the right curve line of the path.

4. When the pointer changes to the arc pointer ▶⌣, drag the **line** in, as shown in Figure 21.

   Your path may be different.

5. Lock the Guide layer, then play the movie.

You altered the motion guide path.

FIGURE 21
Dragging the line to alter the path

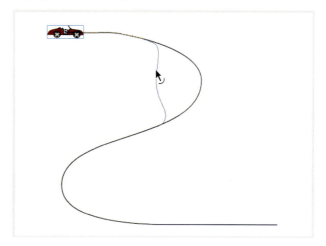

FIGURE 22

FIGURE 22
Setting the Ease value

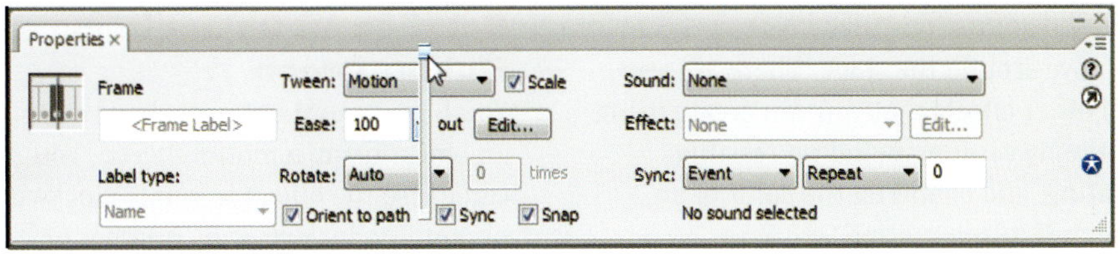

Accelerate an animated object

1. Play the movie and notice the speed of the car is constant.

2. Click **Frame 1** on the carRoute layer.

3. Click the **Ease list arrow** in the Property inspector, drag the slider up to **100**, as shown in Figure 22, then click a **blank area** outside the stage.

4. Play the movie and notice how the car starts out fast and decelerates as it moves toward the end of the path.

5. Click **Frame 1** on the carRoute layer.

6. Click the **Ease list arrow** in the Property inspector, drag the slider down to **–100**, then click a **blank area** outside the stage.

7. Play the movie and notice how the car starts out slow and accelerates as it moves toward the end of the path.

8. Click **Control** on the menu bar, then click **Test Movie.**

9. View the movie, then close the test movie window.

10. Save your work.

You set Ease values to alter the starting and ending speed of the car.

CREATE
ANIMATION EFFECTS

▶ *In this lesson, you will use motion tween-ing to resize, rotate, and change the color of animated objects.*

Creating Motion Animation Effects

Up to this point, you have created motion-tweened animations that cause an object to move around the stage. There are several other effects that you can create using motion tweening, including resizing, rotating, and changing the color of an object as it is in motion.

Resizing an Object Using a Motion Tween

The simplest process for resizing an object during a motion tween is to select a frame as the starting frame, draw or place an object on the stage, and then create a motion tween. You can select an ending frame and resize the object using the resize handles that are displayed when you select the Free Transform tool and the Scale option on the Tools panel. The results of this process are shown in Figure 23. By moving and resizing an object, you can create the effect that it is moving away from you or toward you. If you have the object remain stationary while it is being resized, the effect is similar to zooming in or out.

Rotating an Object Using a Motion Tween

You have several options when rotating an object using a motion tween. You can cause the object to rotate clockwise or counterclockwise any number of degrees and any number of times. You can also stipulate an Ease value to cause the rotation to accelerate or decelerate. These effects can be specified using the Free Transform tool and the Rotate option on the Tools panel, adjusting settings in the Property inspector, or clicking a Transform option on the Modify menu. The Transform options include Flip Vertical and Flip Horizontal. Choosing these options causes the object to slowly flip throughout the length of the animation. You can combine effects so that they occur simultaneously during the animation. For example, you can have a car rotate and get smaller as it moves across the stage. The Scale and Rotate dialog box allows you to specify a percentage for scaling and a number of degrees for rotating.

Changing an Object's Color Using a Motion Tween

Flash provides several ways in which you can alter the color of objects using a motion tween. The most basic change involves starting with one color for the object and ending with another color. The tweening process slowly changes the color across the specified frames. When the movie is played, the colors are blended as the object moves across the stage. If you start with a red color and end with a blue color, at the middle of the anima-tion the object's color is purple with equal portions of the blue and red colors mixed together.

More sophisticated color changes can be made using the Property inspector. You can adjust the brightness; tint the colors; adjust the transparency (Alpha option); and change the red, green, and blue values of an object. One of the most popular animation effects is to cause an object to slowly fade in. You can accomplish this by motion tweening the object, setting the Alpha value to 0 (transparent) in the starting frame, and then setting it to 100 in the ending frame. To make the object fade out, just reverse the values.

Using the Onion Skin Feature

Figure 24 displays an animation using the Onion Skin feature. Normally, Flash displays one frame of an animation sequence at a time on the stage. Turning on the Onion Skin feature allows you to view an outline of the object(s) in any number of frames. This can help in positioning animated objects on the stage. The Edit Multiple Frames feature is also turned on, allowing you to view the objects in the Keyframes in a non-outline form.

FIGURE 23
Resizing an object during a motion tween

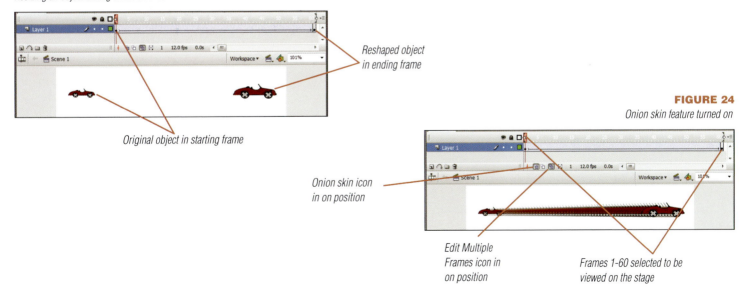

Reshaped object in ending frame

Original object in starting frame

FIGURE 24
Onion skin feature turned on

Onion skin icon in on position

Edit Multiple Frames icon in on position

Frames 1-60 selected to be viewed on the stage

Combining Various Animation Effects

Flash allows you to combine the various motion-tween effects so that you can rotate an object as it moves across the stage, changes color, and changes size. Flash allows you to combine motion-tweened animations to create various effects. For example, if you create an airplane object, you can apply the following aerial effects:

- Enter from off stage and perform a loop
- Rotate the plane horizontally to create a barrel roll effect
- Have the plane grow smaller as it moves across the screen to simulate the effect of the plane speeding away
- Change colors on the fuselage to simulate the reflection of the sun

Creating Timeline Effects

Flash provides several prebuilt Timeline effects, such as having an object fade-in, that allow you to create complex animations with only a few steps. You simply select an object, select an effect, and then specify the settings. You can apply Timeline effects to the following objects:

- Text
- Graphics, including shapes, groups, and graphic symbols
- Bitmap images
- Button symbols

When you apply a Timeline effect to an object, Flash creates a layer and transfers the object to the new layer. The object is placed inside the effect graphic, and all tweens and transformations required for the effect reside in the graphic on the new layer. The new layer automatically receives the same name as the effect, with a number appended that represents the order in which the effect is applied. An effect symbol is created and placed in an Effects Folder that is added to the Library panel. Also, the effect graphic is added to the Library panel.

Adding an Effect to an Object

To add an effect to an object, you select the object and then choose Timeline Effects from the Insert menu. The Timeline Effects menu has three options that name categories of effects available for the type of object you've selected. Each option opens a submenu with additional choices, as shown in Figure 25. When you choose an effect, a

FIGURE 25

The Timeline Effects options on the Insert menu

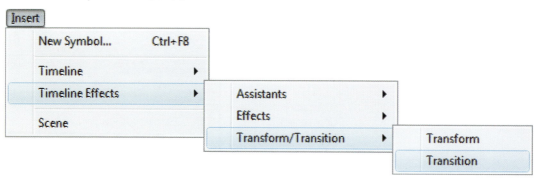

dialog box appears, illustrating the effect and allowing you to modify the default settings. Figure 26 shows the default settings for the Transition Effect – Fade In. These settings allow you to do the following:

- Specify the duration of the effect in number of frames
- Specify the direction (In or Out)
- Specify a motion ease

When you select the object on the stage, you can view properties for the effect in the Property inspector.

Editing a Timeline Effect

To edit a Timeline effect, you select the object associated with the effect on the Stage and click Edit in the Property inspector. This displays the appropriate Effects Setting dialog box.

Deleting a Timeline Effect

When you right-click (Win) or control click (Mac) an object, a menu opens with options specific to the object you clicked. This menu is used to delete Timeline effects. On the Stage, right-click (Win) or control click (Mac) the object, and select Timeline Effects from the context menu, and then select Remove Effect.

FIGURE 26

Default settings for the Transition Effect – Fade In

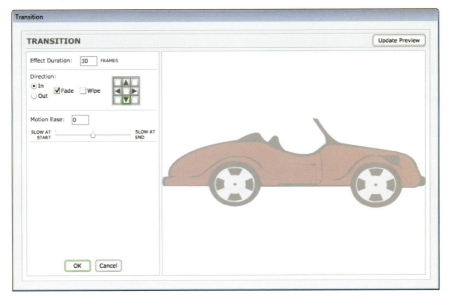

Use motion tweening to resize an object

1. Make sure that the carPath.fla movie is open.

2. Click **Frame 1** on the carRoute layer.

3. Click the **Zoom tool** 🔍 on the Tools panel, then click the **car** to enlarge the view.

4. Make sure the car is selected, click the **Free Transform tool** 🔧 on the Tools panel, then click the **Scale option** 🔲 in the Options section of the Tools panel.

5. Drag the upper-left **corner handle** inward until the car is approximately half the original size, as shown in Figure 27.

6. Change the view to **Fit in Window**.

7. Click **Frame 40** on the carRoute layer.

8. Make sure the car is selected, then click the **Scale option button** 🔲 .

9. Drag the upper-right **corner handle** outward until the car is approximately twice the original size, as shown in Figure 28.

10. Play the movie and notice how the car is resized.

11. Save your work, then close the movie.

You used the Scale option to resize an object in a motion animation.

FIGURE 27

Using the handles to reduce the size of the car

Click and drag the handle toward the car

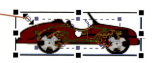

FIGURE 28

Using the handles to increase the size of the car

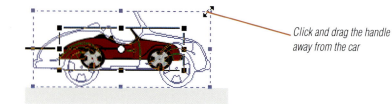

Click and drag the handle away from the car

FIGURE 29
Specifying the rotate settings

Rotation will be
counter-clockwise
1 time

FIGURE 30
Repositioning the motorbike

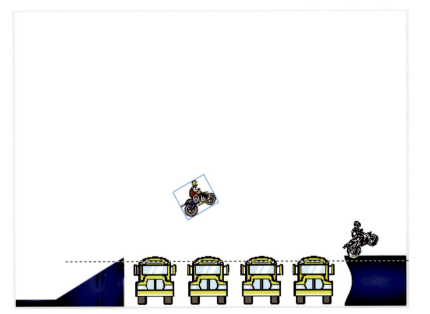

Use motion tweening to rotate an object

1. Open **fl4_4.fla**, save it as **mBikeRotate**, change the view to **Fit in Window**, then play the movie.

2. Click **Frame 10** on the motorBike layer.

3. Make sure the motorbike is selected, click **Insert** on the menu bar, point to **Timeline**, then click **Create Motion Tween**.

4. Click the **Rotate list arrow** on the Property inspector, click **CCW**, then verify 1 is entered into the times box, as shown in Figure 29.

5. Insert a **keyframe** in Frame 20 on the motorBike layer.

6. Play the movie; notice the motorbike moves forward, rotates in place in the middle of the buses, and then disappears.

7. Click **Frame 20** on the motorBike layer, then drag the **motorbike** across the stage to the edge of the landing area, as shown in Figure 30.

8. Insert a **Keyframe** in Frame 21 on the motorBike layer.

9. Verify the motorbike is selected, click **Modify** on the menu bar, point to **Transform**, then click **Scale and Rotate**.

10. Type **30** for the Rotate value, then click **OK**.

11. Insert a **keyframe** in Frame 22, then drag the **motorbike** to the edge of the stage.

12. Play the movie; notice that the motorbike rotates as it moves over the buses to the landing area in the new location.

13. Save your work.

You created a motion animation and used the Property inspector to rotate the object.

Use motion tweening to change the color of an object

1. Click **Frame 20** on the motorBike layer.

2. Click the **Selection tool** ▶ on the Tools panel, then click the **motorbike** to select it.

3. Click the **Color list arrow** in the Property inspector, click **Advanced**, then click the **Settings button**.

4. Click the **x R) + list arrow**, then drag the slider to **86**, as shown in Figure 31.

5. Click **OK**.

6. Click **Frame 1** on the Timeline, then play the movie.

    You can see how the color slowly changes to a red shade.

    > TIP   Because motion tweening is performed on instances of symbols and text blocks, changing the color of a motion-tweened object affects the entire object. To make changes in individual areas of an object, you must first select the object and choose the Break Apart command from the Modify menu.

You used the Property inspector to change the color of an object as it was being animated.

FIGURE 31

Changing the color settings

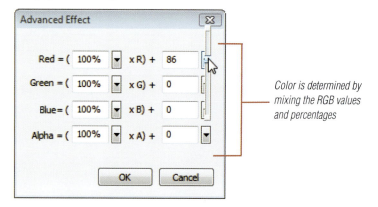

Color is determined by mixing the RGB values and percentages

Click **Frame 1** on the motorBike layer, then click the **Onion Skin button** 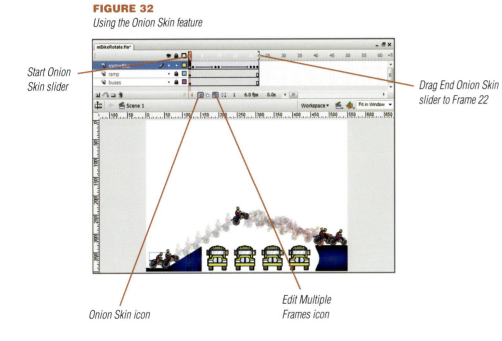 on the Timeline.

2. Click the **Edit Multiple Frames button** on the Timeline.

3. Drag the **End Onion Skin slider** on the Timeline to Frame 22, then compare your Timeline to Figure 32.

   Each frame of the animation is visible on the stage.

4. Play the movie and notice that the animation is not affected by the onion skin feature being turned on.

5. Click the **Onion Skin button** and the **Edit Multiple Frames button** on the Timeline to turn off these features.

6. Save and close the movie.

You displayed the animation using the Onion Skin feature, allowing you to view the object as it appears in each frame of the animation.

FIGURE 32
Using the Onion Skin feature

Start Onion Skin slider

Drag End Onion Skin slider to Frame 22

Onion Skin icon

Edit Multiple Frames icon

Create a Timeline Effect

1. Open fl4_5.fla, save it as **carEffects**, then change the view to **Fit in Window**.

2. Click **Window** on the menu bar, then click **Library** to display the Library panel (if necessary).

   Notice that there is only one item, a graphic named g_car, in the Library.

3. Click the **Selection tool** ➤ on the Tools panel (if necessary), then drag the **g_car graphic** from the Library panel to the upper-left corner of the stage, as shown in Figure 33.

4. Click **Modify** on the menu bar, then click **Break Apart**.

5. Click **Insert** on the menu bar, point to **Timeline Effects**, point to **Transform/ Transition**, then click **Transition**.

   The Transition dialog box opens, allowing you to change the settings for Fade and Wipe effects. The preview shows how the default settings will affect the object on the stage, including a fade, a wipe, and a duration of 30 frames.

6. Click the **Wipe check box** to turn off this effect, then click **Update Preview**. Notice that fade is the only effect.

7. Click **OK** to close the dialog box.

   A new layer was created and given the same name (Transition 1) as the effect, as shown in Figure 34. (Note: The number after the word Transition may vary.)

8. Play the movie.

You created a Fade in Timeline Effect.

FIGURE 33
Positioning the car on the stage

FIGURE 34
The layer name displays the effect name

Car is not visible because the fade in transition effect starts in Frame 1

FIGURE 35

The Library panel displaying the Transition Effect

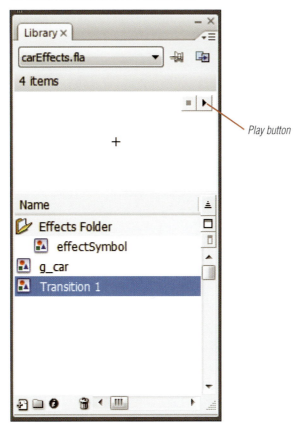

Play button

1. Double-click the **Effects Folder button** 📁 in the Library panel to expand the folder if necessary, then click **effectSymbol** to display the graphic symbol in the Item preview window of the Library panel.

   The effectSymbol was created and added to an Effects Folder in the Library panel when the Timeline effect was specified.

2. Click the **Transition 1 symbol** 📷 in the Library panel.

   The Transition graphic was created and added to the Library panel when the Timeline effect was specified. This graphic holds the effect, which can be viewed in the Library panel.

3. Click the **Play button** ▶ in the Item preview window of the Library panel, as shown in Figure 35.

You viewed the effectSymbol and played the transition using the graphic within the Library panel.

Edit and remove a Timeline Effect

1. Display the Property inspector panel, if necessary.

2. Click **Frame 30** on the Timeline, click the **Selection tool** ▸, then click the **car**.

3. Click the **Edit button** on the Property inspector panel to open the Transition dialog box.

4. Click the **Out option button** to change the direction.

5. Drag the **Motion Ease slider** to the right to set the Motion Ease to **100**, then compare your screen to Figure 36.

6. Click **Update Preview**, then click **OK**.

7. Click **Frame 1** on the Timeline, then play the movie.

8. Click **Frame 1** on the Timeline.

9. Right-click (Win) or control click (Mac) the **car**, point to **Timeline Effects**, then click **Remove Effect**.

10. Play the movie.

You edited a Timeline effect using an Effect Settings dialog box, then removed the effect.

FIGURE 36

The completed Transition dialog box

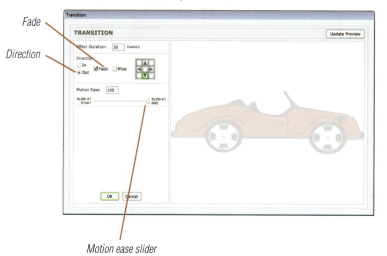

Fade

Direction

Motion ease slider

FIGURE 37

The completed Transform dialog box

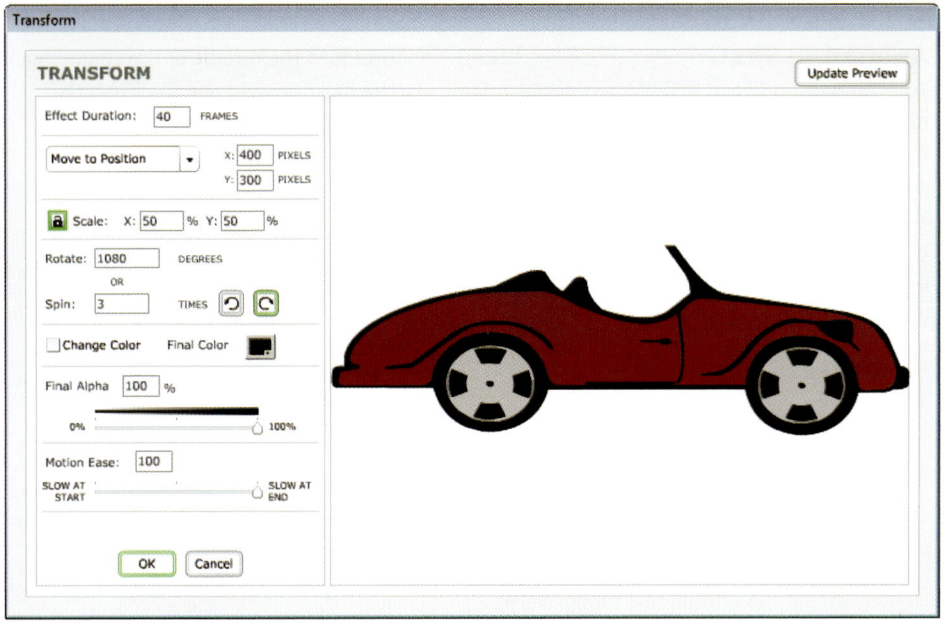

Apply several Timeline Effects to one object

1. Click the **Selection tool** on the Tools panel, then drag a **marquee** around the car to select it.
2. Click **Insert** on the menu bar, point to **Timeline Effects**, point to **Transform/ Transition**, then click **Transform**.
3. Change the effect duration to **40** frames.
4. Click the **Change Position by list arrow**, then click **Move to Position**.
5. Double-click **0** in the X Position PIXELS text box, then type **400**.
6. Double-click **0** in the Y Position PIXELS text box, then type **300**.

   X and Y are the coordinates (in pixels) for the position of the object on the stage. If the stage dimensions are 800 x 600, then 400 (X-width) and 300 (Y-height) position the object in the middle of the stage.
7. Click the **Scale Lock button** to unlock it.
8. Double-click **100** in the Scale X % text box, then type **50**.
9. Double-click **100** in the Scale Y % text box, then type **50**.
10. Change the spin times to **3**.
11. Change the Motion Ease value to **100**, then compare your screen to Figure 37.
12. Click **Update Preview**, then click **OK**.
13. Play the movie, then save and close the movie.

You used the Effect Settings dialog box to apply several effects to a single object.

ANIMATE TEXT

What You'll Do

In this lesson, you will animate text by scrolling, rotating, zooming, and resizing it.

Animating Text

You can motion tween text block objects just as you do graphic objects. You can resize, rotate, reposition, and change their colors. Figure 38 shows three examples of animated text with the Onion Skin feature turned on. When the movie starts, each of the following can occur one after the other:

- The Classic Car Club text block scrolls in from the left side to the top center of the stage. This is done by creating the text block, positioning it off the stage, and creating a motion-tweened animation that moves it to the stage.
- The Annual text block appears and rotates five times. This occurs after you create the Annual text block, posi- tion it in the middle of the stage under the heading, and use the Property inspector to specify a clockwise rota- tion that repeats five times.
- The ROAD RALLY text block slowly zooms out and appears in the middle of the stage. This occurs after you cre- ate the text block and use the Free Transform tool handles to resize it to a small block. You use the Property inspector to specify a transparent value. Finally, the text block is resized to a larger size at the end of the animation.

Once you create a motion animation using a text block, the text block becomes a sym- bol and you are unable to edit individual characters within the text block. You can, however, edit the symbol as a whole.

FIGURE 38

Three examples of animated text

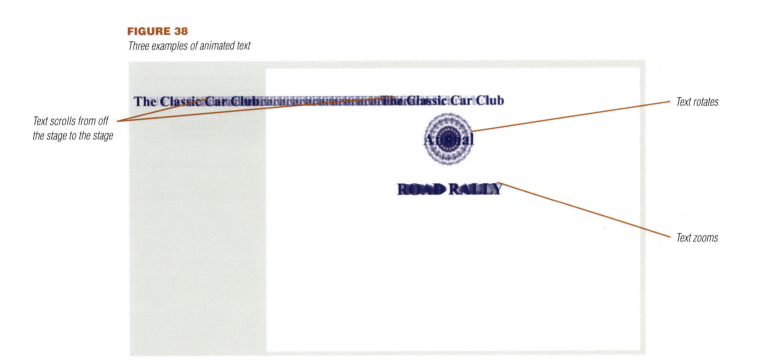

Text scrolls from off
the stage to the stage

Text rotates

Text zooms

Select, copy, and paste frames

1. Open frameAn.fla (the file you created earlier in this chapter), then save the movie as **textAn**.

2. Change the view to **Fit in Window**.

3. Click **Frame 9** on the carGo layer, press and hold **[Shift]**, then click **Frame 1** to select all the frames, as shown in Figure 39.

4. Click **Edit** on the menu bar, point to **Timeline**, then click **Cut Frames**.

5. Click the **Frame View icon** ≡ near the upper right of the Timeline, then click **Small**.

6. Click **Frame 71** on the carGo layer.

7. Click **Edit** on the menu bar, point to **Timeline**, then click **Paste Frames**.

8. Click **Frame 1** of the carGo layer.

9. Play the movie, then save your work.

10. Close all panels except for the Tools panel and Property inspector.

You selected frames, and moved them from one location on the Timeline to another location on the Timeline.

FIGURE 39
Selecting frames

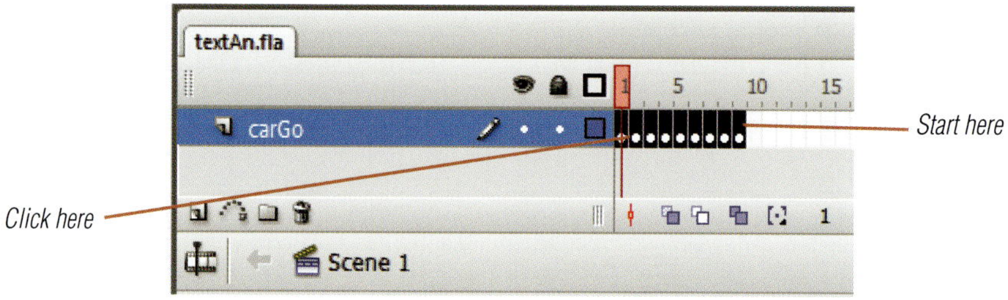

Click here

Start here

FIGURE 40
Positioning the Text tool pointer outside the stage

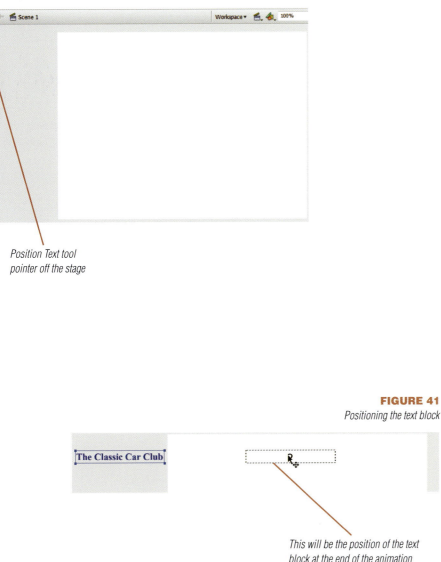

Position Text tool
pointer off the stage

FIGURE 41
Positioning the text block

This will be the position of the text
block at the end of the animation

Create animated text

1. Insert a **new layer**, then name it **scrollText**.

2. Click **Frame 1** on the scrollText layer, then verify that the Property inspector is displayed.

3. Click the **Text tool** **T** on the Tools panel, click the ⊥T pointer outside the stage in the upper-left corner of the workspace, as shown in Figure 40, then click to display a text box.

   | TIP   You may need to scroll the stage to make room for the text box.

4. Click the **Font list arrow** in the Property inspector, then click **Times New Roman** (if necessary).

5. Click the **Font Size list arrow** in the Property inspector, then drag the slider to **20**.

6. Click the **Text (fill) color swatch**, then click the **blue color swatch** on the left column of the color palette.

7. Type **The Classic Car Club**.

8. Click the **Selection tool** , then insert a **keyframe** in Frame 20 on the scrollText layer.

9. Drag the **text block** horizontally to the top center of the stage, as shown in Figure 41.

10. Click **Frame 10** of the scrollText layer, click the **Tween list arrow** in the Property inspector, then click **Motion**.

    This is another way of creating a motion tween.

11. Click **Frame 1** on the Timeline, then play the movie.

    The text moves to center stage from offstage left.

You created a text block object and applied a motion tween animation to it.

Create rotating text

1. Insert a **new layer,** then name it **rotateText**.

2. Insert a **keyframe** in Frame 21 on the rotateText layer.

3. Click the **Text tool** T on the Tools panel, position the pointer beneath the "a" in "Classic," then click to display a blank text box.

4. Verify the Align Left button is selected, click the **Font Size list arrow** on the Property inspector, drag the slider to **24**, click in the new text box (if necessary), type **Annual**, then compare your image to Figure 42.

5. Click the **Selection tool** ▶ on the Tools panel, then insert a **keyframe** in Frame 40 of the rotateText layer.

6. Click **Frame 30** on the rotateText layer, click the **Tween list arrow** in the Property inspector, then click **Motion**.

7. Click **Frame 21** on the rotateText layer, click the **Rotate list arrow** in the Property inspector, click **CW**, type **2** in the times text box, then click anywhere on the stage.

8. Click **Frame 1** on the Timeline, then play the movie.

   The Annual text rotates clockwise two times.

   TIP   If the rotating text crosses the title text, click Frame 21, be sure the Annual text box is selected, then drag it down to provide more space between the two text boxes.

You inserted a new layer, created a rotating text block, and used the Property inspector to rotate the text box.

FIGURE 42

Positioning the Annual text block

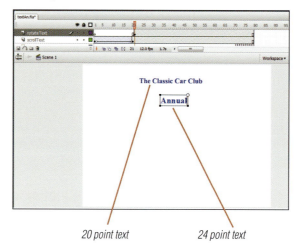

20 point text   24 point text

FIGURE 43

Using the Text Tool to type ROAD RALLY

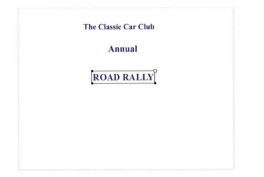

FIGURE 44

Resizing and repositioning the text block

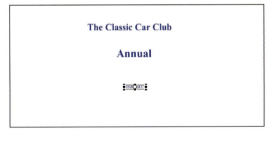

FIGURE 45

Setting the Alpha amount to 0

Your values might differ   *The Alpha amount*

Resize and fade in text

1. Insert a **new layer**, name it **fadeinText**, then insert a **keyframe** in Frame 40 on the layer.

2. Click the **Text tool** **T** , position the pointer beneath the Annual text box, aligning it with the "h" in "The," then type **ROAD RALLY**, as shown in Figure 43.

3. Click **Frame 40** on the fadeinText layer, then click **Insert** on the menu bar, point to **Timeline**, then click **Create Motion Tween**.

4. Insert a **keyframe** in Frame 60 on the fadeinText layer.

5. Click **Frame 40** of the fadeinText layer, select the **Free Transform tool** , then click the **Scale button** in the Options section of the Tools panel.

6. Drag the upper-left **corner handle** inward to resize the text block, as shown in Figure 44.

7. With the text block selected, click the **Color Styles list arrow** on the Property inspector, click **Alpha**, click the **Alpha % list arrow**, then drag the slider to **0**, as shown in Figure 45.

8. Click **Frame 60** on the fadeinText layer, click the **Selection tool** , then click the **text block** on the stage.

9. With the text block selected, verify Alpha is selected in the Color Styles list box, click the **Alpha % list arrow**, then drag the slider to **100**.

10. Click **Frame 70** on the fadeinText layer, right-click (Win) or control click (Mac) **Frame 70**, then click **Remove Tween**.

11. Test the movie in the Flash player.

You created a motion animation that caused a text block to fade in and zoom out.

Make a text block into a button

1. Insert a **new layer**, then name it **continue**.

   | TIP Scroll up the Timeline to view the new layer (if necessary).

2. Insert a **keyframe** in Frame 71 on the continue layer.

3. Click the **Text tool** T on the Tools panel, position the **Text Tool pointer** beneath the back wheel of the car, then type **Click to continue**.

4. Drag the **pointer** over the text to select it, click the **Font Size list arrow** in the Property inspector, drag the slider to **12**, click the **Selection tool** on the Tools panel, then compare your image to Figure 46.

5. Verify that the text box is selected, click **Modify** on the menu bar, click **Convert to Symbol**, type **b_continue** in the Name text box, click the **Button option button** (if necessary), then click **OK**.

6. Click the **Selection tool** (if necessary), then double-click the **text block** to edit the button.

7. Insert a **keyframe** in the Over frame, set the **Fill color** to the **black color swatch** in the left column of the color palette.

8. Insert a **keyframe** in the Down frame, set the **Fill color** to the **bright green color swatch** in the left column of the color palette.

9. Insert a **keyframe** in the Hit frame, select the **Rectangle tool** on the Tools panel, then draw a **rectangle** that covers the text block, as shown in Figure 47.

10. Click **Scene 1** below the Timeline layers to return to the main Timeline.

You made the text block into a button.

FIGURE 46
Adding a button

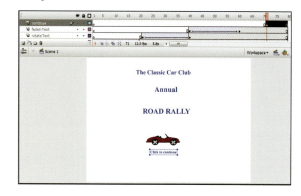

FIGURE 47
The rectangle that defines the hit area

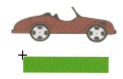

Creating Animations

FIGURE 48

Adding a play action

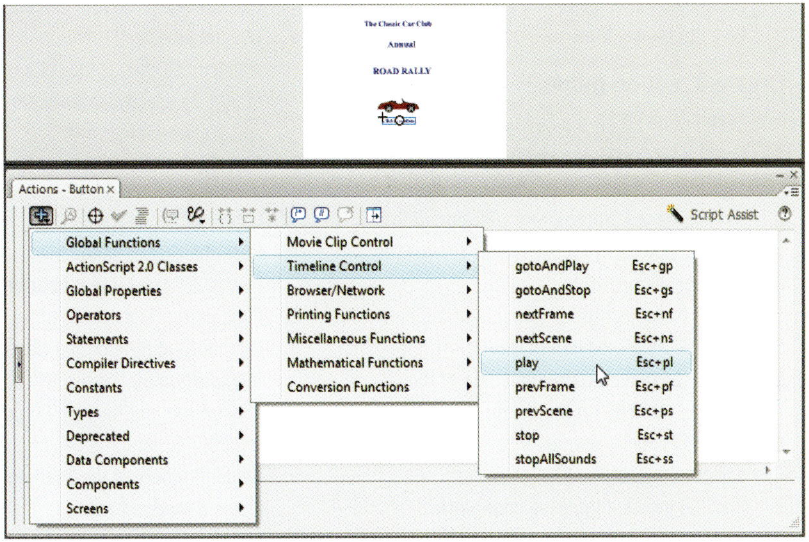

1. Display the Actions panel.

2. Click the **Selection tool** ▶ on the Tools panel, then click the **Click to continue button** on the stage.

3. Verify the Script Assist button ⬚ Script Assist is turned off, then verify b_continue and the button symbol are displayed in the lower-left corner of the Actions panel.

4. Click the **Add a new item to the script button** ⬚ in the Script Assist window, point to **Global Functions**, point to **Timeline Control**, then click **play**, as shown in Figure 48.

5. Insert a new layer, name it **stopmovie**, then insert a **keyframe** in Frame 71 on that layer.

6. Verify that stopmovie:71 is displayed in the lower-left corner of the Actions panel.

7. Click the **Add a new item to the script button** ⬚ in the Script Assist window, point to **Global Functions**, point to **Timeline Control**, then click **stop**.

8. Click **Control** on the menu bar, click **Test Movie**, then click the **Click to continue button** when it appears.

   The movie plays the animated text blocks, then plays the animated car when you click the Click to continue button.

9. Close the test movie window, close the Actions panel, then save and close the movie.

10. Exit Flash.

You inserted a play button and added a stop action to it.

Create a frame animation.

1. Start Flash, open fl4_6.fla, then save it as **skillsdemo4**.
2. Add a background color of **#006666**.
3. Insert a keyframe in Frame 22 on the v-ball layer.
4. Resize the object to approximately one-fourth its original size.
5. Insert a keyframe in Frame 23 on the v-ball layer.
6. Resize the object back to approximately its original size.
7. Insert a keyframe in Frame 24 on the v-ball layer, then drag the object to the upper-left corner of the stage.
8. Insert a keyframe in Frame 25 on the v-ball layer, then drag the object to the lower-left corner of the stage.
9. Insert a keyframe in Frame 26 on the v-ball layer, then drag the object to the upper-right corner of the stage.
10. Insert a keyframe in Frame 27 on the v-ball layer, then drag the object to the lower-right corner of the stage.
11. Change the movie frame rate to 3 frames per second, then play the movie.
12. Change the movie frame rate to 12 frames per second, play the movie, then save your work.

Create a motion-tweened animation.

1. Insert a new layer and name it **ballAn**.
2. Insert a keyframe in Frame 28 on the ballAn layer.
3. Display the Library panel, then drag the g_vball graphic symbol to the lower-left corner of the stage.
4. Make sure the object is selected, then create a Motion Tween.
5. Insert a keyframe in Frame 60 on the ballAn layer.
6. Drag the object to the lower-right corner of the stage.
7. Play the movie, then save your work.

Create a motion guide.

1. Click Frame 28 on the ballAn layer.
2. Insert a Motion Guide layer, then insert a keyframe at Frame 28 of the Guide layer.
3. Use the Pencil tool to draw a motion path in the shape of an arc, then alter the path to resemble Figure 49.
4. Attach the object to the left side of the path in Frame 28 on the ballAn layer.
5. Attach the object to the right side of the path in Frame 60 on the ballAn layer.
6. Use the Property inspector to orient the object to the path.
7. Play the movie, then save your work.

Accelerate the animated object.

1. Click Frame 28 on the ballAn layer.
2. Use the Property inspector to change the Ease value to **–100**.
3. Play the movie, then save your work.

Create motion animation effects.

1. Click Frame 60 on the ballAn layer, and use the Free Transform tool and the Scale option handles to resize the object to approximately one-fourth its original size.
2. Click Frame 28 on the ballAn layer, and use the Property inspector to specify a clockwise rotation that plays five times.
3. Play the movie.
4. Select Frame 60 on the ballAn layer, then use the Selection tool to select the ball.
5. Use the Advanced Color option in the Property inspector to change the color of the object to orange by specifying 20 as the green value and 100 as the red value.
6. Play the movie, then save your work.

Animate text.

1. Click the Guide: ballAn layer, then insert a new layer and name it **heading**.
2. Click Frame 1 on the heading layer.
3. Use the Text tool to type **Having fun with a** in a location off the top-left of the stage.
4. Change the text to Arial, 20 point, light gray (#CCCCCC), and boldface.
5. Select Frame 1 of the heading layer and insert a motion tween.
6. Insert a keyframe in Frame 10 on the heading layer.
7. Use the Selection tool to drag the text to the top-center of the stage.
8. Click Frame 30 on the heading layer, right-click (Win) or control click (Mac) Frame 30, then remove the tween.
9. Play the movie and save your work.
10. Insert a new layer and name it **zoom**.

11. Insert a keyframe in Frame 11 on the zoom layer.
12. Use the Text Tool to type **Volleyball** below the heading, then center it as needed.
13. Select Frame 11 on the zoom layer and create a motion tween.
14. Insert a keyframe in Frame 20 on the zoom layer.

15. Click Frame 11 on the zoom layer and select the text block.
16. Use the Property inspector to set the Alpha color option to **0**.
17. Use the Free Transform tool to resize the text block to approximately one-fourth its original size.

18. Select Frame 20 on the zoom layer, and resize the text block to approximate the size shown in Figure 49.
19. Remove the dashed line tween on the zoom layer.
20. Test the movie, then save your work.
21. Exit Flash.

FIGURE 49
Completed Skills Review

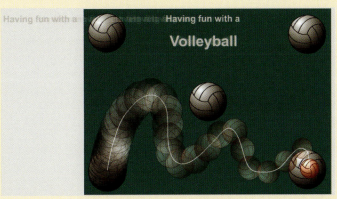

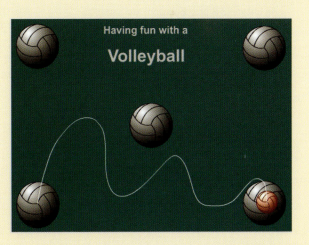

Creating Animations

The Ultimate Tours travel company has asked you to design several sample animations for their Web site. Figure 50 shows a sample home page and the Cruises screen. Using these (or one of the home pages you created in Chapter 3) as a guide, complete the following:

For the Ultimate Tours home page:

(Tip: If you need to insert frames, select the frame where the inserted frame is to go and press [F5] (Win) or use the Timeline command from the Insert menu (Win) (Mac). To insert several frames, select a range of frames and press [F5] (Win), or use the Timeline command from the Insert menu (Win) (Mac)).

1. Open ultimatetours3.fla (the file you created in Chapter 3 Project Builder 1) and save it as **ultimatetours4**.
2. Animate the heading Ultimate Tours on the home page so that it zooms out from a transparent text block.
3. After the heading appears, make the sub-heading We Specialize in Exotic Adventures appear.
4. Make each of the buttons (Treks, Tours, Cruises) scroll from the bottom of the stage to their positions on the stage. Stagger the buttons so that each one scrolls after the other.
5. Have the logo text appear after the buttons appear.
6. Assign a stop action after the home page appears.
7. Assign a go-to action to the Cruises button so it jumps to the frame that has the Cruises screen.
8. Add a Cruises screen, then display the heading, subheading, and logo.
9. To the Library panel, import the graphic file ship.gif from the drive and folder where your Data Files are stored, then rename the graphic file **g_ship**.
   (Hint: To import a graphic to the Library panel, click File on the menu bar, point to Import, then click Import to Library. Navigate to the drive and folder where your Data Files are stored, then select the desired file and click Open (Win) or Import to Library (Mac).)
10. Create a motion-tweened animation that moves the ship across the screen.
11. Add a motion path that has a dip in it.
12. Attach the boat to the motion path, and orient it to the path.
13. Add a new layer, name it **cruise placeholder**, then add three placeholders (Cruise 1, Cruise 2, Cruise 3) to the last frame of the Timeline.
14. Add the Home button.
15. Test the movie, then compare your movie to the example shown in Figure 50.

FIGURE 50

Sample completed Project Builder 1

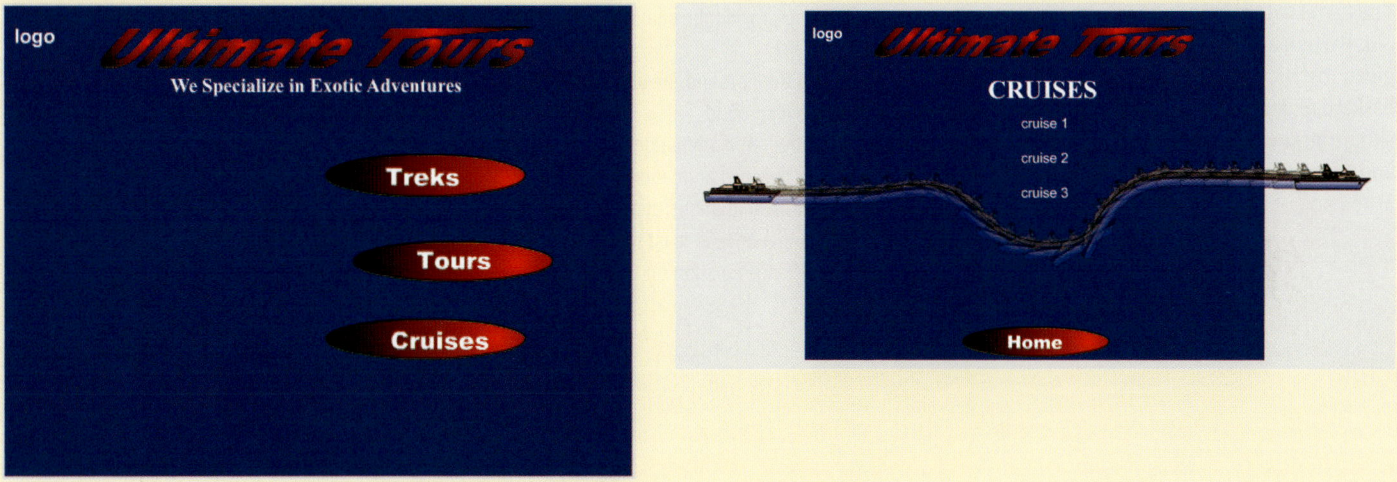

You have been asked to develop a Web site for the school's summer basketball camp. The camp caters to kids aged 6 to 12 years old. Participants are grouped by ability and given instruction on the fundamentals of basketball, such as dribbling, passing, and shooting; the rules of the game; teamwork; and sportsmanship. A tournament is played at the end of the two-week camp.

Include the following on the Web site:

1. An initial screen with information about the camp (you provide the camp name, dates, and so on).
2. A black border around the stage, and add a colored background.
3. A frame-by-frame animation.
4. A motion-tweened animation.
5. One or more animations that has an object(s) that does at least two of the following: change location on the stage, rotate, change size, and change color.
6. One or more animations that has a text block(s) that do two or more of the following: change location on the stage, rotate, change size, change color, zoom in or out, and fade in or out.
7. An animation that uses a motion guide.
8. An animation that changes the Ease setting.
9. Save the movie as **summerBB4**, then compare your image to the example shown in Figure 51.

FIGURE 51
Sample completed Project Builder 2

Figure 52 shows a Web site for kids. Study the figure and complete the following. For each question, indicate how you determined your answer.

1. Connect to the Internet, then go to *www.smokeybear.com/kids*.
2. Open a document in a word processor or open a new Flash document, save the file as **dpc4**, then answer the following questions. (*Hint*: Use the Text tool in Flash.)
   - What seems to be the purpose of this site?
   - Who would be the target audience?
   - How might a frame animation be used in this site?
   - How might a motion-tweened animation be used?
   - How might a motion guide be used?
   - How might motion animation effects be used?
   - How might the text be animated?

FIGURE 52
Design Project

This is a continuation of the Portfolio Project in Chapter 3, which is the development of a personal portfolio. The home page has several categories, including the following:

- Personal data
- Contact information
- Previous employment
- Education
- Samples of your work

In this project, you will create several buttons for the sample animations screen and link them to the animations.

1. Open portfolio3.fla (the file you created in Portfolio Project, Chapter 3) and save it as **portfolio4**.

   (*Hint*: When you open the file, you may receive a missing font message, meaning a font used in this document is not available on your computer. You can choose a substitute font or use a default font.)

2. Display the Sample Animation screen and change the heading to Sample Animations.

3. Add layers and create buttons with labels, as shown in Figure 53, for the tweened animation, frame-by-frame animation, motion path animation, and animated text.

4. Create a tweened animation or use the passing cars animation from Chapter 3, and link it to the appropriate button on the Sample Animations screen.

5. Create a frame-by-frame animation, and link it to the appropriate button on the Sample Animations screen.

6. Create a motion path animation, and link it to the appropriate button on the Sample Animations screen.

7. Create several text animations, using scrolling, rotating, and zooming; then link them to the appropriate button on the Sample Animations screen.

8. Add a layer and create a Home button that links the Sample Animations screen to the Home screen.

9. Create frame actions that cause the movie to return to the Sample Animations screen after each animation has been played.

10. Test the movie.

11. Save your work, then compare sample pages from your movie to the example shown for two of the screens in Figure 53.

FIGURE 53

Sample completed Portfolio Project

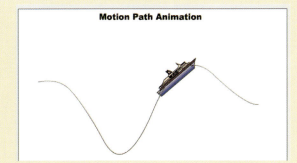

chapter

5

CREATING SPECIAL
EFFECTS

1. Create shape tween animations

2. Create a mask effect

3. Add sound

4. Add scenes

5. Create an animated navigation bar

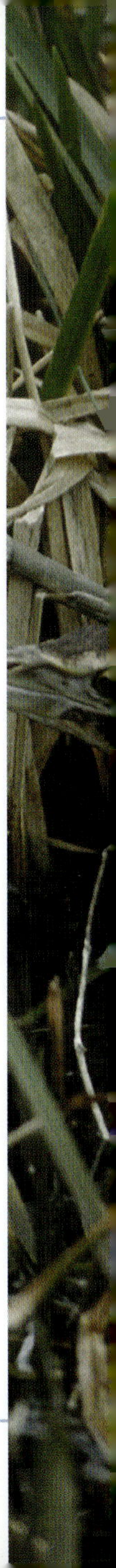

5 CREATING SPECIAL
EFFECTS

Introduction

Now that you are familiar with the basics of Flash, you can begin to apply some of the special features that can enhance a movie. Special effects can provide variety and add interest to a movie, as well as draw the viewer's attention to a location or event in the movie. One type of special effect is an animation that changes the shape of an object. This can be done using the shape tween feature of Flash. Another, related, type of special effect is morphing. The process of morphing makes one shape appear to change into another shape over time, such as an airplane changing into a hot air balloon as it flies across the sky. Another special effect is a spotlight that highlights an area(s) of the movie or

reveals selected content on the stage. You can use sound effects to enhance a movie by creating moods and dramatizing events. Another type of special effect is an animated navigation bar, for example, one that causes a drop-down menu when the user rolls over a button. This effect can be created using masks and invisible buttons.

In addition to working with special effects, you can work with scenes. You have experience in developing several movies around one theme, Classic Car Club, and now you are ready to incorporate these individual movies into a single movie with several scenes. Scenes provide a way to organize a large movie that has several parts, such as a Web site.

Tools You'll Use

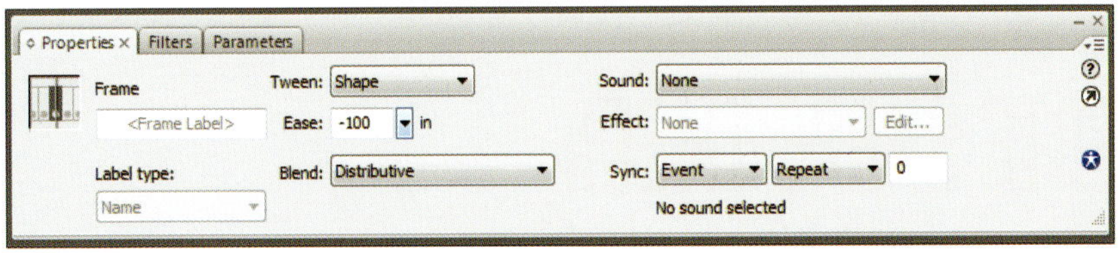

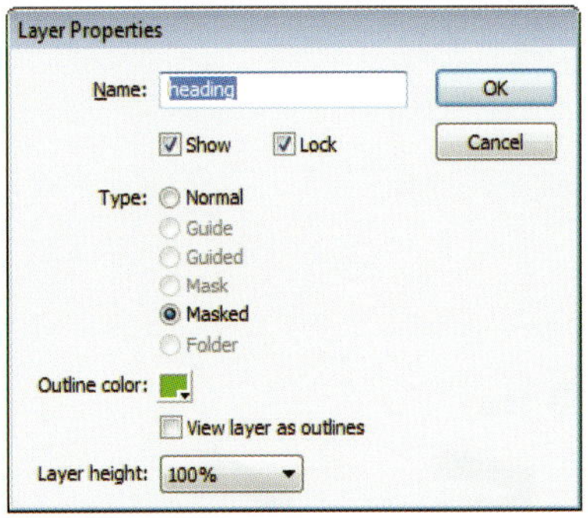

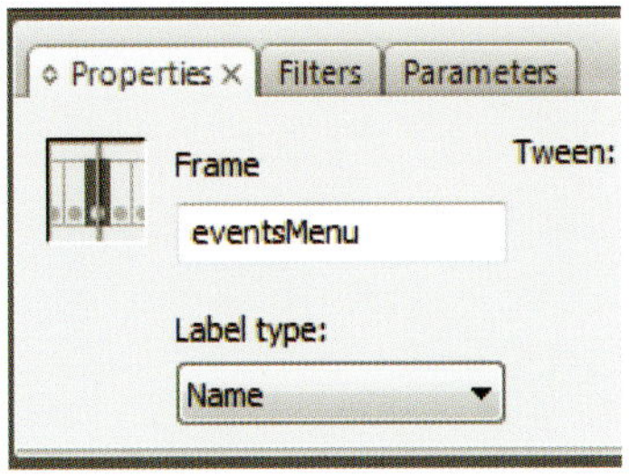

Properties × Filters Parameters

Frame   Tween: Shape   Sound: None

<Frame Label>   Ease: -100 in   Effect: None   Edit...

Label type: Blend: Distributive   Sync: Event   Repeat   0

Name   No sound selected

Layer Properties

Name: heading   OK

☑ Show   ☑ Lock   Cancel

Type: ○ Normal
     ○ Guide
     ○ Guided
     ○ Mask
     ● Masked
     ○ Folder

Outline color:

☐ View layer as outlines

Layer height: 100%

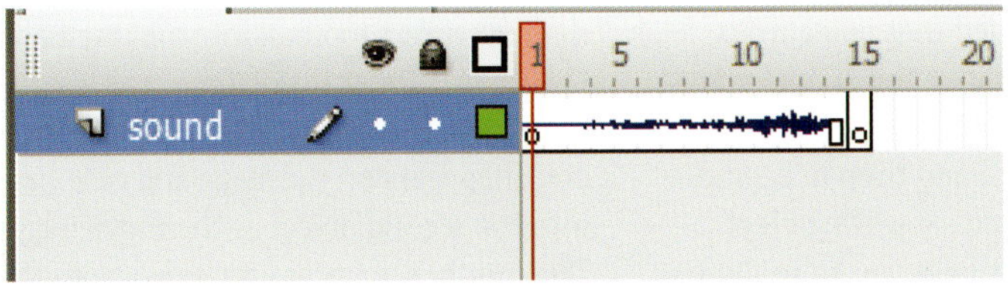

---

1   5   10   15   20

sound

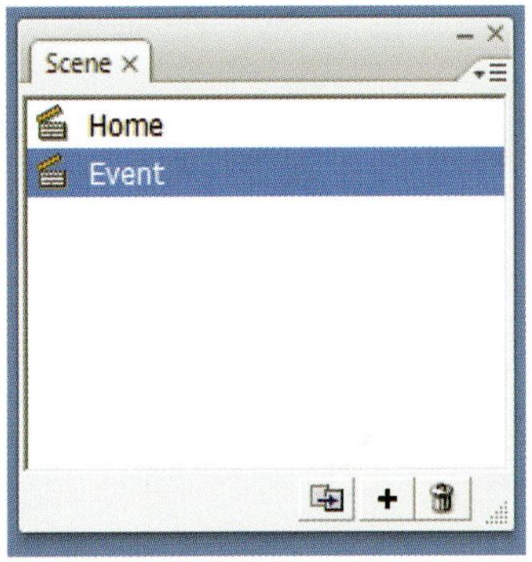

Scene ×

📄 Home
🎬 Event

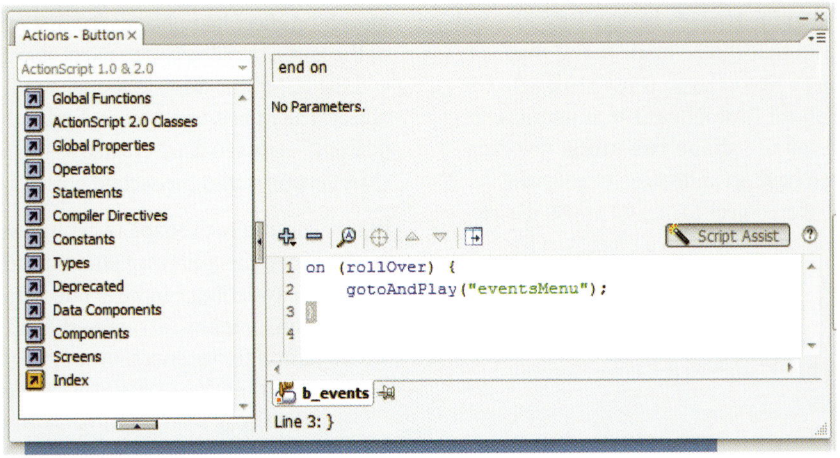

Actions - Button ×

ActionScript 1.0 & 2.0

Global Functions
ActionScript 2.0 Classes
Global Properties
Operators
Statements
Compiler Directives
Constants
Types
Deprecated
Data Components
Components
Screens
Index

end on

No Parameters.

Script Assist

```
1  on (rollOver) {
2      gotoAndPlay("eventsMenu");
3  }
4
```

b_events

Line 3: }

Properties × Filters Parameters

Frame   Tween:

eventsMenu

Label type:

Name

CREATE SHAPE TWEEN
ANIMATIONS

What You'll Do

▶ In this lesson, you will create a shape tween animation and specify shape hints.

Shape Tweening

In Chapter 4, you learned that you can use motion tweening to change the shape of an object. You accomplish this by selecting the Free Transform tool and then dragging the handles to resize and skew the object. While this is easy and allows you to include motion along with the change in shape, there are two drawbacks. First, you are limited in the type of changes (resizing and skewing) that can be made to the shape of an object. Second, you must work with the same object throughout the animation. When you use **shape tweening**, however, you can have an animation change the shape of an object to any form you desire, and you can include two objects in the animation with two different shapes. As with motion tweening, you can use shape tweening to change other properties of an object, such as the color, location, and size.

Using Shape Tweening to Create a Morphing Effect

Morphing involves changing one object into another, sometimes unrelated, object.

For example, you could turn a robot into a man, or turn a football into a basketball. The viewer sees the transformation as a series of incremental changes. In Flash, the first object appears on the stage and changes into the second object as the movie plays. The number of frames included from the beginning to the end of this shape tween animation determines how quickly the morphing effect takes place. The first frame in the animation displays the first object and the last frame displays the second object. The in-between frames display the different shapes that are created as the first object changes into the second object.

When working with shape tweening, you need to keep the following points in mind:

- Shape tweening can be applied only to editable graphics. To apply shape tweening to instances, groups, symbols, text blocks, or bitmaps, you can use the Break Apart command on the Modify menu to break apart an object and make it editable. When you break apart an instance of a symbol, it is no longer linked to the original symbol.

- You can shape tween more than one object at a time as long as all the objects are on the same layer. However, if the shapes are complex and/or if they involve movement in which the objects cross paths, the results may be unpredictable.
- You can use shape tweening to move an object in a straight line, but other options, such as rotating an object, are not available.
- You can use the settings in the Property inspector to set options (such as acceleration or deceleration) for a shape tween.
- Shape hints can be used to control more complex shape changes.

Properties Panel Options

Figure 1 shows the Property inspector options for a shape tween. The options allow you to adjust several aspects of the animation, as described in the following:

- Adjust the rate of change between frames to create a more natural appearance during the transition by setting an ease value. Setting the value between -1 and -100 will begin the shape tween gradually and accelerate it toward the end of the animation. Setting the value between 1 and 100 will begin the shape tween rapidly and decelerate it toward the end of the animation. By default, the rate of change is set to 0, which causes a constant rate of change between frames.
- Choose a blend option. The Distributive option creates an animation in which the in-between shapes are smoother and more irregular. The Angular option preserves the corners and straight lines and works only with objects that have these features. If the objects do not have corners, Flash will default to the Distributive option.

Shape Hints

You can use shape hints to control the shape's transition appearance during animation. Shape hints allow you to specify a location on the beginning object that corresponds to a location on the ending object. Figure 2 shows two shape animations of the same objects, one using shape hints and the other not using shape hints. The figure also shows how the object being reshaped appears in one of the in-between frames. Notice that with the shape hints, the object in the in-between frame is more recognizable.

FIGURE 2

Two shape animations: with and without shape hints

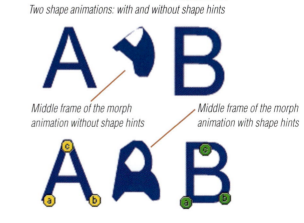

Middle frame of the morph animation without shape hints

Middle frame of the morph animation with shape hints

FIGURE 1

The Property inspector options for a shape tween

Properties ×	Filters	Parameters				− ×
Frame	Tween: Shape ▾		Sound: None ▾		
<Frame Label>	Ease: 0 ▾		Effect: None ▾	Edit...	
Label type:	Blend: Distributive ▾		Sync: Event ▾ Repeat ▾ 0		
Name ▾			No sound selected		

Create a shape tween animation

1. Open fl5_1.fla from the drive and folder where your Data Files are stored, then save it as **antiqueCar**.

2. Close all panels, except for the Tools and Property inspector panels, then change the view to Fit in Window.

   TIP This chapter assumes you always set the magnification to Fit in Window.

3. Click **Frame 30** on the shape layer, then insert a **keyframe**.

4. Click the **selection tool** ▶ on the Tools panel, then click a blank area outside the stage to deselect the car.

5. Point to the right side of the top of the car, then use the arc pointer ▶ to drag the **car top** to create the shape shown in Figure 3.

6. Click anywhere on the shape layer between Frames 1 and 30.

7. Make sure the Property inspector is displayed, click the **Tween list arrow**, then click **Shape**.

8. Click **Frame 1** on the shape layer, then play the movie.

9. Click **Frame 30** on the shape layer.

10. Click the **Selection tool** ▶ on the Tools panel, then drag a **marquee** around the car to select it (if necessary).

11. Drag the **car** to the right side of the stage.

12. Play the **movie**, then save and close it.

You created a shape tween animation, causing an object to change shape as it moves over several frames.

FIGURE 3

The reshaped object

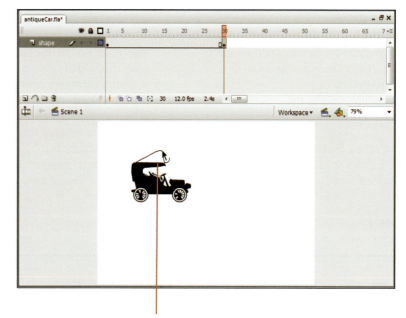

Drag up from here

FIGURE 4

Positioning the car instance on the stage

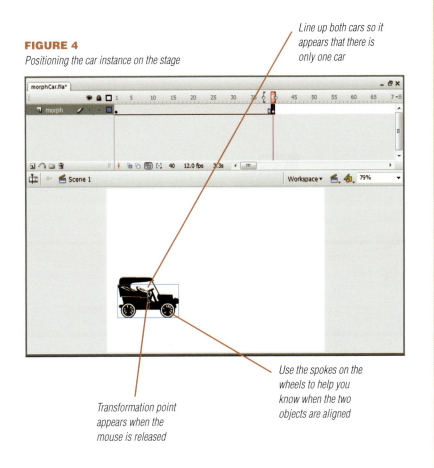

Line up both cars so it appears that there is only one car

Transformation point appears when the mouse is released

Use the spokes on the wheels to help you know when the two objects are aligned

Create a morphing effect

1. Open fl5_2.fla from the drive and folder where your Data Files are stored, then save it as **morphCar**.

2. Click **Frame 40** on the morph layer.

3. Click **Insert** on the menu bar, point to **Timeline**, then click **Blank Key frame**.

   > TIP Inserting a blank keyframe prevents the object in the preceding keyframe from automatically being inserted into the blank key frame.

4. Click the **Edit Multiple Frames icon** on the Timeline.

   Turning on the Edit Multiple Frames feature allows you to align the two objects to be morphed.

5. Open the Library panel.

6. Drag the **g_antiqueCarTopDown** graphic symbol from the Library panel directly on top of the car on the stage, as shown in Figure 4.

   > TIP Use the arrow keys to move the object in small increments as needed.

7. Make sure that the **g_antiqueCarTopDown** object is selected, click **Modify** on the menu bar, then click **Break Apart**.

8. Click the **Edit Multiple Frames icon** to turn off the feature.

9. Click anywhere between Frames 1 and 40 on the morph layer, click the **Tween list arrow** on the Property inspector, then click **Shape**.

10. Click **Frame 1** on the Timeline, then play the movie.

    The first car morphs into the second car.

11. Save the movie.

You created a morphing effect, causing one object to change into another.

Adjust the rate of change in a shape tween animation

1. Click **Frame 40** on the morph layer.

2. Click the **Selection tool** ▸ on the Tools panel, then drag a **marquee** around the car to select it (if necessary).

3. Drag the **car** to the right side of the stage.

4. Click **Frame 1** on the morph layer.

5. Click the **Ease list arrow** on the Property inspector, then drag the slider down to **–100**, as shown in Figure 5.

6. Click the **stage**, then play the movie.

   The car starts out slow and speeds up as the morphing process is completed.

7. Repeat Steps 4 and 5, but change the Ease value to **100**.

8. Click **Frame 1** on the Timeline, then play the movie.

   The car starts out fast and slows down as the morphing process is completed.

9. Save your work, then close the movie.

You added motion to a shape tween animation and changed the Ease values.

FIGURE 5

Changing the Ease value for the morph

FIGURE 6

Positioning a shape hint

FIGURE 7

Adding shape hints

FIGURE 8

Matching shape hints

Use shape hints

1. Open fl5_3.fla from the drive and folder where your Data Files are stored, then save it as **shapeHints**.

2. Play the movie and notice how the L morphs into a Z.

3. Click **Frame 15** on the Timeline, the midpoint of the animation, then notice the shape.

4. Click **Frame 1** on the hints layer to display the first object.

5. Make sure the object is selected, click **Modify** on the menu bar, point to **Shape**, then click **Add Shape Hint**.

6. Drag the **Shape Hint icon** 🔴 to the location shown in Figure 6.

7. Repeat Steps 5 and 6 to set a second and third Shape Hint icon, as shown in Figure 7.

8. Click **Frame 30** on the hints layer.

   The shape hints are stacked on top of each other.

9. Drag the **Shape Hint icons** to match Figure 8.

10. Click **Frame 15** on the hints layer, then notice how the object is more recognizable now that the shape hints have been added.

11. Click **Frame 1** on the Timeline, then play the movie.

12. Save your work, then close the movie.

You added shape hints to a morph animation.

CREATE A
MASK EFFECT

What You'll Do

In this lesson, you will apply a mask effect.

Understanding Mask Layers

A **mask layer** allows you to cover up the objects on one or more layers and, at the same time, create a window through which you can view various objects on the other layer. You can determine the size and shape of the window and specify whether it moves around the stage. Moving the window around the stage can create effects such as a spotlight that highlights certain contents on the stage, drawing the viewer's attention to a specific location. Because the window can move around the stage, you can use a mask layer to reveal only the area of the stage and the objects you want the viewer to see.

You need at least two layers on the Timeline when you are working with a mask layer. One layer, called the mask layer, contains the window object through which you view the objects on the second layer below. The second layer, called the masked layer, contains the object(s) that are viewed through the window. Figure 9 shows how a mask layer works: The top part of the figure shows the mask layer with the window in the shape of a circle. The next part of the figure shows the layer to be masked. The last part of the figure shows the results of applying the mask. Figure 9 illustrates the simplest use of a mask layer. In most cases, you want to have other objects appear on the stage and have the mask layer affect only a certain portion of the stage.

The process for using a mask layer follows:

- Select an original layer that will become the masked layer—it contains the objects that you want to display through the mask layer window.
- Insert a new layer above the masked layer that will become the mask layer. A mask layer always masks the layer(s) immediately below it.
- Draw a filled shape, such as a circle, or create an instance of a symbol that will become the window on the mask layer. Flash will ignore bitmaps, gradients, transparency colors, and line styles on a mask layer. On a mask layer, filled areas become transparent and non-filled areas become opaque.

- Select the new layer and open the Layer Properties dialog box using the Timeline option from the Modify menu, then select Mask. Flash converts the layer to the mask layer.
- Select the original layer and open the Layer Properties dialog box after selecting the Layer command on the Modify menu, and then choose Masked. Flash converts the layer to the masked layer.
- Lock both the mask and masked layers.
- To mask additional layers: Drag an existing layer beneath the mask layer, or create a new layer beneath the mask layer and use the Layer Properties dialog box to convert it to a masked layer.
- To unlink a masked layer: Drag it above the mask layer, or select it and select Normal from the Layer Properties dialog box.

FIGURE 9

A mask layer with a window

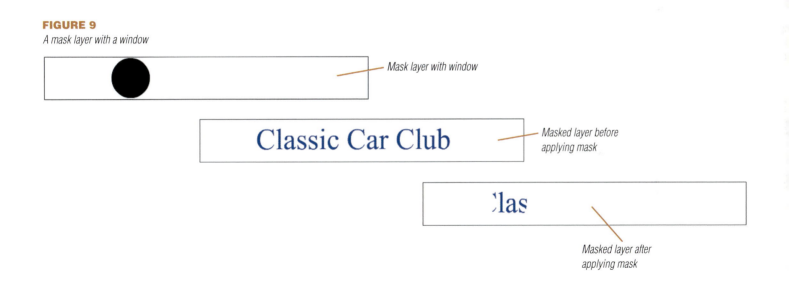

Mask layer with window

Classic Car Club

Masked layer before applying mask

las

Masked layer after applying mask

Create a mask layer

1. Open fl5_4.fla, then save it as **classicCC**.

2. Insert a **new layer**, name it **mask**, then click **Frame 1** of the mask layer.

3. Select the **Oval tool**  on the Tools panel, set the **stroke color** to **No Stroke** on the top row of the color palette.

4. Set the **Fill color** to the **black color swatch** in the left column of the color palette.

5. Draw the **circle** shown in Figure 10, click the **Selection tool** on the Tools panel, draw a **marquee** around the circle to select it, click **Insert** on the menu bar, point to **Timeline**, then click **Create Motion Tween**.

6. Insert a **keyframe** in Frame 40 on the mask layer, then drag the **circle** to the position shown in Figure 11.

7. Click **mask** on the Timeline to select the mask layer, click **Modify** on the menu bar, point to **Timeline**, then click **Layer Properties**.

8. Verify that the Show check box is selected in the Name section, click the **Lock check box** to select it, click the **Mask option button** in the Type section, then click **OK**.

    The mask layer has a shaded mask icon next to it on the Timeline.

9. Play the movie from Frame 1 and notice how the circle object covers the text in the heading layer as it moves across the stage.

You created a mask layer containing a circle object that moves across the stage.

FIGURE 10
Object to be used as the window on a mask layer

FIGURE 11
Repositioning the circle

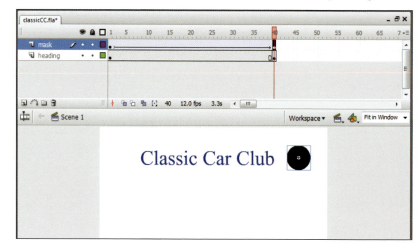

FIGURE 12

The completed Layer Properties dialog box

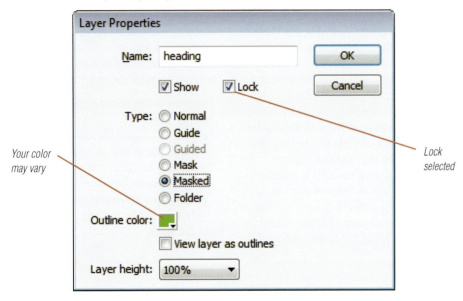

*Your color
may vary*

*Lock
selected*

Create a masked layer

1. Click **heading** on the Timeline to select the heading layer, click **Modify** on the menu bar, point to **Timeline**, then click **Layer Properties** to open the Layer Properties dialog box.

2. Verify that the Show check box is selected in the Name section, click the **Lock check box** to select it, click the **Masked option button** in the Type section, compare your dialog box to Figure 12, then click **OK**.

   The text on the stage seems to disappear. The heading layer title appears indented and has a shaded masked icon next to it on the Timeline.

3. Play the movie and notice how the circle object acts as a window to display the text on the heading layer.

4. Click **Control** on the menu bar, then click **Test Movie**.

5. View the movie in the Flash player window, then close the window.

6. Save your work, then close the movie.

You used the Layer Properties dialog box to create a masked layer.

ADD SOUND

What You'll Do

 In this lesson, you will add sound to an animation.

Incorporating Animation and Sound

Sound can be extremely useful in a Flash movie. Sounds are often the only effective way to convey an idea, elicit an emotion, dramatize a point, and provide feedback to a user's action, such as clicking a button. How would you describe in words or show in an animation the sound a whale makes? Think about how chilling it is to hear the footsteps on the stairway of a haunted house. Consider how useful it is to hear the pronunciation of "buenos dias" as you are studying Spanish. All types of sounds can be incorporated into a Flash movie: for example, CD-quality music that might be used as background for a movie; narrations that help explain what the user is seeing; various sound effects, such as a car horn beeping; and recordings of special events, such as a presidential speech or a rock concert.

The process for adding a sound to a movie follows:

- Import a sound file into a Flash movie; Flash places the sound into the movie's Library.
- Create a new layer.
- Select the desired frame in the new layer and drag the sound symbol to the stage.

You can place more than one sound file on a layer, and you can place sounds on layers with other objects. However, it is recommended that you place each sound on a separate layer so that it is easier to identify and edit. In Figure 13, the sound layer shows a wave pattern that extends from Frame 1 to Frame 15. The wave pattern gives some indication of the volume of the sound at any particular frame. The higher spikes in the pattern indicate a louder sound. The wave pattern also gives some indication of the pitch. The denser the wave pattern, the lower the pitch. You can alter the sound by adding or removing frames. However, removing frames may create undesired effects. It is best to make changes to a sound file using a sound-editing program.

You can use options in the Property inspector, as shown in Figure 14, to synchronize a sound to an event—such as clicking a button—and to specify special effects—such as fade in and fade out. You can import the following sound file formats into Flash:

- WAV (Windows only)
- AIFF (Macintosh only)
- MP3 (Windows or Macintosh)

If you have QuickTime 4 or later installed on your computer, you can import these additional sound file formats:

- AIFF (Windows or Macintosh)
- Sound Designer II (Macintosh only)
- Sound Only QuickTime Movies (Windows or Macintosh)
- Sun AU (Windows or Macintosh)
- System 7 Sounds (Macintosh only)
- WAV (Windows or Macintosh)

FIGURE 13

A sound symbol displayed on the Timeline

FIGURE 14

Sound options in the Property inspector

Add sound to a movie

1. Open fl5_5.fla, then save it as **rallySnd**.

2. Play the movie and notice that there is no sound.

3. Click the **stopmovie layer**, insert a **new layer**, then name it **carSnd**.

4. Insert a **keyframe** in Frame 72 on the carSnd layer.

5. Click **File** on the menu bar, point to **Import**, then click **Import to Library**.

6. Use the Import to Library dialog box to navigate to the drive and folder where your Data Files are stored, click the **CarSnd.wav file**, then click **Open** (Win) or **Import to Library** (Mac).

7. Open the Library Panel (if necessary).

8. Click **Frame 72** of the CarSnd layer.

9. Drag the **CarSnd sound symbol** 🔊 to the stage, as shown in Figure 15.

   After releasing the mouse button, notice the wave pattern that has been placed in the carSnd layer starting in Frame 72.

10. Click **Control** on the menu bar, then click **Test Movie**.

11. Click the **Click to continue text button** to test the sound.

12. Close the test movie window.

You imported a sound and added it to a movie.

FIGURE 15

Dragging the CarSnd symbol to the stage

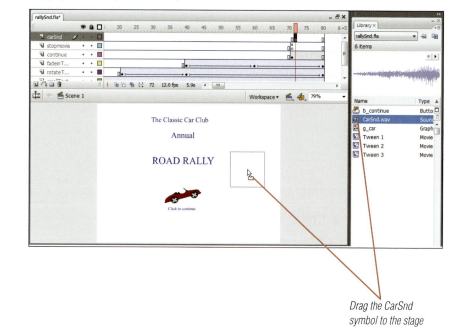

Drag the CarSnd
symbol to the stage

FIGURE 16
The button Timeline with the sound layer

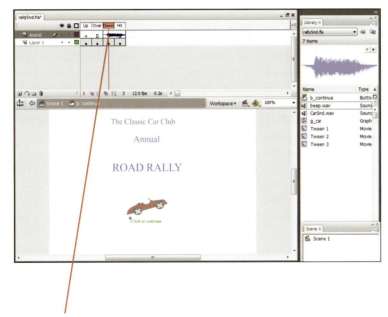

*Sound wave pattern appears
in the selected frame*

Add sound to a button

1. Click **Frame 71** on the carSnd layer.

2. Click the **Selection tool** ▶ on the Tools panel, drag a **marquee** around "Click to continue" to select the button, then double-click the **selection** to display the button's Timeline.

3. Insert a **new layer** above Layer 1, then name it **sound**.

4. Click the **Down frame** on the sound layer, click **Insert** on the menu bar, point to **Timeline**, then click **Blank Keyframe**.

5. Click **File** on the menu bar, point to **Import**, then click **Import to Library**.

6. Use the Import to Library dialog box to navigate to the drive and folder where your Data Files are stored, click the **beep.wav file,** then click **Open** (Win) or **Import to Library** (Mac).

7. Drag the **beep.wav sound symbol** to the stage, then compare your Timeline to Figure 16.

   Dragging the sound symbol to the stage causes the sound to be inserted into the selected frame.

8. Click **Scene 1** below the Timeline layers to display the main Timeline.

9. Click **Control** on the menu bar, then click **Test Movie.**

10. Click the **Click to continue button** and listen to the sounds, then close the test movie window.

11. Save your work, then close the movie.

You added a sound layer to a button, imported a sound, then attached the sound to the button.

ADD SCENES

What You'll Do

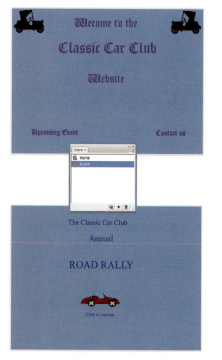

In this lesson, you will add scenes to a movie and combine scenes from multiple movies into one movie.

Understanding Scenes

Until now, you have been working with relatively short movies that have only a few layers and fewer than 100 frames. However, movies can be quite complex and extremely large. One way to help organize large movies is to use scenes. Just as with their celluloid equivalent, Flash scenes are discrete parts of a movie. They have their own Timeline and they can be played in any order you specify, or they can be linked through an interactive process that lets the user navigate to a desired scene.

QUICKTIP

There are no guidelines for the length or number of scenes appropriate for any size movie. The key is to determine how best to break down a large movie so that the individual parts are easier to develop, edit, and combine.

Working with Scenes

To add a scene to a movie, you choose Scene from the Insert menu or use the Scene panel. The Scene panel option is found in the Windows menu. The Scene panel can be used to accomplish the following:

- Rename a scene by double-clicking the scene name, and then typing in the new name.
- Duplicate a scene by selecting it, and then clicking the Duplicate Scene icon.
- Add a scene by clicking the Add Scene icon.
- Delete a scene by selecting it, and then clicking the Delete Scene icon.
- Reorder the scenes by dragging them up or down the list of scenes.

Creating Special Effects

When a movie is played, the scenes are played in the order they are listed in the Scene panel, that is, from top to bottom. You can use the interactive features of Flash, such as buttons with goto actions, to allow the user to jump to various scenes.

The process for combining scenes from several movies into one movie follows:

- Open the movie that will be used as Scene 1.
- Insert a new scene into the movie.
- Open the movie that will be used as Scene 2.

- Copy the frames from the second movie into Scene 2 of the first movie.
- Continue the process until the scenes for all the movies have been copied into one movie.

The home page for the Classic Car Club Web site, shown in Figure 17, will become the first scene of a multi-scene movie.

FIGURE 17
The Classic Car Club home page

Add and name a scene

1. Open fl5_6.fla, then save it as **cccHome**.

2. Click **Window** on the menu bar, point to **Other Panels**, then click **Scene** to open the Scene panel.

   > TIP You may need to drag the panel to have a better view of the stage.

3. Double-click **Scene 1** in the Scene panel, type **Home**, then press **[Enter]** (Win) or **[return]** (Mac).

4. Click the **Add scene icon** ➕ , double-click **Scene 2**, type **Event**, press **[Enter]** (Win) or **[return]** (Mac), then compare your Scene panel with Figure 18.

   When the new scene, Event, is created, the stage and Timeline are blank.

5. Click **Home** in the Scene panel and notice that the Timeline changes to the Home scene.

6. Click **Event** in the Scene panel and notice that the Timeline changes to the Event scene, which is blank.

7. Click **Control** on the menu bar, then click **Test Movie** to test the movie.

   Notice how the movie moves from Scene 1 to the blank Scene 2. There is no content or stop action scripts in the Events scene, so the movie just jumps from one scene to another.

8. Close the test movie window.

You added a scene and used the Scene panel to rename the scenes.

FIGURE 18
Changes to the Scene panel

Creating Special Effects

FIGURE 19

Selecting all the frames

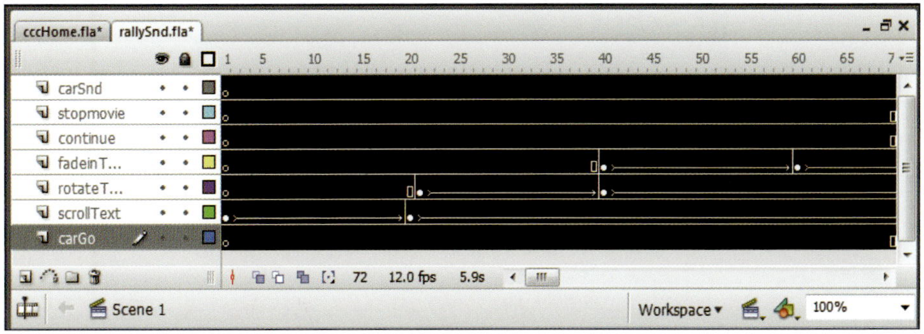

Copying frames to add to a scene

1. Open rallySnd.fla.

   TIP: rallySnd.fla is the file you created in Lesson 3.

2. Click **Edit** on the menu bar, point to **Timeline**, then click **Select All Frames** to select all the frames in all the layers, as shown in Figure 19.
3. Click **Edit** on the menu bar, point to **Timeline**, then click **Copy Frames**.
4. Close rallySnd.fla without saving the changes.
5. Click **Window** on the menu bar, then click **cccHome.fla** (if necessary).
6. Verify the Event scene is selected.
7. Click **Frame 1** on Layer 1 of the Event scene.
8. Click **Edit** on the menu bar, point to **Timeline**, then click **Paste Frames**.

   The layers and frames from rallySnd.fla appear in the Timeline of the Event scene.

9. Click **Home** in the Scene panel.
10. Click **Control** on the menu bar, then click **Test Movie** to test the movie and notice how the Home scene is played, followed by the Event scene.
11. Click the **Click to continue button** to complete the Events scene.
12. Close the test movie window.

You copied frames from one movie into a scene of another movie.

Add interactivity to scenes

1. Make sure that the Home scene is displayed.

2. Drag and resize the **Scene panel** to display the entire stage (if necessary).

3. Click the **Selection tool** on the Tools panel, then click the **Upcoming Event text button** on the stage.

4. Open the Actions panel (if necessary).

5. Verify that ActionScript 1.0 & 2.0 is displayed above the category list.

6. Verify the Script Assist button is selected and the script window is in view.

7. Verify b_event is displayed in the lower-left corner of the Actions panel.

8. Click the **Add a new item to the script icon**, point to **Global Functions**, point to **Movie Clip Control**, then click **on**.

9. Verify on (release) { is selected, click the **Add a new item to the script icon**, point to **Global Functions**, point to **Timeline Control**, then click **goto**.

10. Click the **Scene list arrow**, then click **Event**.

11. Compare your Actions panel with Figure 20.

You used the Actions panel to assign a goto action to a button that causes the movie to jump to another scene.

FIGURE 20
The completed Actions panel

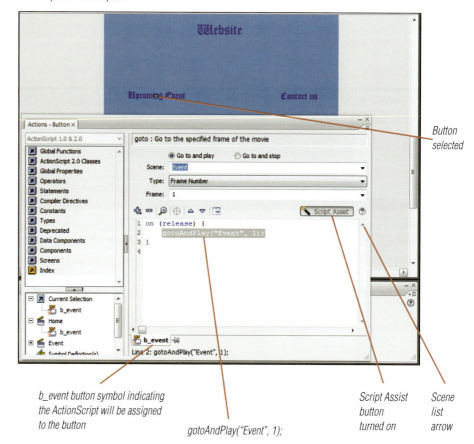

Button selected

b_event button symbol indicating the ActionScript will be assigned to the button

gotoAndPlay("Event", 1);

Script Assist button turned on

Scene list arrow

Creating Special Effects

FIGURE 21
Adding a stop action

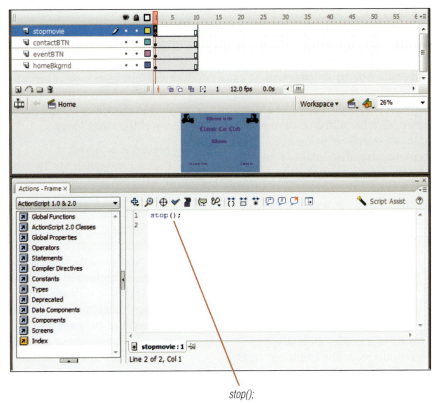

stop();

Add a stop action to a frame

1. Click **Frame 1** of the stopmovie layer.

2. Click **Script Assit** to turn off this feature, then verify stopmovie:1 is displayed in the lower-left corner of the Actions panel.

3. Click the **Add a new item to the script icon** 🔧, point to **Global Functions**, point to **Timeline Control**, then click **stop**.

4. Compare your Actions panel to Figure 21.

5. Click **Control** on the menu bar, then click **Test Movie**.

Notice how the movie stops playing on the Home page. You have to click the Upcoming Event button, which has an action assigned to it, to continue playing the movie.

6. Click the **Upcoming Event button**, then notice how the Event scene plays.

7. Close the test movie window.

8. Close the Scene panel.

9. Close the Actions panel.

10. Save your work, then close the movie.

You added a stop action to a frame to cause the movie to stop playing.

CREATE AN ANIMATED
NAVIGATION BAR

What You'll Do

In this lesson, you will work through the process to create one drop-down menu. The Web site is similar to the one in the previous lesson. However, a navigation bar has been provided as well as the necessary buttons.

Understanding Animated Navigation Bars

A common navigation scheme for a Web site is a navigation bar with drop-down menus, such as the one shown in Figure 22. This scheme has several advantages. First, it allows the developer to provide several menu options to the user without cluttering the screen, thereby providing more screen space for the Web site content. Second, it allows the user to go quickly to a location on the site without having to navigate several screens to find the desired content. Third, it provides consistency in function and appearance, making it easy for users to learn and work with the navigation scheme.

There are several ways to create drop-down menus using the animation capabilities of Flash. One common technique allows you to give the illusion of a drop-down menu by using masks that reveal the menu. When the user points to (rolls over) an option in the navigation bar, a list or "menu" of buttons is displayed ("drops down"). Then the user can click a button to go to another location in the

Web site or trigger some other action. The dropping down of the list is actually an illusion created by using a mask to "uncover" the menu options.

The process is as follows:
- Create a navigation bar. This could be as basic as a background graphic in the shape of a rectangle with navigation bar buttons.
- Position the drop-down buttons. Add a layer beneath the navigation bar layer. Next, place the buttons below the navigation bar beneath their respective menu items on the stage. If the navigation bar has an Events button with two choices, Road Rally and Auction, that you want to have appear on a drop-down menu, you would position these two buttons below the Events button on this drop-down buttons layer.
- Add the animated mask. Add a mask layer above the drop-down buttons layer and create an animation of an object that starts above the drop-down buttons and moves down to reveal them. Then change the layer to a mask

layer and the button layers to masked layers.

- Assign actions to the drop-down buttons. Select each drop-down button and assign an action, such as "on release go to a Frame."
- Assign a roll over action to the navigation bar button. The desired effect is to have the drop-down buttons appear when the user points to a navigation bar button. Therefore, you need to assign an "on rollOver" action to the navigation bar button that causes the playhead to go to the frame that plays the animation on the mask layer. This can be done using the Script Assist feature.
- Create an invisible button. When the user points to a navigation bar button, the drop-down menu appears showing

the drop-down buttons. There needs to be a way to have the menu disappear when the user points away from the navigation bar button. This can be done by creating a button on a layer below the masked layers. This button is slightly larger than the drop-down buttons and their navigation bar button, as shown in Figure 23. A rollOver action is assigned to this button so that when the user rolls off the drop-down or navigation bar buttons, he or she rolls onto this button and the action is carried out. This button should be made transparent so the user does not see it.

Using Frame Labels

Until now, you have worked with frame numbers in ActionScript code when creating a go to action. Frame labels can also

be used in the code. You can assign a label to a frame as an identifier. For example, you could assign the label home to frame 10 and then create a goto home action that will cause the playhead to jump to frame 10. One advantage of using frame labels is that if you insert frames in the Timeline, the label adjusts for the added frames. So, you do not have to change the ActionScript that uses the frame label. Another advantage is that the descriptive labels help you identify parts of the movie as you work with the Timeline. You assign a frame label by selecting the desired frame and typing a label in the Frame text box in the Property inspector.

FIGURE 22

A Web site with a navigation bar with drop-down menus

FIGURE 23

A button that will be assigned a rollOver action

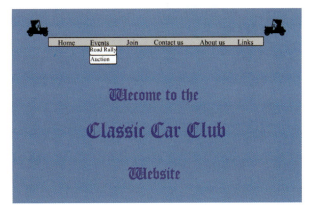

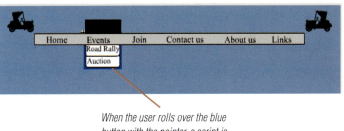

When the user rolls over the blue button with the pointer, a script is executed that causes the drop-down menu to disappear

Position the drop-down buttons

1. Open fl5_7.fla from the drive and folder where your Data Files are stored, then save it as **navBar**.

2. Close all panels, except for the Tools, Library, and Property inspector panels.

3. Set the view to **Fit in Window**.

4. Click the **homeBkgrnd layer**, insert a **new layer**, then name it **roadRally**.

5. Click **Frame 2** of the roadRally layer, then insert a **keyframe**.

6. Expand the Library panel (if necessary), double-click the **Buttons folder**, then drag the **b_roadRally button** to the position just below the Events button on the Navigation bar, as shown in Figure 24.

7. Insert a **new layer** above the homeBkgrnd layer, then name it **auction**.

(continued)

FIGURE 24

Positioning the b_roadRally button

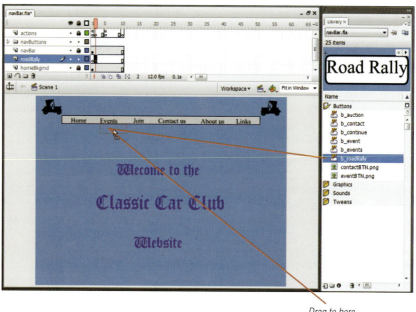

Drag to here

FIGURE 25
Positioning the buttons

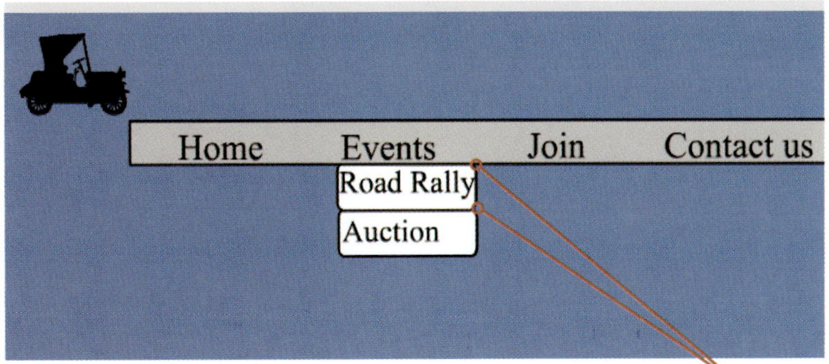

*Make sure the button
borders overlap*

8. Click **Frame 2** of the auction layer, then insert a **keyframe**.

9. Drag the **b_auction button** from the Library panel and position it below the b_roadRally button.

10. Click the **Zoom tool** 🔍 on the Tools panel, then click the **Events button** on the stage to enlarge the view.

11. Click the **Selection tool** 🡤 on the Tools panel, then click each button and use the arrow keys to position them, as shown in Figure 25.

   The top line of the Road Rally button must overlap with the bottom border of the navigation bar. And the bottom border of the Road Rally button must overlap with the top border of the Auction button.

You placed the drop-down buttons on the stage and repositioned them.

Add a mask layer

1. Click the **roadRally layer**, insert a **new layer** above the roadRally layer, then name it **mask**.

2. Click **Frame 2** of the mask layer, then insert a **keyframe**.

3. Select the **Rectangle tool** 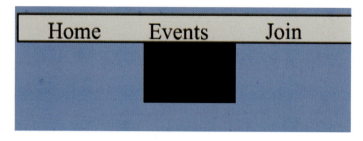 on the Tools panel, set the Stroke color to **none** , then set the Fill color to **black**.

4. Draw a **rectangle** that covers the buttons, as shown in Figure 26.

5. Click the **Selection tool** on the Tools panel, then drag the **rectangle** to above the buttons, as shown in Figure 27.

   The rectangle is below the navigation bar because the mask layer is below the navBar layer in the Timeline.

6. Verify the **rectangle** is selected, click **Insert** on the menu bar, point to **Timeline**, then click **Create Motion Tween**.

7. Click **Frame 5** on the mask layer, then insert a **keyframe**.

(continued)

FIGURE 26
The drawn rectangle that covers the buttons

FIGURE 27
Dragging the rectangle above the buttons

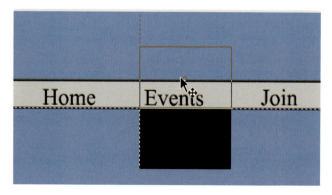

FIGURE 28
The rectangle positioned over the buttons

8. Click the **Selection tool** ⟶ on the Tools panel (if necessary), then drag the **rectangle** down to cover the buttons, as shown in Figure 28.

9. Click **mask** on the Timeline, click **Modify** on the menu bar, point to **Timeline**, click **Layer Properties**, click the **Mask option button**, then click **OK**.

10. Click **roadRally** on the Timeline, click **Modify** on the menu bar, point to **Timeline**, click **Layer Properties**, click the **Masked option button**, then click **OK**.

11. Click **auction** on the Timeline, click **Modify** on the menu bar, point to **Timeline**, click **Layer Properties**, click the **Masked option button**, then click **OK**.

12. Drag the **playhead** in the Timeline and notice how the mask hides and reveals the buttons.

13. Save your work.

You added a mask that animates to hide and reveal the menu buttons.

Assign an action to a drop-down button

1. Click **Frame 2** of the roadRally layer, then click the **Road Rally button** to select it.

2. Open the Actions panel and verify ActionScript 1.0 & 2.0 is displayed above the category list.

3. Verify the Script Assist button is selected and b_roadRally is displayed, as shown in Figure 29.

   b_roadRally in the Actions panel indicates that the b_roadRally button symbol is selected on the stage and that the ActionScript you create will apply to this object.

4. Click the **Add a new item to the script icon** 🖫, point to **Global Functions**, point to **Timeline Control**, then click **goto**.

5. Click the **Scene list arrow**, point to **Scene 2** as shown in Figure 30, then click.

6. Verify the Type is set to Frame Number and the Number is set to 1.

7. Collapse the Actions panel.

You used the Script Assist window to assign a goto action to a menu button.

FIGURE 29
The Actions panel with the b_roadRally button selected

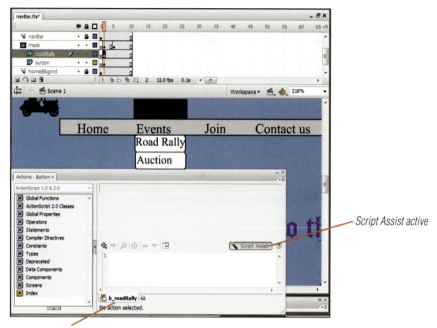

Script Assist active

b_roadRally button indicating the action to be created will be assigned to the button

FIGURE 30
Selecting the scene to go to

Creating Special Effects

FIGURE 31

Specifying a frame label

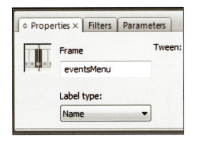

FIGURE 32

The completed Actions panel

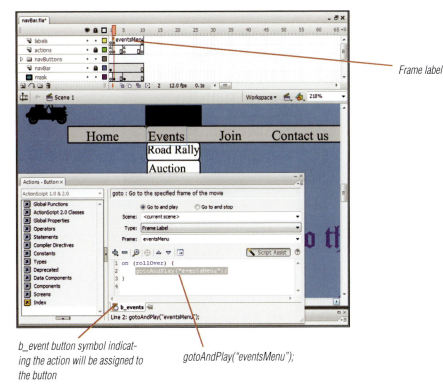

Frame label

b_event button symbol indicating the action will be assigned to the button

gotoAndPlay("eventsMenu");

Add a frame label and assign a rollover action

1. Insert a **new layer** at the top of the Timeline, name it **labels**, then insert a **keyframe** in Frame 2 of the labels layer.

2. Verify that the Property inspector panel is open, click inside the **Frame text box**, then type **eventsMenu**, as shown in Figure 31.

3. Collapse the Property inspector panel, then click the **Events button** on the stage to select it.

4. Expand the Actions panel, then verify b_events is displayed in the lower-left corner of the Actions panel.

5. Click the **Add a new item to the script icon**, point to **Global Functions**, point to **Movie Clip Control**, then click **on**.

6. Click the **Release check box** to deselect it, then click the **Roll Over check box** to select it.

7. Click the **Add a new item to the script icon**, point to **Global Functions**, point to **Timeline Control**, then click **goto**.

8. Click the **Type list arrow**, then click **Frame Label**.

9. Click the **Frame list arrow**, then click **eventsMenu**.

   Your screen should resemble Figure 32.

10. Click **Control** on the menu bar, then click **Test Movie**.

11. Point to **Events**, then click **Road Rally**.

12. Close the test window, collapse the Actions panel, then save your work.

You added a frame label and assigned a rollOver action using the frame label.

Add an invisible button

1. Click **Control** on the menu bar, click **Test Movie**, move the pointer over Events on the navigation bar, then move the pointer away from Events.

   Notice that when you point to Events, the drop-down menu appears. However, when you move the pointer away from the menu, it does not disappear.

2. Close the test window.

3. Insert a **new layer** above the homeBkgrnd layer, then name it **rollOver**.

4. Select the **Rectangle tool** 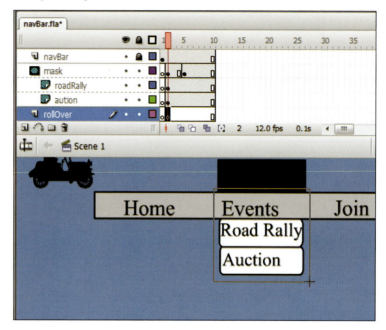 on the Tools panel, verify that the Stroke Color is set to none, then set the Fill Color to blue.

5. Insert a **keyframe** in Frame 2 of the rollOver layer.

6. Draw a **rectangle**, as shown in Figure 33.

7. Click the **Selection tool** on the Tools panel, then click the **blue rectangle** to select it.

8. Click **Modify** on the menu bar, then click **Convert to Symbol**.

9. Type **b_rollOver** for the name, click the **Button option button** (if necessary), then click **OK**.

10. Expand the Actions panel.

(continued)

FIGURE 33
Drawing the rectangle

FIGURE 34

The Actions panel displaying the b_rollOver button symbol

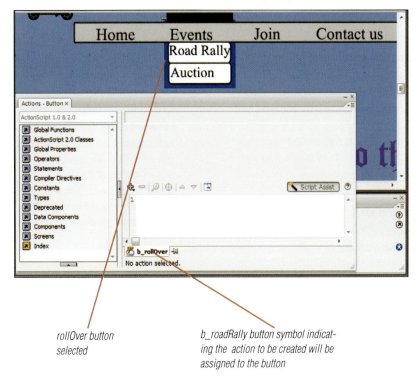

rollOver button
selected

b_roadRally button symbol indicating the action to be created will be
assigned to the button

11. Verify the rollOver button is selected and b_rollOver is displayed in the Actions panel, as shown in Figure 34.

12. Click the **Add a new item to the script icon**, point to **Global Functions**, point to **Movie Clip Control**, then click **on**.

13. Click the **Release check box** to deselect it, then click the **Roll Over check box** to select it.

14. Click the **Add a new item to the script icon**, point to **Global Functions**, point to **Timeline Control**, then click **goto**.

15. Verify Frame 1 is specified.

16. Close the Actions panel.

17. Expand the Property inspector, click the **Color list arrow**, click **Alpha**, then set the percentage to **0**.

18. Click **Control** on the menu bar, then click **Test Movie**.

19. Point to **Events** to display the drop-down menu, then move the pointer away from Events.

   The drop-down menu disappears.

20. Close the test window, then save and close the movie.

21. Exit Flash.

You added a button and assigned a rollOver action to it, then made the button transparent.

Create a shape tween animation.

1. Start Flash, open f15_8.fla, then save it as **skillsdemo5**.
2. Insert keyframes in Frames 45 and 65 on the face2 layer.
3. In frame 65, position the Selection tool at the middle of the mouth of face2, then, when the pointer changes to an arc, drag and reshape the mouth into a smile.
4. Display the Properties panel.
5. Click anywhere between Frames 45 and 65 on the face2 layer.
6. Use the Properties panel to specify a shape tween.
7. Play the movie.
8. Save your work.

Create a morphing effect.

1. Insert a keyframe in Frame 65 on the number1 layer.
2. Use the Selection Tool to select 1, then break it apart twice.
3. Insert a blank keyframe in Frame 85 on the number1 layer.
4. Display the Library panel.
5. Click the Edit Multiple Frames icon on the Timeline to turn on this feature.
6. Drag the g_number2 symbol and place it directly over the 1 so that both graphics are visible.
7. Break apart the 2 symbol twice.
8. Turn off the Edit Multiple Frames feature.
9. Click anywhere between Frames 65 and 85 on the number1 layer.

10. Use the Properties panel to specify a shape tween.
11. Play the movie, then save your work.

Use shape hints.

1. Click Frame 65 of the number1 layer.
2. With the 1 selected, add two shape hints, one at the top and one at the bottom of the 1.
3. Click Frame 85 of the number1 layer, then position the shape hints to match up with the two initial shape hints.
4. Play the movie, then save your work.

Create and apply a mask layer.

1. Insert a new layer above the heading layer, then name it **mask**.
2. Click Frame 1 on the mask layer.
3. Drag the g_face graphic from the Library panel to the left side of the word "How."
4. Insert a keyframe in Frame 45 on the mask layer.
5. Insert a Motion tween.
6. Drag the face to the right side of the word "faces?".
7. Click the mask layer on the Timeline, click Modify on the menu bar, point to Timeline, then click Layer Properties.
8. Use the Layer Properties dialog box to specify a Mask layer that is locked.
9. Click heading in the Timeline, then use the Layer Properties dialog box to specify a Masked layer that is locked.

10. Play the movie, then save your work. At this point, the mask animation should reveal the heading, the face2 smiles, and the number morphs from 1 to 2.

Add and name a scene.

1. Display the Scene panel.
2. Rename Scene 1 **faces**.
3. Add a new scene, then name it **correct**.
4. Type a heading on the stage, **That's correct**, with a red, Arial, 72 pt font, and center it near the middle of the stage.
5. Change the name of Layer 1 to **heading**.
6. Insert a keyframe in Frame 30 on the heading layer.
7. Test the movie.
8. Save your work.

Add interactivity to a scene.

1. Display the faces scene, insert a new layer above the face2 layer, and name it **stopmovie**.
2. Insert a keyframe in Frame 85 on the stopmovie layer and add a stop action to it. (*Hint*: Open the Actions panel. Display ActionScript 1.0 & 2.0 above the category list and verify the stopmovie:1 is displayed. With Script Assist off, click the Add a new item to the script icon, then choose Global Functions, Timeline Control, and stop. *Note*: For simple actions/controls, such as stop, Script Assist is not needed.)
3. Use the Selection tool to select the Continue button on the stage.

4. Use the Actions panel to assign a goto action to the Continue button that jumps the movie to the scene named "correct", when the viewer clicks the button. (*Hint:* Start with Script Assist on.)
5. Test the movie.
6. Save your work.

Add sound to a movie.

1. Use the Scene panel to display the scene named "correct".
2. Insert a new layer and name it **applause**.
3. Click Frame 1 on the applause layer.
4. Display the Library panel and drag the applause sound symbol to the stage.
5. Test the movie.
6. Save your work.

Add a transition effect.

1. Display the scene named "correct" (if necessary).
2. Insert a new layer above the heading layer, name it **mask,** specify it as a mask layer.
3. Click frame 1 of the mask layer.
4. Change the View to **50%**.
5. Draw a rectangle, the size of the stage and position it above the stage.
6. Create a motion tween that causes the rectangle to move from above the stage to cover the stage.

> TIP: You may have to drag the scroll bar at the right of the stage up to provide more room at the top of the stage.

7. Specify the heading layer as a masked layer and lock the layer.
8. Test the movie.
9. Save your work, then compare your images to Figure 35.
10. Exit Flash.

FIGURE 35
Completed Skills Review

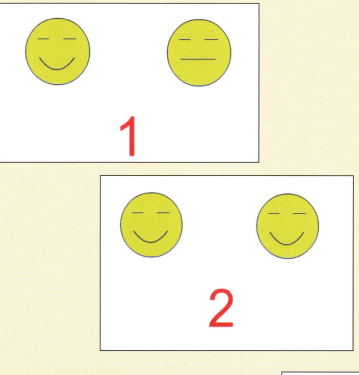

Creating Special Effects

The Ultimate Tours travel company has asked you to design several sample animations for their Web site. Figure 36 shows a sample Cruises screen with morph and shape tween animations, as well as a mask effect. Using these or one of the sites you created in Chapter 4 as a guide, complete the following for the Cruises screen of the Ultimate Tours Web site:

1. Open ultimatetours4.fla (the file you created in Chapter 4 Project Builder 1) and save it as **ultimatetours5**.

2. Create a morph animation, such as the sailboat morphing into a cruise ship, as shown in Figure 36. The animation should play when the Cruises button on the home page is clicked.

3. Create a shape tween animation, such as a light growing out from a lighthouse, as shown in Figure 36.

4. Create a button, such as the words Lighthouse Cruise, that jumps to a second scene.

5. Add a layer and name it **labels**, then add a frame label to the frame where the Cruises screen first appears.

For the new scene:

6. Create a scene and give it an appropriate name.

7. Rename Scene 1 **Home**.

8. Create an animation using a mask effect in the new scene, such as a searchlight effect, as shown in Figure 36.

9. Add a sound to the scene (foghorn.wav is provided for you).

10. Add an action to go to the Cruises screen when the animation is done and the viewer clicks a button. Use the frame label created in Step 5.

11. Test the movie, then compare your image to the example shown in Figure 36.

FIGURE 36
Sample completed Project Builder 1

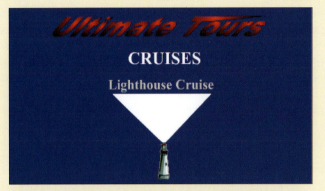

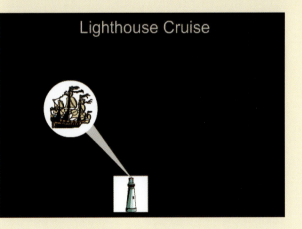

You have been asked to develop a Web site illustrating the signs of the zodiac. The introductory screen should have a heading with a mask effect and 12 zodiac signs, each of which could become a button. Clicking a sign button displays another screen with a different graphic to represent the sign and information about the sign, as well as special effects such as sound, shape animation, and morphing. Each information screen should be linked to the introductory screen.

1. Open a new Flash document, then save it as **zodiac5**.

2. Create an introductory screen for the Web site with the following:
   - A heading, **Signs of the Zodiac**
   - A mask layer that passes across the heading Zodiac
   - Several graphics representing the signs of the Zodiac
   - Two graphics that are buttons and that jump to another scene when clicked.

3. Create a second scene that has the following:
   - A morph animation using two graphics (In the Flash movie represented in Figure 37, the lion morphs into another shape.)

   - A sound (The lion roars.)
   - A Home button with a sound when clicked

4. Create a third scene that has the following:
   - A shape animation using shape hints (In the Flash movie represented in Figure 37, the P in Pisces morphs into an F and the c morphs into an h.)
   - A Home button with a sound when clicked

5. Rename all of the scenes.

6. Test the movie.

7. Save the movie, then compare your scenes to the examples shown in Figure 37.

FIGURE 37
Sample completed Project Builder 2

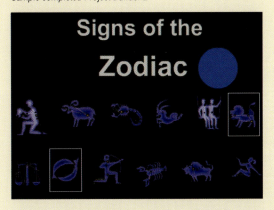

Figure 38 shows the home page of a Web site. Study the figure and complete the following questions. For each question, indicate how you determined your answer.

1. Connect to the Internet, then go to *www.nikeid.com*.

   > TIP: Use Figure 38 to answer the questions. Go to the site and explore several links to get a feeling for how the site is constructed.

2. Open a document in a word processor or open a new Flash document, save the file as **dpc5**, then answer the following questions. (*Hint*: Use the Text tool in Flash.)

   - Who's site is this and what seems to be the purpose of this site?
   - Who would be the target audience?
   - How might a shape tween animation be used in this site?
   - How might a morph animation be used?
   - How might a mask effect be used?
   - How might sound be used?
   - What suggestions would you make to improve the design and why?

FIGURE 38
Design Project

This is a continuation of the Portfolio Project in Chapter 4, which is the development of a personal portfolio. The home page has several categories, including the following:

- Personal data
- Contact information
- Previous employment
- Education
- Samples of your work

In this project, you will create several buttons for the Sample Animations screen and link them to the animations.

1. Open portfolio4.fla (the file you created in Portfolio Project, Chapter 4) and save it as **portfolio5**.

   (*Hint*: When you open the file, you may receive a missing font message, meaning a font used in this document is not available on your computer. You can choose a substitute font or use a default font.)

2. Display the Sample Animations screen. You will be adding buttons to this screen that play various animations. In each case, insert a stop action at the end of the animation and a button to return to the Sample Animations screen.

3. Add layers and create buttons for a shape tween animation, morph animation, and an animation using shape hints.

4. Add shape tween, morph, and shape hint animations that are linked to the buttons.

5. Add a new scene and create a mask animation in this scene.

6. Add a layer with a mask button on the Timeline in Scene 1 so it appears on the Sample Animations screen, as shown in Figure 39. The button should link to the new scene.

7. Rename the new scene and Scene 1 using appropriate names.

8. Add a sound to a scene. For example, add a sound in the mask animation that plays as the mask is revealing the contents of the masked layer.

FIGURE 39
Sample completed Portfolio Project

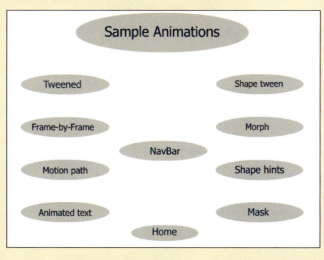

9. Add a new scene with a navigation bar animation and name the scene appropriately. Add a button on the Sample Animations screen that links to this scene.

10. Create frame actions that cause the movie to return to the Sample Animations screen after each animation has been played.

11. Test the movie.

12. Save your work, then compare your image to the example shown in Figure 39.

chapter **1**

GETTING STARTED WITH ADOBE PHOTOSHOP CS3

1. Start Adobe Photoshop CS3

2. Learn how to open and save an image

3. Use organizational and management features

4. Examine the Photoshop window

5. Use the Layers and History palettes

6. Learn about Photoshop by using Help

7. View and print an image

8. Close a file and exit Photoshop

1
GETTING STARTED WITH
ADOBE
PHOTOSHOP CS3

Using Photoshop

Adobe Photoshop CS3 is an image-editing program that lets you create and modify digital images. 'CS' stands for Creative Suite, a complete design environment. The Adobe® Design Premium Creative Design Suite 3 consists of Adobe Photoshop®, Adobe Dreamweaver®, Adobe InDesign®, and Adobe Flash®. A **digital image** is a picture in electronic form. Using Photoshop, you can create original artwork, manipulate color images, and retouch photographs. In addition to being a robust application popular with graphics professionals, Photoshop is practical for anyone who wants to enhance existing artwork or create new masterpieces. For example, you can repair and restore damaged areas within an image, combine images, and create graphics and special effects for the Web.

QUICKTIP

In Photoshop, a digital image may be referred to as a file, document, graphic, picture, or image.

Understanding Platform Interfaces

Photoshop is available in both Windows and Macintosh platforms. Regardless of which type of computer you use, the features and commands are very similar. Some of the Windows and Macintosh keyboard commands differ in name, but they have equivalent functions. For example, the [Ctrl] and [Alt] keys are used in Windows, and the ⌘ and [option] keys are used on Macintosh computers. There is a visual difference between the two platforms due to the user interface found in each type of computer.

Understanding Sources

Photoshop allows you to work with images from a variety of sources. You can create your own original artwork in Photoshop, use images downloaded from the Web, or use images that have been scanned or created using a digital camera. Whether you create Photoshop images to print in high resolution or optimize them for multimedia presentations, Web-based functions, or animation projects, Photoshop is a powerful tool for communicating your ideas visually.

Tools You'll Use

Tools palette

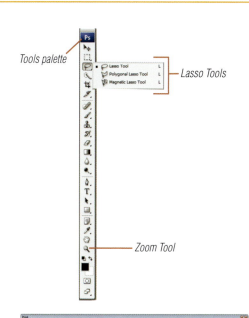

Lasso Tool L
Polygonal Lasso Tool L
Magnetic Lasso Tool L

Lasso Tools

Zoom Tool

Options bar

START ADOBE
PHOTOSHOP CS3

What You'll Do

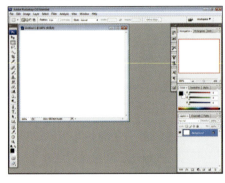

 In this lesson, you'll start Photoshop for Windows or Macintosh, then create a file.

Defining Image-Editing Software

Photoshop is an image-editing program. An **image-editing** program allows you to manipulate graphic images so that they can be reproduced by professional printers using full-color processes. Using windows, various tools, menus, and a variety of techniques, you can modify a Photoshop image by rotating it, resizing it, changing its colors, or adding text to it. You can also use Photoshop to create and open different kinds of file formats, which enables you to create your own images, import them from a digital camera or scanner, or use files (in other formats) purchased from outside sources. Table 1 lists some of the graphics file formats that Photoshop can open and create.

Understanding Images

Every image is made up of very small squares, which are called **pixels**, and each pixel represents a color or shade. Pixels within an image can be added, deleted, or modified.

QUICKTIP
Photoshop files can become quite large. After a file is complete, you might want to **flatten** it, an irreversible process that combines all layers and reduces the file size.

Using Photoshop Features

Photoshop includes many tools that you can use to manipulate images and text. Within an image, you can add new items and modify existing elements, change colors, and draw shapes. For example, using the Lasso Tool, you can outline a section of an image and drag the section onto another area of the image. You can also isolate a foreground or background image. You can extract all or part of a complex image from nearly any background and use it elsewhere.

QUICKTIP
You can create a logo in Photoshop. A **logo** is a distinctive image that you can create by combining symbols, shapes, colors, and text. Logos give graphic identity to organizations, such as corporations, universities, and retail stores.

You can also create and format text, called **type**, in Photoshop. You can apply a variety of special effects to type; for example, you can change the appearance of type and increase or decrease the distance between characters. You can also edit type after it has been created and formatted.

QUICKTIP

Photoshop records each change you make to an image on the History palette. You can undo or redo a recorded action as necessary. Photoshop records actions for the current session only; it discards actions when the program closes.

Adobe Dreamweaver CS3 a Web production software program included in the Design Suite allows you to optimize, preview, and animate images. Because Dreamweaver is part of the same suite as Photoshop, you can jump seamlessly between the two programs.

You can also quickly turn any graphics image into a GIF animation. Photoshop and Dreamweaver let you compress file size (while optimizing image quality) to ensure that your files download quickly from a Web page. Using optimization features, you can view multiple versions of an image and select the one that best suits your needs.

Starting Photoshop and Creating a File

The way that you start Photoshop depends on the computer platform you are using. However, when you start Photoshop in either platform, the computer displays a **splash screen**, a window that displays information about the software, and then the Photoshop window opens.

After you start Photoshop, you can create a file from scratch. You use the New dialog box to create a file. You can also use the New dialog box to set the size of the image you're about to create by typing dimensions in the Width and Height text boxes.

QUICKTIP

There is no one Camera Raw format, as this is determined by your camera manufacturer. Some raw formats you may encounter are:
.raf (Fuji)
.crw .cr2 (Canon)
.kdc .dcr (Kodak)
.mrw (Minolta)
.nef (Nikon)
.orf (Olympus)
.dng (Adobe)
.ptx .pef (Pentax)
.arw .srf (Sony)
.x3f (Sigma)
.erf (Epson)

TABLE 1: Examples of Graphic File Formats Supported in Photoshop

file format	filename extension	file format	filename extension
Photoshop	.PSD	Filmstrip	.VLM
Bitmap	.BMP	Kodak PhotoCD	.PCD
PC Paintbrush	.PCX	Pixar	.PXR
Graphics Interchange Format	.GIF	Scitex CT	.SCT
Photoshop Encapsulated PostScript	.EPS	Photoshop PDF	.PDF
Tagged Image Format	.TIF or .TIFF	Targa	.TGA or .VDA
JPEG Picture Format	.JPG, .JPE, or .JPEG	PICT file	.PCT, .PIC, or .PICT
CorelDraw	.CDR	Raw	varies

Start Photoshop (Windows)

1. Click the **Start button**  on the taskbar.

2. Point to **All Programs**, point to **Adobe Design Premium CS3** as shown in Figure 1, then click **Adobe Photoshop CS3**.

   TIP The Adobe Photoshop CS3 program might be found in the Start menu (in the left pane) or in the Adobe folder, which is in the Program Files folder on the hard drive (Win).

3. Click **File** on the menu bar, then click **New** to open the New dialog box.

4. Double-click the number in the Width text box, type **500**, click the **Width list arrow**, then click **pixels** (if it is not already selected).

5. Double-click the number in the Height text box, type **400**, then specify a resolution of **72** pixels/inch, if necessary.

6. Click **OK**.

7. Click the **arrow** ▶ at the bottom of the image window, point to **Show**, then click **Document Sizes** (if it is not already displayed).

You started Photoshop for Windows, then created a file with custom dimensions. Setting custom dimensions lets you specify the exact size of the image you are creating. You changed the display at the bottom of the image window so the document size is visible.

FIGURE 1

Starting Photoshop CS3 (Windows)

Understanding hardware requirements (Windows)

Adobe Photoshop CS3 has the following minimum system requirements:

- Processor: Intel Based Pentium 4 processor or later
- Operating System: Microsoft® Windows XP SP2 or Windows Vista
- Memory: 512 MB of RAM
- Storage space: 10 GB of available hard-disk space
- Internet connectivity for activation; broadband required for Adobe Stock Photos
- 16-bit video card and Quick Time 7 for Multimedia features

FIGURE 2

Starting Photoshop CS3 (Macintosh)

Hard drive icon

Understanding hardware requirements (Macintosh)

Adobe Photoshop CS3 has the following minimum system requirements:

- Processor: G4, G5, or Intel-based
- Operating System: Mac OS X version 10.2.8 through 10.3.8 (10.3.4 through 10.3.8 recommended)
- Memory: 320 MB of RAM (384 MB recommended)
- Storage space: 750 MB of available hard-disk space
- Monitor: 1024 × 768 or greater monitor resolution with 16-bit color or greater video card
- PostScript Printer PostScript Level 2, Adobe PostScript 3

Start Photoshop (Macintosh)

1. Double-click the **hard drive icon**, double-click the **Applications folder**, then double-click the **Adobe Photoshop CS3 folder**. Compare your screen to Figure 2.

2. Double-click the **Adobe Photoshop CS3 program icon**.

3. Click **File** on the menu bar, then click **New**.

   TIP   If the Color Settings dialog box opens, click No. If a Welcome screen opens, click Close.

4. Double-click the number in the Width text box, type **500**, click the **Width list arrow**, then click **pixels** (if necessary).

5. Double-click the number in the Height text box, type **400**, click the **Height list arrow**, click **pixels** (if necessary), then verify a resolution of **72** pixels/inch.

6. Click **OK**.

7. Click the **arrow** ▶ at the bottom of the image window, click **Show**, then click **Document Sizes** (if is it not already displayed).

You started Photoshop for Macintosh, then created a file with custom dimensions. You changed the display at the bottom of the image window so the document size is visible.

Lesson 1   Start Adobe Photoshop CS3

PHOTOSHOP 1-7

LEARN HOW TO OPEN AND SAVE AN IMAGE

What You'll Do

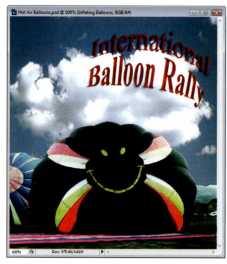

 In this lesson, you'll locate and open files using the File menu and Adobe Bridge, flag and sort files, then save a file with a new name.

Opening and Saving Files

Photoshop provides several options for opening and saving a file. Often, the project you're working on determines the techniques you use for opening and saving files. For example, you might want to preserve the original version of a file while you modify a copy. You can open a file, then immediately save it with a different filename, as well as open and save files in many different file formats. When working with graphic images you can open a Photoshop file that has been saved as a bitmap (.bmp) file, then save it as a JPEG (.jpg) file to use on a Web page.

Customizing How You Open Files

You can customize how you open your files by setting preferences. **Preferences** are options you can set that are based on your work habits. For example, you can use the Open Recent command on the File menu to instantly locate and open the files that you recently worked on, or you can allow others to preview your files as thumbnails. Figure 3 shows the Preferences dialog box options for handling your files in Windows.

TIP In cases when the correct file format is not automatically determined, you can use the Open As command on the File menu (Win).

FIGURE 3
Preferences dialog box

Option for thumbnail preview

Number of files to appear in Open Recent list

Browsing Through Files

You can easily find the files you're looking for by using **Adobe Bridge**: a stand-alone application that serves as the hub for the Adobe Creative Suite. See Figure 4. You can open Adobe Bridge (or just Bridge) by clicking the Go to Bridge button to the left of the Workspace button. You can also open Bridge using the File menu when a Photoshop file is open. When you open Bridge, there are a series of palettes, also called panels, with which you can view the files on your hard drive as hierarchical files and folders. In addition to the Favorites and Folders palettes in the upper-left corner of the Bridge window, there are other important areas. Directly beneath the Favorites and Folders palettes is The Filter panel which allows you to easily change the order of files in the Content panel. Beneath the Preview window is a window containing the Metadata and Keywords palettes, which store information

about a selected file that can then be used as search parameters. You can use this tree structure to find the file you are searching for. When you locate a file, you can click its thumbnail to see information about its size, format, and creation and modification dates.

(Clicking a thumbnail selects the image. You can select multiple non-contiguous images by pressing and holding [Ctrl](Win) ⌘ (Mac) each time you click an image.) You can select contiguous images by clicking

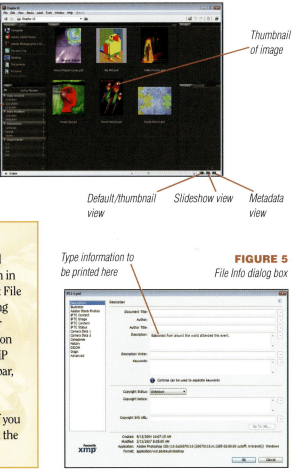

FIGURE 4
Adobe Bridge window

Thumbnail of image

File info

Default/thumbnail view   *Slideshow view*   *Metadata view*

FIGURE 5
File Info dialog box

Type information to be printed here

Using the File Info dialog box

You can use the File Info dialog box to identify a file, add a caption or other text, or add a copyright notice. The Description section allows you to enter printable text, as shown in Figure 5. For example, to add your name to an image, click File on the menu bar, click File Info, then click in the Description text box. (You can move from field to field by pressing [Tab] or by clicking in individual text boxes.) Type your name, course number, or other identifying information in the Description text box. You can enter additional information in the other text boxes, then save all the File Info data as a separate file that has an .XMP extension. To print selected data from the File Info dialog box, click File on the menu bar, then click Print. Click the Color Management list arrow, then click Output. Available options are listed in the right panel. To print the filename, select the Labels check box. You can also select checkboxes that let you print crop marks and registration marks. If you choose, you can even add a background color or border to your image. After you select the items you want to print, click Print.

the first image, then pressing and holding [Shift] and clicking the last image in the group. You can open a file using Bridge by double-clicking its thumbnail, and find out information such as the file's format, and when it was created and edited. You can close Bridge by clicking File (Win) or Bridge CS3 (Mac) on the (Bridge) menu bar, then clicking Exit (Win) or Quit Bridge CS3 (Mac) or by clicking the window's Close button.

Understanding the Power of Bridge

In addition to allowing you to see all your images, Bridge can be used to rate (assign importance), sort (organize by name, rating, and other criteria), and label. Figure 4, on the previous page, contains images that are assigned a rating and shown in Filmstrip view. There are three views in Bridge (Default, Horizontal Filmstrip view, and Metadata Focus view) that are controlled by buttons in the lower-right corner of the window. You can assign a color label or rating to one or more images. Any number of selected images can be assigned a color label by clicking Label on the menu bar, then clicking one of the six options.

Creating a PDF Presentation

Using Bridge you can create a PDF Presentation. Such a presentation can be viewed full-screen on any computer monitor, or in the Adobe Acrobat Reader as a PDF file. You can create such a presentation by opening Bridge, locating and selecting images using the file hierarchy, clicking Tools in the Bridge menu bar, pointing to Photoshop, then clicking PDF Presentation. The PDF Presentation dialog box, shown in Figure 6, opens and lists any figures you have selected. You can add images by clicking the Browse button.

Using Save As Versus Save

Sometimes it's more efficient to create a new image by modifying an existing one, especially if it contains elements and special effects that you want to use again. The Save As command on the File menu creates a copy of the file, prompts you to give the duplicate file a new name, and then displays the new filename in the image's title bar. You use the Save As command to name an unnamed file or to save an existing file with a new name. For example, throughout this book, you will be instructed to open your data files and use the Save As command. Saving your data files with new names keeps them intact in case you have to start the lesson over again or you want to repeat an exercise. When you use the Save command, you save the changes you made to the open file.

FIGURE 6

PDF Presentation dialog box

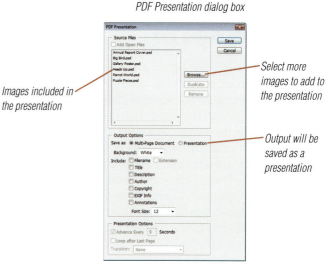

Images included in the presentation

Select more images to add to the presentation

Output will be saved as a presentation

FIGURE 7

Open dialog box for Windows and Macintosh

Look in list arrow
displays list of
available drives

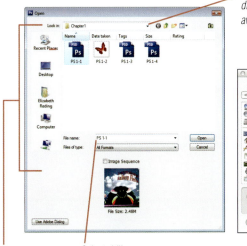

Available folders
and files

Current file location
list arrow

*Available folders
and files may differ
from your list*

Selected filename

FIGURE 8

Bridge window

*Your list may
be different*

Click the Keywords
palette tab to assign
keywords to a selected
file, then click any of the
displayed keywords

Drag to resize
thumbnails

Open a file using the File menu

1. Click **File** on the menu bar, then click **Open**.

2. Click the **Look in list arrow** (Win) or the **From list arrow** (Mac), navigate to the drive and folder where you store your Data Files, then click **Open**.

3. Click **PS 1-1.psd** as shown in Figure 7, then click **Open**.

    TIP   If you receive a message stating that some text layers need to be updated before they can be used for vector-based output, click Update.

You used the Open command on the File menu to locate and open a file.

Open a file using Folders palette in Adobe Bridge

1. Click the **Go to Bridge button** [Br] on the options bar, then click the **Folders palette tab** [Folders] (if necessary).

2. Navigate through the hierarchical tree to the drive and folder where you store your Chapter 1 Data Files.

3. Drag the **slider** (at the bottom of the Bridge window) a third of the way between the Smallest thumbnail size button [□] and the Largest thumbnail size button [□]. Compare your screen to Figure 8.

4. Double-click the **image of a butterfly**, file **PS 1-2.tif**. The butterfly image opens and Adobe Bridge is no longer visible, but still open.

5. Close the butterfly image in Photoshop.

You used the Folders palette tab in Adobe Bridge to locate and open a file. This feature makes it easy to see which file you want to use.

Use the Save As command

1. Verify that the **PS 1-1.psd window** is active.

2. Click **File** on the menu bar, click **Save As**, then compare your Save As dialog box to Figure 9.

3. If the drive containing your Data Files is not displayed, click the **Save in list arrow** (Win) or the **Where list arrow** (Mac), then navigate to the drive and folder where you store your Chapter 1 Data Files.

4. Select the current filename in the File name text box (Win) or Save As text box (Mac) (if necessary); type **Hot Air Balloons**, then click **Save**. Compare your image to Figure 10.

   TIP   Click OK to close the Maximize Compatibility dialog box (if necessary).

You used the Save As command on the File menu to save the file with a new name. This command makes it possible for you to save a changed version of an image while keeping the original file intact.

FIGURE 9
Save As dialog box

Your list of files might be different

New filename

FIGURE 10
Hot Air Balloons image

Duplicate file has new name

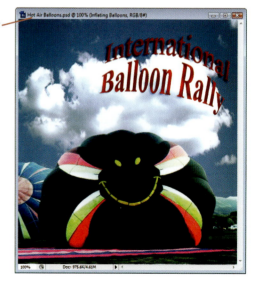

Changing file formats
In addition to using the Save As command to duplicate an existing file, this is a handy way of changing one format into another. For example, you can open an image you created in a digital camera, then make modifications in the Photoshop format. To do this, open the .jpg file in Photoshop, click File on the menu bar, then click Save As. Name the file, click the Format list arrow, click Photoshop (*.PSD, *.PDD), then click OK.

FIGURE 11

Images in Adobe Bridge

Rated and
Approved file

FIGURE 12

Sorted files

Content panel

Filter panel

1. Click the **Go to Bridge button** on the options bar.

2. Click the **Folders palette tab** **Folders** (if necessary), then click the drive and folder where your you store Chapter 1 Data Files on the File Hierarchy tree (if necessary).

3. Click the **butterfly image**, file **PS 1-2.tif** to select it.

4. Press and hold **[Ctrl]** (Win) or **[⌘]** (Mac), click **PS 1-1.psd** (the image of the balloon), then release **[Ctrl]** (Win) or **[⌘]** (Mac).

5. Click **Label** on the menu bar, then click **Approved**.

6. Click **PS 1-1.psd**, click **Label** on the menu bar, then click **★★★**. See Figure 11.

7. Click **View** on the menu bar, point to **Sort**, then click **By Label**. Compare your screen to Figure 12.

   The order of the files is changed.

   > TIP You can also change the order of files (in the Content panel) using the Sort by Filename list arrow in the Filter panel. When you click the Sort by Filename list arrow, you'll see a list of sorting options. Click on the option you want and the files in the Content panel will be rearranged.

8. Click **View** on the menu bar, point to **Sort**, then click **Manually**.

   > TIP You can change the Bridge view at any time, depending on the type of information you need to see.

9. Click **File** (Win) or **Bridge CS3** (Mac) on the (Bridge) menu bar, then click **Exit** or **Quit Bridge CS3** (Mac).

You labeled files using Bridge, sorted the files in a folder, then changed the sort order. When finished, you closed Bridge.

USE ORGANIZATIONAL AND
MANAGEMENT FEATURES

What You'll Do

In this lesson, you'll learn how to use Version Cue and Bridge.

Learning about Version Cue

Version Cue is a file versioning and management feature of the Adobe Creative Suite that can be used to organize your work whether you work in groups or by yourself. Version Cue is accessed through Bridge. You can see Version Cue in Bridge in two different locations: the Favorites tab and the Folders tab. Figure 13 shows Version Cue in the Favorites tab of Bridge. You can also view Version Cue in the Folders tab by collapsing the Desktop, as shown in Figure 14.

Understanding Version Cue Workspaces

Regardless of where in Bridge you access it (the Favorites or Folders tab), Version Cue installs a **workspace** in which it stores projects and project files, and keeps track of file versions. The Version Cue Workspace can be installed locally on your own computer and can be made public or kept private. It can also be installed on a server and can be used by many users through a network.

FIGURE 13
Favorites tab in Adobe Bridge

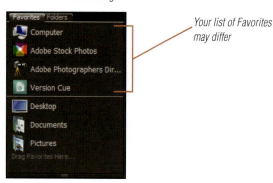

Your list of Favorites may differ

FIGURE 14
Folders tab in Adobe Bridge

Using Version Cue's Administrative Functions

Once you log into Version Cue, you can control who uses the workspace and how it is used with the tabs at the top of the screen. The Content tab, which is shown in Figure 15, lets you open your server, browse projects and other servers, and perform advanced tasks.

Making Use of Bridge

You've already seen how you can use Bridge to find, identify, and sort files. But did you know that you can use Bridge Center to organize, label, and open files as a group? Once you select one or more files, right-click the selection, then click Open, or Open With to display the files in your favorite CS3 program. You can apply label and ratings, or sort the selected files.

QUICKTIP

You can use Bridge to stitch together panoramic photos, rename images in batches, or automate image conversions with the Tools menu. Select the file(s) in Bridge you want to modify, click Tools on the menu bar, point to Photoshop, then click a command and make option modifications.

FIGURE 15
Version Cue CS3 Content tab

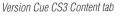
Shortcut key

Using Adobe Stock Photos

You can view and try professional images using Adobe Stock Photos. Available through the Favorites pane in Bridge, an active Internet connection is all you need to browse through a wide variety of images to include in your Photoshop designs. You can download complimentary (comp) low-resolution versions of these images and place them in a Photoshop document to find the perfect fit for your design. Once you find the right image, you can purchase it in a high-resolution format. There are thousands of images to choose from, and you can look at previous downloads and purchases through your Adobe account.

EXAMINE THE
PHOTOSHOP WINDOW

What You'll Do

In this lesson, you'll select a tool on the Tools palette, use a shortcut key to cycle through the hidden tools, select and add a tool to the Tool Preset picker, use the Window menu to show and hide palettes in the workspace, and create a customized workspace.

Learning About the Workspace

The Photoshop **workspace** is the area within the program Photoshop window that includes the entire window, from the command menus at the top of your screen to the status bar (Win) at the bottom. Desktop items are visible in this area (Mac). The workspace is shown in Figure 16.

The **title bar** displays the program name (Win) and, if the active image window is maximized, the filename of the open file (for a new file, **Untitled-1**, because it has not been named). The title bar also contains a Close button, and Minimize, Maximize, and Restore buttons (Win).

The **menu bar** contains the program name (Mac) menu from which you can choose Photoshop commands. You can choose a menu command by clicking it or by pressing [Alt] plus the underlined letter in the menu name (Win). Some commands display shortcut keys on the right side of the menu. Shortcut keys provide an alternative way to activate menu commands. Some commands might appear dimmed, which means they are not currently available. An ellipsis after a command indicates additional choices.

Finding Tools Everywhere

The **Tools palette** contains tools associated with frequently used Photoshop commands.

DESIGNTIP **Overcoming information overload**

One of the most common experiences shared by first-time Photoshop users is information overload. There are just too many places and things to look at! When you feel your brain overheating, take a moment and sit back. Remind yourself that the active image area is the central area where you can see a composite of your work. All the tools and palettes are there to help you, not to add to the confusion.

The face of a tool contains a graphical representation of its function; for example, the Zoom Tool shows a magnifying glass. You can place the pointer over each tool to display a tool tip, which tells you the name or function of that tool. Some tools have additional hidden tools, indicated by a small black triangle in the lower-right corner of the tool.

QUICKTIP

You can view the Tools palette in a 2-column format by clicking the Expand arrow in its upper-left corner.

The **options bar**, located directly under the menu bar, displays the current settings for each tool. For example, when you click the Type Tool, the default font and font size appear on the options bar, which can be changed if desired. You can move the options bar anywhere in the workspace for easier access. The options bar also contains the Tool Preset picker. This is the left-most tool on the options bar and displays the active tool. You can click the list arrow on this tool to select another tool without having to use the Tools palette. The options bar also contains the palette well, an area where you can assemble palettes for quick access.

Palettes, also called panels in other CS3 programs, are small windows used to verify settings and modify images. By default, palettes appear in stacked groups at the right side of the window. A collection of palettes usually in a vertical orientation is called a **dock**. The dock is the dark gray bar above the collection of palettes. The arrows in the dock are used to maximize and minimize the palettes. You can display a palette by simply clicking the palette's name tab, which makes it the active palette. Palettes can be separated and moved

FIGURE 16

Workspace

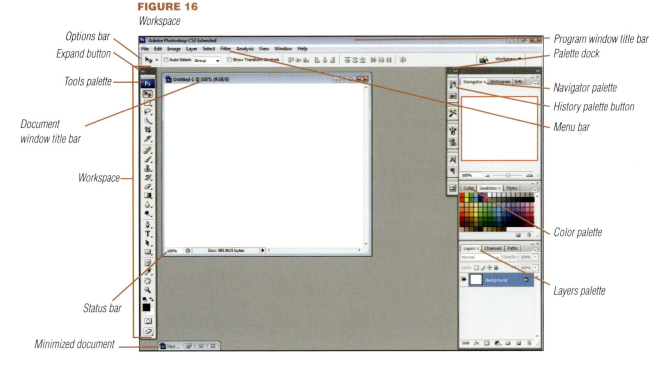

Options bar
Expand button
Tools palette
Document window title bar
Workspace
Status bar
Minimized document

Program window title bar
Palette dock
Navigator palette
History palette button
Menu bar
Color palette
Layers palette

anywhere in the workspace by dragging their name tabs to new locations. You can dock a palette by dragging its tab in or out of a dock. As you move palettes, you'll see blue high-lighted drop zones. A **drop zone** is an area where you can move a palette. You can also change the order of tabs by dragging a tab to a new location within its palette. Each palette contains a menu that you can view by clicking the list arrow in the upper-right corner of the palette.

QUICKTIP
You can reset palettes to their default locations at any time by clicking Window on the menu bar, pointing to Workspace, then clicking Reset Palette Locations.

The **status bar** is located at the bottom of the program window (Win) or work area (Mac). It displays information, such as the file size of the active window and a description of the active tool. You can display other informa-tion on the status bar, such as the current tool, by clicking the black triangle to view a pull-down menu with more options.

Rulers can help you precisely measure and position an object in the workspace. The rulers do not appear the first time you use Photoshop, but you can display them by clicking Rulers on the View menu.

Using Tool Shortcut Keys
Each tool has a corresponding shortcut key. For example, the shortcut key for the Type Tool is T. After you know a tool's shortcut key, you can select the tool on the Tools palette by pressing its shortcut key. To select and cycle through a tool's hidden tools, you press and hold [Shift], then press the tool's shortcut key until the desired tool appears.

Customizing Your Environment
Photoshop makes it easy for you to position elements you work with just where you want them. If you move elements around to make your environment more convenient, you can always return your workspace to its original appearance by resetting the default palette locations. Once you have your work area arranged the way you want it, you can create a customized workspace by clicking Window on the menu bar, pointing to Workspace, then clicking Save Workspace. If you want to open a named workspace, click Window on the menu bar, point to Workspace, then click the workspace you want to use.

QUICKTIP
Click the Workspace button on the options bar to save or delete a workspace, restore the default or any saved workspace.

Creating customized keyboard shortcuts
Keyboard shortcuts can make your work with Photoshop images faster and easier. In fact, once you discover the power of keyboard shortcuts, you may never use menus again. In addition to the keyboard shortcuts that are preprogrammed in Photoshop, you can create your own. To do this, click Edit on the menu bar, then click Keyboard Shortcuts. The Keyboard Shortcuts and Menus dialog box opens, as shown in Figure 17.

FIGURE 17
Keyboard Shortcuts and Menus dialog box

Instructions
to edit
shortcuts

FIGURE 18

Hidden tools

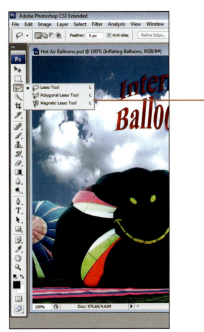

Shortcut key

1. Click the **Lasso Tool** ⟜ on the Tools palette, press and hold the mouse button until a list of hidden tools appears, then release the mouse button. See Figure 18. Note the shortcut key, L, next to the tool name.

2. Click the **Polygonal Lasso Tool** ⟜ on the Tools palette.

3. Press and hold [**Shift**], press [**L**] three times to cycle through the Lasso tools, then release [**Shift**]. Did you notice how the options bar changes for each selected Lasso tool?

   TIP   You can return the tools to their default setting by clicking the Click to open the Tool Preset picker list arrow on the options bar, clicking the list arrow, then clicking Reset All Tools.

You selected the Lasso Tool on the Tools palette and used its shortcut key to cycle through the Lasso tools. Becoming familiar with shortcut keys can speed up your work and make you more efficient.

DESIGNTIP   **Learning shortcut keys**

Don't worry about learning shortcut keys. As you become more familiar with Photoshop, you'll gradually pick up shortcuts for menu commands, such as saving a file, or Tools palette tools, such as the Move Tool. You'll notice that as you learn to use shortcut keys, your speed while working with Photoshop will increase and you'll complete tasks with fewer mouse clicks.

Select a tool from the Tool Preset picker

1. Click the **Click to open the Tool Preset picker list arrow** 🐾 ⃝ on the options bar.

   The name of a button is displayed in a tool tip, descriptive text that appears when you point to the button. Your Tool Preset picker list will differ, and may contain no entries at all. This list can be customized by each user.

2. Deselect the **Current Tool Only check box** (if necessary). See Figure 19.

3. Double-click **Magnetic Lasso 24 pixels** in the list.

You selected the Magnetic Lasso Tool using the Tool Preset picker. The Tool Preset picker makes it easy to access frequently used tools and their settings.

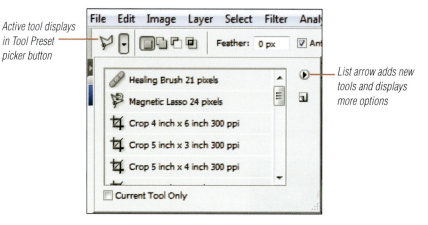

FIGURE 19

Using the Tool Preset picker

Active tool displays in Tool Preset picker button

List arrow adds new tools and displays more options

Using the Full Screen Mode

By default, Photoshop displays images in the Standard Screen Mode. This means that each image is displayed within its own window. You can choose from three other modes: Maximized Screen Mode, Full Screen Mode with Menu Bar, and Full Screen Mode. And why would you want to stray from the familiar Standard Screen Mode? Perhaps your image is so large that it's difficult to see it all in Standard Mode, or perhaps you want a less cluttered screen. Maybe you just want to try something different. You can switch between modes by clicking the Change Screen Mode button (located near the bottom of the Tools palette) or by pressing the keyboard shortcut F. When you click this button, the screen displays changes. Click the Hand Tool (or press the keyboard shortcut H), and you can reposition the active image, as shown in Figure 20.

FIGURE 20

Full screen mode with menu bar

Use hand pointer to reposition image

FIGURE 21
Move Tool added to preset picker

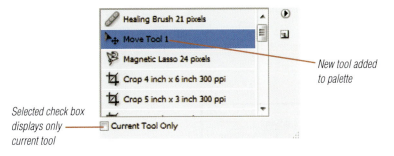

Selected check box
displays only
current tool

*New tool added
to palette*

FIGURE 22
Tool Preset picker list arrow menu

New Tool Preset...
Rename Tool Preset... Delete Tool Preset
✔ Sort By Tool ✔ Show All Tool Presets Show Current Tool Presets
Text Only ✔ Small List Large List
Reset Tool Reset All Tools
Preset Manager...
Reset Tool Presets... Load Tool Presets... Save Tool Presets... Replace Tool Presets...
Art History Brushes Crop and Marquee Text

Add a tool to the Tool Preset picker

1. Click the **Move Tool** ⊹ on the Tools palette.

2. Click the **Click to open the Tool Preset picker list arrow** ⊹ ▾ on the options bar.

3. Click the **list arrow** ▾≡ on the Tool Preset picker.

4. Click **New Tool Preset**, then click **OK** to accept the default name (Move Tool 1). Compare your list to Figure 21.

   TIP   You can display the currently selected tool alone by selecting the Current Tool Only check box.

You added the Move Tool to the Tool Preset picker. Once you know how to add tools to the Tool Preset picker, you can quickly and easily customize your work environment.

Modifying a tool preset

Once you've created tool presets, you'll probably want to know how they can be deleted and renamed. To delete any tool preset, select it on the Tool Preset picker palette. Click the list arrow on the Tool Preset picker palette to view the menu, shown in Figure 22, then click Delete Tool Preset. To rename a tool preset, click the same list arrow, then click Rename Tool Preset.

Show and hide palettes

1. Click **Window** on the menu bar, then verify that **Color** has a check mark next to it, then close the menu.

2. Click the **Swatches tab** next to the Color tab to make the Swatches palette active, as shown in Figure 23.

3. Click **Window** on the menu bar, then click **Swatches** to deselect it.

   TIP   You can hide all open palettes by pressing [Shift], then [Tab], then show them by pressing [Shift], then [Tab] again. To hide all open palettes, the options bar, and the Tools palette, press [Tab], then show them by pressing [Tab] again.

4. Click **Window** on the menu bar, then click **Swatches** to redisplay the Swatches palette.

You used the Window menu to show and hide the Swatches palette. You might want to hide palettes at times in order to enlarge your work area.

FIGURE 23
Active Swatches palette

Swatches tab is active

DESIGN TIP   Considering ethical implications

Because Photoshop enables you to make so many dramatic changes to images, you should consider the ethical ramifications and implications of altering images. Is it proper or appropriate to alter an image just because you have the technical expertise to do so? Are there any legal responsibilities or liabilities involved in making these alterations? Because the general public is more aware about the topic of **intellectual property** (an image or idea that is owned and retained by legal control) with the increased availability of information and content, you should make sure you have the legal right to alter an image, especially if you plan on displaying or distributing the image to others. Know who retains the rights to an image, and if necessary, make sure you have written permission for its use, alteration, and/or distribution. Not taking these precautions could be costly.

FIGURE 24
Save Workspace dialog box

FIGURE 25
Image Size dialog box

Create a customized workspace

1. Click and drag the **Tools palette title bar** so it appears to the right of the image.
2. Click **Window** on the menu bar, point to **Workspace**, then click **Save Workspace**.
3. Type **Sample Workspace** in the Name text box, then verify that only **Palette Locations** has a check mark beside it, as shown in Figure 24.
4. Click **Save**.
5. Click **Window** on the menu bar, then point to **Workspace**.

   The name of the new workspace appears on the Window menu.
6. Click **Reset Palette Locations**.
7. Click **Window** on the menu bar, point to **Workspace**, then click **Sample Workspace**.
8. Click **Window** on the menu bar, point to **Workspace**, then click **Reset Palette Locations**.

You created a customized workspace, reset the palette locations, tested the new workspace, then reset the palette locations again. Customized workspaces provide you with a work area that is always tailored to your needs.

Resizing an image

You may have created the perfect image, but the size may not be correct for your print format. Document size is a combination of the printed dimensions and pixel resolution. With resampling on, you can change the total number of pixels in the image and the print dimensions independently. With resampling off, you can change either the dimensions or the resolution: Photoshop will automatically adjust whichever value you don't ignore. An image designed for a Web site, for example, might be too small for an image that will be printed in a newsletter. You can easily resize an image using the Image Size command on the Image menu. To use this feature, open the file you want to resize, click Image on the menu bar, then click Image Size. The Image Size dialog box, shown in Figure 25, opens. By changing the dimensions in the text boxes, you'll have your image resized in no time.

USE THE LAYERS AND
HISTORY PALETTES

What You'll Do

In this lesson, you'll hide and display a layer, move a layer on the Layers palette, and then undo the move by deleting the Layer Order state on the History palette.

Learning About Layers

A **layer** is a section within an image that can be manipulated independently. Layers allow you to control individual elements within an image and create great dramatic effects and variations of the same image. Layers enable you to easily manipulate individual characteristics within an image. Each Photoshop file has at least one layer, and can contain many individual layers, or groups of layers.

You can think of layers in a Photoshop image as individual sheets of clear plastic that are in a stack. It's possible for your file to quickly accumulate dozens of layers. The **Layers palette** displays all the layers in an open file. You can use the Layers palette to create, copy, delete, display, hide, merge, lock, group or reposition layers.

QUICKTIP

In Photoshop, using and understanding layers is the key to success.

Setting preferences

The Preferences dialog box contains several topics, each with its own settings: General, Interface, File Handling, Performance, Cursors, Transparency & Gamut, Units & Rulers, Guides, Grid, Slices & Count, Plug-Ins, and Type. To open the Preferences dialog box, click Edit (Win) or Photoshop (Mac) on the menu bar, point to Preferences, then click a topic that represents the settings you want to change. If you move palettes around the workspace, or make other changes to them, you can choose to retain those changes the next time you start the program. To always start a new session with default palettes, click Interface on the Preferences menu, deselect the Remember Palette Locations check box, then click OK. Each time you start Photoshop, the palettes will be reset to their default locations and values.

Understanding the Layers Palette

The order in which the layers appear on the Layers palette matches the order in which they appear in the image; the topmost layer in the Layers palette is the topmost layer on the image. You can make a layer active by clicking its name on the Layers palette. When a layer is active, it is highlighted on the Layers palette, the name of the layer appears in parentheses in the image title bar. Only one layer can be active at a time. Figure 26 shows an image with its Layers palette. Do you see that this image contains five layers? Each layer can be moved or modified individually on the palette to give a different effect to the overall image. If you look at the Layers palette, you'll see that the Finger Painting layer is dark, indicating that it is currently active.

QUICKTIP

Get in the habit of shifting your eye from the image in the work area to the Layers palette. Knowing which layer is active will save you time and help you troubleshoot an image.

Displaying and Hiding Layers

You can use the Layers palette to control which layers are visible in an image. You can show or hide a layer by clicking the Indicates layer visibility button next to the layer thumbnail. When a layer is hidden, you are not able to merge it with another, select it, or print it. Hiding some layers can make it easier to focus on particular areas of an image.

Using the History Palette

Photoshop records each task you complete in an image on the **History palette**. This record of events, called states, makes it easy to see what changes occurred and the tools or commands that you used to make the modifications. The History palette, shown in Figure 26, displays up to 20 states and automatically updates the list to display the most recently performed tasks. The list contains the name of the tool or command used to change the image. You can delete a state on the History palette by selecting it and dragging it to the Delete current state button. Deleting a state is equivalent to using the Undo command. You can also use the History palette to create a new image from any state.

QUICKTIP

When you delete a History state, you undo all the events that occurred after that state.

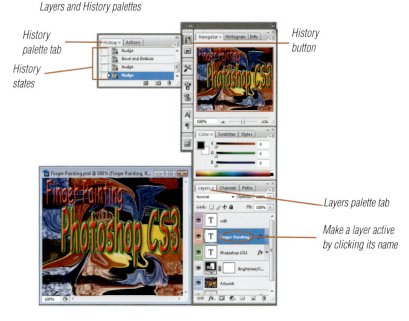

FIGURE 26
Layers and History palettes

History palette tab

History states

History button

Layers palette tab

Make a layer active by clicking its name

Hide and display a layer

1. Click the **Hot Air Balloon layer** on the Layers palette.

   TIP Depending on the size of the window, you might only be able to see the initial characters of the layer name.

2. Verify that the **Show Transform Controls check box** on the options bar is not checked, then click the **Indicates layer visibility button** on the Hot Air Balloon layer to display the image, as shown in Figure 27.

   TIP By default, transparent areas of an image have a checkerboard display on the Layers palette.

3. Click the **Indicates layer visibility button** on the Hot Air Balloon layer to hide the image.

You made the Hot Air Balloon layer active on the Layers palette, then clicked the Indicates layer visibility button to display and hide a layer. Hiding layers is an important skill that can be used to remove distracting elements. Once you've finished working on specific layers, you can display the distracting layers.

FIGURE 27
Hot Air Balloon

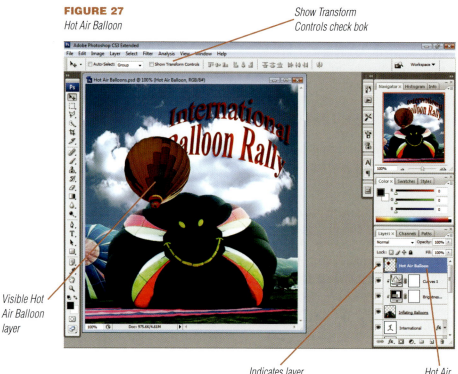

Show Transform Controls check bok

Visible Hot Air Balloon layer

Indicates layer visibility button

Hot Air Balloon layer

FIGURE 28
Layer moved in Layers palette

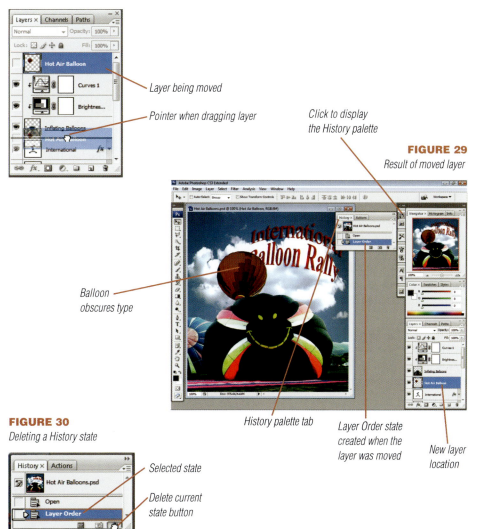

Layer being moved

Pointer when dragging layer

*Click to display
the History palette*

FIGURE 29
Result of moved layer

*Balloon
obscures type*

History palette tab

*Layer Order state
created when the
layer was moved*

*New layer
location*

FIGURE 30
Deleting a History state

Selected state

*Delete current
state button*

Pointer when deleting a history state

1. Click the **Indicates layer visibility button** on the Hot Air Balloon layer on the Layers palette.

2. Click and drag the **Hot Air Balloon layer** on the Layers palette, beneath the Inflating Balloons layer in the palette, as shown in Figure 28.

   The basket of the Hot Air Balloon is hidden by the Inflating Balloons layer. See Figure 29.

3. Click the **History button** in the Dock to display the History palette.

4. Click **Layer Order** on the History palette, then drag it to the **Delete current state button** on the History palette, as shown in Figure 30.

   TIP Each time you close and reopen an image, the History palette is cleared.

   The basket of the hot air balloon is now visible.

5. Click **File** on the menu bar, then click **Save**.

You moved the Hot Air Balloon layer so it was behind the Inflating Balloon layer, then returned it to its original position by dragging the Layer Order state to the Delete current state button on the History palette. You can easily undo what you've done using the History palette.

Lesson 5   Use the Layers and History Palettes

LEARN ABOUT PHOTOSHOP
BY USING HELP

What You'll Do

In this lesson, you'll open Help, then view and find information from the following Help links: Contents, Index, and Search.

Understanding the Power of Help

Photoshop features an extensive Help system that you can use to access definitions, explanations, and useful tips. Help information is displayed in a browser window, so you must have Web browser software installed on your computer to view the information; however, you do not need an Internet connection to use Photoshop Help.

Using Help Topics

The Home page of the Help window has links in the right pane that you can use to retrieve information about Photoshop commands and features. In the left pane, there are two sections: Contents and Index.

The Getting Started link displays the Contents and Index links as shown in Figure 31. The Contents palette tab allows you to browse topics by category; the Index palette tab provides the letters of the alphabet, which you can click to view keywords and topics alphabetically. The Search feature is located on the toolbar (above the left and right panes) in the form of a text box. You can search the Photoshop Help System by entering text in the Type in a word or phrase text box, then click Search.

FIGURE 31
Links in the Getting Started section

Help links

Index link

FIGURE 32

Contents section of the Help window

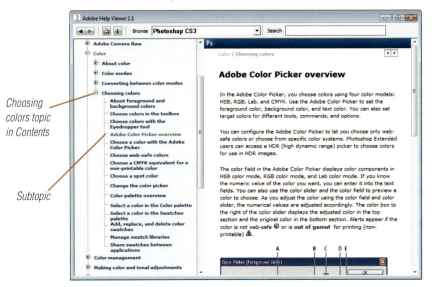

Choosing colors topic in Contents

Subtopic

1. Click **Help** on the menu bar, then click **Photoshop Help**.

   TIP You can also open the Help window by pressing **[F1]** (Win) or ⌘ **[?]** (Mac).

2. If it's not already selected, click the **Contents link**, scroll down the left pane (if necessary), then click **Color**.

3. Click **Choosing colors**, then click **Adobe Color Picker overview** in the left pane. See Figure 32.

   TIP You can maximize the window (if you want to take advantage of the full screen display).

You used the Photoshop Help command on the Help menu to open the Help window and viewed a topic in Contents.

Understanding the differences between monitor, images, and device resolution

Image resolution is determined by the number of pixels per inch (ppi) that are printed on a page. Pixel dimensions (the number of pixels along the height and width of a bitmap image) determine the amount of detail in an image, while image resolution controls the amount of space over which the pixels are printed. High resolution images show greater detail and more subtle color transitions than low resolution images. Device resolution or printer resolution is measured by the ink dots per inch (dpi) produced by printers. You can set the resolution of your computer monitor to determine the detail with which images will be displayed. Each monitor should be calibrated to describe how the monitor reproduces colors. Monitor calibration is one of the first things you should do because it determines whether your colors are being accurately represented, which in turn determines how accurately your output will match your design intentions.

Find information in the Index

1. Click the **Index** link in the left pane of the Help window.

2. Click **E**, scroll down, then click **Eyedropper tool,** click **about**, then click **View color values in an image.** Compare your Help window to Figure 33.

You clicked an alphabetical listing and viewed an entry in the Index.

FIGURE 33

Topics in the Index window

Using How-To Help features

Using Help would always be easy if you knew the name of the feature you wanted up look up. To help you find out how to complete common tasks, Photoshop has a listing of "How-To's" in the Help menu. Click Help in the menu bar, point to the How-To you'd like to read, as shown in Figure 34, then click the item you want information about.

FIGURE 34

How-To Help topics

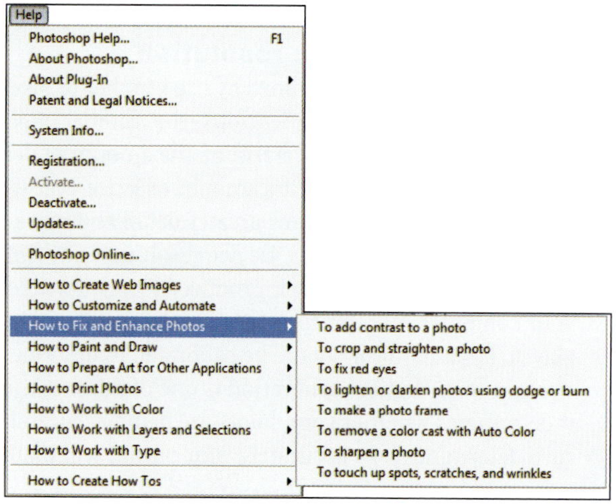

FIGURE 35

Search topic in Help

Search term

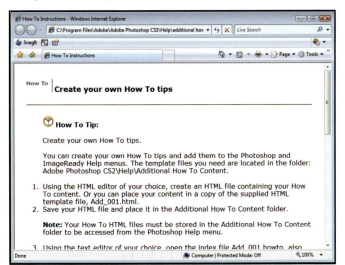

FIGURE 36

Create your own How To tips

Find information using Search

1. Click the **Search text box** in the Help window.

2. Type **print quality**, then press **[Enter]** (Win) or **[return]** (Mac).

   TIP   You can search for multiple words by inserting a space; do not use punctuation in the text box.

3. Scroll down the left pane (if necessary), click **Why colors sometimes don't match**, then compare your Help screen to Figure 35.

4. Click the **Close box** when you are finished reading the topic.

You entered a search term, viewed search results, then closed the Help window.

Creating customized How To's

Photoshop Help is pretty helpful, but perhaps there's a technique you've created, only to return later and think 'How did I do this?' Fortunately, you can create your own How To tips so you'll never wonder how you created a cool effect. To find out more, click Help on the menu bar, point to How to Create How Tos, then click Create your own How To tips. The information shown in Figure 36 walks you through the process.

VIEW AND PRINT
AN IMAGE

What You'll Do

 In this lesson, you'll use the Zoom Tool on the Tools palette to increase and decrease your views of the image. You'll also change the page orientation settings in the Page Setup dialog box, and print the image.

Getting a Closer Look

When you edit an image in Photoshop, it is important that you have a good view of the area that you are focusing on. Photoshop has a variety of methods that allow you to enlarge or reduce your current view. You can use the Zoom Tool by clicking the image to zoom in on (magnify the view) or zoom out of (reduce the view) areas of your image. Zooming in or out enlarges or reduces your *view*, not the actual image. The maximum zoom factor is 1600%. The current zoom percentage appears in the document's title bar, on the Navigator palette, and on the status bar. When the Zoom Tool is selected, the options bar provides additional choices for changing your view as shown in Figure 37. For example, the Resize Windows To Fit check box automatically resizes the window whenever you magnify or reduce the view. You can also change the zoom percentage using the Navigator palette and the status bar by typing a new value in the zoom text box.

Printing Your Image

In many cases, a professional print shop might be the best option for printing a Photoshop image to get the highest quality. You can print a Photoshop image using a standard black-and-white or color printer. The printed image will be a composite of all visible layers. The quality of your printer and paper will affect the appearance of your output. The Page Setup dialog box displays options for printing, such as paper orientation. **Orientation** is the direction in which an image appears on the page. In **portrait orientation**, the image is printed with the shorter edges of the paper at the top and bottom. In **landscape orientation**, the image is printed with the longer edges of the paper at the top and bottom.

Use the Print command when you want to print multiple copies of an image. Use the Print One Copy command to print a single copy without making dialog box selections, and use the Print dialog box when you want to handle color values using color management.

Understanding Color Handling in Printing

The Print dialog box that opens when you click Print on the File menu lets you determine how colors are output. You can click the Color Handling list arrow to choose whether to use color management, and whether Photoshop or the printing device should control this process. If you let Photoshop determine the colors, Photoshop performs any necessary conversions to color values appropriate for the selected printer. If you choose to let the printer determine the colors, the printer will convert document color values to the corresponding printer color values. In this scenario, Photoshop does not alter the color values. If no color management is selected, no color values will be changed when the image is printed.

Viewing an Image in Multiple Views

You can use the New Window command on the Window ➤ Arrange menu to open multiple views of the same image. You can change the zoom percentage in each view so you can spotlight the areas you want to modify, and then modify the specific area of the image in each view. Because you are working on the same image in multiple views, not in multiple versions, Photoshop automatically applies the changes you make in one view to all views. Although you can close the views you no longer need at any time, Photoshop will not save any changes until you save the file.

FIGURE 37
Zoom Tool options bar

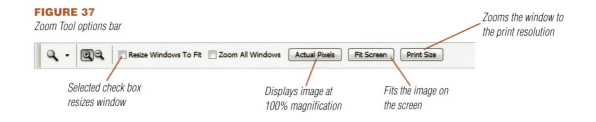

Zooms the window to the print resolution

Selected check box resizes window

Displays image at 100% magnification

Fits the image on the screen

Choosing a Photoshop version

You may have noticed that the title bar on the images in this book say 'Adobe Photoshop CS3 Extended'. What's that about? Well, the release of the Adobe Creative Suite 3 offers two versions of Photoshop: Adobe Photoshop CS3 and Adobe Photoshop CS3 Extended. The Extended version is ideal for multi-media creative professionals, film and video creative professionals, graphic and Web designers who push the limits of 3D and motion, as well as those professionals in the fields of manufacturing, medicine, architecture, engineering and construction, and science and research. Photoshop CS3 is ideal for professional photographers, serious amateur photographers, graphic and Web designers, and print service providers.

Use the Zoom Tool

1. If necessary, click the **Indicates layer visibility button** 👁 on the Layers palette for the Hot Air Balloon layer so the layer is no longer displayed.

2. Click the **Zoom Tool** 🔍 on the Tools palette.

3. Select the **Resize Windows To Fit check box** (if it is not already selected) on the options bar.

4. Position the **Zoom In pointer** ⊕ over the center of the image, then click the **image**.

   TIP   Position the pointer over the part of the image you want to keep in view.

5. Press **[Alt]** (Win) or **[option]** (Mac), then when the Zoom Out pointer appears, click the center of the image twice with the **Zoom Out pointer** ⊖.

6. Release **[Alt]** (Win) or **[option]** (Mac), then compare your image to Figure 38.

   The zoom factor for the image is 66.7%. Your zoom factor may differ.

You selected the Zoom Tool on the Tools palette and used it to zoom in to and out of the image. The Zoom Tool makes it possible to see the detail in specific areas of an image, or to see the whole image at once, depending on your needs.

Using the Navigator palette

You can change the magnification factor of an image using the Navigator palette or the Zoom Tool on the Tools palette. By double-clicking the Zoom text box on the Navigator palette, you can enter a new magnification factor, then press [Enter] (Win) or [return] (Mac). The magnification factor—shown as a percentage—is displayed in the lower-left corner of the Navigator palette, as shown in Figure 39. The red border in the palette, called the Proxy Preview Area, defines the area of the image that is magnified. You can drag the Proxy Preview Area inside the Navigator palette to view other areas of the image at the current magnification factor.

FIGURE 38
Reduced image

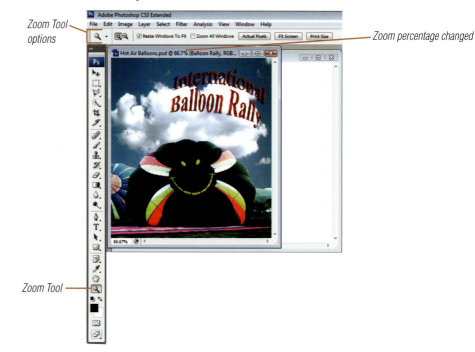

Zoom Tool options

Zoom percentage changed

Zoom Tool

FIGURE 39
Navigator palette

Viewed area of image

FIGURE 40
Page Setup dialog box

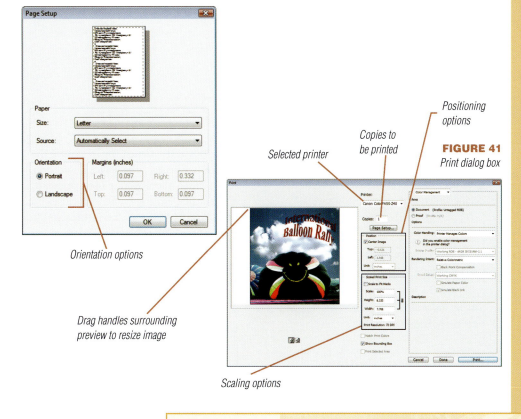

Orientation options

Drag handles surrounding
preview to resize image

Scaling options

Positioning
options

Copies to
be printed

Selected printer

FIGURE 41
Print dialog box

Modify print settings

1. Click **File** on the menu bar, then click **Page Setup** to open the Page Setup dialog box, as shown in Figure 40.

   TIP   If you have not selected a printer using the Print Center, a warning box might appear (Mac).

   Page setup and print settings vary slightly in Macintosh.

2. Click the **Landscape option button** in the Orientation section, then click **OK**.

   TIP   Choose either Landscape option (Mac).

3. Click **File** on the menu bar, click **Print**, then click **Proceed** in the message box that opens. If a PostScript dialog box opens, click **OK** (Mac).

4. Make sure that the **All option button** is selected in the Print range section (Win) or Pages section (Mac), and that **1** appears in the Number of copies text box, then click **OK** (Win) or **Print** (Mac). See Figure 41.

You used the Page Setup command on the File menu to open the Page Setup dialog box, changed the page orientation, then printed the image. Changing the page orientation can make an image fit on a printed page better.

Previewing and creating a Proof Setup
You can create and save a Proof Setup, which lets you preview your image to see how it will look when printed on a specific device. This feature lets you see how colors can be interpreted by different devices. By using this feature, you can decrease the chance that colors will vary from what you viewed on your monitor after they are printed. Create a custom proof by clicking View on the menu bar, pointing to Proof Setup, then clicking Custom. Specify the conditions in the Customize Proof Condition dialog box, then click OK. Each proof setup has the .PSF extension and can be loaded by clicking View on the menu bar, pointing to Proof Setup, clicking Custom, then clicking Load. Use the handles on the image preview in the Print dialog box to scale the print size.

CLOSE A FILE
AND EXIT PHOTOSHOP

What You'll Do

New...	Ctrl+N
Open...	Ctrl+O
Browse...	Alt+Ctrl+O
Open As...	Alt+Shift+Ctrl+O
Open As Smart Object...	
Open Recent	▶
Device Central...	
Close	Ctrl+W
Close All	Alt+Ctrl+W
Close and Go To Bridge...	Shift+Ctrl+W
Save	Ctrl+S
Save As...	Shift+Ctrl+S
Check In...	
Save for Web & Devices...	Alt+Shift+Ctrl+S
Revert	F12
Place...	
Import	▶
Export	▶
Automate	▶
Scripts	▶
File Info...	Alt+Shift+Ctrl+I
Page Setup...	Shift+Ctrl+P
Print...	Ctrl+P
Print One Copy	Alt+Shift+Ctrl+P
Exit	Ctrl+Q

▶ *In this lesson, you'll use the Close and Exit (Win) or Quit (Mac) commands to close a file and exit Photoshop.*

Concluding Your Work Session

At the end of your work session, you might have opened several files; you now need to decide which ones you want to save.

QUICKTIP

If you share a computer with other people, it's a good idea to reset Photoshop's preferences back to their default settings. You can do so when you start Photoshop by clicking Window on the menu bar, pointing to Workspace, then clicking Reset Palette Locations.

Closing Versus Exiting

When you are finished working on an image, you need to save and close it. You can close one file at a time, or close all open files at the same time by exiting the program. Closing a file leaves Photoshop open, which allows you to open or create another file. Exiting Photoshop closes the file, closes Photoshop, and returns you to the desktop, where you can choose to open another program or shut down the computer. Photoshop will prompt you to save any changes before it closes the files. If you do not modify a new or existing file, Photoshop will close it automatically when you exit.

QUICKTIP

To close all open files, click File on the menu bar, then click Close All.

Using Adobe online

Periodically, when you start Photoshop, an Update dialog box might appear, prompting you to search for updates or new information on the Adobe Web site. If you click Yes, Photoshop will automatically notify you that a download is available; however, you do not have to select it. You can also obtain information about Photoshop from the Adobe Photoshop Web site (*www.adobe.com/products/photoshop/main.html*), where you can link to downloads, tips, training, galleries, examples, and other support topics.

FIGURE 42

Closing a file using the File menu

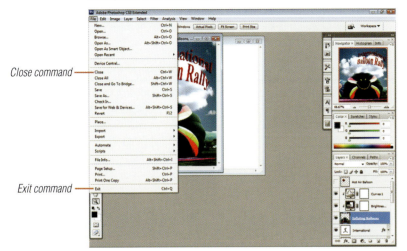

Close command →

Exit command →

Close a file and exit Photoshop

1. Click **File** on the menu bar, then compare your screen to Figure 42.

2. Click **Close**.

   TIP You can close an open file (without closing Photoshop) by clicking the Close button in the image window. Photoshop will prompt you to save any unsaved changes before closing the file.

3. If asked to save your work, click **Yes** (Win) or **Save** (Mac).

4. Click **File** on the menu bar, then click **Exit** (Win) or click **Photoshop** on the menu bar, then click **Quit Photoshop** (Mac).

   TIP To exit Photoshop and close an open file, click the Close button in the program window. Photoshop will prompt you to save any unsaved changes before closing.

5. If asked to save your work, click **No**.

You closed the current file and exited the program by using the Close and Exit (Win) or Quit (Mac) commands.

DESIGNTIP **Using a scanner and a digital camera**

If you have a scanner, you can import print images, such as those taken from photographs, magazines, or line drawings, into Photoshop. Remember that images taken from magazines are owned by others, and that you need permission to distribute them. There are many types of scanners, including flatbed or single-sheet feed. See your instructor to learn how to use the scanner in your facility. You can also use a digital camera to create your own images. A digital camera captures images as digital files and stores them on some form of electronic medium, such as a floppy disk or SmartMedia card. After you upload the images from your camera to your computer, you can work with images in Photoshop.

You can open a scanned or uploaded image (which usually has a .JPG extension or another graphics file format) by clicking File on the menu bar, then by clicking Open. All Formats is the default file type, so you should be able to see all available image files in the Open dialog box. Locate the folder containing your scanned or digital camera images, click the file you want to open, then click Open. A scanned or digital camera image contains all its imagery in a single layer. You can add layers to the image, but you can only save these new layers if you save the image as a Photoshop image (with the extension .PSD).

Power User Shortcuts

to do this:	use this method:	to do this:	use this method:
Close a file	[Ctrl][W] (Win) ⌘ [W] (Mac)	Reset preferences to default settings	[Shift][Alt][Ctrl] (Win) [Shift] [option] ⌘ (Mac)
Create a new file	[Ctrl][N] (Win) ⌘ [N] (Mac)	Save a file	[Ctrl][S] (Win) ⌘ [S] (Mac)
Create a workspace	Window ➤ Workspace ➤ Save Workspace	Show a layer	▢
Drag a layer	🖐	Show hidden lasso tools	[Shift] L
Exit Photoshop	[Ctrl][Q] (Win), ⌘ [Q] (Mac)	Show History palette	▣
Hide a layer	👁	Show or hide all open palettes	[Shift][Tab]
Lasso Tool	⬭ or L	Show or hide all open palettes, the options bar, and the Tools palette	[Tab]
Modify workspace display	Workspace ▼	Show or hide Swatches palette	Window ➤ Swatches
Open a file	[Ctrl][O] (Win), ⌘ [O] (Mac)	Use Save As	[Shift][Ctrl][S] (Win) [Shift] ⌘ [S] (Mac)
Open Bridge	🔍	Zoom in	🔍 [⌘][+]
Open Help	[F1] (Win)	Zoom out	[Alt] 🔍 (Win) [option] ⌘ (Mac) [⌘][–]
Open Preferences dialog box	[Ctrl][K] (Win) ⌘ [K] (Mac)	Zoom Tool	🔍 or Z
Page Setup	[Shift][Ctrl][P] (Win)[Shift] ⌘ [P] (Mac)		
Print File	File ➤ Print [Ctrl][P], (Win) ⌘ [P] (Mac)		

Start Adobe Photoshop CS3.

1. Start Photoshop.
2. Create a new image that is 500 × 500 pixels, accept the default resolution, then name and save it as **Review**.

Open and save an image.

1. Open PS 1-3.psd from the drive and folder where you store your Data Files, and if prompted, update the text layers.
2. Save it as **Zenith Design Logo**.

Use organizational and management features.

1. Open Adobe Bridge.
2. Click the Folders tab, then locate the folder that contains your Data Files.
3. Close Adobe Bridge.

Examine the Photoshop window.

1. Locate the image title bar and the current zoom percentage.
2. Locate the menu you use to open an image.
3. View the Tools palette, the options bar, and the palettes that are showing.
4. Click the Move Tool on the Tools palette, then view the Move Tool options on the options bar.

Use the Layers and History palettes.

1. Drag the Wine Glasses layer so it is above the Zenith layer, then use the History palette to undo the state.
2. Drag the Wine Glasses layer above the Zenith layer again.

3. Use the Indicates layer visibility button to hide the Wine Glasses layer.
4. Make the Wine Glasses layer visible again.
5. Hide the Zenith layer.
6. Show the Zenith layer.
7. Click the Tag Line layer. Notice that the Tag Line layer is now the active layer.
8. Save your work.

Learn about Photoshop by using Help.

1. Open the Adobe Photoshop CS3 Help window.
2. Using the Index, find information about resetting to the default workspace.
3. Print the information you find.
4. Close the Help window.

View and print an image.

1. Make sure that all the layers are visible in the Layers palette.
2. Click the Zoom Tool, then make sure the setting is selected to resize the window to fit.
3. Zoom in on the wine glasses twice.
4. Zoom out to the original perspective.
5. Print one copy of the image.

Close a file and exit Photoshop.

1. Compare your screen to Figure 43, then close the Zenith Design Logo file.
2. Close the Review file.
3. Exit (Win) or Quit (Mac) Photoshop.

FIGURE 43
Completed Skills Review

As a new Photoshop user, you are comforted knowing that Photoshop's Help system provides definitions, explanations, procedures, and other helpful information. It also includes examples and demonstrations to show how Photoshop features work. You use the Help system to learn about image size and resolution.

1. Open the Photoshop Help window.
2. Click the Workspace topic in the Contents link.
3. Click the Working with pop-up palettes in the Palettes and menus subtopic, in the left pane.
4. After you read this topic, click the Display context menus topic, then read this topic.
5. Click the Opening and importing images topic in the left pane.
6. Click the Image size and resolution topic in the left pane, then click About monitor resolution. Print out this topic, then compare your screen to the sample shown in Figure 44.

FIGURE 44
Sample Project Builder 1

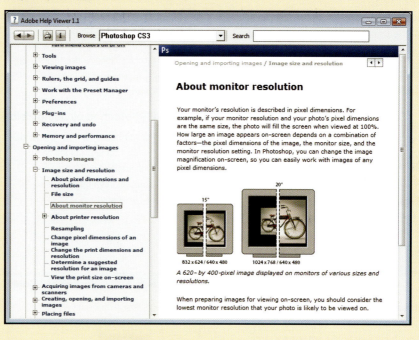

Kitchen Experience, your local specialty cooking shop, has just added herb-infused oils to its product line. They have hired you to draft a flyer that features these new products. You use Photoshop to create this flyer.

1. Open PS 1-4.psd, then save it as **Cooking**.
2. Make the Measuring Spoons layer visible.
3. Drag the Oils layer so the content appears behind the Skillet layer content.
4. Drag the Measuring Spoons layer above the Skillet layer.
5. Save the file, then compare your image to the sample shown in Figure 45.

FIGURE 45
Sample Project Builder 2

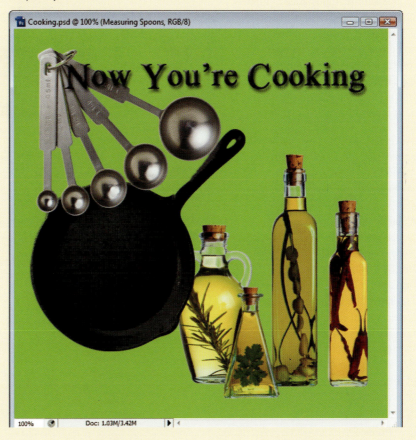

DESIGN PROJECT

As an avid, albeit novice Photoshop user, you have grasped the importance of how layers affect your image. With a little practice, you can examine a single-layer image and guess which objects might display on their own layers. Now, you're ready to examine the images created by Photoshop experts and critique them on their use of layers.

1. Connect to the Internet, and use your browser to find interesting artwork located on at least two Web sites.
2. Review the categories, then download a single-layer image from each Web site.
3. Start Photoshop, then open the downloaded images.
4. Save one image as **Critique-1** and the other as **Critique-2** in the Photoshop format (use the .psd extension).
5. Analyze each image for its potential use of layers.
6. Open the File Info dialog box for Critique-1.psd, then type in the Description section your speculation as to the number of layers there might be in the image, their possible order on the Layers palette, and how moving the layers would affect the image.
7. Close the dialog box.
8. Compare your image to the sample shown in Figure 46, then close the files.

FIGURE 46
Sample Design Project

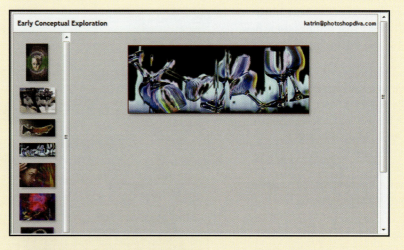

Depending on the size of your group, you can assign individual elements of the project to group members, or work collectively to create the finished product.

You and a select team of graphic artists are preparing to work together on a series of design projects. You want to see what digital imaging options exist. You decide to see what kind of information on this topic is available on the Adobe Web site. You also want to gain familiarity with the Web site so that you can take advantage of its product information, including user tips and feedback, and become more skillful Photoshop users.

1. Connect to the Internet and go to the Adobe Web site at *www.adobe.com*.
2. Point to Products, then find the link for Digital imaging, as shown in Figure 47.
3. Divide into two groups, and let the first group use the links on the Web page to search for information about digital imaging options.
4. Print the relevant page(s).
5. Let the second group start Photoshop and open the Photoshop Help window.

6. Search for information about Adjusting the Monitor Display, then print the relevant page(s).

FIGURE 47
Completed Group Project

7. Let the entire group evaluate the information in the documents, compare any significant differences, and then discuss your findings.

chapter

2

WORKING
WITH LAYERS

1. Examine and convert layers

2. Add and delete layers

3. Add a selection from one image to another

4. Organize layers with layer groups and colors

chapter **2** **WORKING**
WITH LAYERS

Layers Are Everything

You can use Photoshop to create sophisticated images because a Photoshop
image can contain multiple layers. Each
object created in Photoshop can exist on
its own individual layer, making it easy to
control the position and quality of each
layer in the stack. Depending on your
computer's resources, you can have a
maximum of 8000 layers in each
Photoshop image with each layer containing as much or as little detail as
necessary.

> **QUICK**TIP
> The transparent areas in a layer do not increase file size.

Understanding the Importance of Layers

Layers make it possible to manipulate the
tiniest detail within your image, which
gives you tremendous flexibility when you
make changes. By placing objects, effects,
styles, and type on separate layers, you can
modify them individually *without* affecting
other layers. The advantage to using

multiple layers is that you can isolate
effects and images on one layer without
affecting the others. The disadvantage of
using multiple layers is that your file size
might become very large. However, once
your image is finished, you can dramatically reduce its file size by combining all
the layers into one.

Using Layers to Modify an Image

You can add, delete, and move layers in
your image. You can also drag a portion of
an image, called a **selection**, from one
Photoshop image to another. When you do
this, a new layer is automatically created.
Copying layers from one image to another
makes it easy to transfer a complicated
effect, a simple image, or a piece of type.
You can also hide and display each layer, or
change its opacity. **Opacity** is the ability to
see through a layer so that layers beneath
it are visible. You can continuously change
the overall appearance of your image by
changing the order of your layers, until
you achieve just the look you want.

Tools You'll Use

Layer

New	▶	Layer... Shift+Ctrl+N
Duplicate Layer...		Layer From Background...
Delete	▶	Group...
		Group from Layers...
Layer Properties...		
Layer Style	▶	Layer via Copy Ctrl+J
Smart Filter	▶	Layer via Cut Shift+Ctrl+J
New Fill Layer	▶	
New Adjustment Layer	▶	
Change Layer Content	▶	
Layer Content Options...		
Layer Mask	▶	
Vector Mask	▶	
Create Clipping Mask	Alt+Ctrl+G	
Smart Objects	▶	
Video Layers	▶	
3D Layers	▶	
Type	▶	
Rasterize	▶	
New Layer Based Slice		
Group Layers	Ctrl+G	
Ungroup Layers	Shift+Ctrl+G	
Hide Layers		
Arrange	▶	
Align	▶	
Distribute	▶	
Lock All Layers in Group...		
Link Layers		
Select Linked Layers		
Merge Down	Ctrl+E	
Merge Visible	Shift+Ctrl+E	
Flatten Image		
Matting	▶	

Opacity list arrow

Layers × | Channels | Paths

Pass Through   Opacity: 100%

Lock: Fill: 100%

- Type layers
- **Objects**
- Autumn Maple Leaves
- Background

New Layer...	Shift+Ctrl+N
Duplicate Group...	
Delete Group	
Delete Hidden Layers	
New Group...	
New Group from Layers...	
Lock All Layers in Group...	
Convert to Smart Object	
Edit Contents	
Group Properties...	
Blending Options...	
Create Clipping Mask	Alt+Ctrl+G
Link Layers	
Select Linked Layers	
Merge Group	Ctrl+E
Merge Visible	Shift+Ctrl+E
Flatten Image	
Animation Options	▶
Palette Options...	

Color Range

Select: ✎ Sampled Colors

Fuzziness: 40

☐ Invert

○ Selection   ● Image

Selection Preview: None

[OK] [Cancel] [Load...] [Save...]

History × | Actions

PS 2-1.psd

▶ **Open**

Delete current state button

New Group

Name: Group 1

Color: ■ Violet

Mode: Pass Through   Opacity: 100 %

[OK] [Cancel]

Layer Properties

Name: Layer 1

Color: ☐ None

Color list arrow

[OK] [Cancel]

EXAMINE AND
CONVERT LAYERS

What You'll Do

In this lesson, you'll use the Layers palette to delete a Background layer and the Layer menu to create a Background layer from an image layer.

Learning About the Layers Palette

The **Layers palette** lists all the layers within a Photoshop file and makes it possible for you to manipulate one or more layers. By default, this palette is located in the lower-right corner of the screen, but it can be moved to a new location by dragging the palette's tab. In some cases, the entire name of the layer might not appear on the palette. If a layer name is too long, an ellipsis appears, indicating that part of the name is hidden from view. You can view a layer's entire name by holding the pointer over the name until the full name appears. The **layer thumbnail** appears to the left of the layer name and contains a miniature picture of the layer's content, as shown in Figure 1. To the left of the layer thumbnail, you can add color, which allows you to easily identify layers. The Layers palette also contains common buttons, such as the Delete layer button and the Create new layer button.

QUICK TIP
You can hide or resize Layers palette thumbnails to improve your computer's performance. To remove or change the size of layer thumbnails, click the Layers palette list arrow, then click Palette Options to open the Layers Palette Options dialog box. Click the option button next to the desired thumbnail size, or click the None option button to remove thumbnails, then click OK. A paintbrush icon appears in place of a thumbnail.

Recognizing Layer Types

The Layers palette includes several types of layers: Background, type, and image (non-type). The Background layer—whose name appears in italics—is always at the bottom of the stack. Type layers—layers that contain text—contain the type layer icon in the layer thumbnail, and image layers display a thumbnail of their contents. In addition to dragging selections from one Photoshop image to another, you can also drag objects created in other applications, such as Adobe Dreamweaver, Adobe InDesign, or Adobe Flash, onto a Photoshop image, which creates a layer containing the object you dragged from the other program window.

Organizing Layers

One of the benefits of using layers is that you can create different design effects by rearranging their order. Figure 2 contains the same layers as Figure 1, but they are arranged differently. Did you notice that the wreath is partially obscured by the gourds and the title text? This reorganization was created by dragging the Wreath layer below the Gourds layer and by dragging the Fall in New England layer below the Wreath layer on the Layers palette.

FIGURE 1
Image with multiple layers

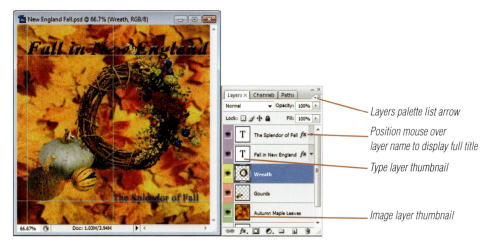

Layers palette list arrow

Position mouse over layer name to display full title

Type layer thumbnail

Image layer thumbnail

FIGURE 2
Layers rearranged

New layer order

Wreath obscured

Converting Layers

When you open an image created with a digital camera, you'll notice that the entire image appears in the Background layer. The Background layer of any image is the initial layer and is always located at the bottom of the stack. You cannot change its position in the stack, nor can you change its opacity or lighten or darken its colors. You can, however, convert a Background layer into an image layer (nontype layer), and you can convert an image layer into a Background layer. You need to modify the image layer *before* converting it to a Background layer. You might want to convert a Background layer into an image layer so that you can use the full range of editing tools on the layer content. You might want to convert an image layer into a Background layer after you have made all your changes and want it to be the bottom layer in the stack.

QUICKTIP

Before converting an image layer to a Background layer, you must first delete the existing Background layer. You can delete a Background layer by clicking it on the Layers palette, then dragging it to the Delete layer button on the Layers palette.

Using rulers and changing units of measurement

You can display horizontal and vertical rulers to help you better position elements. To display or hide rulers, click View on the menu bar, then click Rulers. (A check mark to the left of the Rulers command indicates that the Rulers are displayed.) In addition to displaying or hiding rulers, you can also choose from various units of measurement. Your choices include pixels, inches, centimeters, millimeters, points, picas, and percentages. Pixels, for example, display more tick marks and can make it easier to make tiny adjustments. You can change the units of measurement by clicking Edit [Win] or Photoshop [Mac] on the menu bar, pointing to Preferences, then clicking Units & Rulers. In the Preferences dialog box, click the Rulers list arrow, click the units you want to use, then click OK. The easiest way to change units of measurement, however, is shown in Figure 3. Once the rulers are displayed, right-click (Win) or [Ctrl]-click (Mac) either the vertical or horizontal ruler, then click the unit of measurement you want. The Info palette, located in the upper-right corner of the workspace, also displays your current coordinates. Regardless of the units of measurement in use, the X/Y coordinates are displayed in the Info palette.

FIGURE 3
Changing units of measurement

Right-click (Win) or [Ctrl]-click (Mac) to display measurement choices

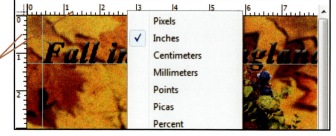

FIGURE 4
Warning box

Adobe Photoshop CS3 Extended

ⓘ Delete the layer "Background"?

[Yes] [No]

☐ Don't show again

FIGURE 5
Background layer deleted

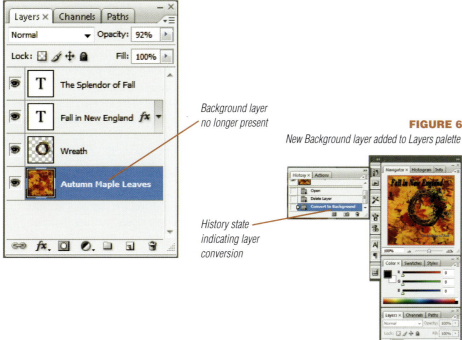

*Background layer
no longer present*

FIGURE 6
New Background layer added to Layers palette

*History state
indicating layer
conversion*

*New
Background
layer*

1. Open PS 2-1.psd from the drive and folder where you store your Data Files, then save it as **New England Fall**.

   TIP If you receive a warning box about maximum compatibility, or a message stating that some of the text layers need to be updated before they can be used for vector-based output, click OK or click Update.

2. Click **View** on the menu bar, click **Rulers** if your rulers are not visible, then make sure that your rulers are displayed in pixels.

   TIP If you are unsure which units of measurement are used, right-click (Win) or [Ctrl]-click (Mac) one of the rulers, then verify that Pixels is selected, or click Pixels (if necessary).

3. On the Layers palette, scroll down, click the **Background layer**, then click the **Delete layer button** 🗑.

4. Click **Yes** in the dialog box, as shown in Figure 4, then compare your Layers palette to Figure 5.

5. Click the **History button** 📑 on the Dock to display the History palette.

6. Click **Layer** on the menu bar, point to **New**, then click **Background From Layer**.

   The Autumn Maple Leaves layer has been converted into the Background layer. Did you notice that in addition to the image layer being converted to the Background layer that a state now appears on the History palette that says Convert to Background? See Figure 6.

7. Save your work.

You displayed the rulers and History palette, deleted the Background layer of an image, then converted an image layer into the Background layer. You can convert any layer into the Background layer, as long as you first delete the existing Background layer.

ADD AND DELETE LAYERS

What You'll Do

 In this lesson, you'll create a new layer using the New command on the Layer menu, delete a layer, create a new layer using buttons on the Layers palette, and relocate a palette tab.

Adding Layers to an Image

Because it's so important to make use of multiple layers, Photoshop makes it easy to add and delete layers. You can create layers in three ways:

- Use the New command on the Layer menu.
- Use the New Layer command on the Layers palette menu.
- Click the Create a new layer button on the Layers palette.

Objects on new layers have a default opacity setting of 100%, which means that objects on lower layers are not visible. Each layer has the Normal (default) blending mode applied to it. (A **blending mode** is a feature that affects a layer's underlying pixels, and is used to lighten or darken colors.)

Merging layers

You can combine multiple image layers into a single layer using the merging process. Merging layers is useful when you want to combine multiple layers in order to make specific edits permanent. (This merging process is different from flattening in that it's selective. Flattening merges *all* visible layers.) In order for layers to be merged, they must be visible and next to each other on the Layers palette. You can merge all visible layers within an image, or just the ones you select. Type layers cannot be merged until they are **rasterized** (turned into a bitmapped image layer), or converted into uneditable text. To merge two layers, make sure that they are next to each other and that the Indicates layer visibility button is visible on each layer, then click the layer in the higher position on the Layers palette. Click Layer on the menu bar, then click Merge Down. The active layer and the layer immediately beneath it will be combined into a single layer. To merge all visible layers, click the Layers palette list arrow, then click Merge Visible. Most layer commands that are available on the Layers menu, such as Merge Down, are also available using the Layers palette list arrow.

Naming a Layer

Photoshop automatically assigns a sequential number to each new layer name, but you can rename a layer at any time. So, if you have four named layers and add a new layer, the default name of the new layer will be Layer 1. After all, calling a layer "Layer 12" is fine, but you might want to use a more descriptive name so it is easier to distinguish one layer from another. If you use the New command on the Layers menu, you can name the layer when you create it. You can rename a layer at any time by using either of these methods:

- Click the Layers palette list arrow, click Layer Properties, type the name in the Name text box, then click OK.
- Double-click the name on the Layers palette, type the new name, then press [Enter] (Win) or [return] (Mac).

Deleting Layers From an Image

You might want to delete an unused or unnecessary layer. You can use four methods to delete a layer:

- Click the name on the Layers palette, click the Layers palette list arrow, then click Delete Layer as shown in Figure 7.
- Click the name on the Layers palette, click the Delete layer button on the Layers palette, then click Yes in the warning box.
- Click the name on the Layers palette, press and hold [Alt] (Win) or [option] (Mac), then click the Delete layer button on the Layers palette.

- Drag the layer name on the Layers palette to the Delete layer button on the Layers palette.

You should be certain that you no longer need a layer before you delete it. If you delete a layer by accident, you can restore it during the current editing session by deleting the Delete Layer state on the History palette.

QUICKTIP

Photoshop always numbers layers sequentially, no matter how many layers you add or delete.

FIGURE 7

Layers palette menu

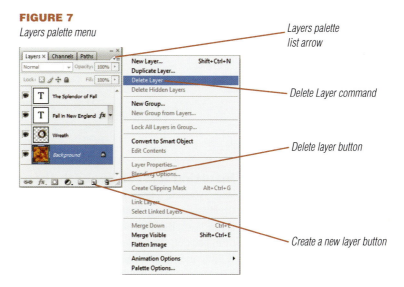

Layers palette list arrow

Delete Layer command

Delete layer button

Create a new layer button

Add a layer using the Layer menu

1. Click the **Fall in New England layer** on the Layers palette.

2. Click **Layer** on the menu bar, point to **New**, then click **Layer** to open the New Layer dialog box, as shown in Figure 8.

   A new layer will be added above the active layer.

   > **TIP** You can change the layer name in the New Layer dialog box before it appears on the Layers palette.

3. Click **OK**.

4. Drag the **History palette tab** over the Color palette until you see the drop zone (the light blue outline indicating where the palette will be placed), then release the mouse button.

5. Click **Window** on the menu bar, point to **Workspace**, click **Save Workspace** then type **History to Colors palette** (capture Palette Locations), then click **OK**.

6. Click the **Actions close button** in the Dock to close the Actions palette.

   The New Layer dialog box closes and the new layer appears above the Fall in New England layer on the Layers palette. The New Layer state is added to the History palette. See Figure 9.

You created a new layer above the Fall in New England layer using the New command on the Layer menu. The layer does not yet contain any content. You also relocated the History palette to make viewing your progress more convenient.

FIGURE 8
New Layer dialog box

Default name determined by existing layer names

Color list arrow

FIGURE 9
Relocated History palette and new layer in Layers palette

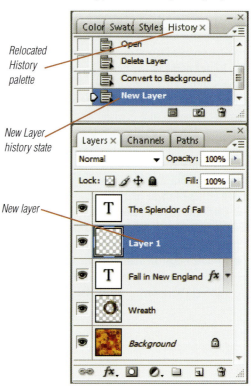

Relocated History palette

New Layer history state

New layer

Inserting a layer beneath the active layer

When you add a layer to an image either by using the Layer menu or clicking the Create a new layer button on the Layers palette, the new layer is inserted above the active layer. But there might be times when you want to insert the new layer beneath, or in back of, the active layer. You can do so easily, by pressing [Ctrl] (Win) or [Command] (Mac) while clicking the Create a new layer button on the Layers palette.

FIGURE 10

New layer with default settings

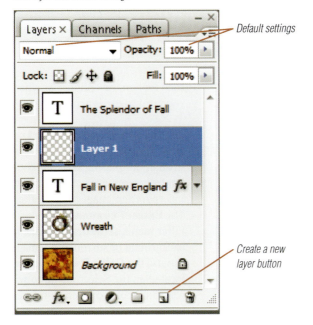

Default settings

Create a new
layer button

Delete a layer

1. Position the **Layer selection pointer** ✋ over Layer 1 on the Layers palette.

2. Drag **Layer 1** to the **Delete layer button** 🗑 on the Layers palette.

   TIP   You can also delete the layer by dragging the New Layer state on the History palette to the Delete current state button.

3. If the Delete the layer "Layer 1" dialog box opens, click the **Don't show again check box**, then click **Yes**.

   TIP   Many dialog boxes let you turn off this reminder feature by selecting the Don't show again check box. Selecting these check boxes can improve your efficiency.

You used the Delete layer button on the Layers palette to delete a layer.

Add a layer using the Layers palette

1. Click the **Fall in New England layer** on the Layers palette, if it is not already selected.

2. Click the **Create a new layer button** ⬛ on the Layers palette, then compare your Layers palette to Figure 10.

3. Save your work.

You used the Create a new layer button on the Layers palette to add a new layer.

Right-clicking for everyone (Mac)

Mac users, are you feeling left out because you can't right-click? If so, you'll welcome this news: anyone (yes, even Mac users!) can right-click simply by replacing the mouse that came with your computer with any two-button mouse that uses a USB connector. OS X was designed to recognize two-button mice without having to add software. Once you've switched mice, just plug and play! You can then right-click using the (Win) instructions in the steps.

ADD A SELECTION FROM ONE
IMAGE TO ANOTHER

What You'll Do

In this lesson, you'll use the Invert check box in the Color Range dialog box to make a selection, drag the selection to another image, and remove the fringe from a selection using the Defringe command.

Understanding Selections

Often the Photoshop file you want to create involves using an image or part of an image from another file. To use an image or part of an image, you must first select it. Photoshop refers to this as "making a selection." A selection is an area of an image surrounded by a **marquee**, a dashed line that surrounds the area you want to edit or move to another image, as shown in Figure 11. You can drag a marquee around a selection using four marquee tools: Rectangular Marquee, Elliptical Marquee, Single Row Marquee, and Single Column Marquee. Table 1 displays the four marquee tools and other selection tools. You can set options for each tool on the options bar when the tool you want to use is active.

Understanding the Extract and Color Range Commands

In addition to using selection tools, Photoshop provides other methods for incorporating imagery from other files. The **Extract command**, located on the Filter menu, separates an image from a background or surrounding imagery. You can use the **Color Range command**, located on the Select menu, to select a particular color contained in an existing image. Depending on the area you want, you can use the Color Range dialog box to extract a portion of an image.

Cropping an image

You might find an image that you really like, except that it contains a particular portion that you don't need. You can exclude, or **crop**, certain parts of an image by using the Crop Tool on the Tools palette. Cropping hides areas of an image from view *without* losing resolution quality. To crop an image, click the Crop Tool on the Tools palette, drag the pointer around the area you *want to keep*, then press [Enter] (Win) or [return] (Mac).

For example, you can select the Invert check box to choose one color and then select the portion of the image that is every color *except* that one. After you select all the imagery you want from another image, you can drag it into your open file.

Making a Selection and Moving a Selection

You can use a variety of methods and tools to make a selection, which can be used as a specific part of a layer or as the entire layer.

You use selections to isolate an area you want to alter. For example, you can use the Magnetic Lasso Tool to select complex shapes by clicking the starting point, tracing an approximate outline, then clicking the ending point. Later, you can use the Crop Tool to trim areas from a selection. When you use the Move Tool to drag a selection to the destination image, Photoshop places the selection in a new layer above the previously active layer.

Defringing Layer Contents

Sometimes when you make a selection, then move it into another image, the newly selected image can contain unwanted pixels that give the appearance of a fringe, or halo. You can remove this effect using a Matting command called Defringe. This command is available on the Layers menu and allows you to replace fringe pixels with the colors of other nearby pixels. You can determine a width for replacement pixels between 1 and 200. It's magic!

FIGURE 11
Marquee selections

Area selected using the Rectangular Marquee Tool

Specific element selected using the Magnetic Lasso Tool

TABLE 1: Selection Tools

tool	tool name	tool	tool name
⬚	Rectangular Marquee Tool	🔾	Lasso Tool
○	Elliptical Marquee Tool	⋈	Polygonal Lasso Tool
⋯	Single Row Marquee Tool	⋈	Magnetic Lasso Tool
┇	Single Column Marquee Tool	⬛	Eraser Tool
⌗	Crop Tool	⬛	Background Eraser Tool
✳	Magic Wand Tool	⬛	Magic Eraser Tool

Make a color range selection

1. Open PS 2-2.psd from the drive and folder where you store your Data Files, save it as **Gourds**, click the **title bar**, then drag the **window** to an empty area of the workspace so that you can see both images.

   TIP When more than one file is open, each has its own set of rulers.

2. Click **Select** on the menu bar, then click **Color Range**.

   TIP If the background color is solid, you can select the Invert check box to pick only the pixels in the image area.

3. Click the **Image option button**, then type **0** in the Fuzziness text box (or drag the **slider** all the way to the left until you see **0**).

4. Position the **Eyedropper pointer** 🖉 in the **white background** of the image in the Color Range dialog box, then click the **background**.

5. Select the **Invert check box**. Compare your dialog box to Figure 12.

6. Click **OK**, then compare your Gourds.psd image to Figure 13.

You opened a file and used the Color Range dialog box to select the image pixels by selecting the image's inverted colors. Selecting the inverse is an important skill in making selections.

FIGURE 12
Color Range dialog box

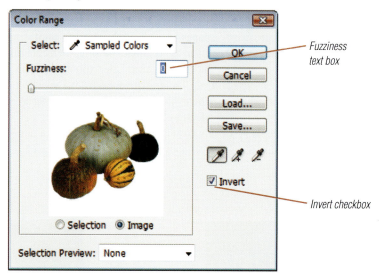

Fuzziness text box

Invert checkbox

FIGURE 13
Marquee surrounding selection

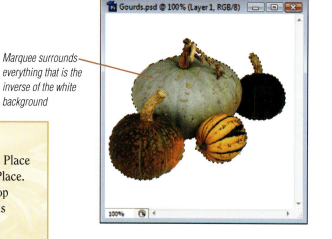

Marquee surrounds everything that is the inverse of the white background

Using the Place command

You can add an image from another image to a layer using the Place command. Place an image in a Photoshop layer by clicking File on the menu bar, then clicking Place. The placed artwork appears inside a bounding box at the center of the Photoshop image. The artwork maintains its original aspect ratio; however, if the artwork is larger than the Photoshop image, it is resized to fit.

FIGURE 14

Gourds image dragged to New England Fall image

White fringe
surrounds object

Document sizes
is selected

FIGURE 15

Gourds layer defringed

Gourds object
in image

Gourds moved to active
layer in image

Move a selection to another image

1. Click the **Move Tool** ⊹ on the Tools palette.

2. Position the **Move Tool pointer** ▶⊰ anywhere over the selection in the Gourds image.

3. Drag the **selection** to the New England Fall image, then release the mouse button.

   The Gourds image moves to the New England Fall file appearing on Layer 1.

4. If necessary, use the **Move Tool pointer** ▶⊹ to drag the **gourds** to the location at the lower-left corner of the wreath.

5. Click the **triangle** ▶ in the document window status bar, point to **Show**, then verify that Document Sizes is selected. Compare your image to Figure 14.

You dragged a selection from one image to another. You verified that the document size is displayed in the window.

Defringe the selection

1. Click **Layer** on the menu bar, point to **Matting**, then click **Defringe**. Defringing a selection gets rid of the halo effect that sometimes occurs when objects are dragged from one image to another.

2. Type **2** in the Width text box, then click **OK**.

3. Save your work.

4. Close **Gourds.psd**, then compare the New England Fall image to Figure 15.

You removed the fringe from a selection.

ORGANIZE LAYERS WITH
LAYER GROUPS AND COLORS

What You'll Do

▶ In this lesson, you'll use the Layers palette menu to create, name, and color a layer group, and then add layers to it. You'll add finishing touches to the image, save it as a copy, then flatten it.

Understanding Layer Groups

A **layer group** is a Photoshop feature that allows you to organize your layers on the Layers palette. A layer group contains individual layers. For example, you can create a layer group that contains all the type layers in your image. To create a layer group, you click the Layers palette list arrow, then click New Group. As with layers, it is helpful to choose a descriptive name for a layer group.

Organizing Layers into Groups

After you create a layer group, you simply drag layers on the Layers palette directly on top of the layer group. You can remove layers from a layer group by dragging them out of the layer group to a new location on the Layers palette or by deleting them. Some changes made to a layer group, such as blending mode or opacity changes, affect every layer in the layer group. You can choose to expand or collapse layer groups, depending on the amount of information you need to see. Expanding a layer group

Duplicating a layer
When you add a new layer by clicking the Create a new layer button on the Layers palette, the new layer contains default settings. However, you might want to create a new layer that has the same settings as an existing layer. You can do so by duplicating an existing layer to create a copy of that layer and its settings. Duplicating a layer is also a good way to preserve your modifications, because you can modify the duplicate layer and not worry about losing your original work. To create a duplicate layer, select the layer you want to copy, click the Layers palette list arrow, click Duplicate Layer, then click OK. The new layer will appear above the original.

shows all of the layers in the layer group, and collapsing a layer group hides all of the layers in a layer group. You can expand or collapse a layer group by clicking the triangle to the left of the layer group icon. Figure 16 shows one expanded layer group and one collapsed layer group.

Adding Color to a Layer

If your image has relatively few layers, it's easy to locate the layers. However, if your image contains many layers, you might need some help in organizing them. You can organize layers by color-coding them, which makes it easy to find the group you want, regardless of its location on the Layers palette. For example, you can put all type layers in red or put the layers associated with a particular portion of an image in blue. To color the Background layer, you must first convert it to a regular layer.

Flattening an Image

After you make all the necessary modifications to your image, you can greatly reduce the file size by flattening the image. **Flattening** merges all visible layers into a single Background layer and discards all hidden layers. Make sure that all layers that you want to display are visible before you flatten the image. Because flattening removes an image's individual layers, it's a good idea to make a copy of the original image *before* it is flattened. The status bar displays the file's current size and the size it will be when flattened. If you work on a Macintosh, you'll find this information in the lower-left corner of the document window.

FIGURE 16
Layer groups

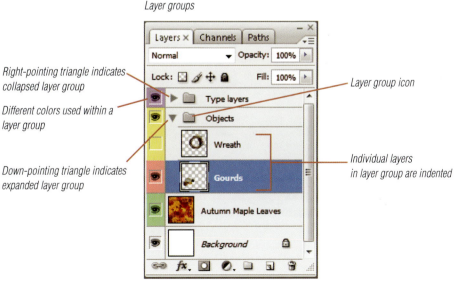

Right-pointing triangle indicates collapsed layer group

Different colors used within a layer group

Down-pointing triangle indicates expanded layer group

Layer group icon

Individual layers in layer group are indented

Understanding Layer Comps

The ability to create a **layer comp**, a variation on the arrangement and visibility of existing layers, is a powerful tool that can make your work more organized. You can create a layer comp by clicking the Layer Comps button on the Dock, then clicking the Create New Layer Comp button on the palette. The New Layer Comp dialog box, shown in Figure 17, opens, allowing you to name the layer comp and set parameters.

Using Layer Comps

Multiple layer comps, shown in Figure 18, make it easy to switch back and forth between variations on an image theme. Say, for example, that you want to show a client multiple arrangements of layers. The layer comp is an ideal tool for this.

FIGURE 17
New Layer Comp dialog box

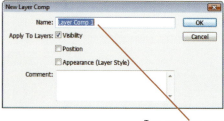

Type new comp name

FIGURE 18
Multiple Layer Comps in image

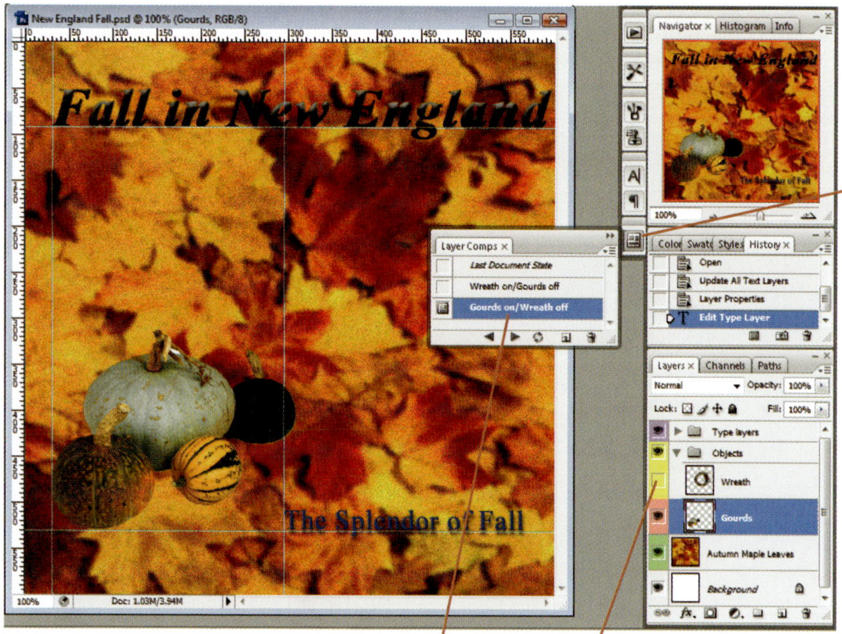

Layer Comps button

Active layer comp

Layer hidden in active layer comp

FIGURE 19
New Group dialog box

New layer group name

Color list arrow

FIGURE 20
New layer group in Layers palette

New layer group

FIGURE 21
Layers added to the All Type layer group

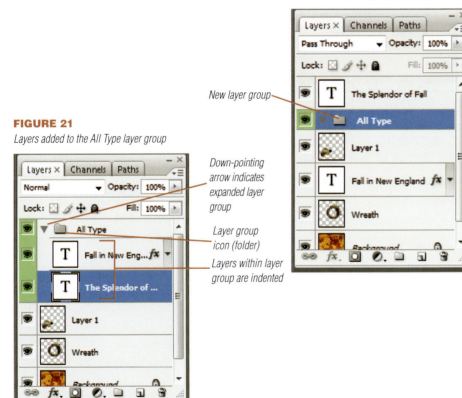

Down-pointing arrow indicates expanded layer group

Layer group icon (folder)

Layers within layer group are indented

Create a layer group

1. Verify that **Layer 1** is active, click the **Layers palette list arrow** ▾☰, then click **New Group**.

   The New Group dialog box opens, as shown in Figure 19.

   TIP Photoshop automatically places a new layer group above the active layer.

2. Type **All Type** in the Name text box.

3. Click the **Color list arrow**, click **Green**, then click **OK**.

   The New Group dialog box closes. Compare your Layers palette to Figure 20.

You used the Layers palette menu to create a layer group, then named and applied a color to it. This new group will contain all the type layers in the image.

Move layers to the layer group

1. Click the **Fall in New England type layer** on the Layers palette, then drag it on to the **All Type layer group**.

2. Click the **The Splendor of Fall type layer**, drag it on to the **All Type layer group**, then compare your Layers palette to Figure 21.

   TIP If the Splendor of Fall layer is not below the Fall in New England layer, move the layers to match Figure 21.

3. Click the **triangle** ▾ to the left of the layer group icon (folder) to collapse the layer group.

You created a layer group, then moved two layers into that layer group. Creating layer groups is a great organization tool, especially in complex images with many layers.

Rename a layer and adjust opacity

1. Double-click **Layer 1**, type **Gourds**, then press **[Enter]** (Win) or **[return]** (Mac).

2. Double-click the **Opacity text box** on the Layers palette, type **75**, then press **[Enter]** (Win) or **[return]** (Mac).

3. Drag the **Gourds layer** beneath the Wreath layer, then compare your image to Figure 22.

4. Save your work.

You renamed the new layer, adjusted opacity, and rearranged layers.

Create layer comps

1. Click the **Layer Comps button** on the Dock.

2. Click the **Create New Layer Comp button** on the Layer Comps palette.

3. Type **Gourds on/Wreath off** in the Name text box, as shown in Figure 23, then click **OK**.

4. Click the **Indicates layer visibility button** on the Wreath layer.

5. Click the **Update Layer Comp button** on the Layer Comps palette. Compare your Layer Comps palette to Figure 24.

6. Save your work, then click the **Layer Comps button** on the Dock to close the Layer Comps palette.

You created a Layer Comp in an existing image.

FIGURE 22
Finished image

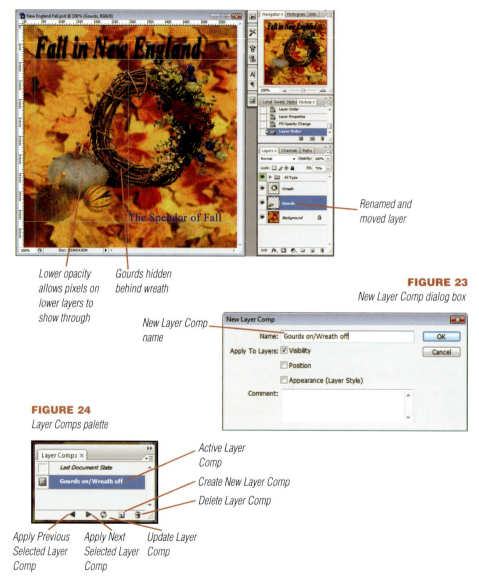

Lower opacity allows pixels on lower layers to show through

Gourds hidden behind wreath

Renamed and moved layer

FIGURE 23
New Layer Comp dialog box

New Layer Comp name

FIGURE 24
Layer Comps palette

Active Layer Comp

Create New Layer Comp

Delete Layer Comp

Apply Previous Selected Layer Comp

Apply Next Selected Layer Comp

Update Layer Comp

FIGURE 25

Save As dialog box

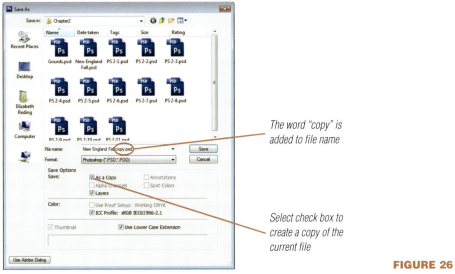

The word "copy" is added to file name

Select check box to create a copy of the current file

FIGURE 26

Flattened image layer

Flattened file size

Flattened image contains one layer

Flatten an image

1. Click **File** on the menu bar, then click **Save As**.

2. Click the **As a Copy check box** to add a checkmark, then compare your dialog box to Figure 25.

   TIP If "copy" does not display in the File name text box, click this text box and type copy to add it to the name.

3. Click **Save**.

   Photoshop saves and closes a copy of the file containing all the layers and effects.

4. Click **Layer** on the menu bar, then click **Flatten Image**.

5. Click **OK** in the warning box, if necessary, then save your work.

6. Compare your Layers palette to Figure 26.

7. Click **Window** on the menu bar, point to **Workspace,** then click **Reset Palette Locations** to Reset palette locations to the workspace.

8. Close all open images, then exit Photoshop.

You saved the file as a copy, and then flattened the image. The image now has a single layer.

Lesson 4   Organize Layers with Layer Groups and Colors

PHOTOSHOP 2-21

Power User Shortcuts

to do this:	use this method:
Adjust layer opacity	Click Opacity list arrow on Layers palette, drag opacity slider or Double-click Opacity text box, type a percentage
Change measurements	Right-click (Win) or [Ctrl]-click (Mac) ruler
Color a layer	Layers palette list arrow, Layer Properties, Color list arrow
Create a layer comp	Click Layer Comps button 🔲
Create a layer group	▾☰, New Group
Delete a layer	🗑
Defringe a selection	Layer ➢ Matting ➢ Defringe

to do this:	use this method:
Flatten an image	Layer ➢ Flatten Image
Move Tool	►⊕ or **V**
New Background layer from existing layer	Layer ➢ New ➢ Background From Layer
New layer	Layer ➢ New ➢ Layer or 🔲
Rename a layer	Double-click layer name, type new name
Select color range	Select ➢ Color Range
Show/Hide Rulers	View ➢ Rulers [Ctrl][R] (Win) ⌘[R] (Mac)
Update a layer comp	🔄

Key: Menu items are indicated by ➢ between the menu name and its command. Blue bold letters are shortcuts for selecting tools on the Tools palette.

Examine and convert layers.

1. Start Photoshop.
2. Open PS 2-3.psd from the drive and folder where you store your Data Files, update any text layers, if necessary, then save it as **Music Store**.
3. Make sure the rulers appear and that pixels are the unit of measurement.
4. Delete the Background layer.
5. Verify that the Rainbow blend layer is active, then convert the image layer to a Background layer.
6. Save your work.

Add and delete layers.

1. Make Layer 2 active.
2. Create a new layer above this layer using the Layer menu.
3. Accept the default name (Layer 4), and change the color of the layer to Red.
4. Delete Layer 4.
5. Make Layer 2 active (if it is not already the active layer), then create a new layer using the Create a new layer button on the Layers palette.
6. Save your work.

Add a selection from one image to another.

1. Open PS 2-4.psd.
2. Reposition this image of a horn by dragging the window to the right of the Music Store image.
3. Open the Color Range dialog box. (*Hint*: Use the Select menu.)

4. Verify that the Image option button is selected, the Invert check box is selected, and that Fuzziness is set to 0.
5. Sample the white background in the preview window in the dialog box, then close the dialog box.
6. Use the Move Tool to drag the selection into the Music Store image.
7. Position the selection so that the upper-left edge of the instrument matches the sample shown in Figure 27.
8. Defringe the horn selection (in the Music Store image) using a 3 pixel width.
9. Close PS 2-4.psd.
10. Drag Layer 4 above Layer 3.
11. Rename Layer 4 **Horn**.
12. Change the opacity for the Horn layer to 55%.
13. Drag the Horn layer so it is beneath Layer 2.
14. Hide Layer 1.
15. Hide the rulers.
16. Save your work.

Organize layers with layer groups and colors.

1. Create a Layer Group called **Type Layers** and assign the color yellow to the group.
2. Drag the following layers into the Type Layers folder: Allegro, Music Store, Layer 2.
3. Delete Layer 2, then collapse the Layer Group folder.
4. Move the Notes layer beneath the Horn layer.
5. Create a layer comp called **Notes layer**.
6. Update the layer comp.
7. Hide the Notes layer.
8. Create a new layer comp called **Notes layer off**, then update the layer comp.
9. Display the previous layer comp, then save your work.
10. Save a copy of the Music Store file using the default naming scheme (add 'copy' to the end of the existing filename).
11. Flatten the original image. (*Hint*: Be sure to discard hidden layers.)
12. Save your work, then compare your image to Figure 27.

FIGURE 27

Completed Skills Review

A credit union is developing a hotline for members to use to help abate credit card fraud as soon as it occurs. They're going to distribute 10,000 refrigerator magnets over the next three weeks. As part of their effort to build community awareness of the project, they've sponsored a contest for the magnet design. You decide to enter the contest.

1. Open PS 2-5.psd, then save it as **Outlaw Fraud**. The Palatino Linotype font is used in this file. Please make a substitution if this font is not available on your computer.
2. Open PS 2-6.psd, use the Color Range dialog box or any selection tool on the Tools palette to select the cell phone image, then drag it to the Outlaw Fraud image.
3. Rename the newly created layer **Cell Phone**, if necessary, then apply a color to the layer on the Layers palette. Make sure the Cell Phone layer is beneath the type layer.
4. Convert the Background layer to an image layer, then rename it **Banner**.
5. Change the opacity of the Banner layer to any setting you like.
6. Defringe the Cell Phone layer using the pixel width of your choice.
7. Save your work, then compare your image to the sample shown in Figure 28.

FIGURE 28
Completed Project Builder 1

Your local 4-H chapter wants to promote its upcoming fair and has hired you to create a promotional billboard commemorating this event. The Board of Directors decides that the billboard should be humorous.

1. Open PS 2-7.psd, then save it as **4H Billboard**. Substitute any missing fonts.
2. Open PS 2-8.psd, use the Color Range dialog box or any selection tool on the Tools palette to create a marquee around the llama, then drag the selection to the 4-H Billboard image.
3. Name the new layer **Llama**.
4. Change the opacity of the Llama layer to 90%.
5. Save your work, then compare your image to the sample shown in Figure 29.

FIGURE 29
Completed Project Builder 2

A friend of yours has designed a new heat-absorbing coffee cup for take-out orders. She is going to present the prototype to a prospective vendor, but first needs to print a brochure. She's asked you to design an eye-catching cover.

1. Open PS 2-9.psd, update the text layers if necessary, then save it as **Coffee Cover**. The Garamond font is used in this file. Please make a substitution if this font is not available on your computer.
2. Open PS 2-10.psd, then drag the entire image to Coffee Cover.
3. Close PS 2-10.psd.
4. Rename Layer 1 with the name **Mocha**.
5. Delete the Background layer and convert the Mocha layer into a new Background layer.
6. Reposition the layer objects so they look like the sample. (*Hint*: You might have to reorganize the layers in the stack so all layers are visible.)
7. Create a layer group above the Love that coffee layer, name it **Java Text**, apply a color of your choice to the layer group, then drag the type layers to it.
8. Save your work, then compare your image to Figure 30.

FIGURE 30
Completed Design Project

Depending on the size of your group, you can assign individual elements of the project to group members, or work collectively to create the finished product.

Harvest Market, a line of natural food stores, and the trucking associations in your state have formed a coalition to deliver fresh fruit and vegetables to food banks and other food distribution programs. The truckers want to promote the project by displaying a sign on their trucks. The only design requirement is that you use the Harvest Market vegetable logo as the background, keeping in mind that it needs to be seen from a distance.

1. Open PS 2-11.psd, then save it as **Organic Market**. Update the text layers as necessary.
2. Have some members of the group obtain at least two images of different-sized produce. You can obtain images by using what is available on your computer, scanning print media, or connecting to the Internet and downloading images.
3. Other members of the group can open one of the produce files, select it, then drag or copy it to the Organic Market image. (*Hint*: Experiment with some of the other selection tools. Note that some tools require you to copy and paste the image after you select it.)
4. Let other members of the group repeat step 3 then close the two produce image files.

5. Set the opacity of the Market layer to 70%.
6. Arrange the layers so that smaller images appear on top of the larger ones.
7. Create a layer group for the type layers, and apply a color to it.
8. Save your work, then compare your image to Figure 31.

9. Be prepared to discuss the advantages and disadvantages of using multiple images. How would you assess the ease and efficiency of the selection techniques you've learned? Which styles did you apply to the type layers, and why?

FIGURE 31
Completed Group Project

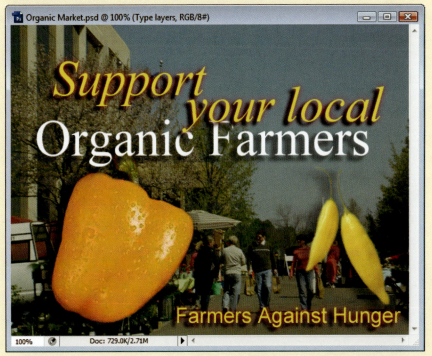

chapter

3

MAKING
SELECTIONS

1. Make a selection using shapes

2. Modify a marquee

3. Select using color and modify a selection

4. Add a vignette effect to a selection

Combining Images

Most Photoshop images are created using a technique called **compositing**—combining images from different sources. These sources include other Photoshop images, royalty-free images, pictures taken with digital cameras, and scanned artwork. How you get all that artwork into your Photoshop images is an art unto itself. You can include additional images by using tools on the Tools palette and menu commands. And to work with all these images, you need to know how to select them—or exactly the parts you want to work with.

Understanding Selection Tools

The two basic methods you can use to make selections are using a tool or using color. You can use three freeform tools to create your own unique selections, four fixed area tools to create circular or rec-tangular selections, and a wand tool to make selections using color. In addition, you can use menu commands to increase or decrease selections that you made with these tools, or you can make selections based on color.

Understanding Which Selection Tool to Use

With so many tools available, how do you know which one to use? After you know the different selection options, you'll learn how to look at images and evaluate selection opportunities. With experience, you'll learn how to identify edges that can be used to isolate imagery, and how to spot colors that can be used to isolate a specific object.

Combining Imagery

After you decide on an object that you want to place in a Photoshop image, you can add the object to another image by cutting, copying, and pasting, dragging and dropping objects using the Move Tool, and using the **Clipboard**, the temporary storage area provided by your operating system.

Tools You'll Use

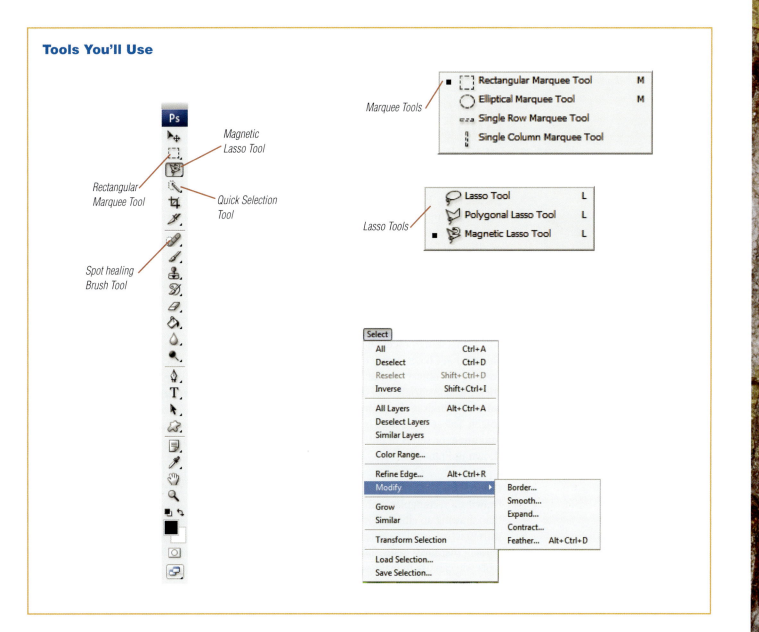

Marquee Tools

- ■ ⬚ Rectangular Marquee Tool   M
- ○ Elliptical Marquee Tool   M
- ⋯ Single Row Marquee Tool
- ▯ Single Column Marquee Tool

Magnetic Lasso Tool

Rectangular Marquee Tool

Quick Selection Tool

Spot healing Brush Tool

Lasso Tools

- ○ Lasso Tool   L
- ▽ Polygonal Lasso Tool   L
- ■ ▽ Magnetic Lasso Tool   L

Select

All	Ctrl+A
Deselect	Ctrl+D
Reselect	Shift+Ctrl+D
Inverse	Shift+Ctrl+I
All Layers	Alt+Ctrl+A
Deselect Layers	
Similar Layers	
Color Range...	
Refine Edge...	Alt+Ctrl+R
Modify	►
Grow	
Similar	
Transform Selection	
Load Selection...	
Save Selection...	

Modify ►
- Border...
- Smooth...
- Expand...
- Contract...
- Feather...   Alt+Ctrl+D

MAKE A SELECTION
USING SHAPES

What You'll Do

▶ *In this lesson, you'll make selections using a marquee tool and a lasso tool, position a selection with the Move Tool, deselect a selection, and drag a complex selection into another image.*

Selecting by Shape

The Photoshop selection tools make it easy to select objects that are rectangular or elliptical in nature. It would be a boring world if every image we wanted fell into one of those categories so fortunately, they don't. While some objects are round or square, most are unusual in shape. Making selections can sometimes be a painstaking process because many objects don't have clearly defined edges. To select an object by shape, you need to click the appropriate tool on the Tools palette, then drag the pointer around the object. The selected area is defined by a **marquee**, or series of dotted lines, as shown in Figure 1.

Creating a Selection

Drawing a rectangular marquee is easier than drawing an elliptical marquee, but with practice, you'll be able to create both types of marquees easily. Table 1 lists the tools you can use to make selections using

shapes. Figure 2 shows a marquee surrounding an irregular shape.

QUICKTIP

A marquee is sometimes referred to as *marching ants* because the dots within the marquee appear to be moving.

Using Fastening Points

Each time you click one of the marquee tools, a fastening point is added to the image. A **fastening point** is an anchor within the marquee. When the marquee pointer reaches the initial fastening point (after making its way around the image), a very small circle appears on the pointer, indicating that you have reached the starting point. Clicking the pointer when this circle appears closes the marquee. Some fastening points, such as those in a circular marquee, are not visible, while others, such as those created by the Polygonal or Magnetic Lasso Tools, are visible.

Selecting, Deselecting, and Reselecting

After a selection is made, you can move, copy, transform, or make adjustments to it. A selection stays selected until you unselect, or **deselect**, it. You can deselect a selection by clicking Select on the menu bar, then clicking Deselect. You can reselect a deselected object by clicking Select on the menu bar, then clicking Reselect.

QUICKTIP

You can select the entire image by clicking Select on the menu bar, then clicking All.

FIGURE 1
Elliptical Marquee Tool used to create marquee

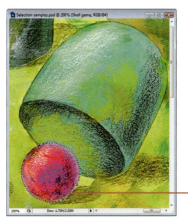

Elliptical Marquee
Tool surrounds
object

QUICKTIP

Correcting a Selection Error

At some point, you'll spend a lot of time making a complex selection only to realize that the wrong layer was active. Remember the History palette? Every action you do is automatically recorded, and you can use the selection state to retrace your steps and recoup the time spent. Your fix may be as simple as selecting the proper History state and changing the active layer in the Layers palette.

TABLE 1: Selection Tools by Shape

tool	button	effect
Rectangular Marquee Tool		Creates a rectangular selection. Press [Shift] while dragging to create a square.
Elliptical Marquee Tool		Creates an elliptical selection. Press [Shift] while dragging to create a circle.
Single Row Marquee Tool		Creates a 1-pixel-wide row selection.
Single Column Marquee Tool		Creates a 1-pixel-wide column selection.
Lasso Tool		Creates a freehand selection.
Polygonal Lasso Tool		Creates straight line selections. Press [Alt] (Win) or [option] (Mac) to create freehand segments.
Magnetic Lasso Tool		Creates selections that snap to an edge of an object. Press [Alt] (Win) or [option] (Mac) to alternate between freehand and magnetic line segments.

FIGURE 2
Marquee surrounding irregular shape

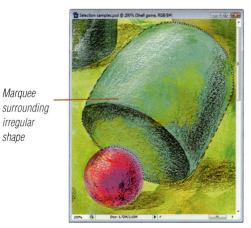

Marquee
surrounding
irregular
shape

Placing a Selection

You can place a selection in a Photoshop image in many ways. You can copy or cut a selection, then paste it to a different location in the same image or to a different image. You can also use the Move Tool to drag a selection to a new location.

QUICKTIP

You can temporarily change *any selected tool* into the Move Tool by pressing and holding [Ctrl] (Win) or ⌘ (Mac). When you're finished dragging the selection, release [Ctrl] (Win) or ⌘ (Mac), and the functionality of the originally selected tool returns.

Using Guides

Guides are non-printing horizontal and vertical lines that you can display on top of an image to help you position a selection. You can create an unlimited number of horizontal and vertical guides. You create a guide by displaying the rulers, positioning the pointer on either ruler, then clicking and dragging the guide into position. Figure 3 shows the creation of a vertical guide in a file that contains two existing guides. You delete a guide by selecting the Move Tool on the Tools palette, positioning the pointer over the guide, then clicking and dragging it back

to its ruler. If the Snap feature is enabled, as you drag an object toward a guide, the object will be pulled toward the guide. To turn on the Snap feature, click View on the menu bar, then click Snap. A check mark appears to the left of the command if the feature is enabled.

QUICKTIP

Double-click a guide to open the Preferences dialog box to change guide colors, width, and other features.

FIGURE 3
Creating guides in image

FIGURE 4
Rectangular Marquee Tool selection

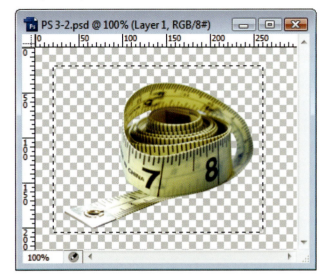

TABLE 2: Working with a Selection

if you want to	then do this
Move a selection (an image) using the mouse	Position the ⊕ over the selection, then drag the marquee and its contents
Copy a selection to the Clipboard	Activate image containing the selection, click Edit ➢ Copy
Cut a selection to the Clipboard	Activate image containing the selection, click Edit ➢ Cut
Paste a selection from the Clipboard	Activate image where you want the selection, click Edit ➢ Paste
Delete a selection	Make selection, then press [Delete] (Win) or [delete] (Mac)
Deselect a selection	Press [Esc] (Win) or [D] (Mac)

Create a selection with the Rectangular Marquee Tool

1. Start Photoshop, open PS 3-1.psd from the drive and folder where you store your Data Files, then save it as **Sewing Box**.

2. Display the rulers (if they are not already displayed) in pixels.

3. Open PS 3-2.psd, then display the rulers in pixels for this image (if they are not displayed).

4. Click the **Rectangular Marquee Tool** ⬚ on the Tools palette.

5. Make sure the value in the Feather text box on the options bar is **0 px**.

   Feathering determines the amount of blur between the selection and the pixels surrounding it.

6. Drag the **Marquee pointer** ╋ to select the tape measure from approximately **20 H/20 V** to **260 H/210 V**. See Figure 4.

   The first measurement refers to the horizontal ruler (H); the second measurement refers to the vertical ruler (V).

   TIP   You can also use the X/Y coordinates displayed in the Info palette (in the group with the Navigator and Histogram palettes).

7. Click the **Move Tool** ⊕ on the Tools palette, then drag the selection to any location in the Sewing Box image.

   The selection now appears in the Sewing Box image on a new layer (Layer 1).

   TIP   Table 2 describes methods you can use to work with selections in an image.

Using the Rectangular Marquee Tool, you created a selection in an image, then you dragged that selection into another image. This left the original image intact, and created a copy of the selection in the image you dragged it to.

Position a selection with the Move Tool

1. Verify that the **Move Tool** ⊕ is selected on the Tools palette.

2. If you do not see guides in the Sewing Box image, click **View** on the menu bar, point to **Show**, then click **Guides**.

3. Drag the **tape measure** so that the top-right corner snaps to the ruler guides at approximately **1030 H/230 V**. Compare your image to Figure 5.

    Did you feel the snap to effect as you positioned the selection within the guides? This feature makes it easy to properly position objects within an image.

    > TIP If you didn't feel the image snap to the guides, click View on the menu bar, point to Snap To, then click Guides.

4. Rename Layer 1 **Tape Measure**.

You used the Move Tool to reposition a selection in an existing image, then you renamed the layer.

FIGURE 5
Rectangular selection in image

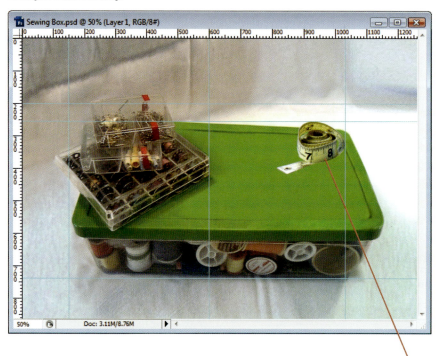

Tape measure

Using Smart Guides

Wouldn't it be great to be able to see a vertical or horizontal guide as you move an object? Using Smart Guides, you can do just that. Smart Guides are turned on by clicking View on the menu bar, pointing to Show, then clicking Smart Guides. Once this feature is turned on, horizontal and vertical purple guide lines appear automatically when you draw a shape or move an object. This feature allows you to align layer content as you move it.

FIGURE 6
Deselect command

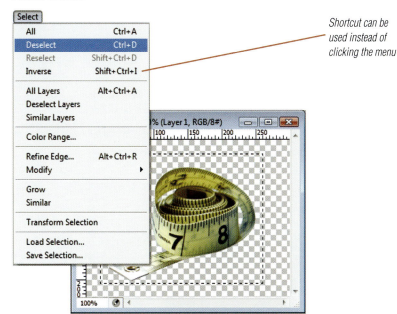

Shortcut can be
used instead of
clicking the menu

Deselect a selection

1. Click **Window** on the menu bar, then click **PS 3-2.psd**.

   TIP   If you can see the window of the image you want anywhere on the screen, you can just click it to make it active instead of using the Window menu.

2. Click **Select** on the menu bar, then click **Deselect**, as shown in Figure 6.

You hid the active layer, then used the Deselect command on the Select menu to deselect the object you had moved into this image. When you deselect a selection, the marquee no longer surrounds it.

FIGURE 7
Save Selection dialog box

Saving and loading a selection

Any selection can be saved independently of the surrounding image, so that if you want to use it again in the image, you can do so without having to retrace it using one of the marquee tools. Once a selection is made, you can save it in the image by clicking Select on the menu bar, then clicking Save Selection. The Save Selection dialog box opens, as shown in Figure 7; be sure to give the selection a meaningful name. When you want to load a saved selection, click Select on the menu bar, then click Load Selection. Click the Channel list arrow, click the named selection, then click OK.

Create a selection with the Magnetic Lasso Tool

1. Click the **Magnetic Lasso Tool** on the Tools palette, then change the settings on the options bar so that they are the same as those shown in Figure 8. Table 3 describes Magnetic Lasso Tool settings.

2. Open PS 3-3.psd from the drive and folder where you store your Data Files.

3. Click the **Magnetic Lasso Tool pointer** once anywhere on the edge of the pin cushion, to create your first fastening point.

    TIP If you click on a spot that is not at the edge of the pin cushion, press [Esc] (win) or ⌘ [Z] (Mac) to undo the action, then start again.

4. Drag the **Magnetic Lasso Tool pointer** slowly around the pin cushion (clicking at the top of each pin may be helpful) until it is almost entirely selected, then click directly over the initial fastening point. See Figure 9.

    Don't worry about all the nooks and crannies surrounding the pin cushion: the Magnetic Lasso Tool will select those automatically. You will see a small circle next to the pointer when it is directly over the initial fastening point, indicating that you are closing the selection. The individual segments turn into a marquee.

    TIP If you feel that the Magnetic Lasso Tool is missing some major details while you're tracing, you can insert additional fastening points by clicking the pointer while dragging. For example, click the mouse button at a location where you want to change the selection shape.

You created a selection with the Magnetic Lasso Tool.

FIGURE 8
Options for the Magnetic Lasso Tool

FIGURE 9
Creating a selection with the Magnetic Lasso Tool

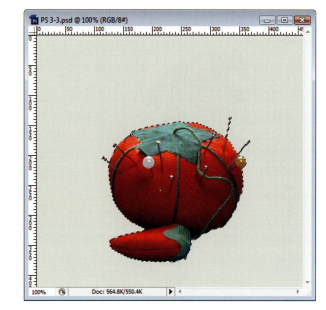

Mastering the art of selections

You might feel that it is difficult when you first start making selections. Making selections is a skill, and like most skills, it takes a lot of practice to become proficient. In addition to practice, make sure that you're comfortable in your work area, that your hands are steady, and that your mouse is working well. A non-optical mouse that is dirty will make selecting an onerous task, so make sure your mouse is well cared for and is functioning correctly.

FIGURE 10

Selection copied into image

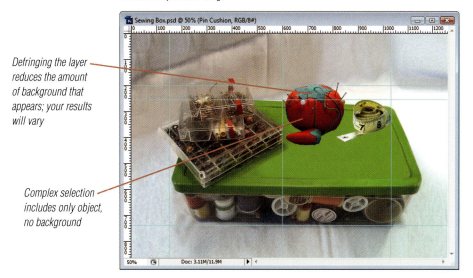

Defringing the layer reduces the amount of background that appears; your results will vary

Complex selection includes only object, no background

TABLE 3: Magnetic Lasso Tool Settings

setting	description
Feather	The amount of blur between the selection and the pixels surrounding it. This setting is measured in pixels and can be a value between 0 and 250.
Anti-alias	The smoothness of the selection, achieved by softening the color transition between edge and background pixels.
Width	The interior width by detecting an edge from the pointer. This setting is measured in pixels and can have a value from 1 to 40.
Edge Contrast	The tool's sensitivity. This setting can be a value between 1% and 100%: higher values detect high-contrast edges.
Frequency	The rate at which fastening points are applied. This setting can be a value between 0 and 100: higher values insert more fastening points.

Move a complex selection to an existing image

1. Click the **Move Tool** ⊕ on the Tools palette.

   TIP   You can also click the Click to open the Tool Preset picker list arrow on the options bar, then double-click the Move Tool.

2. Use the **Move Tool pointer** ▶ to drag the pin cushion selection to the Sewing Box image.

   The selection appears on a new layer (Layer 1).

3. Drag the object so that the left edge of the pin cushion snaps to the guide at approximately **600 Y** and the top of the pin cushion snaps to the guide at **200 X** using the coordinates on the info palette.

4. Use the Layer menu to defringe the new Layer 1 at a width of **1** pixel.

5. Close the PS 3-3.psd image without saving your changes.

6. Rename the new layer **Pin Cushion** in the Sewing Box image.

7. Save your work, then compare your image to Figure 10.

8. Click **Window** on the menu bar, then click **PS 3-2.psd**.

9. Close the PS 3-2.psd image without saving your changes.

You dragged a complex selection into an existing Photoshop image. You positioned the object using ruler guides and renamed a layer. You also defringed a selection to eliminate its white border.

MODIFY A MARQUEE

What You'll Do

In this lesson, you'll move and enlarge a marquee, drag a selection into a Photoshop image, then position a selection using ruler guides.

Changing the Size of a Marquee

Not all objects are easy to select. Sometimes, when you make a selection, you might need to change the size or shape of the marquee.

The options bar contains selection buttons that help you add to and subtract from a marquee, or intersect with a selection. The marquee in Figure 11 was modified into the one shown in Figure 12 by clicking the Add to selection button. After the Add to selection button is active, you can draw an additional marquee (directly adjacent to the selection), and it will be added to the current marquee.

One method you can use to increase the size of a marquee is the Grow command. After you make a selection, you can increase the marquee size by clicking Select on the menu bar, then by clicking Grow. The Grow command selects pixels adjacent to the marquee that have colors

similar to those specified by the Magic Wand Tool. The Similar command selects both adjacent and non-adjacent pixels.

QUICKTIP

While the Grow command selects adjacent pixels that have similar colors, the Expand command increases a selection by a specific number of pixels.

Modifying a Marquee

While a selection is active, you can modify the marquee by expanding or contracting it, smoothing out its edges, or enlarging it to add a border around the selection. These four commands: Border, Smooth, Expand, and Contract are sub-menus of the Modify command, which is found on the Select menu. For example, you might want to enlarge your selection. Using the Expand command, you can increase the size of the selection, as shown in Figure 13.

Moving a Marquee

After you create a marquee, you can move the marquee to another location in the same image or to another image entirely. You might want to move a marquee if you've drawn it in the wrong image or the wrong location. Sometimes it's easier to draw a marquee elsewhere on the page, and then move it to the desired location.

> **QUICK**TIP
>
> You can always hide and display layers as necessary to facilitate making a selection.

FIGURE 12
Selection with additions

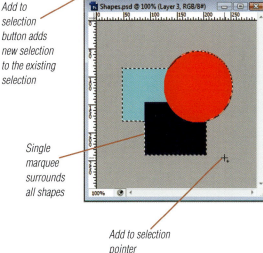

Add to selection button adds new selection to the existing selection

Single marquee surrounds all shapes

Add to selection pointer

FIGURE 11
New selection

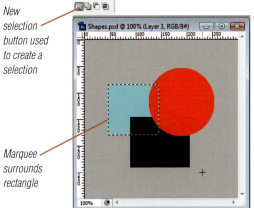

New selection button used to create a selection

Marquee surrounds rectangle

Using the Quick Selection Tool

The Quick Selection Tool lets you paint-to-select an object from the interior using a resizeable brush. As you paint the object, the selection grows. Using the Auto-Enhance check box, rough edges and blockiness are automatically reduced to give you a perfect selection. As with other selection tools, the Quick Selection Tool has options to add and subtract from your selection.

FIGURE 13
Expanded selection

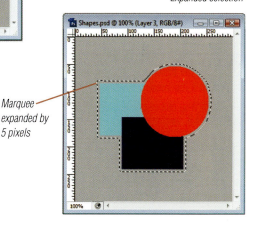

Marquee expanded by 5 pixels

Adding and subtracting from a selection

Of course knowing how to make a selection is important, but it's just as important to know how to make alterations in an existing selection. Sometimes it's almost impossible to create that perfect marquee at first try. Perhaps your hand moved while you were tracing, or you just got distracted. Using the Add to selection, Subtract from selection, and Intersect with selection buttons (which appear with all selection tools), you can alter an existing marquee without having to start from scratch.

Move and enlarge a marquee

1. Open PS 3-4.psd from the drive and folder where you store your Data Files. Change the zoom factor to **200%**.

2. Click the **Elliptical Marquee Tool** on the Tools palette.

   TIP The Elliptical Marquee Tool might be hidden under the Rectangular Marquee Tool.

3. Click the **New selection button** on the options bar (if it is not already selected).

4. Drag the **Marquee pointer** ✛ to select the area from approximately **150 X/50 Y** to **200 X/130 Y**. Compare your image to Figure 14.

5. Position the **pointer** ▷ in the center of the selection.

6. Drag the **Move pointer** ▶ so the marquee covers the thimble, at approximately **100 X/100 Y**, as shown in Figure 15.

   TIP You can also nudge a selection to move it, by pressing the arrow keys. Each time you press an arrow key, the selection moves one pixel in the direction of the arrow.

7. Click the **Magic Wand Tool** ✎ on the Tools palette, then select a Tolerance of **16**, and select the **Anti-alias** and **Contiguous checkboxes**.

8. Click **Select** on the menu bar, then click **Similar**.

9. Click **Select** on the menu bar, point to **Modify**, then click **Expand**.

10. Type **1** in the Expand By text box of the Expand Selection dialog box, then click **OK**.

11. Deselect the selection.

You created a marquee, then dragged the marquee to reposition it. You then enlarged a selection marquee by using the Similar and Expand commands.

FIGURE 14
Selection in image

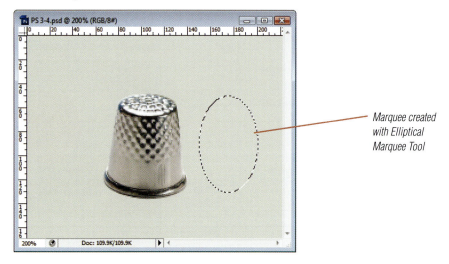

Marquee created with Elliptical Marquee Tool

FIGURE 15
Moved selection

New marquee location

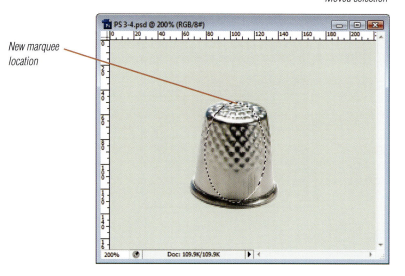

FIGURE 16
Quick Selection Tool settings

FIGURE 17
Selection in file

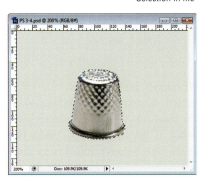

FIGURE 18
Selection moved to the Sewing Box image

Use the Quick Selection Tool

1. Click the **Quick Selection Tool** on the Tools palette, then adjust your settings using Figure 16.

2. Position the pointer in the **center of the thimble,** then slowly drag the pointer until the object is selected. See Figure 17.

3. Click the **Move Tool** on the Tools palette.

4. Position the **Move pointer** over the selection, then drag the **thimble** to the Sewing Box image.

5. Drag the **thimble** so that it is to the left of the pin cushion and snaps to the guides at **600 X/200Y**.

6. Defringe the thimble using a setting of **1** pixel.

7. Rename the new layer **Thimble**.

8. Save your work on the sewing box image, then compare your image to Figure 18.

9. Make PS 3-4.psd active.

10. Close PS 3-4.psd without saving your changes.

You selected an object using the Quick Selection Tool, then you dragged the selection into an existing image.

SELECT USING COLOR AND
MODIFY A SELECTION

What You'll Do

▶ *In this lesson, you'll make selections using both the Color Range command and the Magic Wand Tool. You'll also flip a selection, then fix an image using the Healing Brush Tool.*

Selecting with Color

Selections based on color can be easy to make, especially when the background of an image is different from the image itself. High contrast between colors is an ideal condition for making selections based on color. You can make selections using color with the Color Range command on the Select menu, or you can use the Magic Wand Tool on the Tools palette.

Using the Magic Wand Tool

When you select the Magic Wand Tool, the following options are available on the options bar, as shown in Figure 19:

- The four selection buttons.

- The Tolerance setting, which allows you to specify whether similar pixels will be selected. This setting has a value from 0 to 255, and the lower the value, the closer in color the selected pixels will be.
- The Anti-alias check box, which softens the selection's appearance.
- The Contiguous check box, which lets you select pixels that are next to one another.
- The Sample All Layers check box, which lets you select pixels from multiple layers at once.

Knowing which selection tool to use

The hardest part of making a selection might be determining which selection tool to use. How are you supposed to know if you should use a marquee tool or a lasso tool? The first question you need to ask yourself is, "What do I want to select?" Becoming proficient in making selections means that you need to assess the qualities of the object you want to select, and then decide which method to use. Ask yourself: Does the object have a definable shape? Does it have an identifiable edge? Are there common colors that can be used to create a selection?

Using the Color Range Command

You can use the Color Range command to make the same selections as with the Magic Wand Tool. When you use the Color Range command, the Color Range dialog box opens. This dialog box lets you use the pointer to identify which colors you want to use to make a selection. You can also select the Invert check box to *exclude* the chosen color from the selection. The **fuzziness** setting is similar to tolerance, in that the lower the value, the closer in color pixels must be to be selected.

QUICKTIP

Unlike the Magic Wand Tool, the Color Range command does not give you the option of excluding contiguous pixels.

Transforming a Selection

After you place a selection in a Photoshop image, you can change its size and other qualities by clicking Edit on the menu bar, pointing to Transform, then clicking any of the commands on the submenu. After you select certain commands, small squares called **handles** surround the selection. To complete the command, you drag a handle until the image has the look you want, then press [Enter] (Win) or [return] (Mac). You can also use the Transform submenu to flip a selection horizontally or vertically.

Understanding the Healing Brush Tool

If you place a selection then notice that the image has a few imperfections, you can fix the image. You can fix imperfections such as dirt, scratches, bulging veins on skin, or wrinkles on a face using the Healing Brush Tool on the Tools palette.

QUICKTIP

When correcting someone's portrait, make sure your subject looks the way he or she *thinks* they look. That's not always possible, but strive to get as close as you can to their ideal!

Using the Healing Brush Tool

This tool lets you sample an area, then paint over the imperfections. What is the result? The less-than-desirable pixels seem to disappear into the surrounding image. In addition to matching the sampled pixels, the Healing Brush Tool also matches the texture, lighting, and shading of the sample. This is why the painted pixels blend so effortlessly into the existing image. Corrections can be painted using broad strokes, or using clicks of the mouse.

QUICKTIP

To take a sample, press and hold [Alt] (Win) or [option] (Mac) while dragging the pointer over the area you want to duplicate.

FIGURE 19
Options for the Magic Wand Tool

Select using color range

1. Open PS 3-5.psd from the drive and folder where you store your Data Files.

2. Click **Select** on the menu bar, then click **Color Range**.

3. Click the **Image option button** (if it is not already selected).

4. Click the **Invert check box** to add a check mark.

5. Verify that your settings match those shown in Figure 20, click anywhere in the background area surrounding the sample image, then click **OK**.

   The Color Range dialog box closes and the spool of thread in the image is selected.

6. Click the **Move Tool** ▸⊕ on the Tools palette.

7. Drag the selection into Sewing Box.psd, then position the selection as shown in Figure 21.

8. Rename the new layer **Thread**.

9. Activate **PS 3-5.psd**, then close this file without saving any changes.

You made a selection within an image using the Color Range command on the Select menu, and dragged the selection to an existing image.

FIGURE 20

Completed Color Range dialog box

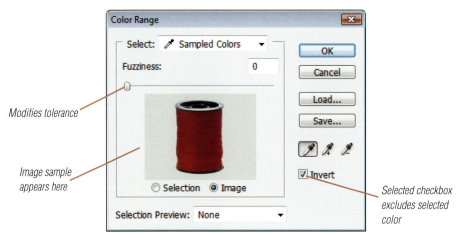

Modifies tolerance

Image sample appears here

Selected checkbox excludes selected color

FIGURE 21

Selection in image

FIGURE 22
Magic Wand Tool settings

FIGURE 23
Selected area

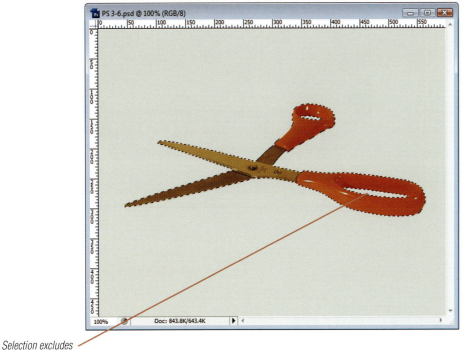

Selection excludes
background color

1. Open PS 3-6.psd from the drive and folder where you store your Data Files.

2. Click the **Magic Wand Tool** ✳ on the Tools palette.

3. Change the settings on the options bar to match those shown in Figure 22.

4. Click anywhere in the background area of the image (such as **50 X/50 Y**).

   TIP Had you selected the Contiguous check box, the pixels within the handles *would not* have been selected. The Contiguous check box is a powerful feature of the Magic Wand Tool.

5. Click **Select** on the menu bar, then click **Inverse**. Compare your selection to Figure 23.

6. Click the **Move Tool** ✥ on the Tools palette, then drag the selection into Sewing Box.psd.

You made a selection using the Magic Wand Tool, then dragged it into an existing image. The Magic Wand Tool is just one more way you can make a selection. One advantage of using the Magic Wand Tool is the Contiguous check box, which lets you choose pixels that are next to one another.

Flip a selection

1. Click **Edit** on the menu bar, point to **Transform**, then click **Flip Horizontal**.

2. Rename Layer 1 as **Scissors**.

3. Defringe **Scissors** using a **1** pixel setting.

4. Drag the flipped selection with the **Move Tool pointer** ▸⊹ so it is positioned as shown in Figure 24.

5. Make **PS 3-6.psd** the active file, then close PS 3-6.psd without saving your changes.

6. Save your work.

You flipped and repositioned a selection. Sometimes it's helpful to flip an object to help direct the viewer's eye to a desired focal point.

FIGURE 24
Flipped and positioned selection

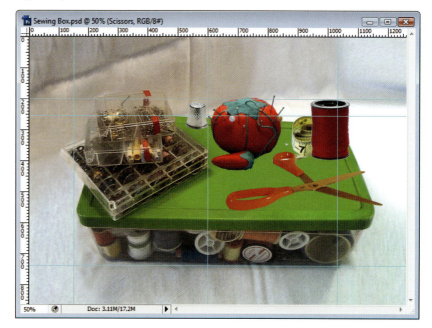

Getting rid of red eye

When digital photos of your favorite people have that annoying red eye, what do you do? You use the Red Eye Tool to eliminate this effect. To do this, select the Red Eye Tool (which is grouped on the Tools palette with the Spot Healing Brush Tool, the Healing Brush Tool, and the Patch Tool), then either click a red area of an eye or draw a selection over one red eye. When you release the mouse button, the red eye effect is removed.

FIGURE 25
Healing Brush Tool options

FIGURE 26
Healed area

Crack removed
from image ————

FIGURE 27
Image after using the Healing brush

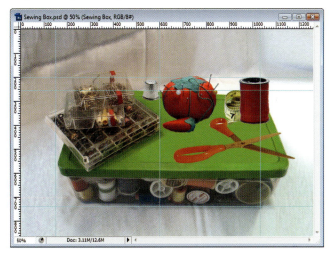

Fix imperfections with the Healing Brush Tool

1. Click the **Sewing Box layer** on the Layers palette, then click the **Zoom Tool** 🔍 on the Tools palette.

2. Click the image with the **Zoom Tool pointer** 🔍 above the pink spool of thread, (in the box) at **750 X/600 Y** until the zoom factor is **200%** and you can see the crack in the lid of the box.

3. Click the **Healing Brush Tool** ✐ on the Tools palette. Change the setting on the options bar to match those shown in Figure 25.

   TIP   If you need to change the Brush settings, click the Brush list arrow on the options bar, then drag the sliders so the settings are 10 px diameter, 0% hardness, 1% spacing, 0° angle, 100% roundness, and pen pressure size.

4. Press and hold **[Alt]** (Win) or **[option]** (Mac), click next to the crack at any location on the green lid, such as **700 X/580 Y**, then release **[Alt]** (Win) or **[option]** (Mac).

   You sampled an area of the box that is not cracked so that you can use the Healing Brush Tool to paint a damaged area with the sample.

5. Click the crack (at approximately **720 X/580 Y**).

6. Repeat steps 4 and 5, each time choosing a new source location, then clicking at a parallel location on the crack.

   Compare the repaired area to Figure 26.

7. Click the **Zoom Tool** 🔍 on the Tools palette press and hold **[Alt]** (Win) or **[option]** (Mac), click the center of the image with the **Zoom Tool pointer** 🔍 until the zoom factor is **50%**, then release **[Alt]** (Win) or **[option]** (Mac).

8. Save your work, then compare your image to Figure 27.

You used the Healing Brush Tool to fix an imperfection in an image.

ADD A VIGNETTE EFFECT
TO A SELECTION

What You'll Do

In this lesson, you'll create a vignette effect, using a layer mask and feathering.

Understanding Vignettes

Traditionally, a **vignette** is a picture or portrait whose border fades into the surrounding color at its edges. You can use a vignette effect to give an image an old-world appearance. You can also use a vignette effect to tone down an overwhelming background. You can create a vignette effect in Photoshop by creating a mask with a blurred edge. A **mask** lets you protect or modify a particular area and is created using a marquee.

Creating a Vignette

A **vignette effect** uses feathering to fade a marquee shape. The **feather** setting blurs the area between the selection and the surrounding pixels, which creates a distinctive fade at the edge of the selection. You can create a vignette effect by using a marquee or lasso tool to create a marquee in an image layer. After the selection is created, you can modify the feather setting (a 10- or 20-pixel setting creates a nice fade) to increase the blur effect on the outside edge of the selection.

Getting that Healing feeling

The Spot Healing Brush Tool works in much the same way as the Healing Brush Tool in that it removes blemishes and other imperfections. Unlike the Healing Brush Tool, the Spot Healing Brush Tool does not require you to take a sample. When using the Spot Healing Brush Tool, you must choose whether you want to use a proximity match type (which uses pixels around the edge of the selection as a patch) or a create texture type (which uses all the pixels in the selection to create a texture that is used to fix the area). You also have the option of sampling all the visible layers or only the active layer.

FIGURE 28
Marquee in image

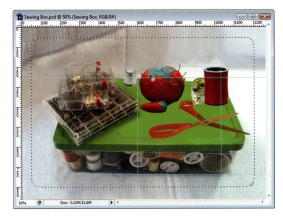

FIGURE 29

Layers palette

FIGURE 30

Vignette in image

Vignette effect
fades border

Feathered mask creates
vignette effect

Create a vignette

1. Verify that the **Sewing Box layer** is selected.

2. Click the **Rectangular Marquee Tool** on the Tools palette.

3. Change the **Feather setting** on the options bar to **20px**.

4. Create a selection with the **Marquee pointer** ╬ from **50 X/50 Y** to **1200 X/800 Y**, as shown in Figure 28.

5. Click **Layer** on the menu bar, point to **Layer Mask**, then click **Reveal Selection**.

   The vignette effect is added to the layer.

   Compare your Layers palette to Figure 29.

6. Click **View** on the menu bar, then click **Rulers** to hide them.

7. Click **View** on the menu bar, then click **Clear Guides**.

8. Save your work, then compare your image to Figure 30.

9. Close the Sewing Box image, then exit Photoshop.

You created a vignette effect by adding a feathered layer mask. You also rearranged layers and defringed a selection. Once the image was finished, you hid the rulers and cleared the guides.

Lesson 4   Add a Vignette Effect to a Selection

Power User Shortcuts

to do this:	use this method:
Copy selection	Click Edit ➤ Copy or [Ctrl][C] (Win) or ⌘[C] (Mac)
Create vignette effect	Marquee or Lasso Tool, create selection, click Layer ➤ Layer Mask ➤ Reveal Selection
Cut selection	Click Edit ➤ Cut or [Ctrl][X] (Win) or ⌘[X] (Mac)
Deselect object	Select ➤ Deselect or [Ctrl][D] (Win) or ⌘[D] (Mac)
Elliptical Marquee Tool	◯ or [Shift] M
Flip image	Edit ➤ Transform ➤ Flip Horizontal
Grow selection	Select ➤ Grow
Increase selection	Select ➤ Similar
Lasso Tool	🔾 or [Shift] L
Magnetic Lasso Tool	🔾 or [Shift] L
Move Tool	⊹ or V

to do this:	use this method:
Move selection marquee	Position pointer in selection, drag ⊹ to new location
Paste selection	Edit ➤ Paste or [Ctrl][V] (Win) or ⌘[V] (Mac)
Polygonal Lasso Tool	🔾 or [Shift] L
Rectangular Marquee Tool	⬚ or [Shift] M
Reselect a deselected object	Select ➤ Reselect, or [Shift][Ctrl][D] (Win) or [Shift] ⌘[D] (Mac)
Select all objects	Select ➤ All, or [Ctrl][A] (Win) or ⌘[A] (Mac)
Select using color range	Select ➤ Color Range, click in sample area
Select using Magic Wand Tool	✳ or W, then click image
Select using Quick Selection Tool	🖊 or [Shift] W, then drag pointer over image
Single Column Marquee Tool	▮
Single Row Marquee Tool	▭

Key: Menu items are indicated by ➤ between the menu name and its command. Blue bold letters are shortcuts for selecting tools on the Tools palette.

Make a selection using shapes.

1. Open PS 3-7.psd from the drive and folder where you store your Data Files, substitute any missing fonts, then save it as **All Cats**.
2. Open PS 3-8.tif.
3. Display the rulers in each image window (if necessary).
4. Use the Rectangular Marquee Tool to select the entire image in PS 3-8.tif. (*Hint*: Reset the Feather setting to 0 pixels, if necessary.)
5. Deselect the selection.
6. Use the Magnetic Lasso Tool to create a selection surrounding only the Block cat in the image. (*Hint*: You can use the Zoom Tool to make the image larger.)
7. Drag the selection into the All Cats image, positioning it so the right side of the cat is at 490 X, and the bottom of the right paw is at 450 Y.
8. Save your work.
9. Close PS 3-8.tif without saving any changes.

Modify a marquee.

1. Open PS 3-9.tif.
2. Change the settings on the Magic Wand Tool to Tolerance = 5, and make sure that the Contiguous check box is selected.
3. Create an elliptical marquee from 100 X/50 Y to 200 X/100 Y, using a setting of 0 in the Feather text box.
4. Use the Grow command on the Select menu.
5. Use the Inverse command on the Select menu.

6. Drag the selection into the All Cats image, positioning it so the upper-left corner of the selection is near 0 X/0 Y.
7. Defringe the new layer using a width of 2 pixels.
8. Save your work.
9. Close PS 3-9.tif without saving any changes.

Select using color and modify a selection.

1. Open PS 3-10.tif.
2. Use the Color Range dialog box to select only the kitten.
3. Drag the selection into the All Cats image.
4. Flip the kitten image (in the All Cats image) horizontally.

FIGURE 31
Completed Skills Review project

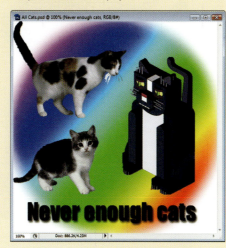

5. Position the kitten image so the bottom right snaps to the ruler guides at 230 X/450 Y.
6. Defringe the kitten using a width of 2 pixels.
7. Save your work.
8. Close PS 3-10.tif without saving any changes.

Add a vignette effect to a selection.

1. Use a 15-pixel feather setting and the Backdrop layer to create an elliptical selection surrounding the contents of the All Cats image.
2. Add a layer mask that reveals the selection.
3. Hide the rulers.
4. Save your work.
5. Compare your image to Figure 31.

As a professional photographer, you often take photos of people for use in various publications. You recently took a photograph of a woman that will be used in a marketing brochure. The client is happy with the overall picture, but wants the facial lines smoothed out. You decide to use the Healing Brush Tool to ensure that the client is happy with the final product.

1. Open PS 3-11.psd, then save it as **Portrait**.
2. Make a copy of the original layer using the default name, or the name of your choice.
3. Use the original copy layer and the Healing Brush Tool to smooth the appearance of facial lines in this image. (*Hint*: You may have greater success if you use short strokes with the Healing Brush Tool than if you paint long strokes.)
4. Save your work, then compare your image to the sample shown in Figure 32.

FIGURE 32
Completed Project Builder 1

The New York Athletic Association, which sponsors the New York Marathon, is holding a contest for artwork to announce the upcoming race. Submissions can be created on paper or computer-generated. You feel you have a good chance at winning this contest, using Photoshop as your tool.

1. Open PS 3-12.psd, then save it as **Marathon Contest**.
2. Locate at least two pieces of appropriate artwork—either on your hard disk, in a royalty-free collection, or from scanned images—that you can use in this file.
3. Use any appropriate methods to select imagery from the artwork.
4. After the selections have been made, copy each selection into Marathon Contest.
5. Arrange the images into a design that you think will be eye-catching and attractive.
6. Deselect the selections in the files you are no longer using, and close them without saving the changes.
7. Add a vignette effect to the Backdrop layer.
8. Display the type layers if they are hidden.
9. Defringe any layers, as necessary.
10. Save your work, then compare your screen to the sample shown in Figure 33.

FIGURE 33
Completed Project Builder 2

DESIGN PROJECT

You are aware that there will be an opening in your firm's design department. Before you can be considered for the job, you need to increase your Photoshop compositing knowledge and experience. You have decided to teach yourself, using informational sources on the Internet and images that can be scanned or purchased.

1. Connect to the Internet and use your browser and favorite search engine to find information on image compositing. (Make a record of the site you found so you can use it for future reference, if necessary.)
2. Create a new Photoshop image, using the dimensions of your choice, then save it as **Sample Compositing**.
3. Locate at least two pieces of artwork—either on your hard disk, in a royalty-free collection, or from scanned images—that you can use.
4. Select the images in the artwork, then copy each into the Sample Compositing image, using the method of your choice.
5. Rename each of the layers using meaningful names.
6. Apply a color to each new layer.
7. Arrange the images in a pleasing design. (*Hint*: Remember that you can flip any image, if necessary.)

8. Deselect the selections in the artwork, then close the files without saving the changes.
9. If desired, create a background layer for the image.
10. If necessary, add a vignette effect to a layer.

11. Defringe any images as you see necessary.
12. Save your work, then compare your screen to the sample shown in Figure 34.

FIGURE 34
Completed Design Project

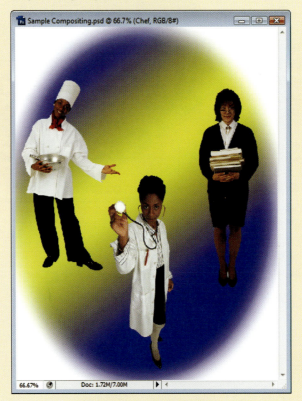

Depending on the size of your group, you can assign individual elements of the project to group members, or work collectively to create the finished product.

At your design firm, a Fortune 500 client plans to start a 24-hour cable sports network called Total Sportz that will cover any nonprofessional sporting events. You and your team have been asked to create some preliminary designs for the network, using images from multiple sources.

1. Open PS 3-13.psd, then save it as **Total Sportz**. (*Hint*: Click Update to close the warning box regarding missing fonts, if necessary.)
2. Assign a few members of your team to locate several pieces of sports-related artwork—either on your hard disk, in a royalty-free collection, or from scanned images. Remember that the images should not show professional sports figures, if possible.
3. Work together to select imagery from the artwork and move it into the Total Sportz image.
4. Arrange the images in an interesting design. (*Hint*: Remember that you can flip any image, if necessary.)
5. Change each layer name to describe the sport in the layer image.
6. Deselect the selections in the files that you used, then close the files without saving the changes.

7. If necessary, add a vignette effect to a layer and/or adjust opacity. (In the sample, the opacity of the Backdrop layer was adjusted to 100%.)

FIGURE 35
Completed Group Project

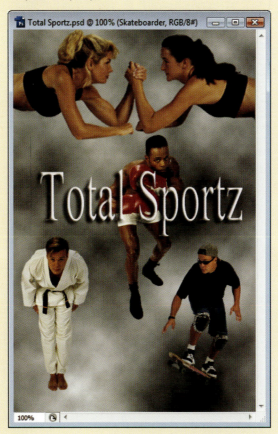

8. Defringe any images (if necessary).
9. Save your work, then compare your image to the sample shown in Figure 35.

chapter

4

INCORPORATING COLOR
TECHNIQUES

1. Work with color to transform an image

2. Use the Color Picker and the Swatches palette

3. Place a border around an image

4. Blend colors using the Gradient Tool

5. Add color to a grayscale image

6. Use filters, opacity, and blending modes

7. Match colors

Using Color

Color can make or break an image. Sometimes colors can draw us into an image; other times they can repel us. We all know what colors we like, but when it comes to creating an image, it is helpful to have some knowledge of color theory and be familiar with color terminology.

Understanding how Photoshop measures, displays, and prints color can be valuable when you create new images or modify existing images. Some colors you choose might be difficult for a professional printer to reproduce or might look muddy when printed. As you become more experienced using colors, you will learn which colors can be reproduced well and which ones cannot.

Understanding Color Modes and Color Models

Photoshop displays and prints images using specific color modes. A **mode** is the amount of color data that can be stored in a given file format, based on an established model. A **model** determines how pigments combine to produce resulting colors. This is the way your computer or printer associates a name or numbers with colors. Photoshop uses standard color models as the basis for its color modes.

Displaying and Printing Images

An image displayed on your monitor, such as an icon on your desktop, is a **bitmap**, a geometric arrangement of different color dots on a rectangular grid. Each dot, called a **pixel**, represents a color or shade. Bitmapped images are *resolution-dependent* and can lose detail—often demonstrated by a jagged appearance—when highly magnified. When printed, images with high resolutions tend to show more detail and subtler color transitions than low-resolution images.

Tools You'll Use

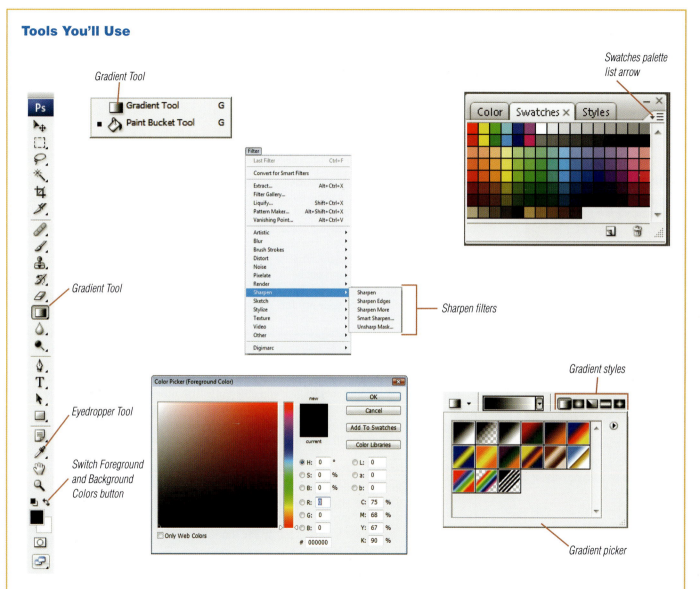

Gradient Tool

Swatches palette list arrow

Gradient Tool

Sharpen filters

Gradient styles

Eyedropper Tool

Switch Foreground and Background Colors button

Gradient picker

WORK WITH COLOR TO
TRANSFORM AN IMAGE

What You'll Do

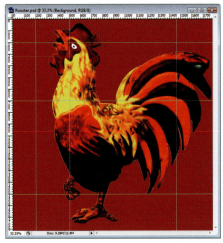

In this lesson, you'll use the Color palette, the Paint Bucket Tool, and the Eyedropper Tool to change the background color of an image.

Learning About Color Models

Photoshop reproduces colors using models of color modes. The range of displayed colors, or **gamut**, for each model available in Photoshop is shown in Figure 1. The shape of each color gamut indicates the range of colors it can display. If a color is out of gamut, it is beyond the color space that your monitor can display or that your printer can print. You select the color mode from the Mode command on the Image menu. The available Photoshop color models are L*a*b, HSB, RGB, CMYK, Bitmap, and Grayscale.

QUICKTIP

A color mode is used to determine which color model will be used to display and print an image.

DESIGNTIP   **Understanding the psychology of color**

Have you ever wondered why some colors make you react a certain way? You might have noticed that some colors affect you differently than others. Color is such an important part of our lives, and in Photoshop, it's key. Specific colors are often used in print and Web pages to evoke the following responses:

- Blue tends to instill a feeling of safety and stability and is often used by financial services.
- Certain shades of green can generate a soft, calming feeling, while others suggest youthfulness and growth.
- Red commands attention and can be used as a call to action; it can also distract a reader's attention from other content.
- White evokes the feeling of purity and innocence, looks cool and fresh, and is often used to suggest luxury.
- Black conveys feelings of power and strength, but can also suggest darkness and negativity.

L*a*b Model

The L*a*b model is based on one luminance (lightness) component and two chromatic components (from green to red, and from blue to yellow). Using the L*a*b model has distinct advantages: you have the largest number of colors available to you and the greatest precision with which to create them. You can also create all the colors contained by other color models, which are limited in their respective color ranges. The L*a*b model is device-independent—the colors will not vary, regardless of the hardware. Use this model when working with photo CD images so that you can independently edit the luminance and color values.

HSB Model

Based on the human perception of color, the HSB (Hue, Saturation, Brightness) model has three fundamental characteristics: hue, saturation, and brightness. The color reflected from or transmitted through an object is called **hue**. Expressed as a degree (between 0° and 360°), each hue is identified by a color name (such as red or green). **Saturation** (or *chroma*) is the strength or purity of the color, representing the amount of gray in proportion to hue. Saturation is measured as a percentage from 0% (gray) to 100% (fully saturated). **Brightness** is the measurement of relative lightness or darkness of a color and is measured as a percentage from 0% (black) to 100% (white). Although you can use the HSB model to define a color on the Color palette or in the Color Picker dialog box, Photoshop does not offer HSB mode as a choice for creating or editing images.

RGB Mode

Photoshop uses color modes to determine how to display and print an image. Each mode is based on established models used in color reproduction. Most colors in the visible spectrum can be represented by mixing various proportions and intensities of red, green, and blue (RGB) colored light. RGB colors are additive colors. **Additive colors** are used for lighting, video, and computer monitors; color is created by light passing through red, green, and blue phosphors. When the values of red, green, and blue are zero, the result is black; when the values are all 255, the result is white. Photoshop assigns each component of the RGB mode an intensity value. Your colors can vary from monitor to monitor even if you are using the exact RGB values on different computers.

FIGURE 1
Photoshop color gamuts

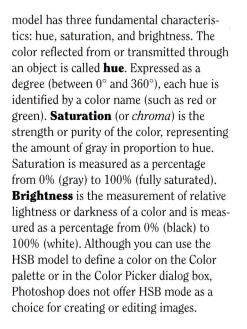
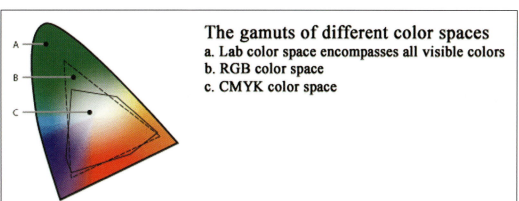

The gamuts of different color spaces
a. Lab color space encompasses all visible colors
b. RGB color space
c. CMYK color space

CMYK Mode

The light-absorbing quality of ink printed on paper is the basis of the CMYK (Cyan, Magenta, Yellow, Black) mode. Unlike the RGB mode—in which components are *combined* to create new colors—the CMYK mode is based on colors being partially *absorbed* as the ink hits the paper and being partially *reflected* back to your eyes. CMYK colors are **subtractive colors**—the *absence* of cyan, magenta, yellow, and black creates white. Subtractive (CMYK) and additive (RGB) colors are complementary colors; a pair from one model creates a color in the other. When combined, cyan, magenta, and yellow absorb all color and produce black. The CMYK mode—in which the lightest colors are assigned the highest percentages of ink colors—is used in four-color process printing. Converting an RGB image into a CMYK image produces a **color separation** (the commercial printing process of separating colors for use with

different inks). Note, however, that because your monitor uses RGB mode, you will not see the exact colors until you print the image, and even then the colors can vary depending on the printer and offset press.

Understanding the Bitmap and Grayscale Modes

In addition to the RGB and CMYK modes, Photoshop provides two specialized color modes: bitmap and grayscale. The **bitmap mode** uses black or white color values to represent image pixels, and is a good choice for images with subtle color gradations, such as photographs or painted images. The **grayscale mode** uses up to 256 shades of gray, assigning a brightness value from 0 (black) to 255 (white) to each pixel. Displayed colors can vary from monitor to monitor even if you use identical color settings on different computers.

Changing Foreground and Background Colors

In Photoshop, the **foreground color** is black by default and is used to paint, fill, and apply a border to a selection. The **background color** is white by default and is used to make **gradient fills** (gradual blends of multiple colors) and fill in areas of an image that have been erased. You can change foreground and background colors

using the Color palette, the Swatches palette, the Color Picker, or the Eyedropper Tool. One method of changing foreground and background colors is **sampling**, in which an existing color is used. You can restore the default colors by clicking the Default Foreground and Background Colors button on the Tools palette, shown in Figure 2. You can apply a color to the background of a layer using the Paint Bucket Tool. When you click an image with the Paint Bucket Tool, the current foreground color on the Tools palette fills the active layer.

FIGURE 2
Foreground and background color buttons

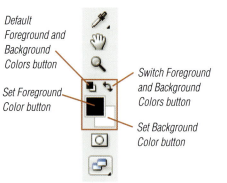

Default Foreground and Background Colors button

Set Foreground Color button

Switch Foreground and Background Colors button

Set Background Color button

FIGURE 3
Image with rulers displayed

FIGURE 4
Color Settings dialog box

Intent list arrow

Set the default foreground and background colors

1. Start Photoshop, open PS 4-1.psd from the drive and folder where you save your Data Files, then save it as **Rooster**.

2. Click the **Default Foreground and Background Colors button** on the Tools palette.

   TIP   If you accidently click the Set foreground color button, the Color Picker (Foreground Color) dialog box opens.

3. Change the status bar so the document sizes display, if necessary.

   TIP   Document sizes will not display in the status bar if the image window is too small. Drag the lower-right corner of the image window to expand the window and display the menu button and document sizes.

4. Display the rulers in pixels (if necessary), then compare your screen to Figure 3.

   TIP   You can right-click (Win) or [control]-click (Mac) one of the rulers to choose Pixels, Inches, Centimeters, Millimeters, Points, Picas, or Percent as a unit of measurement, instead of using the Rulers and Units Preferences dialog box.

You set the default foreground and background colors and displayed rulers in pixels.

Creating a rendering intent

The use of a **rendering intent** determines how colors are converted by a color management system. A **color management system** is used to keep colors looking consistent as they move between devices. Colors are defined and interpreted using a **profile**. You can create a rendering intent by clicking Edit on the menu bar, then clicking Color Settings. Click the More Options button in the Color Settings dialog box, click the Intent list arrow shown in Figure 4, then click one of the four options. Since a gamut is the range of color that a color system can display or print, the rendering intent is constantly evaluating the color gamut and deciding whether or not the colors need adjusting. So, colors that fall inside the destination gamut may not be changed, or they may be adjusted when translated to a smaller color gamut.

Change the background color using the Color palette

1. Click the **Background layer** on the Layers palette.

2. Display the History palette, then click the **Color palette tab** [Color ×] (if it is not already selected).

3. Drag each color slider on the Color palette until you reach the values shown in Figure 5.

   The active color changes to the new color. Did you notice that this image is using the RGB mode?

   TIP   You can also double-click each component's text box on the Color palette and type the color values.

4. Click the **Paint Bucket Tool** on the Tools palette.

   TIP   If the Paint Bucket Tool is not visible on the Tools palette, click the Gradient Tool on the Tools palette, press and hold the mouse button until the list of hidden tools appears, then click the Paint Bucket Tool.

5. Click the image with the **Paint Bucket pointer**.

6. Drag the **Paint Bucket state** on the History palette onto the **Delete current state button**.

   TIP   You can also undo the last action by clicking Edit on the menu bar, then clicking Undo Paint Bucket.

You set new values in the Color palette, used the Paint Bucket Tool to change the background to that color, then undid the change. You can change colors on the Color palette by dragging the sliders or by typing values in the color text boxes.

FIGURE 5
Color palette with new color

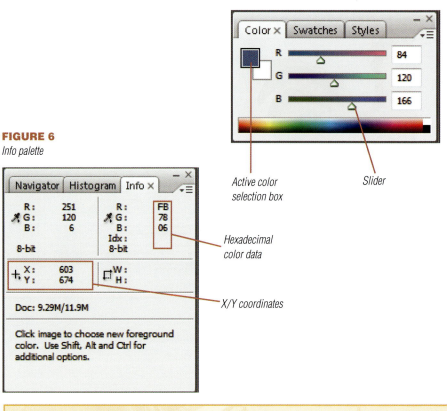

Active color selection box

Slider

Hexadecimal color data

X/Y coordinates

FIGURE 6
Info palette

Using ruler coordinates

Photoshop rulers run along the top and left sides of the document window. Each point on an image has a horizontal and vertical location. These two numbers, called X and Y coordinates, appear on the Info palette (which is located behind the Navigator palette) as shown in Figure 6. The X coordinate refers to the horizontal location, and the Y coordinate refers to the vertical location. You can use one or both sets of guides to identify coordinates of a location, such as a color you want to sample. If you have difficulty seeing the ruler markings, you can increase the size of the image; the greater the zoom factor, the more detailed the measurement hashes.

FIGURE 7
New foreground color applied to Background layer

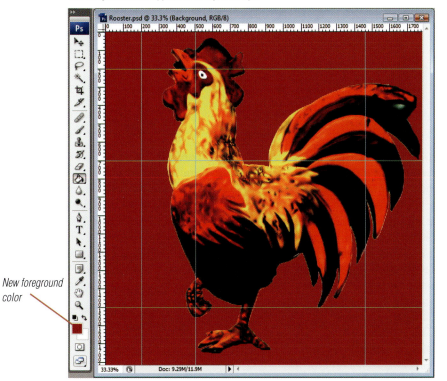

New foreground color

Change the background color using the Eyedropper Tool

1. Click the **Background layer** on the Layers palette.

2. Click the **Eyedropper Tool** 🖋 on the Tools palette.

3. Click the **red part of the rooster's beak** in the image with the **Eyedropper pointer** 🖋, using the Info palette and the blue guides to help ensure accuracy.

   The Set foreground color button displays the red color that you clicked (or sampled).

4. Click the **Paint Bucket Tool** 🪣 on the Tools palette.

5. Close the History palette, click the image, then compare your screen to Figure 7.

   | TIP   Your color values on the Color palette might vary from the sample.

6. Save your work.

You used the Eyedropper Tool to sample a color as the foreground color, then used the Paint Bucket Tool to change the background color to the color you sampled. Using the Eyedropper Tool is a convenient way of sampling a color in any Photoshop image.

Using hexadecimal values in the Info palette

Colors can be expressed in a hexadecimal value, three pairs of letters or numbers that define the R, G, and B components of a color. The three pairs of letters/numbers are expressed in values from 00 (minimum luminance) to ff (maximum luminance). 00 represents the value of black, ffffff is white, and ff0000 is red. To view hexadecimal values in the Info palette, click the Info palette list arrow, then click Palette Options. Click Web Color from either the First Color Readout or Second Color Readout Mode list arrow, then click OK. This is just one more way you can exactly determine a specific color in an image.

USE THE COLOR PICKER AND
THE SWATCHES PALETTE

What You'll Do

In this lesson, you'll use the Color Picker and the Swatches palette to select new colors, then you'll add a new color to the background and to the Swatches palette.

Making Selections from the Color Picker

Depending on the color model you are using, you can select colors using the **Color Picker**, a feature that lets you choose a color from a color spectrum or lets you numerically define a custom color. You can change colors in the Color Picker dialog box by using the following methods:

- Drag the sliders along the vertical color bar.
- Click inside the vertical color bar.
- Click a color in the Color field.
- Enter a value in any of the text boxes.

Figure 8 shows a color in the Color Picker dialog box. A circular marker indicates the active color. The color slider displays the range of color levels available for the active color component. The adjustments you make by dragging or clicking a new color are reflected in the text boxes; when you choose a new color, the previous color appears below the new color in the preview area.

Using the Swatches Palette

You can also change colors using the Swatches palette. The **Swatches palette** is a visual display of colors you can choose from, as shown in Figure 9. You can add your own colors to the palette by sampling a color from an image, and you can also delete colors. When you add a swatch to the Swatches palette, Photoshop assigns a default name that has a sequential number, or you can name the swatch whatever you like. Photoshop places new swatches in the first available space at the end of the palette. You can view swatch names by clicking the Swatches palette list arrow, then clicking Small List. You can restore the default Swatches palette by clicking the Swatches palette list arrow, clicking Reset Swatches, then clicking OK.

FIGURE 8

Color Picker dialog box and Swatches palette

FIGURE 9

Color Picker dialog box and Swatches palette

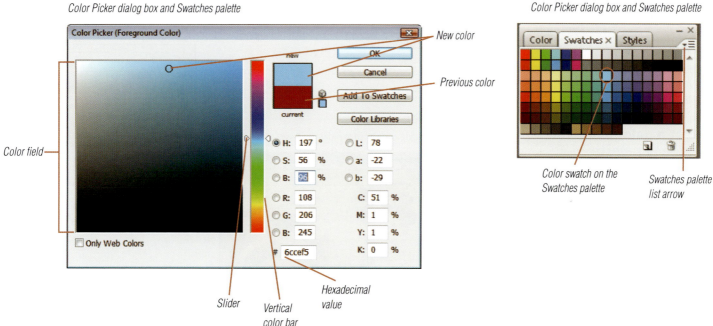

Select a color using the Color Picker dialog box

1. Click the **Set foreground color button** on the Tools palette, then verify that the H: option button is selected in the Color Picker dialog box.

2. Click the **R: option button**.

3. Click the **bottom-right corner** of the Color field (purple), as shown in Figure 10.

   TIP   If the Warning: out-of-gamut for printing indicator appears next to the color, then this color exceeds the printable range.

4. Click **OK**.

You opened the Color Picker dialog box, selected a different color palette, and then selected a new color.

Select a color using the Swatches palette

1. Click the **Swatches palette tab** Swatches ×.

2. Click the **second swatch from the left in the first row** (RGB Yellow), as shown in Figure 11.

   Did you notice that the foreground color on the Tools palette changed to a light, bright yellow?

3. Click the **Paint Bucket Tool** on the Tools palette (if it is not already selected).

4. Click the image with the **Paint Bucket pointer** , then compare your screen to Figure 12.

You opened the Swatches palette, selected a color, and then used the Paint Bucket Tool to change the background to that color.

FIGURE 10
Color Picker dialog box

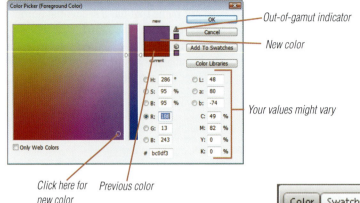

Out-of-gamut indicator

New color

Your values might vary

Click here for new color   Previous color

FIGURE 11
Swatches palette

Your swatches on the last row might vary

FIGURE 12
New foreground color applied to Background layer

FIGURE 13
Swatch added to Swatches palette

New swatch appears
in last row

Add a new color to the Swatches palette

1. Click the **Eyedropper Tool** 🖊 on the Tools palette.

2. Click **above and to the left of the rooster's eye** at coordinates **500 X/200 Y**.

3. Click the empty area to the right of the last swatch in the bottom row of the Swatches palette with the **Paint Bucket pointer** 🪣.

4. Type **Rooster eye surround** in the Name text box.

5. Click **OK** in the Color Swatch Name dialog box.

   TIP   To delete a color from the Swatches palette, press [Alt] (Win) or [option] (Mac), position the pointer over a swatch, then click the swatch.

6. Save your work, then compare the new swatch on your Swatches palette to Figure 13.

You used the Eyedropper Tool to sample a color, and then added the color to the Swatches palette, and gave it a descriptive name. Adding swatches to the Swatches palette makes it easy to reuse frequently used colors.

Maintaining your focus

Adobe Photoshop is probably unlike any other program you've used before. In other programs, there's a central area on the screen where you focus your attention. In Photoshop, there's the workspace containing your document, but you've probably already figured out that if you don't have the correct layer selected in the Layer's palette, things won't quite work out as you expected. In addition, you have to make sure you've got the right tool selected in the Tools palette. You also need to keep an eye on the History palette. As you work on your image, it might feel a lot like negotiating a shopping mall parking lot on the day before Christmas: you've got to be looking in a lot of places at once.

PLACE A BORDER AROUND
AN IMAGE

What You'll Do

 In this lesson, you'll add a border to an image.

Emphasizing an Image

You can emphasize an image by placing a border around its edges. This process is called **stroking the edges**. The default color of the border is the current foreground color on the Tools palette. You can change the width, color, location, and blending mode of a border using the Stroke dialog box. The default stroke width is the setting last applied; you can apply a width from 1 to 16 pixels. The location option buttons in the dialog box determine where the border will be placed. If you want to change the location of the stroke, you must first delete the previously applied stroke, or Photoshop will apply the new border over the existing one.

Locking Transparent Pixels

As you modify layers, you can lock some properties to protect their contents. The ability to lock—or protect—elements within a layer is controlled from within the Layers palette, as shown in Figure 14. It's a good idea to lock transparent pixels when you add borders so that stray marks will

not be included in the stroke. You can lock the following layer properties:

- Transparency: Limits editing capabilities to areas in a layer that are opaque.
- Image: Makes it impossible to modify layer pixels using painting tools.
- Position: Prevents pixels within a layer from being moved.

QUICKTIP

You can lock transparency or image pixels only in a layer containing an image, not in one containing type.

FIGURE 14
Layer palette locking options

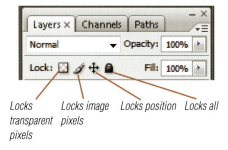

Locks transparent pixels   Locks image pixels   Locks position   Locks all

FIGURE 15

Locking transparent pixels

Lock transparent pixels button

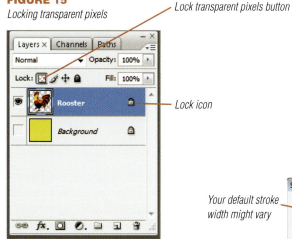

Lock icon

FIGURE 16

Stroke dialog box

Your default stroke
width might vary

Changes
stroke color

Location options

FIGURE 17

Border added to image

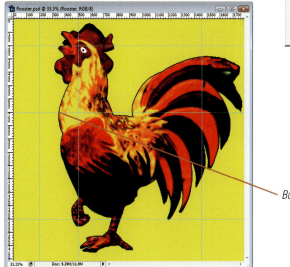

Border

Create a border

1. Click the **Indicates layer visibility button** 👁
    on the Background layer on the Layers palette.

    TIP   You can click the Indicates layer visibil-
    ity button to hide distracting layers.

2. Click the **Default Foreground and Background
    Colors button** ▉.

    The foreground color will become the default
    border color.

3. Click the **Rooster layer** on the Layers
    palette.

4. Click the **Lock transparent pixels button** ▨
    on the Layers palette. See Figure 15.

    The border will be applied only to the pixels
    on the edge of the rooster.

5. Click **Edit** on the menu bar, then click **Stroke** to
    open the Stroke dialog box. See Figure 16.

6. Type **5** in the Width text box, click the **Inside
    option button**, then click **OK**.

    TIP   Determining the correct border location
    can be confusing. Try different settings until
    you achieve the look you want.

7. Click the **Indicates layer visibility button** ☐
    on the Background layer on the Layers palette.

8. Save your work, then compare your image to
    Figure 17.

*You hid a layer, changed the foreground color to
black, locked transparent pixels, then used the
Stroke dialog box to apply a border to the image.
The border makes the image stand out against the
background color.*

BLEND COLORS USING THE
GRADIENT TOOL

What You'll Do

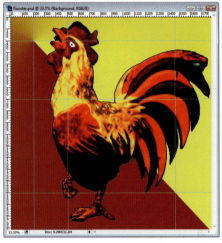

In this lesson, you'll create a gradient fill from a sampled color and a swatch, then apply it to the background.

Understanding Gradients

A **gradient fill**, or simply **gradient**, is a blend of colors used to fill a selection of a layer or an entire layer. A gradient's appearance is determined by its beginning and ending points, and its length, direction, and angle. Gradients allow you to create dramatic effects, using existing color combinations or your own colors. The Gradient picker, as shown in Figure 18, offers multicolor gradient fills and a few that use the current foreground or background colors on the Tools palette.

FIGURE 18
Gradient picker

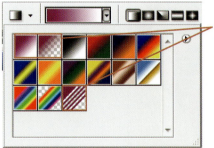

Gradient fills that use current foreground or background colors

Using the Gradient Tool

You use the Gradient Tool to create gradients in images. When you choose the Gradient Tool, five gradient styles become available on the options bar. These styles—Linear, Radial, Angle, Reflected, and Diamond—are shown in Figure 19. In each example, the gradient was drawn from 50 X/50 Y to 100 X/100 Y.

Customizing Gradients

Using the **gradient presets**—predesigned gradient fills that are displayed in the Gradient picker—is a great way to learn how to use gradients. But as you become more familiar with Photoshop, you might want to venture into the world of the unknown and create your own gradient designs. You can create your own designs by modifying an existing gradient using the Gradient Editor. You can open the Gradient Editor, shown in Figure 20, by clicking the selected gradient pattern that appears on the options bar. After it's open, you can use it to make the following modifications:

- Create a new gradient from an existing gradient.
- Modify an existing gradient.
- Add intermediate colors to a gradient.
- Create a blend between more than two colors.
- Adjust the opacity values.
- Determine the placement of the midpoint.

FIGURE 19
Sample gradients

FIGURE 20
Gradient Editor dialog box

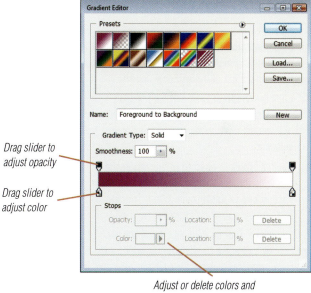

Drag slider to adjust opacity

Drag slider to adjust color

Adjust or delete colors and opacity values

Create a gradient from a sample color

1. Verify that the **Eyedropper Tool** is selected.

2. Click the **yellow neck** in the image at coordinates **500 X/600 Y**.

   | TIP To accurately select the coordinates, adjust the zoom factor as necessary.

3. Click the **Switch Foreground and Background Colors button** on the Tools palette.

4. Click **Rooster eye surround** on the Swatches palette (the new swatch you added) with the **Eyedropper pointer**.

5. Click the **Indicates layer visibility button** on the Rooster layer.

6. Click the **Background layer** on the Layers palette to make it active, as shown in Figure 21.

7. Click the **Paint Bucket Tool** on the Tools palette, then press and hold the mouse button until the list of hidden tools appears.

8. Click the **Gradient Tool** on the Tools palette, then click the **Angle Gradient button** on the options bar (if it is not already selected).

9. Click the **Click to open Gradient picker list arrow** on the options bar, then click **Foreground to Background** (the first gradient fill in the first row), as shown in Figure 22.

You sampled a color on the image to set the background color, changed the foreground color using an existing swatch, selected the Gradient Tool, and then chose a gradient fill and style.

FIGURE 21
Rooster layer hidden

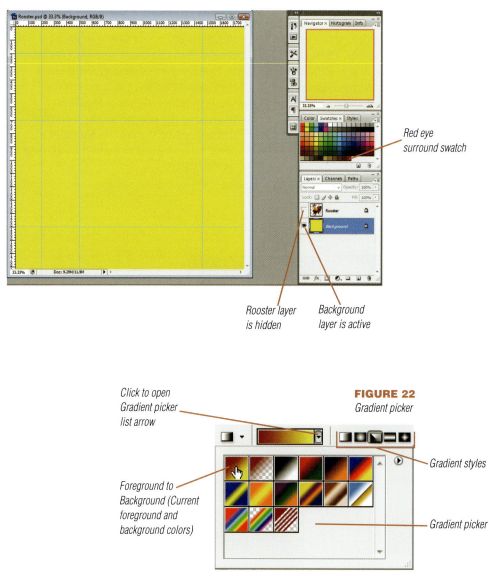

Red eye surround swatch

Rooster layer is hidden

Background layer is active

Click to open Gradient picker list arrow

FIGURE 22
Gradient picker

Gradient styles

Foreground to Background (Current foreground and background colors)

Gradient picker

FIGURE 23
Gradient fill applied to Background layer

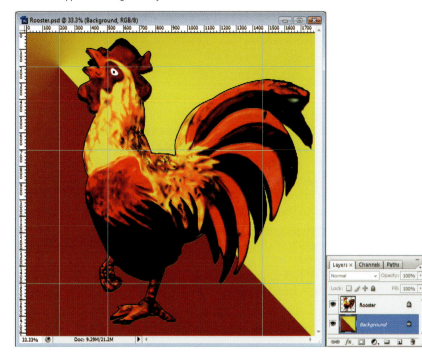

Apply a gradient fill

1. Click the **Click to open Gradient picker list arrow** to close the Gradient picker.

    TIP You can also close the Gradient picker by pressing [Esc] (Win) or [esc] (Mac).

2. Drag the **Gradient pointer** -:- from **200 X/200 Y** to **1430 X/1500 Y** using the Info palette and the guides to help you create the gradient in the work area.

3. Click the **Indicates layer visibility button** on the Rooster layer.

    The Rooster layer appears against the new background, as shown in Figure 23.

    TIP It is a good practice to save your work early and often in the creation process, especially before making significant changes or printing.

4. Save your work.

You applied the gradient fill to the background. You can create dramatic effects using the gradient fill in combination with foreground and background colors.

ADD COLOR TO A
GRAYSCALE IMAGE

What You'll Do

In this lesson, you'll convert an image to grayscale, change the color mode, then colorize a grayscale image using the Hue/Saturation dialog box.

Colorizing Options

Grayscale images can contain up to 256 shades of gray, assigning a brightness value from 0 (black) to 255 (white) to each pixel. Since the earliest days of photography, people have been tinting grayscale images with color to create a certain mood or emphasize an image in a way that purely realistic colors could not. To capture this effect in Photoshop, you convert an image to the Grayscale mode, then choose the color mode you want to work in before you continue. When you apply a color to a grayscale image, each pixel becomes a shade of that particular color instead of gray.

Converting Grayscale and Color Modes

When you convert a color image to grayscale, the light and dark values—called the **luminosity**—remain, while the color information is deleted. When you change from grayscale to a color mode, the foreground and background colors on the Tools palette change from black and white to the previously selected colors.

Converting a color image to black and white

Using the Black & White command, you can easily convert a color image to black and white. This feature lets you quickly make the color to black and white conversion while maintaining full control over how individual colors are converted. Tones can also be applied to the grayscale by applying color tones. To use this feature, click Image on the menu bar, point to Adjustments, then click Black & White. The Black & White command can also be applied as an Adjustment layer.

Colorizing a Grayscale Image

In order for a grayscale image to be colorized, you must change the color mode to one that accommodates color. After you change the color mode, and then adjust settings in the Hue/Saturation dialog box, Photoshop determines the colorization range based on the hue of the currently selected foreground color. If you want a different colorization range, you need to change the foreground color.

QUICKTIP

A duotone is a grayscale image that uses two custom ink colors. The final output is dramatically affected by both the order in which the inks are printed and the screen angles that you use.

Tweaking adjustments

Once you have made your color mode conversion to grayscale, you may want to make some adjustments. You can fine-tune the Brightness/Contrast, filters, and blending modes in a grayscale image.

FIGURE 24
Gradient Map dialog box

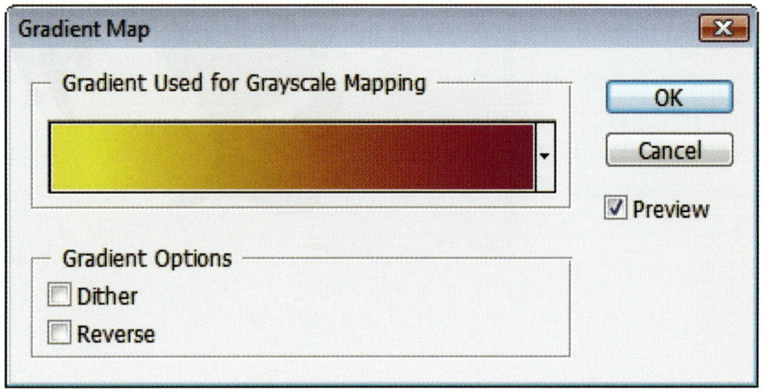

Applying a gradient effect

You can also use the Gradient Map to apply a colored gradient effect to a grayscale image. The Gradient Map uses gradient fills (the same ones displayed in the Gradient picker) to colorize the image, which can produce some stunning effects. You use the Gradient Map dialog box, shown in Figure 24, to apply a gradient effect to a grayscale image. You can access the Gradient Map dialog box using the Adjustments command on the Image menu.

Change the color mode

1. Open PS 4-2.psd from the drive and folder where you store your Data Files, save it as **Rooster Colorized**, then turn off the rulers if they are displayed.

2. Click **Image** on the menu bar, point to **Mode**, then click **Grayscale**.

3. Click **Flatten** in the warning box, then click **Discard**.

   The color mode of the image is changed to grayscale, and the image is flattened so there is only a single layer. All the color information in the image has been discarded.

4. Click **Image** on the menu bar, point to **Mode**, then click **RGB Color**.

   The color mode is changed back to RGB color, although there is still no color in the image. Compare your screen to Figure 25.

You converted the image to Grayscale, which discarded the existing color information. Then you changed the color mode to RGB color.

FIGURE 25
Image with RGB mode

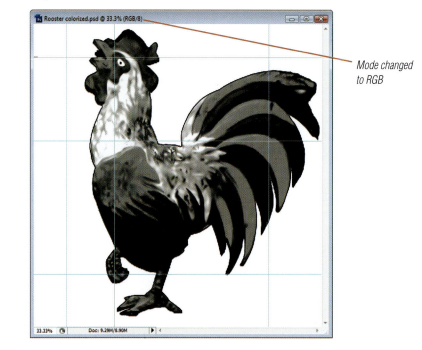

Mode changed to RGB

Understanding the Hue/Saturation dialog box

The Hue/Saturation dialog box is an important tool in the world of color enhancement. Useful for both color and grayscale images, the saturation slider can be used to boost a range of colors. By clicking the Edit list arrow, you can isolate which colors (all, cyan, blue, magenta, red, yellow, or green) you want to modify. Using this tool requires patience and experimentation, but gives you great control over the colors in your image.

FIGURE 26
Hue/Saturation dialog box

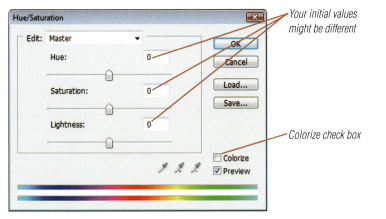

Your initial values might be different

Colorize check box

FIGURE 27
Colorized image

Colorize a grayscale image

1. Click **Image** on the menu bar, point to **Adjustments**, then click **Hue/Saturation** to open the Hue/Saturation dialog box, as shown in Figure 26.

2. Click the **Colorize check box** in the Hue/Saturation dialog box to add a check mark.

3. Drag the **Hue slider** until the text box displays **290**.

   TIP   You can also type values in the text boxes in the Hue/Saturation dialog box. Negative numbers must be preceded by a minus sign or a hyphen. Positive numbers can be preceded by an optional plus sign (+).

4. Drag the **Saturation slider** until the text box displays **40**.

5. Drag the **Lightness slider** until the text box displays **-15**.

6. Click **OK**.

7. Save your work, then compare your screen to Figure 27.

You colorized a grayscale image by adjusting settings in the Hue/Saturation dialog box.

Converting color images to grayscale

Like everything else in Photoshop, there is more than one way of converting a color image into one that is black & white. Changing the color mode to grayscale is the quickest method. You can also make this conversion through desaturation by clicking Image on the menu bar, pointing to Adjustments, then clicking Black & White, or Desaturate. Converting to Grayscale mode generally results in losing contrast, as does the desaturation method.

USE FILTERS, OPACITY, AND BLENDING MODES

What You'll Do

In this lesson, you'll adjust the brightness and contrast in the Chili Shop colorized image, apply a Sharpen filter, and adjust the opacity of the lines applied by the filter. You'll also adjust the color balance of the Chili Shop image.

Manipulating an Image

As you work in Photoshop, you might realize that some images have fundamental problems that need correcting, while others just need to be further enhanced. For example, you might need to adjust an image's contrast and sharpness, or you might want to colorize an otherwise dull image. You can use a variety of techniques to change the way an image looks. For example, you have learned how to use the Adjustments command on the Image menu to modify hue and saturation, but you can also use this command to adjust brightness and contrast, color balance, and a host of other visual effects.

Understanding Filters

Filters are Photoshop commands that can significantly alter an image's appearance. Experimenting with Photoshop's filters is a fun way to completely change the look of an image. For example, the Watercolor filter gives the illusion that your image was

Fixing blurry scanned images

An unfortunate result of scanning a picture is that the image can become blurry. You can fix this, however, using the Unsharp Mask filter. This filter both sharpens and smoothes the image by increasing the contrast along element edges. Here's how it works: the smoothing effect removes stray marks, and the sharpening effect emphasizes contrasting neighboring pixels. Most scanners come with their own Unsharp Masks built into the TWAIN driver, but using Photoshop, you have access to a more powerful version of this filter. You can use Photoshop's Unsharp Mask to control the sharpening process by adjusting key settings. In most cases, your scanner's Unsharp Mask might not give you this flexibility. Regardless of the technical aspects, the result is a sharper image. You can apply the Unsharp Mask by clicking Filter on the menu bar, pointing to Sharpen, then click Unsharp Mask.

painted using traditional watercolors. Sharpen filters can appear to add definition to the entire image, or just the edges. Compare the different Sharpen filters applied in Figure 28. The **Sharpen More filter** increases the contrast of adjacent pixels and can focus a blurry image. Be careful not to overuse sharpening tools (or any filter), because you can create high-contrast lines or add graininess in color or brightness.

Choosing Blending Modes

A **blending mode** controls how pixels are made either darker or lighter based on underlying colors. Photoshop provides a variety of blending modes, listed in Table 1, to combine the color of the pixels in the current layer with those in layer(s) beneath it. You can see a list of blending modes by clicking the Add a layer style button on the Layers palette.

Understanding Blending Mode Components

You should consider the following underlying colors when planning a blending mode: **base color**, which is the original color of the image; **blend color**, which is the color you apply with a paint or edit tool; and **resulting color**, which is the color that is created as a result of applying the blend color.

Softening Filter Effects

Opacity can soften the line that the filter creates, but it doesn't affect the opacity of the entire layer. After a filter has been applied, you can modify the opacity and apply a blending mode using the Layers palette or the Fade dialog box. You can open the Fade dialog box by clicking Edit on the menu bar, then clicking the Fade command.

QUICKTIP
The Fade command appears only after a filter has been applied. When available, the command name includes the name of the applied filter.

Balancing Colors

As you adjust settings, such as hue and saturation, you might create unwanted imbalances in your image. You can adjust colors to correct or improve an image's appearance. For example, you can decrease a color by increasing the amount of its opposite color. You use the Color Balance dialog box to balance the color in an image.

FIGURE 28
Sharpen filters

Original image

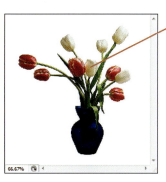
Sharpen filter applied

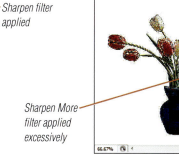
Sharpen More filter applied excessively

TABLE 1: Blending Modes

blending mode	description
Dissolve, Behind, and Clear modes	Dissolve mode creates a grainy, mottled appearance. The Behind mode paints on the transparent part of the layer—the lower the opacity, the grainier the image. The Clear mode paints individual pixels. All modes are available only when the Lock transparent pixels check box is *not* selected.
Multiply and Screen modes	Multiply mode creates semitransparent shadow effects. This mode assesses the information in each channel, then multiplies the value of the base color by the blend color. The resulting color is always *darker* than the base color. The Screen mode multiplies the value of the inverse of the blend and base colors. After it is applied, the resulting color is always *lighter* than the base color.
Overlay mode	Dark and light values (luminosity) are preserved, dark base colors are multiplied (darkened), and light areas are screened (lightened).
Soft Light and Hard Light modes	Soft Light lightens a light base color and darkens a dark base color. The Hard Light blending mode creates a similar effect, but provides greater contrast between the base and blend colors.
Color Dodge and Color Burn modes	Color Dodge mode brightens the base color to reflect the blend color. The Color Burn mode darkens the base color to reflect the blend color.
Darken and Lighten modes	Darken mode selects a new resulting color based on whichever color is darker—the base color or the blend color. The Lighten mode selects a new resulting color based on the lighter of the two colors.
Difference and Exclusion modes	The Difference mode subtracts the value of the blend color from the value of the base color, or vice versa, depending on which color has the greater brightness value. The Exclusion mode creates an effect similar to that of the Difference mode, but with less contrast between the blend and base colors.
Color and Luminosity modes	The Color mode creates a resulting color with the luminance of the base color, and the hue and saturation of the blend color. The Luminosity mode creates a resulting color with the hue and saturation of the base color, and the luminance of the blend color.
Hue and Saturation modes	The Hue mode creates a resulting color with the luminance of the base color and the hue of the blend color. The Saturation mode creates a resulting color with the luminance of the base color and the saturation of the blend color.

FIGURE 29
Brightness/Contrast dialog box

FIGURE 30
Shadow/Highlight dialog box

Adjust brightness and contrast

1. Click **Image** on the menu bar, point to **Adjustments**, then click **Brightness/Contrast** to open the Brightness/Contrast dialog box.

2. Drag the **Brightness slider** until **+15** appears in the Brightness text box.

3. Drag the **Contrast slider** until **+25** appears in the Contrast text box. Compare your screen to Figure 29.

4. Click **OK**.

You adjusted settings in the Brightness/Contrast dialog box. The image now looks much brighter, with a higher degree of contrast, which obscures some of the finer detail in the image.

Correcting shadows and highlights

The ability to correct shadows and highlights will delight photographers everywhere. This image correction feature (opened by clicking Image on the menu bar, pointing to Adjustments, then clicking Shadow/Highlight) lets you modify overall lighting and make subtle adjustments. Figure 30 shows the Shadow/Highlights dialog box with the Show More Options check box selected. Check out this one-stop shopping for shadow and highlight adjustments!

Work with a filter, a blending mode, and an opacity setting

1. Click **Filter** on the menu bar, point to **Sharpen**, then click **Sharpen More**.

   The border and other features of the image are intensified.

2. Click **Edit** on the menu bar, then click **Fade Sharpen More** to open the Fade dialog box, as shown in Figure 31.

3. Drag the **Opacity slider** until **45** appears in the Opacity text box.

   The opacity setting softened the lines applied by the Sharpen More filter.

4. Click the **Mode list arrow**, then click **Dissolve**.

   The Dissolve setting blends the surrounding pixels.

5. Click **OK**.

6. Save your work, then compare your image to Figure 32.

You applied the Sharpen More filter, then adjusted the opacity and changed the color mode in the Fade dialog box. The image looks crisper than before, with a greater level of detail.

FIGURE 31
Fade dialog box

FIGURE 32
Image settings adjusted

FIGURE 33

Color Balance dialog box

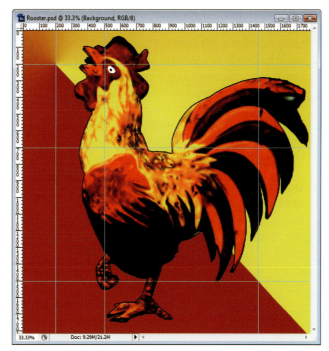

Color Balance

Color Balance

Color Levels: +70   -40   +35

Cyan ———————⊙—— Red
Magenta ——⊙————— Green
Yellow ————⊙——— Blue

OK
Cancel
☑ Preview

Tone Balance
○ Shadows   ⊙ Midtones   ○ Highlights
☑ Preserve Luminosity

FIGURE 34

Image with colors balanced

Rooster.psd @ 33.3% (Background, RGB/8)

33.33%   Doc: 9.29M/21.2M

Adjust color balance

1. Switch to the Rooster image, with the Background layer active.

    The image you worked with earlier in this chapter becomes active.

2. Click **Image** on the menu bar, point to **Adjustments**, then click **Color Balance**.

3. Drag the **Cyan-Red slider** until **+70** appears in the first text box.

4. Drag the **Magenta-Green slider** until **–40** appears in the middle text box.

5. Drag the **Yellow-Blue slider** until **+35** appears in the last text box, as shown in Figure 33.

    Subtle changes were made in the color balance in the image.

6. Click **OK**.

7. Save your work, then compare your image to Figure 34.

You balanced the colors in the Chili Shop image by adjusting settings in the Color Balance dialog box.

MATCH COLORS

What You'll Do

 In this lesson, you'll make selections in source and target images, then use the Match Color command to replace the target color.

Finding the Right Color

If it hasn't happened already, at some point you'll be working on an image and wish you could grab a color from another image to use in this one. Just as you can use the Eyedropper Tool to sample any color in the current image for the foreground and background, you can sample a color from any other image to use in the current one. Perhaps the skin tones in one image look washed out: you can use the Match Color command to replace those tones with skin tone colors from another image. Or maybe the jacket color in one image would look better using a color in another image.

Using Selections to Match Colors

Remember that this is Photoshop, where everything is about layers and selections.

To replace a color in one image with one you've matched from another, you work with—you guessed it—layers and selections.

Suppose you've located the perfect color in another image. The image you are working with is the **target**, and that image that contains your perfect color is the **source**. By activating the layer on which the color lies in the source image, and making a selection around the color, you can have Photoshop match the color in the source and replace a color in the target. To accomplish this, you use the Match Color command, which is available through the Adjustments command on the Image menu.

FIGURE 35

Selection in source image

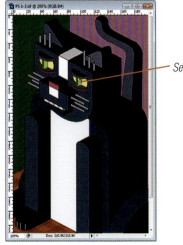

Selected area

FIGURE 36

Match Color dialog box

Name of
target image

Name of
source
image

Layer
containing
selection in
source

FIGURE 37

Image with matched colors

Modified selection

Sample of layer
in source

Match a color

1. Click the **Rooster layer** on the Layers palette, then zoom (once) into the eye of the rooster.

2. Click the **Magic Wand Tool** on the Tools palette.

3. Verify that the **Contiguous check box** on the options bar is selected, then set the **Tolerance** to 10.

4. Click the image with the **Magic Wand pointer** on the white of the eye at approximately **550 X/210 Y**.

5. Open PS 4-3.tif from the drive and folder where you store your Data Files, zoom into the image if necessary, change the tolerance to **40** then click the **light green part of the cat's eye** (at **100 X/95 Y**) with the **Magic Wand pointer**. Compare your selection to Figure 35.

6. Activate the **Rooster image**, click **Image** on the menu bar, point to **Adjustments**, then click **Match Color**.

7. Click the **Source list arrow**, then click **PS 4-3.tif**. Compare your settings to Figure 36.

8. Click **OK**.

9. Deselect the selection, zoom out to **33.3%**, turn off the rulers, save your work, then compare your image to Figure 37.

10. Close all open images, then exit Photoshop.

You used the Match Color dialog box to replace a color in one image with a color from another image. The Match Color dialog box makes it easy to sample colors from other images, giving you even more options for incorporating color into an image.

SKILLS REFERENCE

Power User Shortcuts

to do this:	use this method:
Apply a sharpen filter	Filter ➤ Sharpen
Balance colors	Image ➤ Adjustments ➤ Color Balance
Change color mode	Image ➤ Mode
Choose a background color from the Swatches palette	[Ctrl]Color swatch (Win) ⌘ Color swatch (Mac)
Delete a swatch from the Swatches palette	[Alt], click swatch (Win) [option], click swatch (Mac)
Eyedropper Tool	🖋 or I
Fill with background color	[Shift][Backspace] (Win) ⌘ [delete] (Mac)
Fill with foreground color	[Alt][Backspace] (Win) option [delete] (Mac)
Gradient Tool	▩
Guide pointer	⊩ or ⊥
Hide a layer	👁

to do this:	use this method:
Hide or show rulers	[Ctrl][R] (Win) ⌘ [R] (Mac)
Hide or show the Color Palette	[F6] (Win)
Lock transparent pixels check box on/off	/
Make Swatches palette active	Swatches ×
Paint Bucket Tool	🪣 or G
Return background and foreground colors to default	◼ or D
Show a layer	▢
Show hidden Paint Bucket/ Gradient Tools	[Shift] G
Switch between open files	[Ctrl][Tab] (Win) [control tab] (Mac)
Switch Foreground and Background Colors	⤹ or X

Key: Menu items are indicated by ➤ between the menu name and its command. Blue bold letters are shortcuts for selecting tools on the Tools palette.

Work with color to transform an image.

1. Start Photoshop.
2. Open PS 4-4.psd from the drive and folder where you store your Data Files, then save it as **Firetruck**.
3. Make sure the rulers appear in pixels, and that the default foreground and background colors display.
4. Use the Eyedropper Tool to sample the red color at 90 X/165 Y using the guides to help.
5. Use the Paint Bucket Tool to apply the new foreground color to the Background layer.
6. Undo your last step using either the Edit menu or the History palette.
7. Switch the foreground and background colors.
8. Save your work.

Use the Color Picker and the Swatches palette.

1. Use the Set foreground color button to open the Color Picker dialog box.
2. Click the R:, G:, and B: option buttons, one at a time. Note how the color palette changes.
3. With the B: option button selected, click the palette in the upper-left corner, then click OK.
4. Switch the foreground and background colors.
5. Add the foreground color (red) to the Swatches palette using a meaningful name of your choice.
6. Save your work.

Place a border around an image.

1. Make Layer 1 active (if it is not already active).
2. Revert to the default foreground and background colors.

3. Create a border by applying a 2-pixel outside stroke to the firetruck.
4. Save your work.

Blend colors using the Gradient Tool.

1. Change the foreground color to the fourth swatch from the right in the top row of the Swatches palette (35% Gray).
2. Switch foreground and background colors.
3. Use the new red swatch that you added previously as the foreground color.
4. Make the Background layer active.
5. Use the Gradient Tool, apply the Angle Gradient with its default settings, then using the guides to help, drag the pointer from 145 X/70 Y to 35 X/165 Y.
6. Save your work, and turn off the rulers display.

Add color to a grayscale image.

1. Open PS 4–5.psd, then save it as **Firetruck Colorized**.
2. Change the color mode to RGB Color.
3. Open the Hue/Saturation dialog box, then select the Colorize check box.
4. Drag the sliders so the text boxes show the following values: 175, 56, and –30, then click OK.
5. Save your work.

Use filters, opacity, and blending modes.

1. Use the Sharpen filter to sharpen the image.
2. Open the Fade Sharpen dialog box by using the Edit menu, change the opacity to 40%,

change the mode to Hard Light, then save your work.
3. Open the Color Balance dialog box.
4. Change the color level settings so the text boxes show the following values: +61, –15, and +20.
5. Turn off the rulers display if necessary.
6. Save your work.

Match colors.

1. Open PS 4-6.tif, then select the light green in the cat's eye.
2. Select the white areas of the fire truck in Firetruck.psd. (*Hint:* You can click on multiple areas using the Magic Wand Tool.)
3. Use the Match Color dialog box to change the white in Layer 1 of the Firetruck image to green (in the cat's eye). Compare your images to Figure 38.
4. Save your work.
5. Exit Photoshop.

FIGURE 38
Completed Skills Review

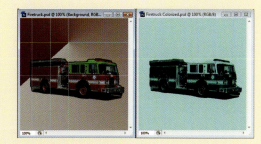

You are finally able to leave your current job and pursue your lifelong dream of opening a furniture repair and restoration business. While you're waiting for the laser stripper and refinisher to arrive, you start to work on a sign design.

1. Open PS 4-7.psd, substitte any missing fonts, then save it as **Furniture Wizard**.
2. Move the objects to any location to achieve a layout you think looks attractive and eye-catching.
3. Sample the blue pliers in the tool belt, then switch the foreground and background colors.
4. Sample the red tape measure in the tool belt.
5. Use any Gradient Tool to create an interesting effect on the Background layer.
6. Save the image, then compare your screen to the sample shown in Figure 39.

FIGURE 39
Completed Project Builder 1

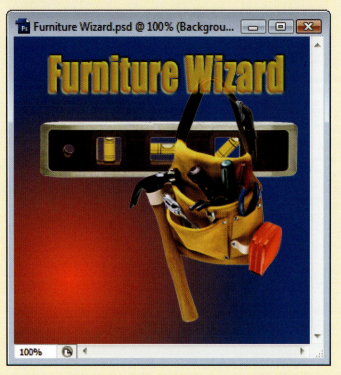

You're painting the swing set at the PB&J Preschool, when you notice a staff member struggling to create a flyer for the school. Although the basic flyer is complete, it doesn't convey the high energy of the school. You offer to help, and soon find yourself in charge of creating an exciting background for the image.

1. Open PS 4-8.psd, update layers as needed, then save it as **Preschool**.
2. Apply a foreground color of your choice to the Background layer.
3. Add a new layer above the Background layer, then select a background color and apply a gradient you have not used before to the layer. (*Hint*: Remember that you can immediately undo a gradient that you don't want.)
4. Add the foreground and background colors to the Swatches palette.
5. Apply a Sharpen filter to the boy at blackboard layer and adjust the opacity of the filter.
6. Save your work.
7. Compare your screen to the sample shown in Figure 40.

FIGURE 40
Completed Project Builder 2

DESIGN PROJECT

A local Top 40 morning radio show recently conducted a survey about chocolate, and discovered that only one in seven people knew about it health benefits. Now everyone is talking about chocolate. An interior designer wants to incorporate chocolates into her fall decorating theme, and has asked you to create a poster. You decide to highlight as many varieties as possible.

1. Open PS 4-9.psd, then save it as **Chocolate**.
2. If you choose, you can add any appropriate images that have been scanned or captured using a digital camera.
3. Activate the Background layer, then sample colors from the image for foreground and background colors. (*Hint*: Try to sample unusual colors, to widen your design horizons.)
4. Add the sampled colors to the Swatches palette.
5. Display the rulers, then move the existing guides to indicate the coordinates of the colors you sampled.
6. Create a gradient fill by using both foreground and background colors and the gradient style of your choice.
7. Defringe the Chocolate layer, if necessary.
8. Hide the rulers, save your work, then compare your image to the sample shown in Figure 41.

FIGURE 41
Completed Design Project

Depending on the size of your group, you can assign individual elements of the project to group members, or work collectively to create the finished product.

An educational toy and game store has hired your team to design a poster announcing this year's Most Unusual Hobby contest. After reviewing the photos from last year's awards ceremony, you decide to build a poster using the winner of the Handicrafts Award. You'll use your knowledge of Photoshop color modes to convert the color mode, adjust color in the image, and add an interesting background.

1. Open PS 4-10.psd, then save it as **Rubberband**.
2. Convert the image to Grayscale mode. (*Hint*: When Photoshop prompts you to flatten the layers, click Don't Flatten.)
3. Convert the image to RGB Color mode. (*Hint*: When Photoshop prompts you to flatten the layers, click Don't Flatten.)
4. Two or more people can colorize the image and adjust the Hue, Saturation, and Lightness settings as desired.
5. Adjust Brightness/Contrast settings as desired.
6. Adjust Color Balance settings as desired.
7. Two or more people can sample the image to create a new foreground color, then add a color of your choice as the background color.
8. Apply any two Sharpen filters and adjust the opacity for one of them.
9. Add a reflected gradient to the Background layer that follows the path of one of the main bands on the ball.
10. Save your work, then compare your image to the sample shown in Figure 42.
11. Be prepared to discuss the color-correcting methods you used and why you chose them.

FIGURE 42
Completed Group Project

chapter

5

PLACING TYPE IN
AN IMAGE

1. Learn about type and how it is created

2. Change spacing and adjust baseline shift

3. Use the Drop Shadow style

4. Apply anti-aliasing to type

5. Modify type with the Bevel and Emboss style

6. Apply special effects to type using filters

7. Create text on a path

5-1

5 PLACING TYPE IN
AN IMAGE

Learning About Type

Text plays an important design role when combined with images for posters, magazine and newspaper advertisements, and other graphics materials that need to communicate detailed information. In Photoshop, text is referred to as **type**. You can use type to express the ideas conveyed in a file's imagery or to deliver an additional message. You can manipulate type in many ways to reflect or reinforce the meaning behind an image. As in other programs, type has its own unique characteristics in Photoshop. For example, you can change its appearance by using different fonts (also called typefaces) and colors.

Understanding the Purpose of Type

Type is typically used along with imagery to deliver a message quickly and with flare. Because type is used sparingly (typically there's not a lot of room for it), its appearance is very important; color and imagery are often used to *complement* or *reinforce* the message within the text. Type should be limited, direct, and to the point. It should be large enough for easy reading, but should not overwhelm or distract from the central image. For example, a vibrant and daring advertisement should contain just enough type to interest the reader, without demanding too much reading.

Getting the Most Out of Type

Words can express an idea, but the appearance of the type is what drives the point home. After you decide on the content you want to use and create the type, you can experiment with its appearance by changing its **font** (characters with a similar appearance), size, and color. You can also apply special effects that make it stand out, or appear to pop off the page.

Tools You'll Use

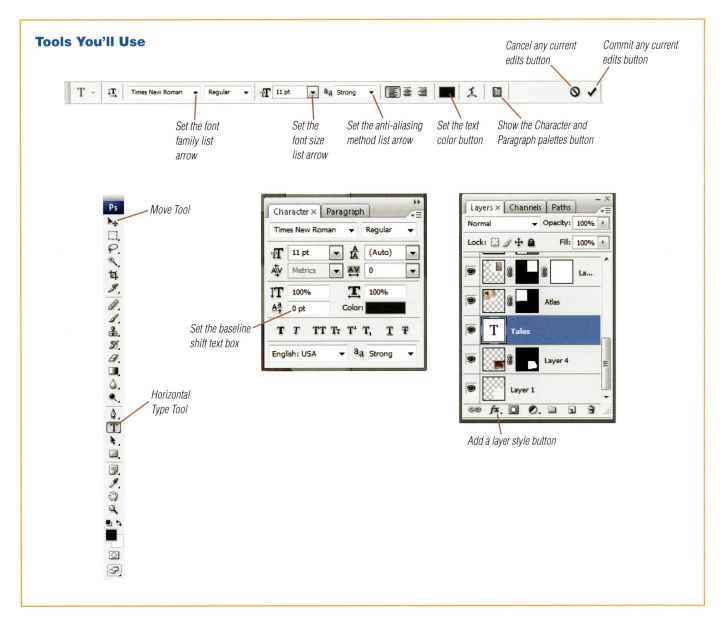

Cancel any current edits button

Commit any current edits button

Set the font family list arrow

Set the font size list arrow

Set the anti-aliasing method list arrow

Set the text color button

Show the Character and Paragraph palettes button

Move Tool

Horizontal Type Tool

Set the baseline shift text box

Add a layer style button

LEARN ABOUT TYPE AND
HOW IT IS CREATED

What You'll Do

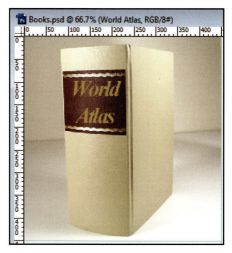

In this lesson, you'll create a type layer, then change the alignment, font family, size, and color of the type.

Introducing Type Types

Outline type is mathematically defined, which means that it can be scaled to any size without losing its sharp, smooth edges. Some programs, such as Adobe Illustrator, create outline type. **Bitmap type** is composed of pixels, and, like images, can develop jagged edges when enlarged. The type you create in Photoshop is initially outline type, but it is converted into bitmap type when you apply special filters. Using the type tools and the options bar, you can create horizontal or vertical type and modify font size and alignment. You use the Color Picker dialog box to change type color. When you create type in Photoshop, it is automatically placed on a new type layer on the Layers palette.

QUICKTIP
Keeping type on separate layers makes it much easier to modify and change positions within the image.

Getting to Know Font Families

Each **font family** represents a complete set of characters, letters, and symbols for a particular typeface. Font families are generally divided into three categories: serif, sans serif, and symbol. Characters in **serif fonts** have a tail, or stroke, at the end of some characters. These tails make it easier for the eye to recognize words. For this reason, serif fonts are generally used in text passages. **Sans serif fonts** do not have tails and are commonly used in headlines.

Symbol fonts are used to display unique characters (such as $, ÷, or ™). Table 1 lists commonly used serif and sans serif fonts. After you select the Horizontal Type Tool, you can change font families using the options bar.

Measuring Type Size

The size of each character within a font is measured in **points**. **PostScript**, a programming language that optimizes printed text and graphics, was introduced by Adobe in 1985. In PostScript measurement, one inch is equivalent to 72 points or six picas. Therefore, one pica is equivalent to 12 points. In traditional measurement, one inch is equivalent to 72.27 points. The default Photoshop type size is 12 points. In Photoshop, you have the option of using PostScript or traditional character measurement.

Acquiring Fonts

Your computer has many fonts installed on it, but no matter how many fonts you have, you probably can use more. Fonts can be purchased from private companies, individual designers, computer stores, catalog companies. Fonts are delivered on CD-ROM, DVDs, or over the Internet. Using your browser and your favorite search engine, you can locate Web sites that let you purchase or download fonts. Many Web sites offer specialty fonts, such as the Web site shown in Figure 1. Other Web sites offer these fonts free of charge or for a nominal fee.

TABLE 1: Commonly Used Serif and Sans Serif Fonts

serif fonts	sample	sans serif fonts	sample
Lucida Handwriting	*Adobe Photoshop*	Arial	Adobe Photoshop
Rockwell	Adobe Photoshop	Bauhaus	Adobe Photoshop
Times New Roman	Adobe Photoshop	Century Gothic	Adobe Photoshop

FIGURE 1
Font Web site

Courtesy of Betterfonts.com - http://betterfonts.com/

Create and modify type

1. Start Photoshop, open PS 5-1.psd from the drive and folder where you store your Data Files, update the text layers if necessary, then save the file as **Books**.

2. Display the document size in the status bar, and the rulers in pixels (if they are not already displayed).

   TIP You can quickly toggle the rulers on and off by pressing **[Ctrl][R]** (Win) or ⌘ **[R]** (Mac).

3. Click the **Default Foreground and Background Colors button** on the Tools palette.

4. Click the **Horizontal Type Tool** T on the Tools palette.

5. Click the **Set the font family list arrow** on the options bar, click **Arial** (a sans-serif font), click the **Set the font style list arrow**, then click **Italic**.

   TIP If Arial is not available, make a reasonable substitution.

6. Click the **Center text button** on the options bar (if it is not already selected).

7. Click the **Set the font size list arrow** on the options bar, then click **24 pt** (if it is not already selected).

8. Click the image with the **Horizontal Type pointer** in the center of the **brown area of the spine** just below the gold leaf at **160 X/130 Y**, then type **World**, press **[Shift] [Enter]** (Win) or **[shift][return]** (Mac), then type **Atlas**, as shown in Figure 2.

You created a type layer by using the Horizontal Type Tool on the Tools palette and modified the font family, alignment, and font size.

FIGURE 2
New type in image

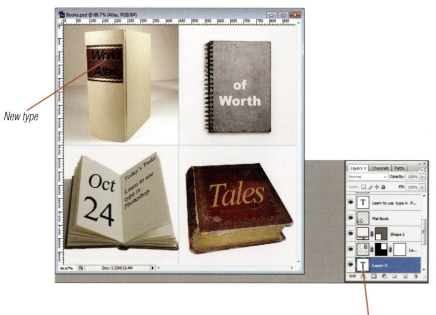

New type

New type layer

Using the active layer palette background (Macintosh)

Icons used in Macintosh to identify type layers are similar to those found in Windows. In Macintosh, the active layer has the same Type and Layer style buttons. The active layer's background color is the same color as the Highlight Color. (In Windows, the active layer's background color is navy blue.)

FIGURE 3
Type with new color

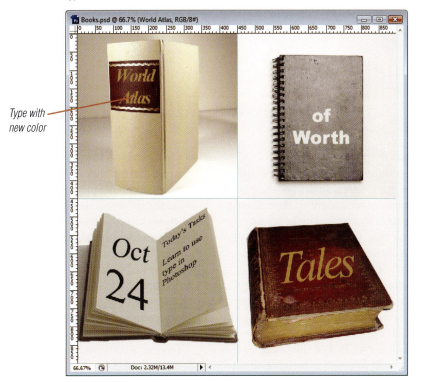

Type with
new color

Books.psd @ 66.7% (World Atlas, RGB/8#)

66.67%   Doc: 2.32M/13.4M

Using the Swatches palette to change type color

You can also use the Swatches palette to change type color. Select the type, then click a color on the Swatches palette. The new color that you click will appear in the Set foreground color button on the Tools palette and will be applied to type that is currently selected.

Change type color using an existing image color

1. Press **[Ctrl][A]** (Win) or ⌘ **[A]** (Mac) to select all the text.

2. Click the **Set the font family list arrow** on the options bar, scroll down, then click **Times New Roman**.

   TIP Click in the Set the font family text box and you can select a different font by typing the first few characters of the font name. Scroll through the fonts by clicking in the Set the font family text box, then pressing the [UpArrow] or [DownArrow].

3. Click the **Set the font style list arrow**, then click **Bold Italic**.

4. Click the **Set the text color button** ■ on the options bar.

   TIP Drag the Set text color dialog box out of the way if it blocks your view of the image.

   As you position the pointer over the image, the pointer automatically becomes an Eyedropper pointer.

5. Click the image with the **Eyedropper pointer** anywhere in the **letter "T"** in the book in the lower-right corner at approximately **600 X/610 Y**.

   The new color is now the active color in the Set text color dialog box.

6. Click **OK** in the Set text color dialog box.

7. Click the **Commit any current edits button** ✔ on the options bar.

   Clicking the Commit any current edits button accepts your changes and makes them permanent in the image.

8. Save your work, then compare your image to Figure 3.

You changed the font family, modified the color of the type by using an existing image color, and committed the current edits.

CHANGE SPACING AND
ADJUST BASELINE SHIFT

What You'll Do

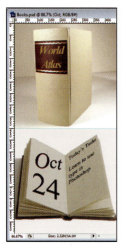

In this lesson, you'll adjust the spacing between characters and change the baseline of type.

Adjusting Spacing

Competition for readers on the visual landscape is fierce. To get and maintain an edge over other designers, Photoshop provides tools that let you make adjustments to your type, thereby making your type more distinctive. These adjustments might not be very dramatic, but they can influence readers in subtle ways. For example, type that is too small and difficult to read might make the reader impatient (at the very least), and he or she might not even look at the image (at the very worst). You can make finite adjustments, called **type spacing**, to the space between characters and between lines of type. Adjusting type spacing affects the ease with which words are read.

Understanding Character and Line Spacing

Fonts in desktop publishing and word processing programs use proportional spacing, whereas typewriters use monotype spacing. In **monotype spacing**, each character occupies the same amount of space. This means that wide characters such as "o" and "w" take up the same real estate on the page as narrow ones such as "i" and "l". In **proportional spacing**, each character can take up a different amount of space, depending on its width. **Kerning** controls the amount of space between characters and can affect several characters, a word, or an entire paragraph. **Tracking** inserts a *uniform* amount of space between selected characters. Figure 4 shows an example of type before and after it has been kerned.

The second line of text takes up less room and has less space between its characters, making it easier to read. You can also change the amount of space, called **leading**, between lines of type, to add or decrease the distance between lines of text.

Using the Character Palette

The **Character palette**, shown in Figure 5, helps you manually or automatically control type properties such as kerning, tracking, and leading. You open the Character palette from the options bar and the Dock.

Adjusting the Baseline Shift

Type rests on an invisible line called a **baseline**. Using the Character palette, you can adjust the **baseline shift**, the vertical distance that type moves from its baseline.

You can add interest to type by changing the baseline shift.

FIGURE 4

Kerned characters

FIGURE 5

Character palette

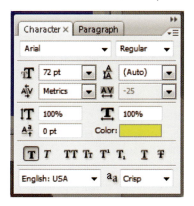

Kern characters

1. Click the **World Atlas type layer** on the Layers palette (if it is not already selected).

2. Click the **Horizontal Type Tool** T on the Tools palette.

3. Click the **Toggle the Character and Paragraph palettes button** on the options bar to open the Character palette.

   > TIP You can close the Character palette by clicking the Collapse button in the upper-right corner of its title bar or by clicking the Character button. You can also open and close the Character palette by clicking the Character button on the vertical dock.

4. Click between "o" and "r" in the word "World."

   > TIP You can drag the Character palette out of the way if it blocks your view.

5. Click the **Set the kerning between two characters list arrow** on the Character palette, then click **–25**.

   The spacing between the two characters decreases.

6. Click between "A" and "t" in the word "Atlas."

7. Click the **Set the kerning between two characters list arrow** , then click **–25**, as shown in Figure 6.

8. Click the **Commit any current edits button** ✓ on the options bar.

You modified the kerning between characters by using the Character palette.

FIGURE 6
Kerned type

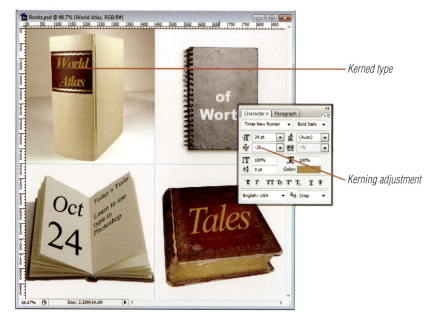

Kerned type

Kerning adjustment

Correcting spelling errors

Are you concerned that your gorgeous image will be ruined by misspelled words? Photoshop understands your pain and has included a spelling checker to make sure you are never plagued by incorrect spellings. If you want, the spelling checker will check the type on the current layer, or all the layers in the image. First, make sure the correct dictionary for your language is selected. English: USA is the default, but you can choose another language by clicking the Set the language on selected characters for hyphenation and spelling list arrow at the bottom of the Character palette. To check spelling, click Edit on the menu bar, then click Check Spelling. The spelling checker will automatically stop at each word not already appearing in the dictionary. One or more suggestions might be offered, which you can either accept or reject.

FIGURE 7
Select text color dialog box

Select text color:

new

current

OK

Cancel

Add To Swatches

Color Libraries

New foreground color

Only Web Colors

○ H: 355 °   ○ L: 18
○ S: 61 %   ○ a: 23
○ B: 29 %   ○ b: 9
○ R: 75   C: 44 %
○ G: 29   M: 83 %
● B: 33   Y: 69 %
4b1d21   K: 63 %

Selects the new
foreground color

FIGURE 8
Type with baseline shifted

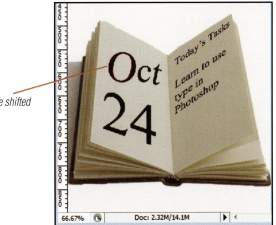

Baseline shifted

66.67%   Doc: 2.32M/14.1M

Shift the baseline

1. Double-click the **layer thumbnail** T. on the Oct type layer, then use the **Horizontal Type Pointer** to select the "O".

2. Click the **Set the text color button** ■ on the options bar.

3. Click anywhere in the maroon area behind the World Atlas type, such as **210 X/180 Y**, compare your Select text color dialog box to Figure 7, then click **OK**.

4. Double-click **36** in the Set the font size text box on the Character palette, type **45**, double-click **0** in the Set the baseline shift text box on the Character palette, then type **–5**.

5. Click the **Commit any current edits button** ✔ on the options bar.

6. Click the **Toggle the Character and Paragraph palettes button** on the options bar.

7. Save your work, then compare your screen to Figure 8.

You changed the type color, then adjusted the baseline of the first character in a word, to make the first character stand out.

USE THE DROP
SHADOW STYLE

What You'll Do

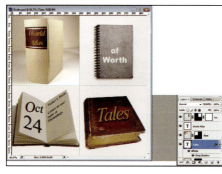

▶ *In this lesson, you'll apply the drop shadow style to a type layer, then modify drop shadow settings.*

Adding Effects to Type

Layer styles (effects which can be applied to a type or image layer) can greatly enhance the appearance of type and improve its effectiveness. A type layer is indicated by the appearance of the T icon in the layer's thumbnail box. When a layer style is applied to any layer, the Indicates layer effects icon (*f*) appears in that layer when it is active. The Layers palette is a great source of information. You can see which effects have been applied to a layer by clicking the arrow to the left of the Indicates layer effects icon on the Layers palette if the layer is active or inactive. Figure 9 shows a layer that has two type layer styles applied to it. Layer styles are linked to the contents of a layer, which means that if a type layer is moved or modified, the layer's style will still be applied to the type.

Using the Drop Shadow

One method of placing emphasis on type is to add a drop shadow to it. A **drop shadow** creates an illusion that another colored layer of identical text is behind the selected type. The drop shadow default color is black, but it can be changed to another color using the Color Picker dialog box, or any of the other methods for changing color.

Applying a Style

You can apply a style, such as a drop shadow, to the active layer, by clicking Layer on the menu bar, pointing to Layer Style, then clicking a style. The settings in the Layer Style dialog box are "sticky," meaning that they display the settings that you last used. An alternative method to using the menu bar is to select the layer that you want to apply the style to, click the Add a layer style button on the Layers palette, then click a style. Regardless of which method you use, the Layer Style dialog box opens. You use this dialog box to add all kinds of effects to type. Depending on which style you've chosen, the Layer Style dialog box displays options appropriate to that style.

QUICKTIP

You can apply styles to objects as well as to type.

Controlling a Drop Shadow

You can control many aspects of a drop shadow's appearance, including its angle, its distance behind the type, and the amount of blur it contains. The **angle** determines where the shadow falls relative to the text, and the **distance** determines how far the shadow falls from the text. The **spread** determines the width of the shadow

text, and the **size** determines the clarity of the shadow. Figure 10 shows samples of two different drop shadow effects. The first line of type uses the default background color (black), has an angle of 160 degrees, distance of 10 pixels, a spread of 0%, and a size of five pixels. The second line of type uses a purple background color, has an angle of 120 degrees, distance of 20 pixels, a spread of 10%, and a size of five pixels. As you modify the drop shadow, the preview window displays the changes.

FIGURE 9
Effects in a type layer

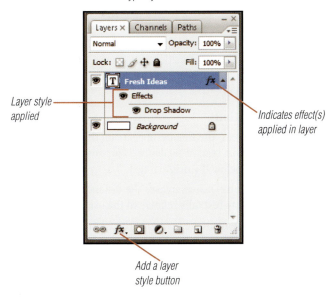

Layer style applied

Indicates effect(s) applied in layer

Add a layer style button

FIGURE 10
Sample drop shadows

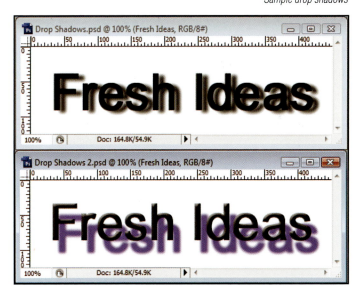

Add a drop shadow

1. Click the **layer thumbnail** on the Tales type layer.

2. Click the **Add a layer style button** *fx* on the Layers palette.

3. Click **Drop Shadow**.

4. Compare your Layer Style dialog box to Figure 11.

   The default drop shadow settings are applied to the type. Table 2 describes the drop shadow settings.

   TIP You can also open the Layer Style dialog box by double-clicking a layer on the Layers palette.

You created a drop shadow by using the Add a layer style button on the Layers palette and the Layer Style dialog box.

FIGURE 11
Drop shadow settings

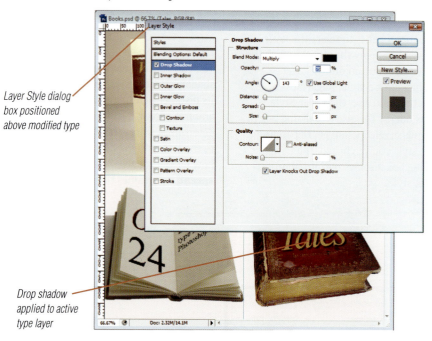

Layer Style dialog box positioned above modified type

Drop shadow applied to active type layer

TABLE 2: Drop Shadow Settings

setting	scale	explanation
Angle	0–360 degrees	At 0 degrees, the shadow appears on the baseline of the original text. At 90 degrees, the shadow appears directly below the original text.
Distance	0–30,000 pixels	A larger pixel size increases the distance from which the shadow text falls relative to the original text.
Spread	0–100%	A larger percentage increases the width of the shadow text.
Size	0–250 pixels	A larger pixel size increases the blur of the shadow text.

FIGURE 12
Layer Style dialog box

Angle text box

Distance text box

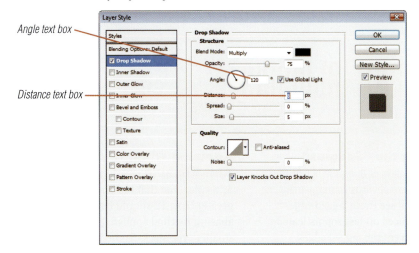

Modify drop shadow settings

1. Double-click the number in the Angle text box, then type **120**.

   Each style in the Layer Styles dialog box shows different options in the center section. These options are displayed as you click each style (in the Styles pane).

   > TIP You can also set the angle by dragging the dial slider in the Layer Style dialog box.

2. Double-click the number in the Distance text box, then type **8**. See Figure 12.

   > TIP You can create your own layer style in the Layer Style dialog box, by selecting style settings, clicking New Style, typing a new name or accepting the default, then clicking OK. The new style appears as a preset in the Styles list of the Layer Style dialog box.

3. Click **OK**, then compare your screen to Figure 13.

4. Click the **list arrow to the right of the Indicates layer effects icon** ▲ on the Tales layer to close the list.

5. Save your work.

You used the Layer Style dialog box to modify the settings for the drop shadow.

FIGURE 13
Drop shadow added to type layer

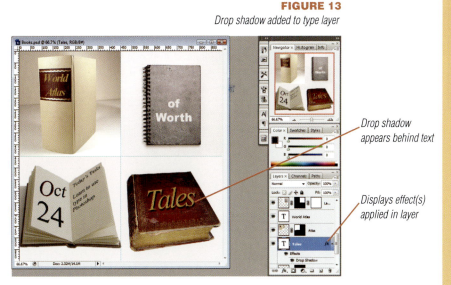

Drop shadow appears behind text

Displays effect(s) applied in layer

Lesson 3   Use the Drop Shadow Style

APPLY ANTI-ALIASING
TO TYPE

What You'll Do

 In this lesson, you'll view the effects of the anti-aliasing feature, then use the History palette to return the type to its original state.

Eliminating the "Jaggies"

In the good old days of dot-matrix printers, jagged edges were obvious in many print ads. You can still see these jagged edges in designs produced on less sophisticated printers. To prevent the jagged edges (sometimes called "jaggies") that often accompany bitmap type, Photoshop offers an anti-aliasing feature. **Anti-aliasing** partially fills in pixel edges with additional colors, resulting in smooth-edge type and an increased number of colors in the image. Anti-aliasing is useful for improving the display of large type in print media; however, this can cause a file to become large.

Knowing When to Apply Anti-Aliasing

As a rule, type that has a point size greater than 12 should have some anti-aliasing method applied. Sometimes, smaller type sizes can become blurry or muddy when anti-aliasing is used. As part of the process, anti-aliasing adds interme-diate colors to your image in an effort to reduce the jagged edges. As a designer, you need to weigh the following factors when determining if you should apply anti-aliasing: type size versus file size and image quality.

Understanding Anti-Aliasing

Anti-aliasing improves the display of type against the background. You can use five anti-aliasing methods: None, Sharp, Crisp, Strong, and Smooth. An example of each method is shown in Figure 14. The **None** setting applies no anti-aliasing, and can result in type that has jagged edges. The **Sharp** setting displays type with the best possible resolution. The **Crisp** setting gives type more definition and makes type appear sharper. The **Strong** setting makes type appear heavier, much like the bold attribute. The **Smooth** setting gives type more rounded edges.

FIGURE 14
Anti-aliasing effects

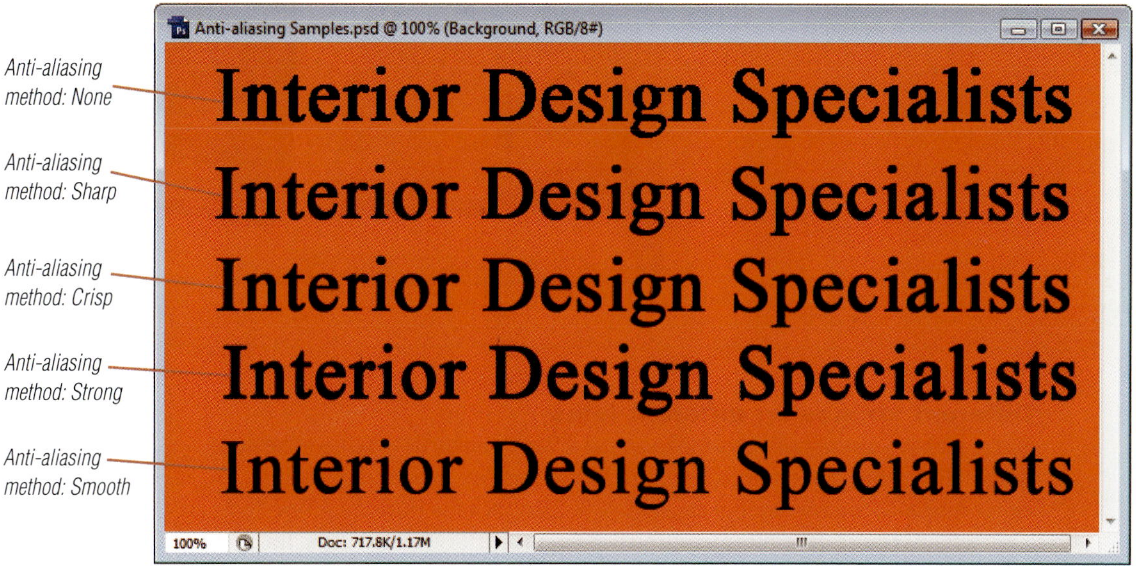

Anti-aliasing method: None

Anti-aliasing method: Sharp

Anti-aliasing method: Crisp

Anti-aliasing method: Strong

Anti-aliasing method: Smooth

Apply anti-aliasing

1. Double-click the **layer thumbnail** on the Tales layer.

2. Click the **Set the anti-aliasing method list arrow** 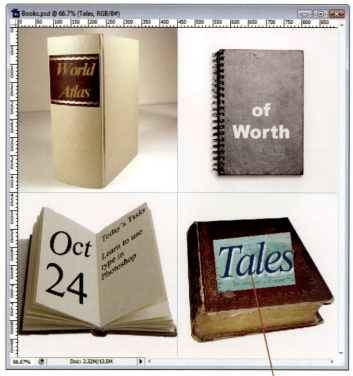 on the options bar.

3. Click **Strong**, then compare your work to Figure 15.

4. Click the **Commit any current edits button** ✔ on the options bar.

You applied the Strong anti-aliasing setting to see how the setting affected the appearance of type.

FIGURE 15
Effect of Strong anti-aliasing

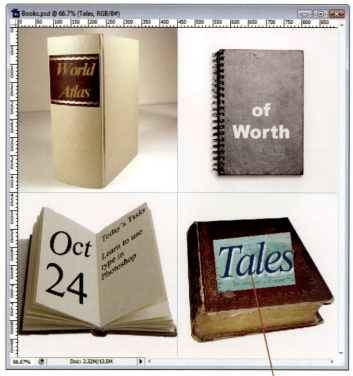

Type appearance altered

Different strokes for different folks

You're probably already aware that you can use different methods to achieve the same goals in Photoshop. For instance, if you want to see the type options bar, you can either double-click a type layer or single-click it, then click the Horizontal Type Tool. The method you use determines what you'll see in the History palette. Using the double-clicking method, a change in the anti-aliasing method will result in the following history state 'Edit Type Layer'. Using the single-clicking method to change to the anti-alias method to Crisp results in an 'Anti Alias Crisp' history state.

FIGURE 16

Deleting a state from the History palette

Delete current
state button

Undo anti-aliasing

1. Click **Window** on the menu bar, point to **Workspace**, then click **Legacy**.

   The palettes display in a format used by the previous version of Photoshop, allowing you to see the History palette.

2. Click the **Edit Type Layer state** listed at the bottom of the History palette, then drag it to the **Delete current state button** 🗑 , as shown in Figure 16.

   | TIP Various methods of undoing actions are reviewed in Table 3.

3. Save your work.

You deleted a state in the History palette to return the type to its original appearance. The History palette offers an easy way of undoing previous steps.

TABLE 3: Undoing Actions

method	description	keyboard shortcut
Undo	Edit ≻ Undo	[Ctrl][Z] (Win)
		⌘ [Z] (Mac)
Step Backward	Click Edit on the menu bar, then click Step Backward	[Alt][Ctrl][Z] (Win)
		[option] ⌘ [Z] (Mac)
History palette	Drag state to the Delete current state button on the History palette	[Alt] 🗑 (Win)
		[option] 🗑 (Mac)

MODIFY TYPE WITH THE
BEVEL AND EMBOSS STYLE

What You'll Do

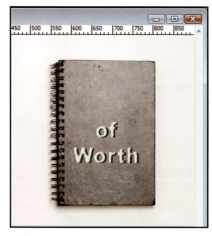

 In this lesson, you'll apply the Bevel and Emboss style, then modify the Bevel and Emboss settings.

Using the Bevel and Emboss Style

You use the Bevel and Emboss style to add combinations of shadows and highlights to a layer and make type appear to have dimension and shine. You can use the Layer menu or the Layers palette to apply the Bevel and Emboss style to the active layer. Like all Layer styles, the Bevel and Emboss style is linked to the type layer that it is applied to.

Understanding Bevel and Emboss Settings

You can use two categories of Bevel and Emboss settings: structure and shading. **Structure** determines the size and physical properties of the object, and **shading** determines the lighting effects. Figure 17 contains several variations of Bevel and Emboss structure settings. The shading used in the Bevel and Emboss style determines how and where light is projected on

Filling type with imagery

You can use the imagery from a layer in one file as the fill pattern for another image's type layer. To create this effect, open a multi-layer file that contains the imagery you want to use (the source), then open the file that contains the type you want to fill (the target). In the source file, activate the layer containing the imagery you want to use, use the Select menu to select all, then use the Edit menu to copy the selection. In the target file, press [Ctrl] (Win) or ⌘ (Mac) while clicking the type layer to which the imagery will be applied, then click Paste Into on the Edit menu. The imagery will appear within the type.

the type. You can control a variety of settings, including the angle, altitude, and gloss contour, to create a unique appearance. The **Angle** setting determines where the shadow falls relative to the text, and the **Altitude** setting affects the amount of visible dimension. For example, an altitude of 0 degrees looks flat, while a setting of 90 degrees has a more three-dimensional appearance. The **Gloss Contour** setting determines the pattern with which light is reflected, and the **Highlight Mode** and **Shadow Mode** settings determine how pigments are combined. When the Use Global Light check box is selected, *all the type* in the image will be affected by your changes.

FIGURE 17

Bevel and Emboss style samples

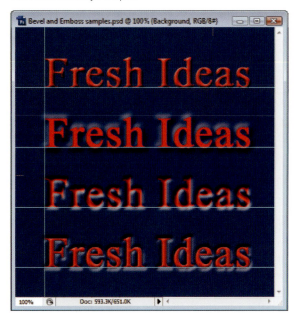

Add the Bevel and Emboss style with the Layer menu

1. Click the **of Worth layer** on the Layers palette.

2. Click **Layer** on the menu bar, point to **Layer Style**, click **Bevel and Emboss,** then click **Bevel and Emboss** in the Styles column (if it is not already selected).

3. Review the Layer Style dialog box shown in Figure 18, then move the Layer Style dialog box (if necessary), so you can see the "of Worth" type.

You applied the Bevel and Emboss style by using the Layer menu. This gave the text a more three-dimensional look.

FIGURE 18
Layer Style dialog box

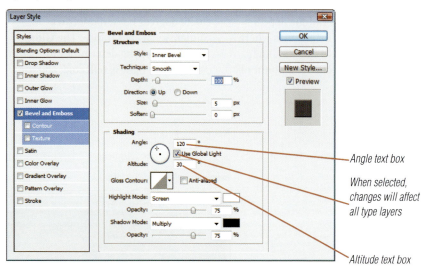

Angle text box

When selected, changes will affect all type layers

Altitude text box

Warping type

You can add dimension and style to your type by using the Warp Text feature. After you select the type layer you want to warp, click the Horizontal Type Tool on the Tools palette. Click the Create warped text button on the options bar to open the Warp Text dialog box. If a warning box opens telling you that your request cannot be completed because the type layer uses a faux bold style, click the Toggle the Character and Paragraph palettes button on the options bar, click the Character palette list arrow, click Faux Bold to deselect it, then click the Create warped text button again. You can click the Style list arrow to select from 15 available styles. After you select a style, you can modify its appearance by dragging the Bend, Horizontal Distortion, and Vertical Distortion sliders.

TABLE 4: Bevel and Emboss Structure Settings

sample	style	technique	direction	size	soften
1	Inner Bevel	Smooth	Up	5	1
2	Outer Bevel	Chisel Hard	Up	5	8
3	Emboss	Smooth	Down	10	3
4	Pillow Emboss	Chisel Soft	Up	10	3

FIGURE 19

Bevel and Emboss style applied to type

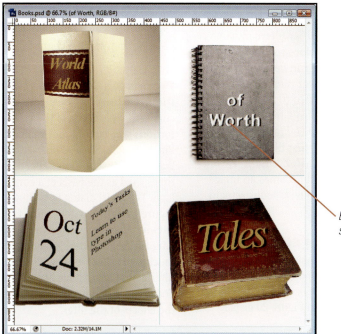

Bevel and Emboss
style applied to layer

Modify Bevel and Emboss settings

1. Double-click the number in the Angle text box, then type **163**.

   Some of the Bevel and Emboss settings are listed in Table 4.

   You can use the Layer Style dialog box to change the structure by adjusting style, technique, direction, size, and soften settings.

2. Double-click the **Altitude text box**, then type **20**.

3. Click **OK**, then compare your type to Figure 19.

4. Save your work.

You modified the default settings for the Bevel and Emboss style. Experimenting with different settings is crucial to achieve the effect you want.

APPLY SPECIAL EFFECTS TO
TYPE USING FILTERS

What You'll Do

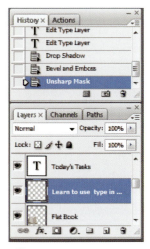

 In this lesson, you'll rasterize a type layer, then apply a filter to it to change its appearance.

Understanding Filters

Like an image layer, a type layer can have one or more filters applied to it to achieve special effects and make your text look unique. Some filter dialog boxes have preview windows that let you see the results of the particular filter before it is applied to the layer. Other filters must be applied to the layer before you can see the results. Before a filter can be applied to a type layer, the type layer must first be **rasterized**, or converted to an image layer. After it is rasterized, the type characters *can no longer be edited* because it is composed of pixels, just like artwork. When a type layer is rasterized, the T icon in the layer thumbnail becomes an image thumbnail while the Effects icons remain on the type layer.

Creating Special Effects

Filters enable you to apply a variety of special effects to type, as shown in Figure 20. Notice that none of the original type layers on the Layers palette in Figure 20 display

the T icon in the layer thumbnail because the layers have all been rasterized.

QUICKTIP

Because you cannot edit type after it has been rasterized, you should save your original type by making a copy of the layer *before* you rasterize it, then hide it from view.

Producing Distortions

Distort filters let you create waves or curves in type. Some of the types of distortions you can produce include Glass, Pinch, Ripple, Shear, Spherize, Twirl, Wave, and Zigzag. These effects are sometimes used as the basis of a corporate logo. The Twirl dialog box, shown in Figure 21, lets you determine the amount of twirl effect you want to apply. By dragging the Angle slider, you control how much twirl effect is added to a layer. Most filter dialog boxes have Zoom In and Zoom Out buttons that make it easy to see the effects of the filter.

Using Textures and Relief

Many filters let you create the appearance of textures and **relief** (the height of ridges within an object). One of the Stylize filters, Wind, applies lines throughout the type, making it appear shredded. The Wind dialog box, shown in Figure 22, lets you determine the kind of wind and its direction. The Texture filter lets you choose the type of texture you want to apply to a layer: Brick, Burlap, Canvas, or Sandstone.

Blurring Imagery

The Gaussian Blur filter softens the appearance of type by blurring its edge pixels. You can control the amount of blur applied to the type by entering high or low values in the Gaussian Blur dialog box. The higher the blur value, the blurrier the effect.

QUICKTIP

Be careful: too much blur applied to type can make it unreadable.

FIGURE 20
Sample filters applied to type

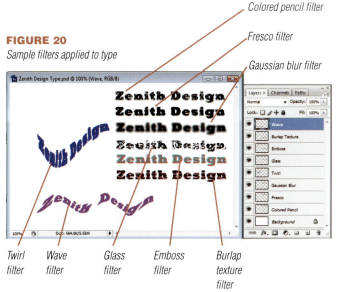

Colored pencil filter

Fresco filter

Gaussian blur filter

Twirl filter Wave filter Glass filter Emboss filter Burlap texture filter

FIGURE 21
Twirl dialog box

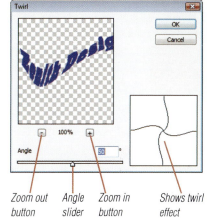

Zoom out button Angle slider Zoom in button Shows twirl effect

FIGURE 22
Wind dialog box

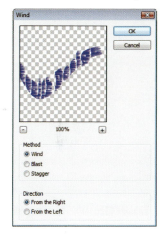

Rasterize a type layer

1. Click the **Learn to use type in Photoshop** layer on the Layers palette.

2. Click **Filter** on the menu bar, point to **Sharpen**, then click **Unsharp Mask**.

3. Click **OK** to rasterize the type and close the warning box shown in Figure 23.

   TIP   You can also rasterize a type layer by clicking Layer on the menu bar, pointing to Rasterize, then clicking Type.

   The Unsharp Mask dialog box opens.

You rasterized a type layer in preparation for filter application.

Adobe Photoshop CS3 Extended

This type layer must be rasterized before proceeding. Its text will no longer be editable. Rasterize the type?

OK   Cancel

DESIGNTIP   Using multiple filters

Sometimes, adding one filter doesn't achieve the effect you had in mind. You can use multiple filters to create a unique effect. Before you try your hand at filters, though, it's a good idea to make a copy of the original layer. That way, if things don't turn out as you planned, you can always start over. You don't even have to write down which filters you used, because you can always look at the History palette to see which filters you applied.

FIGURE 24
Unsharp Mask dialog box

Slider

FIGURE 25
Type with Gaussian blur filter

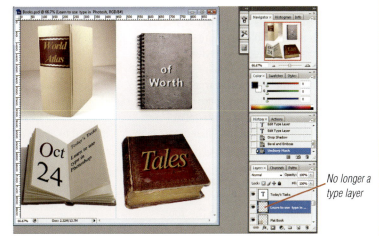

No longer a type layer

Modify filter settings

1. Drag the default background patterns in the preview window of the dialog box to position the type so it is visible.

2. Drag the sliders in the Unsharp Mask dialog box until **250** appears in the Amount text box, **6** appears in the Radius pixels text box, and **85** appears in the Threshold levels text box, as shown in Figure 24.

3. Click **OK**.

4. Save your work. Compare your modified type to Figure 25.

You modified the Unsharp Mask filter settings to modify the appearance of the layer.

Creating a neon glow

Want to create a really cool effect that takes absolutely no time at all, and works on both type and objects? You can create a neon glow that appears to surround an object. You can apply the Neon Glow filter (one of the Artistic filters) to any flattened image. This effect works best by starting with any imagery—either type or objects—that has a solid color background. Flatten the image so there's only a Background layer. Click the Magic Wand Tool on the Tools palette, then click the solid color (in the background). Click Filter on the menu bar, point to Artistic, then click Neon Glow. Adjust the glow size, the glow brightness, and color, if you wish, then click OK. (An example of this technique is used in the Design Project at the end of this chapter.)

CREATE TEXT
ON A PATH

What You'll Do

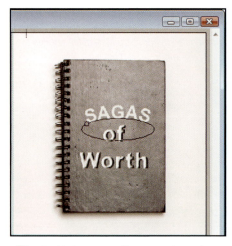

 In this lesson, you'll create a shape, then add type to it.

Understanding Text on a Path

Although it is possible to create some cool type effects by adding layer styles such as bevel, emboss, and drop shadow, you can also create some awesome warped text. Suppose you want type to conform to a shape, such as an oval or a free-form you've drawn? No problem—just create the shape and add the text!

Creating Text on a Path

You start by creating a shape using one of the Photoshop shape tools on the Tools palette, and then adding type to that shape (which is called a path). Add type to a shape by clicking the Horizontal Type Tool. When the pointer nears the path, you'll see that it changes to the Type Tool pointer. Click the path when the Type Tool pointer displays and begin typing. You can change fonts, font sizes, add styles, and any other interesting effects you've learned to apply with type. As you will see, the type is on a path!

QUICKTIP

Don't worry when you see the outline of the path on the screen. The path won't print, only the type will.

FIGURE 26
Type on a path

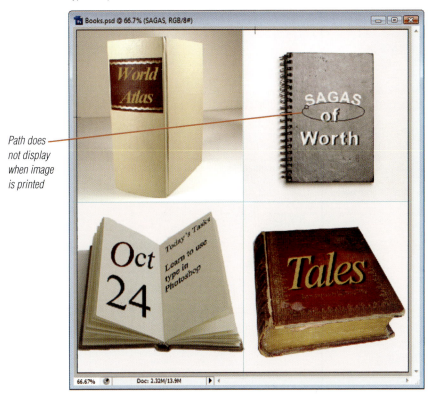

Books.psd @ 66.7% (SAGAS, RGB/8#)

Path does not display when image is printed

66.67%   Doc: 2.32M/13.9M

Create a path and add type

1. Click the **Rectangle Tool** on the Tools palette.

2. Click the **Ellipse Tool** on the options bar.

3. Click the **Paths button** on the options bar.

4. Drag the **Paths pointer** to encircle the word "of" from **610 X/190 Y** to **780 X/240 Y**.

5. Click the **Horizontal Type Tool** on the Tools palette.

6. Change the font to **Arial**, use the Bold font style, set the font size to **20** pt, then verify that the **Left align text button** is selected.

   TIP You can change to any point size by typing the number in the Set the font text box.

7. Click the **Horizontal Type pointer** at approximately **620 X/205 Y** on the left edge of the ellipse.

8. Change the font color by sampling the **white of Worth type**, turn on the Caps Lock, then type **SAGAS**.

9. Commit any current edits, then turn off the Caps Lock.

10. Hide the rulers, reset the palette locations, and save your work. Compare your image to Figure 26.

11. Close the Books.psd file and exit Photoshop.

You created a path using a shape tool, then added type to it.

Power User Shortcuts

to do this:	use this method:
Apply anti-alias method	aa Crisp ▾
Apply Bevel and Emboss style	ƒx ., Bevel and Emboss
Apply blur filter to type	Filter ➤ Blur ➤ Gaussian Blur
Apply Drop Shadow style	ƒx ., Drop Shadow
Cancel any current edits	🚫
Change font family	Times New Roman ▾
Change font size	⁀T 11 pt ▾
Change type color	⬛
Close type effects	▽
Commit current edits	✔
Display/hide rulers	[Ctrl][R] (Win) or ⌘ [R] (Mac)
Erase a History state	Select state, drag to 🗑

to do this:	use this method:
Horizontal Type Tool	T. or T
Kern characters	A͞v -25 ▾
Move Tool	▶⊕ or V
Open Character palette	📋
Save image changes	[Ctrl][S] (Win) or ⌘ [S] (Mac)
See type effects (active layer)	▶
See type effects (inactive layer)	▶
Select all text	[Ctrl][A] (Win) or ⌘ [A] (Mac)
Shift baseline of type	⁀T 100%
Warp type	1

Key: *Menu items are indicated by* ➤ *between the menu name and its command. Blue bold letters are shortcuts for selecting tools on the Tools palette.*

Learn about type and how it is created.

1. Open PS 5-2.psd from the drive and folder where you store your Data Files, then save it as **ZD-Logo**.
2. Display the rulers with pixels.
3. Use the Horizontal Type Tool to create a type layer that starts at 45 X/95 Y.
4. Use a black 35 pt Lucida Sans font or substitute another font.
5. Type **Zenith**.
6. Use the Horizontal Type Tool and a 16 pt type size to create a type layer at 70 X/180 Y, then type **unique and uncompromising**.
7. Save your work.

Change spacing and adjust baseline shift.

1. Use the Horizontal Type Tool to create a new type layer at 205 X/95 Y.
2. Use a 35 pt Myriad font.
3. Type **Design**.
4. Select the Design type.
5. Change the type color to the color used in the lower-left background.
6. Change the type size of the Z and D to 50 pts.
7. Adjust the baseline shift of the Z and D to −5.
8. Save your work.

Use the Drop Shadow style.

1. Activate the Zenith type layer.
2. Apply the Drop Shadow style.
3. In the Layer Style dialog box, set the angle to 150°, then close the Layer Style dialog box.
4. Save your work.

Apply anti-aliasing to type.

1. Activate the Zenith type layer.
2. Change the Anti-Alias method to Smooth.
3. Save your work.

Modify type with the Bevel and Emboss style.

1. Activate the Design type layer.
2. Apply the Bevel and Emboss style.
3. In the Layer Style dialog box, set the style to Inner Bevel.
4. Set the angle to 150° and the altitude to 30°.
5. Close the Layer Style dialog box.
6. Activate the Zenith type layer.
7. Apply the Bevel and Emboss style.
8. Set the style to Inner Bevel.
9. Verify that the angle is set to 150° and the altitude is set to 30°.
10. Close the Layer Style dialog box.
11. Save your work.

Apply special effects to type using filters.

1. Apply a 1.0 pixel Gaussian Blur effect to the "unique and uncompromising" layer.
2. Save your work.

Create text on a path.

1. Use the Ellipse Tool to draw an ellipse from approximately 200 X/120 Y to 370 X/185 Y.
2. Click the line with the Horizontal Type Tool at 210 X/130 Y.
3. Type **Founded in 2002** using the second color swatch in the first row of the Swatches palette (RGB Yellow), in a 16 pt Arial font.
4. Change the anti-aliasing method to Crisp.
5. Change the opacity of the type on the path to 45%.
6. Turn off the ruler display.
7. Save your work, then compare your image to Figure 27.

FIGURE 27
Completed Skills Review Project

A local flower shop, Beautiful Blooms, asks you to design its color advertisement for the trade magazine, *Florists United*. You have already started on the image, and need to add some type.

1. Open PS 5-3.psd, then save it as **Beautiful Blooms Ad**.
2. Click the Horizontal Type Tool, then type **Beautiful Blooms** using a 55 pt Impact font in black.
3. Create a catchy phrase of your choice, using a 24 pt Verdana font.
4. Apply a drop shadow style to the name of the flower shop using the following settings: Multiply blend mode, 75% Opacity, 120%, 5 pixel distance, 0° spread, and 5 pixel size.
5. Apply a Bevel and Emboss style to the catch phrase using the following settings: Inner Bevel style, Smooth technique, 100% depth, Up direction, 5 pixel size, 0 pixel soften, 120° angle, 30° altitude, and using global light.
6. Compare your image to the sample in Figure 28.
7. Save your work.

FIGURE 28
Sample Project Builder 1

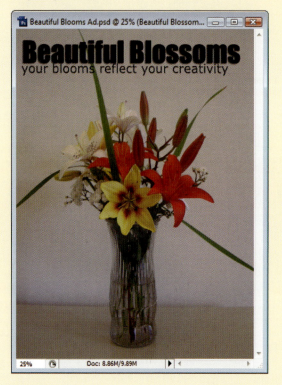

You are a junior art director for an advertising agency. You have been working on an ad that promotes milk and milk products. You have started the project, but still have a few details to finish up before it is complete.

1. Open PS 5-4.psd, then save it as **Milk Promotion**.
2. Create a shape using any shape tool, then use the shape as a text path and type a snappy phrase of your choosing on the shape.
3. Change the font color to any shade of red found in the Swatches palette.
4. Use a 24 pt Arial font in the style and color of your choice for the catch phrase type layer. (If necessary, substitute another font.)
5. Create a Bevel and Emboss style on the type layer, setting the angle to 100° and the altitude to 30°.
6. Compare your image to the sample in Figure 29.
7. Save your work.

FIGURE 29
Sample Project Builder 2

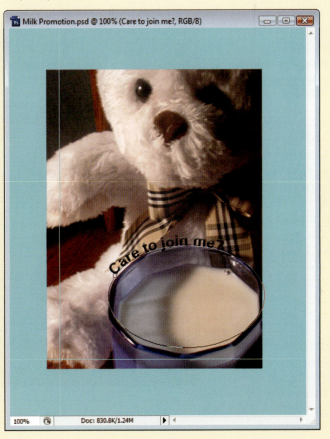

You are a freelance designer. A local clothing store, Attitude, is expanding and has hired you to work on an advertisement. You have already created the file, and inserted the necessary type layers. Before you proceed, you decide to explore the Internet to find information on using type to create an effective design.

1. Connect to the Internet and use your browser to find information about typography. (Make a record of the site you found so you can use it for future reference, if necessary.)
2. Find information about using type as an effective design element.
3. Open PS 5-5.psd, update the layers if necessary, then save the file as **Attitude**.
4. Modify the existing type by changing fonts, font colors, and font sizes.
5. Edit the type, if necessary, to make it shorter and clearer.
6. Rearrange the position of the type to create an effective design.
7. Add a Bevel and Emboss style using your choice of settings, then compare your image to the sample in Figure 30. (The fonts Mistral and Trebuchet MS are used in this image. Make substitutions if you don't have these fonts on your computer.)
8. Save your work.

FIGURE 30
Sample Design Project

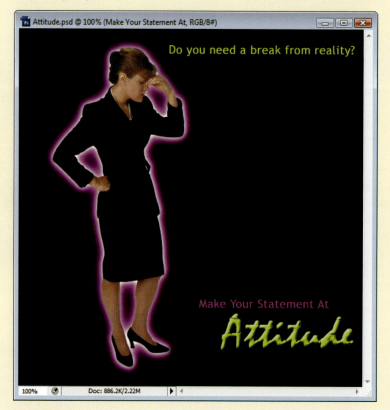

GROUP PROJECT

Depending on the size of your group, you can assign individual elements of the project to group members, or work collectively to create the finished product.

You have been hired by your community to create an advertising campaign that promotes tourism. Assemble a team and decide what aspect of the community you want to emphasize. Locate appropriate imagery (already existing on your hard drive, on the Web, your own creation, or using a scanner), then add type to create a meaningful Photoshop image.

1. Create an image with the dimensions 550 pixels × 550 pixels.
2. Save this file as **Community Promotion**.
3. Work together to locate imagery that exists on your hard drive, or from a digital camera or a scanner.
4. Add at least two layers of type in the image, using multiple font sizes. (Use any fonts available on your computer. You can use multiple fonts if you want.)
5. Add a Bevel and Emboss style to at least one type layer, and add a drop shadow to at least one layer. (*Hint*: You can add both effects to the same layer.)
6. Position type layers to create an effective design.
7. Compare your image to the sample in Figure 31.
8. Save your work.

FIGURE 31
Sample Group Project

INTEGRATING
ADOBE CS3 WEB PREMIUM

1. Insert a Photoshop image into a Dreamweaver document

2. Edit a Photoshop image from a Dreamweaver document

3. Create a Photoshop document and import it into Flash

4. Insert and edit a Flash movie in Dreamweaver

1 INTEGRATING
ADOBE CS3 WEB PREMIUM

Introduction

The Adobe CS3 Web Premium suite of integrated Web development products includes Dreamweaver, Flash, and Photoshop. Used together, these tools allow you to create Web sites that include compelling graphics, animations, and interactivity. Recognizing that developing a Web site often involves team members with varying expertise (graphic designers, animators, programmers, and so on), Adobe has designed these products so that they integrate easily. This integration allows you to move from one product to another as you bring together the elements of a Web site. For example, you can create a graphic image using Photoshop, import the image into Dreamweaver, and then edit the image starting from the Dreamweaver environment. While each of the products can stand alone, they have a similar look and feel, with common features and interface elements, such as the Property inspector,

that allow you to transfer your skills from one product to another. Adobe provides two other products that you can use when working with these Web development tools. Adobe Bridge CS3 provides a quick way to organize, locate, and display the elements used to create Web sites and applications (such as Photoshop images, Flash movies, and Dreamweaver documents). Adobe Version Cue CS3 is used in a workgroup process where team members need access to the latest versions of a file. Using Version Cue, you set up a project, add users and assign permissions, and add files to the project. Then, users can "check out" a file and work on it. The check out process ensures that only one person is working on a file at a time. When the file is saved, a new version is created while the previous versions are maintained. Version Cue is accessed through Adobe Bridge and requires a connection to a server.

Tools You'll Use

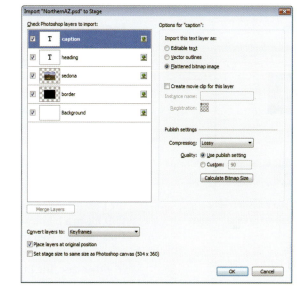

INSERT A PHOTOSHOP IMAGE INTO
A DREAMWEAVER DOCUMENT

What You'll Do

In this lesson, you will integrate a Photoshop image into a Dreamweaver document.

Inserting a Photoshop Image into Dreamweaver

The process for inserting a Photoshop image into a Dreamweaver document is to create the image in Photoshop and save it in the PSD file format. Then, start Dreamweaver and open an existing HTML document or start a new one. Next, select the location in the page where you want the image to appear, and then use the Image command from the Insert menu to insert the PSD file. Alternately, you can save the PSD file to a Library or assets folder in the Dreamweaver Web site and then drag the image from the folder to the document. In either case, the Image Preview dialog box opens, as shown in Figure 1. This dialog box allows you to convert the PSD file to one of the Web-ready file types (PNG, JPEG, or GIF). You can also use the dialog box to change the optimization settings in order to reduce the file size while maintaining the desired quality. For example, a JPEG format would usually result in higher quality for a photograph than a GIF format.

However, the GIF format might have a smaller file size. The Image Preview dialog box allows you to display two or four images at a time and compare the quality of images as the settings are changed.

Another process for inserting Photoshop images into a Dreamweaver document is to copy and paste the image from one application to the other. You can copy the entire image, a portion of the image, a single layer, a group of layers, or a slice of an image.

Setting Photoshop as the Primary External Image Editor

You can import a Photoshop image into a Dreamweaver document. Later on, when desired, you can edit the graphic by launching the Photoshop program from within Dreamweaver. This requires that you set Photoshop as the primary external image editor for PSD, GIF, JPEG, and PNG files in Dreamweaver. You can set the external image editor using settings in the Preferences dialog box in Dreamweaver.

Using Design Notes

When you insert an image or file created in Photoshop or Flash in Dreamweaver, information about the original source file (PSD or FLA) is saved in a Design Notes file (MNO). For example, if in Dreamweaver you import a file named airplane.jpg whose source file is airplane.psd, Dreamweaver creates a Design Notes file named airplane.jpg.mno. The Design Notes file contains references to the source PSD file, which allows you to edit it by opening Photoshop from Dreamweaver. You should save your Photoshop source PSD file and exported files in the Dreamweaver site. Saving in this location ensures that any developer sharing the site can also access the source PSD file. A Design Notes file also contains the optimization settings you specify in the Image Preview dialog box.

Setting up the Dreamweaver Site

Figure 2 shows the structure for the Web site you will be developing in this chapter. You can use the assets folder or create a Library folder as the destination folder when you save a Photoshop image. As you work through the chapter, you will integrate Photoshop images and a Flash movie into the site.

FIGURE 1

The Image Preview dialog box

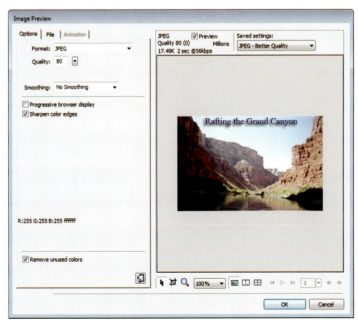

FIGURE 2

Structure of the Web site

Designate the primary external image editor

This lesson requires that you have Dreamweaver CS3 and Photoshop CS3 installed on your computer.

1. Start Dreamweaver CS3, then create a new HTML document.

2. Click **Edit** (Win) or **Dreamweaver** (Mac) on the menu bar, then click **Preferences**.

3. Click **File Types / Editors** to display the options shown in Figure 3.

   TIP Each file type has a default editor.

4. Scroll down the Extensions column, click **.psd**, then verify that Photoshop (Primary) appears in the Editors column.

5. Click **.png** in the Extensions column, click **Photoshop** in the Editors column, then click **Make Primary** (if necessary).

6. Repeat Step 5 for **.gif** and **.jpg .jpe .jpeg** file types in the Extensions column (if necessary).

7. Click **OK** to close the Preferences dialog box.

You used the Preferences dialog box to verify that Photoshop is the primary external editor for .psd, .png, .gif, and .jpg files.

FIGURE 3

Dreamweaver Preferences dialog box

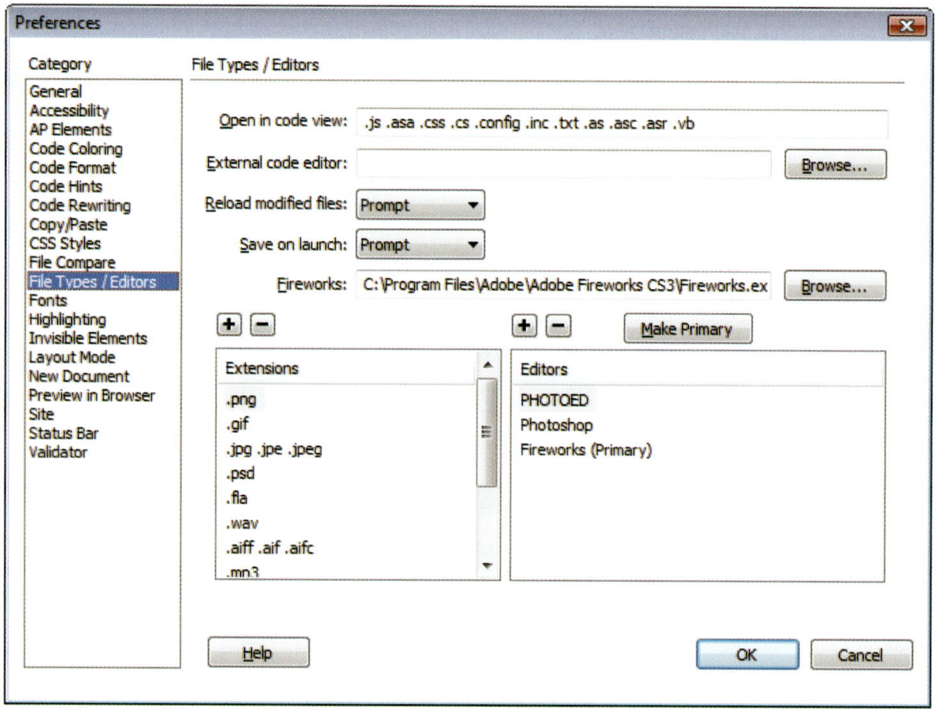

FIGURE 4

Completed Site Definition dialog box

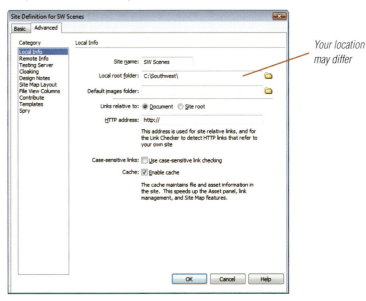

Your location
may differ

FIGURE 5

*The Dreamweaver document with the
insertion line positioned below the heading*

Insertion point

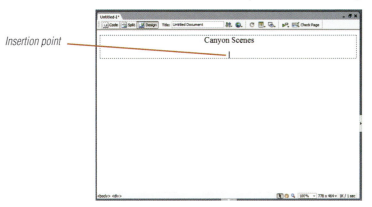

1. Using your operating system file management tool, create a folder where your Data Files are stored, then name it **Southwest**.

2. Create a new folder named **Library** in the Southwest folder.

3. In Dreamweaver, click **Site** on the menu bar, then click **New Site**.

    The Site Definition dialog box opens.

4. If necessary, click the **Advanced tab**.

5. Type **SW Scenes** in the Site name text box.

6. Click the **Browser for file button** 📁 next to the Local root folder text box, then navigate to the Southwest folder.

7. If necessary, double-click the **Southwest folder** to select it in the Choose local root folder for site SW Scenes dialog box, then click **Select** (Win) or **Choose** (Mac).

8. Verify that your Site Definition for SW Scenes dialog box resembles Figure 4, click **OK**, then click **Done** to close the Manage Sites dialog box.

9. Create a new Blank Page HTML document with no layout, type **Canyon Scenes**, change the font to **Times New Roman, Times, serif**, the font size to **24**, the color to **black**, then **center** the text.

10. Point to the right of the text, then click to set the insertion line after the heading.

11. Press and hold **[Shift]**, then press **[Enter]** (Win) or **[return]** (Mac) twice to create two blank lines, as shown in Figure 5.

(continued)

12. Save the document to the Southwest folder with the name **canyon-scenes.html**.

You created a folder for the Dreamweaver site, used the Site Definition dialog box to specify a site name and location, created a new document and added text to it, then saved it.

Edit a Photoshop document

1. Start Photoshop.

2. Open **ic_1.psd** from the drive and folder where you store your Data Files, then save it as **GrandCanyon.psd**.

This document has a single image, a photo of the Grand Canyon.

3. Click the **Text tool T** on the Tools panel, then change the font to **Times New Roman**, the size to **18**, and the color to **blue**.

4. Click the **top-left corner** of the image to create an insertion point, type **Rafting the Grand Canyon**, then position the text as shown in Figure 6.

5. Save your document, specifying Maximize compatibility (if necessary).

6. Exit Photoshop.

You opened a Photoshop PSD file, added a text layer, inserted text, and saved the file.

FIGURE 6
Positioning the text

FIGURE 7

The Image Preview dialog box with two preview windows

Quality set to 60 —

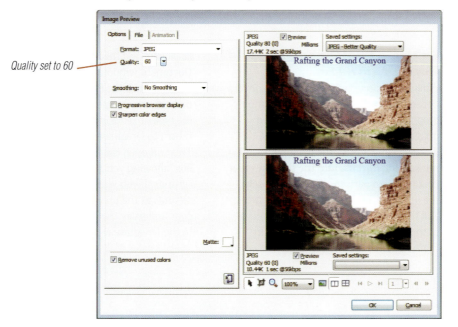

Insert a Photoshop image into a Dreamweaver document

1. Switch to Dreamweaver.

2. Click **Insert** on the menu bar, then click **image**.

3. Use the Select Image Source dialog box to select the **GrandCanyon.psd** file, then click **OK** (Win) or **Choose** (Mac).

   The Image Preview dialog box appears, where you can change various attributes, including Format and Quality.

4. Verify that JPEG is specified for the Format and 80 is specified for the Quality.

5. Click the **2 preview windows icon** ⬛ .

6. Click the **Quality list arrow** ⬛ , use the slider to set the Quality to **60**, click away from the Quality list arrow, then compare your dialog box to Figure 7.

   Notice reducing the quality setting does not affect the quality of the image, but the file size has been reduced from its original size.

7. Click **OK** to apply the changes.

8. Double-click the **Library folder**, then click **Save** in the Save Web Image dialog box.

9. Type **A photo of the Grand Canyon** for the Alternate text in the Image Tab Accessibility Attributes dialog box, then click **OK**.

10. Save your work.

You changed the optimization settings for a Photoshop image and inserted it into a Dreamweaver document.

EDIT A PHOTOSHOP IMAGE
FROM A DREAMWEAVER DOCUMENT

What You'll Do

In this lesson, you will edit a Photoshop image from a Dreamweaver document.

Editing a Photoshop Image from Dreamweaver

When you edit a Photoshop image from a Dreamweaver document, the Photoshop program is launched and the selected image is displayed. You complete the desired changes, save the document, and reinsert the PSD file into the Dreamweaver document. To perform this process, select the image in the Dreamweaver document, and then click the Edit Photoshop button in the Property inspector, as shown in Figure 8. The Photoshop program is launched, and the image appears in the Document window. After making your changes, save the PSD file. If you need to make quick changes such as changing the file type or reducing the file size, you can return to Dreamweaver and insert the file. This will open the Image Preview dialog box, allowing you to make changes in these settings. If you want to maintain the same settings as the previous image, you can copy and paste the image from Photoshop to the Dreamweaver document.

FIGURE 8
Edit button in the Property inspector

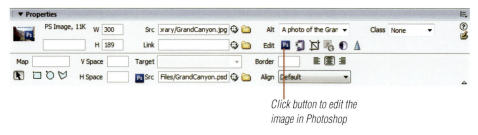

Click button to edit the image in Photoshop

FIGURE 9

The edited Photoshop image

1. Click the **image** to select it, then click the **Photoshop Edit button**  in the Property inspector.

   The GrandCanyon.psd image opens in Photoshop.

2. Verify that the text layer is selected in the Layers panel, click the **Add a layer style icon** *fx.*, then click **Drop Shadow**.

3. Click **OK** in the Layer Style dialog box to accept the default values.

   Your image should resemble Figure 9.

4. Save the document.

   You can also use copy and paste to add the image to the Dreamweaver document.

6. Click **Select** on the menu bar, then click **All**.

7. Click **Edit** on the menu bar, then click **Copy Merged**.

   This ensures that the text will be included with the image.

8. Click **Select** on the menu bar, then click **Deselect**.

9. Display the Dreamweaver document.

10. Verify the image is selected, click **Edit** on the menu bar, then click **Paste**.

11. Complete the Preview dialog box, if necessary.

    The edited image replaces the original image.

12. Save your work, close the document, then exit Dreamweaver.

You used Photoshop to edit an image in a Dreamweaver document.

CREATE A PHOTOSHOP DOCUMENT
AND IMPORT IT INTO FLASH

What You'll Do

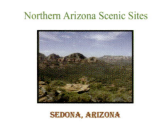

In this lesson, you will create a Photoshop document, import it into Flash, and create an animation.

Importing a Photoshop Document into Flash

Flash allows you to import Photoshop PSD files directly into a Flash document. An advantage of using Photoshop to create graphics and enhance photographs is that the drawing and selection tools, as well as the photo retouching features, allow you to produce more creative and complex images. A key feature of importing PSD files is that you can choose to have the Photoshop layers imported as Flash layers. This allows you to edit individual parts of an image, such as animating text or using a photograph to create a button.

The process for importing Photoshop files into Flash is to open a Flash document and select the Import option from the File menu. Then, choose to import to the stage or to the Library panel and specify which PSD file to import. The Import dialog box appears, as shown in Figure 10, with the following options:

- Check Photoshop layers to import. Allows you to specify which layers to import.
- Options for "Layer . . .". Allows you to specify how the selected layer will be imported. Here you decide whether or not you want to be able to edit the contents (text, image, background, etc.) of the layer. If you choose not to make it editable, the content is flattened as a bitmap image. If you choose to make an image editable, a movie clip symbol is created using the image. The movie clip has its own Timeline, making it easy to animate the image separately from other content in the Flash document.
- Publish settings. Allows you to specify the degree of compression and document quality to apply to the image when it is published as a SWF file. This has no effect on the image that is imported into the Flash document.

- Convert layers to. Allows you to have the content of Photoshop layers be imported as Flash layers or as keyframes.

- Place layers at original position. Allows you to specify that the contents of the PSD file retain the same relative position they had in Photoshop.

- Set stage to same size as Photoshop canvas. Allows you have the Flash stage resize to the same size as the Photoshop document.

FIGURE 10
Import dialog box

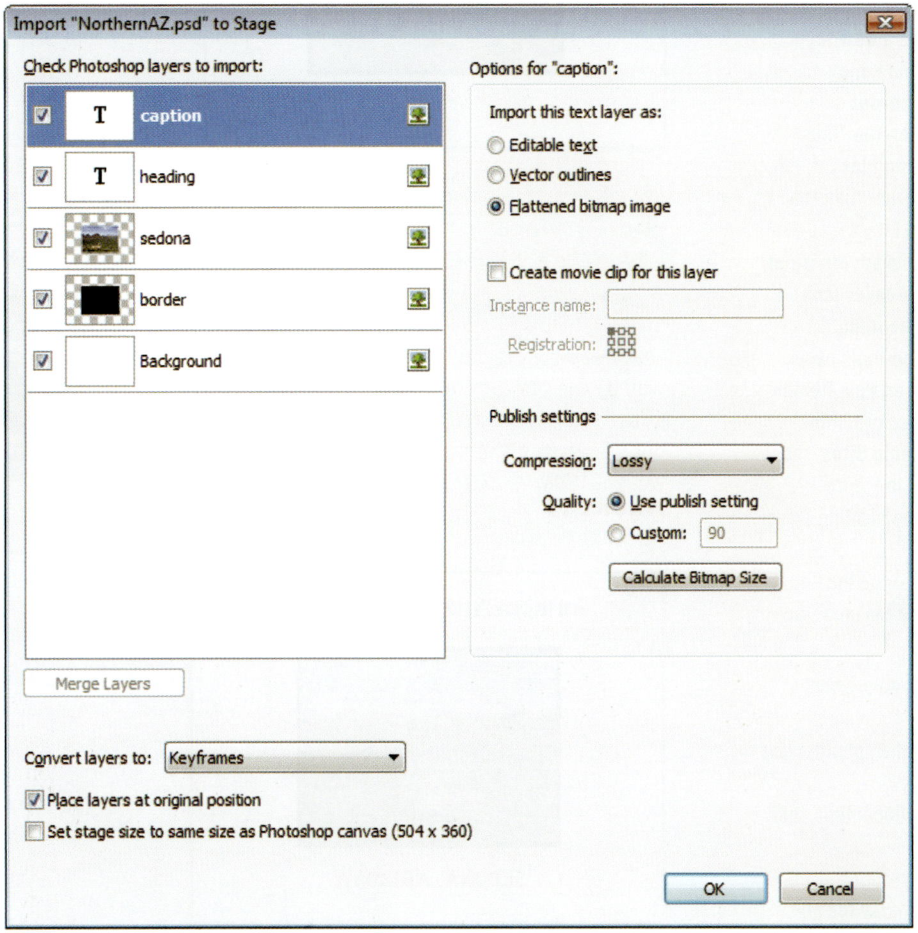

Create a Photoshop image with several layers

1. Start Photoshop.
2. Open **ic_2.psd** from where you store your Data Files, then save it as **NorthernAZ.psd**.

   This document has a single image and a white background.
3. Click the **Background layer** in the Layers panel, then click the **Create a new layer icon** at the bottom of the Layers panel.
4. Change the layer name to **border**.
5. Select the **Rectangle tool** on the Tools panel, change the fill color to **black**, then draw a rectangle slightly larger than the image, as shown in Figure 11.
6. Click the **sedona layer** in the Layers panel, then click the **Create a new layer icon**.
7. Change the layer name to **heading**.
8. Click the **Text tool** **T** on the Tools panel, then change the font to **Times New Roman**, the font size to **30**, and the color to **blue**.
9. Type **Northern Arizona Scenic Sites**, then position the text as shown in Figure 12.
10. Insert a new layer above the heading layer, then name it **caption**.
11. Select the **Text tool**, then change the font to **Algerian**, the size to **24**, and the color to **#993300**.

    TIP If this font is not available, select a different font.
12. Type **SEDONA, ARIZONA**, then position the text as shown in Figure 13.
13. Save your work, close the document, then exit Photoshop.

You opened a Photoshop file and added layers with a shape and text, and positioned the text.

FIGURE 11
The completed rectangle

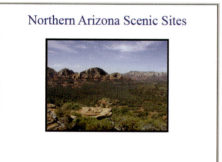

FIGURE 12
Positioning the heading

FIGURE 13
Positioning the caption

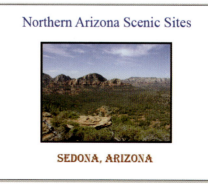

FIGURE 14

Selecting the Editable text option

Click to make text editable

FIGURE 15

The completed Import dialog box

Import a Photoshop document into Flash

1. Start Flash, then click **Flash File (ActionScript 2.0)** in the Create New category.

2. Save the document to where you store your Data Files, with the filename **AZScenes.fla**.

3. Display the Tools, Library, Actions, and Properties panels.

4. Click **View** on the menu bar, point to Magnification, then click **Fit in Window**.

5. Click **File** on the menu bar, click **Import**, then click **Import to Stage**.

6. Navigate to where you store your Data Files, click **NorthernAZ.psd**, then click **Open** (Win) or **Import** (Mac).

7. Click **caption**, then click **Editable text**, as shown in Figure 14.

8. Click **heading**, then click **Editable text**.

9. Click **sedona**, then click **Bitmap image with editable layer styles**.

10. Click **border**, then verify **Flattened bitmap image** is selected.

11. Click the **check box** for the Background layer to deselect the layer so it will not be imported.

12. Verify that the **Convert layers to:** option is set to Flash Layers and the **Place layers at original position** check box is selected.

13. Click the **Set stage size to same size as Photoshop canvas (504 x 360) check box**.

    Your screen should resemble Figure 15.

14. Click **OK**.

You selected a Photoshop file to import, selected which layers to import, and specified whether or not the content could be edited.

Edit a Photoshop image that has been imported into Flash

1. Study the Flash Timeline and notice the four new layers that were created.

   Layer 1 is the default layer that appears when a new document is opened. It does not have any content.

2. Click the **Show/Hide All Layers icon** 👁 to hide all of the objects on the stage.

3. Starting with the border layer, unhide each layer one by one to view its contents.

4. Click Layer 1, then click the **Delete Layer icon** 🗑 to delete the layer.

5. Double-click the **NorthernAZ.psd** Assets folder in the Library panel.

6. Click **border** to display the bitmap image, then click **sedona** to view the movie clip image.

7. Double-click the **Assets folder**, then click **sedona** to view the sedona bitmap image.

   The bitmap image is used to create the sedona movie clip.

8. Click the **Selection tool** ▶ on the Tools panel, click **Frame 1** of the heading layer, then verify the heading is selected.

9. Click the **Text tool** T on the Tools panel, then drag the I-beam pointer I across the text to select it.

10. Click the **Fill color tool** on the Tools panel, then type **#336600** for the color.

11. Click the **Selection tool** ▶ on the Tools panel, then click a blank area of the stage to deselect the heading as shown in Figure 16.

(continued)

FIGURE 16
The completed edits

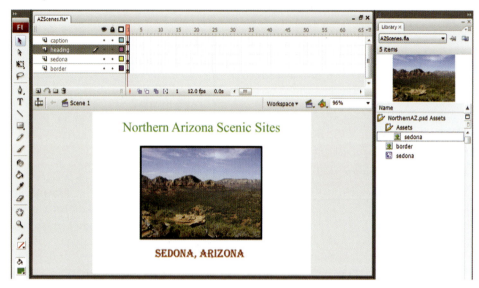

12. Save your work.

Your viewed the contents of the layers that were created when a Photoshop file was imported into Flash, and changed the color of the text heading.

FIGURE 17

The Timeline with keyframes inserted

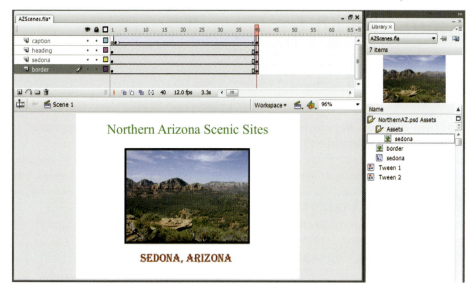

Create an animation using the Photoshop-created text

1. Click **Frame 2** on the caption layer, click **Insert** on the menu bar, click **Timeline**, then click **Keyframe**.

2. Click **Frame 40** on the caption layer, then insert a keyframe.

3. Click **Frame 20** on the caption layer, click **Insert** on the menu bar, click **Timeline**, then click **Create Motion Tween**.

4. Click **Frame 2** on the caption layer, then click the **SEDONA, ARIZONA** text to select it.

5. Click the **Color Styles list arrow** ▾ on the Property inspector, then click **Alpha**.

6. Drag the **Alpha Amount slider** to **0%**.

7. Click **Frame 1** on the caption layer, click **SEDONA, ARIZONA** to select it, then press **[Delete]**.

8. Insert keyframes in Frame 40 of the remaining layers, as shown in Figure 17.

9. Click **Control** on the menu bar, then click **Test Movie**.

10. Close the test movie window.

11. Click **File** on the menu bar, then click **Publish**.

12. Save your work, close the document, then exit Flash.

You created an animation using Photoshop-imported text.

INSERT AND EDIT
A FLASH MOVIE
IN DREAMWEAVER

What You'll Do

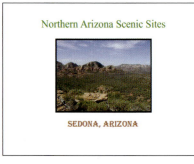

Northern Arizona Scenic Sites

SEDONA, ARIZONA

 In this lesson, you will insert a Flash movie into a Dreamweaver document and edit the movie within Dreamweaver.

Inserting a Flash Movie into a Dreamweaver Document

You can easily insert a Flash movie (.swf) into a Dreamweaver document. To do this, set the insertion point where you want the movie to appear, and then use the Media command on the Insert menu to select Flash as the media to insert. If the file is not in the root folder for the Web site, you are asked whether you would like to copy it into the root folder. It is recommended that you copy the file to the root folder, so that it is accessible when you publish the site. When the insert process is completed, a placeholder appears at the insertion point in the document.

Using the Property Inspector with the Movie

When you click the placeholder to select it, the Property inspector displays information about the movie, including the filename, as shown in Figure 18.

You can use the Property inspector to complete the following:

- Edit the Flash movie
- Play and stop the Flash movie
- Set width and height dimensions
- Cause the movie to loop
- Reposition the placeholder in the document window

FIGURE 18
The Property inspector with a movie selected

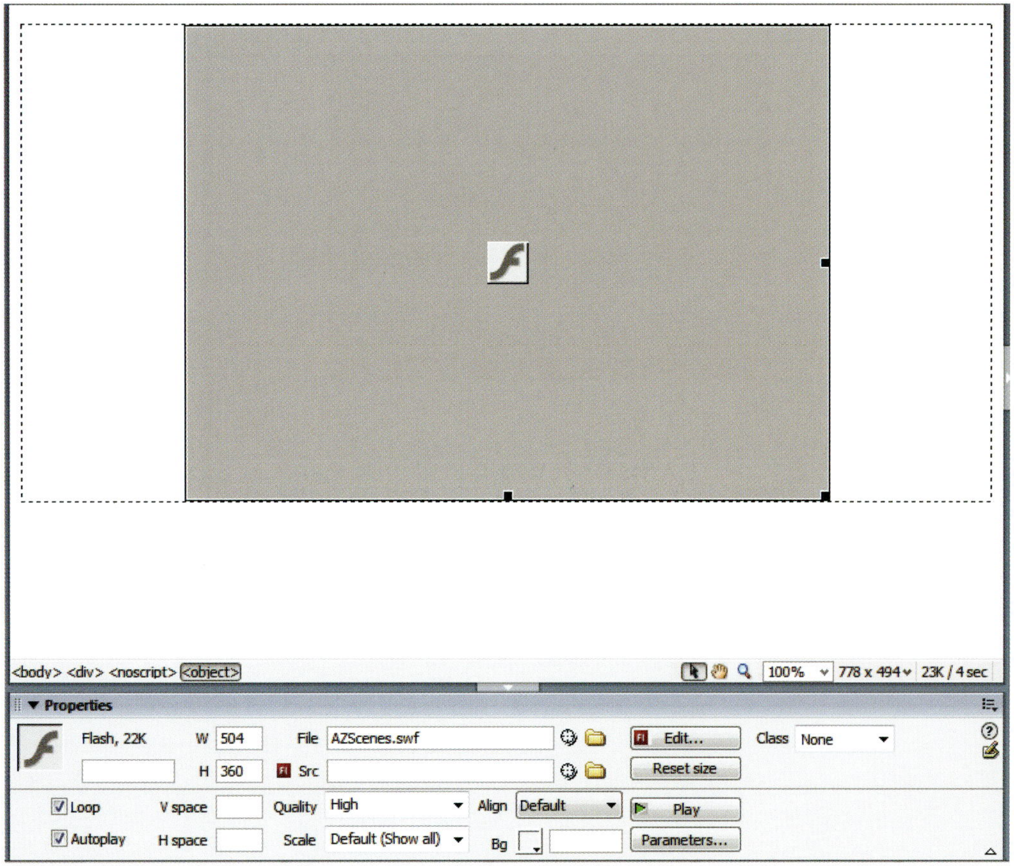

Insert a Flash movie into Dreamweaver

1. Start Dreamweaver.

2. Create a new Blank Page HTML document with no layout, then save it as **NorthernAZ.html** to the Southwest folder in the SW Scenes site.

3. Click the **Align Center button** ≜ on the Property inspector.

4. Click **Insert** on the menu bar, point to **Media**, then click **Flash**.

5. Navigate to the location where you store your Data Files, click **AZScenes.swf**, then click **OK** (Win) or **Choose** (Mac).

6. If a "This file is outside of the root folder..." message appears, click **Yes**, then click **Save** when the Copy File As dialog box appears.

7. Type **Photo of Sedona Arizona** for the title in the Object Tag Accessibility Attributes dialog box, then click **OK**.

   A Flash movie placeholder is inserted at the location of the insertion line, as shown in Figure 19.

8. Save your work.

   If a Copy Dependent Files message box appears, click OK.

You inserted a Flash movie into a Dreamweaver document and copied the Flash movie to the root folder of the Web site.

FIGURE 19
The Flash movie placeholder

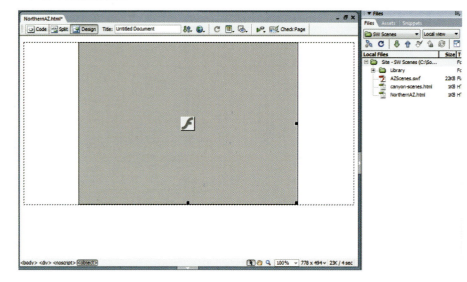

FIGURE 20

Changing the movie height

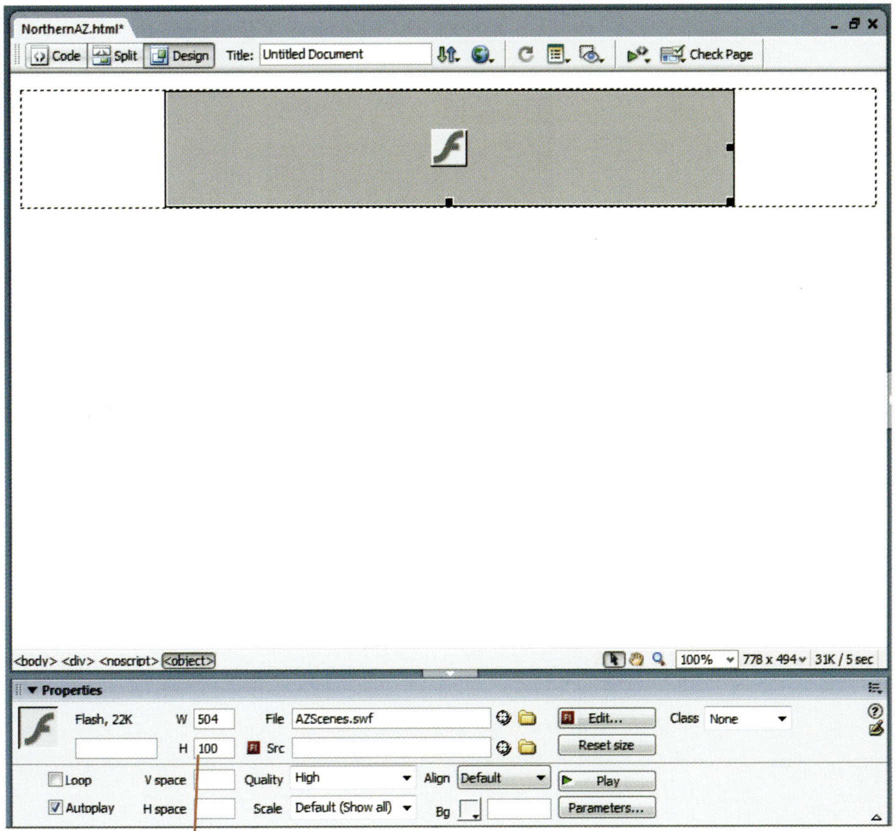

Height text box

Play a Flash movie and change settings from Dreamweaver

1. Click the **Flash movie placeholder** to select it (if necessary).
2. Click **Play** in the Property inspector.
3. Click **Stop** in the Property inspector.
4. Click the **Loop check box** in the Property inspector to deselect it.
5. Double-click the **height box (H)**, type **100**, then press **[Enter]** (Win) or **[return]** (Mac).

   Your screen should resemble Figure 20.
6. Click the **Play button** in the Property inspector.
7. View the resized movie, then click the **Stop button**.
8. Click **Reset size** in the Property inspector to restore the previous setting.
9. Save your work.

You played a Flash movie and changed its settings in Dreamweaver by turning off the Loop option, and then changing and resetting the movie height.

Edit a Flash movie from Dreamweaver

1. Click the **Flash placeholder** to select it, then click **Edit** in the Property inspector.

2. Navigate to the location where you store your Data Files, click **AZScenes.fla**, then click **Open**.

3. Insert a new layer above the caption layer, then name it **stopmovie**.

4. Click **Frame 1** of the stopmovie layer.

5. Display the **Actions panel**, verify ActionScript 1.0 & 2.0 is displayed above the category list, verify the **Script Assist button** Script Assist is off, then verify **stopmovie 1:** is displayed at the bottom of the script pane, as shown in Figure 21.

6. Click the **Add a new item to the script button**, click **Global Functions**, click **Timeline Control**, then click **stop**.

7. Click **Frame 1** on the sedona layer, then click the image to select it.

8. Click **Modify** on the menu bar, then click **Convert to Symbol**.

9. Type **b_sedona** for the name, click **Button** for the Type, then click **OK**.

10. Click the **Script Assist button** Script Assist to turn it on, then verify that **b_sedona** is displayed at the bottom of the script pane.

11. Click the **Add a new item to the script button**, click **Global Functions**, click **Movie Clip Control**, then click **on**.

(continued)

FIGURE 21
Verifying the settings in the Script pane

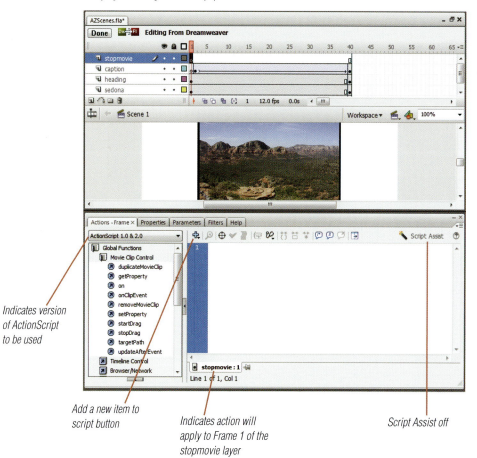

Indicates version of ActionScript to be used

Add a new item to script button

Indicates action will apply to Frame 1 of the stopmovie layer

Script Assist off

FIGURE 22

Specifying the frame to go to

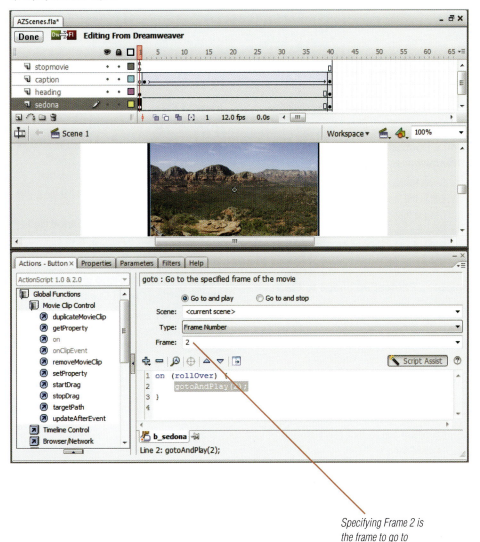

Specifying Frame 2 is
the frame to go to

12. Click **Release** to deselect it, then click **Roll Over** to select it.

13. Click the **Add a new item to the script button**, click **Global Functions**, click **Timeline Control**, then click **goto**.

14. Change the Frame to **2**, as shown in Figure 22.

15. Click **Control** on the menu bar, then click **Test Movie**.

16. Point to the image to view the animation, then close the test movie window.

To save the FLA file and re-export it to Dreamweaver, you can click the Done button above the Timeline (which closes Flash), or use the Update for Dreamweaver command in the File menu (which keeps Flash open).

17. Click the **Done button** above the Timeline to return to Dreamweaver and close Flash.

18. Verify that the Flash placeholder is selected, then click **Play** in the Property inspector.

19. Point to the image to play the animation.

20. Click **File** on the menu bar, point to **Preview in Browser**, then click **IExplore** (Win) or **Internet Explorer** (Mac).

| TIP Your default browser may vary.

21. View the movie, close the browser, then save your work.

You edited a Flash movie from Dreamweaver by creating a rollover action that plays an animation.

Designate the primary external image editor.

1. Start Dreamweaver CS3.
2. Display the Preferences dialog box and display the File Types / Editors option.
3. Verify that Photoshop is set as the default image editor for . psd, .png, .gif, and .jpg files.

Set up the Dreamweaver site.

1. Create a folder where you store your Data Files and name it **Foods**.
2. Add a folder within the Foods folder named **Library**.
3. Create a new Dreamweaver site named **Foods-for-Thought**, using the Foods folder as the root folder.

Edit a Photoshop file.

1. Open bread-heading.psd in Photoshop.
2. Add a layer below the text layer, name it background, then draw a white rectangle for the background.
3. Save the file with the name **bread-heading2.psd**.
4. Close the file.

Insert a Photoshop image into a Dreamweaver document.

1. Open the Foods-for-Thought site in Dreamweaver.
2. Create a new Blank Page HTML document and save it as **food-home.html** in the root folder.

3. Insert the bread-heading2.psd file into the document as a .jpeg file.
4. Type **The Staff of Life heading** for the alternate text.
5. Center-align the heading across the document, then save your work.

Edit a Photoshop image from Dreamweaver.

1. Select the bread-heading2.jpg image and click Edit in the Property inspector.
2. Change the text formatting to italic.
3. Save the document, then copy and paste it in the food-home.html file in Dreamweaver.
4. Close the .psd file in Photoshop.

Import a Photoshop image to Flash.

1. Switch to Photoshop, then open bread-photo.psd.
2. Add a layer below the photo layer and name it **border**.
3. Draw a black rectangle slightly larger than the photo.
4. Save the file as **bread-photo2.psd**.
5. Start Flash and create a new Flash File (ActionScript2).
6. Save the document with the filename **bread-An.fla**.
7. Import the bread-photo2.psd to the stage, making each layer except the background editable and setting the stage size to the same size as the Photoshop canvas.

8. Publish the document.
9. Save your work and close the document.
10. Close the .psd document in Photoshop.

Insert a Flash movie into a Dreamweaver document.

1. Switch to Dreamweaver and set an insertion point below the heading.
2. Insert the bread-An.swf file below the photo image, and accept copying the image to the root folder, if asked.
3. Enter **Animation of the word Bread** for the title.
4. Save your work.

Play a Flash movie and change the movie settings from Dreamweaver.

1. Select the Flash movie placeholder.
2. Click Play, then click Stop.
3. Deselect the Loop feature.
4. Change the movie window height to **250**, then reset the size.
5. Save your work.

Edit a Flash movie from Dreamweaver.

1. Select the movie placeholder, then click Edit.
2. Select the bread-An.fla file.
3. Create a motion animation that causes the word Bread to scroll in from the left side of the stage.
4. Create a rollover action that causes the animation to play when the pointer rolls over the photo.
5. Click Done to return to the document in Dreamweaver.
6. Play the Flash movie in Dreamweaver.
7. Save your work.
8. Display the Web page in a browser, then compare your screen to Figure 23.

FIGURE 23
Completed Skills Review

Ultimate Tours has asked you to develop a Dreamweaver Web site for their travel company. The site will include graphics exported from Photoshop and the Flash animations that were developed in Flash Chapter 5 for the Ultimate Tours Web site.

1. Create a folder on your hard drive and name it **ULTours**, then create a folder within the ULTours folder named **Library**.
2. In Dreamweaver, create a new site named **Ultimate_Tours**, using the ULTours folder as the local root folder.
3. Open ultours_home.html and save it to the root folder for the ULTours folder.
4. Start Photoshop and open ULTours-heading.psd.
5. Change the text formatting to italic and save the document with the filename **ULTours-heading2.psd**.
6. Switch to Dreamweaver and insert the UlTours-heading2.psd image into the ultours_home.html file as a .jpg file.
7. In Dreamweaver, display the ultours_home.html document, insert the ULTours-heading.gif image, and provide alternate text.

8. Edit the heading from Dreamweaver and change the text to white.
9. Save the image and copy and paste it from Photoshop to Dreamweaver.
10. Open ULTours-photo.psd in Photoshop and type **The Islands** as a heading on its own layer.
11. Save the document as ULTours-photo2.psd.
12. Start a new Flash File (ActionScript 2.0) and save it as ULTours-photo-An.fla.
13. Import the ULTours-photo2.psd to the stage with all layers being editable.
14. Add a layer and draw a gray border around the edge of the photo. (*Hint:* Increase the size of the stage a few pixels to accommodate the border.)
15. Convert the photo to a button symbol.
16. Create an animation with a rollover effect that causes the heading to fade in when the viewer points to the photo.
17. Publish and save the movie.
18. Display Dreamweaver and insert the ULTours-photo An.swf file to the right of the heading, provide alternate text, and center the heading and photo across the page.

19. Edit the movie from Dreamweaver. Create an animation that fades in the text when the pointer rolls over the image, then use the Done button to return to the Dreamweaver document.
20. Play the movie in Dreamweaver, then save your work.
21. Insert the ultimatetours5.swf file below the heading and provide a title.
22. Turn off the Loop and Autoplay features, then name the movie **ULTmv**.
23. Select the photo, choose to edit it in Photoshop, and add an inner glow effect.
24. In Dreamweaver, select the photo and set it to play the Flash movie when the user points to the photo.
25. Save your work, view the document in a browser, then compare your image to the sample in Figure 24.

FIGURE 24
Sample Completed Project Builder 1

The Trip of a Lifetime Awaits You...

We Specialize in Exotic Adventures

Treks

Tours

Cruises

This project begins with the Striped Umbrella site created in Dreamweaver Chapter 5.

You have been asked to enhance the Striped Umbrella site by adding a Flash movie and changing a graphic image on the cafe page. Figure 25 shows the completed page for this part of the Web site. The idea is to replace the static crab logo image with a Flash animation that plays in the same space on the page.

1. In Photoshop, open the crab_logo.psd file.
2. Turn the visibility off and on for each layer to see the image is constructed.

3. In Flash, import the crab_logo.psd file to the stage, specifying that each layer is editable.
4. In Flash, create an animation using the cafe_logo.psd image. You decide on the type of animation, which could be a zoom or fade in; the entire crab moving; the crab claws moving; and so forth. (*Hint*: The crab image is made up of a body and left and right claws. If you want to animate these as one object, you can press and hold [Shift] to select all three, then convert them to a graphic symbol. Include a rollover effect or some other form of user interaction.) Save the movie as **crab_Anim.fla** and publish it.
5. In Dreamweaver, open the Striped Umbrella site on the Site panel.

6. Open the cafe.html page and delete the cafe_logo graphic on the page.
7. Insert the crab_Anim.swf file in the cell where the cafe_logo graphic had been.
8. Select the Flash movie placeholder and use the Property inspector to play and stop the animation.
9. Save your work.
10. View the Web page in your browser.

FIGURE 25
Sample Completed Project Builder 2

Crab is animated on mouse over

Figure 26 shows the home page of a Web site. Study the figure and complete the following questions. For each question, indicate how you determined your answer.

1. Connect to the Internet, and go to *www.memphiszoo.org*.
2. Open a document in a word processor or in Flash, save the file as **dpcIntegration**, then answer the following questions.

- What seems to be the purpose of this site?
- Who would be the target audience?
- Identify three elements within the Web page that could have been created or enhanced using Photoshop.
- Identify two elements on the page and indicate how you would use Photoshop to enhance them.
- Identify an animation that could have been developed by Flash.

- Indicate how you would use Flash to enhance the page.
- What would be the value of using Flash, Dreamweaver, and Photoshop to create the Web site?
- What suggestions would you make to improve on the design, and why?

FIGURE 26
Design Project

PORTFOLIO PROJECT

This is a continuation of the Portfolio Project in Flash Chapter 5. You will create a Web site in Dreamweaver, import graphic files from Photoshop, and import portfolio5.swf into the site. The home page of the Web site will include a heading and photo image (of your choice), as shown in Figure 27.

1. Create a folder on your hard drive and name it **Portfoliowebsite**, then create a folder within the Portfoliowebsite folder named **Library**.
2. In Dreamweaver, create a new site named **PortfolioWeb**, using the Portfoliowebsite folder as the local root folder.
3. Open portfoliohome.html and save it to the Portfoliowebsite site.

4. In Photoshop, open portfolio-heading.psd and save it as a .jpg file to the Portfoliowebsite folder.
5. In Dreamweaver, display the portfolio-home.html document, insert the portfolio-heading.jpg image, and provide alternate text.
6. Insert the portfolio-photo.psd to the right of the heading, provide alternate text, and center the heading and photo across the page. (*Hint*: You can use a photo of your choice, if desired.)
7. Insert portfolio5.swf below the heading and provide a title.
8. Select the heading and edit it in Photoshop to apply a drop shadow, then save it and copy and paste it into the Dreamweaver document.

9. Select the photo, choose to edit it in Photoshop, and add an inner glow effect, then save it and copy and paste it into the Dreamweaver document.
10. Switch to Dreamweaver, then choose to edit the Flash movie.
11. In Photoshop, create a graphic that resembles a portfolio case and name it portfolioCase.psd.
12. In Flash, import portfolioCase.psd to the stage, specifying all the layers to be editable.
13. Center the portfolioCase image on the stage.
14. Use the Done button to update the Flash movie and return to Dreamweaver.
15. In Dreamweaver, save your work, display the document in a browser, then compare your image to the sample in Figure 27.

FIGURE 27

Sample Completed Portfolio Project

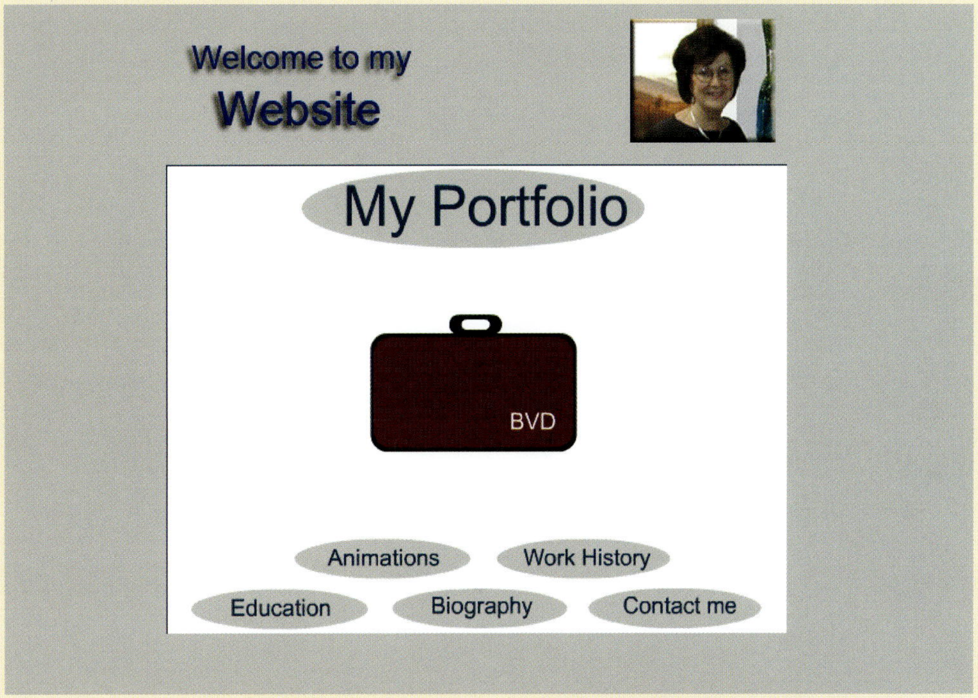

Read the following information carefully!!

Find out from your instructor the location where you will store your files.

- To complete many of the chapters in this book, you need to use the Data Files on the CD at the back of this book.

- All of the Data Files are organized in folders named after the chapter in which they are used. You should leave all the Data Files in these folders; do not move any Data File out of the folder in which it is originally stored.

- Your instructor will tell you where you will store the files you create and modify.

Copy and organize your Data Files.

- Use the Data Files List to organize your files to a USB storage device, network folder, hard drive, or other storage device.

- **Special instructions for Dreamweaver chapters:**

  - As you build each Web site, the exercises in this book will guide you to copy the Data Files you need from the appropriate Data Files folder to the folder where you are storing the Web site. Your Data Files should always remain intact because you are copying (and not moving) them to the Web site.

  - Because you will be building a Web site from one chapter to the next, sometimes you will need to use a Data File that is already contained in the Web site you are working on.

Find and keep track of your Data Files and completed files.

- Use the **Data File Supplied** column to make sure you have the files you need before starting the chapter or exercise indicated in the **Chapter** column.

  - **Special instructions for Dreamweaver chapters:** Some of the files listed in the **Data File Supplied** column are ones that you created or used in a previous chapter, and that are already part of the Web site you are working on.

- Use the **Student Creates File** column to determine the filename you use when saving your new file for the exercise.

- The **Used in** column tells you where a file is used in a chapter.

DATA FILES LIST

Files used in this book

Adobe Dreamweaver CS3

Chapter	Data File Supplied	Student Creates File	Used In
1	dw1_1.html about_us.swf accommodations.swf activities.swf cafe.swf index.swf shop.swf spa.swf assets/pool.jpg assets/su_background.jpg assets/su_banner.gif		Lesson 2
	dw1_2.html assets/su_banner.gif	about_us.html activities.html cafe.html cruises.html fishing.html spa.html	Lesson 4
	dw1_3.html dw1_4.html assets/blooms_banner.jpg assets/blooms_logo.jpg	annuals.html classes.html newsletter.html perennials.html plants.html tips.html water_plants.html	Skills Review
	dw1_5.html assets/tripsmart_banner.jpg	amazon.html catalog.html destinations.html kenya.html newsletter.html services.html	Project Builder 1
	dw1_6.html assets/cc_banner.jpg	adults.html catering.html children.html classes.html recipes.html shop.html	Project Builder 2

Adobe Dreamweaver CS3 (continued)

Chapter	Data File Supplied	Student Creates File	Used In
	none		Design Project
	none		Group Project
2	dw2_1.html spa.doc assets/su_banner.gif assets/the_spa.jpg		Lesson 2
	dw2_2.html gardening_tips.doc assets/blooms_banner.jpg assets/garden_tips.jpg		Skills Review
	none		Project Builder 1
	none		Project Builder 2
	none		Design Project
	none		Group Project
3	questions.doc		Lesson 1
		su_styles.css	Lesson 2
	dw3_1.html assets/boardwalk.jpg assets/club_house.jpg assets/pool.jpg assets/sago_palm.jpg assets/sports_club.jpg assets/su_banner.gif		Lesson 4
	assets/stripes_back.gif assets/umbrella_back.gif		Lesson 6
	dw3_2.html assets/blooms_banner.jpg assets/daisies.jpg assets/lantana.jpg assets/petunias.jpg assets/verbena.jpg	blooms_styles.css	Skills Review
	dw3_3.html dw3_4.html assets/tripsmart_banner.jpg assets/lion.jpg assets/zebra_mothers.jpg	tripsmart_styles.css	Project Builder 1

Adobe Dreamweaver CS3 (continued)

Chapter	Data File Supplied	Student Creates File	Used In
	dw3_5.html dw3_6.html assets/cc_banner.jpg assets/pot_knives.jpg	cc_styles.css	Project Builder 2
	none		Design Project
	none		Group Project
4	dw4_1.html assets/heron_waiting_small.jpg assets/su_banner.gif assets/two_dolphins_small.jpg		Lesson 1
		top.swf	Lesson 3
	assets/about_us_down.gif assets/about_us_up.gif assets/activities_down.gif assets/activities_up.gif assets/cafe_down.gif assets/cafe_up.gif assets/home_down.gif assets/home_up.gif assets/spa_down.gif assets/spa_up.gif		Lesson 4
	dw4_2.html dw4_3.html assets/boats.jpg assets/heron_small.jpg		Lesson 6
	dw4_4.html dw4_5.html dw4_6.html dw4_7.html assets/b_classes_down.jpg assets/b_classes_up.jpg assets/b_home_down.jpg assets/b_home_up.jpg assets/b_newsletter_down.jpg assets/b_newsletter_up.jpg assets/b_plants_down.jpg assets/b_plants_up.jpg	top.swf	Skills Review

Adobe Dreamweaver CS3 (continued)

Chapter	Data File Supplied	Student Creates File	Used In
	assets/b_tips_down.jpg assets/b_tips_up.jpg assets/blooms_banner.jpg assets/fuchsia.jpg assets/iris.jpg assets/water_hyacinth.jpg		
	dw4_8.html dw4_9.html dw4_10.html assets/giraffe.jpg assets/parrot.jpg assets/sloth.jpg assets/tripsmart_banner.jpg assets/water_lily.jpg		Project Builder 1
	dw4_11.html dw4_12.html dw4_13.html assets/cc_banner.jpg assets/cc_banner_with_text.jpg assets/children_cooking.jpg assets/cookies_oven.jpg assets/dumplings1.jpg assets/dumplings2.jpg assets/dumplings3.jpg assets/fish.jpg		Project Builder 2
	none		Design Project
	none		Group Project
5	assets/cafe_logo.gif assets/cafe_photo.jpg assets/cheesecake.jpg		Lesson 3
	cafe.doc		Lesson 4
	gardeners.doc registration.doc assets/flower_bed.jpg		Skills Review

Adobe Dreamweaver CS3 (continued)

Chapter	Data File Supplied	Student Creates File	Used In
	assets/hat.jpg assets/pants.jpg assets/vest.jpg		Project Builder 1
	menu items.doc assets/muffins.jpg		Project Builder 2
	none		Design Project
	none		Group Project
6		The Striped Umbrella.ste	Lesson 4
		blooms & bulbs.ste	Skills Review
		TripSmart.ste	Project Builder 1
		Carolyne's Creations.ste	Project Builder 2
	none		Design Project
	none		Group Project

Adobe Flash CS3

Chapter	Data File Supplied	Student Creates File	Used In
1		workspace.fla	Lesson 1
	fl1_1.fla		Lesson 2
		tween.fla	Lesson 3
		layers.fla	Lesson 4
	*layers.fla		Lesson 5
	fl1_2.fla		Skills Review
		demonstration.fla	Project Builder 1
	fl1_3.fla		Project Builder 2
		dpc1.fla	Design Project
			Portfolio Project
2		tools.fla	Lessons 1-4
	fl2-1.fla		Lesson 5
		skillsdemo2.fla	Skills Review
		ultimatetours2.fla	Project Builder 1
		thejazzclub2.fla	Project Builder 2
		dpc2.fla	Design Project
		portfolio2.fla	Portfolio Project
3	fl3-1.fla		Lesson 1
	fl3-2.fla		Lessons 2-4
	fl3_3.fla		Skills Review
	**ultimatetours2.fla		Project Builder 1
		isa3.fla	Project Builder 2
		dpc3.fla	Design Project
	**portfolio2.fla		Portfolio Project

*Created in a previous Lesson or Skills Review in current chapter

**Created in a previous chapter

Adobe Flash CS3 (continued)

Chapter	Data File Supplied	Student Creates File	Used In
4	fl4-1.fla		Lesson 1
	fl4-2.fla		Lesson 2
	fl4-3.fla		Lesson 3
	fl4-4.fla fl4-5.fla		Lesson 4
	*frameAn.fla		Lesson 5
	fl4-6.fla		Skills Review
	**ultimatetours3.fla ship.gif		Project Builder 1
		summerBB4.fla	Project Builder 2
		dpc4.fla	Design Project
	**portfolio3.fla		Portfolio Project
5	fl5-1.fla fl5-2.fla fl5-3.fla		Lesson 1
	fl5-4.fla		Lesson 2
	fl5-5.fla CarSnd.wav beep.wav		Lesson 3
	fl5-6.fla *rallySnd.fla		Lesson 4
	fl5-7.fla		Lesson 5
	fl5-8.fla		Skills Review
	**ultimatetours4.fla foghorn.wav		Project Builder 1
		zodiac5.fla	Project Builder 2
		dpc5.fla	Design Project
	**portfolio4.fla		Portfolio Project

*Created in a previous Lesson or Skills Review in current chapter

**Created in a previous chapter

Adobe Photoshop CS3

Chapter	Data File Supplied	Student Creates File	Used in
Chapter 1	PS 1-1.psd PS 1-2.tif		Lessons 2–8
		Review.psd	Skills Review
	PS 1-3.psd		Skills Review
	PS 1-4.psd		Project Builder 2
		Critique-1.psd Critique-2.psd	Design Project
Chapter 2	PS 2-1.psd PS 2-2.psd		Lessons 1–4
	PS 2-3.psd PS 2-4.psd		Skills Review
	PS 2-5.psd PS 2-6.psd		Project Builder 1
	PS 2-7.psd PS 2-8.psd		Project Builder 2
	PS 2-9.psd PS 2-10.psd		Design Project
	PS 2-11.psd		Group Project
Chapter 3	PS 3-1.psd PS 3-2.psd PS 3-3.psd PS 3-4.psd PS 3-5.psd PS 3-6.psd		Lessons 1–4
	PS 3-7.psd PS 3-8.tif PS 3-9.tif PS 3-10.tif		Skills Review
	PS 3-11.psd		Project Builder 1
	PS 3-12.psd		Project Builder 2
		Sample Compositing.psd	Design Project
	PS 3-13.psd		Group Project

Adobe Photoshop CS3 (continued)

Chapter	Data File Supplied	Student Creates File	Used in
Chapter 4	PS 4-1.psd		Lessons 1–4, 6-7
	PS 4-2.psd		Lessons 5–6
	PS 4-3.tif		Lesson 7
	PS 4-4.psd		Skills Review
	PS 4-5.psd		
	PS 4-6.tif		
	PS 4-7.psd		Project Builder 1
	PS 4-8.psd		Project Builder 2
	PS 4-9.psd		Design Project
	PS 4-10.psd		Group Project
Chapter 5	PS 5-1.psd		Lessons 1–7
	PS 5-2.psd		Skills Review
	PS 5-3.psd		Project Builder 1
	PS 5-4.psd		Project Builder 2
	PS 5-5.psd		Design Project
		Community Promotion.psd	Group Project

Integration

Chapter	Data File Supplied	Student Creates File	Used In
1	ic_1.psd	canyon-scenes.html	Lesson 1
	*GrandCanyon.psd		Lesson 2
	ic_2.psd	AZScenes.fla AZScenes.swf	Lesson 3
	*AZScenes.swf	NorthernAZ.html	Lesson 4
	bread-heading.psd bread-photo.psd	food-home.html bread-An.fla bread-An.swf	Skills Review
	ultours_home.html ULTours-photo.psd ULTours-heading.psd **ultimatetours5.fla **ultimatetours5.swf	ULTours-photo-An.fla ULTours-photo-An.swf	Project Builder 1
	cafe_logo.psd cafe.html Striped Umbrella site files	crab_Anim.fla crab_Anim.swf	Project Builder 2
	none	dpcIntegration	Design Project
	portfoliohome.html portfolio-heading.psd portfolio-photo.psd **portfolio5.swf **portfolio5.fla	portfolioCase.psd	Portfolio Project

Absolute path
A path containing an external link that references a link on a Web page outside of the current Web site, and includes the protocol "http" and the URL, or address, of the Web page.

ActionScript
The Flash scripting language used by developers to add interactivity to movies, control objects, exchange data, and create complex animations.

Actions Panel
The Flash panel used when you create and edit actions for an object or frame.

Adobe Version Cue
Version Cue is used to track versions of a file and monitor file check-in and check-out, which helps ensure efficient workgroup collaboration when sharing files.

Additive colors
A color system in which, when the values of R, G, and B are 0, the result is black; when the values are all 255, the result is white.

Adobe Bridge
A stand-alone application that serves as the hub for the Adobe Create Suite 3. Can be used for file management tasks such as opening, viewing, sorting, and rating files.

Aligning an image
Positioning an image on a Web page in relation to other elements on the page.

Alternate text
Descriptive text that can be set to appear in place of an image while the image is downloading or when users place a mouse pointer over an image.

Altitude
A Bevel and Emboss setting that affects the amount of visible dimension.

Anchor point
Joins path segments to delineate changes in direction.

Angle
In the Layer Style dialog box, the setting that determines where a drop shadow falls relative to the text.

Animation
The perception of motion caused by the rapid display of a series of still images.

Anti-aliasing
Partially fills in pixel edges, resulting in smooth-edge type. This feature lets your type maintain its crisp appearance and is especially useful for large type.

Assets folder
A subfolder in which you store most of the files that are not Web pages, such as images, audio files, and video clips.

Assets panel
A panel that contains nine categories of assets, such as images, used in a Web site. Clicking a category button displays a list of those assets.

Background color
A color that fills the entire Web page, a frame, a table, a cell, or a document.

In Photoshop, used to make gradient fills and to fill in areas of an image that have been erased. The default background color is white.

Background image
A graphic file used in place of a background color.

Balance
In screen design, balance refers to the distribution of optical weight in the layout. Optical weight is the ability of an object to attract the viewer's eye, as determined by the object's size, shape, color, and so on.

Banners
Graphics that generally appear across the top of the screen that can incorporate a company's logo, contact information, and navigation bars.

Base color
The original color of an image.

Base layer
The bottom layer in a clipping group, which serves as the group's mask.

Baseline
An invisible line on which type rests.

Baseline shift
The distance type appears from its original position.

Behavior
A preset piece of JavaScript code that can be attached to page objects. A behavior tells the page object to respond in a

specific way when an event occurs, such as when the mouse pointer is positioned over the object.

Bitmap
A geometric arrangement of different color dots on a rectangular grid.

Bitmap mode
Uses black or white color values to represent image pixels; a good choice for images with subtle color gradations, such as photographs or painted images.

Bitmap type
Type that may develop jagged edges when enlarged.

Blend color
The color applied to the base color when a blending mode is applied to a layer.

Blending mode
Affects the layer's underlying pixels or base color. Used to darken or lighten colors, depending on the colors in use.

BMP
Bitmapped file. A file format used for images that is based on pixels.

Body
The part of a Web page that is seen when the page is viewed in a browser window.

Border
An outline that surrounds a cell, a table, or a frame.

Brightness
The measurement of relative lightness or darkness of a color (measured as a percentage from 0% [black] to 100% [white]).

Broken links
Links that cannot find the intended destination file for the link.

Browser
Software used to display Web pages, such as Microsoft Internet Explorer, Mozilla Firefox, or Safari.

Bullet
A small dot or similar icon preceding unordered list items.

Bulleted list
An unordered list that uses bullets.

Button Symbols
Objects in Flash that appear on the stage and that are used to provide interactivity, such as jumping to another frame on the Timeline.

Cascading Style Sheet
A file used to assign sets of common formatting characteristics to page elements such as text, objects, and tables.

Cell padding
The distance between the cell content and the cell walls in a table.

Cell spacing
The distance between cells in a table.

Cell walls
The edges surrounding a cell in a table.

Cells
Small boxes within a table that are used to hold text or graphics. Cells are arranged horizontally in rows and vertically in columns.

Character palette
Helps you control type properties. The Toggle the Character and Paragraph palette button is located on the options bar when you select a Type tool.

Child page
A page at a lower level in a Web hierarchy that links to a parent page.

Class style
See Custom style.

Clipboard
Temporary storage area, provided by your operating system, for cut and copied data.

Code and Design Views
A Web page view that is a combination of Code View and Design View.

Code Inspector
A window that works just like Code view, except that it is a floating window.

Code View
A Web page view that shows a full screen with the HTML code for the page. Use this view to read or directly edit the code.

Color Picker
A feature that lets you choose a color from a color spectrum.

Color Range command
Used to select a particular color contained in an existing image.

Color separation
Result of converting an RGB image into a CMYK image; the commercial printing process of separating colors for use with different inks.

Columns
Table cells arranged vertically.

Comments
Helpful text describing portions of the HTML code, such as a JavaScript function, that are inserted in the code and are not visible in the browser window.

Compositing
Combining images from sources such as other Photoshop images, royalty-free images, pictures taken from digital cameras, and scanned artwork.

Contents
The Adobe Help feature that lists topics by category.

Controller
A toolbar that contains the playback controls for a movie.

Crisp
Anti-aliasing setting that gives type more definition and makes it appear sharper.

Crop
To exclude part of an image. Cropping hides areas of an image without losing resolution quality.

Custom style
A style that can contain a combination of formatting attributes that can be applied

to a block of text or other page elements. Custom style names begin with a period (.). Also known as a class style.

Debug
To find and correct coding errors.

Declaration
The property and value of a style in a Cascading Style Sheet.

Default base font
Size 3 (Dreamweaver). The default font that is applied to any text without an assigned size that is entered on a Web page.

Default font color
The color the browser uses to display text, links, and visited links if no other color is assigned.

Default link color
The color the browser uses to display links if no other color is assigned. The default link color is blue.

Defining a Web site
Specifying the site's local root folder location to help Dreamweaver keep track of the links among Web pages and supporting files.

Definition lists
Lists made up of terms with indented descriptions or definitions.

Delimited files
Database or spreadsheet files that have been saved as text files with delimiters.

Delimiter
A comma, tab, colon, semicolon, or similar character that separates tabular data.

Description
A short summary of Web site content that resides in the Head section.

Deselect
A command that removes the marquee from an area, so it is no longer selected.

Design notes
A file (.mno) that contains the original source file (.psd, .png or .fla) when a Photoshop, Fireworks, or Flash file is inserted in to Dreamweaver.

Design View
The view that shows a full-screen layout and is primarily used when designing and creating a Web page.

Diagonal symmetry
A design principle in which page elements are balanced along the invisible diagonal line of the page.

Digital image
A picture in electronic form. It may be referred to as a file, document, picture, or image.

Distance
Determines how far a shadow falls from the text. This setting is used by the Drop Shadow and Bevel and Emboss styles.

Distort filters
Create three-dimensional or other reshaping effects. Some of the types of distortions you

can produce include Glass, Pinch, Ripple, Shear, Spherize, Twirl, Wave, and ZigZag.

Dock
A collection of palettes or buttons surrounded by a dark gray bar. The arrows in the dock are used to maximize and minmize the palettes.

Document toolbar
A toolbar that contains buttons for changing the current Web page view, previewing and debugging Web pages, and managing files.

Document-relative path
A path referenced in relation to the Web page that is currently displayed.

Documents
Flash, Photoshop, Fireworks, and Dreamweaver files.

Document window
The large white area in the Dreamweaver workspace where you create and edit Web pages.

Domain name
An IP address expressed in letters instead of numbers, usually reflecting the name of the business represented by the Web site.

Down Image state
The state of a page element when the element has been clicked with the mouse pointer.

Download time
The time it takes to transfer a file to another computer.

Drop Shadow
A style that adds what looks like a colored layer of identical text behind the selected type. The default shadow color is black.

Drop Zone
A blue outline area that indicates where a palette can be moved.

DSL
Digital Subscriber Line. A type of high-speed Internet connection.

Embedded CSS style sheet
Styles that are part of an HTML page rather than comprising a separate file.

Enable Cache
A setting to direct the computer system to use space on the hard drive as temporary memory, or cache, while you are working in Dreamweaver.

Expanded Tables Mode
A Dreamweaver mode that displays tables with temporary cell padding and spacing to make it easier to see the table cells.

Export data
To save data that was created in Dreamweaver in a special file format so that you can bring it into another software program.

External CSS style sheet
Collection of rules stored in a separate file that control the formatting of content in a

Web page. External CSS style sheets have a .css file extension.

External links
Links that connect to Web pages in other Web sites or to an e-mail address.

Extract feature
Used to isolate a foreground object from its background.

Fastening point
An anchor within the marquee. When the marquee pointer reaches the initial fastening point, a small circle appears on the pointer, indicating that you have reached the starting point.

Favorites
Assets that are used repeatedly in a Web site and are included in their own category in the assets panel.

Feather
A method used to control the softness of a selection's edges by blurring the area between the selection and the surrounding pixels.

Files panel
A window similar to Windows Explorer (Windows) or Finder (Macintosh), where Dreamweaver stores and manages files and folders. The Files panel contains a list of all the folders and files in a Web site.

Fill
A solid color, a pattern, or a gradient applied to an object.

Filters
Used to alter the look of an image and give it a special, customized appearance by applying special effects, such as distortions, changes in lighting, and blurring.

Flash Button Objects
Flash graphic and text objects that you can insert onto a Web page without having the Flash program installed.

Flash Player
A program that allows Flash movies (.swf and .exe formats) to be viewed on a computer. This a free program from Adobe.

Flash text
A vector-based graphic that contains text.

Flattening
Merges all visible layers into one layer, named the Background layer, and deletes all hidden layers, greatly reducing file size.

Floating workspace
A feature of Adobe products that allows each document and panel to appear in its own window.

Font combination
A set of three fonts that specifies which fonts a browser should use to display the text on a Web page.

Font
Characters with a similar appearance.

Font family
Represents a complete set of characters, letters, and symbols for a particular typeface. Font families are generally divided into three categories: serif, sans serif, and symbol.

Foreground color
Used to paint, fill, and stroke selections. The default foreground color is black.

Frame animation
An animation created by specifying the object that is to appear in each frame of a sequence of frames (also called a frame-by-frame animation).

Frame-by-frame animation
Animation that creates a new image for each frame (also called Frame animation).

Frame label
A text name for a keyframe that can be referenced within ActionScript code.

Frames
Individual cells that make up the Timeline in Flash.

Frameset
Multiple Web pages displayed together using more than one frame or window.

FTP
File Transfer Protocol. The process of uploading and downloading files to and from a remote site.

Fuzziness
Similar to tolerance, in that the lower the value, the closer the color pixels must be to be selected.

Gamut
The range of displayed colors in a color model.

GIF file
Graphics Interchange Format file. A GIF is a type of file format used for images placed on Web pages that can support both transparency and animation.

Gloss Contour
A Bevel and Emboss setting that determines the pattern with which light is reflected.

Gradient
Two or more colors that blend into each other in a fixed design.

Gradient fill
A type of fill in which colors appear to blend into one another. A gradient's appearance is determined by its beginning and ending points. Photoshop contains five gradient fill styles.

Gradient presets
Predesigned gradient fills that are displayed in the Gradient picker.

Graphic
Picture or design element that adds visual interest to a page.

Graphic Symbols
Objects in Flash, such as drawings, that are converted to symbols and stored in the Library panel. A graphic symbol is the original object. Instances (copies) of a symbol can be made by dragging the symbol from the Library to the stage.

Grayscale image
Can contain up to 256 shades of gray. Pixels can have brightness values from 0 (black) to white (255).

Grayscale mode
Uses up to 256 shades of gray, assigning a brightness value from 0 (black) to 255 (white) to each pixel.

Group
A command that manipulates multiple objects as a single selection.

Guide layers
Layers used to align objects on the stage in a Flash document.

Guides
Horizontal and vertical lines that you create to help you align objects. Guides appear as light blue lines.

Handles
Small boxes that appear along the perimeter of a selected object and are used to change the size of an image.

Head content
The part of a Web page that is not viewed in the browser window. It includes meta tags, which are HTML codes that include information about the page, such as keywords and descriptions.

Headings
Six different styles that can be applied to text: Heading 1 (the largest size) through Heading 6 (the smallest size).

Hexadecimal value
A value that represents the amount of red, green, and blue in a color and is based on the Base 16 number system.

Highlight Mode
A Bevel and Emboss setting that determines how pigments are combined.

History palette
Contains a record of each action performed during a Photoshop session. Up to 1000 levels of Undo are available through the History palette (20 levels by default).

History panel
A panel that lists the steps that have been performed in an Adobe application while editing and formatting a document.

Home page
Usually, the first Web page that appears when users visit a Web site.

Horizontal symmetry
A design principle in which page elements are balanced side-to-side across the page.

Horizontal and vertical space
Blank space above, below, and on the sides of an image that separates the image from the text or other elements on the page.

Hotspot
An area that you define in your document to which you can assign a URL (Web address) or other type of interactivity. A clickable area on a graphic that, when clicked, links to a different location on the page or to another Web page.

HTML
Hypertext Markup Language. A language Web developers use to create Web pages.

Hue
The color reflected from/transmitted through an object and expressed as a degree (between 0° and 360°). Each hue is identified by a color name (such as red or green).

Hyperlinks
Graphic or text elements on a Web page that users click to display another location on the page, another Web page on the same Web site, or a Web page on a different Web site. Hyperlinks are also known as links.

Image-editing program
Used to manipulate graphic images that can be reproduced by professional printers using full-color processes.

Image map
A graphic that has one or more hotspots defined on it that, when clicked, serve as a link that will take the viewer to another location.

Import data
To bring data created in one software program into another application.

Index
The Adobe Help feature that displays topics in alphabetical order.

Insert bar
Groups of buttons for creating and inserting objects arranged by category.

Instances

Editable copies of symbols after you drag them from the Library panel to the canvas or stage (in Flash).

Intellectual property

An image or idea that is owned and retained by legal control.

Interactivity

Allows visitors to your Web site to interact with and affect content by moving or clicking the mouse.

Internal links

Links to Web pages within the same Web site.

IP address

An assigned series of numbers, separated by periods, that designates an address on the Internet.

ISP

Internet Service Provider. A service to which you subscribe to be able to connect to the Internet with your computer.

JavaScript

A Web-scripting code that interacts with HTML code to create dynamic content, such as rollovers or interactive forms.

JPEG file

Joint Photographic Experts Group file. A JPEG is a type of file format used for images that appear on Web pages. Many photographs are saved with the JPEG file format.

Kerning

Controlling the amount of space between two characters.

Keyframe

A frame that signifies a change in the Timeline of a Flash movie, such as an object being animated.

Keywords

Words that relate to the content of the Web site and reside in the Head section.

Landscape orientation

An image with the long edge of the paper at the top and bottom.

Layer

A section within an image on which objects can be stored. The advantage: Individual effects can be isolated and manipulated without affecting the rest of the image. The disadvantage: Layers can increase the size of your file.

Layers (Flash)

Rows on the Timeline that are used to organize objects and that allow the stacking of objects on the stage.

Layer comp

A variation on the arrangement and visibility of existing layers within an image; an organizational tool.

Layer group

An organizing tool you use to group layers on the Layers palette.

Layer (Photoshop)

An element that functions like a folder divided into sections that contain objects. A document can be made up of many layers.

Layers (Flash)

Rows on the Timeline that are used to organize objects and that allow the stacking of objects on the stage.

Layers palette

Displays all the layers within an active image. You can use the Layers palette to create, delete, merge, copy, or reposition layers.

Layer style

An effect that can be applied to a type or image layer.

Layer thumbnail

Contains a miniature picture of the layer's content, and appears to the left of the layer name on the Layers palette.

Layout Mode

A Dreamweaver mode that is used when you draw your own table.

Leading

An adjustment to the amount of vertical space between lines of text.

Library

A panel containing graphic symbols, button symbols, and animation symbols. You can use multiple Libraries in a document and share Libraries between documents.

Logo

A distinctive image used to identify a company, project, or organization. You can create a logo by combining symbols, shapes, colors, and text.

Local root folder

A folder on your hard drive, Zip disk, or floppy disk that holds all the files and folders for the Web site.

Looping

The number of times an animation repeats.

Luminosity

The remaining light and dark values that result when a color image is converted to grayscale.

Mailto: link

An e-mail address that is formatted as a link that opens the default mail program with a blank, addressed message.

Main Timeline

The primary Timeline for a Flash movie. The main Timeline is displayed when you start a new Flash document.

Marquee

A series of dotted lines indicating a selected area that can be edited or dragged into another image.

Mask

A feature that lets you protect or modify a particular area; created using a marquee.

Mask layer

A layer in a Flash document that is used to cover the objects on another layer(s) and, at the same time, create a window through which you can view various objects on the other layer.

Menu bar

A bar across the top of the program window that is located under the program title bar and lists the names of the menus that contain commands.

Merge cells

To combine multiple cells in a table into one cell.

Merge Drawing Model

A drawing mode that causes overlapping drawings (objects) to merge, so that a change in the top object, such as moving it, may affect the object beneath it.

Meta tags

HTML codes that include information about the page such as keywords and descriptions. Meta tags reside in the head section.

Mode

Represents the amount of color data that can be stored in a given file format, and determines the color model used to display and print an image.

Model

Determines how pigments combine to produce resulting colors; determined by the color mode.

Monotype spacing

Spacing in which each character occupies the same amount of space.

Morphing

The animation process of changing one object into another, sometimes unrelated, object.

Motion guide layer

A path used to specify how an animated object moves around the Flash stage.

Motion tweening

The process used in Flash to automatically fill in the frames between keyframes in an animation that changes the properties of an object such as the position, size, or color. Motion tweening works on groups and symbols.

Movement

In screen design, movement refers to the way the viewer's eye moves through the objects on the screen.

Named anchor

A specific location on a Web page that is used to link to that portion of the Web page.

Navigation bar

A set of text or graphic links that viewers can use to navigate between pages of a Web site.

Nested table
A table within a table.

Non-breaking space
A space that is left on the page by a browser.

None
Anti-aliasing setting that applies no anti-aliasing, resulting in jagged edges.

Object Drawing Model
A drawing mode that allows you to overlap objects which are then kept separate, so that changes in one object do not affect another object. You must break apart these objects before you can select their stroke and fills.

Objects
The individual elements in a document, such as text or images. In Flash, objects are placed on the stage and can be edited or manipulated.

Onion skinning
A setting that allows you to view one or more frames before and after in the current frame.

Opacity
Determines the percentage of transparency. Whereas a layer with 100% opacity will obstruct objects in the layers beneath it, a layer with 1% opacity will appear nearly transparent.

Options bar
Displays the settings for the active tool. The options bar is located directly under the menu bar but can be moved anywhere in the workspace for easier access.

Ordered lists
Lists of items that must be placed in a specific order and are preceded by numbers or letters.

Orientation
Direction an image appears on the page: portrait or landscape.

Orphaned files
Files that are not linked to any pages in the Web site.

Outline type
Type that is mathematically defined and can be scaled to any size without its edges losing their smooth appearance.

Over Image state
The state of a page element when the mouse pointer is over the element.

Over While Down Image state
The state of a page element when the mouse pointer is clicked and held over the element.

Palettes
Floating windows that can be moved and are used to modify objects. Palettes contain named tabs, which can be separated and moved to another group. Each palette contains a menu that can be viewed by clicking the list arrow in its upper-right corner.

Panel groups
Groups of panels such as Design, Code, Application, and Files that are displayed through the Window menu. Sets of related panels are grouped together.

Panels (Dreamweaver)
Individual windows in Dreamweaver that display information on a particular topic, such as Answers or History.

Panels (Flash)
Components in Flash used to view, organize, and modify objects and features in a movie.

Parent page
A page at a higher level in a Web hierarchy that links to other pages on a lower level.

Pasteboard
The gray area surrounding the Flash stage where objects can be placed and manipulated. Neither the pasteboard, nor objects placed on it appear in the movie unless the objects move onto the stage during the playing of the movie.

Path (vector object)
An open or closed line consisting of a series of anchor points.

Path (file location)
The location of an open file in relation to any folders in the Web site.

Persistence of vision
The phenomenon of the eye capturing and holding an image for one-tenth of a second before processing another image.

PICS
Platform for Internet Content Selection. This is a rating system for Web pages.

Pixels

Small squares of color used to display a digital image on a rectangular grid, such as a computer screen. Each dot in a bitmapped image that represents a color or shade.

Playhead

An indicator specifying which frame is playing in the Timeline of a Flash movie.

Plug-in

A module that adds features or enhancements to an application.

PNG file

Portable Network Graphics file. A PNG is a file format used for images placed on Web pages that is capable of showing millions of colors but is small in file size. The native file format in Fireworks.

Point of contact

A place on a Web page that provides viewers a means of contacting a company.

Points

Unit of measurement for font sizes. Traditionally, 1 inch is equivalent to 72.27 points. The default Photoshop type size is 12 points.

Portrait orientation

An image with the short edge of the paper at the top and bottom.

PostScript

A programming language created by Adobe that optimizes printed text and graphics.

PPI

Pixels per inch.

Preferences

Used to control the Photoshop environment using your specifications.

Projector

In Flash, a standalone executable movie, such as a Windows .exe file.

Property inspector

A panel where properties and options specific to a selected tool or command appear. In Dreamweaver, a panel that displays the properties of the selected Web page object. In Flash, the Property inspector displays the properties of the selected object on the stage or the selected frame. You can change an object's properties using the text boxes, drop-down menus, and buttons on the Property inspector. The contents of the Property inspector vary according to the object currently selected.

Proportional spacing

The text spacing in which each character takes up a different amount of space, based on its width.

Publish

The process used to generate the files necessary for delivering Flash movies on the Web.

Publish a Web site

To make a Web site available for viewing on the Internet or on an intranet.

QuickTime

A file format used for movies and animations that requires a QuickTime Player.

Radial symmetry

A design principle in which page elements are balanced from the center of the page outward, like the petals of a flower.

Rasterize

Converts a type layer to an image layer.

Reference panel

A panel used to find answers to coding questions, covering topics such as HTML, JavaScript, and Accessibility.

Refresh Local File List Automatically option

A setting that directs Dreamweaver to automatically reflect changes made in your file listings.

Registration point

The point on an object that is used to position the object on the stage in a Flash movie.

Relative path

A path used with an internal link to reference a Web page or graphic file within the Web site. In Flash, a path for an external link or to an object that is based on the location of the movie file.

Relief

The height of ridges within an object.

Remote server

A Web server that hosts Web sites and is not directly connected to the computer housing the local site.

Remote site

A Web site that has been published to a remote server.

Rendering intent

The way in which a color-management system handles color conversion from one color space to another.

Resolution

The number of pixels per inch in an image. Also refers to an image's clarity and fineness of detail.

Resulting color

The outcome of the blend color applied to the base color.

Rollover

An effect that changes the appearance of an object when the mouse rolls over it.

Root folder (local root folder)

A folder used to store all folders and files for a Web site.

Root-relative path

A path referenced from a Web site's root folder.

Rows

Table cells arranged horizontally.

Rule of Thirds

The rule of thirds is a design principle that entails dividing a page into nine squares and then placing the page elements of most interest on the intersections of the grid lines.

Rules

Sets of formatting attributes in a Cascading Style Sheet.

Rulers

On screen markers that help you precisely measure and position an object. Rulers can be displayed using the View menu.

Sampling

A method of changing foreground and background colors by copying existing colors from an image.

Sans serif fonts

Fonts that do not have tails or strokes at the end of characters; commonly used in headlines and on Web pages.

Saturation

The strength or purity of the color, representing the amount of gray in proportion to hue (measured as a percentage from 0% [gray], to 100% [fully saturated]). Also known as *chroma*.

Scene

A Timeline designated for a specific part of a Flash movie. Scenes are a way to organize long movies by dividing the movie into sections.

Screen reader

A device used by the visually impaired to convert written text on a computer monitor to spoken words.

Script Assist

A feature found in the Actions panel which can be used to generate ActionScript without having to write programming code.

Seamless image

A tiled image that is blurred at the edges so that it appears to be all one image.

Search

The Adobe Help feature that allows you to enter a keyword to begin a search for a topic.

Selection

An area in an image that is surrounded by a selection marquee.

Selector

The name or the tag to which style declarations have been assigned.

Serif fonts

Ornate fonts that have a tail, or stroke, at the end of some characters. These tails make it easier for the eye to recognize words; therefore, serif fonts are generally used in text passages.

Shading

Bevel and Emboss setting that determines lighting effects.

Shadow Mode

Bevel and Emboss setting that determines how pigments are combined.

Shape hints

Indicators used to control the shape of an object as it changes appearance during an animation.

Shape tweening

The process of animating an object so that its shape changes. Shape tweening requires editable graphics.

Sharp
Anti-aliasing setting that displays type with the best possible resolution.

Sharpen More filter
Increases the contrast of adjacent pixels and can focus blurry images.

Site map
A graphical representation of how Web pages relate to each other within a Web site.

Slices
A Web element that divides an image into different sections, which allows you to apply rollover behaviors, animation, and URLs to those areas.

Size
Determines the clarity of a drop shadow.

Smooth
Anti-aliasing setting that gives type more rounded edges.

Soft return
A shortcut key combination that forces text to a new line without creating a new paragraph by creating a <BR> tag.

Source
The image containing the color that will be matched.

Splash screen
A window that displays information about the software you are using.

Split cells
To divide cells into multiple cells.

Spread
Determines the width of drop shadow text.

Stage
That area of the Flash workspace that contains the objects that are part of the movie and that will be seen by the viewers.

Standard toolbar
A toolbar that contains icons for some frequently used commands that are also available on the File and Edit menus.

Standard Mode
A Dreamweaver mode that is used when you insert a table using the Insert Table icon or command.

State
Represents the button's appearance based on a mouse action. These include: Up, Over, Down, and Over While Down.

Status bar
The area located at the bottom of the program window (Win) or the image window (Mac) that displays information such as the file size of the active window and a description of the active tool. In Dreamweaver, bar that appears at the bottom of the Dreamweaver document window. The left end of the status bar displays the tag selector, which shows the HTML tags being used at the insertion point location. The right end displays the window size and estimated download time for the page displayed.

Stroking the edges
The process of making a selection or layer stand out by formatting it with a border.

Strong
Anti-aliasing setting that makes type appear heavier, much like the bold attribute.

Storyboard
A small sketch that represents each page in a Web site. Like a flowchart, a storyboard shows the relationship of each page to the other pages in the site.

Structure
A Bevel and Emboss setting that determines the size and physical properties of the object.

Style Rendering toolbar
A toolbar that allows you to render a Web page as different media types (e.g., handheld).

Subtractive colors
A color system in which the full combination of cyan, magenta, and yellow absorb all color and produce black.

Swatches palette
Contains available colors that can be selected for use as a foreground or background color. You can also add your own colors to the Swatches palette.

Symbol
A graphic, animation, or button that represents an object, text, or combination group.

Symbol fonts
Used to display unique characters (such as $, ÷, or ™).

Table header
Text placed at the top or sides of a table on a Web page that is read by screen readers.

Tables
Grids of rows and columns that can be used either to hold tabular data on a Web page or as a basic design tool for page layout.

Tabular data
Data arranged in columns and rows and separated by a delimiter.

Tag Selector
A location on the status bar that displays HTML tags for the various page elements, including tables and cells.

Target (Dreamweaver)
The location on a Web page that the browser displays in full view when an internal link is clicked or the frame that opens when a link is clicked.

Target (image editing)
When sampling a color, the image that will receive the matched color.

Templates
Web pages that contain the basic layout for similar pages in the site.

Title bar
Displays the program name and filename of the open image. The title bar also contains buttons for minimizing, maximizing, and closing the image.

Tiled image
A small graphic that repeats across and down a Web page, appearing as individual squares or rectangles.

Timeline
The component of Flash used to organize and control the movie's contents over time, by specifying when each object appears on the stage.

Timeline Effect
Pre-built animation effects (such as rotating, fading, and wiping) that can be applied to objects using a dialog box.

Tools panel
A panel in Flash, Dreamweaver, and Photoshop separated into categories containing tools and their options.

Transformation point
The point on an object that is used to orient the object as it is being animated and the point that snaps to a motion guide.

Tracking
The insertion of a uniform amount of space between characters.

Tweening
The process of adding tweened instances and distributing them to frames so that the movement appears more fluid.

Type
Text, or a layer containing text. Each character is measured in points. In PostScript measurement, 1 inch is equivalent to

72 points. In traditional measurement, 1 inch is equivalent to 72.27 points.

Type spacing
Adjustments you can make to the space between characters and between lines of type.

Unity
In screen design, intra-screen unity has to do with how the various screen objects relate. Inter-screen unity refers to the design that viewers encounter as they navigate from one screen to another.

Unordered lists
Lists of items that do not need to be placed in a specific order and are usually preceded by bullets.

Unvisited links
Links that have not been clicked by the viewer.

Up Image state
The state of a page element when the mouse pointer is not on the element.

Upload
The process of transferring files from a local drive to a Web server.

URL
Uniform Resource Locator. An address that determines a route on the Internet or to a Web page.

Vector graphics
Mathematically calculated objects composed of anchor points and straight or curved line segments.

Version Cue
See Adobe Version Cue.

Vignette
A feature in which the border of a picture or portrait fades into the surrounding color at its edges.

Vignette effect
A feature that uses feathering to fade a marquee shape.

Visited links
Links that have been previously clicked, or visited. The default color for visited links is purple.

Web design program
A program for creating interactive Web pages containing text, images, hyperlinks, animation, sound, and video.

Web server
A computer dedicated to hosting Web sites that is connected to the Internet and configured with software to handle requests from browsers.

Web site
Related Web pages stored on a server that users can download using a Web browser.

Web safe Colors
Colors that display consistently in all browsers and on Macintosh, Windows, and Unix platforms.

White space
An area on a Web page that is not filled with text or graphics.

Workspace
The entire window, from the menu bar at the top of the window, to the status bar at the bottom border of the program window. The area in the Dreamweaver program window where you work with documents, movies, tools, and panels.

WYSIWYG
An acronym for What You See Is What You Get, meaning that your Web page should look the same in the browser as it does in the Web editor.

XHTML
eXtensible HyperText Markup Language. The most current standard for developing Web pages.

advantages of, DREAMWEAVER
3-11
attaching, DREAMWEAVER 3-16–19
CSS style sheet code,
DREAMWEAVER 3-11–15
CSS styles panel, DREAMWEAVER
3-10
overview, DREAMWEAVER 3-10
.CDR files, PHOTOSHOP 1-5
cells in HTML tables
formatting, DREAMWEAVER
5-23–29
formatting cell content,
DREAMWEAVER 5-22
graphics in, DREAMWEAVER
5-16–21
merging, DREAMWEAVER 5-11–15
padding, DREAMWEAVER 5-4, 17
spacing, DREAMWEAVER 5-4, 17
splitting, DREAMWEAVER
5-11–15
walls, DREAMWEAVER 5-4
Change Position by list arrow, FLASH
4-33
Character palette, PHOTOSHOP 5-9, 30
Check In button, DREAMWEAVER
6-23–24
Check Links Sitewide feature,
DREAMWEAVER 4-32–33; 6-6
Check Out File(s) button,
DREAMWEAVER 6-22–24
Check out files when opening check
box, DREAMWEAVER 6-24
Check Page button, DREAMWEAVER
6-5
child pages, DREAMWEAVER 1-16
chroma, PHOTOSHOP 4-5
Class style, DREAMWEAVER 3-10

Clean Up button, DREAMWEAVER 6-12
Clean Up Word HTML command,
DREAMWEAVER 2-15
Clear Cell Heights command,
DREAMWEAVER 5-12
Clear Cell Widths command,
DREAMWEAVER 5-12
Clear mode, PHOTOSHOP 4-26
Cloak files ending with check box,
DREAMWEAVER 6-28
cloaking files, DREAMWEAVER 6-26–29
folders, DREAMWEAVER 6-26–27
overview, DREAMWEAVER 6-26
selected file types, DREAMWEAVER
6-27–29
Close panel group, DREAMWEAVER 2-28
closing
Bridge, PHOTOSHOP 1-10
files, PHOTOSHOP 1-36–38
CMYK mode, PHOTOSHOP 4-6
code, HTML, DREAMWEAVER 1-5;
2-25–29; 6-7
Code inspector, DREAMWEAVER
2-25–29
Coding toolbar, DREAMWEAVER 1-4–5
Collapse button, FLASH 1-8
Collapse to Icons button, FLASH
1-8, 10
Collapse to show only local or remote
site button, DREAMWEAVER 1-33;
2-23; 4-7, 9; 6-19, 33
color, PHOTOSHOP 4-1–37. See also
background color; foreground color
adding to Swatches palette,
PHOTOSHOP 4-13
additive, PHOTOSHOP 4-5–6
balancing, PHOTOSHOP 4-25,
29, 32

base, PHOTOSHOP 4-25
blend, PHOTOSHOP 4-25
blending using Gradient Tool,
PHOTOSHOP 4-16–19
changing using motion tween,
FLASH 4-23
converting grayscale and color
modes, PHOTOSHOP 4-20
layers, PHOTOSHOP 2-17, 22
matching, PHOTOSHOP
4-30–31
models, PHOTOSHOP 4-2, 4–5
modes, PHOTOSHOP 4-2, 5–6,
22, 32
overview, FLASH 2-11
printing images, PHOTOSHOP
1-33
psychology, PHOTOSHOP 4-4
removing from Web sites,
DREAMWEAVER 3-33–37
resulting, PHOTOSHOP 4-25
sample, creating gradients,
PHOTOSHOP 4-18
selections based on, PHOTOSHOP
3-16–18, 24
separation, PHOTOSHOP 4-6
subtractive, PHOTOSHOP 4-6
type, PHOTOSHOP 5-7, 30
Color Balance dialog box, PHOTOSHOP
4-29
Color Burn mode, PHOTOSHOP 4-26
Color Cubes, DREAMWEAVER 2-4
Color Dodge mode, PHOTOSHOP 4-26
Color list arrow, FLASH 3-7,
PHOTOSHOP 2-3
color models, PHOTOSHOP 4-2, 4–5
Color modes, PHOTOSHOP 4-2,
5–6, 22, 26, 32

Delete Layer icon, FLASH 2-35
deleting
 layers, PHOTOSHOP 2-9, 11, 22
 selections, PHOTOSHOP 3-7
 states, PHOTOSHOP 1-27
 Timeline effect, FLASH 4-25–33
delimited files, DREAMWEAVER 5-24
dependent files, DREAMWEAVER 6-15
derivative works, DREAMWEAVER 6-35
Description text box, FLASH 1-11
descriptions, DREAMWEAVER 2-5
deselecting selections, PHOTOSHOP
 3-5, 7, 9
design guidelines, FLASH 1-32–33
Design Notes, DREAMWEAVER
 6-10–11
Design-time Style Sheets button,
 DREAMWEAVER 3-14
Design view, DREAMWEAVER 1-5;
 2-25; 6-7
destination link, DREAMWEAVER 4-17
devices, resolution, PHOTOSHOP 1-29
diagonal symmetry, DREAMWEAVER
 2-32
Difference mode, PHOTOSHOP 4-26
digital cameras, PHOTOSHOP 1-37.
 See also Camera Raw images
digital images, PHOTOSHOP 1-2.
 See also files; graphics; images
digital subscriber line (DSL),
 DREAMWEAVER 1-17
Direction list arrow, DREAMWEAVER
 6-21
displaying. *See also* viewing
 Color Palette, PHOTOSHOP 4-32
 Gradient Tool, PHOTOSHOP 4-32
 gridlines, guides, and rulers,
  FLASH 2-5–9

hidden lasso tools, PHOTOSHOP
 1-38
History palette, PHOTOSHOP 1-38
layers, PHOTOSHOP 1-25–26, 38;
 4-32
open palettes, PHOTOSHOP 1-38
options bar, PHOTOSHOP 1-38
palettes, PHOTOSHOP 1-22
rulers, PHOTOSHOP 2-6, 22;
 4-32; 5-30
Swatches palette, PHOTOSHOP 1-38
Tools palette, PHOTOSHOP 1-38
Dissolve mode, PHOTOSHOP 4-26
distance, drop shadows, PHOTOSHOP
 5-13–14
Distance list arrow, FLASH 2-27
Distort filters, PHOTOSHOP 5-24
Distort option, FLASH 2-17
distortion, FLASH 2-17
distributing movies, FLASH
 1-26–29
Distributive option, FLASH 5-5
Div tags, DREAMWEAVER 5-21
.dng files, PHOTOSHOP 1-5
docks, PHOTOSHOP 1-17
Document command, FLASH 1-8
Document properties button,
 FLASH 1-11
Document Properties dialog box,
 FLASH 1-8
document-relative paths,
 DREAMWEAVER 4-5
Document toolbar, DREAMWEAVER
 1-4; 2-31; 6-5
Document window, DREAMWEAVER
 1-4, 7
documents. *See* files; graphics;
 images

domain name, DREAMWEAVER 1-20
Down image state, DREAMWEAVER
 4-20
Down state, FLASH 3-16
downloading media, DREAMWEAVER
 6-34
Drag Over button, FLASH 3-23
dragging layers, PHOTOSHOP 1-38
Draw Layout Cell button,
 DREAMWEAVER 5-4–5
Draw Layout Table button,
 DREAMWEAVER 5-4–5
drawing
 HTML tables, in Layout mode,
  DREAMWEAVER 5-5–9
 model modes, FLASH 2-10–11
drawing tools, FLASH 1-16; 2-4–9
 displaying gridlines, guides, and
  rulers, FLASH 2-5–9
 overview, FLASH 2-4–5
 using guide layers, FLASH 2-5–9
drawn objects, FLASH 2-16–23
 copying and moving, FLASH
  2-16
 distorting, FLASH 2-17
 flipping, FLASH 2-17–23
 reshaping segment of, FLASH
  2-17
 resizing, FLASH 2-16
 rotating and skewing, FLASH
  2-17
 transforming, FLASH 2-16
drop-down menus, DREAMWEAVER
 1-4
drop shadows, PHOTOSHOP
 5-12–15
 adding, PHOTOSHOP 5-14, 30
 settings, PHOTOSHOP 5-13–15

Web Collection Premium Chapter Opener Art Credits

Web Collection Premium Chapter #	Credit
Dreamweaver 1	© Chris Gomersall/Alamy
Dreamweaver 2	© Art Wolfe/Getty Images
Dreamweaver 3	© Martin Siepmann/RF/Alamy
Dreamweaver 4	© Jose B. Ruiz/Nature Picture Library/Alamy
Dreamweaver 5	© Keren Su/China Span/Alamy
Dreamweaver 6	© Mervyn Rees/Alamy
Flash 1	© David Davis Productions/RF/Alamy
Flash 2	© Hal Beral/Corbis
Flash 3	© Veer
Flash 4	© Michale & Patricia Fogden/Corbis
Flash 5	© Nature Picture Library/Alamy
Photoshop 1	© Kevin Schafer/Corbis
Photoshop 2	© Don Hammond/Design/Corbis
Photoshop 3	© Ralph A. Clevenger/Corbis
Photoshop 4	© Dave Marsden/RF/Alamy
Photoshop 5	© Chris Mattison/Frank Lane Picture Agency/Corbis
Integration	© Hal Beral/Corbis
End matter	© Darren Matthews/RF/Alamy